Brief contents

contents

Contents | ix

A UNIQUE INTEGRATED LEARNING SYSTEM

The Integrated Learning System helps students learn quickly by driving home key chapter concepts and providing a framework for studying. It links all of the instructor and student materials to each chapter's learning goals.

Learning goals are listed at the beginning of each chapter and then major headings within the chapter are identified by the relevant chapter learning goal. Each section ends with **Concept Checks** that can be used to self-test understanding of the material.

The chapter **Summary of Learning Goals** provides easy review of the chapter's content.

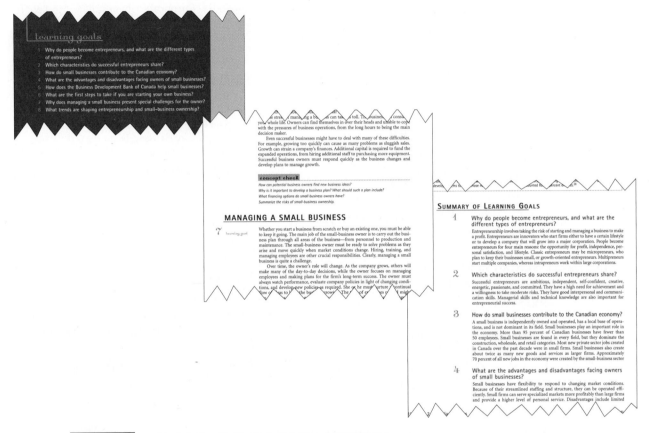

learning goals

1 Why do people become entrepreneurs, and what are the different types of entrepreneurs?
2 Which characteristics do successful entrepreneurs share?
3 How do small businesses contribute to the Canadian economy?
4 What are the advantages and disadvantages facing owners of small businesses?
5 How does the Business Development Bank of Canada help small businesses?
6 What are the first steps to take if you are starting your own business?
7 Why does managing a small business present special challenges for the owner?
8 What trends are shaping entrepreneurship and small–business ownership?

...the stress of managing a business can take a toll. The business consumes your whole life. Owners can find themselves in over their heads and unable to cope with the pressures of business operations, from the long hours to being the main decision maker.

Even successful businesses might have to deal with many of these difficulties. For example, growing too quickly can cause as many problems as sluggish sales. Growth can strain a company's finances. Additional capital is required to fund the expanded operations, from hiring additional staff to purchasing more equipment. Successful business owners must respond quickly as the business changes and develop plans to manage growth.

concept check

How can potential business owners find new business ideas?
Why is it important to develop a business plan? What should such a plan include?
What financing options do small business owners have?
Summarize the risks of small-business ownership.

MANAGING A SMALL BUSINESS

7 *learning goal*

Whether you start a business from scratch or buy an existing one, you must be able to keep it going. The main job of the small-business owner is to carry out the business plan through all areas of the business—from personnel to production and maintenance. The small-business owner must be ready to solve problems as they arise and move quickly when market conditions change. Hiring, training, and managing employees are other crucial responsibilities. Clearly, managing a small business is quite a challenge.

Over time, the owner's role will change. As the company grows, others will make many of the day-to-day decisions, while the owner focuses on managing employees and making plans for the firm's long-term success. The owner must always watch performance, evaluate company policies in light of changing conditions, and develop new policies as required. She or he must nurture a continual flow of ideas to keep the business growing...

SUMMARY OF LEARNING GOALS

1 Why do people become entrepreneurs, and what are the different types of entrepreneurs?

Entrepreneurship involves taking the risk of starting and managing a business to make a profit. Entrepreneurs are innovators who start firms either to have a certain lifestyle or to develop a company that will grow into a major corporation. People become entrepreneurs for four main reasons: the opportunity for profit, independence, personal satisfaction, and lifestyle. Classic entrepreneurs may be micropreneurs, who plan to keep their businesses small, or growth-oriented entrepreneurs. Multipreneurs start multiple companies, whereas intrapreneurs work within large corporations.

2 Which characteristics do successful entrepreneurs share?

Successful entrepreneurs are ambitious, independent, self-confident, creative, energetic, passionate, and committed. They have a high need for achievement and a willingness to take moderate risks. They have good interpersonal and communication skills. Managerial skills and technical knowledge are also important for entrepreneurial success.

3 How do small businesses contribute to the Canadian economy?

A small business is independently owned and operated, has a local base of operations, and is not dominant in its field. Small businesses play an important role in the economy. More than 95 percent of Canadian businesses have fewer than 50 employees. Small businesses are found in every field, but they dominate the construction, wholesale, and retail categories. Most new private sector jobs created in Canada over the past decade were in small firms. Small businesses also create about twice as many new goods and services as larger firms. Approximately 70 percent of all new jobs in the economy were created by the small-business sector

4 What are the advantages and disadvantages facing owners of small businesses?

Small businesses have flexibility to respond to changing market conditions. Because of their streamlined staffing and structure, they can be operated efficiently. Small firms can serve specialized markets more profitably than large firms and provide a higher level of personal service. Disadvantages include limited

NEW TEXT ORGANIZATION

Chapters are now organized into four parts:

- Trends and the Business Environment
- Canadian Business
- Business Management
- Functional Areas of Business

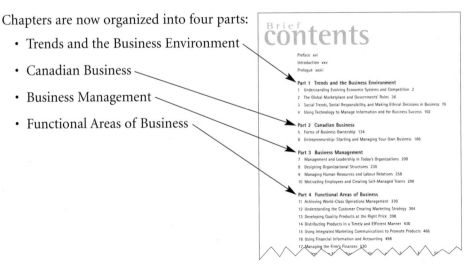

Brief
contents

PROLOGUE

Fast Forward to the Future

The new prologue offers practical and inspiring advice for getting the most out of your post-secondary education experience as well as offering suggestions for finding the right career and succeeding in your first job.

CHAPTER ORGANIZATION MATTERS!

Each chapter has been organized in a unique three-part structure that links principles, trends, and ideas:

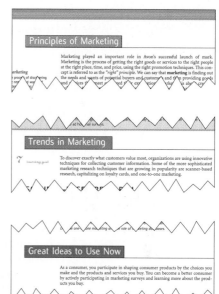

Principles of Business

Gives students a comprehensive overview of current business practices and teaches key principles through real-life examples.

Trends in Business

Explores fundamental factors and emerging trends that are reshaping today's business world and altering tomorrow's competitive environment.

Great Ideas to Use Now

Brings chapter topics to life with relevant and interesting tips for making the most of a professional career or becoming a smart consumer.

OPENING VIGNETTES THAT CONNECT

Making the Connection

Making the Connection introduces the chapter's content and is designed to help students connect the chapter concepts to business as a whole.

TWO NEW BOXES

Customer Satisfaction and Quality

Because customer satisfaction and quality are essential to attracting and keeping customers, the **Customer Satisfaction and Quality box** addresses how these concepts are illustrated and applied in actual companies.

Making Ethical Choices

These new ethical activites boxes present real-world ethical challenges to stimulate discussion regarding ethical issues faced by organizations.

HOT LINKS

Provide an opportunity to connect to relevant Web sites to expand on chapter information.

KEY TERMS

Every business term is carefully defined and is conveniently located in the text margins beside the section where the term is first introduced. A complete glossary of all key terms is included at the end of the text.

END-OF-CHAPTER SKILL-BUILDING ACTIVITIES, EXERCISES, AND RESOURCES

Experiential Exercises

This new feature allows students to practice and apply the chapter concepts and to expand on the chapter topics. These exercises can be used as assessments, assignments, and to add a real-world application.

Review Questions

Review questions confirm student learning
and understanding of chapter topics.

REVIEW QUESTIONS
1. Define production and operations management.
2. What is production planning? What is the production process, and what options are available to manufacturers?
3. What are some of the considerations when determining the location of production facilities?
4. After management has decided on a location for the facilities, they need to design the facilities' layout. What are some options in the design?
5. What are the considerations when we are formulating our resource planning?

300 | Part 4 Functional Areas of Business

Cases

These three types of chapter-ending cases
encourage the exploration and analysis of business strategies. Many of these cases
are new to this edition.

Creative Thinking Cases

10. ____ss th___mport__ce of ____manag____t.
11. What is modular production?

CREATIVE THINKING CASE
Shipshape Quality at Bombardier

Bombardier, a Montreal-based manufacturer of jets, railcars, and snowmobiles with revenues of $14 billion a year, knew it was taking on a big risk when it bought the manufacturing operations of Outboard Marine Corporation (OMC) for $55 million in 2001. OMC, maker of Evinrude and Johnson outboard boat engines, was in a tailspin. Product quality had declined so severely that the company's share of the $2-billion-a-year outboard engine market had plummeted from 55 percent in 1995 to just 23 percent in 2000.

OMC manufactured its components and parts at nine production facilities scattered around the United States, Mexico, and China. Engine transmission housings die-cast in Waukegan, Illinois, were shipped to Andrews, North Carolina, for machining and subassembly and then sent to the Calhoun, Georgia, plant for final assembly. It often took three weeks or more for component parts to move between plants, boosting production costs and delaying production.

Bombardier did not want to wait for OMC to turn around on its own. It sent a cross-functional team of specialists from its plant maintenance, operations, marketing, finance, and quality control departments to determine how to improve OMC's quality and operations. The first recommendation? Shut down two plants, and reduce production in a third to consolidate operations and drastically shorten parts supply routes. OMC would now concentrate final assembly at its four-year-old Sturtevant, Wisconsin, plant. Bombardier would spend $50 million upgrading the plant with new technology and equipment. The team next hired a new workforce, carefully selecting workers who were team players with problem-solving skills.

The Bombardier team studied all of OMC's engineering drawings and recommended that OMC redesign many parts to improve quality control. Defective parts stored in inventory were identified and eliminated. Bombardier now requires that all assembly workers spend as much as 20 percent of their time inspecting engines for quality defects. Bombardier also set what it calls DQR—durability, quality, and reliability—standards for each unit produced.

Bombardier implemented these and other changes within 78 days of acquiring OMC. The results have been dramatic. Quality has improved enough that Bombardier offers a three-year warranty on its engines, the longest in the industry. Market share is almost back to previous levels. Bombardier plans to expand the Sturtevant plant to boost production to 60,000 engines a year, including many new models—2 times the current rate.

Video Cases

CBC20___ Byline: "Blue Function: The ___setting Life__Standards ___Quality ___ol, Previ___ Maintenance and Automation," *Fortune*, September 2, 2002, 172B; "Bombardier First-Built Outboard Engine Delivered to Worldwide Market," Bombardier company press release, October 17, 2001.

VIDEO CASE
Big Blue Turns Small Businesses into Large Competitors

"It is like music, once it is in place and working," says Susan Jain, a marketing executive with IBM Global Services. She is talking about Enterprise Resource Planning, or ERP, complex software modules that do just about everything to help companies run more efficiently and competitively.

"The old systems couldn't relate one piece of information to another," she says. Separate databases meant information systems weren't integrated, so day-to-day operations were cumbersome and management reporting often inaccurate. With ERP, information is accessible immediately, greatly improving overall operating efficiency and speeding up and shortening internal reporting procedures, and even reducing the time it takes to bring new products to market.

ERP is a "relational database" that ties all aspects of information gathering and dissemination together in a tidy package. For example, ERP software modules can receive an order, check raw material stocks to make sure the order can be produced, order any additional materials that might be needed, place the order in the production schedule, and send it to shipping and invoicing. Its human resources module will even help hire and train the staff needed to produce and fulfill the order.

Companies no longer need to predict what products customers might want, or keep tons of product on warehouse shelves gathering dust. ERP literally allows companies to "build to order"—in fact, IBM has an automobile customer that does just that. It builds to order, one car at a time, eliminating the customary guessing games of what colours or styles might be popular at a given time.

Even small companies are investing in ERP systems to enable them to grow and compete, despite the substantial investment in time and dollars that is required. Jain is candid about the costs involved. The software costs about $1 million dollars, with an equal expenditure required for new hardware. Implementation, training, and education can cost two to three times that amount and take years in the case of very large companies.

IBM Global Financing supports all elements of an ERP acquisition with a broad array of financing offerings with flexible payment options. But after all that expense, return on investment is difficult to measure. With so many variables driving business success, good results could be due to other factors, such as changes in working styles or a general upswing in the current business environment. IBM's promotional material asks "Are You Ready for IBM?" It's a big decision for small companies to make.

E-Commerce Cases

E-COMMERCE CASE
GM Goes Digital

Six years ago, General Motors was an e-commerce dinosaur. The giant automaker was bogged down with 7,000 different information technology (IT) systems spread across the company. Communications with suppliers, dealers, and customers—as well as between the company's own divisions—often stumbled, resulting in long product development delays and an inefficient supply chain.

To solve these problems, GM had to go digital. It started by consolidating the company's telecommunications infrastructure to increase Internet bandwidth. This allowed GM to support connectivity between the company and its business partners. The next step was to reduce the number of company IT systems by nearly half, so that communications could flow freely from computer to computer via the Internet.

GM chose a single CAD program that allows 3-D design documents to be shared on-line by the company's 18,000 designers and engineers at its 14 global design labs. GM also hooked more than 1,000 of its key suppliers' engineers into the same system. Now, all parties involved in the design and development process are able to view and discuss design plans on-line in real time. The time required to bring a new vehicle to market has been cut to just 18 months. GM purchases many of its raw materials and parts through the Internet as well, through an on-line joint procurement effort formed with other automakers, further streamlining production and operations.

GM also launched a consumer on-line shopping and buying site in 40 countries, **http://www.GMBuyPower.com**. U.S. consumers can visit the site, choose which options they want their car to have, find a dealer that has it in inventory, and shop for the best price.

Brazilian consumers can actually complete their entire sales transaction on-line through **http://www.GMBuyPower.com**. GM worked with its Brazilian dealers to develop a special Chevrolet model, the Celta, specifically for Internet sales. Since GM began selling the Celta on-line in Brazil, more than 80,000 of the cars have been sold entirely over the Internet. GM hopes to expand on-line sales to other countries within the next few years.

CRITICAL THINKING QUESTIONS

1. What are the benefits and disadvantages for suppliers who are connected to GM's Internet-based CAD system? How do you think GM decides which suppliers should be included?
2. If you were GM's information technology manager, __at oth__ _ses of the Int___

preface

The Future of Business, Second Canadian Edition, provides a personal roadmap for understanding and navigating the future of business. The second Canadian edition builds on the success of the first edition with thorough coverage of business principles and leading-edge practices adopted by business innovators, all illustrated with relevant and interesting business examples. Because the future of business is approaching us at warp speed, the second Canadian edition has been written with the goal of making you the winner in tomorrow's fast-paced marketplace. Each chapter will help you understand what is happening and what will happen in the sometimes chaotic and always exciting world of business.

THE INTERACTIVE PERSPECTIVE: MAJOR BUSINESS TOPICS UP CLOSE

Today's most important business topics and trends are thoroughly covered in the second Canadian edition—this means more insight into the key economic and business developments that shape the future. Topics at the forefront of business covered in this edition include:

- Customer satisfaction and quality
- Relationship management
- Changing Canadian population
- Corporate ethics scandals
- Enlargement of the European Union
- Managing multinational cultures in the workplace
- Crisis management
- Virtual teams and corporations
- Protecting whistle blowers
- Nurturing knowledge workers
- Global management skills
- Executive compensation
- Concession bargaining
- Internet marketing research
- E-retailing
- Category management
- Database marketing
- Growth in Web advertising
- Guerrilla marketing
- One-to-one marketing
- E-procurement

Through extensive reviews, we discovered that instructors teaching the introduction to business course place considerable importance on the topics of ethics, customer satisfaction and quality, the role of technology in business, e-commerce, entrepreneurship and small business management, global business opportunities, and careers. Therefore, we gave these topics special emphasis.

The Future of Business is supported by real-world examples to introduce today's students to tomorrow's business careers. The text is written in a friendly and conversational style and helps prepare students of all interests and abilities for future achievements with the information, skills, and techniques they need to get to work and jump on the fast-track to success.

WHAT'S NEW IN THE SECOND CANADIAN EDITION

Highlights of new content to the second Canadian edition include the following:

- The chapters have been re-organized into the following four parts: Trends and the Business Environment, Canadian Business, Business Management, and Functional Areas of Business.

- A new prologue, *Fast Forward to the Future: Strategies for Success in School and Business,* offers practical and inspiring advice for developing test-taking, interpersonal, time management, and planning skills. The prologue also features suggestions for finding the right career and succeeding in that first professional job.

- For instructors who discuss Canadian law and taxation, we have included an appendix "Corporate Governance, the Legal Environment, and Taxation."

- Two new boxed features have been added:

  Customer Satisfaction and Quality
  This new boxed feature demonstrates how these concepts are applied in actual companies.

  Making Ethical Choices
  This new boxed feature can be used by instructors to stimulate discussions regarding ethical issues faced by organizations.

- More coverage of financial issues. This includes three chapters that focus on accounting, managing the firm's finances, and understanding money, financial institutions, and securities markets.

- New discussion of unions and their role in Canadian business.

- New end-of-chapter content includes:

  Experiential Exercises
  The new Experiential Exercises feature offers the instructor yet another resource that can be used to expand the chapter topics, to use as assessments or assignments, or simply for general interest. Each chapter has various experiential exercises that instructors can choose from.

  Review Questions
  To supplement the concept checks that are used throughout the chapter to test students' comprehension of the material, there are now review questions at the end of the chapter. These can be used by the students to confirm their learning and by the instructor as assessments or assignments.

- Three types of end-of-chapter cases have been included. Creative Thinking Cases, Video Cases, and E-Commerce Cases invite you to explore business strategies of various companies, analyze business decisions, and prepare open-response comments.

- Organization matters! Each chapter of *The Future of Business,* Second Canadian Edition has been organized into a unique three-part structure that links principles, trends, and ideas:

Principles of Business
Gives students a comprehensive overview of current business practices, and teaches key principles through real-world examples from the largest global corporate giants to the smallest family start-ups.

Trends in Business
Explores the fundamental factors and emerging trends that are reshaping today's business world and altering tomorrow's competitive environment. This preview of the future gives students a keen advantage when entering the workplace.

Great Ideas to Use Now
Brings chapter topics to life with relevant and interesting tips for making the most of a professional career or becoming a smart consumer. Students develop skills that are applicable immediately.

GREAT FEATURES RETAINED FROM THE FIRST CANADIAN EDITION

In the **Introduction,** students learn the basic terms that are associated with organizations and business. They are given the foundation of what a business is, how risk can affect the business (more comprehensive discussion in Chapter 17), revenues, expenses and profits, etc. Here, too, the students are first introduced to the *Integrated Model of a Successful Business.*

Making the Connection introduces each chapter. This section shows how the chapter concepts relate to "The Integrative Model" to help students connect the chapter concepts to business as a whole.

Learning Goals (lg) are provided at the beginning of each chapter to highlight the learning expectations for students as they read the chapter. These help to guide students' learning by providing key concepts that are presented in the chapter.

Each chapter begins with an **opening vignette** about a prominent, student-friendly company or a business professional that actually previews that chapter's content. We then provide several questions to prompt critical thinking.

Unlike most traditional textbooks that have review or study questions at the end of each chapter only, *The Future of Business* has **Concept Checks** throughout the chapter. These concept checks are meant to challenge the students' learning as they progress through the chapter. If they are unable to respond to the concept checks, they can simply review the previous few pages instead of trying to search through the entire chapter to locate the information.

Hot Links give the student an opportunity to connect to various Web sites to expand on the information presented in the chapter. Instructors may also choose to send students to the Web site links to fulfill assignments.

Key Terms help students to master the business vocabulary. Every key business term is carefully defined within the text. Each term appears in bold type and is defined in the margin where the term is first introduced. A complete glossary of all key terms is also included at the end of the book.

A **Summary of Learning Goals** at the end of each chapter helps students to focus on the relevant material in a concise manner. As a supplement to this summary, the Key Terms that were used in the chapter are listed along with their page numbers.

The **Integrated Learning System** anchors chapter concepts, provides a framework for study, and links all of the instructor and student supplements. The

Integrated Learning System helps you learn quickly and study efficiently. It also helps ease lecture preparation. Learning goals at the beginning of each chapter outline the key concepts in the chapter and provide structure for lesson plans and help exam preparation. Learning goals are tied to major headings within the chapter and are supported with concept checks and a chapter summary. Every supplement is also organized by learning goal to ensure that each piece of the Integrated Learning System reinforces the other components.

ORGANIZATION

In Part One of *The Future of Business,* Second Canadian Edition students learn how the PEST model works and its impact on any business. In these first four chapters to either introduce or refresh the students' awareness of certain elementary, but critical components, the book discusses understanding *Evolving Economic Systems and Competition* (Chapter 1), *The Global Marketplace and Governments' Roles* (Chapter 2), *Social Trends, Social Responsibility, and Making Ethical Decisions in Business* (Chapter 3), and *Using Technology to Manage Information and for Business Success* (Chapter 4) including the role of MIS in the organization.

Part Two introduces the concepts of Canadian business by discussing the *Forms of Business Ownership* (Chapter 5) and *Entrepreneurship: Starting and Managing Your Own Business* (Chapter 6).

Business Management (Part Three) examines *Management and Leadership in Today's Organizations* (Chapter 7), *Designing Organizational Structures* (Chapter 8), *Managing Human Resources and Labour Relations* (Chapter 9), and *Motivating Employees and Creating Self-Managed Teams* (Chapter 10). This section was revised considerably from the first edition to reflect the reviewers' thoughts of how the subject matter was covered and placed in the book.

The final section, Part Four, gives the students the basic understanding of the functional areas of business. The eight chapters include: *Achieving World-Class Operations Management, understanding the customer creating marketing strategy, Developing Quality Products at the Right Price, Distributing Products in a Timely and Efficient Manner, Using Integrated Marketing Communications to Promote Products, Using Financial Information and Accounting, Managing the Firms Finances, and Understanding Money, Financial Institutions, and the Securities Markets.*

SUPPLEMENTS

Business success is stimulated by access to and mastery of vital resources. The same is true for the classroom. Whether teaching an on-line course or simply enhancing your course with Web resources, *The Future of Business,* Second Canadian Edition offers a vast, complementary system of teaching and learning resources.

Comprehensive Instructor's Manual. At the core of the integrated learning system for *The Future of Business* is the Instructor's Manual prepared by textbook author Norm Althouse. Developed in response to numerous suggestions from instructors teaching this course, each chapter is designed to provide maximum guidance for delivering the content in an interesting and dynamic manner. Each chapter begins with learning goals that anchor the integrated learning system. A lecture outline guides instructors through key terminology and concepts. Each chapter includes lecture support for teaching the cases and guidance for integrating PowerPoint™ slides and other visuals that illustrate and reinforce the lecture. A comprehensive video guide is included in the Instructor's Manual and includes the running time of each video, concepts illustrated in the video, teaching objectives for the case, and solutions for video case study questions.

PowerPoint™ Lecture System. The PowerPoint™ Lecture System includes hundreds of slides that illustrate key chapter concepts and actual business examples, many not included in the text. These slides will help improve lecture organization and reduce preparation time. The PowerPoint™ slides were prepared textbook author Norm Althouse.

Test Bank. The comprehensive test bank, written by textbook author Shirley Rose, is organized by learning goal to support the integrated learning system. With over 2,000 true/false, multiple-choice, fill-in-the-blank, and short-answer questions, tests can be customized to support a variety of course objectives.

ExamView® Testing Software. Create, deliver, and customize print and online tests in minutes with this easy-to-use Windows-based testing and assessment system. ExamView® offers both a Quick Test Wizard and an Online Test Wizard that guide you step-by-step through the process of creating tests. With ExamView®'s complete word processing capabilities, you can enter an unlimited number of new questions or edit existing questions.

Instructor's Resource CD (ISBN 0-17-644191-3). For maximum convenience, the Instructor's Manual, the PowerPoint™ slides, the Test Bank, and the ExamView® Testing System are all available on CD.

JoinIn™ on Turning Point®. Now you can author, deliver, show, assess, and grade all in PowerPoint™ ... with NO toggling back and forth between screens! JoinIn™ on TurningPoint® is the only classroom response software tool that gives you true PowerPoint™ integration. With JoinIn™ on TurningPoint®, you are no longer tied to your computer ... you can walk about your classroom as you lecture, showing slides and collecting and displaying responses with ease. There is simply no easier or more effective way to turn your lecture hall into a personal, fully interactive experience for your students. If you can use PowerPoint™, you can use JoinIn™ on TurningPoint®!

Videos and Video Guide. Designed to enrich and support chapter concepts, each of the 18 video segments presents real business issues faced by a variety of service and manufacturing organizations. The video cases challenge you to study business issues and develop solutions to business problems. The instructor's video guide, included in the instructor's manual, outlines the key teaching objectives of each video case and suggests answers to the critical thinking questions.

The Future of Business **Web Site (www.futureofbusiness2e.nelson.com).** The Web site for *The Future of Business* provides rich content to maximize student learning and build on-line skills. Each text chapter is supported by an on-line Test Yourself quiz (written by Angela Davis of the University of Winnipeg) that tests student understanding and offers clear, customized feedback for incorrect answers. Also included on the Web site are Web Links, Collaborative Exercises, a business plan template, downloadable supplements, and much more.

ThomsonNOW™. This on-line diagnostic tool identifies each student's unique needs with a Pre-Test that generates a personalized Study Plan for each chapter, helping students focus on concepts they're having the most difficulty mastering. Students then take a Post-Test to measure their understanding of the material. An instructor Gradebook is available to track and monitor student progress. A key component of the Study Plan is the inclusion of visually and pedagogically rich modules that begin with clearly stated learning objectives followed by knowledge-building animations with audio to present key concepts. Modules also include discovery activities and self-check quizzes that confirm students understanding of the module material.

InfoTrac College Edition™. Now you can give your students an entire library for the price of one book. With InfoTrac College Edition™, students gain complete, 24-hour-a-day access to full-text articles from hundreds of scholarly journals and popular periodicals such as *Canadian Business, Business Week, Canadian Business Review,* and *HR Professional.* Thousands of full-length, substantive articles spanning the past four years are updated daily, indexed, and linked. And because they're online, the articles are accessible from any computer with Internet access. InfoTrac College Edition™ is perfect for all students, from dorm-dwellers to commuters and distance learners.

ACKNOWLEDGMENTS

We are exceedingly grateful to the many reviewers who offered suggestions and recommendations for enhancing the coverage, pedagogy, and support package of *The Future of Business.* The feedback from these instructors helped guide our efforts and ensure that this textbook surpassed expectations for customer satisfaction and quality. We are deeply appreciative of the insights of the following reviewers:

Barry Boothman, University of New Brunswick

F. Alex Boultbee, Seneca College

Elisabeth Carter, Douglas College

Angela Davis, University of Winnipeg

Johan de Rooy, University of British Columbia

Vic de Witt, Red River College

Dave Fleming, George Brown College

Jane Forbes, Seneca College

Robert Fournier, Red Deer College

Walter Isenor, Acadia University

Ed Leach, Dalhousie University

Valerie Miceli, Seneca College

Alan McGee, Acadia University

Erica Morrill, Fanshawe College

Richard Powers, University of Toronto

John Purcell, Sheridan College

Carson Rappell, Dawson College

Cynthia Riley, Seneca College

Frank Saccucci, Grant MacEwan College

Bob Sproule, University of Waterloo

William Thurber, Brock University

Leslie Wilder, Red River College

We would also like to recognize the contribution of Lawrence Gitman and Carl McDaniel, authors of the U.S. edition of *The Future of Business.* Their original work served as the foundation for our writing and set a standard of excellence we conscientiously followed.

We have benefited from the detailed and constructive contributions of many individuals. Specifically, we would like to thank the following people for their insight and contributions to *The Future of Business*:

Janice Bodnarchuk	Leanne McDonald
Victoria Calvert	Doug McDonnell
Gordon Campbell	Fred (Scoop) McKay
Bob Channing	Tim Morgan
Carl Cheverie	Ron Munaweera
Doug Dokis	Ron Murch
Randall Gossen	Albert Nasaar
Christopher Halpin	Margaret Nemeth
Donna Harlamow	Gino Panucci
Karina Hope	Barry Sadrehashemi
Marc Jerry	Frank Thirkettle
Robin Lynas	Elizabeth Watson
Robert Malach	Justine Wheeler
Sandra E. Malach	Kim Wilson
Arden Matheson	Claire Wright

And, of course, our talented and patient editorial and production staff at Thomson Nelson.

Norm R. Althouse	Lawrence J. Gitman
Shirley A. Rose	Carl McDaniel
Laura A. Allan	

ABOUT THE AUTHORS

Norm R. Althouse

Norm Althouse received his Bachelor of Business Administration (Accounting) and worked in the public sector for ten years before returning to continue studies in the Master of Business Program. He has studied in Canada, Australia, Ireland, and Hungary. Currently, Norm teaches at the Haskayne School of Business at the University of Calgary. He has also taught at the University of Lethbridge and Mount Royal College.

After several years of teaching in the Human Resource area at the University of Calgary, Norm transferred to the Strategy and Global Management Area and currently teaches in the Business and Environment Area. Initially, Norm's primary responsibility was to develop a required core-course in business for first- and second-year business students. His commitment to "continuous improvement" has resulted in many new developments, including the integration of materials and changes in the pedagogy of the course.

Norm's research activities include: team building, the changing nature of management and managers, and, most currently, studying values and diversity in the workplace. Additionally, Norm has presented at conferences such as the Administrative Sciences Association of Canada ("*The Gendering Component of*

Diversity: How is it Faring?") and has been published in a book of readings from the Global Business and Technology Association—Budapest, Hungary ("*Hierarchies in Transition: Hungary and Canada*"). Also, Norm is an active member of the Academy of Management (Management Education and Development Division).

Shirley A. Rose

Shirley Rose received her Bachelor of Business Administration from the University of New Brunswick in 1980. She then moved to Alberta to assume a position with the Alberta Provincial Government in the Department of Advanced Education. After some time in industry, Shirley returned to university and completed an MBA at the University of Calgary in 1989. Upon completion of the MBA, Shirley taught in a variety of full- and part-time positions at the University of New Brunswick, Athabasca University, Simon Fraser University, University of Calgary, University of Lethbridge, and the University College of the Cariboo. She was accepted into a Ph.D. program at the University of Bath in the UK and completed two years of study. Shirley's research and consulting activities are in the fields of health care, oil and gas, union-government relations, and unemployment.

Shirley Rose has been with the Bissett School of Business at Mount Royal College since 1998. During that time she has taught in the areas of management, organizational behaviour, and general business. She served as Program Chair from 2000 to 2003 and was responsible for programs in marketing, human resources, general business, and aviation. Shirley is on the Board of Directors for Aviation Alberta and is Vice President of the Canadian Association of Aviation Colleges. She has authored test banks and study guides, as well as served as a contributing author for textbooks in management and introduction to business.

Laura A. Allan

Laura Allan received her Honours Bachelor of Business Administration from Wilfrid Laurier University, and after a brief stint in the private sector working for an advertising agency, she went on to get her Masters of Business Administration in Marketing at York University. Laura went back to her alma mater to teach in 1984, and apart from taking brief time off to have her two children, she has been there ever since. Laura teaches primarily first-year undergraduate classes, but has also taught a second-year decision-making course. She also teaches executive development seminars for the Laurier Institute. Laura has been academic editor on another introductory text, written a study guide, and contributed chapters for two introductory textbooks. She has also co-authored the lab manual for the two first-year courses each semester since 1998, and has developed an on-line version of both courses for the university's distance education department.

Laura's commitment to the integrative approach to teaching business led to a complete redesign of the first-year courses. Most recently, she helped design the annual New Venture Competition for first-year students. Currently, Laura serves as co-coordinator for the first-year program at Wilfrid Laurier University, and has been recognized as one of the "most popular profs" in *MacLean's* magazine since 2000.

Lawrence J. Gitman

Lawrence J. Gitman is a professor of finance at San Diego State University. He received his bachelor's degree from Purdue University, his M.B.A. from the University of Dayton, and his Ph.D. from the University of Cincinnati. Professor Gitman is a prolific textbook author and has over 50 articles appearing in *Financial Management, Financial Review, Financial Services Review, Journal of Financial Planning, Journal of Risk and Insurance, Journal of Financial Research, Financial Practice and Education, Journal of Financial Education,* and other publications.

His singly authored major textbooks include *Principles of Managerial Finance: Brief,* Third Edition, *Principles of Managerial Finance,* Tenth Edition, and *Foundations of Managerial Finance,* Fourth Edition. Other major textbooks include *Personal Financial Planning,* Tenth Edition, and *Fundamentals of Investing,* Ninth Edition, both co-authored with Michael D. Joehnk. Gitman and Joehnk also wrote *Investment Fundamentals: A Guide to Becoming a Knowledgeable Investor,* which was selected as one of 1988's ten best personal finance books by *Money* magazine. In addition, he co-authored *Introduction to Finance* with Jeff Madura and *Corporate Finance* with Scott B. Smart and William L. Meggison.

An active member of numerous professional organizations, Professor Gitman is a former president of the Academy of Financial Services, the San Diego Chapter of the Financial Executives Institute, the Midwest Finance Association, and the FMA National Honor Society. In addition, he is a Certified Financial Planner (CFP)® and a Certified Cash Manager (CCM). Gitman served as Vice President, Financial Education of the Financial Management Association, as a Director of the San Diego MIT Enterprise Form, and on the CFP® Board of Standards. He and his wife have two children and live in La Jolla, California, where he is an avid bicyclist.

Carl McDaniel

Carl McDaniel is a professor of marketing at the University of Texas–Arlington, where he is Chairman of the Marketing Department. He has been an instructor for more than 20 years and is the recipient of several awards for outstanding teaching. McDaniel has also been a District Sales Manager for Southwestern Bell Telephone Company. Currently, he serves as a board member of the North Texas Higher Education Authority, a 1.5 billion member organization that provides immediate financing for student loans across America.

In addition to this text, McDaniel has also co-authored a number of textbooks in marketing. McDaniel's research has appeared in publications such as *Journal of Marketing, Journal of Business Research, Journal of the Academy of Marketing Science,* and *California Management Review.*

McDaniel is a member of the American Marketing Association, Academy of Marketing Science, Society for Marketing Advances, and Southwestern Marketing Association.

Besides his academic experience, McDaniel has business experience as the co-owner of a marketing research firm. Recently, McDaniel served as senior consultant to the International Trade Centre (ITC), Geneva, Switzerland. The ITC's mission is to help developing nations increase their exports. McDaniel also teaches international business each year in France. He has a bachelor's degree from the University of Arkansas and his master's degree and doctorate from Arizona State University.

Introduction

This text on business is important whether you are working in a business today or hope to work in one in the future. Even if your major is in the arts or sciences, you will likely work in an organization that is considered to be a business. Profit or nonprofit, the same principles apply.

First let's look at the nature of business.

A **business** is an organization that strives for a profit by providing goods and services desired by its customers. Businesses meet the needs of consumers by providing movies, medical care, autos, and countless other goods and services. **Goods** are tangible items manufactured by businesses, such as laptop computers and BlackBerries. **Services** are intangible offerings of businesses that can't be held, touched, or stored. Accountants, lawyers, restaurants, car washes, and airlines all provide services. Businesses also serve other organizations, such as hospitals, retailers, and governments, by providing machinery, goods for resale, computers, and thousands of other items.

Thus, businesses create the goods and services that are the basis of our standard of living. The **standard of living** of any country is measured by the output of goods and services people can buy with the money they have. This includes not only privately purchased goods and services but also collectively consumed goods and services, such as those provided by public utilities and governments.

Businesses play a key role in determining our quality of life by providing jobs and goods and services to society. **Quality of life** refers to the general level of human happiness based on such things as life expectancy, educational standards, health, sanitation, and leisure time. Zurich, Switzerland, is ranked as having the world's highest quality of life, followed by Vienna, Austria, and Vancouver, Canada.[1] Building a high quality of life is a combined effort of businesses, government, and not-for-profit organizations.

Creating a high quality of life is not without risks, however. **Risk** is the potential for losing time and money or otherwise not being able to accomplish an organization's goals. Without enough blood donors, for example, the Canadian Blood Services faces the risk of not meeting the demand for blood by victims of disaster. Businesses like BCE face the risk of falling short of their revenue goals. **Revenue** is the money a company earns from providing services or selling goods to customers. **Costs** are expenses for rent, salaries, supplies, transportation, and many other items that a company incurs from creating and selling goods and services. Some of the costs incurred by Research in Motion (featured in our opening) include expenses for research and development, building rental or purchase, advertising, and transportation. **Profit** is the money left over after all expenses are paid.

When a company like Research in Motion uses its resources intelligently, it can often increase sales, hold costs down, and earn a profit. Not all companies earn profit, but that is the risk of being in business. In Canadian business today, there is generally a direct relationship between risks and profit: the greater the risks, the greater the potential profit (or loss).

Not all organizations strive to make a profit. A **not-for-profit organization** is an organization that exists to achieve some goal other than the usual business goal of profit. The United Way, the Canadian Cancer Society, and Greenpeace are all not-for-profit organizations.

Successful not-for-profit organizations follow sound business principles. These groups have goals they hope to accomplish, but the goals are not focused on profits. For example, a not-for-profit organization's goal might be feeding the poor, stopping destruction of the environment, increasing attendance at the ballet, or preventing drunk driving. Reaching such goals takes good planning, management, and control. Not-for-profit organizations do not compete directly with each other as, for example, Ford and Honda do, but they do compete for people's scarce volunteer time and donations.

business
An organization that strives for a profit by providing goods and services desired by its customers.

goods
Tangible items manufactured by businesses.

services
Intangible offerings of businesses that can't be held, touched, or stored.

standard of living
A country's output of goods and services that people can buy with the money they have.

quality of life
The general level of human happiness based on such things as life expectancy, educational standards, health, sanitation, and leisure time.

risk
The potential for losing time and money or otherwise not being able to accomplish an organization's goals.

revenue
The money a company earns from providing services or selling goods to customers.

costs
Expenses incurred in creating and selling goods and services.

profit
The money left over after all expenses are paid.

not-for-profit organization
An organization that exists to achieve some goal other than the usual business goal of profit.

If you want to be as successful as you can be, and make your business as successful as it can be, then it is critical that you understand how a successful business works. Most introductory textbooks and courses do a good job of introducing you to the different elements of a business, but often fail to show you how these elements fit together. This objective is achieved mostly in senior business courses. The problem is that by that point, you are so used to studying each piece separately that it's very difficult to see them working together to create the business entity as a whole. And what's important to see is that *"the whole" really is greater than the sum of its parts.* To truly understand what makes a business successful, you must accept it as a fully integrated entity and, as you study each of its parts, study them with the whole in mind.

To this end, we have used an integrative model (shown on the next page) of a successful business as the framework, or basis, of this book. Each chapter will focus on a specific part of this model, and you will be reminded of where and how each piece fits with the other aspects of the model at the beginning of each chapter.

Before we get into the model in detail, take a look at the title—*The Integrated Model of a Successful Business.* Why is this important? What does it tell you?

It Is *Integrative.*

All the elements of the model work together to create a unified whole. Each piece depends on the others, and they all affect one another. One of the most important lessons to learn about business is that you can't make a decision in one area of a business without considering the impact that it will have on other areas of the business.

For example, according to *Report on Business Magazine's* 2005 Top 1000, General Motors was the number one–ranked private company in Canada (wholly owned by General Motors Corp. U.S.) on the basis of revenue. This company has clearly shown that it knows what it takes to be successful. If the *operations* department of GM was to find a new, less-expensive source for a material that it uses in the making of its cars, could it use this material without any impact on other areas of the business? If the material was also of lesser quality, or was perceived to be of lesser quality, this would affect the image of the product in the mind of the consumer, making it difficult for the *marketing* department to sell the cars. Therefore, the marketing department would be affected in terms of the sales of the product, which, in turn, means that the *finance* department would be affected, as it would affect the expected income for the year, and this might mean that the salaries negotiated in future labour contracts by the *human resources* department might be lower, and so on. All the elements of the business or areas of its *internal environment* (shown by the green circle on the model) affect one another.

By the same token, what if new *technology* was developed that would allow GM to produce its cars by way of machine only, with no human input? Then layoffs would likely result and affect the *economy* of the towns where the plants were located. This, in turn, would have an impact on the *social* environment of the business with respect to the relationship it has with the residents of the community, and might lead to the government's stepping in to enact a *political* solution for the community.

All the areas of the *external environment* (shown by the pink circle on the model) have an impact on each other as well as on the business as a whole. These four areas of the external environment together can be remembered as the acronym PEST—for political, economic, social, and technological. The external environment can, indeed, be a pest to business! But it can also create enormous opportunities, as you will see.

To make our model more fully integrated, changes in this external environment set off another chain reaction inside the internal environment of the business. For example, what if GM's supplier can sell materials to GM for less because it uses this new technology? The interactions are endless. It's not necessary that you see all these connections. What is necessary is that you understand, as we go through the material section by section, that these sections of material cannot be treated as if they are separate areas of a business that can act on their own. They all work together.

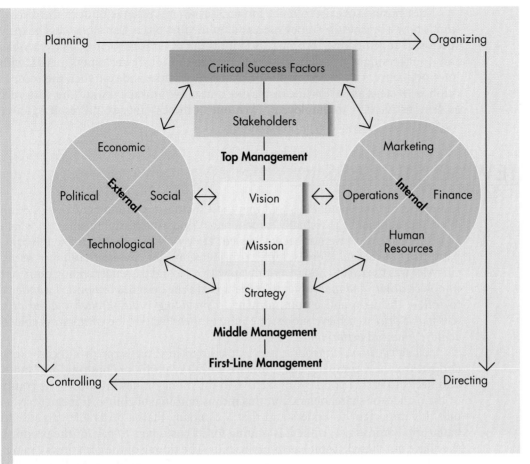

SOURCE: LAURA ALLAN AND JIM MCCUTCHEON, *BUSINESS 111 LAB MANUAL*, 18TH ED. (CAPTUS PRESS).

The Integrated Model of a Successful Business

It Is a *Model*

This means several things. A model represents reality—this is how a real business works! A model simplifies reality—you are learning how a successful business works, and that's very complicated. A model summarizes the essential elements in a simple form to give you a base on which to build your knowledge. A model integrates ideas into a whole, as we discussed. And finally, a model provides a framework, so that you can see how the pieces fit together and how you can build on it in later business courses.

It Is a Model of a *Successful* Business

We're not discussing what all businesses do. We are discussing what successful businesses do that makes them successful over time—not just one year but consistently outperforming year after year. That's how we learn about business—by studying those successful businesses that are leaders in their fields.

What does it mean to be truly successful? Is it simply making money? What does it take to make money? The *critical success factors* for any business, or the factors that indicate success, are

- achieving financial performance,
- meeting and exceeding customer needs,
- providing value—quality products at a reasonable price,
- encouraging creativity and innovation, and
- gaining employee commitment.[2]

Most businesses exist to make money, but what is often left out of the discussion is how a business becomes successful in the first place. Can a business be truly successful at generating income if it ignores the other four factors? For example, can it make money by selling products that do not satisfy customers' needs, with inferior quality at an unreasonable price, using yesterday's ideas (when the competition is 10 steps ahead), while displaying a negative attitude toward the customer as demonstrated by its employees? Even one of these points would result in lower income and a less successful business.

ACHIEVING SUCCESS

It's important to remember as well that these factors are also integrative—they all affect one another. It is virtually impossible to find a successful business in which all of these factors have not been achieved. They work together to make the company truly successful. For example, consider Chrysler. To *meet customer needs,* Chrysler was the first to design a minivan with a second passenger sliding door, but it took *creativity and innovation* to come up with the design, a *committed workforce* to follow through, and a commitment to *providing value through quality at a reasonable price* to achieve success. Because of these factors, the company is able to achieve *financial performance.*

Achieving financial performance is measured in three ways: profit, cash flow, and net worth. A company needs to have a healthy profit, or "bottom line," but it also needs to earn a good profit relative to the money it has invested—the equity of the owners or shareholders. But this means nothing, of course, if it can't pay its bills. It's important to understand that a company that is profitable can still go bankrupt. For instance, while it is waiting for its customers to pay for the products they have purchased, it still has to pay its bills. The timing of the cash flows can put an otherwise profitable business into a very precarious position. And finally, the net worth of the company is important, measured either by its stock price multiplied by the number of shares outstanding, or in terms of its assets (what it owns) relative to its liabilities (what it owes).

Meeting and exceeding customer needs means that companies must be sensitive to the needs of customers, anticipate changes in their needs, and, of course, work to meet these needs in a proactive fashion—before a customer complains. However, today companies cannot just provide what the customer wants. They need to satisfy customers beyond their expectations, or the competition will.

Providing value means that a business must constantly strive to improve the quality of its products and services, and do so at a reasonable cost. Customers demand quality and will stand for nothing less, but they want value for their dollar. They will pay a price that gives them value for their money—the quality that they demand at a price that makes it worthwhile or valuable to them.

Encouraging creativity and innovation involves the process of being creative (or "thinking outside the box"), as well as harnessing that creativity to generate the innovations that keep the company one step ahead of the competition. Danger exists when the company becomes comfortable with its level of success, as it might resist the change needed to stay ahead. But remember, there are only two kinds of businesses—those that constantly innovate and those that go out of business. In today's business world, one of the only constants is change. The status quo doesn't work any more. Companies need to become "learning organizations," proactively seeking to learn and move ahead every day in everything they do.

And finally, probably the most important success factor is *gaining employee commitment.* Employees need to be empowered to act and motivated to meet the company's objectives in each of the first four factors, or those objectives won't be met. Therefore, every company needs to understand the needs of its employees.

Only then can it gain their commitment, for they will be committed to meeting the goals of the company only if their own goals are met at the same time. It is, again, an integrative relationship.

Underneath the critical success factors are the *stakeholders* of the business. These are individuals and groups that have a "stake" in what the business does. They are affected by the decisions that the business makes, and therefore the business has a responsibility to consider them in those decisions.

The three most critical and obvious stakeholder groups are the owners of the business (or shareholders in the case of a corporation), the employees of the business (and their union if represented by one), and the customers. But there is a much wider world out there that must be considered—the government, special interest groups, the community surrounding the business, its suppliers, and so on. All of these groups interact with the business and keep it operating.

The business cannot operate in a vacuum, as if these groups did not exist. They must be considered in every decision the business makes. If we change this material, how will our customers react? Will they keep buying our product? If we move the business, how will it affect the community? How many employees will we lose? If we cut down these trees to build the new plant, how will the environmentalist groups respond? How will the community and the local government respond? If earnings drop in the fourth quarter as expected, will our shareholders sell their shares, making the share price fall even lower? Achieving the critical success factors clearly depends on an intimate knowledge of and relationship with the stakeholders of the business.

It is primarily *top management's* external focus that keeps the business looking at the stakeholders. It is the responsibility of the top management of the company to look outward and chart a course for the company. They examine the external environment of the business and match the threats and opportunities in the external environment with both the expectations of the stakeholders and the strengths and weaknesses of the company, to determine the direction the company should take in the future—their *vision* for the future of the company. This is further refined into a *mission* statement for the company. Next they determine the *strategy* for the company to pursue to achieve this mission—how to go about achieving the company's goals in the future.

For example, perhaps opportunities exist in the external environment to take the company global. Perhaps needs exist within foreign countries for the type of product the company sells, and little competition exists from other firms at the present time. If the company has the internal marketing, operations, human, and financial strength to achieve this objective, then top management might determine that the vision for the future of the company is to make it a strong global competitor. The strategy would then need to take into account such decisions as what countries to enter first, whether to search out foreign firms with which to form a joint venture, and whether to pursue a licensing arrangement with a foreign firm or build its own plants.

It is then *middle management's* job within each of the functional areas of the business to determine and plan out what each area needs to do to help achieve this overall corporate strategy. For example, what type of marketing campaigns will be most successful in these new foreign markets? Do we build new plants or lease/purchase and renovate existing plants? What new skills and attributes are needed to staff our operations in these new foreign markets? Where will the money come from, and how will the budgets be realigned?

First-line management manages the workers that do the actual work in each of the functional areas. It is their job to make sure the plans at the higher levels are implemented, and—most important—by committed workers who are motivated to achieve the goals of the company.

Top managers, middle managers, and first-line managers are responsible for managing the company and its employees to ensure that all five of the critical success factors are achieved. They do this by

- *planning* what the goals are (to achieve the critical success factors) and how to achieve them,
- *organizing* the resources of the company—human, physical, and financial—to achieve the goals,
- *motivating* the workers to gain their commitment to the goals, and then
- *measuring* results and making any changes necessary to continue to steer the company in the direction of the goals, thus maintaining control over the achievement of these five critical success factors.

This is the model we will use in this text to help you integrate the different topics covered into an understanding of how a successful business works as a whole. By studying the topics presented in this textbook, you will gain a solid foundation on which to build your further understanding of successful business practices.

Prologue

Fast Forward to the Future: Strategies for Success in School and Business

Your Future in Business: Begin with a Diploma or Degree

What makes someone a winner in life? Winners are people who go through the various stages of life content in knowing that they have done their best. Their best at work, at home, and in all pursuits of life. And a big part of having a happy life is pursuing a career that offers job satisfaction and financial rewards. If you are going to "be all that you can be," you need a good education.

A diploma or degree unlocks doors to economic opportunity. Why get a diploma or degree?

- *Get and keep a better job.* Because the world is changing rapidly, and many jobs rely on new technology, more jobs require education beyond high school. With a postsecondary education, you will have more jobs from which to choose.

- *Earn more money.* People who go to postsecondary institutions usually earn more than those who do not. For example, currently a bachelor's degree is worth a minimum of $25,000 a year more than a high school diploma. If your career spans 45 years, you will earn $1,125,000 more than a high school graduate!

- *Get a good start in life.* A postsecondary education helps you acquire a wide range of knowledge in many subjects as well as an advanced understanding of your specialized area of business. Postsecondary institutions also train you to express your thoughts clearly in speech and in writing and to make informed decisions.

Simply stated, a diploma or degree gives you the chance to achieve the quality of life you deserve. The lifestyle, the new friends, the purchasing power of a diploma or degree won't guarantee happiness but will put you well on the road to finding it.

LEARNING THE BASICS OF BUSINESS

You might want to pursue a career as a physician, florist, game warden, systems analyst, or any of a thousand other opportunities. One thing that all careers have in common is that you need to have a basic understanding of business. Your success in whatever you choose will depend partially on your basic business skills. And that is why this course is so important.

Few courses present all the fundamental areas of business and then link them together the way this course does. This is where you get the big picture as well as an introduction to fundamental components of business. Learn it well, because it will be invaluable throughout your life.

CHOOSING A CAREER

Because this course gives you a detailed overview of all of the areas of business, it will guide you in selecting a major should you select to get a diploma or degree in business. Choosing a major is one of life's true milestones. Your major essentially determines how you will spend the next four decades of your life!

A marketing major will find a career in sales, marketing research, advertising, or other marketing-related field. An accounting major (you guessed it) will become an accountant. Never take selecting a major lightly. If you work 40 hours a week for the next 45 years (less vacations), you will put in about 90,000 hours on the job. Don't you think that you should choose something that you will enjoy?

Success in Business: Improving Your Interpersonal Skills

A diploma or degree in business is going to offer you many great career opportunities. Once you take your first job, how rapidly you move up the ladder is up to you. People with great interpersonal skills will always do better on and off the job than those who lack them. It has been estimated that up to 95 percent of our workplace success depends on an understanding of other people.[1] Here's how to enhance your interpersonal skills:

1. *Build your people skills.* Learn to build alliances in a group and establish harmony. Make a concerted effort to know what is happening in the lives of those on your team at school and work. About once a month get together with your group and pass out a list of issues, concerns, fears, and potential problems. Then invite everyone to give input to solve little problems before they become big. If something goes wrong, try to find out where things are not running smoothly and improve them. Be sure to compliment someone in your group who is doing an exemplary job.

2. *Become a good listener.* When you listen well, you are, in effect, telling the other person that he or she is worth listening to. Listening well includes listening to both what is said and what is not said. Learn to read unspoken gestures and expressions. When giving feedback, plan what you will say in advance. Be positive and be specific. Ask the person receiving the feedback if he or she would like to discuss your comments further.

3. *Understand how to persuade others.* Remember, we all must sell ourselves and our ideas to get ahead in life and business. Influencing others means overcoming objectives, igniting passions, or changing minds. The first step is to build *esprit de corps*, a shared enthusiasm and devotion to the group. Make your vision their vision, so that everyone is working toward a common goal. Praise the team as a whole, but recognize the unique contributions different team members have made. The trick is to praise everyone, yet for different reasons. When you and your team successfully solve a problem, change will result.

Persuasion rests on trust. You can build trust by being honest, fulfilling your commitments, being concerned about others, and minimizing problems and pain for others whenever possible. In short, if you have integrity, building trust becomes a simple task.

When people raise objections to your plans or ideas, try to understand fully their comments and their motivation for making them. When you feel that you understand the true objection, answer the objection in the form of a benefit: "Yes, you will need to work next Saturday, but then you can have compensatory time off anytime you wish next month."

4. *Learn to think on your feet.* Top executives, like former Chrysler Chairman Lee Iacocca, say that "speaking well on your feet" is the best thing that you can do for your career. If you cannot quickly express yourself with confidence, others will lose confidence in you.

It will not happen overnight, but you can become an outstanding thinker and speaker. A simple technique is to set a timer for two minutes and ask a friend to begin speaking. When the timer goes off, your friend stops speaking and you begin talking. The challenge is to use the final thought that your friend spoke as the first word of your two-minute talk. Another technique is to have someone supply you with a series of quotes. Then, without hesitation, give your interpretation.

5. *Empower yourself.* No matter who you are, what position you will hold, or where you will work, you probably will have to report to somebody. If you are fortunate enough to work in a culture of empowerment, you will be allowed control over your job (not complete control, but enough to make you feel your opinion matters). When you are not given an opportunity to provide input, you will eventually lose interest in your job. When empowered, you have the confidence to do something to alter your circumstances. On the job, empowerment means that you can make decisions to benefit the organization and its customers.

If you want to gain empowerment in your life and work, here are a few tips: Be assertive, ask for credit for yourself when it is due, propose ideas to your group and your supervisor, initiate projects without being asked, tie your personal goals to those of the organization, develop your leadership skills, plan to learn on a continuing basis, be informed, don't let others intimidate you, and don't complain about a bad situation. Instead, take action to improve it.

6. *Acquire political savvy.* Politics is an inevitable part of every organization in Canada, including your school. Politics has always been a part of the workplace and always will be. The trick is to learn to play the political game to your own advantage and to the advantage of others without causing harm to anyone else. Being political means getting along with others to move them toward accomplishing a specific goal. It does not mean manoeuvring for selfish purposes, manipulating to deceive, or scheming so that others lose while you win.

Here are some tips and techniques for being an effective player in the political game.

- *Think about what you say.* Understand the effect your words will have on others before you say or write them.
- *Empathize.* Try to think of a situation from the other person's perspective.
- *Suggest a trial period, if you meet opposition to an idea you're proposing.* If you are as successful as you are confident, you can then ask to have the trial period extended.
- *Learn about the political climate in which you are working.* This means knowing, among other things, what actions have led to failure for others, knowing who is "in" and why, determining who is "out" and why, and learning what behaviours lead to promotion.
- *Volunteer to do the jobs no one else wants to do.* Occasionally pitching in shows your willingness to get the job done. However, do not make this your trademark; you do not want others to think they can take advantage of you.
- *Work hard to meet the needs of those in authority.* Make certain you fully understand management's requirements; then go out of your way to meet them. If in time you do not think you are getting the recognition or respect you deserve, make your own needs known.

If you are asked to lead a team, you will need to involve all members in discussions, know how to manage conflict, understand team dynamics, and assess the team's success.

- *Give credit.* You never know who might be in a position to hurt or harm you. Consequently, the best policy is to treat everyone with respect and dignity. Show your appreciation to everyone who has helped you. Don't steal credit that belongs to someone else.
- *Learn your supervisor's preferences.* The more you are in sync with your supervisor's style, wishes, and preferences, the better you can do your job. However, don't be a rubber stamp. Rather, work the way your manager works. When necessary, suggest better ways of doing things.
- *Keep secrets—your own and others'.* Resist the temptation to tell all. Not only do you run the risk of being labelled a gossip, but if you share too much about yourself, your words can come back to haunt you. If you are revealing information told to you in confidence, you are bound to lose the trust and respect of those who originally confided in you.

7. *Become a team builder.* Throughout your postsecondary and business career, you will participate on teams. Most Canadian business organizations employ teamwork. An effective team is one that meets its goals on time and, if a budget is involved, within budget. The first step in creating an effective team is to have goals that are clear, realistic, supported by each team member, and parallel the larger organization goals. We have listed the questions that teams should answer to ensure their success.

8. *Handle conflict well.* Let's face it. The world is not a perfect place, and there are no perfect people inhabiting it. The best we can hope for is people's willingness to improve life's circumstances. If we are truly committed to the idea of reducing school and workplace conflict, there is much we can do to inspire such willingness in others. Bringing conflict into the open has its advantages. Talking about conflict often helps to clear the air, and thinking about the possibility of conflict often helps to avoid it.

Key Questions That Teams Should Answer before Starting a Project

1. What are the goals?
2. Who provides the mission statement?
3. What are our limits?
4. Where will support come from? Who will be our sponsor?
5. Who will be team leader? How is he or she selected?
6. What are the deadlines we face?
7. What resources are available?
8. What data will we need to collect?
9. For how long will our team exist?
10. Who are the customers for our team results? What do they expect of us?
11. Will our team responsibilities conflict with our regular jobs?
12. What is the reward for success?
13. How will decisions be made?
14. How will our efforts be measured?
15. Will our intended success be replicated? If so, how and by whom?

When conflicts occur, try the K-I-N-D technique. The letters stand for

K = Kind

I = Informed

N = New

D = Definite

As an example, this technique can be used when requesting a meeting with a difficult person, whether he or she is having a conflict with you or with others. Start off with kind words, words that encourage cooperation, words that show your determination to make the conflict situation better. Next, demonstrate that you have taken the time to learn more about the person, what is important to him or her, and what he or she prefers in terms of work. Show by your words that you have taken the time to become informed about the individual.

The third step requires you to do something novel, something you have not tried before. Put your creativity to work, and discover a plan to which you can both subscribe (for example, keeping a journal regarding the problem and possible solutions).

Finally, do not permit the exchange to conclude until you have made a definite overture to ensure future success. What can you promise the other person you will do differently? What are you asking him or her to do differently? Set a time to meet again and review your individual attempts to achieve collective improvement.

Make Your Future Happen: Learn to Plan²

There is a natural conflict between planning and being impulsive, between pursuing a long-range goal and doing what you feel like doing right now. If you have ever had to study while the rest of the family was in the living room watching television, you know what that conflict feels like. If you have ever been invited to go to the mall to eat pizza and hang out with friends but stayed home to work on a class assignment, you know that sticking to a plan is not easy.

Of course, planning and being impulsive are both good. Each has a place in your life, you need to balance them. Having a plan does not mean that you can't act on the spur of the moment and do something that was not planned. Spontaneous events produce some of the happiest, most meaningful times of your life. Problems arise only when you consistently substitute impulsive actions for goal-oriented planning. Success in life requires a balance between the two.

If you do not engage in long-range planning and lack the discipline for it, you might limit your opportunities to be impulsive. You are not going to take a weekend fun trip just because you need a break, if you haven't saved the money to do it. In the short run, planning involves sacrifice, but in the long run, it gives you more options.

WHAT IS A PLAN?

A plan is a method or process worked out in advance that leads to the achievement of some goal. A plan is systematic, which means it relies on using a step-by-step procedure. A plan also needs to be flexible, so that it can be adapted to gradual changes in your goal.

THE PLANNING PROCESS

Whether choosing a postsecondary institution or finding financial aid, you should understand how the planning process helps you accomplish your goals. The following steps outline the planning process.

Step 1: Set a goal. Identify something you want to achieve or obtain: your goal. The goal, which is usually longer term in nature, will require planning, patience, and discipline to achieve. Just living in the present moment is not a goal.

Step 2: Acquire knowledge. Gain an understanding of your goal and what will be required to achieve it. Gather information about your goal through research, conversation, and thought.

Step 3: Compare alternatives. Weigh your options, which are the different paths you might take to achieve your goal. Analyze the pluses and minuses of each—the costs, the demands, and the likelihood of success.

Step 4: Choose a strategy. Select one option as the best plan of action. The choice is based on sound information, the experience of others, and your own interests and abilities.

Step 5: Make a commitment. Resolve to proceed step-by-step toward achieving your goal. Keep your eyes on the prize.

Step 6: Stay flexible. Evaluate your progress and, when necessary, revise your plan to deal with changing circumstances and new opportunities.

AN EXAMPLE OF PLANNING

The following example illustrates the process of buying a new stereo using this planning process.

Step 1: Set a goal. Purchase a wireless media player.

Step 2: Acquire knowledge. Visit friends to hear their systems. Study standards and specifications. Check on dealers, brands, models, and prices. Consult various consumer reports.

Step 3: Compare alternatives.

Alternative 1: Purchase a stereo from an on-line auction such as eBay.

Pro: Affordable high-end equipment. Can buy right now.

Con: Uncertain condition of equipment. Limited warranty.

Alternative 2: Buy a compact shelf system for $325.

Pro: Can afford now. New equipment with warranty.

Con: Unsuitable for adding extra speakers or using with television. Not the best sound quality.

Alternative 3: Buy a high-quality component system for $775.

Pro: Excellent sound. Greatest flexibility. New equipment with warranty.

Con: Costs more than prepared to pay now.

Step 4: Choose a strategy. Decide to buy the high-quality system but, rather than use a credit card and paying interest, will delay the purchase for six months to save for it.

Step 5: Make a commitment. Give up going to the movies for the six-month period, carry a lunch and stop eating out, and place the savings in a stereo fund.

Step 6: Keep flexible. Four months into the plan, a model change sale provides an opportunity to buy comparable equipment for $550. Make the purchase, paying cash.

PLANNING FOR YOUR LIFE

Using the planning process to make a buying decision is a simple exercise. Making a decision about major parts of your life is far more complex. You will see that no part of life is exempt from the need for planning. It is important to apply thought, creativity, and discipline to all the interrelated phases of our lives. These phases include the following.

Career. Choosing a field of work and developing the knowledge and skills needed to enter and move ahead in that field. We will offer you some tips to get started on a great career later in the Prologue.

Every aspect of your life deserves some type of planning. One decision you will need to make is how to spend your time and money. Will volunteering be one of your priorities?

Self. Deciding who you are and what kind of person you want to be, working to develop your strengths and overcome your weaknesses, and refining your values.

Lifestyle. Expressing yourself in the nature and quality of your everyday life, your recreation and hobbies, and how you use your time and money.

Relationships. Developing friendships and learning to get along with people in a variety of contexts. Building family and community ties.

Finances. Building the financial resources and the economic security needed to pursue all the other dimensions of your life.

Dreams and Plans

People are natural dreamers. Dreams give us pleasure. They are also part of making a future. If you don't have dreams or think that you are not worthy of dreaming, something very important might be missing from your life. You have a right to your dreams, and you need them—even if there is little possibility that they will ever come true.

Planning is not the same as dreaming, but it uses dreams as raw materials. It translates them into specific goals. It tests them. It lays out a course of action that moves you toward realizing these goals and sets up milestones you need to achieve. Planning brings dreams down to earth and turns them into something real and attainable. For example, assume you have a dream to visit Spain as an exchange student. To translate this dream into a specific goal, you will need to follow the planning process—gather information about the exchange process, discuss the program with parents and teachers, and improve your Spanish-language skills.

Directions for Your Life

One of the best things about pursuing your dreams is that even when you fall short, the effort leads to growth and opens a path to other opportunities. The person who practices the piano every day might not achieve the dream of becoming a concert pianist but might eventually put appreciation of music to work as the director of an arts organization. A hockey player might not make it to a professional team but might enjoy a satisfying career as a coach or a sportswriter. Without a plan, dreams simply dissolve. With a plan, they give shape and direction to our lives.

Planning involves a lot of thinking and finding answers to lots of questions. The answers, and even the plan, will change over time as you gain more knowledge and life experience. Planning is a skill that is useful in every area of your life. It is something you have to pursue consciously and thoughtfully. When you plan, you translate your goals and dreams into step-by-step strategies, specific things you can do to test your goals and bring them to reality. You often have to revise your plans, but even when your plans are not fulfilled, planning will have a positive effect on the course of your life.

Going to a Postsecondary Institution Is an Opportunity of a Lifetime—Grab It, and Don't Let Go[3]

You have already had one of your dreams come true—you are in a postsecondary institution. It is, indeed, a rare privilege, because far less than 1 percent of traditional postsecondary-age people around the world get to attend a postsecondary institution. You're lucky! So make the best of it by learning the following skills.

LEARN TO CONCENTRATE

Concentration is the art of being focused, the ability to pay attention. Without concentration, you have no memory of what you hear, see, and read. Concentration is a frame of mind that enables you to stay centred on the activity or work you are doing. You know when you're concentrating, because time seems to go by quickly, distractions that normally take you off task don't bother you, and you have a lot of mental or physical energy for the task.

You are ultimately in charge of how well you concentrate. Here are some ways to make it happen.

- *Choose a workplace.* Avoid the bed—you associate it with relaxing or sleeping. Try a desk or table for studying; you will concentrate better and accomplish more in less time. You will also have a convenient writing space and plenty of space to spread out. Be sure to have good lighting.

- *Feed your body right.* What you eat plays an important role in how well or how poorly you concentrate. Protein foods (such as cheese, meat, fish, and vegetables) keep the mind alert, whereas carbohydrates (such as pasta, bread, and processed sugars) make you sleepy. Caffeine (commonly found in coffee, tea, soft drinks, and chocolate) acts as a stimulant in low doses.

- *Avoid food.* Food and serious learning don't mix well. Think about it. When you try to eat and study at the same time, which gets more of your concentration? The food, of course! You will be more effective if you eat first and then study.

- *Listen to your thoughts.* Listening to anything but your own thoughts interferes with good concentration. Eliminating distractions such as music, television, cell phones, e-mail beeps, and other people can greatly increase the amount of studying you can accomplish. Hold all calls, and let e-mail wait.

Choose a study location that is free from distractions, so you can concentrate better and accomplish more in less time.

- *Make a to-do list.* If you are trying to study but get distracted by all of the things you need to do, take time to make a to-do list. Keeping track of your thoughts on paper and referring to the paper from time to time can be very effective for clearing your mind and focusing on your task.
- *Take short, frequent breaks.* Since people concentrate for about 20 minutes or less at a time, it would make sense to capitalize on your natural body rhythms and take a short break every 20 to 30 minutes. If you feel you are fully concentrating and involved in a task, then work until a natural break occurs.

LEARN TO MANAGE YOUR TIME

There are two ways to make sure you have more time in a day. *The first and most important way to gain more time is to plan it!* It's like getting in a car and going somewhere. You need to know where you are going and have a plan to get there. Without a plan, you will waste your time and take longer to get to your destination—if you get there at all!

A **weekly project planner** will allow you to keep track of your assignments in more detail. It contains a to-do list specific to one day. It looks like a calendar but is divided into five one-day periods with plenty of space to write. Using a weekly project planner is an effective way of keeping track of assignments and planning study time according to the school calendar. Free calendars are available at **http://www.calendar.yahoo.com.**

A second way to gain more time in a day is to do more in less time. This can be as simple as doubling up on activities. For example, if you have three errands, you might try to combine them instead of doing one at a time, making one round-trip instead of three. If you commute on a bus or train, or carpool, you can study during your ride. At lunch, you can review notes. Use your imagination as to how you can get more done in less time.

Here are some ideas to help you master your time.

- *Prepare for the morning the evening before.* Put out your clothes, make lunches, and pack your books.
- *Get up 15 minutes earlier in the morning.* Use the time to plan your day, review your assignments, or catch up on the news.
- *Schedule a realistic day.* Avoid planning for every minute. Leave extra time in your day for getting to appointments and studying.
- *Leave room in your day for the unexpected.* This will allow you to do what you need to do, regardless of what happens. If the unexpected never happens, you will have more time for yourself.
- *Do one thing at a time.* If you try to do two things at once, you become inefficient. Concentrate on the here and now.
- *Learn to say "No!"* Say no to social activities or invitations when you don't have the time or energy.

SOLVE THE MONEY PROBLEM

You can get postsecondary money from three different sources.

- *Grants and scholarships.* This refers to aid you do not have to repay. Grants are usually based on need, whereas scholarships are frequently based on academic merit and other qualifying factors.

- *Student loans.* The mission of the Canada Student Loans Program (CSLP) is to promote accessibility to postsecondary education for students with a demonstrated financial need by lowering financial barriers through the provision of loans and grants, and to ensure that Canadians have an opportunity to develop the knowledge and skills to participate in the economy and society.
- *Work aid.* This is financial aid you have to work for, frequently 10 or 15 hours a week on campus.

There are many ways to cut the cost of going to a postsecondary institution. Consider:

- going to a community college for the first two years and then transferring to a four-year institution,
- attending a nearby postsecondary institution and living at home,
- enrolling in one of the postsecondary institutions that offer cooperative educational programs that alternate between full-time studies and full-time employment, or
- taking a full-time job at a company that offers free educational opportunities as a fringe benefit.

Check with your postsecondary institution for the various sources of financial aid that are available to you.

STUDY SMART

The first key to doing well in a subject is completing your assignments on time. Most instructors base their assignments on what they will be discussing in class on a given day. Therefore, if you read the pages you are assigned for the day they are due, you will understand the day's lecture better. If you don't complete an assignment when it is due, not only will you be at a disadvantage in the class, you will also have twice as much work to do for the following class.

Second, know what material to study. This might sound simple, but all too often, students don't ask what material they should study and find out too late that they studied the wrong information. The easiest and most accurate way to learn what will be covered on a test is to ask your instructor or read the syllabus.

Tests measure your working memory and knowledge base. To help yourself remember, you can use several **memory devices** to recall the information you need to study. Here are a few that have been proven to work:

- *Recite information using your own words.* You will learn more when you reinforce your learning in as many ways as possible. You can reinforce your learning through hearing, writing, reading, reviewing, and reciting.
- *Develop acronyms.* **Acronyms** are words or names formed from the first letters or groups of letters in a phrase. Acronyms help you remember, because they organize information according to the way you need or want to learn it. When you study for a test, be creative and make up your own acronyms. For example, COD means "cash on delivery," and GDP refers to "gross domestic product."
- *Try mnemonic sentences, rhymes, or jingles.* **Mnemonic sentences** are similar to acronyms; they help you organize your ideas, but instead of creating a word, you make up a sentence. Creating a rhyme, song, or jingle can make the information even easier to remember. The more creative and silly the sentence, the easier it is to remember. For example, if you are learning to read sheet music, the notes on the lines of the treble clef are EGBDF—you could remember this as Every Good Boy Deserves Fudge.

- *Visualize.* Visualization refers to creating or recalling mental pictures related to what you are learning. Have you ever tried to remember something while taking a test and visualized the page the information was on? This is your visual memory at work. Approximately 90 percent of your memory is stored visually in pictures, so visualizing what you want to remember is a powerful study tool.

BECOME A MASTER AT TAKING TESTS

Taking a formal test is like playing a game. The object is to get as many points as possible in the time that you are allowed. Tests are evaluations of what you know and what you can do with what you know. Here are the rules of the test-taking game:

Rule 1: Act as if you will succeed. Thought is powerful. When you think negative thoughts, your stress level rises. Your confidence level might drop, which often leads to feelings of failure. When this happens, think about success. Smile and take deep, slow breaths. Close your eyes, and imagine getting the test back with a good grade written at the top.

Rule 2: Arrive ahead of time. Being on time or early for a test sets your mind at ease. You will have a better chance of getting your favourite seat, relaxing, and preparing yourself mentally for the game ahead.

Rule 3: Bring the essential testing tools. Don't forget to bring the necessary testing tools along with you, including extra pens, sharpened pencils, erasers, a calculator, a dictionary, and other items you might need.

Rule 4: Ignore panic pushers. Some people become nervous before a test and hit the panic button, afraid they don't know the material. **Panic pushers** are people who ask you questions about the material they are about to be tested on. If you know the answers, you will feel confident; however, if you don't, you might panic and lose your confidence. Instead of talking with a panic pusher before a test, spend your time concentrating on what you know, not on what you don't know.

Rule 5: Preview the playing field. Here's how to do a preview.

- **Listen to instructions,** and **read directions carefully.**
- Determine the point spread. Look at the total number of questions and the point value of each. Decide how much time you can spend on each question and still finish the test on time.
- Budget your time. If you budget your time and stick to your time limits, you will always complete the test in the amount of time given.
- Use the test as an information tool. Be on the lookout for clues that answer other questions. Frequently, instructors will test you on a single topic in more than one way.

Rule 6: Write in the margin. Before you begin the test, write key terms, formulas, names, dates, and other information in the margin, so you don't forget them.

Rule 7: Complete the easy questions first. Answering easy questions first helps build your confidence. If you come across a tough question, mark it so you can come back to it later. Avoid spending so much time on a challenging question that you run out of time to answer the questions you do know.

Rule 8: Know if there is a guessing penalty. Chances are your tests will carry no penalty for guessing. If your time is about to run out and there is no penalty, take a wild guess. On the other hand, if your test carries a penalty for guessing, choose your answers wisely, and leave blank the answers you do not know.

Rule 9: Avoid changing your answers. Have you ever chosen an answer, changed it, and learned later that your first choice was correct? Research indicates that three out of four times, your first answer will be correct; therefore, you should avoid changing an answer unless you are absolutely sure the answer is wrong.

Rule 10: Write clearly and neatly. If you are handwriting your test (versus using a computer), imagine your instructor reading your writing. Is it easy to read or difficult? The easier your test is for the instructor to read, the better your chances of getting a higher grade.

Here are some Web sites to help you learn more about taking tests:

- *Essay tests and a checklist for essay tests*
  http://www.calpoly.edu/~sas/asc/ael/tests.essay.html
- *Checklist for essay tests*
  http://www.mtsu.edu/~studskl/essay.html
- *General test taking*
  http://www.calpoly.edu/~sas/asc/ael/tests.general.html
- *Post-test analysis*
  http://www.calpoly.edu/~sas/asc/ael/tests.post.test.analysis.html
- *Objective tests*

Getting Your Career Off on the Right Track

Mark this section of the text with a permanent bookmark, because you are going to want to refer back to it many times during the remainder of your postsecondary institution career. Yes, we are going to give you a roadmap to find, keep, and advance in that job that is perfect for you.

THINK POSITIVELY

To be successful in life and in a career, you need to be positive. Positive thinking is making a conscious effort to think with an optimistic attitude and to anticipate positive outcomes. *Positive behaviour* means purposely acting with energy and enthusiasm. When you think and behave positively, you guide your mind toward your goals and generate matching mental and physical energy.

Positive thinking and behaviour are often deciding factors in landing top jobs: your first job, a promotion, a change of jobs—whatever career step you are targeting. That's because the subconscious is literal; it accepts what you regard as fact.

Follow these steps to form the habit of positive thinking and to boost your success.

1. *Deliberately motivate yourself every day.* Think of yourself as successful, and expect positive outcomes for everything you attempt.

2. *Project energy and enthusiasm.* Employers hire people who project positive energy and enthusiasm. Develop the habit of speaking, moving, and acting with these qualities.

3. *Practice this positive expectation mind-set until it becomes a habit.* Applicants who project enthusiasm and positive behaviour generate a positive chemistry

that rubs off. Hiring decisions are influenced largely by this positive energy. The habit will help you reach your peak potential.

4. *Dwell on past successes.* Focusing on past successes to remind yourself of your abilities helps in attaining goals. For example, no one is born knowing how to ride a bicycle or how to use a computer software program. Through training, practice, and trial and error, you master new abilities. During the trial-and-error phases of development, remind yourself of past successes; look at mistakes as part of the natural learning curve. Continue until you achieve the result you want, and remind yourself that you have succeeded in the past and can do so again. You fail only when you quit trying![4]

TAKE A GOOD LOOK AT YOURSELF

Once you've developed a positive, "can do" attitude, the next step is to understand yourself better. Ask yourself two basic questions: "Who am I?" and "What can I do?"

Who Am I? The first step is to ask "Who am I?" This question is the start of *self-assessment,* examining your likes and dislikes and basic values. You might want to ask yourself the following questions:

- Do I want to help society?
- Do I want to help make the world a better place?
- Do I want to help other people directly?
- Is it important for me to be seen as part of a big corporation?
- Do I prefer working indoors or outdoors?
- Do I like to meet new people, or do I want to work alone?

What Can I Do? After determining what your values are, take the second step in career planning by asking, "What can I do?" This question is the start of *skill assessment,* evaluating your key abilities and characteristics for dealing successfully with problems, tasks, and interactions with other people. Many skills—for instance, the ability to speak clearly and strongly—are valuable in many occupations.

Part-time jobs can teach you valuable business skills that will make you more attractive to employers. Choose a job, if possible, that gives you experience related to your chosen field.

© AP / WIDE WORLD PHOTOS

Be sure to consider the work experience you already have, including part-time jobs while going to school, summer jobs, volunteer jobs, and internships (short-term jobs for students, related to their major field of study). These jobs teach you skills and make you more attractive to potential employers. It's never too early or too late to take a part-time job in your chosen field. For instance, someone with an interest in accounting would do well to try a part-time job with an accountancy firm.

In addition to examining your job-related skills, you should also look at your leisure activities. Some possible questions: Am I good at golf? Do I enjoy sailing? Tennis? Racquetball? In some businesses, transactions are made during leisure hours. In that case, being able to play a skillful, or at least adequate, game of golf or tennis might be an asset.

It's hard to like your job if you don't like the field that you're in. Most career counsellors agree that finding work you're passionate about is one of the critical factors behind career success. That's why so many career counsellors love all those diagnostic tools that measure your personality traits, skill levels, professional interests, and job potential.

The Web is virtually exploding with tests and assessments that you can take. Try, for example, **http://www.self-directed-search.com.** This test is based on the theory that people and work environments can be classified into six basic types: realistic, investigative, artistic, social, enterprising, and conventional. The test determines which three types best describe you, and it suggests occupations that could be a good match. The **Keirsey Character Sorter** (**http://www.keirsey.com**) is a first cousin of Myers-Briggs. It sorts people into four temperaments: idealists, rationalists, artisans, and guardians. Like Myers-Briggs, it not only places you in an overall category but also offers a more detailed evaluation of your personality traits. To find a bunch of tests in one place, visit **Yahoo!** and type "on-line personality tests" in the search field.

UNDERSTAND WHAT EMPLOYERS WANT[5]

Employers want to hire people who will make their businesses more successful. The most desirable employees have the specific skills, transferable career competencies, work values, and personal qualities necessary to be successful in the employers' organizations. The more clearly you convey your skills as they relate to your job target, the greater your chance of landing your ideal job.

Job-specific skills. Employers seek job-specific skills (skills and technical abilities that relate specifically to a particular job). Two examples of job-specific skills are using specialized tools and equipment and using a custom-designed software program.

Transferable skills and attitudes. Change is a constant in today's business world. Strong transferable career skills are the keys to success in managing your career through change. The most influential skills and attitudes are the abilities to

- work well with people,
- plan and manage multiple tasks,
- maintain a positive attitude, and
- show enthusiasm.

Employers need workers who have transferable career competencies—basic skills and attitudes that are important for all types of work. These skills make you highly marketable, because they're needed for a wide variety of jobs and can be transferred from one task, job, or workplace to another. Examples include

- planning skills,
- research skills,
- communication skills,

- human relations and interpersonal skills,
- critical thinking skills, and
- management skills.

Take, for example, a construction supervisor and an accountant. Both must work well with others, manage time, solve problems, read, and communicate effectively—all transferable competencies. They both must be competent in these areas, even though framing a house and balancing a set of books (the job-specific skill for each field, respectively) are not related. In every occupation, transferable competencies are as important as technical expertise and job-specific skills.[6]

FINDING MY FIRST PROFESSIONAL JOB

The next step is landing the job that fits your skills and desires. You need to consider not only a general type of work but also your lifestyle and leisure goals. If you like to be outdoors most of the time, you might be very unhappy spending eight hours a day in an office. Someone who likes living in small towns might dislike working at the headquarters of a big corporation in Toronto, Calgary, or Vancouver. But make sure that your geographic preferences are realistic. Some parts of the country will experience much greater growth in jobs than others.

You might start answering the question "What will I do" by searching various Internet sites that offer job counselling or job offers.

USING THE INTERNET TO JUMP-START YOUR JOB SEARCH

You must start with a great résumé—a written description of your education, work experience, personal data, and interests. Professional Web résumé software (available through http://webresume.com) can make the task a lot easier. WebResume software not only helps you format your résumé but also lets you control who sees it. A "confidential" option enables you to create a two-tiered résumé. The first tier offers professional information but doesn't include your name or address. The second contains contact information but is password protected—and you decide who can get the password. WebResume understands what's different about looking for a job on-line. Its "Search Engine Keywords" function inserts the "tags" that major search engines use to index résumés. We offer seven tips for preparing your cyber résumé.

Once you have created a great résumé, the next step is to get it noticed. Here are a few tips for getting noticed.

- Post a digital version of your résumé with examples of past work experience on your own home page. Many postsecondary institutions and professional associations offer free or low-cost Web space and resources for posting résumés.
- Place the word *résumé* in the Web site address to increase your chances of being caught by Internet recruiters.
- Place plenty of links to Web sites of present and former employers, postsecondary institutions, professional associations, and publications on your digital résumé.
- Create a simpler version of your résumé to send to a recruiter or potential employer, and let them know a longer version is available.
- Read the privacy policies of on-line job boards to prevent unwanted eyes from viewing your résumé. Some companies have "Web scavengers," who check for

their own employees' résumés on-line. In turn, some job boards let users "block" certain companies from seeing their postings.

- Use niche job boards in your field. Smaller, targeted boards can sometimes be more effective than the big brand-name sites.[7]

There are thousands of places to send your résumé. Don't neglect using the Internet; 83 percent of the corporate recruiters use the Internet to advertise their jobs.[8]

OH MY GOSH—I'VE GOT A JOB INTERVIEW

If some of the companies you contacted want to speak with you, your résumé achieved its goal of getting you a job interview. Look at the interview as a chance to describe your knowledge and skills and interpret them in terms of the employer's specific needs. To make this kind of presentation, you need to do some research on the company. A great place to start looking is **http://www.hoovers.com.** This site offers profiles and financial data on more than 12,000 companies worldwide. It also provides links to other sites where you can dig further. Hoovers.com allows you to search for companies by

- company name,
- geographic location,
- industry,
- stock index, or
- news stories.

As you do your information search, you should build your knowledge in these three areas.

1. *General information about the industry.* Learn about the current and predicted industry trends, general educational requirements, job descriptions, growth outlook, and salary ranges in the industry.

Tips for Preparing Your Cyber Résumé

- Use key words to define your skills, experience, education, professional affiliations, and so on.
- Use concrete words rather than vague descriptions to describe your experience. For example, use "managed a team of software engineers" rather than "responsible for managing and training."
- Be concise and truthful.
- Use jargon and acronyms specific to your industry (spell out the acronyms for a human reader).
- Increase your list of key words by including specifics. For example, list the names of software that you use, such as Microsoft Word.

- Use common headings, such as Objective, Experience, Work History, Skills, Education, Professional Affiliations, Licenses, and References.
- Describe your interpersonal traits and attitude. Key words can include *dependable, high energy, leadership, sense of responsibility,* and *good memory.*

SOURCE: "Resume Tool Kit," http://www.thespectrum.com (accessed January 2003).

One-on-one interviews are the most common type and might include interviews with managers in different departments. Showing enthusiasm and interest in the job projects a positive impression.

© DIGITAL VISION / GETTY IMAGES

2. *Information about prospective employers.* Learn whether the organization is publicly or privately owned. Verify company names, addresses, products or services (current and predicted, as well as trends); history; culture; reputation; performance; divisions and subsidiaries; locations (Canada and global); predicted growth indicators; number of employees; company philosophies and procedures; predicted job openings; salary ranges; and listings of managers of your targeted department within the organization. Also learn about the competitors and customers.

3. *Information about specific jobs.* Obtain job descriptions; identify the required education and experience; and determine prevalent working conditions, salary, and fringe benefits.[9]

INTERVIEW LIKE A PRO

An interview tends to have three parts: icebreaking (about five minutes), in which the interviewer tries to put the applicant at ease; questioning (directly or indirectly) by the interviewer; and questioning by the applicant. Almost every recruiter you meet will be trying to rate you in 5 to 10 areas. The questions will be designed to assess your skills and personality.

Many firms start with a *screening interview,* a rather short interview (about 30 minutes) to decide whether to invite you back for a second interview. Only about 20 percent of job applicants are invited back. The second interview is a half day or a day of meetings set up by the human resource department with managers in different departments. After the meetings, someone from the human resource department will discuss other application materials with you and tell you when a letter of acceptance or rejection is likely to be sent. (The wait might be weeks or even months.) Many applicants send follow-up letters in the meantime to show they are still interested in the firm.

For the interview you should dress conservatively. Plan to arrive about 10 to 15 minutes ahead of time. Try to relax. Smile and make eye contact with (but do not stare at) the interviewer. Body language is an important communicator. The placement of your hands and feet and your overall posture say a good deal about you. Here are some other tips for interviewing like a pro.

1. *Concentrate on being likable.* As simplistic as it seems, research proves that one of the most essential goals in successful interviewing is to be liked by the interviewer. Interviewers want to hire pleasant people that others will like working

with on a daily basis. Pay attention to the following areas to project that you are highly likable.

- Be friendly, courteous, and enthusiastic.
- Speak positively.
- Smile.
- Use positive body language.
- Make certain your appearance is appropriate.

2. *Project an air of confidence and pride.* Act as though you want and deserve the job, not as though you are desperate.

3. *Demonstrate enthusiasm.* The applicant's level of enthusiasm often influences employers as much as any other interviewing factor. The applicant who demonstrates little enthusiasm for a job will never be selected for the position.

4. *Demonstrate knowledge of and interest in the employer.* "I really want this job" is not convincing enough. Explain why you want the position and how the position fits your career plans. You can cite opportunities that might be unique to a firm or emphasize your skills and education that are highly relevant to the position.

5. *State your name and the position you're seeking.* When you enter the interviewer's office, begin with a friendly greeting, and state the position you're interviewing for: "Hello, Ms. Levine, I'm Bella Reyna. I'm here to interview for the accounting position." If someone has already introduced you to the interviewer, simply say, "Good morning, Ms. Levine." Identifying the position is important, because interviewers often interview for many different positions.

6. *Focus on how you fit the job.* Near the beginning of your interview, as soon as it seems appropriate, ask a question similar to this: "Could you describe the scope of the job and tell me what capabilities are most important in filling the position?" The interviewer's response will help you focus on emphasizing your qualifications that best match the needs of the employer.

7. *Speak correctly.* Grammatical errors can cost applicants the job. Use correct grammar, word choice, and a businesslike vocabulary, not an informal, chatty one. Avoid slang. When under stress, people often use pet phrases (such as *you know*) too often. This is highly annoying and projects immaturity and insecurity. Don't use *just* or *only.* "I just worked as a waiter." Don't say "I guess." Avoid the word *probably,* because it suggests unnecessary doubt. Ask a friend or family member to help you identify any speech weaknesses you have. Begin eliminating these speech habits now.[10]

In addition, you should avoid these "disqualifiers" at all costs. Any one of these blunders could cost you your dream job:

1. Don't sit down until the interviewer invites you to; waiting is courteous.

2. Don't bring anyone else to the interview; it makes you look immature and insecure.

3. Don't smoke.

4. Don't put anything on or read anything on the interviewer's desk; it's considered an invasion of personal space.

5. Don't chew gum or have anything else in your mouth; this projects immaturity.

6. If you are invited to a business meal, don't order alcohol. When ordering, choose food that's easy to eat while carrying on a conversation.

7. Don't offer a limp handshake; it projects weakness. Use a firm handshake.[11]

SELECTING THE RIGHT JOB FOR YOU

Hard work and a little luck can pay off with multiple job offers. Your happy dilemma is deciding which one is best for you. Start by considering the FACTS:

- *Fit.* Do the job and the employer fit your skills, interests, and lifestyle?
- *Advancement and growth.* Will you have the chance to develop your talents and move up within the organization?
- *Compensation.* Is the employer offering a competitive salary and benefits package?
- *Training.* Will the employer provide you with the tools needed to be successful on the job?
- *Site.* Is the job location a good match for your lifestyle and your pocketbook?

A great way to evaluate a new location is through HOMEFAIR (http://www.homefair.com). This site offers tools to help you calculate the cost of moving, the cost of living, and the quality of life in various places in Canada and the United States. The **Moving Calculator** helps you figure out how much it will cost to ship your worldly possessions to a particular city. The **Relocation Crime Lab** compares crime rates in various locations. The **City Snapshots** feature compares demographic, economic, and climate information for two cities of your choosing. The **Salary Calculator** computes cost-of-living differences between hundreds of Canadian and international cities and tells you how much you'd need to make in your new city to maintain your current standard of living.

STARTING YOUR NEW JOB

No time is more crucial, and possibly nerve-racking, than the first few months at a new job. During this breaking-in period, the employer decides whether a new employee is valuable enough to keep and, if so, in what capacity. Sometimes the employee's whole future with the company rides on the efforts of the first few weeks or months.

Most firms offer some sort of formal orientation, but generally speaking, they expect employees to learn quickly—and often on their own. You will be expected to become familiar with the firm's goals; its organization, including your place in the company; and basic personnel policies, such as coffee breaks, overtime, and parking.

Here are a few tips on making your first job rewarding and productive.

Listen and Learn

When you first walk into your new job, let your eyes and ears take everything in. Do people refer to one another by first names, or is the company more formal? How do people dress? Do the people you work with drop into one another's open offices for informal chats about business matters? Or have you entered a "memo mill," where anything of substance is put on e-mail and talks with other employees are scheduled through secretaries? Size up where the power lies. Who seems to assume a leadership role most often? Who is the person others turn to for advice? Why has that person achieved that position? What traits have made this person a "political leader"? Don't be misled by what others say, but also don't dismiss their evaluations. Make your own judgments based on what you see and hear.

Do unto Others

Be nice. Nice people are usually the last to be fired and among the first to be promoted. Don't be pleasant only with those who can help you in the company. Be nice to everyone. You never know who can help you or give you information that will turn out to be useful. Genuinely nice people make routine job assignments, and especially pressure-filled ones, more pleasant. And people who are dealt with pleasantly usually respond in kind.

Don't Start Out as a Maverick

If every new employee tried to change tried-and-true methods to suit his or her whims, the firm would quickly be in chaos. Individual needs must take a back seat to established procedures. Devote yourself to getting things done within the system. Every manager realizes that it takes time for a new person to adjust. But the faster you start accomplishing things, the faster the boss will decide that you were the right person to hire.

Find a Great Mentor

The leading cause of career unhappiness is working for a bad boss. Good jobs can easily be ruined by supervisors who hold you back. In contrast, your career will soar (and you will smile every day) when you have a great mentor helping you along the way. If you find a job with a super mentor, jump at the chance to take it.

MOVIN' ON UP

Once you have been on the job for a while, you will want to get ahead and be promoted. We offer several suggestions for improving your chances of promotion. The first item might seem a bit strange, yet it's there for a practical reason. If you don't really like what you do, you won't be committed enough to compete with those who do. The passionate people are the ones who go the extra mile, do the extra work, and come up with fresh outside-the-box ideas.

So there you have it! In the next chapter we will begin our journey through the world of business, so that you can determine what areas are most interesting to you. Remember, it's never too early to begin planning your career—the future is now.

How to Move Up

- Love what you do, which entails first figuring out who you are.
- Never stop learning about new technologies and new management skills.
- Try to get international experience, even if it is only a short stint overseas.

- Create new business opportunities—they could lead to a promotion.
- Be really outstandingly terrific at what you're doing now, this week, this month.

The Future of Business

Second Canadian Edition

Chapter 1

Making the Connection

Understanding Evolving Economic Systems and Competition

In this chapter, you'll learn about different economic systems, basic economic concepts you need to understand how the economy works, and the role of competition in the economic environment. But first, you might be wondering, "Where does all this fit into our understanding of a successful business?" Take a look at the model below.

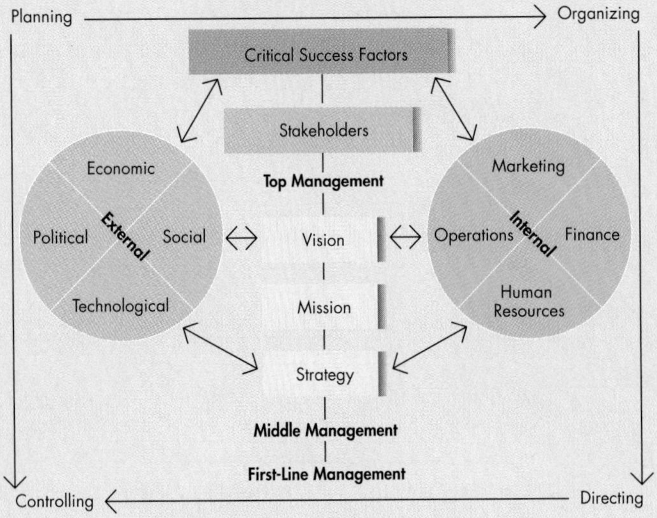

SOURCE: LAURA ALLAN AND JIM McCUTCHEON, *Business 111 Lab Manual*, 18TH EDITION (CONCORD, ON: CAPTUS, 2003).

The most obvious relationship between this chapter and the model of a successful business is in the external environment. The PEST model of the external environment is an acronym for the **p**olitical, **e**conomic, **s**ocial, and **t**echnological environments that interact with business.

The *economic* environment is part of our PEST model of the external environment. In this chapter, we will describe the economic system of a country as a combination of policies, laws, and choices made by its government. Remember, this is an integrative model. Here we see a direct link between the *political* and economic environments. But as you'll see throughout the chapter, the economy has an impact on all the other aspects of the external environment, as well as on the internal environment of a business and how it operates.

Take, for example, any of the new hybrid cars, such as Toyota's Prius. You might have seen these sleek, trendy machines racing around your neighbourhood. As a result of pressure from governments and *society* to reduce fuel emissions that cause pollution and increase the threat of global warming, as well as economic pressure from foreign oil companies raising gas prices, Toyota has worked to create the *technology* for hybrid cars that run on gasoline and electricity. This affects the

A diagram showing the business model. Across the top: Planning → Organizing. The left side: External circle with Economic, Political, Social, Technological. Center column (top to bottom): Critical Success Factors, Stakeholders, Top Management, Vision, Mission, Strategy, Middle Management, First-Line Management. Right side: Internal circle with Marketing, Operations, Finance, Human Resources. Across the bottom: Controlling ← Directing.

economic environment, because it is an action that other companies need to respond to if they are going to remain competitive—and many have. The internal environment of the business interacted by creating the product to *meet the needs of the customer*—a critical success factor. *Marketing* worked with *operations* to design and build the product through the *human resources* of the company and with the *financial resources* of the company. This was a very innovative move on the part of the company that would take several years to create a return. But it is this commitment to *innovation* in response to an environmental threat that has allowed companies like Toyota to remain competitive and turn what would have been a threat into an opportunity for the business. That is what competition and success are all about.

In this chapter, we describe economic systems as differing based on how they manage the factors of production—the resources needed to produce a company's products. These factors are provided by the **stakeholders** of the business: Employees provide human resources, and owners provide financial resources, for example. The economic system that exists in a society depends partly on the relationship between the stakeholders, business, and the government. This stakeholder relationship to the economic environment can also be seen in the discussion of **economics** as a "circular flow": Resources are provided by the stakeholders, who then receive something in return from the business. This circular flow also clearly demonstrates the integrative nature of a business, as changes in one flow affect the others.

We have provided numerous examples of the integrative nature of business. One such example is the "crowding out" that occurs when government spending replaces private sector spending. This is an excellent example of how the political and economic environments affect one another as well as affecting the internal environments of companies. When the government spends more on libraries, for example, and individuals spend less on books, how does that affect all the different functional areas of a company? As described in this chapter, this crowding out also occurs when the governments raises funds for spending, making corporate financing more expensive and thus crowding out private investment, which, in turn, slows economic growth in the private sector.

All the examples in the chapter of news stories that deal with economic matters demonstrate the extent to which the economic environment creeps into the daily workings of a business. Consider the following.

- *"The Bank of Canada lowers interest rates."* This would affect the financial decisions of the company, perhaps making it more feasible financially to expand—affecting the company's overall strategy, as well as its ability to meet the needs of the customer by offering better financing packages.
- *"The Minister of Finance proposes a cut in income taxes."* Lower personal income taxes result in customers' having more disposable income to spend on the company's products. Lower corporate taxes make the economic environment more favourable to business investment domestically and make it easier for Canadian enterprises to compete with companies from countries with lower taxes.

We will use numerous examples throughout the chapter to demonstrate how factors in the economy affect business decisions: what to produce (marketing and operations), how to price these products (marketing and finance), and how many people to employ and how much to pay them (human resources and finance). The impact of inflation, business cycles, and government policy all provide examples of how economics affects business. But if you look at the factors that cause demand and supply curves to shift, you can also see many other aspects of the environment at play; for example, technology shifts the supply curve, but buyers' preferences (social environment) shift the demand curve.

The economy also affects critical success factors of the business. Many trends in the economic environment relate to these success factors. The chapter describes how "companies are focusing on relationship management, which involves building, maintaining, and enhancing interactions with customers … so as to develop long-term satisfaction." This comes, in part, as a result of better educated and more demanding customers from the social environment; new technology, which allows customers to find companies that meet their needs and switch to them at the click of a mouse; and the globalization of markets in the economic environment, creating more competition. These environmental factors, combined with an understanding that financially it's better on the bottom line to keep an existing customer than find a new one, results in a trend toward meeting customer needs that takes on more long-term significance. We will describe how "creating and building long-term relationships require a world-class work force." Better training and better technology to improve worker productivity help to build a *workforce committed* to meeting the *quality* needs of the customer and to building long-term relationships with them. And, of course, satisfied long-standing customers and more productive and committed workers result in both higher revenues and cost savings, which help the company achieve better *financial performance*.

Chapter 1

SHIRLEY A. ROSE

Understanding Evolving Economic Systems and Competition

learning goals

1   What is an economic system, and what economic systems are prevalent in the world today?

2   What is economics, what are the three sectors of the economy, and how are these three sectors linked?

3   How do economic growth, full employment, and price stability indicate a nation's economic health?

4   What is inflation, how is it measured, and what causes it?

5   How does the Bank of Canada use monetary policy, and how do governments use fiscal policy to achieve their macroeconomic goals?

6   What are the basic microeconomic concepts of demand and supply, and how do they establish prices?

7   What are the four types of market structure?

8   Which trends are reshaping micro- and macroeconomic environments?

Canada's Rise to Fiscal Respectability: What's Next?

Gordon Ritchie has been with RBC Capital markets for 27 years and currently holds the position of vice chairman. Gordon summarized Canada's rise to the position of a financially stable member of the G8.

For years Canada struggled in the global capital markets with a less-than-appealing balance sheet. A lot of borrowing was needed to finance the deficits and this approach to fiscal responsibility was a concern to the international markets, many of whom wanted to reduce their investments in Canada. As a result of this international political pressure, Ottawa adopted a fiscal policy requiring a balanced budget. To attain this goal, the expenses and revenues of the Federal Government had to be brought into balance by the revising of cost strategies and the pushing down of costs to the provinces.

Today, Canada has one of the strongest balance sheets in the G8, with trade and budget surpluses but at the same time we face many challenges. Canada is a small player on the world stage, with only 1 to 2 percent of global GDP, which tends to limit the degree of our influence. Our close ties with the United States impact our economy. While the Canadian dollar is strong, imports will be cheaper and the federal government will be watching closely to monitor interest rates, employment rates, and inflation rates, all of which impact our quality of life. With our strong rate of economic growth, increased immigration, relatively low interest rates, and strong dollar, what else would we be looking at?

Mr. Ritchie feels that the government should look at the taxation on capital in Canada. As well, Canada has one of the highest tax rates in the world, and to increase the availability of capital for additional investment, it might be time to look at corporate and personal income taxes. This could free up funds for additional investments by businesses and individuals, but maintaining the balanced budget would require a federal strategy to replace the lost revenue or to further reduce costs.

Critical Thinking Questions

1. If the federal government were to reduce income taxes, what would be the effect on the circular flow illustrated in Exhibit 1.1?

2. What other strategies might be employed to help our economic growth continue?

economic system
The combination of policies, laws, and choices made by a nation's government to establish the systems that determine what goods and services are produced and how they are allocated.

A nation's **economic system** is the combination of policies, laws, and choices made by its government to establish the systems that determine what goods and services are produced and how they are allocated. Economic systems found in the world today include market economy (private enterprise or market system), command (planned economies), socialism, and mixed economies, all of which are discussed below.

Reading this chapter will help you understand how economies provide jobs for workers and also create and deliver products to consumers and businesses. You will also learn how governments attempt to influence economic activity through policies such as lowering or raising taxes. Next, we discuss how supply and demand determine prices for goods and services. We conclude by examining trends in evolving economic systems and competition.

EVOLVING GLOBAL ECONOMIC SYSTEMS

1 learning goal

factors of production
The resources used to create goods and services, including natural resources, labour, capital, entrepreneurship, and knowledge.

As noted above, there are four primary types of economic systems in the world today: market economies, command economies, socialism, and mixed economies. The primary difference between the types of economic systems is how they manage the **factors of production**. Managers must understand and adapt to the factors of production and the economic system or systems in which they operate to be successful.

Factors of Production: The Building Blocks of Business

Factors of production are the resources used to create goods and services. By using the factors of production efficiently, a company can produce more output with the same resources. Four traditional factors of production are common to all productive activity: natural resources, labour, capital, and entrepreneurship. A fifth factor, knowledge, is gaining in importance.

Commodities that are useful inputs in their natural state are known as **natural resources**. They include farmland, forests, mineral and oil deposits, and water. Sometimes natural resources are simply called *land*, although, as you can see, the term means more than just land. Today, urban sprawl, pollution, and limited resources have raised questions about resource use. Conservationists, ecologists, and government bodies are proposing laws to require land use planning and resource conservation.

The economic contributions of people working with their minds and muscles are called **labour**. This input includes the talents of everyone—from a restaurant cook to a nuclear physicist—who performs the many tasks of manufacturing and selling goods and services. The tools, machinery, equipment, and buildings used to produce goods and services and get them to the consumer are known as **capital**. Sometimes the term *capital* is also used to mean the money that buys machinery, factories, and other production and distribution facilities. However, because money itself produces nothing, it is *not* one of the basic inputs. Rather, it is a means of acquiring the inputs. Therefore, in this context, capital does not include money.

Entrepreneurs are people who combine the inputs of natural resources, labour, and capital to produce goods or services with the intention of making a profit. These people make all the decisions that set the course for their firms; they create products and production processes. Because they are not guaranteed a profit in return for their time and effort, they must be risk takers. Of course, if their firms succeed, the rewards can be great.

Today, many Canadians want to start their own businesses. They are attracted by the opportunity to be their own boss and reap the financial rewards of owning a successful firm.

A number of outstanding managers and noted academics are beginning to emphasize a fifth factor of production—knowledge. **Knowledge** is the combined talents and skills of the workforce. As the world becomes ever more uncertain, the very nature of work, organizations, and management is changing. The new competitive environment places a premium on knowledge and learning. Lester Thurow, a leading world expert on economic issues, says, "the dominant competitive weapon of the twenty-first century will be the knowledge of the work force."[1] The companies that will become and remain successful will be the ones that can learn quickly, assimilate this learning, and develop new insights.

concept check

Explain the concepts of revenue, costs, and profit.

What are the five factors of production?

What is the role of an entrepreneur in society?

Market Economy

A remarkable trend in global economies today is the move toward market economies. Sometimes, as in the case of the former East Germany, the transition to a market economy has been painful but fairly quick. In other countries, such as Russia, the movement has been characterized by false starts and backsliding. A **market economy,** also known as the *private enterprise system* or *capitalism,* is based on competition in the marketplace and private ownership of the factors of production (resources). In a competitive economic system, a large number of people and businesses buy and sell products freely in the marketplace. In a pure market economy all the factors of production are owned privately, and the government does not try to set prices or coordinate economic activity.

A market economy guarantees certain economic rights: the right to own property, the right to make a profit, the right to make free choices, and the right to compete. The right to own property is central to a market economy. The main incentive in this system is profit, which encourages entrepreneurship. Profit is also necessary for producing goods and services, building plants, paying dividends and taxes, and creating jobs. The freedom to choose whether to become an entrepreneur or to work for someone else means that people have the right to decide what they want to do on the basis of their own drive, interest, and training. The government does not create job quotas for each industry or give people tests to determine what they will do.

In a market economy, competition is good for both businesses and consumers. It leads to better and more diverse products, keeps prices stable, and increases the efficiency of producers. Producers try to produce their goods and services at the lowest possible cost and sell them at the highest possible price. But when profits are high, more firms enter the market to seek those profits. The resulting competition among firms tends to lower prices. Producers must then find new ways of operating more efficiently if they are to keep making a profit—and stay in business.

The Command Economy

The complete opposite to a market economy is a command economy. A **command economy,** or planned economy, is characterized by government ownership of virtually all resources and economic decision-making by central-government planning. The government decides what will be produced, where it will be produced, how much

market economy

An economic system based on competition in the marketplace and private ownership of the factors of production (resources); also known as the *private enterprise system* or *capitalism.*

command economy

An economic system characterized by government ownership of virtually all resources and economic decision-making by central-government planning; also known as *planned economy.*

will be produced, where the raw materials and supplies will come from, and who will get the output.

Pure market economy and the command economy are extremes; real-world economies fall somewhere between the two. The Canadian economy leans toward a market economy, but government policies are used to promote economic stability and growth. As well, through policies and laws, the government transfers money to those with lower incomes, the unemployed, and the elderly. In the United States, the market economy has produced some very powerful organizations in the form of huge corporations, such as General Motors and Microsoft. On the other hand, laws have been enacted to help smaller firms and entrepreneurs by requiring that the giants compete fairly against weaker competitors.

Before the Soviet Union collapsed in 1991, it had a command economy, but even so it relied to some extent on market-determined prices and allowed some private ownership. Recent reforms in Russia, China, and most of the Eastern European nations have moved these economies toward more capitalistic, market-oriented systems. North Korea and Cuba are the best remaining examples of command economies.

Socialism

socialism

An economic system in which the basic industries are owned either by the government or by the private sector under strong government control.

Socialism is an economic system in which the basic industries are owned by the government or by the private sector under strong government control. A socialist state controls critical large-scale industries such as transportation, communications, and utilities. Smaller businesses may be privately owned. To varying degrees, the state also determines the goals of businesses, the prices and selection of goods, and the rights of workers. Socialist countries typically provide their citizens with a higher level of services, such as health care and unemployment benefits, than do most capitalist countries. As a result, taxes and unemployment can also be quite high in socialist countries.

Many countries, including Great Britain, Denmark, Israel, and Sweden, have socialist systems, but the systems vary from country to country. In Denmark, for example, most businesses are privately owned and operated, but two-thirds of the population is sustained by the state through government welfare programs.

Socialism is proving to be surprisingly resilient in Western Europe. France, for example, inched toward a capitalistic form of government after the presidency of François Mitterrand ended in 1995. Yet several years later, the country elected Lionel Jospin, who won the election based on a pledge of more government control and intervention in the workplace. Now, Jacques Chirac has moved the country back toward a more capitalistic type of government. In Great Britain, Labour Prime Minister Tony Blair nationalized industry, advanced extraordinary social regulation, and promoted massive taxation to support it all.

Mixed Economic Systems

mixed economies

Economies that combine several economic systems; for example, an economy in which the government owns certain industries but the private sector owns others.

Canada, Great Britain, and Sweden, among others, are also called **mixed economies**; that is, they use more than one economic system. Sometimes, the government is basically socialist and owns basic industries. In Canada, some industries are at least partly owned by the government (e.g., communications, transportation, and utilities industries), but most activities are carried on by private enterprises, as in a capitalist system.

The few factors of production owned by the government include some public lands, Canada Post, and some water resources. But the government is extensively involved in the economic system through taxing, spending, and welfare activities. The economy is also mixed in the sense that the country tries to achieve many social goals—income redistribution (transfer payments) and Canada Pension Plan, for example—that might not be attempted in purely capitalist systems. Exhibit 1.1 summarizes key factors of the world's economic systems.

What is a market economy, and why is it growing?
What is socialism, and why is it still popular?
Why are most economies mixed?

Exhibit 1.1 | The Basic Economic Systems of the World

	MARKET ECONOMY	COMMAND ECONOMY	SOCIALISM	MIXED ECONOMY
Ownership of Business	Businesses are privately owned with minimal government ownership or interference	Governments own all or most enterprises	Basic industries such as railroads and utilities are owned by government; very high taxation as government redistributes income from successful private businesses and entrepreneurs	Private ownership of land and businesses but government control of some enterprises; the private sector is typically large
Control of Markets	Complete freedom of trade; no or little government control	Complete government control of markets	Some markets are controlled and some are free; significant central-government planning; state enterprises are managed by bureaucrats; these enterprises are rarely profitable	Some markets, such as nuclear energy and the post office, are controlled or highly regulated
Worker Incentives	Strong incentive to work and innovate because profits are retained by owners	No incentive to work hard or produce quality products	Private-sector incentives the same as a market and public-sector incentives the same as a planned economy	Private-sector incentives the same as capitalism; limited incentives in the public sector
Management of Enterprises	Each enterprise is managed by owners or professional managers with little government interference	Centralized management by the government bureaucracy; little or no flexibility in decision making at the factory level	Significant government planning and regulation; bureaucrats run government enterprises	Private-sector management similar to capitalism; public sector similar to socialism
Forecast for 2020	Continued steady growth	No growth and perhaps disappearance	Stable with probable slight growth	Continued growth

HOW BUSINESS AND ECONOMIES WORK

2 *learning goal*

economics

The study of how a society uses scarce resources to produce and distribute goods and services.

Economics is the study of how a society uses scarce resources to produce and distribute goods and services. The resources of a person, a firm, or a nation are limited. Hence, economics is the study of choices—what people, firms, or nations choose from among the available resources. Every economy is concerned with what types and amounts of goods and services should be produced, how they should be produced, and for whom. These decisions are made by the marketplace, the government, or both. In Canada the government and the free-market system together guide the economy.

You probably know more about economics than you realize. Every day, many news stories deal with economic matters: A union wins wage increases at General Motors; the Bank of Canada raises interest rates; Toronto Stock Exchange has a record day; the federal government proposes a cut in income taxes; consumer spending rises as the economy grows; or retail prices are on the rise, to mention just a few examples.

Macroeconomics and Microeconomics

The state of the economy affects both people and businesses. How you spend your money (or save it) is a personal economic decision. Whether you continue in school and whether you work part-time are also economic decisions. Every business also operates within the economy. Based on their owners' and managers' economic expectations, businesses decide what products to produce, how to price them, how many people to employ, how much to pay these employees, how much to expand the business, and so on.

macroeconomics

The sub-area of economics that focuses on the economy as a whole by looking at aggregate data for large groups of people, companies, or products.

Economics has two main sub-areas. **Macroeconomics** is the study of the economy as a whole. It looks at *aggregate* data, data for large groups of people, companies, or products considered as a whole. In contrast, **microeconomics** focuses on individual parts of the economy, such as households or firms.

microeconomics

The sub-area of economics that focuses on individual parts of the economy, such as households or firms.

Both macro- and microeconomics offer valuable outlooks on the economy. For example, Ford might use both to decide whether to introduce a new line of cars. The company would consider such macroeconomic factors as the national level of personal income, the unemployment rate, interest rates, fuel costs, and the national level of sales of new cars. From a microeconomic viewpoint, Ford would judge consumer demand for new cars versus the existing supply, competing models, labour and material costs and availability, and current prices and sales incentives.

Economics as a Circular Flow

circular flow

The movement of inputs and outputs among households, businesses, and governments; a way of showing how the sectors of the economy interact.

Another way to see how the sectors of the economy interact is to examine the **circular flow** of inputs and outputs among households, businesses, and governments, as shown in Exhibit 1.2. Let's review the exchanges by following the purple circle around the inside of the diagram. Households provide inputs (natural resources, labour, capital, entrepreneurship) to businesses, which convert these inputs into outputs (goods and services) for consumers. In return, consumers receive income from rent, wages, interest, and ownership profits (green circle). Businesses receive income from consumer purchases of goods and services.

The other important exchange in Exhibit 1.2 takes place between governments (federal, provincial, and municipal) and both individuals and businesses. Governments supply many types of publicly provided goods and services (highways, schools, police, courts, health services, unemployment insurance, Canada Pension Plan) that benefit individuals and businesses. Government purchases from businesses also contribute to business profits. The contractor who repairs a local stretch of highway, for example, is paid by government for the work. As the diagram shows, government receives taxes from individuals and businesses to complete the flow.

Changes in one flow affect the others. If the government raises taxes, households have less to spend on goods and services. Lower consumer spending causes businesses to reduce production, and economic activity declines; unemployment might rise. In contrast, cutting taxes can stimulate economic activity. Keep the circular flow in mind as we continue our study of economics. The way economic sectors interact will become more evident as we explore macroeconomics and microeconomics.

concept check

What is economics?

What is the difference between macroeconomics and microeconomics?

How do resources flow among the household, business, and government sectors?

Exhibit 1.2 | Economics as a Circular Flow

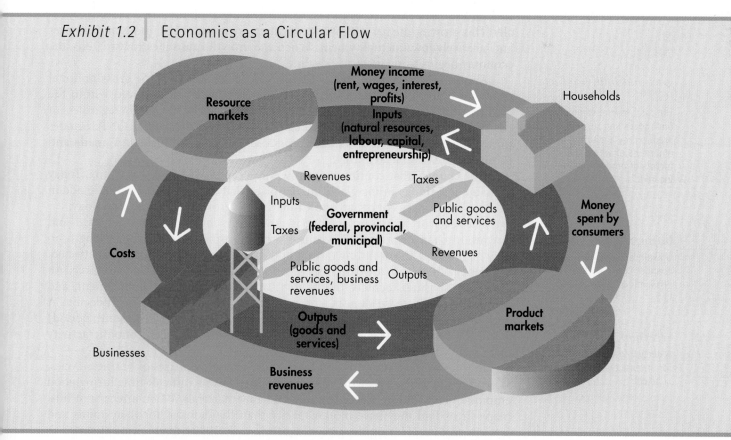

MACROECONOMICS: THE BIG PICTURE

3   *learning goal*

HOT *Links*

The Canadian Government follows national and regional economic statistics, including the GDP. For the latest economic overview of the Canadian economy, visit http://www.canadianeconomy.gc.ca.

economic growth

An increase in a nation's output of goods and services.

gross domestic product (GDP)

The total market value of all final goods and services produced within a nation's borders in a year.

gross national product (GNP)

The total market value of all final goods and services produced by a country regardless of where the factors of production are located.

business cycles

Upward and downward changes in the level of economic activity.

recession

A decline in GDP that lasts for at least two consecutive quarters.

Have you ever looked at CBC Newsworld (http://www.cbc.ca/newsworld) or turned on the radio or television and heard something like, "Today the government reported that for the second straight month the unemployment rate has declined"? Statements like this are macroeconomic news. Understanding the national economy and how changes in government policies affect households and businesses is a good place to begin our study of economics.

Let's look first at macroeconomic goals and how they can be met. Canada and most other countries have three main macroeconomic goals: economic growth, full employment, and price stability. A nation's economic well-being depends on carefully defining these goals and choosing the best economic policies to reach them.

Striving for Economic Growth

Perhaps the most important way to judge a nation's economic health is to look at its production of goods and services. The more the nation produces, the higher its standard of living. An increase in a nation's output of goods and services is **economic growth.**

Economic growth is usually a good thing, but it also has a bad side. Increased production yields more pollution. Growth can strain public facilities, such as roads, electricity, schools, and hospitals. Thus, the government tries to apply economic policies that will keep growth to a level that does not reduce the quality of life.

The most basic measure of economic growth is the **gross domestic product (GDP)**. GDP is the total market value of all final goods and services produced within a nation's borders each year. It is reported quarterly and is used to compare trends in national output. When GDP rises, the economy is growing.

The *rate* of growth in real GDP (GDP adjusted for inflation) is also important. Recently, the Canadian economy has been growing at about 2 to 3 percent annually. This growth rate has meant a steady increase in output of goods and services and relatively low unemployment. When the growth rate slides toward zero, the economy begins to stagnate and decline.

Another measurement that is often used by economist is the **gross national product (GNP)**. Unlike the GDP, which calculates what is produced within the countries borders, the GNP measures what is produced by the nation regardless of where the factors of production are located. Therefore the Canadian GNP includes the value of the goods and services produced by Canadian firms in Canada and profits from capital held abroad.

One country that continues to grow more rapidly than most is China. Today there are few things in the global marketplace that are not or cannot be made in China. The primary contributor to China's rapid growth has been technology.

The level of economic activity is constantly changing. These upward and downward changes are called **business cycles.** Business cycles vary in length, in how high or low the economy moves, and in how much the economy is affected. Changes in GDP trace the patterns as economic activity expands and contracts. An increase in business activity results in rising output, income, employment, and prices. Eventually, these all peak, and output, income, and employment decline. A decline in GDP that lasts for two consecutive quarters (each a three-month period) is called a **recession.** It is followed by a recovery period, when economic activity once again increases.

Businesses must monitor and react to the changing phases of business cycles. When the economy is growing, companies often have a difficult time hiring good employees and finding scarce supplies and raw materials. When a recession hits, many firms find they have more capacity than the demand for their goods and services requires. During the recession of the early 1990s, many firms operated at

The housing industry is a leading economic indicator. A rise in new home construction typically translates into a robust economy.

© KIM STEELE/PHOTODISC/GETTY IMAGES

HOT *Links*

For the latest information about the Canadian population numbers and the unemployment rate in Canada see http://www.statscan.ca.

75 percent or less of their capacity. When plants use only part of their capacity, they operate inefficiently and have higher costs per unit produced. Let's say that Nestlé has a plant that can produce 1 million Aero chocolate bars a day, but because of a recession, Nestlé can sell only half a million candy bars a day. Nestlé has a huge plant with large, expensive machines designed to produce a million candy bars a day. Producing Aero chocolate bars at 50 percent capacity does not use Nestlé's investment in the plant and equipment efficiently.

Keeping People on the Job

full employment
The condition when all people who want to work and can work have jobs.

Another macroeconomic goal is **full employment,** or having jobs for all who want to and can work. Full employment doesn't actually mean 100 percent employment. Some people choose not to work for personal reasons (attending school, raising children) or are temporarily unemployed while they wait to start a new job. Thus, the government defines full employment as the situation when about 94 to 96 percent of those available to work actually have jobs.

unemployment rate
The percentage of the total labour force that is actively looking for work but is not actually working.

Measuring Unemployment To determine how close we are to full employment, the government measures the **unemployment rate.** This rate indicates the percentage of the total labour force that is not working but is *actively looking for work.* It excludes "discouraged workers," those not seeking jobs because they think no one will hire them. Each month the government releases statistics on employment. These figures help us understand how well the economy is doing.

concept check

What are the three (3) main macroeconomic objectives of Canada?

What is GDP? GNP?

What are business cycles?

Types of Unemployment Economists classify unemployment into four types: frictional, structural, cyclical, and seasonal. The categories are of small consolation to someone who is unemployed, but they help economists understand the problem of unemployment in our economy.

Frictional unemployment is short-term unemployment that is not related to the business cycle. It includes people who are unemployed while waiting to start a better job, those who are reentering the job market, and those entering for the first time, such as new college graduates. This type of unemployment is always present and has little impact on the economy.

Structural unemployment is also unrelated to the business cycle but is involuntary. It is caused by a mismatch between available jobs and the skills of available workers in an industry or a region. For example, if the birthrate declines, fewer teachers will be needed. Or the available workers in an area might lack the skills that employers want. Retraining and skill-building programs are often required to reduce structural unemployment.

Cyclical unemployment, as the name implies, occurs when a downturn in the business cycle reduces the demand for labour throughout the economy. In a long recession, cyclical unemployment is widespread, and even people with good job skills can't find jobs. The government can partly counteract cyclical unemployment with programs that boost the economy.

In the past, cyclical unemployment affected mainly less skilled workers and those in heavy manufacturing. Typically, they would be rehired when economic growth increased. During the 1990s and early 2000s, however, competition forced many Canadian companies to downsize so they could survive in the global marketplace.

The last type is **seasonal unemployment**, which occurs during specific seasons in certain industries. Employees subject to seasonal unemployment include retail workers hired for the Christmas buying season, road construction, and restaurant employees in ski areas in the winter.

Keeping Prices Steady

The third macroeconomic goal is to keep overall prices for goods and services fairly steady. The situation in which the average of all prices of goods and services is rising is called **inflation.** Inflation's higher prices reduce **purchasing power**, the value of what money can buy. If prices go up but income doesn't rise or rises at a slower rate, a given amount of income buys less. For example, if the price of a basket of groceries rises from \$30 to \$40 but your salary remains the same, you can buy only 75 percent as many groceries (\$30 ÷ \$40). Your purchasing power declines by 25 percent (\$10 ÷ \$40).

Inflation affects both personal and business decisions. When prices are rising, people tend to spend more—before their purchasing power declines further. Businesses that expect inflation often increase their supplies, and people often speed up planned purchases of cars and major appliances.

From the years 2000 to 2005 the average inflation rate in Canada was approximately 2.16 percent. This level is generally viewed as quite low. Some nations have had triple-digit or even higher inflation in recent years. In the late 1990s, Bulgaria had an annual rate of inflation of 123 percent; Turkmenistan, 992 percent; and Angola, 4,145 percent!

Types of Inflation There are two types of inflation. **Demand-pull inflation** occurs when the demand for goods and services is greater than the supply. In this case, would-be buyers have more money to spend than the amount needed to buy available goods and services. Their demand, which exceeds the supply, tends to pull prices up. This situation is sometimes described as "too much money chasing too

---

frictional unemployment
Short-term unemployment that is not related to the business cycle.

structural unemployment
Unemployment that is caused by a mismatch between available jobs and the skills of available workers in an industry or region; it is not related to the business cycle.

cyclical unemployment
Unemployment that occurs when a downturn in the business cycle reduces the demand for labour throughout the economy.

seasonal unemployment
Unemployment that occurs during specific seasons in certain industries.

4 learning goal

inflation
The situation in which the average of all prices of goods and services is rising.

purchasing power
The value of what money can buy.

demand-pull inflation
Inflation that occurs when the demand for goods and services is greater than the supply.

few goods." The higher prices lead to greater supply, eventually creating a balance between demand and supply.

Cost-push inflation is triggered by increases in production costs, such as expenses for materials and wages. These increases push up the prices of final goods and services. Wage increases are a major cause of cost-push inflation, creating a "wage-price spiral." For example, assume the Canadian Auto Workers Union negotiates a three-year labour agreement that raises wages 3 percent per year and increases overtime pay. Car makers will then raise car prices to cover their higher labour costs. These higher wages will also give auto workers more money to buy goods and services, and this increased demand might pull up other prices. Workers in other industries will demand higher wages to keep up with the increased prices, and the cycle will push prices even higher.

How Inflation Is Measured Economists most commonly measure the rate of inflation by looking at changes in the **consumer price index** (CPI), an index of the prices of a "shopping basket" of goods and services purchased by consumers. It tracks the retail price of a representative shopping basket of approximately 300 goods and services that an average household would purchase and is published monthly by Statistics Canada. Some of the expenditures include food, housing, transportation, furniture, clothing, and recreation. The index is weighted to reflect typical spending patterns. For instance, greater importance is given to housing than to recreation. Statistics Canada updates the CPI basket to reflect broad changes in consumer spending habits and to acknowledge changes in products and services.

The CPI sets prices in a base period at 100. The base period, which now is 1992, is chosen for its price stability. Current prices are then expressed as a percentage of prices in the base period. A rise in the CPI means prices are increasing. For example, the CPI was 127.08 in 2005, meaning that prices had increased 1.86 percent per year on average between 1992 and 2005.

HOT Links

For historical and current information on the CPI visit Statistics Canada's Web site at http://www.statcan.ca.

The consumer price index (CPI) provides a broad measure of cost of living in Canada. Currently the base year is 1992 and subsequent years are compared to the prices in 1992.

© AP/WORLD WIDE PHOTOS

producer price index (PPI)

An index of the prices paid by producers and wholesalers for various commodities such as raw materials, partially finished goods, and finished products.

Changes in wholesale prices are another important indicator of inflation. The **producer price index** (PPI) measures the prices paid by producers and wholesalers for such commodities as raw materials, partially finished goods, and finished products. The PPI is actually a family of indexes for many different product categories. Examples of PPI indexes are raw materials and industrial products. Because the PPI measures prices paid by producers for raw materials, energy, and other commodities, it might foreshadow subsequent price changes for businesses and consumers.

The Impact of Inflation Inflation has several negative effects on people and businesses. For one thing, it penalizes people who live on fixed incomes. Let's say that a couple receives $1,000 a month retirement income beginning in 2004. If inflation is 10 percent in 2005, then the couple can buy only 90 percent of what they could purchase in 2004. Similarly, inflation hurts savers. As prices rise, the real value, or purchasing power, of savings deteriorates.

concept check

What is a business cycle? How do businesses adapt to periods of contraction and expansion?

Why is full employment usually defined as a target percentage below 100 percent?

What is the difference between demand-pull and cost-push inflation?

ACHIEVING MACROECONOMIC GOALS

 5 *learning goal*

HOT Links

For more information on the Bank of Canada and its importance, see http://www.bankofcanada.ca.

Bank of Canada

Canada's central bank, which has as its objective to "promote the economic and financial well-being of Canada."

monetary policy

The measures taken by the Bank of Canada to regulate the amount of money in circulation to influence the economy.

To reach macroeconomic goals, countries must often choose among conflicting alternatives. Sometimes political needs override economic ones. For example, bringing inflation under control might call for a politically difficult period of high unemployment and low growth. Or, in an election year, politicians might resist raising taxes to curb inflation. Still, the federal government and the **Bank of Canada** must try to guide the economy to a sound balance of growth, employment, and price stability. The two main tools used are the fiscal policy and **monetary policy**. By having a separation of fiscal and monetary policymakers (i.e., the federal government and the Bank of Canada, respectively), Canada has separated the power to spend money (i.e., fiscal policy) from the power to create money (i.e., monetary policy).

Monetary Policy

Monetary policy refers to the Bank of Canada's programs for controlling the amount of money circulating in the economy and interest rates. Changes in the money supply affect both the level of economic activity and the rate of inflation. According to the Bank of Canada Act of 1934, the Bank of Canada is the central banking system that prints money and controls how much of it will be in circulation to "promote the economic and financial well-being of Canada."

The Bank of Canada increases or decreases in the amount of money in circulation affect interest rates (the cost of borrowing money and the reward for lending it). The Bank of Canada can change the interest rate on money it lends to banks, signalling to the banking system and financial markets that it has changed its monetary policy. Banks, in turn, may pass along this change to consumers and businesses that receive loans from the banks. If the cost of borrowing increases, the economy slows because interest rates affect consumer and business decisions to spend or invest. The housing industry, business, and investments react the most strongly to changes in interest rates.

contractionary policy
The use of monetary policy by the Bank of Canada to tighten the money supply by selling government securities or raising interest rates.

expansionary policy
The use of monetary policy by the Bank of Canada to increase the growth of the money supply.

fiscal policy
The government's use of taxation and spending to affect the economy.

As you can see, the Bank of Canada can use monetary policy to contract or expand the economy. With **contractionary policy**, the Bank of Canada restricts, or tightens, the money supply by selling government securities or raising interest rates. The result is slower economic growth and higher unemployment. Thus, contractionary policy reduces spending and, ultimately, lowers inflation. With **expansionary policy**, the Bank of Canada increases, or loosens, growth in the money supply. An expansionary policy stimulates the economy. Interest rates decline, so business and consumer spending go up. Unemployment rates drop as businesses expand. But increasing the money supply also has a negative side: More spending pushes prices up, increasing the inflation rate.

Fiscal Policy

The other economic tool used by the government is **fiscal policy**, its program of taxation and spending. By increasing government spending or by cutting taxes, the government can stimulate the economy. Look again at Exhibit 1.2 on page 11. The more government buys from businesses, the greater business revenues and output are. Likewise, if consumers or businesses have to pay less in taxes, they will have more income to spend for goods and services. Tax policies in Canada therefore affect business decisions. High corporate taxes can make it harder for Canadian firms to compete with companies in countries with lower taxes. As a result, companies may choose to locate facilities in other countries to reduce their tax burden.

The interest rate set by the Bank of Canada is passed on to consumers and businesses by the banking system.

federal budget deficit
The condition that occurs when the federal government spends more for programs than it collects in taxes.

national debt
The accumulated total of all of the federal government's annual budget deficits.

HOT *Links*

Want to know the current public deficit and debt? Head to http://www.fin.gc.ca.

crowding out
The situation that occurs when government spending replaces spending by the private sector.

bonds
Securities that represent long-term debt obligations (liabilities) issued by corporations and governments

If the government spends more for programs (social services, education, etc.) than it collects in taxes, the result is a **federal budget deficit**. To balance the budget, the government can cut its spending, increase taxes, or do some combination of the two. When it cannot balance the budget, the government must make up any shortfalls by borrowing (just like any business or household). The accumulated total of all of the federal government's annual budget deficits is known as the **national debt**.

Since 1991 the Government of Canada and the Bank of Canada have jointly been fighting inflation. In that year, they agreed to target inflation to a long-term objective of a 2 percent midpoint. By December of 1993, they were successful, and this focus is needed in the short and medium term to maintain a relatively stable price environment. By keeping inflation between 1 and 3 percent, the Canadian economy should see an economic growth at a sustainable pace and avoid the "boom-and-bust" periods seen in the 1980s and 1990s.

Although fiscal policy has a major impact on businesses and consumers, continual increases in government spending raise another important issue. When government takes more money from businesses and consumers (the private sector) and uses these funds for increased government spending (the public sector), a phenomenon known as **crowding out** occurs. Here are three examples of crowding out:

1. The government spends more on public libraries, and individuals buy fewer books at bookstores.

2. The government spends more on public education, and individuals spend less on private education.

3. The government spends more on public transportation, and individuals spend less on private transportation.

In other words, government spending is crowding out private spending.

Crowding out Private Investment Of concern is the effect of the national debt on private investment. If, to sell its **bonds**, the government raises the interest rate on the bonds it offers, it forces private businesses, which must stay competitive as suppliers of bonds in the bond market, to raise the rates they offer on their corporate bonds (long-term debt obligations issued by a company). In other words, financing government spending by government debt makes it more costly for private industry to finance its own investment. As a result, government debt can end up crowding out private investment and slowing economic growth in the private sector.

Another concern is that there is limited supply of investment capital. If is the government borrows heavily, there is less for private investment and, therefore, private growth.

concept check

What is a monetary policy? Who is responsible for this policy in Canada? What are its main objectives?

What is fiscal policy? What fiscal policy tools can the government use to achieve its macroeconomic goals?

What problems can a large national debt present?

Governments' Other Roles in the Economy

We have mentioned that the government uses its fiscal policy to determine public spending and taxation, but it has other roles within our economy. The three levels of governments (federal, provincial, and local) use their many roles to influence businesses and the Canadian economy. Briefly, some of the more important roles are the following.

- *Customer.* Governments purchase thousands of products and services to carry out their functions. Some businesses (e.g., road construction companies) rely on governments for most, if not all, of their revenues.
- *Competitor.* Through Crown corporations, governments compete directly with private companies.
- *Provider of incentives.* Governments use many programs to stimulate economic growth, development, and employment. "Team Canada" (as illustrated in Chapter 2) is just one example.
- *Provider of essential services.* Governments have traditionally supplied and continue to supply services that private enterprises do not. The armed forces and Statistics Canada are two examples.
- *Regulator.* Governments are responsible for the safety and well-being of the citizens of Canada. This includes the protection of consumers (e.g., consumer rights, as discussed in Chapter 3), protecting businesses and competition (e.g., tariffs and quotas), protection of social goals (e.g., Canadian content laws), environmental protection (e.g., the Fisheries Act and antipollution laws), and so on.
- *Taxation agent.* Taxes are necessary for governments to employ people to provide goods and services. Taxes are the responsibility not only of individuals but also of businesses.

MICROECONOMICS: ZEROING IN ON BUSINESSES AND CONSUMERS

6 learning goal

Now let's shift our focus from the whole economy to *microeconomics*, the study of households, businesses, and industries. This field of economics is concerned with how prices and quantities of goods and services behave in a free market. It stands to reason that people, firms, and governments try to get the most from their limited resources. Consumers want to buy the best quality at the lowest price. Businesses want to keep costs down and revenues high to earn larger profits. Governments also want to use their revenues to provide the most effective public goods and services possible. These groups choose among alternatives by focusing on the prices of goods and services.

As consumers in a free market, we influence what is produced. If Vietnamese food is popular, the high demand attracts entrepreneurs, who open more Vietnamese restaurants. They want to compete for our dollars by supplying Vietnamese food at a lower price, of better quality, or with different menu choices. This section explains how business and consumer choices influence the price and availability of goods and services.

demand
The quantity of a good or service that people are willing to buy at various prices.

demand curve
A graph showing the quantity of a good or service that people are willing to buy at various prices.

The Nature of Demand

Demand is the quantity of a good or service that people are willing to buy at various prices. The higher the price, the lower the quantity demanded, and vice versa. A graph of this relationship is called a **demand curve**.

Let's assume you own a store that sells jackets for snowboarders. From experience, you know how many jackets you can sell at different prices. The demand curve in Exhibit 1.3 depicts this information. The x-axis (horizontal axis) shows the quantity of jackets, and the y-axis (vertical axis) shows the related price of those jackets. For example, at a price of $60, customers will buy (demand) 500 jackets.

In the graph, the demand curve slopes downward and to the right. This means that as the price falls, people will want to buy more jackets. Some people who were not going to buy a jacket will purchase one at the lower price. Also, some snowboarders who already have a jacket will buy a second one. The graph also shows that if you put a large number of jackets on the market, you will have to reduce the price to sell all of them.

Understanding demand is critical to businesses. This is because demand tells you how much you can sell and at what price—in other words, how much money the firm will take in that can be used to cover costs and hopefully earn a profit. Predicting demand is often difficult even for the very largest corporations but is particularly challenging for small firms.

The Nature of Supply

supply

The quantity of a good or service that businesses will make available at various prices.

supply curve

A graph showing the quantity of a good or service that a business will make available at various prices.

Demand alone is not enough to explain how the market sets prices. We must also look at **supply**, the quantity of a good or service that businesses will make available at various prices. The higher the price, the greater the amount a jacket manufacturer is willing to supply, and vice versa. A graph of the relationship between various prices and the quantities a manufacturer will supply is a **supply curve.**

We can again plot the quantity of jackets on the x-axis and the price on the y-axis. As Exhibit 1.4 shows, 900 jackets will be available at a price of $60. Note that the supply curve slopes upward and to the right, the opposite of the demand curve. If snowboarders are willing to pay higher prices, manufacturers of jackets

| Exhibit 1.3 | Demand Curve for Jackets for Snowboarders |

Exhibit 1.4 | Supply Curve for Jackets for Snowboarders

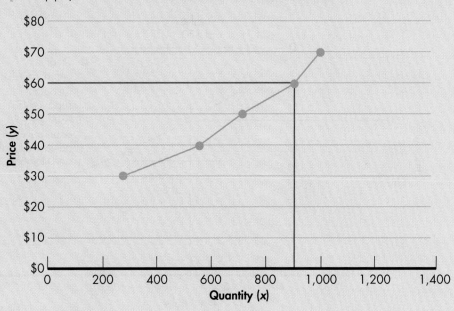

will buy more inputs (Gore-Tex, dye, machinery, labour, etc.) and produce more jackets. The quantity supplied will be higher at higher prices, because producers can earn higher profits.

How Demand and Supply Interact to Determine Prices

In a stable economy, the number of jackets that snowboarders demand depends on the jackets' price. Likewise, the number of jackets that suppliers provide depends on price. But at what price will consumer demand for jackets match the quantity suppliers will produce?

To answer this question, we need to look at what happens when demand and supply interact. By plotting both the demand curve and the supply curve on the same graph (Exhibit 1.5), we see that they cross at a certain quantity and price. At that point, labelled E, the quantity demanded equals the quantity supplied. This is the point of **equilibrium**. The equilibrium price is $50; the equilibrium quantity is 700 jackets. At that point there is a balance between the amount consumers will buy and the amount the manufacturers will supply.

Market equilibrium is achieved through a series of quantity and price adjustments that occur automatically. If the price increases to $70, suppliers produce more jackets than consumers are willing to buy, and a surplus result. To sell more jackets, prices will have to fall. Thus, a surplus pushes prices downward until equilibrium is reached. When the price falls to $40, the quantity of jackets demanded rises above the available supply. The resulting shortage forces prices upward until equilibrium is reached at $50.

equilibrium
The point at which quantity demanded equals quantity supplied.

Exhibit 1.5 | Equilibrium Price and Quantity

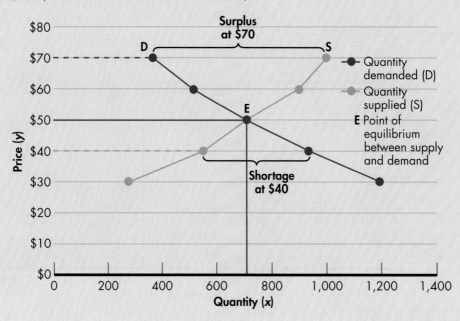

The number of snowboarder jackets produced and bought at $50 will tend to rest at equilibrium unless there is a shift in either demand or supply. If demand increases, more jackets will be purchased at every price, and the demand curve shifts to the right (as illustrated by line D₂ in Exhibit 1.6). If demand decreases, fewer will be bought at every price, and the demand curve shifts to the left (D₁). When demand decreased, snowboarders bought 500 jackets at $50 instead of 700 jackets. When demand increased, they purchased 800.

Exhibit 1.6 | Shifts in Demand

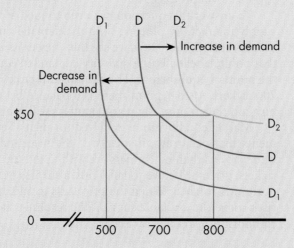

Changes in Demand A number of things can increase or decrease demand. For example, if snowboarders' incomes go up, they might decide to buy a second jacket. If incomes fall, a snowboarder who was planning to purchase a jacket might wear an old one instead. Changes in fashion or tastes can also influence demand. If snowboarding were suddenly to go out of fashion, demand for jackets would decrease quickly. A change in the price of related products can also influence demand. For example, if the average price of a snowboard rises to $1,500, some people will quit snowboarding, and jacket demand will fall.

Another factor that can shift demand is expectations about future prices. If you expect jacket prices to increase significantly in the future, you might decide to go ahead and get one today. If you think prices will fall, you will postpone your purchase. Finally, changes in the number of buyers will affect demand. Snowboarding is a young person's sport. The number of teenagers will increase in the next few years. Therefore, the demand for snowboarding jackets should increase.

Changes in Supply New technology typically lowers the cost of production. For example, North Face, a manufacturer of ski and snowboarder jackets, has just purchased laser-guided pattern-cutting equipment and computer-aided pattern-making equipment. Each jacket is now cheaper to produce, resulting in a higher profit per jacket. This becomes an incentive to supply more jackets at every price. On the other hand, if the price of resources, such as labour or fabric, goes up, North Face will earn a smaller profit on each jacket, and the amount supplied will decrease at every price. The reverse is also true. Changes in the prices of other goods can also affect supply.

Let's say that snow skiing becomes a really hot sport. The number of skiers jumps dramatically, and the price of ski jackets soars. North Face can use its machines and fabrics to produce either ski or snowboard jackets. If the company can make more profit from ski jackets, it will produce fewer snowboarding jackets at every price. Also, simply a change in the number of producers will shift the supply curve. If the number of manufacturers increases, more jackets will be placed on the market at every price, and vice versa. Taxes can also affect supply. If the government decides, for some reason, to tax the manufacturer for every snowboard jacket produced, then profits will fall and fewer jackets will be offered at every price. Exhibit 1.7 summarizes the factors that can shift demand and supply curves.

Exhibit 1.7 | Factors That Cause Demand and Supply Curves to Shift

	SHIFT DEMAND	
FACTOR	**TO THE RIGHT IF:**	**TO THE LEFT IF:**
Buyers' incomes	increase	decrease
Buyers' preferences/tastes	increase	decrease
Prices of substitute products	increase	decrease
Expectations about future prices	will rise	will fall
Number of buyers	increases	decreases
	SHIFT SUPPLY	
Technology	lowers cost	increases cost
Resource prices	fall	increase
Changes in prices of other products that can be produced with the same resources	profit of other product falls	profit of other product increases
Number of suppliers	increases	decreases
Taxes	lowered	increased

COMPETING IN A FREE MARKET

 learning goal

market structure
The number of suppliers in a market.

One of the characteristics of a free-market system is that suppliers have the right to compete with one another. The number of suppliers in a market is called **market structure.** Economists identify four types of market structures: (a) perfect competition, (b) pure monopoly, (c) monopolistic competition, and (d) oligopoly.

Perfect Competition

perfect (pure) competition
A market structure in which a large number of small firms sell similar products, buyers and sellers have good information, and businesses can be easily opened or closed.

Characteristics of **perfect (pure) competition** include

- a large number of small firms are in the market;
- the firms sell similar products; that is, each firm's product is very much like the products sold by other firms in the market;
- buyers and sellers in the market have good information about prices, sources of supply, and so on; and
- it is easy to open a new business or close an existing one.

In a perfectly competitive market, firms sell their products at prices determined solely by forces beyond their control. Because the products are very similar, and because each firm contributes only a small amount to the total quantity supplied by the industry, price is determined by supply and demand. A firm that raised its price even a little above the going rate would lose customers.

Monopolistic Competition

monopolistic competition
A market structure in which many firms offer products that are close substitutes and in which entry is relatively easy.

Three characteristics define the market structure known as **monopolistic competition:**

- Many firms are in the market.
- The firms offer products that are close substitutes but still differ from one another.
- It is relatively easy to enter the market.

Under monopolistic competition, firms take advantage of product differentiation. Industries in which monopolistic competition occurs include clothing, food, and similar consumer products. Firms under monopolistic competition have more control over pricing than do firms under perfect competition, because consumers do not view the products as exactly the same. Nevertheless, firms must demonstrate those product differences to justify their prices to customers. Consequently, companies use advertising to distinguish their products from others. Such distinctions may be significant or superficial. For example, Nike says, "Just Do It," and Tylenol is advertised as being easier on the stomach than aspirin.

Oligopoly

oligopoly
A market structure in which a few firms produce most or all of the output and in which large capital requirements or other factors limit the number of firms.

An **oligopoly** has two characteristics:

- A few firms produce most or all of the output.
- Large capital requirements or other factors limit the number of firms.

Boeing and Lockheed Martin (aircraft manufacturers) and Stelco Incorporated (Canada's largest and most diversified Canadian steel producer) are major firms in different oligopoly industries.

With so few firms in an oligopoly, what one firm does has an impact on the other firms. Thus, the firms in an oligopoly watch one another closely for new technologies, product changes and innovations, promotional campaigns, pricing, production, and other developments. Sometimes they go as far as coordinating their pricing and output decisions, which is illegal. Many antitrust cases—legal challenges arising out of laws designed to control anticompetitive behaviour—occur in oligopolies. Exhibit 1.8 summarizes the primary types of market structures.

Pure Monopoly

pure monopoly
A market structure in which a single firm accounts for all industry sales and in which there are barriers to entry.

barriers to entry
Factors, such as technological or legal conditions, that prevent new firms from competing equally with a monopoly.

At the other end of the spectrum is **pure monopoly,** the market structure in which a single firm accounts for all industry sales. The firm is the industry. This structure is characterized by **barriers to entry**—factors that prevent new firms from competing equally with the existing firm. Often the barriers are technological or legal conditions. Polaroid, for example, has held major patents on instant photography for years. When Kodak tried to market its own instant camera, Polaroid sued, claiming patent violations. Polaroid collected millions of dollars from Kodak. Another barrier might be one firm's control of a natural resource. De Beers Group, for example, controls most of the world's supply of uncut diamonds.

Public utilities such as natural gas and water are pure monopolies (although many public utilities are being privatized, and competition is being encouraged). Some monopolies have been created by government regulations that prohibit competition. Canada Post Corporation's direct mail service is one such monopoly.

Making Ethical Choices

PURCHASING POWER

As a child, you treasured your weekly allowance and delighted in scouting out the best deals. You ended up with more toys than your friends while spending the same amount of money. Your keen sense of the price of goods and ability to buy more quality products for the same money made your college friends envious. Finally, they convinced you to take their money to purchase needed items. You were a natural purchasing agent.

You understood the relationship between supply and demand and the price you were willing to pay for goods. Shortly after graduating, you accepted a position as chief purchasing agent for a public health facility (i.e., hospital).

In the hospital, you became concerned that prices paid for pharmaceutical goods seemed out of alignment with the laws of supply and demand. No more best deals. Perhaps even "a crisis with regard to the cost of prescription drugs." Two pharmaceutical companies seemed to be inflating their drug prices. Your sense about overcharging proved correct. The provincial government filed a lawsuit against the companies, accusing them of offering drugs to pharmacists at deeply discounted prices as a way of selling more. Part of the issue involved the government's wholesale price system. Could the government be impeding your purchasing power at the hospital? The companies' pricing policy seems to involve inflating the price reported to the government and then offering the pharmacists an opportunity to make money on the difference between the higher reimbursements and promised lower prices from the companies.

All of this is troubling, because you haven't been able to identify manufacturers of equivalent drugs at competitive prices.

ETHICAL DILEMMA

Would you purchase drugs that were not exactly the same to save the hospital money?

SOURCES: Christopher Bowe, "NY Attorney General Targets Drugmakers," *FT.com*, February 23, 2003, http://www.FT.com; and Hollister H. Hovey, "New York State Sues Pharmacia, Glaxo, Alleging Pricing Scheme," *Wall Street Journal*, February 14, 2003. Note: This case has been amended from its earlier publication.

Exhibit 1.8 | Types of Market Structures

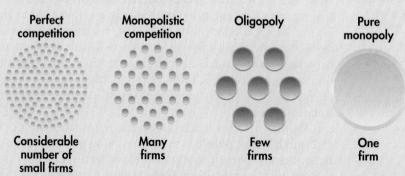

Perfect competition — Considerable number of small firms

Monopolistic competition — Many firms

Oligopoly — Few firms

Pure monopoly — One firm

Trends in Economics and Competition

8 *learning goal*

Trends in business occur at both the macroeconomic and the microeconomic levels. We will begin by taking a look at some microeconomic trends: the focus on relationship management and the creation of a competitive workforce. We will conclude with a look at the macroeconomic trend of increased entrepreneurial spirit in former command economies.

Starbucks strives to build strong customer relationships and retain loyal customers with the Starbucks Card. It offers the convenience of shopping on-line and making purchases with a quick, easy-payment method.

© TERRI L. MILLER / E-VISUAL COMMUNICATIONS, INC.

CREATING LONG-TERM RELATIONSHIPS

relationship management

The practice of building, maintaining, and enhancing interactions with customers and other parties to develop long-term satisfaction through mutually beneficial partnerships.

Today, companies are focusing on **relationship management,** which involves building, maintaining, and enhancing interactions with customers and other parties so as to develop long-term satisfaction through mutually beneficial partnerships. In general, the longer a customer stays with a company, the more that customer is worth. Long-term customers buy more, take less company time, are less sensitive to price, and bring in new customers. Best of all, they require no acquisition or start-up costs. Good long-standing customers are worth so much that in some industries, reducing customer defections by as little as five points—from, say, 15 percent to 10 percent per year—can double profits.

Travelodge practices relationship management by launching Travelodge Miles, a guest rewards program featuring swipe-card technology. The program thanks frequent Travelodge and Thriftlodge guests for their patronage with value-added rewards such as frequent-flyer miles, free hotel nights, free rental cars, and other travel perks. Guests earn one Travelodge Mile for each qualified lodging dollar spent at participating economy Travelodge and Thriftlodge properties. When 250 Miles have been accumulated, members can redeem them for Sleepy Bear dolls, T-shirts, or a road atlas, or keep saving the Miles for other rewards at higher levels. The enhanced level is already paying off with an increase in the average stay of preferred guests—almost a full night longer per stay. The system makes it easy to track and gather data on the company's best customers and enabled the creation of a "Gold Level" for preferred customers. These Gold Level customers receive preferred rates and free local phone calls.

Relationship management also means creating long-term relationships with suppliers. Suppliers are making major adjustments in their thinking, management styles, and methods of responding to purchasers' standards and operational requirements. A satisfied customer is one of the best sources of new business, because the customer already knows that the supplier can meet expectations and deliver on its promises. Thus, the supplier has created trust, and trust is the foundation of most successful relationships.

strategic alliance

A cooperative agreement between business firms; sometimes called a strategic partnership.

A **strategic alliance,** sometimes called a *strategic partnership*, is a cooperative agreement between business firms. The trend toward forming strategic alliances is accelerating rapidly, particularly among high-tech firms. These companies have realized that strategic partnerships are more than just important—they are critical. Nike, the largest producer of athletic footwear in the world, does not manufacture a single shoe. Gallo, the largest wine company on earth, does not grow a single grape. The Boeing Company, the preeminent aircraft manufacturer, makes little more than cockpits and wing bits. "How can this be?" you ask. These companies, like many other companies these days, have entered into strategic alliances with their suppliers to do much of their actual production and manufacturing for them.

CREATING A COMPETITIVE WORKFORCE

Creating and building long-term relationships require a world-class workforce. The goal of leading companies such as McCain Foods Limited and Mark's Work Wearhouse is for all workers to add value to every job they do every day. Such firms place a strong emphasis on training and the use of technology to improve worker productivity. Mark's Work Wearhouse, for example, values the investment in the training of its workers and enjoys significant savings as a result (see Chapter 4).

ENTREPRENEURIAL SPIRIT IN FORMER COMMAND ECONOMIES

A key trend in macroeconomics is the surprising entrepreneurial spirit among many citizens of former command economies.

Russia and China have inched away from planned economies. Today, China has a population of 1.3 billion, and they all want more and better goods and services. Already there are 21 million *ge-ti-hu* (entrepreneurs) in China.

One example of a Russian entrepreneur is Olga Chudakova, who founded Epic Rus, a software firm in Moscow. Olga has a PhD in economics from Moscow State University. She thinks that Russian entrepreneurs are broader, more intuitive, and more philosophical than those in North America.[2] This, she claims, is because of their mind-set. Russian education is more comprehensive, whereas education in North America is more specialized. Olga notes that her staff of 150 are loyal and highly trained. Recently Epic Rus moved to a large, beautifully renovated building and invested in the most advanced computers for all its employees.

concept check

How do businesses provide customer value?

How does relationship management make a business more competitive?

Explain the entrepreneurial movement in former command economies.

Great Ideas to Use Now

As you study micro- and macroeconomics, remember that economics is not something you should learn for an exam and then forget. Economics is an analytical science that will help you understand the world around you. It can help you be more imaginative and insightful in everyday life. You should now better understand why prices are going up or down, when interest rates will fall, and when and why the unemployment rate will fall.

Understanding these basic economic concepts can help you decide whether to change jobs (and how much money to ask for) and whether to buy a car now or wait until next year. When you hear that an automobile manufacture has 115 days of inventory, understanding supply and demand will tell you that now might be the time to buy that new car.

Similarly, economics will help you become a better informed citizen. Almost every political issue is, in some way, grounded in economic concepts. You should now know what it means to balance the budget and what problems occur with monopoly power. In short, economics can help you make more thoughtful and informed decisions.

Economics not only can help you understand what is happening in other countries but also can help raise your awareness of opportunities in those countries. As more and more countries have moved away from command economies, Canadian and foreign multinational firms are moving in to take advantage of ground-floor opportunities. Consider accepting a foreign assignment. It's a wonderful way to experience other cultures and, at the same time, get ahead in your career. More and more large organizations are requiring that their middle and upper level managers have foreign field experience. When you have an opportunity for a foreign assignment, don't let it slip by.

In today's business world, if a firm doesn't deliver customer value, it doesn't survive. Firms that provide customer value end up with satisfied customers. Some companies that are especially good at satisfying customers are Mercedes-Benz, H. J. Heinz, Lexus, Colgate-Palmolive, Mars, Maytag, Quaker Oats, Hershey Foods, Toyota, and Cadbury Schweppes. All of the companies have won either quality or customer satisfaction awards at one time or another.

Customer Satisfaction and Quality

We spoke earlier in this chapter about China's tremendous growth as a producer of goods and services for the world marketplace. The reason for that growth is that buyers are willingly purchasing the Chinese products because they deliver quality and value.

Customer value is the customer's perception of the ratio of benefits to the sacrifice necessary to obtain those benefits. Customers receive benefits in the form of functionality, performance, durability, design, ease of use, and serviceability. To receive those benefits, they give up money, time, and effort.

Customer value is not simply a matter of high quality. A high-quality product that is available only at a high price will not be perceived as a value. Nor will bare-bones service or low-quality goods selling for a low price. Instead, customers value goods and services of the quality they expect that are sold at prices they are willing to pay. Value marketing can be used to sell a $150,000 Rolls Royce as well as a $5 frozen chicken dinner.

Businesses provide customer value by ...

* *offering products that perform.* This is the bare minimum. Consumers have lost patience with shoddy merchandise.
* *giving consumers more than they expect.* Soon after Toyota launched Lexus, the company had to order a recall. The weekend before the recall, dealers personally phoned all the Lexus owners in North America and arranged to pick up their cars and provide replacement vehicles.
* *avoiding unrealistic pricing.* Consumers couldn't understand why Kellogg's cereals commanded a premium over other brands, so Kellogg's market share fell 5 percent.
* *giving the buyer facts.* Today's sophisticated consumer wants informative advertising and knowledgeable salespeople.

SUMMARY OF LEARNING GOALS

1 What is an economic system, and what economic systems are prevalent in the world today?

An economic system is the combination of policies, laws, and choices made by a nation's government to establish the systems that determine what goods and services are produced and how they are allocated. The main economic systems in the world today include market economies (capitalism), command (planned) economies, socialism, and mixed economies.

2 What is economics, what are the three sectors of the economy, and how are the three sectors of the economy linked?

Economics is the study of how individuals, businesses, and governments use scarce resources to produce and distribute goods and services. The two major areas in economics are macroeconomics, the study of the economy as a whole, and microeconomics, the study of households and firms. The individual, business, and government sectors of the economy are linked by a series of two-way flows. The government provides public goods and services for the other two sectors and receives income in the form of taxes. Changes in one flow affect the other sectors.

3 How do economic growth, full employment, and price stability indicate a nation's economic health?

A nation's economy is growing when the level of business activity, as measured by gross domestic product, is rising. GDP is the total value of all goods and services produced in a year. The goal of full employment is to have a job for all who can and want to work. How well a nation is meeting its employment goals is measured by the unemployment rate. There are four types of unemployment: frictional, structural, cyclical, and seasonal. With price stability, the overall prices of goods and services are not moving very much either up or down.

4 What is inflation, how is it measured, and what causes it?

Inflation is the general upward movement of prices. When prices rise, purchasing power falls. The rate of inflation is measured by changes in the consumer price index (CPI) and the producer price index (PPI). There are two main causes of inflation. If the demand for goods and services exceeds the supply, prices will rise. This is called demand-pull inflation. With cost-push inflation, higher production costs, such as expenses for materials and wages, increase the final prices of goods and services.

5 How does the Bank of Canada use monetary policy, and how do governments use fiscal policy to achieve their macroeconomic goals?

Monetary policy refers to actions by the Bank of Canada to control the money supply. When the Bank of Canada restricts the money supply, interest rates rise, the inflation rate drops, and economic growth slows. By expanding the money supply, the Bank of Canada stimulates economic growth.

The government uses fiscal policy—changes in levels of taxation and spending—to control the economy. Reducing taxes or increasing spending stimulates the economy; raising taxes or decreasing spending does the opposite. When the government spends more than it receives in tax revenues, it must borrow to finance the deficit. Some economists favour deficit spending as a way of stimulating the economy; others worry about our high level of national debt.

6 What are the basic microeconomic concepts of demand and supply, and how do they establish prices?

Demand is the quantity of a good or service that people will buy at a given price. Supply is the quantity of a good or service that firms will make available at a given price. When the price increases, the quantity demanded falls but the quantity supplied rises. A price decrease leads to increased demand but a lower supply. At the point where the quantity demanded equals the quantity supplied, demand and supply are in balance. This equilibrium point is achieved by market adjustments of quantity and price.

7. What are the four types of market structure?

Market structure is the number of suppliers in a market. Perfect competition is characterized by a large number of buyers and sellers, very similar products, good market information for both buyers and sellers, and ease of entry into and exit from the market. In a pure monopoly, there is a single seller in a market. In monopolistic competition, many firms sell close substitutes in a market that is fairly easy to enter. In an oligopoly, a few firms produce most or all of the industry's output. An oligopoly is also difficult to enter, and what one firm does will influence others.

8. Which trends are reshaping the micro- and macroeconomic environments?

Companies are establishing long-term relationships with both customers and suppliers. To compete in today's environment, companies and industries must build a competitive workforce. At the macro level, budding entrepreneurial spirit in former command economies is sparking wealth among individual business owners and fuelling the growth of market economies.

EXPERIENTIAL EXERCISES

1. Understand your tax commitment. Soon you will enter the permanent job market, if you are not there already. Typically, your earnings will rise over the next 35 years, but as your earnings increase, so will your taxes. The average Canadian works five to six months out of every year just to cover taxes. Are taxes too high in our country? As taxes will be a major part of your financial life for the next 35 to 45 years, you need to be informed. Visit the Web sites of a few organizations that advocate tax reform, such as the Canadian Taxpayers Federation at **http://www.taxpayer.com**.

2. Learn a new language. Consider taking a job outside of Canada for a while. If you decide to work overseas, having basic skills in a second language will go a long way toward ensuring that you have a rewarding and pleasant experience. Learning a second language can also bring a lot of self-satisfaction. Go to **http://www.learnalanguage.com** and learn more about learning a foreign language.

3. Use the Internet or go to the library and determine the current trends in GDP growth, unemployment, and inflation. What do these trends tell you about the level of business activity and the business cycle? If you owned a personnel agency, how would this information affect your decision-making?

4. As a manufacturer of in-line skates, you are questioning your pricing policies. You note that over the past five years, the CPI increased an average of 2 percent per year, but the price of a pair of skates increased an average of 8 percent per year for the first three years and 2 percent for the next two years. What does this information tell you about demand, supply, and other factors influencing the market for these skates?

5. Write a paper describing an occasion on which you received outstanding customer value and an occasion when you received very poor customer value.

6. Divide the class into four teams. One pair of teams will debate the pros and cons of airline deregulation. The other pair will debate electric-utility deregulation. One team should take the pro and the other the con for each issue. If you have Internet access, use the Dow Jones news service, ABI, or another database to obtain current articles on the subjects.

REVIEW QUESTIONS

1. What are the factors of production? How do they work together to produce goods and services?
2. What are the four types of economies? How do they differ regarding the ownership and allocation of the factors of production?
3. Distinguish between macro- and microeconomics. What are the three main macro goals?
4. How do GDP and GNP differ?
5. What are the various types of unemployment?
6. What are monetary policy and fiscal policy? Who is responsible for each?
7. What are contractionary policy and expansionary policy?
8. What is relationship management? How can it be achieved?
9. What is a strategic alliance? What are its benefits to the companies involved?
10. Why is it important for companies to create a competitive workforce?
11. How can understanding economics help you as a consumer? As a business manager or owner?

CREATIVE THINKING CASE
Inside Intel: It's about Copying—Exactly

Intel Corporation has more than 2,000 PhDs on staff to cultivate new ideas. But innovation also depends on people like Trish Roughgarden, an Air Force veteran whose job is to copy slavishly. Ms. Roughgarden is known inside Intel as a "seed," an unofficial title for technicians who transfer manufacturing know-how from one Intel chip factory to another. Her job: to help ensure that Intel's latest plant works just like an identical plant in Hillsboro, Oregon. Several hundred other seeds will copy the same techniques to a third plant in Ireland.

It is all part of a major Intel strategy known as "Copy Exactly," which discourages experimentation at individual factories. Instead, engineers and technicians painstakingly clone proven Intel manufacturing techniques from one plant to the next—down to the colour of workers' gloves and wall paint, or other features that would seem to have no bearing on efficiency.

The strategy emerged after Intel's most recent disastrous slump, when maddening variations between factories in the early 1980s hurt productivity and product quality. Japanese competitors nearly drove Intel out of business. Today, Copy Exactly shapes Intel's response to the latest economic downturn, helping accelerate the relentless pace of technology improvements known as Moore's Law, after former Intel chairman Gordon Moore.

Intel's newest plant contains 200,000 square feet of new factory space, linked to an existing 300,000-square-foot facility to create what Intel believes is the world's largest semiconductor "clean room." One corridor stretches 900 feet, an avenue of white, ventilated flooring intersecting side streets called bays and chases. The price: more than $2 billion, roughly the same as the Oregon and Ireland additions.

Although it prohibits willy-nilly changes, the Copy Exactly methodology encourages Intel workers to come up with ideas to boost productivity or make chip features smaller. But the ideas must pass a committee called the Process Change Control Board, which requires workers to come up with tests to prove the value of their suggestions.

Intel's bureaucracy "creates frustration" for some engineers, concedes Youssef Aly El-Mansy, an Intel vice president in charge of developing manufacturing processes. "We've lost some people from that."[3]

CRITICAL THINKING QUESTIONS

1. Explain the link between quality and "Copy Exactly."

2. How important is technology to a global competitor like Intel? What about product quality?

3. Most management consultants claim that employees are happiest when they have freedom to make decisions in the work environment. How does this fit with Copy Exactly? What can be done to let employees exercise their creativity?

SOURCE: Adapted from Don Clark, "In Setting Up It's New Plants, Chip Maker Clones Older Ones Down to the Paint on the Wall," Wall Street Journal (October 28, 2002), pp. B1, B4. Reprinted by permission of the Wall Street Journal, Copyright © 2002 Dow Jones & Company, Inc. All Rights Reserved Worldwide.

VIDEO CASE

Black Forest Motors: A Triple Whammy that Works

Headquartered in Germany, Mercedes-Benz (http://www.mercedes-benz.com) manufactures luxury automobiles for distribution in Germany, the United States, and elsewhere. To increase sales and perceived customer value in the United States, Mercedes-Benz initiated the "Customer Value Triad," a corporate strategy comprising three key components: quality goods, quality service, and value-based pricing. Although quality goods and value-based pricing are generated by the manufacturer, the 310 independently owned U.S. dealerships and their 16,000 employees are the most important element when it comes to providing customers with quality service.

Black Forest Motors, a Mercedes-Benz dealership in North Acme, Michigan, is a prime example of Mercedes-Benz's corporate strategy in action. Black Forest prides itself on exceeding customers' expectations with fair pricing and quality goods and services. Dedicated employees, who have been with Black Forest Motors since its founding, translate directly into quality customer service, ensuring that the dealership is not only a great place to work but "a great place to buy a car." Enjoying the benefits of the Customer Value Triad initiative, Black Forest's customer base, their "family of owners," continues to grow.

The sales, service, and parts departments all powerfully demonstrate Black Forest's commitment to quality service, quality goods, and value-based pricing. The sales department's sole purpose is to exceed customer expectations, from test drive to vehicle delivery. Customers can schedule their test drive on-line through Black Forest's Web site, meet with a sales staff committed to providing the information they need to make an educated buying decision, and drive away in the Mercedes-Benz perfect for them.

The service department is a state-of-the-art facility featuring the latest diagnostic and repair equipment used by highly trained factory technicians. This department operates on the basis that "you and your vehicle deserve only the best of care." Quality goods and quality service are also emphasized in the parts department, which is stocked with a large inventory of the same high-quality parts used in manufacturing Mercedes-Benz vehicles.

Committed to the Customer Value Triad of quality goods, quality service, and value-based pricing, Black Forest Motors asks only one thing of its clients: "If you were treated well, your expectations met, and the service good, please tell your friends."

SOURCE: http://www.mercedes-benz.com (accessed February 2003).

CRITICAL THINKING QUESTIONS

1. Do you think the Mercedes-Benz Customer Value Triad is an effective corporate strategy?

2. How might a strategy based on the Customer Value Triad help Mercedes-Benz and its dealerships compete effectively in the North American marketplace?

3. Why are product and service quality important elements of operating a successful business? What is the impact on the price of cars?

4. Does Mercedes-Benz operate in an oligopolistic marketplace?

E-COMMERCE CASE
Travels with Orbitz

In 2000, five major airlines—American, United, Continental, Delta, and Northwest—announced plans to launch a new on-line travel site called Orbitz (**http://www.orbitz.com**). Like on-line travel pioneer sites Travelocity and Expedia, Orbitz would let consumers search for the best airfares. Thirty other airlines quickly agreed to post their fares on the Orbitz site. Each participating airline had to agree to publish its lowest fares on the Orbitz site. The airlines, however, weren't prevented from offering the same low fares elsewhere on the Internet. One airline that decided not to join Orbitz was Southwest. The company explained that it didn't feel comfortable providing information on its fares to a company run by its top competitors.

Even before Orbitz officially opened, controversy arose. The Interactive Travel Services Association (ITSA), a trade association of on-line travel sites whose membership includes both Travelocity and Expedia, said the airline industry was jealous of the profits made by on-line travel sites and that Orbitz was an organized effort by the airlines to "cash in" on those profits by wiping out competitive travel-booking sites. Orbitz would give airlines an unfair advantage, said the ITSA, by encouraging price fixing between airlines.

After an initial investigation, the U.S. Department of Transportation agreed that Orbitz could provide the potential for unfair competition, but it didn't stop the company's launch. Instead, it agreed to review the case again after Orbitz was in operation for six months. At that point, the Department of Transportation said it hadn't found any unfair trade practices in the Orbitz operation, nor did it see any negative effect on competition or consumer choice. At the ITSA's urging, Orbitz has come under federal scrutiny several times since then, but the government has not found Orbitz in violation of any anticompetition laws.

Antonella Pianalto, ITSA executive director, is unconvinced. "The evidence is clear: Orbitz is harming competition. Prior to Orbitz, both consumers and airlines benefited from independent distributors who fiercely negotiated for the best available fares and placed downward pressure on those fares by forcing the airlines to compete. Now airlines have little incentive to compete because they don't have to use other on-line sites."

Nonsense, counters Orbitz CEO Jeff Katz. "The on-line travel marketplace was already dominated by a 'Big Two'—Travelocity and Expedia. Their complaints about us are a little like Coke and Pepsi teaming up to run Dr Pepper out of the market."

Although still third in size behind Travelocity and Expedia, Orbitz is currently the fastest-growing on-line travel site, with revenues topping $1 billion a year. On-line air ticket purchases continue to grow, with over $14 billion worth of tickets purchased last year. However, the company has not yet turned a profit.

CRITICAL THINKING QUESTIONS

1. Do you agree with the ITSA's position or that of Orbitz CEO Jeff Katz about the effect Orbitz is having on competition and consumer choice? Defend your answer.

2. Explain how supply and demand affect the price of airline tickets. How could a change in either supply or demand affect the growth of on-line travel sites? Would Orbitz be in a better position to deal with these changes than Travelocity or Expedia? Why?

SOURCES: Greg Sandoval, "Competitors Call Orbitz Tactics into Question," CNet/News.com, November 20, 2001, http://www.news.com; Rachel Konrad, "Lawmakers Urge Stronger Orbitz Probe," CNet/News.com, April 25, 2002, http://www.news.com; Greg Sandoval, "Agency: Orbitz Could Harm Competition," CNet/News.com, June 27, 2002, http://www.news.com; and David Wessel, Airlines' Orbitz: Consumers' Friend or Foe?" *Wall Street Journal*, August 29, 2002.

2

Making the Connection

The Global Marketplace and Governments' Roles

In Chapter 1 we looked at economic systems and competition as one factor in the external economic environment of a business. In this chapter you will learn about global trade and the role of the government in promoting global trade as well as protecting domestic trade. This chapter deals directly with the interrelationship between the *political* environment (the government's role) and the *economic* environment (the global marketplace), two factors in our PEST model. As we saw in Chapter 1, and will see again in this chapter, these two factors are related to each other, and they impact the success of the business.

For example, the external environment presents opportunities and threats for a business. The business considers these opportunities and threats when determining its *strategy* for the future. In this chapter, we discuss Team Canada, a partnership between government and industry to promote global trade. Team Canada is an initiative of the political environment that presents opportunities for Canadian business to gain access to international markets. This opportunity is one that many businesses have capitalized on to develop and expand exposure for their products in global markets. Expanding their businesses globally is one strategy that these companies have chosen to meet their growth objectives. One environmental factor

that has affected global trade negatively is the threat of terrorism. As discussed in the chapter, this factor will not stop globalization, but it will likely slow its growth and make it costlier because of tighter controls.

We will also discuss free trade zones in this chapter. This is another way in which government helps to create opportunities for business to expand. How a business capitalizes on these political initiatives depends on its strategy, and so we will explore different strategies for expanding in the global marketplace: exporting, licensing, joint ventures, and so on.

Other political initiatives result in threats to business. Tariff and non-tariff barriers are obvious examples. In an attempt to protect domestic trade, governments set up obstacles for foreign competition by making foreign goods more expensive through tariffs or by restricting the import of foreign goods through quotas. These barriers are meant to create opportunities for domestic companies to grow within a protected domestic environment; however, they may very well stifle these companies instead, because they don't have to *innovate* (one of the critical success factors) and improve their operations to compete with this foreign competition.

These opportunities and threats exist in the economic environment as well. Companies need to have a global *vision* to recognize and react to international business opportunities, as well as to remain competitive at home. In relation to our model of a successful business, what this means is that the *vision* that is created for the company must take the global economic environment in which it operates into account to survive and prosper. The environment affects the business. Opportunities exist in the global economic environment—that is sure. But even if a business decides not to pursue a strategy that involves selling in the global marketplace, it cannot ignore the fact that foreign firms can and will still compete in the domestic marketplace. This foreign competition presents a threat to a Canadian enterprise—one that, if ignored, can easily put it out of business.

This chapter also gives several examples of how the other aspects of the external environment affect or are affected by global trade. Technological factors, such as transportation improvements and the Internet, make physical distances less of a barrier to global trade than they used to be. Companies like Federal Express, as discussed later in the chapter, can take advantage of both these factors, as transportation improvements have greatly increased efficiency and advanced computerized tracking software can communicate where packages are at any time. Other barriers still exist, however. Language and cultural differences, and a sense of nationalism, are natural barriers to trade with foreign countries. These differences are part of the *social* environment of these countries that must be considered in terms of the products that are sold and the way business is conducted.

All of these external environmental factors interact when a business enters the global marketplace. They affect the vision for the company and its strategy for competing. They also affect the internal environment. The *marketing* department must consider the different needs of customers in different countries in which a company's products are sold. The *operations* department must consider the logistics of operating in a global environment depending on the strategic option chosen—exporting to the country or investing in its own facilities in that country, for example. The *human resources* department must consider the skills needed of its employees to do business effectively in foreign countries, language being an obvious example. And the *finance* department must consider differences in exchange rates to maintain the company's profitability.

If a company considers its external environment carefully and develops a global vision for doing business, it can work toward achieving the critical success factors. It can *achieve financial performance* by *meeting the needs* of foreign *customers* with *products of value* to their unique tastes and circumstances. And whether its strategy is to expand into foreign markets or not, it will be forced to innovate to stay ahead of foreign competition. These critical factors of success are, of course, achieved through a *committed workforce*.

© AP/WORLD WIDE PHOTOS

The Global Marketplace and Governments' Roles

learning goals

The Viennese Lap up Starbucks

It takes some hubris to bring a North American coffee shop to Vienna, the city of cafés, and then to ban smoking in it. But no one has ever considered Starbucks (**http://www.starbucks.com**) humble. And the move, a keystone of Starbucks's rapid expansion in Europe, appears to have paid off. Since the Karntnerstrasse coffeehouse opened in December 2001, in the smoky, beating heart of Vienna, near the Opera House, it has been a resounding success.

Many Viennese believe that their culture has been infected, that Viennese use their 1,900 or so coffee shops to linger and meet, smoke and drink, savour the wonders of pastries with cream and marzipan, ponder the world, write books, and read free newspapers. They drink from china cups and order from a waiter, usually in a stained black dinner jacket.

Some Austrians say a caramel macchiato is worse than a Coca-Cola, likely to do more damage to European values (and waistlines) than a Big Mac. There was also skepticism about the Starbucks brand, associated with globalization and mass North American culture.

"It was the hardest part," said Franz Holzschuh, who leads the Starbucks joint venture in Austria. "People would say, 'You're the McDonald's of coffee, with paper cups.' I'd explain a hundred times that we're not McDonald's, that we're high quality and not cheap, and only use paper cups to go."

The smoking issue loomed large as well. Holzschuh, a heavy smoker, originally argued that no Austrian coffee shop could possibly ban cigarettes. "Some 40 percent of Europeans smoke and 60 percent of Italians," he said. "That's half your market!" Starbucks' bosses were unfazed. "They said that we have 3,000 nonsmoking stores and the 3,001st will be nonsmoking too." Holzschuh conceded, but kept thinking, "OK, friends, let's wait and see."

In Austria, there is a coffeehouse for every 530 people, and Austrians drink 1,000 cups of coffee a year outside homes and offices. This is, quite simply, the densest coffee market in the world. One of the most competitive, too. "Austrians love their coffee," Holzschuh said. "We go three or four times a day to a coffeehouse to meet friends or do business."[1]

Critical Thinking Questions

1. What are some factors that can make success difficult in the global marketplace?
2. What can governments do to protect domestic competitors from firms like Starbucks?
3. What cultural differences should Starbucks consider when entering other European markets?

SOURCE: Erlanger, Steven J., "The Viennese Lap Up Starbucks," *International Herald Tribune*, June 03, 2002, p. 1, 4. Copyright © 2002 by The New York Times Co. Reprinted with permission.

global vision

The ability to recognize and react to international business opportunities, be aware of threats from foreign competition, and effectively use international distribution networks to obtain raw materials and move finished products to customers.

Today, global revolutions are under way in many areas of our lives: management, politics, communications, and technology, to name a few. The word global has assumed a new meaning, referring to a boundless mobility and competition in social, business, and intellectual arenas. No longer just an option, having a global vision has become a business imperative. Having a **global vision** means recognizing and reacting to international business opportunities, being aware of threats from foreign competitors in all markets, and effectively using international distribution networks to obtain raw materials and move finished products to the customer.

Canadian managers must develop a global vision if they are to recognize and react to international business opportunities, as well as remain competitive at home. Often a Canadian firm's toughest domestic competition comes from foreign companies. Moreover, a global vision enables a manager to understand that customer and distribution networks operate worldwide, blurring geographic and political barriers and making them increasingly irrelevant to business decisions. The purpose of this chapter is to explain how global trade is conducted. We also discuss the barriers to international trade and the organizations that foster global trade. We conclude the chapter with a discussion of trends in the global marketplace.

CANADA GOES GLOBAL

1 learning goal

Over the past two decades, world trade has climbed from $200 billion (USD) a year to more than $4 trillion (USD). Countries and companies that were never considered major players in global markets are now contributing to this growth in world trade. In 2005 Canada exported over $450 billion and imported almost $390 billion in goods and services.[2]

On the Champs Élysées, this McDonald's is the most frequented restaurant in France. Designed to appeal to local customers, the restaurant offers a cozy Parisian atmosphere.

© AP/WORLD WIDE PHOTOS

Go into a Paris McDonald's, and you might not recognize where you are. There are no utilitarian chairs and tables and other plastic features. The restaurants have exposed brick walls, hardwood floors, and armchairs. Some French McDonald's even have faux marble walls. Most restaurants have TVs with continuous music videos. You can even order an espresso, beer, or chicken sandwich made with focaccia bread.[3]

Global business is not a one-way street, where only Canadian companies sell their wares and services throughout the world. Foreign competition in the domestic market used to be relatively rare but now occurs in almost every industry. Nevertheless, the global market has created vast, new business opportunities for many Canadian firms.

The Importance of Global Business to Canada

One reason the United Nations has ranked Canada as one of the best countries in which to live is because of our ability to do business with the "outside world." According to the Department of Foreign Affairs and International Trade, "trade enhances the quality of Canadian life" and helps give Canadians the economic energy we need to create the nation we want.[4]

Just how important is international trade to Canada? Canada's population, at approximately 33 million, is relatively small versus the 6.5 billion people worldwide. This translates into roughly 200 times more potential customers for Canadian business. Canada exports approximately 45 percent of what Canadians produce. In terms of a dollar value, we export more than $15,000 in goods and services of what we produce for each Canadian resident. Every $1 billion increase in Canada's exports translates into more than 10,000 jobs, and approximately 33 percent of all jobs rely on exports.[5] We can see that exports are vital to the Canadian economy.

But can we maintain this advantage and keep our economy growing? The simple answer is no—not unless we continue to develop outside markets. Canada has seen international trade increase, helped in part by its proactive partnership between government and industry known as "Team Canada Missions." These missions are led by the prime minister with participation by the provincial premiers, territorial government leaders, and the minister of international trade and have as their aim to increase international trade and create or sustain jobs for Canadians. Similar to the Team Canada Missions are the Canada Trade Missions, which are led by the Minister of International Trade with the provincial trade ministers invited to participate.

HOT Links
For more information about Team Canada Inc see http://www.exportsource.ca.

Successful missions have included Russia, Germany, India, China, Brazil, Mexico, Saudi Arabia, and the United Arab Emirates, to name just a few. The focus of the missions is to emphasize Canadian commercial, political, educational, and cultural links with the countries visited. The presence and support of prominent government leaders facilitates access to crucial economic decision makers for Canadian firms and provides a much greater public profile for the business participants, helping them network with the international business community.[6]

"Team Canada missions send a strong message to prospective partners that Canada is committed to doing business with them. The missions help build prestige and credibility for Canada while helping new exporters, particularly small- and medium-sized firms, to position themselves in markets where competition is fierce. This is important when you consider that smaller businesses create most new jobs in Canada but only about 10 percent of them are currently involved in international markets."[7]

International trade refers to imports as well as exports. If we expect countries to purchase our products, they will need the dollars that are generated by their exports to do so. Imports offer Canadians a wider range and choice of products and services to purchase. Our economy has become more sophisticated in recent decades (see Chapter 1), developing into a knowledge-based economy. Canada's technological potential is ranked first among nations according to the Global *Competitiveness Report*.[8] If Canada is to capitalize on its technical potential, we must convert this potential into global success.

Not only does international trade affect the Canadian economy and provide employment for Canadians, other benefits have been identified. These include

- economies of scale in production and marketing;
- ease of the transfer of experience, technology, and know-how across borders;
- global recognition of products and brand names, allowing for easier introduction of new products and services; and
- the possibility of a uniform global image for the companies.

concept check

What is a global vision, and why is it important?

What impact does international trade have on the Canadian economy and Canadians?

The Impact of Terrorism on Global Trade

The terrorist attacks on the United States on September 11, 2001, changed forever the way the world conducts business. The immediate impact was a short-term shrinkage of global trade. Globalization will continue because the world's major markets are too vitally integrated for globalization to stop. Nevertheless, the growth will be slower and costlier than anticipated.

Companies are paying more for insurance and to provide security for overseas staff and property. Heightened border inspections slow movements of cargo, forcing companies to stock more inventory. Tighter immigration policies have curtailed the former liberal inflows of skilled and blue-collar workers that allowed companies to expand while keeping wages in check. Meanwhile, greater concern about political risk is causing companies to narrow their horizons greatly when making new investments.[9] The impact of terrorism will lessen over time, but multinational firms will always be on guard.

MEASURING TRADE BETWEEN NATIONS

International trade improves relationships with friends and allies, helps ease tensions among nations, and—economically speaking—bolsters economies, raises people's standard of living, provides jobs, and improves the quality of life. The value of international trade is more than $4.6 trillion (USD) a year and growing. In this section, we take a look at some key measures of international trade: exports and imports, the balance of trade, the balance of payments, and exchange rates.

Exports and Imports

The developed nations (those with mature communication, financial, educational, and distribution systems) are the major players in international trade, accounting for about 70 percent of the world's exports and imports. **Exports** are goods and services made in one country and sold to others. **Imports** are goods and services that are bought from other countries. Canada is both an exporter and importer. The main countries (based on dollar amounts) that Canada trades with are listed in Exhibit 2.1.

Many Canadian exports and imports are transported between Canada and the United States by the rail systems.

PHOTO BY LINDA CRAIG

As Exhibit 2.1 illustrates, approximately 81 percent of Canada's exports are to the United States, and approximately 67 percent of imports come from the United States. This heavy reliance that Canada has on the United States for trade is one rationale for Canada's seeking other international trading partners. Recent studies have shown that Canadian imports are coming less and less from the United States and Japan. In 2005 about 40 percent of Canada's imports came from other countries, with China providing much in the consumer and investment goods areas. It should be noted that although these imports are from China, many of these products are assembled in China from part manufactured elsewhere in Asia.[10] For the most part, Canada increases its exports and imports each year.

Exhibit 2.1	Chart of Canada's Main Trading Partners Based on Dollar Amounts					
	2000	**2001**	**2002**	**2003**	**2004**	**2005**
			$ millions			
Exports	**429,372.2**	**420,730.4**	**414,056.0**	**400,175.4**	**429,134.2**	**453,600.**
United States[1]	359,021.2	352,165.0	347,072.1	330,468.3	350,769.3	369,284.1
Japan	11,297.4	10,120.8	10,146.9	9,770.3	9,958.0	10,488.1
United Kingdom	7,273.3	6,910.3	6,182.2	7,699.7	9,439.7	9,692.0
Other European Economic Community countries	16,846.3	16,688.9	16,353.0	16,423.6	17,461.7	19,211.9
Other OECD[2]	12,059.0	12,172.5	12,460.5	12,679.6	14,394.4	15,238.4
Other countries[3]	22,875.1	22,672.9	21,841.3	23,134.0	27,111.0	29,685.7
Imports	**362,336.7**	**350,071.2**	**356,758.6**	**342,608.0**	**363,075.8**	**386,906.9**
United States[1]	266,511.1	254,330.7	255,259.7	240,291.9	250,064.4	258,430.0

Continued

	2000	2001	2002	2003	2004	2005
			$ millions			
Japan	11,729.8	10,571.9	11,732.6	10,644.9	10,018.9	11,182.6
United Kingdom	12,289.3	11,954.1	10,180.9	9,166.1	9,461.2	9,111.6
Other European Economic Community countries	21,136.5	23,197.1	25,862.1	25,999.7	27,014.6	29,247.7
Other OECD[2]	19,067.6	18,649.8	19,685.6	19,692.0	22,217.1	24,115.2
Other countries[3]	31,602.5	31,367.6	34,037.6	36,813.4	44,299.6	54,819.8
Balance	**67,035.5**	**70,659.2**	**57,297.4**	**57,567.4**	**66,058.4**	**66,693.3**
United States[1]	92,510.1	97,834.3	91,812.4	90,176.4	100,704.9	110,854.1
Japan	-432.4	-451.1	-1,585.7	-874.6	-60.9	-694.5
United Kingdom	-5,016.0	-5,043.8	-3,998.7	-1,466.4	-21.5	580.4
Other European Economic Community countries	-4,290.2	-6,508.2	-9,509.1	-9,576.1	-9,552.9	-10,035.8
Other OECD[2]	-7,008.6	-6,477.3	-7,225.1	-7,012.4	-7,822.7	-8,876.8
Other countries[3]	-8,727.4	-8,694.7	-12,196.3	-13,679.4	-17,188.6	-25,134.1

1. Includes also Puerto Rico and Virgin Islands.
2. Organization for Economic Co-operation and Development excluding the United States, Japan, United Kingdom and the other European Economic Community countries.
3. Countries not included in the European Economic Community or the OECD.

SOURCE: Adapted from the Statistics Canada CANSIM database "http://cansim2.statcan.ca/"

Making Ethical Choices

THE IMPACT OF MOVING OPERATIONS?

As one of the leading strategists for your company, you have been assigned to a project that is examining the possibility of moving the company's production operations to China. You are looking at the advantages and disadvantages of doing so before reporting to the project team. Whatever you recommend will have ramifications both in Canada and internationally.

Currently production is in Ontario, which is close to your primary customer base. Your company has been successful with Team Canada in China and has negotiated for the right to sell your products in China. As there is an opportunity for a larger Chinese market for your products, much greater than your existing Canadian customer base, one option would be to move the production closer to your "new primary customer base." The other option is to maintain the Canadian production operations. Costs will not allow you to have two production facilities.

Here are some of the considerations:

1. Your present customer base for your "consumer" products (those products bought by the end user) is in Canada, but with the new opportunity in China you believe that the customer base will shift to China.

2. Your history has been as a Canadian producer. How will your existing Canadian customers view your move?

3. If your company moves production to China, it will have to lay off about 300 Canadian workers.

4. The labour is abundant in China and is considerably less expensive than in Canada.
5. In addition to labour costs, you can cut other production costs by moving the operations to China.
6. Moving production to China will give your company more control over workers because of the lack of labour laws and employee rights.

7. You have concerns about the human rights issues that have been raised concerning China in recent years.

ETHICAL DILEMMA
What would you recommend? Why?

Balance of Trade

balance of trade
The difference between the value of a country's exports and the value of its imports during a certain time.

trade surplus
A favourable balance of trade that occurs when a country exports more than it imports.

trade deficit
An unfavourable balance of trade that occurs when a country imports more than it exports.

balance of payments
A summary of a country's international financial transactions showing the difference between the country's total payments to and total receipts from other countries.

The difference between the value of a country's exports and the value of its imports during a certain time is the country's **balance of trade**. A country that exports more than it imports is said to have a *favourable* balance of trade, called a **trade surplus**. A country that imports more than it exports is said to have an *unfavourable* balance of trade, or a **trade deficit**. When imports exceed exports, more money from tradebox flows out of the country than flows into it.

Balance of Payments

Another measure of international trade is called the **balance of payments**, which is a summary of a country's international financial transactions showing the difference between the country's total payments to and total receipts from other countries. The balance of payments includes imports and exports (balance of trade), long-term investments in overseas plants and equipment, government loans to and from other countries, gifts and foreign aid, military expenditures made in other countries, and money transfers into and out of foreign banks.

Although Canada has a favourable balance of trade, it is due to our trade with the United States (i.e., if we exclude our trade with the United States, Canada would have an unfavourable balance of trade). The lower section of Exhibit 2.1 shows that our overall favourable balance of trade is increasing, but as the United States increases its trade with other countries, Canada's balance of trade might become unfavourable.

The Changing Value of Currencies

HOT Links

Export Development Canada provides Canadian exporters with financing, insurance, and bonding services as well as foreign market expertise. Visit its Web site (http://www.edc.ca).

HOT Links

Check out the current Canadian balance of trade with various countries by going to http://www.statcan.ca and then, using the search menu, typing in "balance of trade" for the latest URL.

The exchange rate is the price of one country's currency in terms of another country's currency. If a country's currency *appreciates*, less of that country's currency is needed to buy another country's currency. If a country's currency *depreciates*, more of that currency will be needed to buy another country's currency.

How do appreciation and depreciation affect the prices of a country's goods? If, say, the Canadian dollar depreciates relative to the Japanese yen, Canadian residents will have to pay more dollars to buy Japanese goods. To illustrate, suppose the dollar price of a yen is $0.012 and a Toyota is priced at 2 million yen. At this exchange rate, a Canadian resident pays $24,000 for a Toyota ($0.012 × 2 million yen = $24,000). If the dollar depreciates to $0.018 to one yen, then the Canadian resident will have to pay $36,000 for a Toyota.

As the dollar depreciates, the prices of Japanese goods rise for Canadian residents, so they buy fewer Japanese goods—thus, Canadian imports decline. At the same time as the dollar depreciates relative to the yen, the yen appreciates relative to the dollar. This means prices of Canadian goods fall for the Japanese, so they buy more Canadian goods—and Canadian exports rise.

floating exchange rates

A system in which prices of currencies move up and down based on the demand for and supply of the various currencies.

devaluation

A lowering of the value of a nation's currency relative to other currencies.

HOT Links

Get up-to-the-minute exchange rates at http://xe.net/currency.

Currency markets operate under a system called **floating exchange rates**. Prices of currencies "float" up and down based on the demand for and supply of each currency. Global currency traders create the supply of and demand for a particular currency based on that currency's investment, trade potential, and economic strength. If a country decides that its currency is not properly valued in international currency markets, the government may step in and adjust the currency's value. In a **devaluation**, a nation lowers the value of its currency relative to other currencies. In 2002 Argentina was forced to devalue its currency, prompting a spike in inflation, and a rise in unemployment and food prices coupled with a fall in wages. By June 2002, 56 percent of Argentineans were living below the poverty level. The economy is recovering as the unemployment rate of 25 percent in 2002 declined to 13 percent in 2004, but the recovery is gradual. Many new jobs are in the lower paying category, leading to a greater gap between the haves and the have-nots. In 1999, the richest worker made 26 times as much as the poorest. In 2005, the richest now earns 33 times as much as the poorest worker. Unless this gap is narrowed, other problems will soon emerge.[11]

concept check

What is the difference between balance of trade and balance of payments?

What impact does international trade have on the Canadian economy?

Explain the impact of a currency devaluation.

WHY NATIONS TRADE

2 learning goal

One might argue that the best way to protect workers and the domestic economy is to stop trade with other nations. Then the whole circular flow of inputs and outputs would stay within our borders. But if we decided to do that, how would we get resources like cotton and coffee beans? Canada simply can't produce some things, and it can't manufacture some products, such as steel and most clothing, at the low costs we're used to. The fact is that nations—like people—are good at producing different things: You might be better at balancing a ledger than repairing a car. In that case, you benefit by "exporting" your bookkeeping services and "importing" the car repairs you need from a good mechanic. Economists refer to specialization like this as *advantage*.

Absolute Advantage

absolute advantage

The situation when a country can produce and sell a product at a lower cost than any other country or when it is the only country that can provide the product.

A country has an **absolute advantage** when it can produce and sell a product at a lower cost than any other country or when it is the only country that can provide a product. Canada, for example, has an absolute advantage in softwood and certain technologies.

Suppose that Canada has an absolute advantage in air traffic control systems for busy airports and that Brazil has an absolute advantage in coffee. Canada does not have the proper climate for growing coffee, and Brazil lacks the technology to develop air traffic control systems. Both countries would gain by exchanging air traffic control systems for coffee.

principle of comparative advantage

The concept that each country should specialize in the products that it can produce most readily and cheaply and trade those products for those that other countries can produce more readily and cheaply.

Comparative Advantage

Even if Canada had an absolute advantage in both coffee and air traffic control systems, it should still specialize and engage in trade. Why? The reason is the **principle of comparative advantage**, which says that each country should specialize in the products that it can produce most readily and cheaply and trade those products for goods that foreign countries can produce most readily and cheaply. This specialization ensures greater product availability and lower prices.

For example, Mexico and China have a comparative advantage in producing clothing because of low labour costs. Japan has long held a comparative advantage in consumer electronics because of technological expertise. America has an advantage in computer software, airplanes, some agricultural products, heavy machinery, and jet engines.

Thus, comparative advantage acts as a stimulus to trade. When nations allow their citizens to trade whatever goods and services they choose without government regulation, free trade exists. **Free trade** is the policy of permitting the people of a country to buy and sell where they please without restrictions. The opposite of free trade is **protectionism**, in which a nation protects its home industries from outside competition by establishing artificial barriers such as tariffs and quotas. In the next section, we'll look at the various barriers, some natural and some created by governments, that restrict free trade.

free trade
The policy of permitting the people of a country to buy and sell where they please without restrictions.

protectionism
The policy of protecting home industries from outside competition by establishing artificial barriers such as tariffs and quotas.

The Fear of Trade and Globalization

The protests in Genoa and Seattle during meetings of the World Trade Organization and the protests in New York during the convocation of the World Bank and the International Monetary Fund (the three organizations are discussed later in the chapter) showed that many people fear world trade and globalization. What do they fear? The negatives of global trade are as follows:

- Canadians have lost jobs because of imports or production shifts abroad. Most find new jobs, but those jobs often pay less.
- Others fear losing their jobs, especially at those companies operating under competitive pressure.
- Employers often threaten to export jobs if workers do not accept pay cuts.
- Service and white-collar workers are increasingly vulnerable to seeing their operations moving offshore.[12]

Benefits of Globalization

A closer look, however, reveals that globalization has been the engine that creates jobs and wealth. Benefits of global trade include the following:

- In China and the rest of East Asia, more than 300 million people rose out of poverty between 1990 and 2000. The main reason was global trade.[13]
- In Africa, with its many developing economies, per capita income rose 3.6 percent per year during the 1990s, double the 1.8 percent of developed countries, and trade was the single biggest reason.[14]
- Productivity grows more quickly when countries produce goods and services in which they have a comparative advantage. Living standards can go up faster.
- Global competition and cheap imports keep down prices, so inflation is less likely to arrest economic growth.
- An open economy spurs innovation with fresh ideas from abroad.
- Export jobs often pay more than other jobs.[15]

concept check

Describe the policy of free trade and its relationship to comparative advantage.

Why do people fear globalization?

What are the benefits of globalization?

BARRIERS TO TRADE

3 *learning goal*

International trade is carried out by both businesses and governments—as long as no one puts up trade barriers. In general, trade barriers keep firms from selling to one another in foreign markets. The major obstacles to international trade are natural barriers, tariff barriers, and non-tariff barriers.

Natural Barriers

Natural barriers to trade can be either physical or cultural. For instance, even though raising beef in the relative warmth of Argentina might cost less than raising beef in the bitter cold of Siberia, the cost of shipping the beef from South America to Siberia might drive the price too high. *Distance* is thus one of the natural barriers to international trade.

Some other natural barriers include

- *language differences*—people who can't communicate effectively might not be able to negotiate trade agreements or might ship the wrong goods;
- *cultural differences*—companies that wish to pursue business with countries whose culture is different from theirs must consider these differences and adjust their operations, products, services, and so on, to account for the differences; and
- *legal and regulatory differences*—Canadian companies have to consider not only Canadian laws and regulations but also the laws and regulations of the host country.

Tariff Barriers

tariff
A tax imposed on imported goods.

A **tariff** is a tax imposed by a nation on imported goods. It might be a charge per unit, such as per barrel of oil or per new car; it might be a percentage of the value of the goods, such as 5 percent of a $500,000 shipment of shoes; or it might be a combination. No matter how it is assessed, any tariff makes imported goods more costly, so they are less able to compete with domestic products.

protective tariffs
Tariffs that are imposed to make imports less attractive to buyers than domestic products are.

Protective tariffs make imported products less attractive to buyers than domestic products. The United States, for instance, has at times imposed protective tariffs on imported softwood from Canada. On the other side of the world, Japan imposes a tariff on U.S. cigarettes that makes them cost 60 percent more than Japanese brands. U.S. tobacco firms believe they could get as much as a third of the Japanese market if there were no tariffs on cigarettes. With tariffs, they have less than 2 percent of the market.

ARGUMENTS FOR AND AGAINST TARIFFS

Tariffs are not a new concept. For centuries industries have tried to protect their products and services and countries have used tariffs to protect employment. The main argument against tariffs is that they discourage free trade, and free trade lets the principle of comparative advantage work most efficiently. The main argument for tariffs is that they protect domestic businesses and workers.

One of the oldest arguments in favour of protectionism is the *infant industry argument*. By protecting new domestic industries from established foreign competitors, so this argument goes, a tariff can give a struggling industry time to become an effective competitor.

A second argument for tariffs is the *job protection argument*. Supporters—especially unions—say we should use tariffs to keep foreign labour from taking away Canadian jobs. Canadian jobs are lost, they say, when low-wage countries sell products at lower prices than those charged in Canada. The higher prices charged by the Canadian firms help pay the higher wages of Canadian workers.

An argument against tariffs is that they cause an increase in prices, thereby decreasing consumers' purchasing power. Over the long run, tariffs can also be too protective if they cause domestic companies to stop innovating and fall behind technologically. An example is the Italian car builder Fiat. Protective tariffs helped keep Fiat's Italian market share very high, but as Europe's trade barriers fell, foreign competitors moved in with cars that Italian drivers preferred. Fiat is now desperately spending billions of dollars to revamp its factories and design new models.

Non-Tariff Barriers

Governments use many tools in addition to tariffs to restrict trade. Among them are import quotas, embargoes, buy-national regulations, custom regulations, and exchange controls.

Import Quotas One type of non-tariff barrier is the **import quota**, or limit on the quantity of a certain good that can be imported. The goal of setting quotas is to limit imports to the optimum amount of a given product.

Embargoes A complete ban against importing or exporting a product is an **embargo**. For instance, Canada does not allow the export of "military goods to countries that threaten Canada's security, are under UN (United Nations) sanction, are threatened by internal or external conflict, and/or abuse the human rights of their citizens."[16]

Customs Regulations In a more subtle move, a country may make it hard for foreign products to enter its markets by establishing **customs regulations** that are different from generally accepted international standards, such as requiring bottles to be litre size rather than quart size. The French seem particularly adept at using this tactic. For example, to reduce imports of foreign VCRs, at one time France ruled that all VCRs had to enter through the customs station at Poitiers. This customs house was located in the middle of the country, was woefully understaffed, and was open only a few days each week. What's more, the few customs agents at Poitiers opened each package separately to inspect the merchandise. Within a few weeks, imports of VCRs in France came to a halt.

Exchange Controls **Exchange controls** are laws that require a company earning foreign exchange (foreign currency) from its exports to sell the foreign exchange to a control agency, usually a central bank. For example, assume that Rolex, a Swiss company, sells 300 watches to a Canadian retailer for $120,000. If Switzerland had exchange controls, Rolex would have to sell its Canadian dollars to the Swiss central bank and would receive Swiss francs. If Rolex wants to buy goods from abroad, it must go to the central bank and buy foreign exchange (currency). By controlling the amount of foreign exchange sold to companies, the government controls the amount of products that can be imported. Limiting imports and encouraging exports helps a government to create a favourable balance of trade.

Tariffs on the imported goods arriving on this foreign ship make the products more expensive than those of Canadian competitors.

import quota
A limit on the quantity of a certain good that can be imported; also known as a *quantitative restraint.*

embargo
A total ban on imports or exports of a product.

customs regulations
Regulations on products that are different from generally accepted international standards.

exchange controls
Laws that require a company earning foreign exchange (foreign currency) from its exports to sell the foreign exchange to a control agency, such as a central bank.

concept check

Discuss the concept of natural trade barriers.

Describe several tariff and non-tariff barriers to trade.

FOSTERING GLOBAL TRADE

4   learning goal

From our discussion so far, it might seem that governments act only to restrain global trade. On the contrary, governments and international financial organizations work hard to increase it, as we explain in this section.

Antidumping Laws

dumping

The practice of charging a lower price for a product in foreign markets than in the firm's home market.

Canadian firms don't always get to compete on an equal basis with foreign firms in international trade. To level the playing field, the federal government has passed antidumping laws. **Dumping** is the practice of charging a lower price for a product (perhaps below cost) in foreign markets than in the firm's home market. The company might be trying to win foreign customers, or it might be seeking to get rid of surplus goods.

When the variation in price can't be explained by differences in the cost of serving the two markets, dumping is suspected. Most industrialized countries have antidumping regulations. They are especially concerned about *predatory dumping*, the attempt to gain control of a foreign market by destroying competitors with impossibly low prices.

The legal test for product dumping is based on two criteria. First, the product must be priced unfairly low—either below its production costs or below the selling price in the home country. Second, the imported product must harm the domestic industry.

The Uruguay Round and the World Trade Organization

Uruguay Round

A 1994 agreement by 117 nations to lower trade barriers worldwide.

The **Uruguay Round** of trade negotiations is an agreement to lower trade barriers dramatically worldwide. Adopted in 1994, the agreement had been signed by 149 nations as of December 11, 2005. The most ambitious global trade agreement ever negotiated, the Uruguay Round reduced tariffs by one-third worldwide, a move that is expected to increase global income by $235 billion (USD) annually. Perhaps the most notable aspect of the agreement is its recognition of new global realities. For the first time, an agreement covers services, intellectual property rights, and trade-related investment measures, such as exchange controls.

World Trade Organization (WTO)

An organization established by the Uruguay Round in 1994 to oversee international trade, reduce trade barriers, and resolve disputes among member nations.

The **World Trade Organization (WTO)** replaces the old General Agreement on Tariffs and Trade (GATT), which was created in 1948. The GATT contained extensive loopholes that enabled countries to evade agreements to reduce trade barriers. Today, all WTO members must comply fully with all agreements under the Uruguay Round. The WTO also has an effective dispute settlement procedure with strict time limits to resolve disputes.

The WTO has emerged as the world's most powerful institution for reducing trade barriers and opening markets. The advantage of WTO membership is that member countries lower trade barriers among themselves. Countries that don't belong must negotiate trade agreements individually with all their trading partners. To date, Russia is the largest country that has not qualified for WTO membership.

HOT Links

The World Trade Organization tracks the latest trade developments between countries and regions around the world. For the most recent global trading news, visit the WTO's site (http://www.wto.org).

World Bank

An international bank that offers low-interest loans, as well as advice and information, to developing nations.

The World Bank and International Monetary Fund

Two international financial organizations are instrumental in fostering global trade. The **World Bank** offers low-interest loans to developing nations. Originally, the purpose of the loans was to help these nations build infrastructure such as roads, power plants, schools, drainage projects, and hospitals. Now the World Bank offers loans to help developing nations relieve their debt burdens. To receive the loans, countries must pledge to lower trade barriers and aid private enterprise. In addition to making loans, the World Bank is a major source of advice and information for developing nations.

The **International Monetary Fund (IMF)** was founded in 1945, one year after the creation of the World Bank, to promote trade through financial cooperation and eliminate trade barriers in the process. The IMF makes short-term loans to member nations that are unable to meet their budgetary expenses and operates as a lender of last resort for troubled nations. In exchange for these emergency loans, IMF lenders frequently obtain significant commitments from the borrowing nations to address the problems that led to the crises. These steps can include curtailing imports or even devaluing the currency.

Some global financial problems do not have a simple solution. One option would be to pump a lot more funds into the IMF, giving it enough resources to bail out troubled countries and put them back on their feet. In effect, the IMF would be turned into a real lender of last resort for the world economy.

The danger of counting on the IMF, though, is the "moral hazard" problem. Investors would come to assume that the IMF would bail them out and might therefore be tempted to take bigger and bigger risks in emerging markets, leading to the possibility of even deeper financial crises in the future.

International Monetary Fund (IMF)

An international organization, founded in 1945, that promotes trade, makes short-term loans to member nations, and acts as a lender of last resort for troubled nations.

HOT Links

Gain additional insight into the workings of the International Monetary Fund at http://www.imf.org.

concept check

Describe the purpose and role of the WTO.

What are the roles of the World Bank and the IMF in world trade?

INTERNATIONAL ECONOMIC COMMUNITIES

5 learning goal

Nations that trade with each other frequently might decide to formalize their relationship. In this case, their governments meet and work out agreements for a common economic policy. The result is an economic community or, in other cases, a bilateral trade agreement (an agreement between two countries to lower trade barriers). For example, two nations might agree on a **preferential tariff**, which gives advantages to one nation (or several nations) over others. When members of the British Commonwealth trade with Great Britain, for example, they pay lower tariffs than do other nations. In other cases, nations may form free trade associations. In a **free trade zone**, few duties or rules restrict trade among the partners, but nations outside the zone must pay the tariffs set by the individual members.

preferential tariff

A tariff that is lower for some nations than for others.

free trade zone

An area where the nations allow free, or almost free, trade among each other while imposing tariffs on goods of nations outside the zone.

North American Free Trade Agreement (NAFTA)

A 1993 agreement creating a free-trade zone including Canada, Mexico, and the United States.

North American Free Trade Agreement (NAFTA)

The **North American Free Trade Agreement (NAFTA)** created one of the world's largest free trade zones. It includes Canada, the United States, and Mexico, with a combined population of more than 430 million and an economy of approximately $14 trillion (USD). Canada and the United States entered a free-trade agreement in 1988. Thus, as NAFTA was established in 1994, most of the new long-run opportunities opened for Canadian business under NAFTA are in Mexico.

The real test of NAFTA will be whether it can continue to deliver rising prosperity to its three members. For Mexicans, NAFTA must provide rising wages, better benefits, and an expanding middle class with enough purchasing power to keep buying goods from Canada and the United States. As of 2005, that scenario was working.

HOT Links

Want to learn the latest info about NAFTA? Go to http://www.nafta-customs.org.

Mercosur

Mercosur

Trade agreement between Brazil, Argentina, Uruguay, and Paraguay.

The largest new trade agreement is **Mercosur**, which includes Brazil, Argentina, Uruguay, and Paraguay, with Bolivia, Columbia, Ecuador, and Peru as associate member states. Venezuela was accepted as a new member in December 2005. The elimination of most tariffs among the trading partners has resulted in trade revenues that currently exceed $16 billion annually. Unfortunately, recent recessions in Mercosur countries have limited economic growth, although trade among Mercosur countries has continued to grow.

HOT Links

See the latest news about Mercosur at http://www.mercosur.int.

European Union

Trade agreement among 25 European nations.

The European Union

In 1993, the member countries of the European Community (EC) ratified the Maastricht Treaty, which proposed to take the EC further toward economic, monetary, and political union. Although the heart of the treaty deals with developing a unified European Market, Maastricht was also intended to increase integration among **European Union** (EU) members.

The EU has helped increase this integration by creating a borderless economy for these 27 European nations, shown on the map in Exhibit 2.2. The two newest members, Bulgaria and Romania were admitted in 2007.

Exhibit 2.2 | The European Union Gets Bigger

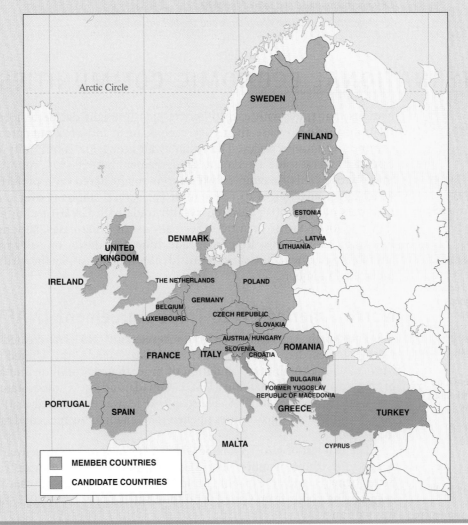

The Eurodollar replaced the individual currencies of many of the European Union nations. The common currency enables the countries to do business as a single trading bloc.

© MATTHIAS KULKA / CORBIS

One of the principal objectives of the European Union is to promote the economic progress of all member countries. The EU has stimulated economic progress by eliminating trade barriers, differences in tax laws, and differences in product standards, and by establishing a common currency. A new European Community Bank was created along with a common currency called the euro.

ASEAN

ASEAN
The Association of Southeast Asian Nations, which, as of 2006, included 10 member states.

The **Association of Southeast Asian Nations** was initially established in 1967, with the original members being Indonesia, Malaysia, the Philippines, Singapore, and Thailand. Today the association has 10 members, the original 5 plus Brunei Darussalam, Vietnam, Laos, Myanmar, and Cambodia. The region has a population of about 500 million, a combined GDP of the $737 billion (USD), and a total trade of $720 billion (USD).[17]

HOT Links

For further in-depth information on ASEAN see http://www.aseansec.org.

concept check

Explain the pros and cons of NAFTA.
What is Mercosur?
What is the European Union?

PARTICIPATING IN THE GLOBAL MARKETPLACE

6 *learning goal*

Companies decide to "go global" for a number of reasons. Perhaps the most urgent is to earn additional profits. If a firm has a unique product or technological advantage not available to other international competitors, this advantage should result in major business successes abroad. In other situations, management might have exclusive market information about foreign customers, marketplaces, or market situations not known to others. In this case, although exclusivity can provide an initial motivation

Procter & Gamble introduced Swiffer to a global market, appealing to consumers who share a universal desire for a simple cleaning system.

© TERRI L. MILLER / E-VISUAL COMMUNICATIONS, INC.

for going global, managers must realize that competitors will eventually catch up. Finally, saturated domestic markets, excess capacity, and potential for cost savings can also be motivators to expand into international markets. A company can enter global trade in several ways, as we describe in this section.

Exporting

exporting
The practice of selling domestically produced goods to buyers in another country.

When a company decides to enter the global market, usually the least complicated and least risky alternative is **exporting,** or selling domestically produced products to buyers in another country. A company, for example, can sell directly to foreign importers or buyers. Exporting is not limited to huge corporations.

Licensing

licensing
The legal process whereby a firm agrees to allow another firm to use a manufacturing process, trademark, patent, trade secret, or other proprietary knowledge in exchange for the payment of a royalty.

One effective way for a firm to move into the global arena with relatively little risk is to sell a license to manufacture its product to a firm in a foreign country. **Licensing** is the legal process whereby a firm (the *licensor*) agrees to let another firm (the *licensee*) use a manufacturing process, trademark, patent, trade secret, or other proprietary knowledge. The licensee, in turn, agrees to pay the licensor a royalty or fee agreed on by both parties.

Many companies have eagerly embraced the licensing concept. For instance, Philip Morris licensed Labatt Brewing Company to produce Miller High Life in Canada. The Spalding Company receives more than $2 million annually from license agreements on its sporting goods. Fruit-of-the-Loom lends its name through licensing to 45 consumer items in Japan alone, for at least 1 percent of the licensee's gross sales.

The licensor must make sure it can exercise sufficient control over the licensee's activities to ensure proper quality, pricing, distribution, and so on. Licensing might also create a new competitor in the long run, if the licensee decides to void the license agreement. International law is often ineffective in stopping such actions. Two common ways in which a licensor can maintain effective control over its licensees are by shipping one or more critical components from Canada and by registering patents and trademarks locally in its own name.

Franchising, which we will discuss in Chapter 5, is a form of licensing that has grown rapidly in recent years. The Canadian Franchise Association publishes a bimonthly magazine for entrepreneurs wanting to establish a successful franchise and an annual comprehensive directory listing franchises available in Canada.

Contract Manufacturing

contract manufacturing

The practice in which a foreign firm manufactures private label goods under a domestic firm's brand name.

In **contract manufacturing**, a foreign firm manufactures private label goods under a domestic firm's brand. Marketing may be handled by either the domestic company or the foreign manufacturer. Levi Strauss, for instance, entered into an agreement with the French fashion house of Cacharel to produce a new Levi's line called "Something New" for distribution in Germany.

The advantage of contract manufacturing is that it lets a company "test the water" in a foreign country. By allowing the foreign firm (e.g., Cacharel) to produce a certain volume of products to specification and put the domestic firm's brand name on the goods (e.g., Levi's), the domestic firm can broaden its global marketing base without investing in overseas plants and equipment. After establishing a solid base, the domestic firm may switch to a joint venture or direct investment, explained below.

Joint Ventures

joint venture

An agreement in which a domestic firm buys part of a foreign firm or joins with a foreign firm to create a new entity.

Joint ventures are somewhat similar to licensing agreements. In a **joint venture**, the domestic firm buys part of a foreign company or joins with a foreign company to create a new entity. A joint venture is a quick and relatively inexpensive way to enter the global market. It can also be very risky. Many joint ventures fail; others fall victim to takeovers, in which one partner buys out the other.

Recently, General Motors entered into a joint venture with Avtovaz, a Soviet-era auto manufacturer in Russia, to produce a car to be called the Chevrolet Niva. Russia is expected to be one of the top 10 growth markets for cars during this decade, and GM wants to be a player. The assembly and engineering will be done at low cost in Russia. GM is providing $333 million and technology. Avtovaz offers skilled workers and a distribution system.[18]

In a successful joint venture, both parties gain valuable skills from the alliance. In the General Motors–Suzuki joint venture in Canada, for example, both parties have contributed and gained. The alliance, CAMI Automotive, was formed to manufacture low-end cars for the U.S. market. The plant, which is run by Suzuki management, produces the Geo Metro/Suzuki Swift—the smallest, most fuel-efficient GM car sold in North America—as well as the Geo Tracker/Suzuki Sidekick sport utility vehicle. Through CAMI, Suzuki has gained access to GM's dealer network and an expanded market for parts and components. GM avoided the cost of developing low-end cars and obtained models it needed to revitalize the lower end of its product line and its average fuel economy rating. The CAMI factory might be one of the most productive plants in North America. There GM has learned how Japanese automakers use work teams, run flexible assembly lines, and manage quality control.

In 2006, Wal-Mart sold its 85 German stores. Wal-Mart had spent years trying to compete in a market in which strong local competitors proved to have a better understanding of German tastes.

Direct Foreign Investment

direct foreign investment

Active ownership of a foreign company or of manufacturing or marketing facilities in a foreign country.

Active ownership of a foreign company or of overseas manufacturing or marketing facilities is referred to as **direct foreign investment**. Direct investors have either a controlling or a large minority interest in the firm. Thus, they stand to receive the greatest potential reward but also face the greatest potential risks. A firm may make a direct foreign investment by acquiring an interest in an existing company or by building new facilities. It might do so because it has trouble transferring some resources to a foreign operation or obtaining that resource locally. One important resource is personnel, especially managers. If the local labour market is tight, the firm might buy an entire foreign firm and retain all its employees instead of paying higher salaries than competitors.

Sometimes firms make direct investments because they can find no suitable local partners. Direct investments also help businesses avoid the communication problems and conflicts of interest that can arise with joint ventures. IBM, for instance, insists on total ownership of its foreign investments, because it does not want to share control with local partners.

Wal-Mart has now made direct investments in nine countries with more than 1,100 stores. International sales now top $32 billion (USD).[19] In Mexico alone, it had 579 grocery stores, wholesale club outlets, and restaurants in 2002. Wal-Mart spent some $600 million to open 63 new Mexican units in 2003.[20] Just a decade after entering the country, Wal-Mart now captures half of all Mexican supermarket sales, and Wal-Mart's strategy of offering low prices every day is drawing more and more consumers.

Not all of its global investments have been successful, however. In Germany, Wal-Mart bought the 21-store Wertkauf hypermarket chain in 1997 and then 74 unprofitable and often decrepit Interspar stores in 1998. Problems in integrating and upgrading the stores resulted in at least $200 million (USD) in losses. Like all other stores, Wal-Mart stores in Germany are required by law to close at 8 p.m. on weekdays and 4 p.m. on Saturdays, and they cannot open at all on Sundays. Furthermore, costs are astronomical. Derek Rowe, an American brought over to supervise the $5 million renovation of the Dortmund store, estimated that construction costs in Germany are five times what they are in the United States.[21]

Now Wal-Mart seems to be turning the corner on its international operations. It is pushing operational authority down to country managers better to respond to local cultures. Wal-Mart enforces certain core principles, such as "everyday low prices," but country managers handle their own buying, logistics, building design, and other operational decisions.

Countertrade

countertrade

A form of international trade in which part or all of the payment for goods or services is in the form of other goods and services.

International trade does not always involve cash. Today, **countertrade** is a fast-growing way to conduct international business. In countertrade, part or all of the payment for goods or services is in the form of other goods or services. Countertrade is a form of barter (swapping goods for goods), an age-old practice whose origins have been traced back to cave dwellers.

Atwood Richards Inc. is the world's largest countertrade organization. Atwood reviews a client's unsold products and issues trade credits in exchange. The credits can be used to obtain other products and services Atwood has acquired everything from hotel rooms and airline tickets to television advertising time, forklift trucks, carpeting, wood pulp, envelopes, steel castings, or satellite tracking systems.

concept check

Discuss several ways that a company can enter international trade.

Explain the concept of countertrade.

THREATS AND OPPORTUNITIES IN THE GLOBAL MARKETPLACE

learning goal

To be successful in a foreign market, companies must fully understand the foreign environment in which they plan to operate. Politics, cultural differences, and the economic environment can represent both opportunities and pitfalls in the global marketplace.

Political Considerations

We have already discussed how tariffs, exchange controls, and other governmental actions threaten foreign producers. The political structure of a country can also jeopardize a foreign producer's success in international trade.

Intense nationalism, for example, can lead to difficulties. **Nationalism** is the sense of national consciousness that boosts the culture and interests of one country over those of all other countries. Strongly nationalistic countries, such as Iran and New Guinea, often discourage investment by foreign companies. In other, less radical forms of nationalism, the government may take actions to hinder foreign operations. France, for example, requires that pop music stations play at least 40 percent of their songs in French. This law was enacted because the French love American rock and roll. Without airtime, American CD sales suffer. Coca-Cola recently attempted to purchase Orangina, France's only domestically owned and distributed soft drink, but the French government blocked the sale, saying that it would be "anticompetitive." The real reason was nationalism.

In a hostile climate, a government might *expropriate* a foreign company's assets, taking ownership and compensating the former owners. Even worse is *confiscation*, when the owner receives no compensation. This happened during rebellions in several African nations during the 1990s and 2000s.

nationalism
A sense of national consciousness that boosts the culture and interests of one country over those of all other countries.

Cultural Differences

Central to any society is the common set of values shared by its citizens that determine what is socially acceptable. Culture underlies the family, educational system, religion, and social class system. The network of social organizations generates overlapping roles and status positions. These values and roles have a tremendous effect on people's preferences and thus on marketers' options. Inca Kola, a fruity, greenish-yellow carbonated drink, is the largest-selling soft drink in Peru. It was invented in Peru and contains only fruit indigenous to the country. Despite being described as "liquid bubble gum," the drink has become a symbol of national pride and heritage. A local consumer of about a six-pack a day says, "I drink Inca Kola because it makes me feel like a Peruvian." He tells his young daughter, "This is our drink, not something invented overseas. It is named for your ancestors, the great Inca warriors."

Language is another important aspect of culture. Marketers must take care in selecting product names and translating slogans and promotional messages so as not to convey the wrong meaning. For example, Mitsubishi Motors had to rename its Pajero model in Spanish-speaking countries, because in Spanish, the term refers to a sexual activity. Toyota Motors' MR2 model dropped the number 2 in France because the combination sounds like a French swearword. The literal translation of Coca-Cola in Chinese characters means "bite the wax tadpole."

Each country has its own customs and traditions that determine business practices and influence negotiations with foreign customers. In many countries, personal relationships are more important than financial considerations. For instance, skipping social engagements in Mexico might lead to lost sales. Negotiations in Japan often include long evenings of dining, drinking, and entertaining; only after a close personal relationship has been formed do business negotiations begin. See page 58 for some cultural "dos and don'ts."

Cultural Dos and Don'ts

DO:

- Always present your business card with both hands in Asian countries. It should also be right-side up and print-side showing so that the recipient can read it as it is being presented. If you receive a business card, accept it with gratitude and examine it carefully. Don't quickly put it into your pocket.

- Dress to the culture. If you are in Switzerland, always wear a coat and tie. In other countries, wearing a coat and tie might be viewed as over-dressing and make you appear snobbish.

- Use a "soft sell" and subtle approach when promoting a product in Japan. Japanese people do not feel comfortable with North America's traditional hard-selling style.

- Understand the role of religion in business transactions. In Muslim countries, Ramadan is a holy month when most people fast. During this time, everything slows down, including business.

- Have a local person available to interpret culturally and linguistically any advertising that you plan to do. When American Airlines wanted to promote its new first-class seats in the Mexican market, it translated the "Fly in Leather" campaign literally, which meant "Fly Naked" in Spanish.

DON'T:

- Glad-hand, back-slap, or use first names on your first business meeting in Asia. If you do, you will be considered a lightweight.

- Fill a wine glass to the top if dining with a French businessperson. It is considered completely uncouth.

- Begin your first business meeting in Asia by talking business. Be patient. Let your clients get to know you first.

- Kiss someone on the cheek or pat them on the shoulder in Spain before you get to know them. In Chile, expect women to greet you with a kiss on the cheek even if you are a stranger. Offer a kiss on both cheeks after you become friends with a French woman (even if you are a woman). In Switzerland, offer three kisses.

- Be on time for your appointment in some Latin American countries, but always be on time in Germany.

The Economic Environment

The level of economic development varies considerably worldwide, ranging from countries where everyday survival is a struggle, such as the Sudan and Eritrea, to those that are highly developed, such as Switzerland and Japan. In general, complex, sophisticated industries are found in developed countries, and more basic industries are found in less developed nations. Average family incomes are higher in the more developed countries than in the least developed markets. Larger incomes mean greater purchasing power and demand not only for consumer goods and services but also for the machinery and workers required to produce consumer goods. Exhibit 2.3 provides a glimpse of what families earn throughout the world.

Business opportunities are usually better in countries that have an economic **infrastructure** in place. Infrastructure is the basic institutions and public facilities on which an economy's development depends. It includes the money and banking system that provides the major investment loans to our nation's businesses; the educational system that turns out the incredible varieties of skills and basic research that actually run our nation's production lines; the extensive transportation and

infrastructure
The basic institutions and public facilities on which an economy's development depends.

Exhibit 2.3 | What the World Earns

High consumption levels are concentrated in a small share of households worldwide.

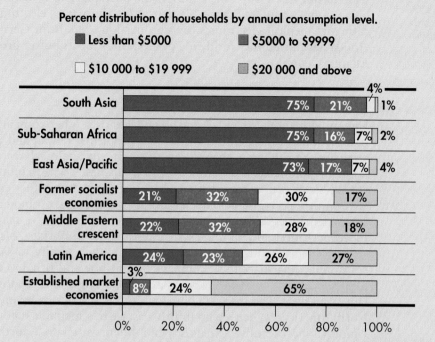

Percent distribution of households by annual consumption level.

- ■ Less than $5000
- ■ $5000 to $9999
- □ $10 000 to $19 999
- ■ $20 000 and above

South Asia	75% 21% 4% 1%
Sub-Saharan Africa	75% 16% 7% 2%
East Asia/Pacific	73% 17% 7% 4%
Former socialist economies	21% 32% 30% 17%
Middle Eastern crescent	22% 32% 28% 18%
Latin America	24% 23% 26% 27%
Established market economies	3% 8% 24% 65%

NOTE: Consumption is in U.S. dollars on a purchase power–parity basis. Some percentages add up to more than 100 percent because of rounding.

SOURCE: © International Bank for Reconstruction and Development / The World Bank.

communications systems—highways, railroads, airports, canals, telephones, Internet sites, postal systems, television stations—that link almost every piece of our geography into one market; the energy system that powers our factories; and, of course, the market system itself, which brings our nation's goods and services into our homes and businesses. When we think about how our own economy works, we tend to take our infrastructure for granted.

concept check

Explain how political factors can affect international trade.

Describe several cultural factors that a company involved in international trade should consider.

How can economic conditions affect trade opportunities?

THE IMPACT OF MULTINATIONAL CORPORATIONS

8 learning goal

Corporations that move resources, goods, services, and skills across national boundaries without regard to the country in which their headquarters are located are **multinational corporations**. Some are so rich and have so many employees that they resemble small countries. The successful ones take political and cultural differences into account.

multinational corporations
Corporations that move resources, goods, services, and skills across national boundaries without regard to the country in which their headquarters are located.

A multinational company can have several headquarters worldwide, depending on the location of its markets or technologies. Britain's APV, a maker of food-processing equipment, has a different headquarters for each of its worldwide businesses. HP recently moved the headquarters of its personal computer business to Grenoble, France. Siemens A.G., Germany's electronics giant, is relocating its medical electronics division headquarters from Germany to Chicago. Honda has moved the worldwide headquarters for its power products division to Atlanta, Georgia.

The Multinational Advantage

Large multinationals have several advantages over other companies. For instance, multinationals can often overcome trade problems. Taiwan and South Korea have long had an embargo against Japanese cars for political reasons and to help domestic automakers. Yet Honda USA, a Japanese-owned company based in the United States, sends Accords to Taiwan and Korea. In another example, when the environmentally conscious Green movement challenged the biotechnology research conducted by BASF, a major German chemical and drug manufacturer, BASF moved its cancer and immune system research to Cambridge, Massachusetts.

Another advantage for multinationals is their ability to sidestep regulatory constraints. Pharmaceutical company SmithKline and Britain's Beecham decided to merge, in part so that they could avoid licensing and regulatory hassles in their largest markets. The merged company can say it's an insider in both Europe and North America. "When we go to Brussels, we're a member state [of the European Union]," one executive explains. "And when we go to Canada, we're a North American company."

Multinationals can also shift production from one plant to another as market conditions change. When European demand for a certain solvent declined, Dow Chemical instructed its German plant to switch to manufacturing a chemical that had been previously imported from outside the European Union. Computer models help Dow make decisions like these, so it can run its plants efficiently and keep costs down.

Multinationals can also tap new technology from around the world. Xerox has introduced some 80 different office copiers in Canada that were designed and built by Fuji Xerox, its joint venture with a Japanese company. Versions of the super-concentrated detergent that Procter & Gamble first formulated in Japan in response to a rival's product are now being sold under the Ariel brand name in Europe and being tested under the Cheer and Tide labels in Canada. Also, consider Otis Elevator's development of the Elevonic 411, an elevator that is programmed to send more cars to floors where demand is high. It was developed at six research centres in five countries. Otis's group in the United States handled the systems integration, a Japanese group designed the special motor drives that make the elevators ride smoothly, a French group perfected the door systems, a German group handled the electronics, and a Spanish group took care of the small-geared components. Otis says the international effort saved more than $10 million (USD) in design costs and cut the process from four years to two.

Finally, multinationals can often save a lot in labour costs, even in highly unionized countries. For example, when Xerox started moving copier-rebuilding work to Mexico to take advantage of the lower wages, its union objected because it saw that members' jobs were at risk. Eventually, the union agreed to change work styles and to improve productivity to keep the jobs at home.

concept check

What is a multinational corporation?

What are the advantages of multinationals?

9 *learning goal*

In this section we will examine several underlying trends that will continue to propel the dramatic growth in world trade. These trends are market expansion, resource acquisition, the Internet, technological change, and government actions.

MARKET EXPANSION

The need for businesses to expand their markets is perhaps the most fundamental reason for the growth in world trade. The limited size of domestic markets often motivates managers to seek markets beyond their national frontiers. The economies of large-scale manufacturing demand big markets. Domestic markets, particularly in smaller countries like Denmark and the Netherlands, simply can't generate enough demand. Nestlé was one of the first businesses to "go global," because its home country, Switzerland, is so small. Nestlé was shipping milk to 16 countries as early as 1875. Today, hundreds of thousands of businesses are recognizing the potential rich rewards to be found in international markets.

The emergence of China and India as economic powers has had a major global impact on both imports and exports. China is the sixth largest economy in the world, with a growth rate of 9.5 percent in 2004. It is the world's largest consumer of grain, meat, coal, and steel.[22] However, its future is uncertain. The political system will need to support the country's economic growth in a manner that satisfies other world powers. Issues such as the education and health care systems, the banking system, the land-ownership system, and rural unrest will demand the attention of those in power.[23]

India has been less than enthralled with the multinationals, however, and has chosen to support its own entrepreneurs to foster economic growth, with strength in the information technology (IT) and IT-enabled services fields. India's protectionist tariff is above the developing country average of 13.4 percent, with peak tariff levels of 22 percent. With India's strong democracy behind the economic growth, it has the potential to outpace China.[24]

RESOURCE ACQUISITION

More and more companies are going to the global marketplace to acquire the resources they need to operate efficiently. These resources might be cheap or skilled labour, scarce raw materials, technology, or capital. Nike, for example, uses manufacturing facilities in many Asian countries to take advantage of cheap labour.

THE IMPACT OF THE INTERNET

In many respects, going global is easier than it has ever been before. Opening an e-commerce site on the Internet immediately puts a company in the international marketplace, and sophisticated language translation software can make any site accessible to persons around the world. Global shippers such as UPS, FedEx, and DHL help solve international e-commerce distribution complexities. E4X, Inc., offers software to ease currency conversions. Sites that use E4X's software can post prices in U.S. dollars and then ask their customers what currency they wish to use for payment. If the answer is anything but dollars, E4X takes over the transaction and translates the price into any of 22 currencies, collects the payment from the customer, and pays the site in dollars, just as though it were any other transaction. Customers never realize they're dealing with a third party.[25]

Nevertheless, the promise of "borderless commerce" and the new "Internet economy" are still being restrained by the old brick-and-mortar rules, regulations, and habits. For example, many Japanese people don't even have a credit card. So how do they pay for e-commerce purchases? Seven-Eleven Japan, with more than 8,000 convenience stores, has come to the rescue. eS-Books, the Japanese Web site partner of Yahoo! Japan, lets shoppers buy books and videos on the Internet, then specify to which 7-Eleven the merchandise is to be shipped. The buyer goes to that specific store and pays cash for the e-purchase.

In Germany it is typically cheaper to buy books from Amazon.com in the United Kingdom than from the local site. Why? Germany, France, and several other European states allow publishing cartels through which groups of book publishers can legally dictate retail prices to booksellers—both on-line and on the ground. When *Galileo's Daughter,* a biography by Dava Sobel, for example, was selling at the list price of 50.24 Euros on Germany's Amazon.de, at Amazon.co.uk, it cost 40 percent less.

The e-commerce site for the clothing retailer Lands' End in Germany is not allowed to mention its unconditional refund policy, because German retailers, which normally do not allow returns after 14 days, sued and won a court ruling blocking mention of it.

TECHNOLOGICAL CHANGE

Both new technology in transportation systems and the expanded nature of information processing fosters continued growth in international trade. Transportation improvements from computerized container ships to cargo jetliners have dramatically improved the efficiency of distribution throughout the world. Moreover, Federal Express and other shippers use advanced computerized tracking software to tell shippers where their packages are at any point in time. Shippers can use special software that enables them to enter FedEx's database and track the packages themselves, if they so desire. It's a far cry from the sailing ships of yesteryear, when voyages took weeks or months, and there was no way to communicate with the ship once it left port.

The Internet opens up the world to any seller with a Web site. Markets no longer have geographic boundaries. E-mail enables a manager in London to receive reports from Toronto, Moscow, Capetown, and Tokyo in a matter of minutes rather than days. Thus, coordinating global business strategies is now a workable reality.

GOVERNMENT ACTIONS

Governments around the globe, working with the WTO, have significantly lowered barriers to world trade. Sellers in the global marketplace have a more level playing field than ever before. Regional trade organizations, such as the European Union, NAFTA, and Mercosur, also have reduced trade barriers in large geographic areas. As these governmental actions continue to make it easier to go global, world trade will continue to grow.

concept check

What trends will foster continued growth in world trade?

Describe some of the ways businesses can take advantage of these trends to "go global."

CONTINUE YOUR EDUCATION

The handwriting is on the wall. Low-skilled jobs are rapidly disappearing in Canada. Canadian businesses know that to compete globally, they must find cheap labour for labour-intensive businesses. This means establishing plants in Mexico, Asia, or other places in the world where labour is inexpensive. It also means that unskilled or low-skilled Canadian workers will find it increasingly difficult to secure permanent jobs. By continuing your education, you can avoid falling into this very undesirable trap.

CUSTOMER SATISFACTION AND QUALITY

Determining *quality* is not always easy in the global marketplace. For example, a manufacturer of garden tools used very high-quality tempered steel to make shovel blades and aged hickory wood for the handles. The shovel is a market leader in Canada but sold poorly in Asia despite a competitive price. The company was puzzled, so it undertook a research project to find out why the shovels weren't selling. The answer proved to be quite simple: People in Asia were of shorter stature than Canadians, making the handles too long to use comfortably! The company shortened the handles and sales skyrocketed.

Quality in developing countries might mean simplifying product features and/or making the parts more durable to withstand a tougher environment. In some cases, a quality sewing machine is one that is foot pedal operated, because buyers don't have access to or can't afford electricity. Yet, companies should not assume that even the poorest people won't pay for quality. Nomads who wander the northern Sahara Desert always buy the highest quality of cloth available to make their clothes. Their garments are all that stand between them and 120 degrees plus in the summer and 10 below zero in the winter.

So to understand quality in the global marketplace, a business must understand the local culture and listen to the voice of the consumer. A good example is when Universal Studios decided to build a theme park in Japan.

By surveying Japanese visitors at Universal parks in Orlando and Los Angeles, Universal gradually drew a picture of what the Japanese did and didn't like about the parks. For example, cramped in their small homes, they loved the expansive space, but accustomed to modest portions of food, many were turned off by the mountainous servings at restaurants.

A marketing survey in Japan catalogued Japanese expectations for every aspect of Universal Studios Japan, from bathrooms to souvenir sales. One theme was clear, if a bit contradictory: Japanese people wanted an authentic American experience while expecting the park to cater to their cultural preferences.

Searching for the right formula required painstaking attention to detail. Universal set up a test kitchen in Japan, where 10 Japanese and U.S. chefs tested 4,000 recipes to develop U.S.-style dishes with a touch of Japanese flavour. A seafood pizza and gumbo-style soup made the cut. A fried-shrimp concoction with coloured rice crackers didn't. American tasters liked it. Japanese simply found it gross.

In a musical number based on the movie *Beetlejuice*, the main character banters away in Japanese while his sidekicks speak and sing in English. Snippets of Japanese and a Japanese stuntman were injected into a Wild West show to make the gunfight story more understandable to Japanese without ruining the effect of the U.S. performers.

Other features are uniquely Japanese. The nation's penchant for buying edible souvenirs inspired a 6,000-square-foot confection shop packed with Japanese sweets such as dinosaur-shaped bean cakes. Restrooms include Japanese-style squat toilets. Even the park layout caters to the tendency of Japanese crowds to flow clockwise in an orderly manner, contrary to more chaotic U.S. crowds, which steer right.

SOURCE: Adapted from Bill Spindle, "Cowboys and Samurai: The Japanizing of Universal," Wall Street Journal (March 22, 2002), pp. B1, B6. Reprinted by permission of the Wall Street Journal, Copyright © 2002 Dow Jones & Company, Inc. All Rights Reserved Worldwide.

STUDY THE ROLE OF A GLOBAL MANAGER

Business is becoming more global, and so chances are that you might become a global manager. Start learning right now what this means and if it's right for you. The life of a global manager can be hectic, as these examples illustrate.

Top overseas performers at Secure Computing, a software developer, are treated to a dinner for two by Christine Hughes, senior vice president of marketing and business development. Ms. Hughes supervises a 24-person staff in North and

South America and Asia. One of her missions on trips is to combat the tendency of foreign-based employees to think the organization is "North American–centric," she says. Because they take much longer flights than the typical corporate road warrior, global managers wind up turning airplanes into offices. When she is overseas, Ms. Hughes has her office ship a package of paperwork overnight to her, so she can work on the flight home.

Indeed, a global manager's workday never really ends. Wherever he or she is, it's still business hours somewhere else. When she's working in Australia, Ms. Hughes usually ends her day in a hotel room, talking with someone at the home office. "I'm on the phone until two in the morning dealing with issues," she says. "You just have to accept that."[26]

Your position might not be as hectic as that of Hughes, but you can easily see the differences between a person who is a global manager and one who is not. Is this the life for you? Would you enjoy living abroad? Can you adapt easily to other cultures?

One way to see if you might be cut out to be a global manager is to spend some time abroad. The ideal situation is to find a job overseas during the summer months. This experience will help you decide if you want to be a global manager. Also, it will look good on your résumé. One source of international jobs information is **http://www.internationaljobs.org**.

If you can't find a job overseas, save your money and travel abroad. Seeing how others live and work will broaden your horizons and give you a more enlightened view of the world. Even international travel can help you decide what you want to do in the global marketplace.

SUMMARY OF LEARNING GOALS

1   Why is global trade important to Canada, and how is trade measured?

International trade improves relations with friends and allies, eases tensions among nations, helps bolster economies, raises people's standard of living, and improves the quality of life. With Canada's small population, to meet the economies of scale, we must produce more than we can consume. Approximately a third of all jobs in Canada are supported by exports.

Two concepts important to global trade are the balance of trade (the difference in value between a country's exports and its imports over some period) and the balance of payments (the difference between a country's total payments to other countries and its total receipts from other countries). Canada currently has both a positive balance of trade and a positive balance of payments. Another import concept is the exchange rate, which is the price of one country's currency in terms of another country's currency. Currencies float up and down based upon the supply of and demand for each currency. Sometimes a government steps in and devalues its currency relative to those of other countries.

2   Why do nations trade?

Nations trade because they gain by doing so. The principle of comparative advantage states that each country should specialize in the goods it can produce most readily and cheaply and trade them for those that other countries can produce most readily and cheaply. The result is more goods at lower prices than if each country produced everything it needed. Free trade allows trade among nations without government restrictions.

3   What are the barriers to international trade?

The three major barriers to international trade are natural barriers, such as distance and language; tariff barriers, or taxes on imported goods; and non-tariff barriers. The non-tariff barriers to trade include import quotas, embargoes, buy-national regulations, customs regulations, and exchange controls. The main argument against tariffs is that they discourage free trade and keep the principle of comparative advantage from working efficiently. The main argument for using tariffs is that they help protect domestic companies, industries, and workers.

4   How do governments and institutions foster world trade?

The World Trade Organization created by the Uruguay Round has dramatically lowered trade barriers worldwide. For the first time, a trade agreement covers services, intellectual property rights, and exchange controls. The World Bank makes loans to developing nations to help build infrastructures. The International Monetary Fund makes loans to member nations that cannot meet their budgetary expenses. Despite efforts to expand trade, terrorism can have a negative impact on trade growth.

5   What are international economic communities?

International economic communities reduce trade barriers among themselves while often establishing common tariffs and other trade barriers toward non-member countries. The best-known economic communities are the European Union, NAFTA, and Mercosur.

6   How do companies enter the global marketplace?

There are a number of ways to enter the global market. The major ones are exporting, licensing, contract manufacturing, joint ventures, and direct investment.

7   What threats and opportunities exist in the global marketplace?

Domestic firms entering the international arena need to consider the politics, economies, and culture of the countries where they plan to do business. For example, government trade policies can be loose or restrictive, countries can be nationalistic, and governments can change. As well, many products fail because companies don't understand the culture of the country where they are trying to sell their products. Some developing countries also lack an economic infrastructure, which can make it very difficult to conduct business.

8   What are the advantages of multinational corporations?

Multinational corporations have several advantages. First, they can frequently side-step restrictive trade and licensing restrictions because they have headquarters in more than one country. Multinationals can also move their operations from one country to the next, depending on which location offers more favourable economic conditions. In addition, multinationals can tap into a vast source of technological expertise by drawing on the knowledge of a global workforce.

9   What are the trends in the global marketplace?

Global business activity will continue to escalate for several reasons. Firms that desire a larger customer base or need additional resources will continue to seek opportunities outside their country's borders. The Internet offers an excellent way for firms to go global. In addition, technological improvements in communication and transportation will continue to fuel growth in global markets by making it easier to sell and distribute products internationally.

EXPERIENTIAL EXERCISES

1. Know the exchange rate between the Canadian dollars and the currencies of the countries you plan to visit before you go. Go to **http://www.cnnfn.com/markets/currencies/** for the latest quotations. Keep up with the changing rates by reading your local paper. Explain the implication in the change of the exchange rate for your next vacation to Mexico.

2. When you travel, avoid changing money at airports, train stations, and hotels. These places usually have the worst rates. Ask local people where they change money. Locals know where the best rates are.

3. Discuss the rise of the Indian and Chinese economies. Investigate what the future might hold for these countries from a political and economic perspective.

4. How can a country's traditions create barriers to trade? Ask foreign students to describe such barriers in their country. Students should give examples of problems that foreign businesspeople might experience with Canadian customs.

5. Should the United Kingdom be admitted to NAFTA? Why might Britain not wish to join?

6. Write a paper on how international economic communities might affect Canadian business.

7. What do you think is the best way for a small company to enter international trade? Why?

8. What impact have foreign multinationals had on the Canadian economy? Give some examples.

9. Identify some Canadian multinational companies that have been successful in world markets. How do you think they have achieved their success?

REVIEW QUESTIONS

1. What is a global vision?

2. What is the importance of global business to Canada?

3. What impact has terrorism had on international trade?

4. Define exports and imports.

5. What is the balance of trade? What is the difference between a trade surplus and a trade deficit?

6. What is a country's balance of payments?

7. How does changing values of currencies affect imports and exports?

8. Why do nations trade? What is the principle of comparative advantage?

9. What are some natural barriers to trade?

10. What are tariffs? What are some arguments for and against tariffs?

11. What is the role of the World Bank and the International Monetary Fund?

12. What are some of the main international economic communities?

13. What are some options for Canadian companies that want to participate in the global marketplace?

CREATIVE THINKING CASE
Going Global Has Glitches

The Canadian-U.S. lumber dispute has been an issue for Canadian softwood lumber producers since May 2002, when the United States began applying punitive duties to lumber imports from Canada. The Americans claimed that Canadian lumber was unfairly subsidized because of the artificially low Crown timber fees, which allowed producers to sell at below-market price. If you are a major lumber producer, this political issue in the global environment is completely out of the control of your company. By April 27, 2006, a tentative framework for a new Canadian-U.S. softwood lumber deal had been announced. However, many details remained to be worked out. The deal gave exporters the choice of two strategies to placate the Americans. First, if lumber prices fall below a predetermined level, significant export duties must be paid to Ottawa. Second, quotas will be put in place based on Canada's 34 percent share of the U.S. market, plus a small tax would be required. The tentative deal also includes penalties for subverting the spirit of the agreement by the inclusion of an anti-circumvention clause.

As this represents only the *framework* for a *tentative* deal, the uncertainty for Canadian lumber producers wishing to export to the United States is immense.

CRITICAL THINKING QUESTIONS

1. As a Canadian softwood lumber producer who exports to the United States, what are the implications of this political issue?
2. Given that this issue represents only one factor in the overall environment of Canadian softwood lumber producers, what other issues do you see as being of similar importance?

SOURCE: "B.C. Lumber Industry Supports Canada-U.S. Softwood Deal," *Times-Colonist*, May 20, 2006.

VIDEO CASE
ESPN Goes Global

If your passion is Indian cricket, Argentinean soccer, or Scottish links golf, tune in to ESPN International for live coverage of your favourite international sports events. The company's initial 1989 foray into international sports broadcasting was in South America, a market that still represents 40 percent of its international business. But ESPN's international programming has since expanded to include 150 to 160 million households worldwide.

"Minimal data was available on basic demographics like household cable penetration, markets, or advertising," said Managing Director of ESPN International Operations, Willy Burkhart. But ESPN followed pioneers CNN and HBO into the international broadcast arena, convinced that sporting events would carry the same global appeal for viewers as news and movies. Their goal was to bring quality programming and journalistic integrity in American sports to a global audience.

Initial distribution partnerships were established with broadcast companies in Europe, Canada, and Asia, followed by penetration into Japan, Australia, New Zealand, the Middle East, Africa, and Antarctica, under ESPN's own banner. Unlike CNN, whose international coverage focuses on bringing news to an American expatriate and tourist audience, ESPN soon realized that sports viewers were mainly interested in local events. As a result, they invested in the "localization" of their coverage, which included being sensitive to different languages and dialects, and hired announcers with accents unlikely to offend or insult any of their viewers.

ESPN's sales pitch to cable operators was the lure of enticing new subscribers to cable and the promise of retaining existing users unwilling to relinquish access to first-rate, up-to-the-minute sports programming. ESPN's two revenue streams are generated from cable operators and the companies that buy ESPN advertising airtime.

Initially ESPN's advertising was designed to encourage viewer tune-in for specific events, with little focus on building the ESPN brand or image. That has changed, however, and the company now features stunts in their own airtime that help build ESPN brand awareness.

As the worldwide leader in sports entertainment, ESPN also recognized the need to identify and even create trends in the world of sports by producing some of its own events. Its phenomenally successful X-Games, staged each year in Thailand, feature edgy "evolving sports" like ramp boarding. Retaining rights to some events is an ongoing challenge for ESPN, but its own production capability provides it with greater control over some of these events.

After 10 years of successfully investing in establishing a worldwide presence, ESPN has now turned its focus to building its brand value and brand name, a name the company hopes worldwide sports viewers will continue to see as synonymous with excellence in sports broadcasting.

CRITICAL THINKING QUESTIONS

1. Why did ESPN take the risk of moving into the international broadcast arena, even though it did not have solid demographic data available?

2. What were some of the main challenges ESPN experienced in this new venture?

3. How has ESPN's international presence evolved over the past 10 years? What trends have helped it grow?

SOURCES: Adapted from material contained in the video *ESPN International* and the company Web site, http://www.international.espn.com.

E-COMMERCE CASE
Auto Manufacturing in China for the Chinese Market

A May 2006 report on Canada's auto industry suggested that there is a trend emerging to assemble automobiles in the country for which they are ultimately intended. As a result, competition among assemblers of automobiles will be intense. One way to keep costs down is, of course, cheap labour. Assembling the product at its ultimate destination also serves to lower delivery costs. China represents a massive potential market. New car sales in China were 3.1 million in 2005 and from the first quarter 2006 increased 74 percent to 890,000.

Can Canadian manufacturers take advantage of this? China has many domestic manufacturers who provide low-cost cars of reasonable quality, but the higher end automobiles are generally produced through joint ventures with foreign companies. The Chinese manufacturers might decide to focus on their domestic market, which would create competition for Canadian firms looking to assemble in China to access the huge Chinese market. On the other hand, the Chinese might try to move into the export market. Moving into foreign markets will create several problems for the Chinese. Issues such as environmental and safety concerns will arise, as will the desire to protect domestic manufacturers in Canada, the United States, and Europe. Also, Chinese auto brands are virtually unknown outside China, and service support could be a problem.

Given the advantages of staying domestic and the challenges of exporting globally, the Chinese might choose to focus on the local market. Hence, Canadian manufacturers attempting to assemble in China would be in direct competition with local auto manufacturers.

CRITICAL THINKING QUESTIONS

1. Do you see a place for Canadian automobile manufacturers in China?

2. Do you see a potential for Chinese automakers to export to Canada, the United States and Europe? Do a Google search on "Chery," a Chinese automaker, and look at its M14.

SOURCES: Nicholas Van Preet, "Carmakers to Stay Local, TD Says," *National Post*, May 19, 2006. Jim Hemerling, "China's Carmakers at the Crossroads," *Business Week Online*, May 31, 2006, http://msnbc.msn.com (accessed June 7, 2006).

Making the Connection

Social Trends, Social Responsibility, and Making Ethical Decisions in Business

In this chapter you'll be learning about some very important trends in the social environment. One such trend is the changing demographic composition of the Canadian population, resulting in changing patterns in the workforce and in consumer wants and needs. Another is one of the most important and newsworthy trends in the social environment: the trend toward better ethics, or, at least, higher expectations with regard to business ethics and increased corporate responsibility.

Just as the other trends in the PEST environment model affect and are affected by one another, so are these trends. For example, demographic changes in the population—both in age and in multicultural diversity—lead to changing consumer wants and needs (another social trend), as well as to changes in government/*political* policy (such as to extend the mandatory retirement age to hold off the damage to the Canada Pension Plan that is inevitable as the large bulge of boomers retires, as well as increasing immigration to offset a shrinking labour force). Demographic changes also lead to changes in *technology* as businesses look for ways to make up for a shrinking labour force. This has even helped lead to the *economic* trend toward entrepreneurship (which we'll discuss in Chapter 6), as those born at the latter part of the baby boom have difficulty finding jobs at higher levels in companies because the early boomers have taken all of those jobs, and

the numbers of visible minorities starting their own businesses increase. This trend toward increased diversity is one that can have a very positive impact on a business if it embraces this diversity in its hiring, making it much more capable of understanding and meeting its increasingly diverse customer base.

Business ethics and corporate responsibility are examples of other social factors that have integrative implications for businesses. In this chapter, we will show how the different elements in the environment affect and are affected by trends in ethics and corporate responsibility. Many recent news articles demonstrate how economic factors relate to ethics and corporate responsibility. Market forces and market failures have motivated greater corporate responsibility for organizations wishing to promote consumer confidence. Technology is also related, as the Internet often creates the perception of anonymity, prompting less-than-ethical behaviour in some businesspeople because they have less fear of getting caught. And the political factor is always present, because if business does not act ethically and take its social responsibility voluntarily, governments are likely to step in and enact legislation, as we have seen in response to the Enron and WorldCom scandals in the United States.

Research done by the Canadian Centre for Social Performance and Ethics at the University of Toronto shows how a company's commitment to ethical and responsible behaviour affects the success of the company and helps to meet the critical success factors in our model. For example, it leads to reduced operating costs (helping the company *achieve financial success*); enhanced brand and image reputation and increased sales and customer loyalty (helping to achieve financial success, because the company gains the trust of customers and better *meets their needs* in the long term); and increased ability to attract and retain employees (helping to gain *employee commitment*).[1]

An interesting piece of evidence to support the assertion that ethical and socially responsible corporate behaviour improves the financial performance of a company can be found in the first issue of the magazine *Corporate Knights*. The *Corporate Knights* organization undertook the first-ever ranking of the 50 best corporate citizens in Canada in 2002. Its research shows that when you compare the historical returns of the 50 best corporate citizens in Canada against the Toronto Stock Exchange (TSE) 300 Composite Index, the more socially responsible companies come out on top by a margin of 21.6 percent for the year ended December 31, 2001, 10.8 percent for the previous three years, and 14.9 percent for the previous five years.

Thus, acting in an ethical and responsible fashion creates a key opportunity for businesses to be more financially successful; furthermore, not doing so creates enormous threats to the survival of the business—just look at WorldCom and Enron. In fact, all environmental trends create both threats and opportunities. The environment changes constantly and uncontrollably, but if seen early enough and handled proactively, these changes can be exploited as opportunities. For example, the social trend of the growth of dual-income families has resulted in the economic effect of increased purchasing power. As we indicate in this chapter, the "phenomenon of working women has probably had a greater effect on marketing than has any other social change." As women's earnings have grown, so has their impact on purchase decisions, particularly big-ticket items. Working women create opportunities for items such as childcare and eldercare, home-cleaning services, and other convenience items and services. The impact on items such as car sales, however, has created huge market opportunities that many companies have taken advantage of, changing their sales messages to attract female customers.

One of the more interesting and challenging opportunities discussed in this chapter is the trend toward component lifestyles. This makes meeting customer needs very difficult but full of opportunities. Businesses must use technology to track customer needs and then focus on *innovation* to develop products of *value* to customers while keeping *operations* extremely flexible to meet changes as they occur and adjust to the differing demands of the consumer.

One of the major social trends discussed in this chapter is the shift in the demographic composition of the Canadian population created by the baby boom. Pay close attention to the impact of this trend, as it has definite implications for business. (A good reference to understanding the impact of demographics is David Foot's *Boom, Bust and Echo*.) As the chapter indicates, demographic changes definitely affect the market for products, as well as the size and composition of the workforce, so shifts in demographics have implications for the overall *strategy* of a business as well as its functional areas. Some products will find demand declining, whereas others will experience increased demand as demographics shift—important concerns for *marketing*. The size and composition of the workforce will change, and that's important for *human resources* to understand and plan for. This changing composition of the workforce might necessitate moving operations to other countries in search of labour with the required skills. Clearly, all of these implications have a direct impact on the *finance* area, but the demographic shifts we are experiencing in Canada, coupled with a declining birth rate, have also caused the government to respond with changes in economic policy, as discussed earlier, and this inevitably affects the finance area of the business.

Without a doubt, there is also a connection between functional areas and ethical and responsible corporate behaviour. According to Canadian Business for Social Responsibility (CBSR), companies that practice corporate social responsibility develop and practice policies and programs in areas such as employee relations (human resources), international relations (operations), marketplace practices (marketing), and fiscal responsibility and accountability (finance). In fact, if a business is to be truly responsible, commitment must come from the top, and it must be part of the *mission* and culture of the company, and therefore part of the decisions made within all functional areas.

Add to this list community development and environmental stewardship, and you've covered the major *stakeholder* groups. Clearly, behaving ethically and responsibly involves operating in a manner that recognizes and balances the competing expectations of all the various stakeholders of the business, and building a relationship of trust with them. Furthermore, meeting the company's obligations to its stakeholders helps the company achieve its critical success factors. For example, meeting its responsibility to employees helps gain employee commitment, meeting its responsibility to customers helps meet customer needs, and meeting its responsibility to investors helps achieve financial performance by providing needed capital. In fact, social investing theory would suggest that this is a very big factor. More and more investment funds are moving toward socially responsible companies, and as we can see from the *Corporate Knights* survey, they are doing very well.

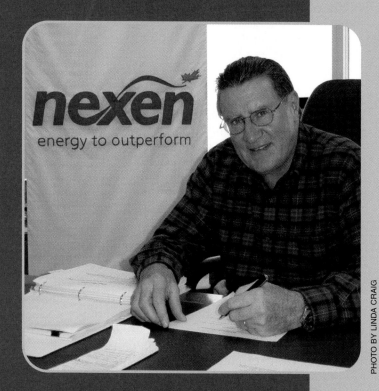

PHOTO BY LINDA CRAIG

Social Trends, Social Responsibility, and Making Ethical Decisions in Business

learning goals

1 How are current social trends affecting business?

2 How are demographic trends creating new opportunities for business?

3 What philosophies and concepts shape personal ethical standards?

4 How can organizations encourage ethical business behaviour?

5 What is social responsibility?

6 How do businesses meet their social responsibilities to various stakeholders?

7 What are the global and domestic trends in ethics and social responsibility?

Business Integrity at Nexen, Inc.

Dr. Randall Gossen is the vice president of safety, environment, and social responsibility for Nexen, Inc., and the current president of the World Petroleum Council. Randy describes business integrity as "the human face of business." He suggests that the term *business integrity* tends to be more palatable to business than the more commonly used *corporate responsibility*. Nexen supports five pillars of corporate social responsibility: business practices, employee relations, community investment, safety and environment, and supplier and customer relations. Exhibit 3.1 illustrates the five pillars.

Nexen operates internationally, and several locations would be considered high risk. Many of the risks faced by Nexen include the obvious social, environmental, political, legal, economic, and security risks, but there are also problems with drug cartels, terrorists, corruption, and kidnapping. The approach taken by Nexen is to improve the quality of life in the communities and the societies of the host countries. Nexen believes that if the company is to enjoy sustainable success, the communities in which it operates must also experience success. With reference to Nexen's operations in Colombia, Randy says, "Community support is the cornerstone of risk management." Nexen designs and implements community-based and supported programs, such as developing computer literacy in the local schools, protecting the water supplies, and training local leaders in formulating projects. In Yemen, Nexen has steadily increased the number of locals employed by the company. The company provides English language and technical training, and a scholarship program for Yemeni students to study in Canada at post-secondary institutions. "In order to operate in this way, we need the management structure and system to support it," explains Randy. This structure includes knowledgeable employees who are prepared to "walk the talk." Nexen's continuous improvement model for business integrity involves "(1) knowing what we stand for, (2) taking action, (3) measuring performance, and (4) verifying." With respect to "knowing what we stand for," Nexen's statement of vision, beliefs, values, and principles is made available to employees and any

Exhibit 3.1 | The Five Pillars of Corporate Responsibility

Community Investment
Community Affairs Programs
Public Consultation
Capacity Building
Technology Transfer
Cash Donations
Matching Gifts
Employee Secondment
Aboriginal Relations
Volunteerism
Sponsorship

Business Practices
Ethics
Governance
Government Relations
Risk and Crisis Management
Public Policy
Anti-Corruption
Human Rights
Verification

Employee Relations
Training
Pay and Benefits
Freedom of Association
Labour Relations
Diversity
Satisfaction
Turnover

CORPORATE SOCIAL RESPONSABILITY

Safety and Environment
Management Systems
Emergency Preparedness
Regulatory Compliance
Air, Water, and Land Quality
Site Remediation and Land Reclamation
Occupational Health
Waste Management
Emissions

Supplier and Customer Relations
Global Sourcing
Fair Handling of Contracts
Fair Prices
Service Reliability
Products Labelling
Products Safety

member of the general public who wishes to read it. "How can a company practise business integrity without transparency?" asks Randy. Take a look at Nexen's code of ethics on pages 86-88.

Randy explains that Nexen believes there is a strong business case for practising business integrity and behaving in a socially responsible manner but, more important, it's the right thing to do. The rewards, according to Randy, include "stronger financial performance, meeting expectations of the investment community, employee commitment, motivation and morale, decreased vulnerability and risk, and improved reputation." The bottom line for Nexen is "Good business practices are the best insurance."[2]

Critical Thinking Questions

As you read this chapter, consider the following questions as they relate to Nexen:

1. How have trends affected Nexen, and what opportunities and threats have these trends offered the company?
2. How has Nexen shown that it is socially responsible, and how does this impact on their profits in the short and long terms?
3. Why is ethical behaviour important to companies such as Nexen?

Principles of Social Trends, Social Responsibilities, and Ethics

No one business is large or powerful enough to create major changes in the external environment. Thus, managers are basically adapters to, rather than agents of, change. For example, despite the huge sizes of General Motors, Ford, and DaimlerChrysler, these companies have only recently been able to stem the competitive push by the Japanese for an ever-growing share of the North American automobile market. Global competition is basically an uncontrollable element in the external environment, as discussed in Chapter 2. In this chapter, we examine the social trends in the business environment that are reshaping today's business landscape. Most important are the trends for companies to consider their social responsibility and the expectation that they will act in an ethical manner.

Every day, managers and business owners make business decisions based on what they believe to be right or wrong. Through their actions, they demonstrate to their employees what is and is not acceptable behaviour and shape the moral standard of the organization. **Ethics** is a set of moral standards for judging whether something is right or wrong. As you will see in this chapter, personal and professional ethics are important cornerstones of an organization and shape its ultimate contributions to society. Let's consider first the important social trends and then how individual business ethics are formed.

ethics
A set of moral standards for judging whether something is right or wrong.

SOCIAL TRENDS

1 *learning goal*

Social change is perhaps the most difficult environmental factor for owners and managers to forecast, influence, or integrate into business plans. Social factors include our attitudes, values, and lifestyles. Social factors influence the products people buy, the prices paid for products, the effectiveness of specific promotions, and how, where, and when people expect to purchase products.

The Growth of Component Lifestyles

component lifestyle
A lifestyle made up of a complex set of interests and choices.

People in Canada today are piecing together component lifestyles. A lifestyle is a mode of living; it is the way people decide to live their lives. A **component lifestyle** is a lifestyle made up of a complex set of interests and choices. In other words, people are choosing products and services that meet diverse needs and interests rather than conforming to traditional stereotypes.

In the past, a person's profession—for instance, banker—defined that person's lifestyle. Today a person can be a banker, gourmet, fitness enthusiast, dedicated single parent, and conservationist—all at once. Each of these lifestyles is associated with different goods and services and represents a unique market. For example, businesses advertise cooking utensils, wines, and exotic foods through magazines like *Bon Appétit* and *Gourmet* for the gourmets. The fitness enthusiast buys Adidas equipment and special jogging outfits, and reads *Runner's World* magazine. Component lifestyles increase the complexity of consumers' buying habits. The banker may own a BMW, but she may change the oil herself. She may buy fast food for lunch but French wine for dinner, own sophisticated photographic equipment and a low-priced home stereo, and shop for hosiery at Wal-Mart and for business suits at Holt Renfrew.

Two-Income Families

Component lifestyles have evolved because consumers can choose from a growing number of goods and services, and most have the money to exercise more options. As well, the growth of dual-income families has resulted in increased purchasing power. Of the more than 16 million Canadians in the workforce today, 53 percent are men and 47 percent are women.[3] The phenomenon of working women has probably had a greater effect on marketing than has any other social change. As women's earnings grow, so do their levels of expertise, experience, and authority. Working-age women are not the same group businesses targeted 30 years ago. They expect different things in life—from their jobs, from their spouses, and from the products and services they buy.

The automotive industry has finally begun to recognize the power of women in vehicle purchase decisions. Women are the principal buyers or influencers of purchases for 54 percent of all cars and trucks sold in North America.[4] Toyota has found that women influence 8 out of 10 vehicle purchases. Armed with this information, Toyota has set up a hotline just for women. It has also created a Web site just for female car buyers and owners. The site avoids male-oriented jargon and offers helpful hints on safety, maintenance, and financing. The limited-edition Toyota Roxy Echo is targeted at female buyers aged 18 to 32.[5]

Saturn honours outstanding women with its Saturn Women at Their Best Awards. Saturn is also highly responsive to women customers, who are the principal buyers for more than 54 percent of all cars and trucks sold in Canada.

© AP/WORLD WIDE PHOTOS

In a recent survey, two-thirds to three-fourths of women said they are making many major economic decisions either independently or equally with a spouse. Few of the women said they left important marketplace decisions to others.[6] When it comes to big-ticket, long-term items, women remain active in the decision-making process, though most say they are more likely to make these decisions with a spouse. Life experience is an important factor in women's independence in long-term planning; married women over age 55 are more likely to make these decisions on their own than their younger counterparts are.

The income level, and often the disposable income, varies greatly by economic family type. For example, the average total income for a two-earner married couple was approximately $80,000 in 2003. A one-earner family had an average of income of approximately $60,000. Despite huge strides for women in the world of work, a large wage discrepancy, which is only partially explainable by the type of work being done, still exists. The average income for a male lone-parent family was approximately $57,000, whereas the female lone-parent family income was $33,000.[7]

concept check

Why are social changes the most difficult environmental factor to predict?

How do component lifestyles make it more difficult to predict a consumer's buying habits?

What social change has had the greatest impact on business?

DEMOGRAPHIC TRENDS

2 *learning goal*

Demographic trends—another uncontrollable factor in the business environment—are also extremely important to managers. **Demography** is the study of people's vital statistics, such as their age, race and ethnicity, and location. Demographics are significant, because the basis for any market is people. Demographics also determine the size and composition of the workforce. For the following discussion, we will use the 2006 population of 33 million people (rounded for simplicity). Let's begin by taking a closer look at key age groups.

Generation Y

Those designated by demographics as **Generation Y** were born between 1979 and 1994. Although Generation Y is much smaller than the baby boom, which lasted nearly 20 years, its members are plentiful enough to put their own footprints on society.

The marketing impact of Generation Y has been immense. Companies that sell toys, videos, software, and clothing to kids have boomed in recent years. Nine of the 10 best-selling videos of all time are animated films from the Walt Disney Company. Club Med, the French vacation company, now earns half its revenues from family resorts. The members of Generation Y were born into a world vastly different from the one their parents entered. The changes in family, the workforce, technology, and demographics in recent decades will no doubt affect their attitudes, but often in unpredictable ways.

Generation Y, born between 1979 and 1994, is brand and fashion conscious. Smart marketers will monitor this segment of the market and continue to develop products that appeal to them.

Unlike the "party a-go-go" ads aimed at them, Gen Yers lead relatively quiet lives: "listening to music, hanging with friends, going to movies, dining out, and watching TV. They rarely participate in high-action activities such as tennis and motorcycling." Most are pragmatic, like convenience, and are value oriented.

Gen Y appears to be a "notoriously fickle" consumer group, demanding the latest trends in record time. Communicators wanting to reach these teens have "to embrace that type of fast change." A critical consumer group, they "don't like a hard sell." They are "brand and fashion-conscious," but as one advertising manager has learned, you have to get the "merchandise in front of them without being in their face."[8] Many Gen Yers are still in their teenage years, and they have money to spend on things they like.

Generation X

Generation X is made up of people born between 1965 and 1978. It is the first generation of latchkey children—products of dual-career households or, in roughly half of the cases, of divorced or separated parents. Gen Xers have been bombarded by multiple media since their cradle days; thus they are savvy and cynical consumers.

With careers launched and families started, Generation X is at the stage in life when there is suddenly a host of demands competing for their time—and their budgets. As a result, Gen X spending is quite diffused: food, housing, and transportation. Time is at a premium for harried Gen Xers, so they're outsourcing the tasks of daily life, which include everything from domestic help to baby-sitting. Xers spend 78 percent more than average on personal services, more than any other age group, and therefore spend 15 percent less than average on housekeeping supplies.[9]

Baby Boomers—Canada's Mass Market

People born between the late 1940s (after World War II) and the mid-1960s are called **baby boomers**. Many baby boomers are now over 50, but most continue to live very active lives. This group cherishes convenience, which has resulted in a growing demand for home delivery of large appliances, furniture, groceries, and other items. In addition, the spreading culture of convenience explains the tremendous appeal of prepared take-out foods, VCRs, DVDs, cordless telephones, and the Internet.

Baby boomers' parents raised their children to think for and of themselves. Studies of child-rearing practices show that parents of the 1950s and 1960s consistently ranked "to think for themselves" as the number one trait they wanted to nurture in their children. Postwar affluence also enabled parents to indulge their children as never before. They invested in their children's skills by sending them to university. They also encouraged their children to succeed in a job market that rewarded competitive drive more than cooperative spirit, and individual skills more than teamwork.

In turn, the sheer size of the generation encouraged businesses to play to the emerging individuality of baby boomers. Even before the oldest boomers started earning a living more than three decades ago, astute businesspeople anticipated the profits that could come from giving millions of young people what they wanted. Businesses offered individualistic baby boomers a growing array of customized products and services—houses, cars, furniture, appliances, clothes, vacations, jobs, leisure time, and even beliefs.

Older Consumers—Not Just Grandparents

The oldest baby boomers have already crossed the 60-year threshold that many demographers use to define the "mature market." Yet today's mature consumers are wealthier, healthier, and better educated than those of earlier generations. Fixed incomes mean tighter budgets, however, and as many seniors make the transition into their retirement years, average household income and spending decline substantially. But although spending among seniors reflects this reality, they are far from being out of the consumer marketplace. Seniors spend money maintaining what they've already accumulated. Given the amount of time they now spend at home, these consumers direct a larger chunk of their budgets to food to be eaten there.

Businesspeople who want to actively pursue the mature market must understand it. Aging consumers create some obvious opportunities. For example, some manufacturers and retailers provide clothes featuring Velcro fasteners for women with arthritis or other ailments, who might have difficulty with zippers or buttons. Furthermore, as these Canadians near retirement, many make non-financial preparations before leaving the workforce. These preparations include increasing participation in hobbies, physical activities, volunteerism, and general information gathering about what to expect in retirement (see Exhibit 3.2).

Canadians on the Move

As employment opportunities change by region, Canadians often follow the opportunities. This trend has implications for business. A large influx of new people into an area creates many new opportunities for all types of businesses. Conversely, significant out-migration from a city or town can force many of its businesses to move or close down because they can't find qualified employees.

See Exhibit 3.3 for the changes of employment numbers from March 2005 to March 2006 in Canada and the provinces.

Diversity in Canada

According to the Canadian Policy Research Network, in 2001, 13 percent of the Canadian population identified themselves as belonging to a visible minority group. It is estimated that by 2017, that percentage will rise to between 19 and 23 percent, excluding First Nations peoples, who are expected to increase their proportion of the Canadian population from 3.4 to 4.1 percent during the same period.[10]

multiculturalism
The fundamental belief that all citizens are equal regardless of their racial or ethnic backgrounds.

Multiculturalism is fundamental to Canada and our belief that all citizens are equal regardless of their racial and ethnic backgrounds. Multiculturalism encourages racial cross-cultural understanding and discourages hatred, discrimination, and violence.[11] Because of the current demographic transition, the trend in Canada is toward greater multiculturalism, although the degree varies in different parts of the country. Half the residents of both Toronto and Vancouver might be members of what are now considered visible minorities by 2017.[12]

Exhibit 3.2 | Type of Non-Financial Preparation by Recent Retirees (in Percentages)

OCCUPATION TYPE	PHYSICAL ACTIVITIES	LEISURE ACTIVITIES AND HOBBIES	VOLUNTEERISM	GATHERING INFORMATION
Managerial	28	38	28	42
Professional	30	42	38	63
Technical	41	40	31	54
Clerical	29	37	34	53
Sales and service	26	31	27	38
Trades and transportation	21	34	22	39
Other blue collar	28	36	20	36

SOURCE: Adapted from the Statistics Canada publication "Canadian Social Trends," Preparing for retirement, Catalogue 11-008, Fall 2005, no. 78, page 10, released September 13, 2005.

Exhibit 3.3	Changes of Employment Numbers in Canada from March 2005 to March 2006	
	EMPLOYMENT NUMBERS (THOUSANDS) MARCH 2006 NUMBERS	PERCENTAGE CHANGE FROM MARCH 2005 TO MARCH 2006
Canada	16,396.2	2.1
Newfoundland	211.9	−1.9
Prince Edward Island	67.9	−0.9
Nova Scotia	443.7	0.3
New Brunswick	359.6	2.8
Quebec	3,752.9	1.6
Ontario	6,463.0	1.8
Manitoba	583.0	1.2
Saskatchewan	483.2	−1.1
Alberta	1,841.9	3.7
British Columbia	2,189.0	4.0

SOURCE: Adapted from the Statistics Canada website http://www40.statcan.ca/101/cst01/labr66a.htm, accessed April 18, 2006.

Changing demographics affect the marketing of goods and services. As Canadians are becoming more health conscious, for instance, companies should promote the "healthiness" of goods and services. As our population ages and becomes more technically sophisticated, organizations need to search for new marketing streams that will encourage the target market to purchase goods and services.

Organizations need to be responsive to the customers, and as they change, the organizations need to change their marketing efforts. This includes the goods and services that they are providing, the price at which they offer them, the place where the customer can have access to them, and how the organizations promote the goods and services.

If organizations fail to monitor the changing demographics of their customers, they will not be able to respond to these changes and will most likely lose sales.

The Impact of Immigration

Part of the reason for the tremendous shift in Canadian demographics is immigration. Canada's relativity small population simply cannot maintain the current high standard of living. From July 2004 to June 2005, there were approximately 340,000 births in Canada.[13] This rate cannot sustain our economic growth. The federal government, along with the provinces, is trying to determine the level of need for immigration and various ways to encourage people to move to Canada. For instance, Canada has initiated discussions on the free movement of labour between the NAFTA countries (Canada, United States, and Mexico).

The most important contributing factor to this desired increase is immigration; however, other factors such as higher fertility and higher life expectancy are also being considered. With increased immigration, the largest visible minority group would continue to be South Asians and Chinese, with the South Asian population growth projected at 72 to 137 percent between 2001 and 2017. The Chinese population growth is expected to be 51 to 111 percent for the same period.[14]

There is no doubt that immigrant entrepreneurs, from the corner grocer to the local builder, are creating jobs for other immigrants and for those born in Canada.

Employees from different ethnic and racial backgrounds will continue to enrich the workplace with their diverse views and ideas.

© PHOTODISC / GETTY IMAGES

Vibrant immigrant communities are revitalizing cities and older suburbs that would otherwise be suffering from a shrinking tax base. And the immigrants' links to their countries of origin are boosting Canadian exports to fast-growing regions such as Asia and Latin America.

Canada is also reaping a bonanza of highly educated foreign-born citizens. High-tech industries, which deal in everything from semiconductors to biotechnology, are depending on immigrant scientists, engineers, and entrepreneurs to remain competitive.

concept check

How has the changing role of women affected business?

Explain how Generation X, Generation Y, and baby boomers differ.

How is diversity changing the marketplace?

INDIVIDUAL BUSINESS ETHICS

3 learning goal

Individual business ethics are shaped by personal choices and the environments in which we live and work. In addition, the laws of our society are guideposts for choosing between right and wrong. In this section, we describe personal philosophies and legal factors that influence the choices people make when confronting ethical dilemmas.

Utilitarianism—Seeking the Best for the Majority

utilitarianism

A philosophy that focuses on the consequences of an action to determine whether it is right or wrong, and holds that an action that affects the majority adversely is morally wrong.

One of the philosophies that might influence choices between right and wrong is **utilitarianism**, which focuses on the consequences of an action taken by a person or organization. The notion that "people should act so as to generate the greatest good for the greatest number" is derived from utilitarianism. When an action affects the majority adversely, it is morally wrong. One problem with this philosophy is that it is nearly impossible to determine accurately how a decision will affect a large number of people.

Another problem is that utilitarianism always involves both winners and losers. If sales are slowing, and a manager decides to fire 5 people rather than putting everyone on a 30-hour workweek, the 20 people who keep their full-time jobs are winners, but the other 5 are losers.

A final criticism of utilitarianism is that some "costs," although small relative to the potential good, are so negative that some segments of society find them unacceptable. Reportedly, the backs of up to 3,000 animals a year are deliberately broken so that scientists can conduct research that might someday lead to a cure for spinal cord injuries. To a number of people, however, the "costs" are simply too horrible for this type of research to continue.

Individual Rights

In our society, individuals and groups have certain rights that exist under certain conditions regardless of the external circumstances. These rights serve as guides when individuals make ethical decisions. The term *human rights* implies that certain rights are conveyed at birth and cannot be arbitrarily taken away. Denying the rights of an individual or group is considered to be unethical and illegal in most, though not all, parts of the world. Certain rights are guaranteed by the various levels of government and their laws, and these are considered legal rights. The **Canadian Charter of Rights and Freedoms** was enacted in 1982 to guarantee the rights and freedoms of Canadians and is superordinate to any other laws that affect Canadians' rights and freedoms.

Some of the freedoms listed in the Charter include

- freedom of conscience and religion;
- freedom of thought, belief, opinion, and expression (e.g., press and other media of communication);
- freedom of peaceful assembly; and
- freedom of association.

Charter rights include

- democratic rights (right to vote at the age of majority),
- mobility rights (the right to enter, remain in, and leave Canada),
- legal rights (the right to life, liberty, and security),
- equality rights (everyone is equal under the law), and
- minority language educational rights (the right to be educated in either English or French).

HOT Links

For more about the Canadian Charter of Rights and Freedoms and other Canadian legislation, go to http://laws.justice.gc.ca/en/charter/index.html.

Justice—The Question of Fairness

justice
What is considered fair according to the prevailing standards of society; in the 20th century, an equitable distribution of the burdens and rewards that society has to offer.

A factor that influences individual business ethics is **justice**, or what is fair according to prevailing standards of society. We all expect life to be reasonably fair. You expect your exams to be fair, the grading to be fair, and your wages to be fair, based on the type of work being done.

In the 21st century, we take justice to mean an equitable distribution of the burdens and rewards that society has to offer. The distributive process varies from society to society. Those in a democratic society believe in the "equal pay for equal work" doctrine, in which individuals are rewarded based on the value that the free market places on their services. Because the market places different values on different occupations, the rewards, such as wages, are not necessarily equal. Nevertheless, many regard the rewards as just. At the other extreme, communist theorists have argued that justice would be served by a society in which burdens and rewards were distributed to individuals according to their abilities and their needs, respectively.

Stages of Ethical Development

We can view an individual's ethical development as having reached one of three levels: preconventional, conventional, or postconventional. The behaviour of a person at the level of **preconventional ethics** is childlike in nature; it is calculating, self-centred, and even selfish, and is based on the possibility of immediate punishment or reward. Thus, a student might not cheat on an exam because he or she is afraid of getting caught and therefore receiving a failing grade for the course. The student's behaviour is based not on a sense of what's right or wrong but, instead, on the threat of punishment.

Conventional ethics moves from an egocentric viewpoint toward the expectations of society. Loyalty and obedience to the organization (or society) become paramount. At the conventional ethics level, a businessperson might say, "I know that our advertising is somewhat misleading, but as long as it will increase sales we should continue the campaign." Right or wrong is not the issue; the only question is whether the campaign will benefit the organization.

Postconventional ethics represents the ethical standards of the mature adult. At the postconventional level, businesspeople are concerned less about how others might see them and more about how they see and judge themselves over the long run. A person who has attained this ethical level might ask, "Even though this action is legal and will increase company profits, is it right in the long run? Might it do more harm than good in the end?" A manager at a fast-food restaurant might refuse to offer Styrofoam cups because they are nonbiodegradable. An advertising agency manager might refuse a tobacco account because of the health hazards of smoking. A lab technician might refuse to recommend a new whitener for a detergent because it could harm the environment. All of these individuals are exhibiting postconventional morality.

Many people believe that the Internet is a vast anonymous place where they can say and do just about anything. When they think that they can't be caught, they sometimes revert to preconventional ethics. Yet e-mail servers owned by businesses and governmental agencies can quickly tell what is being sent and to whom. The Computer Ethics Institute has proposed the "Ten Commandments of Computer Ethics."

Computers and Ethics

The Computer Ethics Institute (CEI) is a research, education, and policy study organization focusing on the interface of information technologies, ethics, and corporate and public policy. Its objective is to undertake research about the actual and potential effects of information technology, and to provide advice to various interested parties (individuals, organizations, communities, etc.) regarding ethical and social responsibilities.

Until recently, there has been a very laissez-faire approach to ethics when it comes to cyberspace, coupled with a great reluctance to restrict information on the Internet, but this is changing in the 21st century. The increased use of the information highway has encouraged more policing. First presented in Dr. Ramon C. Barquin's paper "In Pursuit of a 'Ten Commandments' for Computer Ethics," the CEI has created the "Ten Commandments of Computer Ethics," shown on the next page.

preconventional ethics
A stage in the ethical development of individuals in which people behave in a childlike manner and make ethical decisions in a calculating, self-centred, selfish way, based on the possibility of immediate punishment or reward; also known as self-centred ethics.

conventional ethics
The second stage in the ethical development of individuals in which people move from an egocentric viewpoint to consider the expectations of an organization of society; also known as social ethics.

postconventional ethics
The third stage in the ethical development of individuals in which people adhere to the ethical standards of a mature adult and are less concerned about how others view their behaviour than about how they will judge themselves in the long run; also known as principled ethics.

concept check

Define ethics.

What is utilitarianism?

Discuss the stages of ethical development.

Ten Commandments of Computer Ethics

1. Thou shalt not use a computer to harm other people.
2. Thou shalt not interfere with other people's computer work.
3. Thou shalt not snoop around in other people's computer files.
4. Thou shalt not use a computer to steal.
5. Thou shalt not use a computer to bear false witness.
6. Thou shalt not copy or use proprietary software for which you have not paid.
7. Thou shalt not use other people's computer resources without authorization or proper compensation.
8. Thou shalt not appropriate other people's intellectual output.
9. Thou shalt think about the social consequences of the program you are writing or the system you are designing.
10. Thou shalt always use a computer in ways that ensure consideration and respect for your fellow humans.

SOURCE: Computer Ethics Institute, The Brookings Institution, "Ten Commandments of Computer Ethics," http://www.brook.edu/its/cei/overview/Ten_Commandments_of_Computer_Ethics.htm (accessed July 3, 2003). Reprinted by permission of The Computer Ethics Institute.

HOT Links

The Canadian Information Processing Society is a professional association providing leadership in information systems and technologies fields. Find out more about their code of ethics at http://www.cips.ca.

Recognizing Unethical Business Activities

Researchers from Brigham Young University state that all unethical business activities will fall into one of the following categories:

1. *Taking things that don't belong to you.* The unauthorized use of someone else's property or taking property under false pretences is taking something that does not belong to you. Even the smallest offence, such as using the postage meter at your office for mailing personal letters or exaggerating your travel expenses, belongs in this category of ethical violations.

2. *Saying things you know are not true.* When trying for a promotion and advancement, employees might be tempted to discredit their coworkers. Falsely assigning blame or inaccurately reporting conversations is lying. Although "This is the way the game is played around here" is a common justification, saying things that are untrue is an ethical violation.

3. *Giving or allowing false impressions.* The salesperson who permits a potential customer to believe that cardboard boxes will hold the customer's tomatoes for long-distance shipping when the salesperson knows the boxes are not strong enough has given a false impression. A car dealer who fails to disclose that a car has been in an accident is misleading potential customers.

4. *Buying influence or engaging in a conflict of interest.* A conflict of interest occurs when the official responsibilities of an employee or government official are influenced by the potential for personal gain. Suppose a company awards a construction contract to a firm owned by the father of a provincial politician while the attorney general's office is investigating that company. If this construction award has the potential to shape the outcome of the investigation, a conflict of interest has occurred.

After the Ford Explorer was linked to rollover accidents and 271 deaths, the Ford Motor Company reached a nationwide settlement that includes a national SUV safety campaign that advises consumers on safe SUV driving and loading.

5. *Hiding or divulging information.* Failing to disclose the results of medical studies that indicate your firm's new drug has significant side effects is the ethical violation of hiding information that the product could be harmful to purchasers. Taking your firm's product development or trade secrets to a new place of employment constitutes the ethical violation of divulging proprietary information.

6. *Taking unfair advantage.* Many current consumer protection laws were passed because so many businesses took unfair advantage of people who were not educated or were unable to discern the nuances of complex contracts. Credit disclosure requirements, truth-in-lending provisions, and new regulations on auto leasing all resulted because businesses misled consumers who could not easily follow the jargon of long, complex agreements.

7. *Committing improper personal behaviour.* Although the ethical aspects of an employee's right to privacy are still debated, it has become increasingly clear that personal conduct outside the job can influence performance and company reputation. Thus, a company driver must abstain from substance abuse because of safety issues. Even the traditional company Christmas party and picnic have come under scrutiny because of the possibility that employees at and following these events might harm themselves or others through alcohol-related accidents.

8. *Abusing another person.* Suppose a manager sexually harasses an employee or subjects employees to humiliating corrections in the presence of coworkers or customers. In some cases, laws protect employees. Many situations, however, are simply interpersonal abuse that constitutes an ethical violation.

9. *Permitting organizational abuse.* Many companies with operations outside of their own country have faced issues of organizational abuse. The unfair treatment of workers in international operations appears in the form of child labour, demeaning wages, and excessive work hours. Although a business cannot change the culture of another country, it can perpetuate—or stop—abuse through its operations there.

10. *Violating rules.* Many organizations use rules and processes to maintain internal controls or to respect the authority of managers. Although these rules might seem burdensome to employees trying to serve customers, a violation might be considered an unethical act.

11. *Condoning unethical actions.* What if you witnessed a fellow employee embezzling company funds by forging her signature on a cheque that was to be voided? Would you report the violation? A winking tolerance of others' unethical behaviour is itself unethical.[15]

HOT Links

Visit the Canadian Resources for Business Ethics site at http://www.businessethics.ca.

concept check

How are individual business ethics formed?

How can you recognize unethical activities?

HOW ORGANIZATIONS INFLUENCE ETHICAL CONDUCT

4 *learning goal*

People choose between right and wrong based on their personal code of ethics. Ethical behaviours (or unethical behaviours) are also influenced by the ethical environment created by their employers. Consider the following newspaper headlines that announce legal claims against organizations that failed to manage their employees ethically:

- "Home Depot Pays $87.5 Million for Not Promoting More Women"
- "Home Depot's Agreement to Settle Suit Could Cut 3rd-Quarter Earnings by 21%"[16]

As these headlines illustrate, poor business ethics can be very expensive for a company. Organizations can reduce the potential for these types of liability claims by educating their employees about ethical standards through various informal and formal programs. The first step in making a good ethical decision, however, is to recognize unethical business activities when they occur.

Leading by Example

Employees often follow the examples set by their managers. That is, leaders and managers establish patterns of behaviour that determine what's acceptable and what's not within the organization. While Ben Cohen was president of Ben & Jerry's ice cream, he followed a policy that no one could earn a salary more than seven times that of the lowest-paid worker. He wanted all employees to feel that they were equal. At the time he resigned, company sales were $140 million (USD) and the lowest-paid worker earned $19,000 (USD) per year. Ben Cohen's salary was $133,000 (USD) based on the "seven times" rule. A typical top executive of a $140 million (USD) company might have earned 10 times Cohen's salary. Ben Cohen's actions helped shape the ethical values of Ben & Jerry's.

Offering Ethics Training Programs

In addition to providing a system to resolve ethical dilemmas, organizations also provide formal training for employees to help them to develop an awareness of questionable business activities and practice appropriate responses. Many Canadian companies have some type of ethics training program. The ones that are most effective begin with techniques for solving ethical dilemmas such as those discussed earlier. Next, employees are presented with a series of situations and are asked to come up with the "best" ethical solution. One of these ethical dilemmas is shown on the next page. Some companies have tried to add a bit of excitement and fun to their ethics training programs by presenting them in the form of games. Citigroup, for example, has created The Work Ethic, a board game in which participants strive to answer legal, regulatory, policy-related, and judgment ethics questions correctly.

Bill Gannon was a middle manager of a large manufacturer of lighting fixtures in Newark, New Jersey. Bill had moved up the company ladder rather quickly and seemed destined for upper management in a few years. Bill's boss, Dana Johnson, had been pressuring him about the semiannual reviews concerning Robert Talbot, one of Bill's employees. Dana, it seemed, would not accept any negative comments on Robert's evaluation forms. Bill had found out that a previous manager who had given Robert a bad evaluation was no longer with the company. As Bill reviewed Robert's performance for the forthcoming evaluation period, he found many areas of substandard performance. Moreover, a major client had called recently, complaining that Robert had filled a large order improperly and then had been rude to the client when she called to complain.

DISCUSSION QUESTIONS

1. What ethical issues does the situation raise?
2. What courses of action could Bill take? Describe the ethics of each course.
3. Should Bill confront Dana? Dana's boss?
4. What would you do in this situation? What are the ethical implications?

Establishing a Formal Code of Ethics

code of ethics

A set of guidelines prepared by a firm to provide its employees with the knowledge of what the firm expects in terms of their responsibilities and behaviour toward fellow employees, customers, and suppliers.

Most large companies and thousands of smaller ones have created, printed, and distributed codes of ethics. In general, a **code of ethics** provides employees with the knowledge of what their firm expects in terms of their responsibilities and behaviour toward fellow employees, customers, and suppliers. Some ethical codes offer a lengthy and detailed set of guidelines for employees. Others are not really codes at all but rather summary statements of goals, policies, and priorities. Some companies have their codes framed and hung on office walls or printed on cards to be carried at all times by executives. The code of ethics for Nexen, Inc., is shown below.

INTERNATIONAL CODE OF ETHICS FOR CANADIAN BUSINESS[1]

Nexen helped develop this code in 1997 as a template for Canadian businesses to follow when conducting business at home and abroad. Since then, many businesses have adopted the code to ensure they operate ethically.

VISION

Canadian business has a global presence that is recognized by all stakeholders[2] as

- economically rewarding to all parties;
- acknowledged as being ethically, socially, and environmentally responsible;

- welcomed by the communities in which we operate; and
- facilitates economic, human resource, and community development within a stable operating environment

WE BELIEVE THAT

- we can make a difference within our sphere of influence (stakeholders);
- business should take a leadership role through the establishment of ethical business practices;
- national governments have the prerogative to conduct their own government and legal affairs in accordance with their sovereign rights;
- all governments should comply with international treaties and other agreements that they have committed to, including the areas of human rights and social justice;
- while reflecting cultural diversity and differences, we should do business throughout the world consistent with the way we do business in Canada;
- the business sector should show ethical leadership;
- we can facilitate the achievement of wealth generation and a fair sharing of economic benefits;
- our principles will assist in improving relations between the Canadian and host governments;
- open, honest and transparent relationships are critical to our success;
- local communities need to be involved in decesion-making for issues that affect them;
- multi-stakeholder processes need to be initiated to seek effective solutions;
- confrontation should be tempered by diplomacy;
- wealth maximization for all stakeholders will be enhanced by resolution of outstanding human rights and social justice issues; and
- doing business with other countries is good for Canada, and vice versa.

WE VALUE

- human rights and social justice;
- wealth maximization for all stakeholders;

- operation of a free market economy;
- public accountability by governments;
- a business environment that militates against bribery and corruption;
- equality of opportunity;
- a defined code of ethics and business practice;
- protection of environmental quality and sound environmental stewardship;
- community benefits;
- good relationships with all stakeholders; and
- stability and continuous improvement within our operating environment.

PRINCIPLES

A. CONCERNING COMMUNITY PARTICIPATION AND ENVIRONMENTAL PROTECTION, WE WILL

- strive within our sphere of influence to ensure a fair share of benefits to stakeholders impacted by our activities;
- ensure meaningful and transparent consultation with all stakeholders and attempt to integrate our corporate activities;
- ensure our activities are consistent with sound environmental management and conservation practices; and
- provide meaningful opportunities for technology cooperation, training, and capacity building within the host nation.

B. CONCERNING HUMAN RIGHTS, WE WILL

- support and respect the protection of international human rights within our sphere of influence, and
- not be complicit in human rights abuses.

C. CONCERNING BUSINESS CONDUCT, WE WILL

- not make illegal and improper payments and bribes and will refrain from participating in any corrupt business practices;
- comply with all applicable laws and conduct business activities with integrity; and
- ensure contractors,' suppliers', and agents' activities are consistent with these principles.

D. CONCERNING EMPLOYEE RIGHTS AND HEALTH AND SAFETY, WE WILL

- ensure health and safety of workers is protected;
- strive for social justice and respect freedom of association and expression in the workplace; and
- ensure consistency with other universally accepted labour standards related to exploitation of child labour, forced labour, and non-discrimination in employment.

NOTES

1. The Code is a statement of values/principles designed to facilitate and assist individual firms in developing their policies and practices that are consistent with the visions, beliefs, and principles contained herein.

2. Should include local communities, Canadian and host governments, local governments, shareholders, the media, customers and suppliers, interest groups, and international agencies.

Source: Reprinted by permission of Nexen, Inc.

Do codes of ethics make employees behave in a more ethical manner? Some people believe that they do. Others think that they are little more than public relations gimmicks. If senior management abides by the code of ethics and regularly emphasizes the code to employees, then it will likely have a positive influence on behaviour.

concept check

What is the role of top management in organizational ethics?
What is a code of ethics?

MANAGING A SOCIALLY RESPONSIBLE BUSINESS

5 *learning goal*

social responsibility
The concern of businesses for the welfare of society as a whole; consists of obligations beyond those required by law or contracts.

Acting in an ethical manner is one of the four components of the pyramid of corporate social responsibility. **Social responsibility** is the concern of businesses for the welfare of society as a whole. It consists of obligations beyond those required by law or union contract. This definition makes two important points. First, social responsibility is voluntary. Beneficial action required by law, such as cleaning up factories that are polluting air and water, is not voluntary. Second, the obligations of social responsibility are broad. They extend beyond investors in the company to include workers, suppliers, consumers, and communities.

Exhibit 3.4 portrays economic performance as the foundation for the other three responsibilities. At the same time that a business pursues profits (economic responsibility), however, it is expected to obey the law (legal responsibility); to do what is right, just, and fair (ethical responsibility); and to be a good corporate citizen (philanthropic responsibility). These four components are distinct but together constitute the whole.

Understanding Social Responsibility

Peter Drucker, a management expert, says to look first at what an organization does *to* society and second at what it can do *for* society. This idea suggests that social responsibility has two basic dimensions: legality and responsibility.

Exhibit 3.4 | The Pyramid of Corporate Social Responsibility

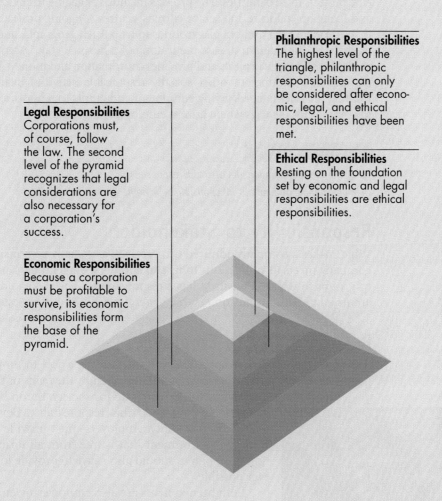

Philanthropic Responsibilities
The highest level of the triangle, philanthropic responsibilities can only be considered after economic, legal, and ethical responsibilities have been met.

Legal Responsibilities
Corporations must, of course, follow the law. The second level of the pyramid recognizes that legal considerations are also necessary for a corporation's success.

Ethical Responsibilities
Resting on the foundation set by economic and legal responsibilities are ethical responsibilities.

Economic Responsibilities
Because a corporation must be profitable to survive, its economic responsibilities form the base of the pyramid.

Illegal and Irresponsible Behaviour The idea of social responsibility is so widespread today that it is hard to conceive of a company continually acting in illegal and irresponsible ways. Nevertheless, such actions do sometimes occur. Of course, the acts of managers of Enron and WorldCom created financial ruin for their organizations, extreme financial hardships for many former employees, and general hardships for the communities in which they operated. Yet top executives walked away with millions. Some, however, will ultimately pay large fines and be sentenced to jail. Federal, provincial, and local laws determine whether an activity is legal or not.

Irresponsible but Legal Behaviour Sometimes companies act irresponsibly, yet their actions are legal. The governments are pressuring the advertising industry and the automobile industry for more responsible advertising. The government is concerned about advertisements that place an emphasis on speed and that show vehicles engaging in dangerous driving practices. "It seems that some ads work against road safety rather than for it," according to one spokesperson.

Legal and Responsible Behaviour The vast majority of business activities fall into the category of behaviour that is both legal and responsible. Most firms act legally, and most try to be socially responsible. Lucent Technologies (formerly Bell Labs) each year has 10,000 employees participate in "Global Days of Caring," assisting community projects worldwide. A recent Global Days of Caring found employees working on specific projects in 20 countries. The projects included engaging in environmental cleanup and fixing up childcare and senior citizens' centres. Ongoing projects include painting maps on elementary school playgrounds to help teach geography and making "smart" teddy bears for children to ease the trauma of a hospital stay. Lucent gives employees paid time off for the projects and provides coordination and money. The company also engages in a number of other socially responsible activities including hiring and training the unemployed, giving equipment and grants to schools, and making grants to community agencies where Lucent employees volunteer.

concept check

What are the four components of social responsibility?

Give an example of legal but irresponsible behaviour.

6   learning goal

stakeholders
Individuals or groups to whom a business has a responsibility; include employees, customers, the general public, and investors.

Responsibility to Stakeholders

What makes a company admired or perceived as socially responsible? This type of company meets its obligations to its **stakeholders.** Stakeholders are the individuals or groups to whom a business has a responsibility. The stakeholders of a business are its employees, its customers, the general public, and its investors.

Responsibility to Employees

An organization's first responsibility is to provide a job to employees. Keeping people employed and letting them have time to enjoy the fruits of their labour is the

CIBC's sponsorship of the Run for the Cure represents a legal and socially responsible activity that also enhances the image of the bank in the eyes of many consumers.

finest thing business can do for society. Enron is an example of a company that violated this responsibility. Beyond this fundamental responsibility, employers must provide a clean and safe working environment that is free from all forms of discrimination. Companies should also strive to provide job security whenever possible.

Enlightened firms are also empowering employees to make decisions on their own and suggest solutions to company problems. Empowerment contributes to an employee's self-worth, which, in turn, increases productivity and reduces absenteeism.

Responsibility to Customers

A central theme of this text is that to be successful today, a company must satisfy its customers. A firm must deliver what it promises. It must also be honest and forthright with its clients. We will discuss this in more detail in the, "Customer Satisfaction and Quality" section later in the chapter.

Responsibility to Investors

Companies' relationships with investors also entail social responsibility. Although a company's economic responsibility to make a profit might seem to be its main obligation to its shareholders, many investors increasingly are putting emphasis on other aspects of social responsibility.

CP PHOTO/TORONTO STAR/STUART NIMMO

social investing

The practice of limiting investments to securities of companies that behave in accordance with the investor's beliefs about ethical and social responsibility.

Some investors are limiting their investments to securities that fit within their beliefs about ethical and social responsibility. This is called **social investing.** For example, a social investment fund might eliminate from consideration the securities of all companies that make tobacco products or liquor, manufacture weapons, or have a history of polluting.

Investors who are dissatisfied with corporate managers tend to be less passive than in the past. They are pressuring corporations with tactics such as exposés on television and in other media and calling government attention to perceived wrongdoings. Groups of owners are pressuring companies to increase profits, link executive pay to performance, and oust inefficient management. Consequently, executives and managers are giving more weight to the concerns of owner stakeholders in the decision-making process.

HOT Links

Each year the Financial Post lists the best companies to work for. See the latest at http://working.canada.com/toronto/resources/topemployers/index.html.

Responsibility to Suppliers

As noted in Chapter 2, many companies rely on other companies for their survival. Often companies hire other companies to provide products or perform services for them. These suppliers (or business partners) are usually contracted because they can provide the products or perform the service more cheaply. Mark's Work Wearhouse, for example, does not produce its own line of clothing for resale but instead contracts it out to its suppliers. These suppliers are employing people, in turn providing more money to fuel the economy. It is important that businesses support their suppliers (e.g., giving contracts, paying supplier invoices). As we will see in Chapter 4, many companies are tying the e-business technology to their suppliers to realize many of the efficiencies that this can provide.

Responsibility to Governments

Governments in Canada rely on tax dollars to operate and provide their services to Canadians. Much of the tax revenue that the governments collect is in the form of corporate taxes. Corporations are responsible for accurately reporting their earnings and fulfilling their tax obligations.

Responsibility to Society

A business must also be responsible to society. A business provides a community with jobs, goods, and services. It also pays taxes that go to support schools, hospitals, and better roads. Most companies try to be good citizens in their communities.

HOT Links

Want to see how the global environment is changing and learn the latest about global warming? Check out http://www.climatehotmap.org.

Environmental Protection Business is also responsible for protecting and improving the world's fragile environment. The world's forests are rapidly being destroyed. Every second, an area the size of a football field is laid bare. Plant and animal species are becoming extinct at the rate of 17 per hour. A continent-sized hole is opening in the Earth's protective ozone shield. Each year we throw out more refuse than we did in 1960; as a result, more of our landfills are filled to capacity. To maintain sustainable development, business must be more sensitive to our environment (e.g., recycling, land management, pollution controls).

To slow the erosion of the world's resources, many companies are becoming more environmentally responsible. Canadian Tire, for example, strives to divert as much waste as possible from landfills. Since 1990, it has implemented aggressive pallet reuse and packaging recycling programs.[17]

corporate philanthropy

The practice of charitable giving by corporations; includes contributing cash, donating equipment and products, and supporting the volunteer efforts of company employees.

Corporate Philanthropy Companies also display their social responsibility through **corporate philanthropy,** which includes cash contributions, donations of equipment and products, and support for the volunteer efforts of company employees. For example, in 2005, Manulife Financial assisted approximately 500 nonprofit companies with community building in four main areas: health care, education, community services, and local volunteerism. Its contribution was not only in the form of cash donations and sponsorship but also included more than 44,000 hours of employees time globally.[18]

concept check

How do businesses carry out their social responsibilities to consumers?

What is corporate philanthropy?

Is a company's only responsibility to its investors to make a profit? Why or why not?

Trends in Ethics and Social Responsibility

learning goal

Four important trends related to ethics and social responsibility are increased protection for whistle blowers, changes in corporate philanthropy, a new social contract between employers and employees, and the growth of global ethics and social responsibility.

MORE PROTECTION FOR WHISTLE BLOWERS

whistle blower

An employee, former employee, or any other member of an organization that reports misconduct by others in the organization that have the power to take corrective action.

In the recent past there have been many instances of whistle blowing in Canada. A **whistle blower** is an employee, former employee, or any other stakeholder of an organization that reports misconduct by others in the organization of harmful or illegal acts.

In Canada various federal and provincial statutes are designed to protect employees who provide information to law enforcement offices (especially related to health and safety standards). However, little has been done until recently to protect those that have "blown the whistle" on corrupt and/or unethical behaviours of an organization or its employees or directors.

TRENDS IN CORPORATE PHILANTHROPY

strategic giving

The practice of tying philanthropy closely to the corporate mission or goals and targeting donations to regions where a company operates.

Corporate philanthropy has typically involved seeking out needy groups and then giving them money or company products. Today the focus is shifting to **strategic giving,** which ties philanthropy more closely to the corporate mission or goals and targets donations to regions where a company operates.

Stan Litow, IBM's vice president of corporate community relations, notes that the company knows it takes more than just money—chequebook philanthropy (the old model)—to have a successful giving program. "With check book philanthropy you could contribute a lot of money and accomplish very little," he says.

> I think that in the new model, being generous is incredibly important, but the most important aspect of this new model is using our many resources to achieve something of lasting value in the communities where we live, work and do business.[19]

HOT Links

What does IBM Corporation require from its employees in terms of ethical business conduct? It's all presented in the Business Conduct Guidelines, which you will find at http://www.ibm.com/us/.

A NEW SOCIAL CONTRACT TREND BETWEEN EMPLOYER AND EMPLOYEE

Another trend in social responsibility is the effort by organizations to redefine their relationship with their employees. Many people have viewed social responsibility as a one-way street that focuses on the obligations of business to society, employees, and others. Now companies are telling employees that they also have a responsibility when it comes to job security. The new contract goes like this:

> There will never be job security. You will be employed by us as long as you add value to the organization, and you are continuously responsible for finding ways to add value. In return, you have the right to demand interesting and important work, the freedom and resources to perform it well, pay that reflects your contribution, and the experience and training needed to be employable here or elsewhere.

HOT Links

How is the International Business Ethics Institute working to promote business ethics worldwide? Find out at http://www.business-ethics.org.

Coca-Cola, for example, requires extensive employee retraining each year. The idea, according to a Coke executive, is to become a more valuable employee by adding 25 percent to your existing knowledge every year.

GLOBAL ETHICS AND SOCIAL RESPONSIBILITY

As Canadian businesses expand into global markets, their corporate codes of ethics and policies on social responsibility must travel with them. As a citizen of several countries, a multinational corporation has several responsibilities. These include respecting local practices and customs, ensuring that there is harmony between the organization's staff and the host population, providing management leadership, and developing a cadre of local managers who will be a credit to their community. When a multinational makes an investment in a foreign country, it should commit to a long-term relationship. That means involving all stakeholders in the host country in decision-making. Finally, a responsible multinational will implement ethical guidelines within the organization in the host country. By fulfilling these responsibilities, the company will foster respect for both local and international laws.

Computer firms that link their product donations to schools with their corporate goals represent the corporate philanthropic trend of strategic giving.

© GEOSTOCK/PHOTODISC/GETTY IMAGES

Making Ethical Choices

BLOWING THE WHISTLE OR BLOWING A CAREER

As the female head of household, you've put two of your three children through college. Your youngest is now in high school. She wants to enter a six-year joint premed-MBA program. At 50, you are financially comfortable, having worked in the same job for Tyco's CEO, Dennis Kozlowski, handling his and his predecessor's expenses for 24 years. Over the past 18 months you've noticed several large out-of-the-ordinary expenses and you want to discuss them with Kozlowski, with whom you have an open and honest working relationship.

In fact, Kozlowski knows of your plans to retire in eight years, coinciding with the graduation of your youngest. You believe that Tyco, a conglomerate of various types of industries, will always be in business and that the company's stock and retirement plan are "sacred." However, as you've paid out such large sums of money for items that you can't tie directly to the business, such as art masterpieces that do not grace any of the walls at Tyco and a private plane that isn't being used for corporate travel, you feel you must raise your concerns directly with Kozlowski. At the same time, you fear that raising these concerns might jeopardize your plans to retire at 58. In fact, Kozlowski seems to have changed, making talking with him even more troublesome.

ETHICAL DILEMMA

Would you raise your concerns about the expenses directly with Kozlowski, knowing that doing so could create serious problems for you or for the company?

SOURCES: Anthony Bianco, William Symonds, and Nanette Byrnes, "The Rise and Fall of Dennis Kozlowski," *Business Week*, December 23, 2002, 64–77; and Andrew Hill, "Kozlowski Speaks Out on Tyco Loan Deal," *Financial Times*, February 10, 2003, http://www.FT.com

Multinational corporations often must balance conflicting interests of stakeholders when making decisions regarding social responsibilities, especially in the area of human rights. Questions involving child labour, forced labour, minimum wages, and workplace safety can be particularly difficult. Levi Strauss was strongly praised when it announced it was leaving China in 1993 because of the country's poor human rights record. However, China is an inexpensive place to manufacture clothing, and the temptation to stay there was simply too great. In fact, Levi Strauss never stopped making clothes in China; its Hong Kong subsidiary continues to manufacture clothes on a contract basis. Levi recently announced that it would begin selling clothes in China. One might argue that Levi Strauss must remain competitive and profitable, or it will not be able to be a leader in the cause of social responsibility. When the announcement came, however, human rights activists quickly set up a picket at Levi's San Francisco headquarters.

HOT Links

Levi Strauss's unique corporate culture rewards and recognizes employee achievements. To learn about working for a company that values employee efforts, go to the Levi Strauss home page (http://www.levistrauss.com).

concept check

Describe strategic giving.

What role do employees have in improving their job security?

How do multinational corporations demonstrate social responsibility in a foreign country?

Great Ideas to Use Now

In many situations, there are no right or wrong answers. Instead, organizations must provide a process to resolve the dilemma quickly and fairly. Two approaches for resolving ethical problems are the "three-questions test" and the newspaper test.

RESOLVING ETHICAL PROBLEMS IN BUSINESS

In evaluating an ethical problem, managers can use the three-questions test to determine the most ethical response: "Is it legal?" "Is it balanced?" and "How does it make me feel?" Companies such as Texas Instruments, Marriott, and McDonald's rely on this test to guide employee decision-making. If the answer to the first question is "no," then don't do it. Many ethical dilemmas, however, involve situations that aren't illegal. For example, the sale of tobacco is legal in Canada, but given all the research that shows that tobacco use is dangerous to one's health, is it an ethical activity?

The second question, "Is it balanced?" requires you to put yourself in the position of other parties affected by your decision. For example, as an executive, you might not favour a buyout of your company, because you will probably lose your job. Shareholders, however, might benefit substantially from the price to be paid for their shares in the buyout. At the same time, the employees of the business and their community might suffer economically if the purchaser decides to close the business or focus its efforts in a different product area. The best situation, of course, is when everybody wins or shares the burden equally.

HOT *Links*

Discover what Texas Instruments's "Ethics Quick Test" includes at http://www.ti.com/corp/docs/company/citizen/ethics/quicktest.shtml.

Customer Satisfaction and Quality

Ethics and social responsibility play important roles in customer satisfaction and quality. Acting in an unethical manner, such as overcharging a client or failing to service a product properly after the sale, will normally mean losing that customer for life. Moreover, a dissatisfied customer will often tell other potential customers, resulting in further lost sales. Using cheaper, less reliable parts in the manufacturing process, for example, might save money in the short run but will drive off customers in the long term.

People like to do business with organizations that they feel are good corporate citizens. For example, members of the Retail Council of Canada have a voluntary scanner code, which includes the following policy:

1. THE ITEM FREE SCANNER POLICY

Retailers will implement an Item Free Scanner Policy as follows:

1.1 On a claim being presented by the customer, where the scanned price of a product at checkout is higher than the price displayed in the store or than advertised by the store, the lower price will be honoured; and

(a) if the correct price of the product is $10 or less, the retailer will give the product to the customer free of charge; or

(b) if the correct price of the product is higher than $10, the retailer will give the customer a discount of $10 off the corrected price.

SOURCE: Courtesy the Retail Council of Canada.

The final question, "How does it make me feel?" asks you to examine your comfort with a particular decision. Many people find that after reaching a decision on an issue, they still experience discomfort that can manifest itself in a loss of sleep or appetite. Those feelings of conscience can serve as a guide in resolving ethical dilemmas.

FRONT PAGE OF THE NEWSPAPER TEST

Many managers use the "front page of the newspaper test" for evaluating ethical dilemmas. The question to be asked is how a critical and objective reporter would report your decision in a front-page story. Some managers rephrase the test for their employees: How will the headline read if I make this decision? This test is helpful in spotting and resolving potential conflicts of interest. Obviously, executives from firms like Enron and WorldCom didn't consider the front-page test when they took their actions.

SUMMARY OF LEARNING GOALS

1 How are current social trends affecting business?

The business environment consists of social, demographic, economic, technological, and competitive trends. In addition, terrorism has had a negative impact on business and has resulted in a major increase in government spending and activities. Managers cannot control environmental trends. Instead, they must understand how the environment is changing and the impact of those changes on the business. Several social trends are currently influencing businesses. First, people of all ages have a broader range of interests, defying traditional consumer profiles. Second, changing gender roles are bringing more women into the workforce. This trend is increasing family incomes, heightening demand for time-saving goods and services, and changing family shopping patterns.

2 How are demographic trends creating new opportunities for business?

Businesses today must deal with the unique shopping preferences of Generations X and Y and the baby boomers. Each must be appealed to in a different way with different goods and services. Generation Y, for example, is the most computer literate and the most interested in computers and accessories. Furthermore, because the population is growing older, businesses are offering more products that appeal to middle-aged and older markets.

3 What philosophies and concepts shape personal ethical standards?

Ethics is a set of moral standards for judging whether something is right or wrong. A utilitarianism approach to setting personal ethical standards focuses on the consequences of an action taken by a person or organization. According to this approach, people should act so as to generate the greatest good for the greatest number. Every human is entitled to certain rights such as freedom and the pursuit of happiness. Another approach to ethical decision-making is justice, or what is fair according to accepted standards.

4 How can organizations encourage ethical business behaviour?

Top management must shape the ethical culture of the organization. They should lead by example, offer ethics training programs, and establish a formal code of ethics.

5 What is social responsibility?

Social responsibility is the concern of businesses for the welfare of society as a whole. It consists of obligations beyond just making a profit. Social responsibility also goes beyond what is required by law or union contract. Companies can engage in illegal and irresponsible behaviour, irresponsible but legal behaviour, or legal and responsible behaviour. The vast majority of organizations act legally and try to be socially responsible.

6 How do businesses meet their social responsibilities to various stakeholders?

Stakeholders are individuals or groups to whom business has a responsibility. Businesses are responsible to employees. They should provide a clean and safe working environment. Organizations can build employees' self-worth through empowerment programs. Businesses also have a responsibility to customers to provide good, safe products and services. Organizations are responsible to the general public to be good corporate citizens. Firms must help protect the environment and provide a good place to work. Companies also engage in corporate philanthropy, which includes contributing cash, donating goods and services, and supporting volunteer efforts of employees. Finally, companies are responsible to investors. They should earn a reasonable profit for the owners.

7 What are the global and domestic trends in ethics and social responsibility?

Today, corporate philanthropy is shifting away from simply giving to any needy group and is focusing instead on strategic giving, in which the philanthropy relates more closely to the corporate mission or goals and targets donations to areas where the firm operates. Corporate philanthropy is coming under increasing attacks from special-interest groups, however.

A second trend is toward a new social contract between employer and employee. Instead of the employer having the sole responsibility for maintaining jobs, now the employee must assume part of the burden and find ways to add value to the organization.

As the world increasingly becomes a global community, multinational corporations are now expected to assume a global set of ethics and responsibility. Global companies must understand local customs. They should also involve local stakeholders in decision-making. Multinationals must also make certain that their suppliers are not engaged in human rights violations.

EXPERIENTIAL EXERCISES

1. **Support a good cause.** You don't have to wait until you graduate to start demonstrating your social responsibility. It will also look good on your résumé when you need to differentiate yourself from all of the other job seekers. Go to **http://www.volunteer.ca/index-eng.php** and find organizations in your area looking for volunteers. Find one that meets your interest and that is related to your career goals, and go to work.

2. **Know your ethical values.** To get a better idea of your own level of ethical development, take an ethics test. Go to **http://www.ethicsandbusiness.org/stylequiz.htm.** This test will give you better insight into yourself.

3. If you are thinking about giving money to a charity, check it out first. Find out what charities are registered in Canada at **http://www.cra-arc.gc.ca/tax/charities/online_listings/charity_listings-e.html.**

4. **Work for a firm that cares about its social responsibilities.** When you enter the job market, make certain that you are going to work for a socially responsible organization. Ask a prospective employer "how the company gives back to society." If you plan to work for a large company, check out *Financial Post's* current list of Canada's most admired corporations.

5. Professor Joseph Badaracco of Harvard Business School believes that "real ethical dilemmas are not choices between right and wrong, but choices between right and right—cases in which both options seem correct for different reasons, yet one must be chosen and one rejected." Here is an example: Many CEOs sell shares of their stock when prices were near their high points. Even though their actions were legal, it soon became apparent that they knew that the stock was significantly overpriced. Was the CEO ethically obligated to tell the public that this was the case—even knowing that doing so could cause the stock price to plummet, thereby hurting someone who bought the stock earlier that day?

SOURCE: Geoffrey Colvin, "Between Right and Right," *Fortune*, October 30, 2002, http://www.fortune.com.

6. Your company has decided to create a new position for an ethics officer and has asked you to be part of the team that is writing the job description. Using resources such as the Web site of the Ethics and Compliance Officer Association (ECOA), **http://www.theecoa.org,** and other materials, draft a list of job responsibilities for this new role.

7. The Boeing Company makes business ethics a priority, asking employees to take refresher training every year. It encourages employees to take the Ethics Challenge with their work groups and to discuss the issues with their peers. You can take the challenge, too, by going to **http://www.boeing.com/ companyoffices/aboutus/ethics/education.htm.** Each question presents an ethical dilemma, together with three or four potential answers. Taking the challenge will show you how Boeing approaches workplace ethics. Summarize your findings. Did any answers surprise you?

8. You'll find a comprehensive list of business ethics sites at **http://www. web-miner.com/busethics.htm.** Once at the site, go to the section on Corporate Codes of Ethics. Look at three examples of codes in different industries. What elements do they have in common? How are they different? Suggest how one of the codes could be improved.

9. What ethical issues arise as companies add e-business to their operations? Go to *Information Week*'s site, **http://www.informationweek.com,** and perform a search for business ethics. What topics did you find? Identify three areas where the potential for ethical breaches could occur, and briefly discuss each.

10. Visit the Fur Is Dead Web site from the People for the Ethical Treatment of Animal (PETA), **http://furisdead.com.** Read about PETA's view of the fur industry. Do you agree with this view? Why or why not? How do you think manufacturers of fur clothing would justify their actions to someone from PETA? Would you work for a store that sold fur-trimmed clothing? Explain your answer.

11. *Green Money Journal,* **http://www.greenmoneyjournal.com,** is a bimonthly on-line journal that promotes social responsibility investing. What are the current topics of concern in this area? Visit the archives to find articles on socially responsible investing and find two areas of corporate social responsibility. Summarize what you have learned.

REVIEW QUESTIONS

1. What are some of the social trends affecting Canadian business? Discuss how each of these is affecting business.

2. What are the major demographic groups by age? What are some characteristics of each group?

3. How does diversity and multiculturalism impact Canadian business?

4. What is utilitarianism?

5. What are some of the individual rights we enjoy in Canada?

6. How does the idea of justice affect business?

7. What are some unethical business activities discussed in the chapter?

8. What can organizations do to influence ethical conduct?

9. Define social responsibility.

10. Give examples of legal but irresponsible business behaviours.

11. List the various stakeholders of an organization.

12. What responsibilities does a company have to the various stakeholders?

13. How can being philanthropic help the bottom line of a company?

CREATIVE THINKING CASE
Got Milk, California?

The California Milk Processor Board, creator of the "Got Milk?" advertising campaign, decided to launch a new promotion. To celebrate 10 years of "Got Milk?" advertising, the Board asked 24 small California towns to consider changing their name to Got Milk? The town would become the centrepiece of a national advertising campaign and receive free school computers, new playgrounds, a Got Milk? museum, and other goodies in exchange for changing its name.

The California towns approached by the Board were: Biggs, Vernon, Sand City, Amador, Trinidad, Point Arena, Tehama, Fort Jones, Industry, Plymouth, Etna, Isleton, Dorris, Loyalton, Bradbury, Tulelake, Maricopa, Colma, Blue Lake, Ferndale, Montague, Colfax, San Juan Bautista, and Del Rey Oaks.

Jeff Manning, the Board's executive director, stated that all he wants is to "pick up a newly printed California map and run my finger down a road and see Got Milk? California."

Officials in several towns said it would take millions of dollars to convince a town to change its name—and even then they're hesitant. Sand City Administrator Kelly Morgan, for example, said, "We're on the Monterey Peninsula and it would surely cause us to come in for some ridicule." Pam DeYoung, a resident of Industry since 1977, was even more caustic in dismissing the idea.

Not all towns are so picky. In 2000, Halfway, Oregon, changed its name to Half.com for a year in exchange for a mere $93,000 and some computers.[15]

CRITICAL THINKING QUESTIONS

1. Do you think that the California Milk Producer Board is acting unethically? What criteria are you using to claim that their behaviour is ethical or unethical? Are they being socially responsible?

2. If a town's administrators decided to accept the offer, would they be acting unethically? Would they be acting socially responsibly?

3. How would you feel about living in Got Milk? Why?

SOURCES: Used with permission of the Associated Press copyright 2006. All Rights Reserved.

VIDEO CASE
Fair Trade Sweetens the Coffee

When you sip your morning coffee, you probably don't wonder who grew the beans. Rink Dickinson did, and when he learned that small coffee growers were at the mercy of agents and middlemen, who paid them the lowest possible prices, he decided to do something about it.

Coffee growers, receiving only 40 cents on each $8 to $9 pound of gourmet coffee sold, were fleeing their farms to seek jobs in overcrowded cities. Others were planting illegal crops such as marijuana or coca to generate cash for their next coffee crop. The 20 million coffee farmers who lived in poverty called the middlemen "coyotes," because they preyed on the poor.

Dickinson decided to change these unfair practices and engage in more ethically and socially responsible ways of doing business. In 1986, he cofounded Equal Exchange, a worker-owned cooperative gourmet coffee company. By buying direct and thereby eliminating middlemen, Equal Exchange was able to pay growers 50 cents per pound more than the previous rate.

Coffee is the leading source of foreign currency in Latin America, so this price increase had a significant impact on the economy and lifestyle of the region. Coffee growing provides jobs for people who would otherwise be unemployed. The growers' entire region benefits from projects the farm cooperatives undertake with the additional income, from reforestation programs to building new schools, daycare centers, and carpentry workshops. "We used to live in houses made of corn husks," recalls Don Miguel Sifontes, a farmer in El Salvador. "Now we have better work, better schools, homes of adobe, and a greater brotherhood of decision makers."

Fair trade underscores the idea that businesses are accountable to employees, customers, and the general public. Under exclusive agreements with farming cooperatives, Equal Exchange growers receive better prices, and customers are guaranteed high-quality coffee at fair prices. Receiving a guaranteed minimum price per pound for coffee, even when the market is lower, assures farmers of a living wage during downturns.

Following strict fair-trade guidelines, Equal Exchange enters into long-term relationships with growers, buying directly from cooperatives owned and run by farmers. The farmers govern the even distribution of income and services, such as education and health care. Making credit available to farmers helps them avoid the cycle of debt. "When we sign a contract with growers, we pay up to 50 percent of the contract six months in advance," notes marketing manager Erbin Crowell. "If a hurricane hits, we share the risk." The company pays a premium price for certified organic and shade-grown coffee, and by helping growers use environmentally friendly farming methods, the environment and consumers are protected from toxic chemicals.

When specialty coffee giants Starbucks and Green Mountain announced they were entering into fair-trade agreements with farmers, Equal Exchange congratulated them. "We know these farmers and their struggles. They urgently need more importers to pay a just price, so we encourage our fellow roasters." With this statement, Dickinson raised the bar of ethical standards in the coffee business, knowing that his company can clear it with ease. With $7 million in sales, he is clearly supported by many coffee-loving consumers who do care where their beans come from.

CRITICAL THINKING QUESTIONS

1. Has Equal Exchange gone beyond other organizations in being socially and ethically responsible? Explain.

2. What are the key components of Equal Exchange's fair-trade agreement with coffee growers? How do they support the company's goals and affect coffee growers' regions and lifestyles?

3. How might Equal Exchange encourage other companies to adopt fair-trade agreements? Suggest an approach the company could use to launch such a campaign.

SOURCES: Adapted from material in the video case *The Rewards of Paying Fair: Ethics and Social Responsibility at Equal Exchange* and company Web site, http://www.equalexchange.com (accessed February 8, 2003).

E-COMMERCE CASE
Geekcorps: Spreading the (IT) Gospel

A Peace Corps for techies? Ethan Zuckerman had a mission: to bring the technology revolution to developing countries such as Rwanda, Mongolia, Lebanon, Bulgaria, and Ghana, via techno-savvy volunteers. Zuckerman, a 1993 graduate of Williams College, became an instant millionaire in 1999 when Lycos bought the on-line company where he served as vice president of research and development. A self-confessed Net head, he wanted to do something he believed was important.

Geekcorps (**http://www.geekcorps.com**) was started in February 2000 with $100,000 of Zuckerman's own money. Seven months later, its first team of volunteers was at work in Accra, Ghana, where Zuckerman had spent time on a Fulbright fellowship. Geekcorps now delves into a database of 3,500 volunteers from 11 countries to select teams of seven or eight rigorously screened volunteers, who are given four months to prepare for their stint abroad. Geekcorps pays for travel and provides lodging and a small stipend. On sabbatical from their jobs for periods of one to four months, volunteers are trained to teach their skills to people with different backgrounds.

"We never tell the volunteers to go in and do the project; they teach the in-country staff and company members to do it themselves," says Ana Marie Harkins, Geekcorps's director of programs. In return, each business agrees to transfer the skills it acquires to the community, free of charge. "The number one asset for a Geekcorps volunteer is a good sense of humor and the ability to roll with the punches," says Peter Beardsley, 26, who spent six months in Accra. "If you let power outages and leaky roofs get to you, you're going to have a hard time." But it is not all work and no play for the volunteers, who spend their free time exploring the host country and meeting its people.

After the dot-com bubble burst, corporate donations dwindled. The United Nations and other organizations provided some grants to help keep Geekcorps afloat. In 2002, Zuckerman joined forces with the International Executive Service Corps (IESC), an organization with a history of sending business professionals to developing countries. "We both believe that the way to transform an economy is by building small business, by bringing over skills volunteers," says Zuckerman. Thanks to the IESC partnership and private donations, Geekcorps had enough funding for the next year and a half.

CRITICAL THINKING QUESTIONS

1. Ethan Zuckerman still hopes to attract donations from corporate sponsors. If you were Ethan Zuckerman, how would you explain to a high-technology firm why contributing to Geekcorps would be a strategic giving choice?

2. Do you think other consumer goods firms—for instance, a maker of breakfast cereals or a clothing company—would see donating to Geekcorps as an opportunity to meet their social responsibilities to employees, customers, or investors? Explain.

3. Why do you think corporate donations dwindled after the dot-com bubble burst? Do you think companies have a moral obligation to continue corporate sponsorship programs during economic downturns? Defend your answer.

SOURCES: Dawn Calleja, "Heart of Geekness," *Canadian Business Magazine*, April 20, 2002; Laurie O'Connell, "Geekcorps' Savvy Volunteers Bring the Benefits of IT to Developing Countries," *Software Development*, October 2002, http://www.sdmagazine.com; material from Geekcorps Web site, http://www.geekcorps.org (accessed February 25, 2003); and John Yaukey, "Geekcorps Spread Computer Skills Worldwide," *Gannet News Service, HonoluluAdvertiser.com*, March 26, 2002, http://www.honoluluadvertiser.com (accessed February 25, 2003).

Making the Connection

Using Technology to Manage Information and for Business Success

In this chapter, you'll learn about the last piece of our PEST model puzzle—the *technological* environment.

This is a wonderful example of the integrative nature of business, because technology permeates just about every aspect of our model. To begin with, it affects a company's ability to meet its critical success factors. *Financial performance* is affected by technology, because a firm can operate more efficiently and, therefore, increase its bottom line using technology. Technology also gives businesses quicker and better access to information on customer needs. In addition, *customer needs* are better met through the speed with which technology helps us deliver on our promises and provide customer service. In fact, as you'll see in the chapter, a company's technology-based information system can "track new orders" to speed order processing; "determine what products are selling best," which can help a company to develop products to meet customer needs; "identify high-volume customers" to focus on enhancing those relationships; "or contact customers about new or related products" to help form relationships. In fact, even greater needs can be met with expanded product offerings, because the Internet does not have the physical limits of a typical store—any number of items can be sold through a single Web

site. *Quality* is also enhanced through the use of technology. In fact, *innovations* have allowed us to improve quality and make it a priority at all levels of an organization. The rate of these and other innovations has been boosted up to "warp speed" because of technology. Finally, *employees are more committed* to meeting company goals, because companies can make their jobs more interesting by having the most repetitive and monotonous jobs completed through the use of technology instead of valuable human resources. So technology can definitely help a business be more successful, and given that the rapid pace of technological change is a reality for today's business, it is, in fact, a necessity for success.

Technology as an environmental factor affects the other aspects of our PEST model as well. For example, in the *political* environment, the government issues patents on new technology, preventing other firms from copying that technology. This gives a company an advantage over other firms for years to come. From the point of view of *economics*, we have recently seen how the rapid growth of technological firms can fuel the stock market to the point of overvalue and then rapid adjustment, to the shock of many investors. Technology also changes the nature of competition. The Internet has removed the geographic and time-related limits to doing business. Customers no longer have to visit a store during business hours—companies don't even need to have a store! And the traditional relationship between manufacturers, distributors, and retailers has changed, because companies can bypass these channels by selling directly over the Internet. From a *social* perspective, it is clear that technology has changed how we, as consumers, see the world—it has given us much more access to information, making us better equipped to make buying decisions and more demanding in terms of the speed with which we expect our needs to be met. It is also important to understand that as new technologies are adopted, they promote other waves of technological innovation. In this way, technology enhances our ability to create more technology.

Technology also affects how companies operate. As we emphasize in this chapter, it affects the way businesses communicate and share information in all areas of the company. The company's information system can gather and provide information on what customers want directly to *marketing* to enhance its sales efforts. The order information can then be provided directly to *operations*, so that managers can obtain the correct inventory needed, when it's needed, and schedule production to meet the customer's needs exactly and on time. Information is also provided to *human resources* to ensure that the skilled workers are available as the production schedule requires. The final sales information can also be provided directly to *finance* to prepare financial statements. This integration of information brings together the functional areas in an essential way, so that they can work together more efficiently to achieve the company's goals and ensure its success.

Technology also affects each specific functional area. For example, on the operational side, it affects how products are built (using computers to help design products and guide manufacturing) as well as what products are built (as technology allows for greater customization to meet customer needs). It affects how products are marketed (such as through the Internet, using e-commerce) and financed. Technology has had such an impact on capital markets that it's becoming very difficult for new technology firms to sell their stock to the public and generate much-needed funds for expansion to raise money. Even the human resource function is affected by technology, because computers can take over many tasks done by humans, and companies have the added demand of finding the best people with the necessary skills to use technology and manage technology workers.

The very nature of business has changed dramatically with technology. E-business has revolutionized the way business is done, affecting the overall *strategies* of many organizations as it has created a new paradigm for business. We have moved beyond the individual enterprise to an interconnected economy through interconnected information systems. As businesses become more interconnected between suppliers, manufacturers, and retailers, they operate more as one company. This allows them to meet the needs of the customer better, providing a seamless integration from the beginning of the business chain to the ultimate consumer.

4

SHIRLEY A. ROSE

Using Technology to Manage Information and for Business Success

learning goals

1   How has information technology transformed business and managerial decision-making?

2   Why are computer networks an important part of today's information technology systems?

3   What types of systems make up a typical company's management information system?

4   How can technology management and planning help companies optimize their information technology systems?

5   What are the best ways to protect computers and the information they contain?

6   What are the leading trends in information technology?

Mark's Work Wearhouse: An E-Business Success Story

According to Robin Lynas, the chief information officer for Mark's Work Wearhouse (MWW), the company's e-business strategy is to "build an integrated multi-channel retailing environment." This strategy is based on the key customer requirements of convenience, access to products, brand loyalty, selection, and information. The main challenges for MWW are the dynamic retail environment and rapidly changing technologies. With more than 340 stores, and sales exceeding $780 million per year, these challenges require a comprehensive understanding of the organization and its strategies.

MWW is one of Canada's largest retail clothing chains, and its customers include both individuals and corporations. Its target market is built on the philosophy of "Clothes That Work," with the company selling traditional work wear, casual and business casual, and casual outdoor clothing and footwear. The company has been successful, in part, by developing computer applications that put timely customer information in the hands of its sales force. Every MWW store is linked to a database via portal technology that provides information on sales and inventory levels, replenishes inventories at the SKU (stock-keeping unit—the bar code attached to each product) level by store, and reports gross margins as well as expenses by individual store.

"We have become less 'techie' and much more strategic in our approach to e-business and have become very successful," says Lynas. E-commerce (the actual exchange of transactions using electronic technology, and part of e-business) accounts for less than 10 percent of their e-business. "Our philosophy has been to understand our business, including our customers, and develop an infrastructure that responds to the needs of our stakeholders."

The electronic culture (or e-culture) at MWW incorporates three primary focuses: business to business (B2B), business to consumer (B2C), and business to enterprise (B2E), as shown in Exhibit 4.1.

B2B incorporates both its suppliers and its corporate customers. Each of the stores maintains its minimal level of stock according to product and size. Once the inventory of a particular product reaches its minimal service level in the store, an automatic replenishment system sends an EDI (electronic data interchange) message to the supplier (40 percent of suppliers are domestic and concentrated in the Toronto-Montreal corridor). The supplier completes the order, and all stock for each particular store is then packaged together and transported to the

Exhibit 4.1 | Mark's Work Wearhouse's E-Commerce Focuses

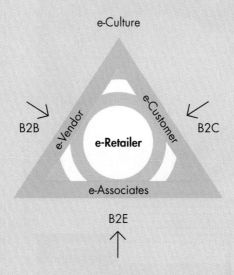

distribution centre, where the packages are sorted and sent to the appropriate stores. (MWW picks up the orders from its domestic suppliers two or three times per week and receives a thousand overseas containers per year from its foreign suppliers) This procedure ensures that stock levels are maintained (therefore maximizing sales) and markdowns are kept to a minimum.

MWW has been very responsive to its corporate customers. The "Product Knowledge Database" and catalogues specific to a particular customer have been very successful. The applications allow customers (i.e., the corporations) to manage their programs on-line and track employee purchases with customized purchase vouchers. As each employee of the corporate customer is registered, and purchases are recorded, it is impossible for the employee to purchase more than the authorized amount.

Critical Thinking Questions

As you read this chapter, consider the following questions as they relate to Mark's Work Wearhouse:

1. What is the difference between e-business and e-commerce? How does MWW use each to satisfy customers' requirements?

2. What are the advantages and disadvantages to the company and the customer of on-line retailing?

3. Identify some of the reasons why MWW has been successful in the retail market.

4. Are clothes and footwear well suited for Web sales? Why or why not?

Principles of Information Technology

information technology (IT)
The equipment and techniques used to manage and process information.

HOT Links

If you want to know the definition of a computer term or more about a particular topic, Webopedia (http://www.webopedia.com) has the answer.

Manufacturers are constantly pushing the limits on innovation. Semiconductor chips have decreased in size to a fraction of a millimetre! Hitachi's tiny radio frequency identification chip takes security and authentication capabilities to a higher level. These chips could be used on passports, charge cards, and bank notes.

Harnessing the power of information technology gives a company a significant competitive advantage. **Information technology** (IT) includes the equipment and techniques used to manage and process information.

Information is at the heart of all organizations. Without information about the processes of and participants in an organization—including orders, products, inventory, scheduling, shipping, customers, suppliers, and employees—a business cannot operate.

In less than 60 years, we have shifted from an industrial society to a knowedge-based economy driven by information. Businesses depend on information technology for everything from running daily operations to making strategic decisions. Computers are the tools of this information age, performing or helping workers perform extremely complex operations as well as everyday jobs like word processing and creating spreadsheets. The pace of change has been rapid since the personal computer became a fixture on most office desks. Individual units became part of small networks, followed by more sophisticated enterprise-wide networks. Now the Internet makes it effortless to connect quickly to almost anyplace in the world. A manager can share information with hundreds of thousands of people worldwide almost as easily as with a colleague on another floor of the same office

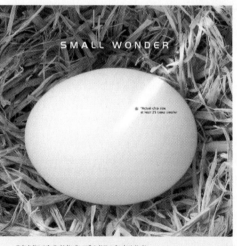

SMALL WONDER

Actual chip size at least 25 times smaller

You're looking at the Mu (μ)-chip, the smallest chip** on the planet. Mu-chip can be attached to most things, including passports and bank notes. It is revolutionizing security and authentication technologies with its intelligent data storage abilities. As an egg brings new life, so Hitachi is always looking to bring a new quality to life. Hitachi is working throughout the various fields of life sciences, this includes all human protein analysis through which lives can be saved and prolonged. Small wonders building big futures.

Visit Hitachi on the web and see how we're inspiring the next with our advanced technologies and innovative solutions.

*Actual chip size measures 0.4mm x 0.4mm. **Smallest RFID (radio frequency identification) chip

HITACHI
Inspire the Next

chief information officer (CIO)
An executive with responsibility for managing all information resources and processes in an organization.

knowledge worker
A worker who develops or uses knowledge, contributing to and benefiting from information used in performing various tasks, including planning, acquiring, searching, analyzing, organizing, storing, programming, producing, distributing, marketing, or selling functions.

building. The Internet and the Web have become indispensable business tools that facilitate communication within companies as well as with customers. Like MWW, many companies entrust an executive called the **chief information officer** (CIO) with the responsibility of managing all information resources and processes.

Today most of us are **knowledge workers** who develop or use knowledge. Knowledge workers contribute to and benefit from information they use in performing various tasks, including planning, acquiring, searching, analyzing, organizing, storing, programming, producing, distributing, marketing, or selling functions. We must know how to gather and use information from the many resources available to us.

Because most jobs today depend on information—obtaining, using, creating, managing, and sharing it—we begin this chapter with the role of information in decision-making and then go on to discuss computer networks and management information systems. The management of information technology—planning and protection—follows. Finally, we'll look at the latest trends in information technology. Throughout the chapter, we will use examples to show how managers and their companies are using computers to make better decisions in a highly competitive world.

TRANSFORMING BUSINESSES THROUGH INFORMATION

1 learning goal

management information system (MIS)
The methods and equipment that provide information about all aspects of a firm's operations

database
An electronic filing system that collects and organizes data and information.

Information systems and the computers that support them are so much a part of our lives that we almost take them for granted. These **management information systems (MIS)**, methods, and equipment that make available information about all aspects of a firm's operations provide managers with the information they need to make decisions. They help managers properly categorize and identify ideas, which results in substantial operational and cost benefits.

Businesses collect a great deal of *data*—raw, unorganized facts that can be moved and stored—in their daily operations. Only through well-designed IT systems and the power of computers can managers process these data into meaningful and useful *information*, which they can use for specific purposes, such as making business decisions. One such form of business information is the **database,** an electronic filing system that collects and organizes data and information. Using software called a *database management system (DBMS)*, you can quickly and easily enter, store, organize, select, and retrieve data in a database. These data are then turned into information to run the business and to perform business analysis.

Databases are at the core of business information systems. For example, a customer database containing name, address, payment method, products ordered, price, order history, and similar data provides information to many departments. Marketing teams can track new orders and determine what products are selling best, salespeople can identify high-volume customers or contact customers about new or related products, operations managers need order information to obtain inventory and schedule production of the ordered products, and financial personnel need sales data to prepare financial statements. Later in the chapter, we will see how companies use very large databases called data warehouses and data marts. The data warehouse will help the retailer in many ways, from cutting inventory costs to identifying market trends more quickly.

Companies are discovering that they can't operate well with a series of separate information systems geared to solving specific departmental problems. It takes a team effort to integrate the systems described in Chapter 11 throughout the firm. Company-wide *enterprise resource planning (ERP)* systems that bring together human resources, operations, and technology are becoming an integral part of business strategy. So is managing the collective knowledge contained in

HOT *Links*

Darwin.com is an on-line magazine that offers helpful articles and Executive Guides that provide a good introduction to key IT topics (http://www .darwinmag.com).

an organization using data warehouses and other technology tools. Technology experts are learning more about the way the business operates, and business managers are learning to use information systems technology effectively to create new opportunities and reach their goals.

concept check

What are management information systems? Why are they important to today's business organizations?

Distinguish between data and information. How are they related?

How does systems integration benefit a company?

LINKING UP: COMPUTER NETWORKS

2 learning goal

computer network
A group of two or more computer systems linked together by communications channels to share data and information.

Today most businesses use networks to deliver information to employees, suppliers, and customers. A **computer network** is a group of two or more computer systems linked together by communications channels to share data and information. Today's networks often link thousands of users and can transmit audio and video as well as data.

Networks include clients and servers. The *client* is the application that runs on a personal computer or workstation. It relies on a *server,* which manages network resources or performs special tasks, such as storing files, managing one or more printers, or processing database queries. Any user on the network can access the server's capabilities.

By making it easy and fast to share information, networks have created new ways to work and increase productivity. They provide more efficient use of resources, permitting communication and collaboration across distance and time. With file sharing, all employees, regardless of location, have access to the same information. Shared databases also eliminate duplication of effort. Employees at different sites can "screen share" computer files, working on data as if they were in the same room. Their computers are connected by phone or cable lines, they all see the same thing on their display, and anyone can make changes, which are seen by the other participants. The employees can also use the networks for videoconferencing.

Networks make it possible for companies to run enterprise software, large programs with integrated modules that manage all of the corporation's internal operations. Enterprise resource planning systems run on networks. Typical subsystems include finance, human resources, engineering, sales and order distribution, and order management and procurement. These modules work independently and then automatically exchange information, creating a company-wide system that includes current delivery dates, inventory status, quality control, and other critical information. Let's now look at the basic types of networks companies use to transmit data—local area networks and wide area networks—and popular networking applications like intranets and extranets.

Connecting Near and Far with Networks

local area network (LAN)
A network that connects computers at one site, enabling the computer users to exchange data and share the use of hardware and software from a variety of computer manufacturers.

wide area network (WAN)
A network that connects computers at different sites via telecommunications media such as phone lines, satellites, and microwaves.

Two basic types of networks are distinguished by the area they cover. A **local area network (LAN)** lets people at one site exchange data and share the use of hardware and software from a variety of computer manufacturers. LANs offer companies a more cost-effective way to link computers than linking terminals to a mainframe computer. The most common uses of LANs at small businesses, for example, are office automation, accounting, and information management. LANs can help companies reduce staff, streamline operations, and cut processing costs. LANs can be set up with wired or wireless connections.

A **wide area network (WAN)** connects computers at different sites via telecommunications media such as phone lines, satellites, and microwaves. A modem connects

Private Lines: Virtual Private Networks

Many companies use **virtual private networks (VPNs)** to connect two or more private networks (such as LANs) over a public network, such as the Internet. VPNs include strong security measures to allow only authorized users to access the network and its sensitive corporate information. Companies with widespread offices might find that a VPN is a more cost-effective option than purchasing equipment and private lines for that purpose alone. This type of private network is more limited than a VPN, because it doesn't allow users to connect to the corporate network when they are at home or travelling.

As Exhibit 4.2 shows, the VPN uses existing Internet infrastructure and equipment to connect remote users and offices almost anywhere in the world—without long-distance charges. In addition to saving on telecommunications costs, companies using VPNs don't have to buy or maintain special networking equipment and can outsource management of remote access equipment. VPNs are useful for salespeople and telecommuters, who can access the company's network as if they were on-site at the company's office. On the downside, the VPN's availability and performance, especially when it uses the Internet, depend on factors largely outside of an organization's control.[4]

Exhibit 4.2 | Virtual Private Networks (VPNs)

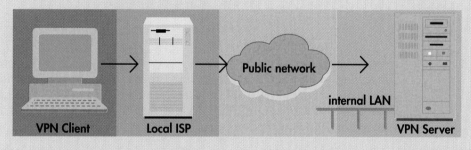

Software on Demand: Application Service Providers

As software developers release new types of application programs and updated versions of existing ones every year or two, companies have to analyze whether they can justify buying or upgrading to the new software in terms of both cost and implementation time. **Application service providers (ASPs)** offer a different approach to this problem. Companies subscribe to an ASP and use the applications much like you'd use telephone voice mail, the technology for which resides at the phone company. Exhibit 4.3 shows how the ASP interfaces with software and hardware vendors and developers, the IT department, and users.

The simplest ASP applications are automated. For example, a user might use one to build a simple e-commerce site. ASPs provide three major categories of applications to users:

- enterprise applications, including customer relationship management, enterprise resource planning (ERP), e-commerce, and data warehousing;
- collaborative applications for internal communications, e-mail, groupware, document creation, and management messaging; and
- applications for personal use, for example, games, entertainment software, and home office applications.

The basic idea behind subscribing to an ASP is compelling. Users can access any of their applications and data from any computer, and IT can avoid purchasing,

Exhibit 4.3 | Structure of an ASP Relationship

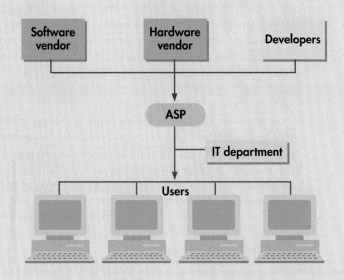

installing, supporting, and upgrading expensive software applications. ASPs buy and maintain the software on their servers and distribute it through high-speed networks. Subscribers rent the applications they want for a set period and price. The savings in infrastructure, time, and staff could be significant.

concept check

What is a computer network? What benefits do companies gain by using networks?

How do LANs and WANs differ? Why would a company use a wireless network?

What advantages do VPNs offer a company? ASPs?

MANAGEMENT INFORMATION SYSTEMS

3 *learning goal*

Whereas individuals use business productivity software such as word-processing, spreadsheet, and graphics programs to accomplish a variety of tasks, the job of managing a company's information needs falls to *management information systems*: users, hardware, and software that support decision-making. Information systems collect and store the company's key data and produce the information managers need for analysis, control, and decision-making.

Many companies use computer-based information systems to automate production processes and to order and monitor inventory. Most companies use them to process customer orders and handle billing and vendor payments. Banks use a variety of information systems to process transactions such as deposits, ATM withdrawals, and loan payments. Most consumer transactions also involve information systems. When you check out at the supermarket, book a hotel room using a toll-free hotel reservations number, or buy CDs over the Internet, information systems record and track the transaction and transmit the data to the necessary places. Health care providers and insurers use information systems to speed up claims processing.

Computer modeling helps Aventis, a major pharmaceutical company, save time and money on later-stage clinical drug trials. When the simulation results in one study indicated that the drug's side effects outweighed its benefits, Aventis saved approximately $50 to $100 million by stopping the trial and using that funding for another project that had greater potential for success.

Companies typically have several types of information systems, starting with systems to process transactions. Management support systems are dynamic systems that allow users to analyze data to make forecasts, identify business trends, and model business strategies. Office automation systems improve the flow of communication throughout the organization. Each type of information system serves a particular level of decision-making: operational, tactical, or strategic. Exhibit 4.4 shows the relationship between transaction-processing and management support

Exhibit 4.4 | A Company's Integrated Information System

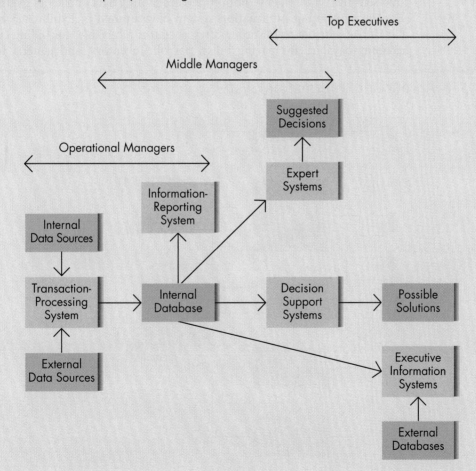

systems as well as the management levels they serve. Let's now take a more detailed look at how companies and managers use transaction-processing and management support systems to manage information.

Transaction-Processing Systems

The firm's integrated information system starts with its **transaction-processing system (TPS)**. The TPS receives raw data from internal and external sources and prepares these data for storage in a database similar to a microcomputer database but vastly larger. In fact, all the company's key data are stored in a single huge database, which becomes the company's central information resource. As noted earlier, the *database management system* tracks the data and allows users to query the database for the information they need.

The database can be updated in two ways: **batch processing**, whereby data are collected over some time period and processed together, and **on-line** (or **real-time**), **processing**, in which data are processed as they become available. Batch processing uses computer resources very efficiently and is well suited to applications such as payroll processing that require periodic rather than continuous processing. On-line processing keeps the company's data current. When you make an airline reservation, the agent enters your reservation directly into the airline's computer and quickly receives confirmation. On-line processing is more expensive than batch processing, so companies must weigh the cost versus the benefit. For example, a factory that operates around the clock might use real-time processing for inventory and other time-sensitive requirements, but process accounting data in batches overnight.

The accounting information system diagrammed in Exhibit 4.5 is a typical TPS. It has subsystems for order entry, accounts receivable (for billing customers), accounts payable (for paying bills), payroll, inventory, and general ledger (for

transaction-processing system (TPS)

An information system that handles the daily business operations of a firm. The system receives and organizes raw data from internal and external sources for storage in a database using either batch or on-line processing.

batch processing

A method of updating a database in which data are collected over some time period and processed together.

on-line (real-time) processing

A method of updating a database in which data are processed as they become available.

Exhibit 4.5 | Accounting Information System

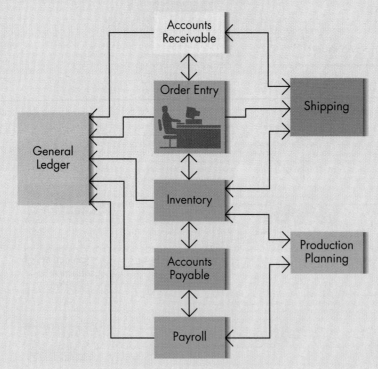

NEL

determining the financial status and profitability of the business). The accounting information system provides input to and receives input from the firm's other information systems, such as manufacturing (production planning data, for example) and human resources (data on hours worked and salary increases to generate paycheques).

Decisions, Decisions: Management Support Systems

Transaction-processing systems automate routine and tedious back-office processes such as accounting, order processing, and financial reporting. They reduce clerical expenses and provide basic operational information quickly. **Management support systems (MSSs)** use the internal master database to perform the higher-level analyses that help managers make better decisions.

Information technologies such as data warehousing are part of more advanced MSSs. A **data warehouse** combines many databases across the whole company into one central database that supports management decision-making. Data warehouses include software to extract data from operational databases, maintain the data in the warehouse, and provide data to users. Data warehouses may contain many **data marts**, special subsets of a data warehouse that each deal with a single area of data. Data marts are organized for quick analysis. Companies use data warehouses for many purposes, including customer relationship management systems, fraud detection, product line analysis, and corporate asset management. Retailers might wish to identify customer demographic characteristics and shopping patterns to improve direct-mailing responses. Banks can more easily spot credit card fraud, as well as analyze customer usage patterns. Telecommunications firms tap into their data warehouses to determine which customers are likeliest to switch service providers so they can offer special pricing incentives to maintain their loyalty.[5]

At the first level of an MSS is an *information-reporting system*, which uses summary data collected by the TPS to produce both regularly scheduled and special reports. The level of detail would depend on the user. A company's payroll personnel might get a weekly payroll report showing how each employee's paycheque was determined. Higher-level managers might receive a payroll summary report that shows total labour cost and overtime by department, and a comparison of current labour costs with those in the prior year. Exception reports show cases that fail to meet some standard. An accounts receivable exception report that lists all customers with overdue accounts would help collection personnel focus their work. Special reports are generated only when a manager requests them; for example, a report showing sales by region and type of customer can highlight reasons for a sales decline.

Decision Support Systems

A **decision support system (DSS)** helps managers make decisions using interactive computer models that describe real-world processes. The DSS also uses data from the internal database but looks for specific data that relate to the problems at hand. It is a tool for answering "what if" questions about what would happen if the manager made certain changes. In simple cases, a manager can create a spreadsheet and try changing some of the numbers. For instance, a manager could create a spreadsheet to show the amount of overtime required if the number of workers increases or decreases. With models, the manager enters into the computer the values that describe a particular situation, and the program computes the results. Marketing executives at a furniture company could run DSS models that use sales data and demographic assumptions to develop forecasts of the types of furniture that would appeal to the fastest-growing population groups.

management support system (MSS)

An information system that uses the internal master database to perform high-level analyses that help managers make better decisions.

data warehouse

An information technology that combines many databases across a whole company into one central database that supports management decision-making.

data mart

Special subset of a data warehouse that deals with a single area of data and is organized for quick analysis.

decision support system (DSS)

A management support system that helps managers make decisions using interactive computer models that describe real-world processes.

Medical professionals use expert systems to analyze patients' medications, ensuring that they do not cause allergic reactions or potentially dangerous interactions with the patients' other prescriptions.

© MICHAEL NEWMAN / PHOTO EDIT

Executive Information Systems

executive information system (EIS)

A management support system that is customized for an individual executive; provides specific information for strategic decisions.

Although similar to a DSS, an **executive information system (EIS)** is customized for an individual executive. These systems provide specific information for strategic decisions. For example, a CEO's EIS might include special spreadsheets that present financial data comparing the company to its principal competitors, and graphs showing current economic and industry trends.

Expert Systems

expert system

A management support system that gives managers advice similar to what they would get from a human consultant; it uses artificial intelligence to enable computers to reason and learn to solve problems in much the same way that humans do.

An **expert system** gives managers advice similar to what they would get from a human consultant. Artificial intelligence enables computers to reason and learn to solve problems in much the same way humans do, using what-if reasoning. Although they are expensive and difficult to create, expert systems are finding their way into more companies as more applications are found. Lower-end expert systems can even run on PDAs (personal digital assistants) like the Palm Pilot. Top-of-the-line systems help airlines appropriately deploy aircraft and crews, critical to the carriers' efficient operations. The cost of hiring enough people to do these ongoing analytical tasks would be prohibitively expensive. Expert systems have also been used to help explore for oil, schedule employee work shifts, and diagnose illnesses. Some expert systems take the place of human experts, whereas others assist them.

Office Automation Systems

office automation system

An information system that uses information technology tools such as word-processing systems, e-mail systems, cell phones, personal digital assistants (PDAs), pagers, and facsimile (fax) machines to improve communications throughout an organization.

Today's **office automation systems** make good use of the computer networks in many companies to improve communications. Office automation systems assist all levels of employees and enable managers to handle most of their own communication. Many of the newer devices now combine multiple functions. The key elements, many of which have been around for years but others of which are fairly new, include

- word-processing systems for producing written messages;
- e-mail systems for communicating directly with other employees and customers, and transferring computer files;
- departmental scheduling systems for planning meetings and other activities;

- cell phones for providing telephone service away from the office, as in cars, with newer models able to receive and send e-mail, text messages, and graphics, and browse the Web;
- PDAs, which replace paper personal planners and address books but can also transfer data to and from the user's PC and run some software, with newer models also able to handle e-mail and Web browsing;
- wireless e-mail devices, such as the BlackBerry;
- pagers, which notify employees of phone calls and can, in some cases, display more extensive written messages sent from a computer network;
- voice mail systems for recording, storing, and forwarding phone messages;
- fax systems for delivering messages on paper within minutes; and
- electronic bulletin boards and computer conferencing systems for discussing issues with others who are not present.

Office automation systems also make telecommuting and home-based businesses possible. Instead of spending time on the road twice a day, telecommuters work at home two or more days a week. This can save time for workers while increasing their flexibility. Companies can save costs by eliminating the need to provide a physical structure for employees.

concept check

What are the main types of management information systems, and what does each do?

Discuss how the different types of management support systems can be used in companies.

How can office automation systems help employees work more efficiently?

TECHNOLOGY MANAGEMENT AND PLANNING

4 *learning goal*

With the help of computers, people have produced more data in the past 30 years than in the previous 5,000 years combined. Companies today make sizable investments in information technology to help them manage this overwhelming amount of data, convert the data into knowledge, and deliver it to the people who need it. In many cases, however, the companies do not reap the desired benefits from these expenditures. Among the typical complaints from senior executives are: the company is spending too much and not getting adequate performance and payoff from IT investments, these investments do not relate to business strategy, the firm seems to be buying the latest technology for technology's sake, and communications between IT specialists and IT users are poor.

Optimize IT!

Managing a company's enterprise-wide IT operations, especially when those often stretch across multiple locations, software applications, and systems, is no easy task. Not only must IT managers deal with on-site systems, they must also oversee the networks that connect staff working at locations ranging from the next town to another continent. What makes the IT manager's job even more difficult is providing this technology for remote employees in the face of time constraints and lower budgets, while maintaining a cohesive corporate culture.[6] Add to these concerns the increasing use by employees of handheld devices like PDAs and cell phones that handle e-mail messaging, and you have an overwhelming management task!

Growing companies might find themselves with a decentralized IT structure that includes many separate systems and much duplication of efforts. A company that wants to enter or expand into e-commerce needs systems that are flexible enough to adapt to this changing marketplace. Security for equipment and data, which we will cover later in the chapter, is another critical area.

The goal is to develop an integrated, company-wide technology plan that balances business judgment, technology expertise, and technology investment. IT planning requires a coordinated effort among a firm's top executives, IT managers, and business-unit managers to develop a comprehensive plan. Such plans must take into account the company's strategic objectives and how the right technology will help managers reach those goals.

Technology management and planning are not just about buying new technology. Today companies are cutting IT budgets, so managers are being asked to do more with less. For that reason, they are implementing projects that leverage their investment in the technology they already have. MIS specialists must continually evaluate the company's existing technology infrastructure to make sure that it is optimized for maximum system availability and service levels. This is an important component in achieving a formal Six Sigma quality certification (see Chapter 11).

Managing Knowledge Resources

As a result of the proliferation of information, we are seeing a major shift from information management to a broader view that focuses on finding opportunities in and unlocking the value of intellectual rather than physical assets. Whereas *information management* involves collecting, processing, and condensing information, the more difficult task of **knowledge management (KM)** focuses on researching, gathering, organizing, and sharing an organization's collective knowledge to improve productivity, foster innovation, and gain a competitive advantage. Some companies have even created a new position, *chief knowledge officer*, to head up this effort. The goal of KM is to allow organizations to generate value from their intellectual assets—not just documents but also the knowledge in their employees' heads.[7]

Companies use their IT systems to facilitate the physical sharing of knowledge, but better hardware and software are not the answers to KM. KM is not technology based but, rather, is a business practice that uses technology. Effective KM calls for a major change in behaviour as well as technology to leverage the power of information systems, especially the Internet, and a company's human capital resources. The first step is creating, through organizational structure and rewards, an information culture that promotes a more flexible, collaborative way of working and communicating. Moving an organization toward KM is no easy task, but it is well worth the effort in terms of creating a more collaborative environment, reducing duplication of effort, and increasing shared knowledge. The benefits can be significant in terms of growth, time, and money. A study of leading technology companies by InMomentum, Inc., a research and consulting firm, revealed that companies with advanced networks that enabled people to share ideas both within and outside the company grew faster than companies that lacked these resources. These companies had more network interconnectivity. This strong communications system was part of a larger package of cultural characteristics that included a customer-centred culture, strong leadership, and a lean bureaucracy. The payoff can be significant.

Technology Planning

A good technology plan provides employees with the tools they need to perform their jobs at the highest levels of efficiency. The first step is a general needs assessment, followed by ranking of projects and the specific choices of hardware and software. The Questions for IT Project Planning section lists some basic questions departmental managers and IT specialists should ask when planning technology purchases.

knowledge management (KM)

The process of researching, gathering, organizing, and sharing an organization's collective knowledge to improve productivity, foster innovation, and gain competitive advantage.

Once managers identify the projects that make business sense, they can choose the best products for the company's needs. The final step is to evaluate the potential benefits of the technology in terms of efficiency and effectiveness. For a successful project, you must evaluate and restructure business processes, choose technology, develop and implement the system, and manage the change processes to serve your organizational needs in the best possible way. Installing a new IT system on top of inefficient business processes is a waste of time and money!

Questions for IT Project Planning

- What are the company's overall objectives?
- What problems does the company want to solve?
- How can technology help meet those goals and solve the problems?
- What are the company's IT priorities, both short- and long-term?
- What type of technology infrastructure (centralized or decentralized) best serves the company's needs?
- Which technologies meet the company's requirements?

- Are additional hardware and software required? If so, will they integrate with the company's existing systems?
- Does the system design and implementation include the people and process changes, in addition to the technological ones?
- Do you have the in-house capabilities to develop and implement the proposed applications, or should you bring in an outside specialist?

concept check

What are some ways in which a company can manage its technology assets to its advantage?

Differentiate between information management and knowledge management. What steps can companies take to manage knowledge?

List the key questions managers need to ask when planning technology purchases.

PROTECTING COMPUTERS AND INFORMATION

Have you ever lost a term paper you'd worked on for weeks because your hard drive crashed or you deleted the file by mistake? You were upset, angry, and frustrated. Multiply that paper and your feelings hundreds of times over, and you can understand why companies must protect computers, networks, and the information they store and transmit, from a variety of potential threats. For example, security breaches of corporate information systems—from human hackers or electronic assailants such as viruses and worms—are growing in number at an alarming rate. The ever-increasing dependence on computers requires plans that cover human error, power outages, equipment failure, and—since September 11, 2001—terrorist attacks. To withstand natural disasters such as major fires, earthquakes, and floods, for example, many companies install specialized fault-tolerant computer systems.

Disasters are not the only threat to data. A great deal of data, much of it confidential, can easily be tapped into or destroyed by anyone who knows about computers. Keeping your networks secure from unauthorized access—from internal as well as external sources—requires formal security policies and enforcement procedures. The increasing popularity of mobile devices—laptops, handheld computers, PDAs, and digital cameras—and wireless networks requires calls for new types of security provisions. Rob Clyde, chief technology officer at computer security software firm Symantec, reports that half of the chief executives at a recent round-table event cited Wi-Fi, a wireless networking technology, as a top security concern. Wireless networks with open access points, for example, can permit unauthorized entry—even if a company has methods in place to prevent this.[8]

Data Security Issues

Unauthorized access to a company's computer systems can be expensive, and not just in monetary terms. A recent study reported that 90 percent of the participating corporations had experienced a computer break-in in the previous year. In the 10-year period from 1993 to 2002, the number of crimes reported to the CERT Coordination Center, a U.S. federally financed information centre for computer security information, has climbed from 1,334 to more than 82,000. Most of the increase occurred since 1998, when the number of reported crimes was only 3,734.[9]

Firms are taking steps to prevent these costly computer crimes and problems, which fall into several major categories.

- *Unauthorized access and security breaches.* Whether from internal or external sources, unauthorized access and security breaches are a top concern of IT managers. These can create havoc with a company's systems and damage customer relationships. Unauthorized access also includes that of employees, who can copy confidential new-product information and provide it to competitors or use company systems for personal business that might interfere with systems operation. Networking links make it easier for someone outside the organization to gain access to a company's computers. Computer crooks are getting more sophisticated all the time and find new ways to get into ultra-secure sites. For example, in December 2000, hackers accessed the customer database of on-line software retailer Egghead.com, which held 3.7 million credit card account numbers. Although Egghead maintained that its security measures prevented the hackers from stealing the data, customers and shareholders were not convinced. The stock's price quickly dropped 25 percent, customers defected to other companies, and Egghead filed for bankruptcy in August 2001.[10]

- *Software piracy.* The copying of copyrighted software programs by people who haven't paid for them is another form of unauthorized use. Piracy takes revenue away from the company that developed the program—usually at great cost. It includes making counterfeit CDs to sell as well as personal copying of software to share with friends. Software firms take piracy seriously and go after the offenders. Many also make special arrangements, so that large companies can get multiple copies of programs at a lower cost, to encourage them not to use illegal copies. Companies are continually adding features such as anti-piracy codes and "shells" to limit the use of the software on other computers and prevent unauthorized copying of CDs. Recent versions of Microsoft's Windows XP and Office require "activation" to get full use. The user is limited in the number of times he or she can start up a system without registering the software. "That's been very helpful in making it tough for counterfeiters," says Patrick Mueller, senior investigator for Microsoft.[11] Intuit requires customers to obtain a special product activation number before using its TurboTax software to prepare income taxes. Although customers can use the program on other computers, only the original computer can be used to print and electronically file tax returns.[12]

- *Deliberate damage to equipment or information.* For example, an unhappy employee in the purchasing department could get into the computer system and delete information on past orders and future inventory needs. The sabotage could severely disrupt production and the accounts payable system. Wilful acts to destroy or change the data in computers are hard to prevent. To lessen the damage, companies should back up critical information.

- *Computer viruses.* In a recent survey, network managers ranked new computer viruses their top security/business threat.[13] A program or piece of code that is loaded onto a computer without the user's knowledge, runs automatically, and is designed to replicate itself, a **computer virus** can destroy the contents of a computer's hard drive or damage files. Another form is called a "worm," because it spreads itself automatically from computer to computer. Unlike a virus, a worm doesn't require e-mail to replicate and transmit itself into other systems. It can enter through valid access points. The January 25, 2003, "Slammer" worm entered computer systems through a standard entry point for queries to a Microsoft database. It not only affected computers but caused so much additional traffic volume that it clogged up the Internet as well. This brought down some types of telephone service, bank networks, and other critical Net-dependent communications systems.[14]

Viruses can hide for weeks or months before starting to damage information. A virus that "infects" one computer or network can be spread to another computer through the sharing of disks or the downloading of infected files over the Internet. To protect data from virus damage, virus protection software automatically monitors computers to detect and remove viruses. Program developers make regular updates available to guard against newly created viruses. In addition, experts are becoming more proficient at tracking down virus authors, who are then subject to criminal charges.

- *Spam.* Although you might think that *spam*, or unsolicited and unwanted e-mail, is just a nuisance, it also poses a security threat to companies. Viruses spread through e-mail attachments that can accompany spam e-mails. Spam presents other threats to a corporation as well, including the cost of time lost in dealing with spam: opening the messages, searching for legitimate messages that special spam filters keep out, etc.

Preventing Problems

Firms that take a proactive approach can prevent security and technical problems before they start. They begin by creating formal written security policies to set standards and provide the basis for enforcement. These should have the support of top management. Then they follow with procedures to implement the security policies. Because IT is a dynamic field with ongoing changes to equipment and processes, it's important to review security policies often. Some security policies can be handled automatically, by technical measures, whereas others involve administrative policies that rely on humans to perform them. Examples of administrative policies are "Users must change their passwords each quarter" and "End users will update their virus signatures at least once a week."[15]

Preventing costly problems can be as simple as backing up applications and data regularly. Companies should have systems in place that automatically back up the company's data every day and store copies of the backups off-site. In addition, employees should back up their work regularly. Another good policy is to maintain a complete and current database of all IT hardware, software, and user details to make it easier to manage software licenses and updates, and diagnose problems. In many cases, IT staff can use remote access technology to monitor and fix problems automatically, as well as update applications and services.

computer virus
A program or piece of code that is loaded onto a computer without the user's knowledge, runs automatically, and is designed to replicate itself.

HOT Links

How can you "inoculate" your computer against viruses? Symantec's Security Response has the latest details on virus threats and security issues: http://www.symantec.com/avcenter/.

Companies should never overlook the human factor in the security equation. As Kevin Mitnick, the infamous convicted hacker, was quoted as saying, "Companies spend millions of dollars on firewalls, encryption and secure access devices, and it's money wasted, because none of these measures address the weakest link in the security chain." He first used what he called a "social engineering" attack—convincing someone over the phone through deception to reveal a password—to get into the computer systems. One of the most common ways in which outsiders get into company systems is by getting the staffer's full name and user name from an e-mail message, then posing as that employee and calling the help desk to ask for a forgotten password. Other practices that allow thieves to obtain passwords include employees' keeping them on sticky notes attached to their desk or computer monitor, leaving machines logged on when they are away from their desks, and leaving laptop computers with sensitive information unsecured in public places.[16]

Handheld computers and PDAs pose security risks as well. They are often used to store sensitive data such as passwords, bank details, and calendars. Imagine the problems that could arise if an employee saw a calendar entry like "meeting re: layoffs" or an outsider saw "meeting about merger with ABC Company." As well, PDAs can spread viruses when users download virus-infected documents to their company computers.

Companies have many other ways to avoid an IT meltdown, as the Procedures to Protect IT Assets box demonstrates.

Keep IT Confidential: Privacy Concerns

The very existence of huge electronic file cabinets full of personal information presents a threat to our personal privacy. Until recently, our financial, medical, tax, and other records were stored in separate computer systems. Now computer networks

Procedures to Protect IT Assets

- Protect the equipment with stringent physical security measures to the premises.
- Protect data using special *encryption* technology to encode confidential information, so only the recipient can decipher it.
- Stop unwanted access from inside or outside with special authorization systems. These can be as simple as a password or as sophisticated as fingerprint or voice identification.
- Install *firewalls*—hardware or software designed to prevent unauthorized access to or from a private network.
- Monitor network activity with intrusion-detection systems that signal possible unauthorized access and document suspicious events.

- Train employees to troubleshoot problems in advance rather than just react to them.
- Hold frequent staff training sessions to teach correct security procedures, such as logging out of networks when they go to lunch and changing passwords often.
- Make sure employees choose sensible passwords, of at least six and ideally eight characters long, containing numbers, letters, and punctuation marks. Avoid dictionary words and personal information.
- Establish a database of useful information and FAQs (frequently asked questions) for employees so they can solve problems themselves.
- Develop a healthy communications atmosphere.

make it easy to pool these data into data warehouses. Companies also sell the information they collect about you from sources like warranty registration cards, credit card records, registration at Web sites, personal data forms required for on-line purchases, and grocery store discount club cards. Telemarketers can combine data from different sources to create fairly detailed profiles of consumers. With information about their buying habits, advertisers can target consumers for specific marketing programs.

Increasingly, consumers are fighting to regain control of personal data and how that information is used. Privacy advocates are working to block sales of information collected by governments and corporations. For example, they want to prevent governments from selling driver's license information, and supermarkets from collecting and selling information gathered when shoppers use bar-coded plastic loyalty cards.

The challenge to companies is to find a balance between collecting the information they need and protecting individual consumer rights. Most registration and warranty forms that ask questions about income and interests have a box for consumers to check to prevent the company from selling their names. Many companies now state their privacy policies to ensure consumers that they will not abuse the information they collect.

In Canada the *Personal Information Protection and Electronic Documents Act*, which was enacted in 2000, is intended to support and promote electronic commerce by protecting personal information. In an era of technology that is used to facilitate the exchange of information, the Government of Canada recognized a need for rules that governed the collection, use, and disclosure of personal information in a manner that recognizes the right of privacy of individuals with respect to their personal information.[17]

HOT Links

For more information about personal information protection in Canada, see the Web site of the Office of the Privacy Commissioner of Canada (http://www.privcom.gc.ca/).

concept check

Describe the various threats to data security.

How can companies protect information from destruction and from unauthorized use?

Why are privacy rights advocates alarmed over the use of techniques such as data warehouses?

Trends in Information Technology

6 *learning goal*

HOT Links

For the latest in technology news see http://www.zdnet.com or http://www.news.com.com.

Information technology is a continually evolving field. The fast pace and amount of change, coupled with IT's broad reach, make it especially challenging to isolate industry trends. From the time we write this chapter to the time you read it—as little as six months—new trends will appear, and some of those that seemed important will have faded. However, some trends that are reshaping today's IT landscape are enterprise portals and on-demand computing.

ENTERPRISE PORTALS OPEN THE DOOR TO PRODUCTIVITY

Improving communications with employees was a top priority for global information technology giant HP. Not only was the company reinventing itself, it was also in the process of integrating its acquisition of computer manufacturer Compaq—situations that called for good channels for the CEO to communicate with employees about these changes. Add to that systems and procedures that differed across company divisions and geographic locations, and you have a major IT challenge on your hands.

The answer for HP was a business-to-employee (B2E) enterprise portal that has become the company's primary source for employee information. A **web portal** is a Web site that provides a starting point, or gateway, to other resources on the Internet or on an intranet. An **enterprise portal** is an internal Web site that provides proprietary corporate information to a defined user group. By evaluating, streamlining, and standardizing a host of separate manual transactions, the portal development team at HP created a cohesive, unified framework for employee communications. Although the initial portal project cost about $20 million (US), HP saved $50 million in just the first year by reducing staffing in call centres, outsourcing benefits administration, and consolidating Web sites and servers.[18]

Portals can take one of three forms: business to employee (B2E), business to business (B2B), and business to consumer (B2C). Although this might sound much like an intranet, an enterprise portal allows individuals or user groups to customize the portal page. They can select from the available information sources and applications exactly what they need for their particular job situations and don't have to waste time searching for them. The portal gathers everything into one place, helping employees to do their jobs more quickly and efficiently.

web portal

A Web site that provides a starting point, or gateway, to other resources on the Internet or on an intranet.

enterprise portal

A customizable internal Web site that provides proprietary corporate information to a defined user group, such as employees, supply chain partners, or customers.

Technology is responsible for the rapidly increasing flow of information. It can also provide solutions to prevent serious communication errors and improve productivity. For example, automated order fulfillment software reduces errors, improves turnaround time, and increases customer satisfaction.

Why are more companies adopting portal technology? Portals provide

- a consistent, simple user interface across the company;
- integration of disparate systems and multiple sets of data and information;
- a single source for accurate and timely information that integrates internal and external information;
- a shorter time to perform tasks and processes;
- cost savings through the elimination of "information intermediaries"; and
- improved communications within the company and with customers, suppliers, dealers, and distributors.

HOT Links

For more information about the history of portals and their use, see http://en.wikipedia.org/wiki/Portals.

ON-DEMAND COMPUTING SOLVES GRIDLOCK

What do you do with 8,000 demonstration desktop computers sitting idle in your 272 retail stores? If you are Gateway Computers, you link together the processing power they represent into a grid that produces more than 14 trillion floating point operations per second at peak capacity—creating a virtual supercomputer that ranks above the world's second fastest supercomputer. Then you offer businesses Gateway Processing on Demand (POD), a cost-effective way of accessing high-end computing resources on an as-needed basis at a fraction of what it would cost to have a supercomputer on-site. As a result, smaller companies and those that don't have an ongoing need for super-computer capacity can perform extremely complex calculations in hours or days instead of months.

With *grid computing*, users work collaboratively on a virtual supercomputer using a hardware and software infrastructure that clusters and integrates computers and applications from multiple sources, harnessing unused power in their existing PCs and networks. The grid structure distributes computational resources but maintains central control of the process. A central server acts as a team leader and traffic monitor. The controlling cluster server divides a task into subtasks, assigns the work to computers on the grid with surplus processing power, combines the results, and moves on to the next task until the job is finished. Exhibit 4.6 shows how a typical grid setup works.

HOT Links

To learn more about clusters and grid computing, see The Grid Computing Information Centre Web site (http://www.gridcomputing.com).

Gateway is not alone in pursuing this largely untapped market. IBM, Sun Microsystems, and HP are among the companies that have announced on-demand services. IBM is hoping to generate a significant new revenue stream for the company with its on-demand e-business unit. In March 2003, Petroleum Geo-Services (PGS) became IBM's first on-demand customer. PGS needs massive computing power to analyze sonar data in searching for oil deposits. When it signed on with IBM, PGS expected to obtain about one-third of its supercomputing capacity from the company. "PGS has been looking for a more flexible business model which addresses peak computing requirements," said PGS's Chris Usher. By outsourcing its peak needs and buying IT infrastructure sufficient to serve only its average demand, PGS and other companies don't have lots of unused capacity going to waste.

Irving Wladawsky-Berger, vice president of IBM's Technical Strategy and Innovation, expects on-demand computing to become increasingly popular. Businesses will be able to choose whether to own the hardware and applications or acquire them from a service provider on a fixed- or variable-cost basis. Several factors are coming together to make on-demand computing delivered via a grid more feasible: ever-present connectivity via the Internet, improved network performance, and greater acceptance of collaborative work methods. Several industry groups are currently developing standards and security protocols to protect data.

Exhibit 4.6 | How Grid Computing Works

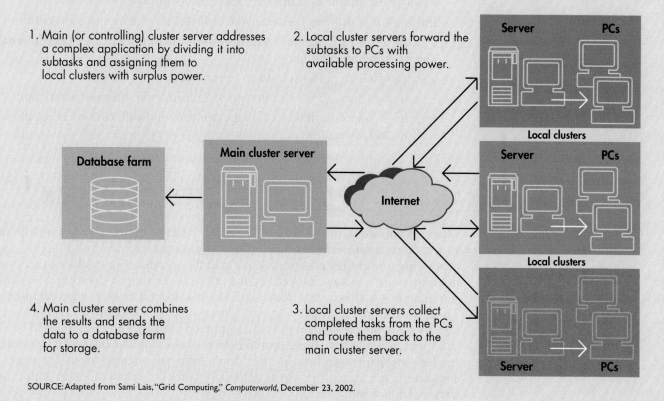

1. Main (or controlling) cluster server addresses a complex application by dividing it into subtasks and assigning them to local clusters with surplus power.

2. Local cluster servers forward the subtasks to PCs with available processing power.

4. Main cluster server combines the results and sends the data to a database farm for storage.

3. Local cluster servers collect completed tasks from the PCs and route them back to the main cluster server.

SOURCE: Adapted from Sami Lais, "Grid Computing," *Computerworld*, December 23, 2002.

Companies are setting up internal grids as well as tapping into the on-demand services offered by these companies. Monsanto company scientists analyze plant genes to determine traits characteristic leading to better crop yields. Because this process requires the manipulation of huge amounts of data, researchers were able to analyze only 10 to 50 genes each year before 2000, when Monsanto decided to use grid computing rather than invest in its own supercomputers. It created a grid from hundreds of computers in its St. Louis, Missouri, headquarters and the Cambridge, Massachusetts, offices of its Cereon subsidiary. In between doing other tasks, these computers perform small calculations. Instead of six weeks, the gene analysis process now takes less than a day, enabling Monsanto to investigate thousands of genes each year.[19]

concept check

How do enterprise portals differ from intranets? What additional benefits do they provide to a company?

What advantages does grid computing offer a company? What are some of the downsides to using this method?

Great Ideas to Use Now

Computer literacy is no longer a luxury. To succeed in business today, almost everyone must develop technological competence. Whether you have a part-time job in a fast-food restaurant that uses computerized ordering systems, or perform financial analyses that guide the future of your company, you will depend on computers. The more you increase your knowledge of technology, the more valuable you will be as an employee in today's information-driven businesses. In addition, the shortage of qualified IT personnel opens up new career avenues to those who enjoy working with technology. You will also have the knowledge to be able to take steps to protect your privacy.

PREPARATION PAYS OFF

Whether you are an employee or a business owner, you need to be aware of how technology affects the way your firm operates. New applications can change fundamental company operations and employees' roles. For example, companies that install ERP systems want individual employees to make more strategic, far-reaching decisions than before. This requires a dramatic shift in employees' roles and the way they should view their jobs. For example, an accountant's responsibilities might now include analyzing budgets, not just auditing expenses. A salesperson's role might expand to include more strategic decision-making about customer issues. Your company will see the business benefits sooner if you prepare for these changing roles. A manager should begin teaching employees operational procedures before implementing the new system and help them acquire the necessary analytical skills. As an employee, you can take the initiative to learn as much as possible about the new technology and how it operates.

PROTECT YOUR GOOD NAME

Identity theft is on the rise. Recent developments in telecommunications and computer processing make it easier for companies and the public to reach each other; they also cause your personal information to be more widely circulated. If identity theft happens, you could be held responsible for bills and other charges.

Customer Satisfaction and Quality

Information technology can be used in many ways to satisfy customers and improve quality. In fact, most IT systems, from customer relationship management systems to enterprise portals, are at the heart of satisfying employees, vendors, and customers. For example, with accurate and timely information, company managers can make decisions that add new products in response to customer requests. Customer databases and order fulfillment systems speed products on their way to customers. Internally, better information allows production managers to forecast inventory accurately, so that it is on-site when needed and the company can avoid paying for rush delivery. Automated systems improve the quality of production, ordering, administration, and finance. Pharmaceutical companies use computer modeling systems to simulate clinical trials, saving time and money when developing new drugs.

Quality, of course, has another side. IT systems must be planned, designed, and implemented to meet the highest quality standards. Many companies have rushed to implement new systems without allowing adequate time to test them before "going live"—with disastrous results.

HOT *Links*

For a more complete list of recommendations of the Office of the Privacy Commissioner of Canada, see http://www.privcom.gc.ca.

Often you have no idea that your identity has been stolen, and you might not be able to prevent it. To protect your identity, the Office of the Privacy Commissioner of Canada has some recommendations.

1. Be careful about sharing information.

2. Ask how your personal information is to be used.

3. Give only the minimum required personal information.

4. Be very careful with giving out your SIN.

5. Don't give out your credit card number on the telephone, electronically, or voice mail unless you know the person on the other end.

6. Use technologies that can enhance your security.

7. Pay attention to your billing cycle.[20]

SUMMARY OF LEARNING GOALS

1 How has information technology transformed business and managerial decision-making?

Businesses depend on information technology for everything from running daily operations to making strategic decisions. Companies must have management information systems that gather, analyze, and distribute information to the appropriate parties, including employees, suppliers, and customers. These systems collect data and process it into usable information for decision-making. Managers tap into databases to access the information they need, whether for placing inventory orders, scheduling production, or preparing long-range forecasts. They can compare information about the company's current status to its goals and standards. Company-wide enterprise resource planning systems that bring together human resources, operations, and technology are becoming an integral part of business strategy.

2 Why are computer networks an important part of today's information technology systems?

Computer networks link computers so they can share. Today companies use networks of computers that share data and expensive hardware to improve operating efficiency. Types of networks include local area networks (LANs), wide area networks (WANs), and wireless local area networks (WLANs). Intranets are private WANs that allow a company's employees to communicate quickly with each other and work on joint projects, regardless of their location. Companies are finding new uses for wireless technologies, such as handheld computers, cell phones, and e-mail devices. Virtual private networks (VPNs) give companies a cost-effective, secure connection between remote locations using public networks such as the Internet.

3 What types of systems make up a typical company's management information system?

A management information system consists of a transaction-processing system, management support systems, and an office automation system. The transaction-processing system (TPS) collects and organizes operational data on the firm's activities. Management support systems help managers make better decisions. They include an information-reporting system, which provides information based on the data collected by the TPS to the managers who need it; decision support systems, which use models to assist in answering "what if" types of questions; and expert systems, which give managers advice similar to what they would get from a human consultant. Executive information systems are customized to the needs of top management. All employees benefit from office automation systems, which facilitate communication by using word processing, e-mail, fax machines, and similar technologies.

4 How can technology management and planning help companies optimize their information technology systems?

To get the most value from information technology (IT), companies must go beyond simply collecting and summarizing information. Technology planning involves evaluating the company's goals and objectives and using the right technology to reach them. IT managers must also evaluate existing infrastructure to get the best return on the company's investment in IT assets. Knowledge management (KM) focuses on sharing an organization's collective knowledge to improve productivity and foster innovation. Some companies establish the position of chief knowledge officer to head up KM activities.

5 What are the best ways to protect computers and the information they contain?

Because companies are more dependent on computers than ever before, they need to protect data and equipment from natural disasters and computer crime. Types of computer crime include unauthorized use and access, software piracy, malicious damage, and computer viruses. To protect IT assets, companies should prepare written security policies. They can use technology, such as virus protection and firewalls, and employee training in proper security procedures. They must also take steps to protect customers' personal privacy rights.

6 What are the leading trends in information technology?

IT is a dynamic industry, and companies must stay current with the latest trends to identify those that help them maintain their competitive edge. Enterprise portals and on-demand grid computing are two trends that help users work more quickly and efficiently, increase employee productivity, and improve communications inside and outside the company. An enterprise portal provides users with a single source for information and applications. They can customize this internal Web page to gather everything into one place, helping users to do their jobs more quickly and efficiently. Portals can take one of three forms: business to employee (B2E), business to business (B2B), and business to consumer (B2C). Grid computing harnesses the idle power of desktop PCs and other computers to create a virtual supercomputer. A company can access the grid on an as-needed basis instead of investing in its own supercomputer equipment. Outsourcing a portion of the company's computing needs provides additional flexibility. Companies can also set up internal grids.

EXPERIENTIAL EXERCISES

1. **Stay current.** Keeping up with the fast pace of technology change is a real challenge, but it is necessary if you wish to remain up-to-date on the latest IT developments. The Internet has simplified this task, however. Get into the habit of visiting news sites such as ZDNet (**http://www.zdnet.com**) for current tech news. You can also link to Ziff Davis publications such as *PC Magazine*, read product reviews, find on-line classes, and even compare prices on technology products. Another excellent site is CNet's News.com (**http://www.news.com**), which updates the technology news headlines throughout the day. It has sections on enterprise computing, e-business, communications, media, personal technology, and investing, among others.

2. **What jobs are hot?** Managing information is an emerging career area. There are jobs for people to enter the information, for people to "mine" it to find the best markets as well as to assess the interest and need for new products, and for specialists who understand the complex hardware and software needed to facilitate the loading, maintenance, and use of information. As a result of the increase in outsourcing of some IT functions and the shift of many IT jobs overseas, where labour costs are lower, companies now are hiring business analysts (BAs), also called subject area experts, or SAEs. BAs serve as the business liaisons and interface with the company to which the project is outsourced and with offshore personnel. To learn more about these areas and the wide range of other IT positions currently available, read the classified employment ads in your local newspaper and *The Wall Street Journal*. Go on-line to browse the employment ads from almost any major newspaper and surf through the Web sites with job listings. Many technology company Web sites also post job openings. Make a list of jobs that interest you. In addition, read the general job listings to see how many require computer skills.

3. How has information technology changed your life? Describe at least three areas (both personal and school/work related) where having access to better information has improved your decisions. Are there any negative effects? What steps can you take to manage information more effectively?

4. Your school wants to automate the class registration process. Prepare a memo to the Dean of Information Systems describing an integrated information system that would help a student choose and register for courses. Make a list of the various groups that should be involved, and questions to ask during the planning process. Include a graphic representation of the system similar to that in Exhibit 4.4 showing how the data become useful information. Indicate the information a student needs to choose courses and its sources. Explain how several types of management support systems could help students make better course decisions. Include ways in which the school could use the information it collects from this system. Have several students present their plans to the class, which will take the role of university management in evaluating them.

5. Should companies outsource IT? According to an interview in the December 9, 2002, San Jose *Mercury News*, Craig Conway, president and chief executive of PeopleSoft, believes that IT is too important to outsource and that application service providers (ASPs) don't have a future. What's your position? Divide the class into groups designated "for" or "against" outsourcing and/or ASPs. Have them research the current status of ASPs using publications like *CIO* and *Computerworld* and Web sites like ASPnews.com (**http://www.aspnews.com**).

6. One of the fastest-growing areas of business software is enterprise resource planning (ERP) applications. Visit the site of one of the following companies: SAP (**http://www.sap.com**), PeopleSoft (http://www.oracle.com/index.html), or Baan (http://www.ssaglobal.com/solutions/erp/ln.aspx). Prepare a short presentation for the class about the company's ERP product offerings and capabilities. Include examples of how companies use the ERP software.

7. What can an intranet accomplish for a company? Find out by using such resources as Brint.com's Intranet Portal (**http://www.brint.com/Intranets.htm**) and *Intranet Journal* (**http://www.intranetjournal.com**). Look for case studies that show how companies apply this technology. Summarize the features an intranet provides.

8. Learn more about the CERT Coordination Center (CERT/CC), which serves as a center of Internet security expertise. Explore its Web site (**http://www.cert.org**). What are the latest statistics on incidents reported, vulnerabilities, security alerts, security notes, mail messages, and hotline calls? What other useful information does the site provide to help a company protect IT assets?

9. Research the latest developments in computer security at Computerworld's site (**http://computerworld.com/securitytopics/security**). What types of information can you find here? Pick one area, such as security for mobility/wireless devices, and summarize your findings.

REVIEW QUESTIONS

1. How has technology been incorporated to help manage business?
2. What is the role of the CIO?
3. What is an MIS, and what are its roles?
4. How do LANs and WANs help in business?
5. How does a transaction-processing system (TPS) help to manage information?
6. Compare data warehouses and data marts.
7. Discuss the role of decision support systems (DSS).
8. How have office automation systems helped businesses?
9. How can we manage knowledge resources?
10. Why is protecting computers and information so important?
11. What are some ways in which computer and information security issues can be breached?
12. How can we prevent security and technical problems?

CREATIVE THINKING CASE
Canada Takes the Lead

The 2006 Canadian census information formed the basis for the February 2007 release of data by Statistics Canada. The census provided data for such important facts as characteristics of the population, households, dwellings, and families. This information is used to inform government planning and decision-making as well as planning and decision-making in the private sector, both profit and not-for-profit.

The census represented a massive project six years in the making, with the census Web site to handle on-line responses being more successful than any other in the world. The system had the capacity to handle 15,000 respondents at once and did not go down even during the busiest time of the response activity. Director-general Anil Arora stated that the security was so sophisticated that it exceeded even the level of security on most banking transactions. If respondents were unable to get through because of capacity problems, they were asked to try again later, and they did. About 20 percent of the 13 million households completed the census on-line, resulting in huge savings in labour, postage, and other costs. For example, having the data already in digital form when submitted eliminates the necessity of someone keying it in and also eliminates the potential for error. The cost to the government for census administration is about $15 per person, whereas in the United States it is more than $90 per household, three times the Canadian cost. Canadians also had access to a toll-free hotline number that handled a million calls over three days.

The main cost incurred in collecting the data is the follow-up process for those who do not submit their information. Approximately 30,000 field staff are hired to complete the collection of the data. Even so, Canada has one of the highest response rates in the world, with initial responses of 75 to 80 percent of households. The total cost for administering the census was approximately $567 million.

CRITICAL THINKING QUESTIONS

1. Given the importance of the data collected by the administration of the census, is there any way costs could be lowered further using technology?

2. If so, how could the census office encourage more respondents to use the on-line system?

SOURCE: The Ottawa Citizen, "Counter Spin," May 21, 2006, pg. A. 7. Reprinted with permission.

VIDEO CASE
Scammed

What exactly is phishing? Are you one of the 84 percent of Canadians who do not know? It is probably in your best interests to understand what is going on in the Internet crime scene before you become a victim of it.

Phishing is just as its homonym suggests … fishing for unsuspecting e-mail users to—you guessed it—reel them in.

Just how extensive are these phishing expeditions? Estimates suggest that one out of every 125 e-mails is a phishing attempt, with an estimated 5.7 million such e-mails sent out every day. The average life of these attempts is 5.5 days, which makes catching the perpetrators very difficult.

The dangers of this crime range from charges on your credit card to complete identity theft, with identity theft increasing at a rate of 25 to 50 percent per month. There are chat rooms where information is sold and credit cards traded. A member can buy a credit card for $2.

What can we do? Be smart. Don't be a sucker for an e-mail that suggests an incredible deal or easy money or credit. Watch for the following warning signs: spelling errors, grammatical errors, and/or a sense of urgency. And remember: Banks NEVER ask for personal information via e-mail.

CRITICAL THINKING QUESTIONS

1. Given the proliferation of phishing e-mails, how do you see this as an issue for legitimate information gathering by reputable companies?

2. What might be a reasonable course of action on receiving one of these e-mails?

SOURCE: CBC, *Marketplace*, "Sc@mmed," November 6, 2005.

E-COMMERCE CASE
Opening the Bottleneck in On-Line Wine Sales

E-commerce wine sites appeal to connoisseurs and novices alike. The wealth of information and search features available on-line make it easy for wine lovers to get helpful advice and product information. Consumers can find a large selection of wines—from rare vintages to moderately priced bottles—and then conveniently order them.

Despite the obvious appeal of buying wine on-line, the growth of Internet wine sales has been hampered by legal restrictions. Archaic liquor laws dating back to Prohibition allow each state to determine who can sell alcohol directly to residents. Even counties within a state might have special laws. Some states have reciprocal agreements, so that wineries, retailers, and dot-coms based within them can ship directly to consumers in those states. Other states require retailers to obtain the right sales permit to ship across state lines, or they make direct shipping illegal. Montana even requires the customer to buy a $50 "connoisseur's permit"! Some states have unique rules: Pennsylvanians can order wine on-line as long as they pick it up at a state-controlled wine and spirits store. Wine e-tailers face a logistical tangle in trying to keep track of each jurisdiction. In fact, no one can sell wine nationally; Wine.com, one of the largest wine wholesalers, operates in just 31 states plus Washington, D.C.

Creative wine dot-coms have figured out how to serve customers in many states. Wineaccess.com (**http://www.wineaccess.com**), an on-line mall of individual shops, uses a consolidated search engine to identify stores with the desired wines. Wine.com operates as a "buyers' agent" through in-state networks that join wholesalers and retailers into one large on-line store. It arranges order delivery or pickup with a wholesaler and retailer located in a jurisdiction that can legally sell to the customer. At the Web site (**http://www.wine.com**), the consumer enters the state to which the wine will be shipped; the on-line customer information system tells the buyer whether he or she can proceed. It then follows up with specific screens and ordering forms based on the recipient's place of residence. Other databases and site links provide extensive reviews and recommendations as well as searches by region and type of wine. Developing the information system for the networks was no easy task, however. In addition to different state liquor laws, each distributor used different inventory-tracking and -coding systems.

CRITICAL THINKING QUESTIONS

1. What advantages do on-line wine sales offer wine merchants? Their customers? Are there any drawbacks to buying via the Internet?

2. Assume that you are working with Wine.com to develop its information systems project. Prepare a list of the types of information Wine.com should include in its distributor and customer databases.

3. How can Wine.com use the information in its customer and distributor databases to increase sales?

SOURCES: Katy McLaughlin, "Merlot by Mail: Ordering Wine On-line Gets Easier," The Wall Street Journal, August 21, 2002; Wine.com Web site, http://www.wine.com (accessed May 20, 2003); and the Wine Institute Web site, http://www.wineinstitute.org.

Making the Connection

Forms of Business Ownership

In this chapter you'll learn about the different forms of organization taken by business owners. How does an owner set the business up legally, and what does this imply for the business and its owner(s)? This is related directly to our *political* environment in the PEST model, because the government regulates the options for business ownership and the rules to follow. However, you will see that the form of business ownership has implications for all aspects of the integrative business model and thus, ultimately, for the success of the business.

Let's look at the critical success factors. First, the form of business ownership chosen will affect the *financial performance* of the company, because it affects its costs (costs of setting up the organization, for example) and the level of taxes that it must pay. It also affects how much profit is available or distributed to the owner(s). The form of business ownership can also indirectly affect the business's ability to *meet customer needs*, as the degree of flexibility and control for the owner(s) tends to decrease as the business grows larger, which is often when the form of ownership is changed. More directly, the owner is restricted in terms of how to meet the needs of the customer if he or she is under a franchise agreement, for example. This, in turn, will affect the amount of *innovation and creativity* that is possible. Finally, it is perhaps easier to *gain employee commitment* in

some forms of business organization, as they offer the possibility of direct ownership beyond purchasing a minority interest in the company's stock.

So the form of business ownership, like all the decisions made in a business, has an integrative impact. It must be chosen with the company's overall goals and *strategy* in mind; for example, it would be difficult for a sole proprietorship to raise sufficient capital to build a chain of hotels worldwide. The form of business ownership also affects how the external environment treats the business and how that business, in turn, affects the environment, in addition to affecting the decisions that are made internally.

Looking back at our PEST model of the external environment, we can examine the effect that the form of business ownership has with regard to those dealing with the business from the outside. For example, within the political environment, the government tends to regulate larger businesses more heavily, especially large public corporations that have a greater impact on society. As well, the amount of legal liability that the owners have for business debts depends on the form of ownership. This might lead to a situation in which a loan is turned down because the lender doubts that the debt can be satisfied out of business assets, and yet the form of ownership chosen (namely, incorporation) does not allow for the debt to be satisfied from the personal assets of the owner(s) unless they are specifically used as collateral.

The form of business ownership chosen affects the amount of taxes paid to the government as well, which, in turn, affects the *economic* environment: Paying less tax allows for greater spending to grow the business. Within the *social* environment, society is becoming ever more demanding of businesses to be socially responsible and act ethically. This extends to all forms of business organization, but perhaps the highest expectations rest on the larger public corporations because of their visibility and resources. The trends in business ownership, as discussed later in this chapter, also have relationships to the social environment. For example, the changing demographics in society—the increasingly prominent role of women in business and the influence women have over purchase decisions—along with political pressure from various groups—have led many franchisors to encourage women to own their own franchises and to facilitate the process for them.

The *technological* environment is perhaps the only area not directly impacted by the form of business organization. Small and large organizations, whether sole proprietorships, partnerships, or corporations, have equal access to technology. This access to technology has allowed different forms of business to compete on more of a level playing field, leading to the creation of many new businesses. These new businesses usually start small, as sole proprietorships, partnerships, or small private corporations—creating a trend that we will discuss in Chapter 6.

When looking at the advantages and disadvantages of each form of ownership, you will see many examples of the integration of the form of ownership and the decisions made within the functional areas. For example, in the *finance* area, the form of ownership directly affects the degree of capital that the business has access to, and the options it has to raise that capital. This, in turn, will affect the size of its *operations*. In the *human resource* area, taking the large corporation as an example, this form of ownership affects the organization's ability to find and keep quality employees as well as the incentives available to them—the larger the company, the greater the opportunities for employees to advance and the greater the resources to attract and hold onto them.

In a broader sense, the form of ownership affects the ability of the business to make good decisions in all areas. It is very unlikely for a sole proprietor, for example, to be an expert at every function, and thus the business will be weak where he or she is weak unless expert assistance is brought in. This is why businesses often develop partnerships, preferably with people who have complementary skills, and/or create corporations that can, as they grow larger, attract professional talent to round out the company's needs. A good example is Research In Motion (RIM), the maker of the famous BlackBerry pager. The company was built on the strength of its technology, but a major weakness early on was in the area of marketing. Because of the success and visibility of this publicly traded corporation, it was able to attract very strong talent in that area to continue the success of the company. A sole proprietorship would have had much more difficulty.

This issue is the same with respect to the basic tasks of a manager in any of the functional areas or levels of the company. A sole proprietor may be good at *planning*, but bad at executing (*organizing*, *leading*, and *controlling*), or vice versa. Bringing other people into the company to balance those needs is important to the success of the company, and it is easier as the business grows, which often necessitates a change in the form of ownership.

5

PHOTO BY LINDA CRAIG

Forms of Business Ownership

learning goals

1 What are the advantages and disadvantages of the sole proprietorship form of business organization?

2 What are the advantages of operating as a partnership, and what downside risks should partners consider?

3 How does the corporate structure provide advantages and disadvantages to a company, and what is a special type of corporation?

4 Does a venture have other business organization options in addition to sole proprietorships, partnerships, and corporations?

5 What makes franchising an appropriate form of organization for some types of business, and why is it growing in importance?

6 Why are mergers and acquisitions important to a company's overall growth?

7 How will current trends affect the business organizations of the future?

The Freedom of Ownership

For six years, Christopher Halpin, owner of Manna Catering Services, was frustrated by what he describes as "the lack of respect for employees and lack of choices for the customers." During these six years, Christopher worked for numerous catering companies to supplement his art consulting business. The frustration that Christopher felt convinced him that he could become a successful business owner and demonstrate respect for his employees, all while delivering professional service and products to his customers.

His philosophy is simple: "create the right atmosphere and allow the customers to feel comfortable. The customers must see that the events are flexible, creative, unique, remarkable, and memorable." He says that people in our culture are generally not comfortable with being "served," so this has been his major challenge.

Since Christopher started Manna Catering Services in 1995, he has used his prior knowledge of the industry but has also learned some valuable lessons along the way. Because of what he saw while working for other people, he believed that the catering industry was not viewed as being professional or "white collared." Since opening his business, his approach has been to "treat the industry from a professional aspect and others will see it as being professional."

First he had to design flexible menu choices. "Not all customers want the same experience. By offering a variety of menus and a unique atmosphere around these menus, each event is seen as special and memorable," he says. He was also very aware that it was important to keep his costs to a minimum, without sacrificing quality, so that these savings could be passed on to the customer. With the combination of a variety of experiences and savings to the customers, Christopher ensures that they are receiving the quality and service they want.

Christopher also believes that to be truly customer focused, he must also be considerate of his employees and their needs. "Employees must enjoy their job and the customer must be made to realize that it is okay to be served." Christopher continued to share his philosophy about employees:

Typically, employees in the small catering businesses are part time, supplementing their regular income. This often results in employees being very transient. I wanted to have a more secure and stable part-time group. I pay well (about 50 percent more than the standard), I allow the staff to eat the same food as the clients (therefore there is no thieving), they dress professionally (basic black, and of course, the Manna Catering signature natural linen apron, always freshly laundered), I provide training to ensure consistency in the service and to respect the customers and make them feel comfortable and, most importantly, I respect my employees.

Because of Christopher's respect for his employees and his fair and equitable treatment of them, the turnover rate of his staff has been very low, and they do not work for other caterers.

Being customer focused has been a very valuable and profitable lesson for Christopher. He warns those who are considering starting their own business not to forget to do their homework. He recommends that after you decide to start a business and determine what the business focus is, you should think about what the legal structure of your enterprise is going to be. "I researched the various types of business ownership and decided to form the simplest, the sole proprietorship, for many reasons," says Christopher.

"I looked into incorporating," he says, "but did not think the added expense and regulations were worth the investment; I could do better things with the money. The limited liability appealed to me, but in this business if you are customer-focused and careful (e.g., handling of food), there is little risk."

The partnership form, on the other hand, held very little interest for him. Christopher sat down and wrote out his qualifications for the catering business. Based on the day-to-day operations, there were no skills that he felt he did not possess or could not learn quickly, so there was no need to have a partner from that perspective. He did acknowledge that he was weak in the accounting and financial management area, but to overcome this situation, he found an accounting firm to help with financial and tax advice. Christopher sums up his sense about the possibility of forming a partnership:

Besides, I had no interest in sharing the profits with anyone. The sole proprietorship appealed to me the best. I am able to make the decisions by myself and control the growth of the enterprise. I don't ever think that I will take on a partner, but I can see the day that if I want the enterprise to grow to a certain point, I will have to incorporate it.

Today, Christopher enjoys a successful business, the flexibility it offers him, and the respect of both his employees and his customers. He is happy in his venture and suggests that if you want to start a business—"Do your homework."[1]

Critical Thinking Questions

As you read this chapter, consider the following questions as they relate to Christopher Halpin and Manna Catering Services:

1. What factors did Christopher consider when selecting a form of business organization?

2. What are some of the pros and cons of operating the business as a sole proprietorship? If Christopher decided to include a partner, what should that partner bring to the business?

3. What would be the benefits of incorporating the business?

Principles of Business Ownership

So you've decided to start a business. You have a good idea and some cash in hand, but before you get going, you need to decide what form of business organization will best suit your needs.

So first ask yourself some questions. Would you prefer to go it alone as a *sole proprietorship*, or do you want others to share the burdens and challenges of a *partnership*, or do you prefer the limited liability protection of a *corporation*?

Here are some other questions you need to consider: How easy will it be to find financing? Can you attract employees? How will the business be taxed, and who will be liable for the business's debts? If you choose to share ownership with others, how much operating control will they want, and what costs will be associated with that or other forms of ownership? Most start-up businesses select one of the major ownership categories.

In the following pages, we will discover the advantages and disadvantages of each form of business ownership and the factors that might make it necessary to change from one form of organization to another as the needs of the business change. As your business expands from a small to midsize or larger venture, the form of business structure you selected in the beginning might no longer be appropriate. We will also look at specialized forms of business.

GOING IT ALONE: SOLE PROPRIETORSHIPS

1 *learning goal*

sole proprietorship
A business that is established, owned, operated, and often financed by one person.

Mike Robson was working full time, just finishing a bachelor's degree and starting work on his master's, when having lunch with a fellow student changed everything. His friend mentioned that the company he worked for had trouble obtaining "toppers," metal boxes for ATM (automatic teller machine) modems. Before lunch was over, Robson decided to start a business—building toppers.

Eight months after Robson had set up business as a **sole proprietorship,** a business established, owned, operated, and often financed by one person, his $20,000 home equity loan financing was gone without his having sold a single box! Then he made a fateful sales call at a local credit union, where it needed someone to spruce up a dilapidated ATM. Robson drew on his chemical engineering background to clean, polish, and paint the machine until it looked like new, and so his new business restoring and maintaining ATMs was born!

Robson thrived as a sole proprietor. He liked the independence of being his own boss and controlling all business decisions. When he realized that his initial idea was headed nowhere, he was able to change direction quickly when a new opportunity presented itself. Many businesses in your neighbourhood, including florists, dry cleaners, and beauty salons, are sole proprietorships, as are many service providers, such as lawyers, accountants, and real estate agents.[2]

Advantages of Sole Proprietorships

Sole proprietorships have several advantages that make them popular:

- *They are easy and inexpensive to form.* As Mike Robson discovered, sole proprietorships have few legal requirements and are not expensive to form, making them the business organization of choice for many small companies and start-ups.
- *Profits all go to the owner.* The owner of a sole proprietorship obtains the start-up funds and gets all the profits earned by the business.
- The owner has *direct control of the business.* All business decisions are made by the sole proprietorship owner, without having to consult anyone else. This was beneficial for Mike Robson when he needed to change the direction of his business.
- They are relatively free *from government regulations.* Sole proprietorships have more freedom than other forms of business with respect to government controls.
- There is no *corporate taxation.* Sole proprietorships do not pay corporate taxes. Profits are taxed as personal income and are reported on the owner's individual tax return.
- They are easy to dissolve. With no co-owners or partners, the sole proprietor can sell the business or close the doors at any time, making this form of business organization an ideal way to test new business ideas.

Disadvantages of Sole Proprietorships

Along with the freedom to operate the business as they wish, sole proprietors face several disadvantages:

- *Unlimited liability.* From a legal standpoint, the sole proprietor and the business he or she owns are one and the same, making the business owner personally responsible for all debts the business incurs, even if they exceed the business's value. The owner might need to sell other personal property— his or her car, home, or other investments—to satisfy claims against the business.
- *Difficulty in raising capital.* Business assets are unprotected against claims of personal creditors, and business lenders view sole proprietorships as high risk because of the owner's unlimited liability. Owners often must use personal funds—borrowing on credit cards, securing assets (collateral) for loans or lines of credit, or selling investments—to finance their business, and expansion plans can also be affected by an inability to raise additional funding.
- *Limited managerial expertise.* The success of a sole proprietorship rests solely with the skills and talents of the owner, who must wear many different hats and make all decisions. Owners are often not equally skilled in all areas of running a business. A graphic designer might be a wonderful artist but may not know bookkeeping, how to manage production, or how to market his or her work.
- *Trouble finding qualified employees.* Sole proprietors often cannot offer the same pay, fringe benefits, and opportunities for advancement as larger companies

can, making them less attractive to employees seeking the most favourable employment opportunities.

- *Personal time commitment.* Running a sole proprietorship business requires personal sacrifices and a huge time commitment, often dominating the owner's life with 12-hour workdays and 7-day workweeks.
- *Unstable business life.* The life span of a sole proprietorship can be uncertain. The owner might lose interest, experience ill health, retire, or die. The business will cease to exist unless the owner makes provisions for it to continue operating or puts it up for sale.
- *Losses are the owner's responsibility.* The sole proprietor is responsible for all losses, although tax laws allow these to be deducted from other personal income.

The sole proprietorship might be a suitable choice for a one-person start-up operation with no employees and little risk of liability exposure. For many sole proprietors, however, this is a temporary choice, and as the business grows, the owner might be unable to operate with limited financial and managerial resources. At this point, he or she might decide to take in one or more partners to ensure that the business continues to flourish.

concept check

What is a sole proprietorship?

Why is this such a popular form of business organization?

What are the drawbacks to being a sole proprietor?

PARTNERSHIPS: SHARING THE LOAD

2 *learning goal*

partnership
An association of two or more individuals who agree to operate a business together for profit.

general partnership
A partnership in which all partners share in the management and profits. Each partner can act on behalf of the firm and has unlimited liability for all its business obligations.

limited partnership
A partnership with one or more general partners, who have unlimited liability, and one or more limited partners, whose liability is limited to the amount of their investment.

general partners
Partners who have unlimited liability for all of the firm's business obligations and who control its operations.

Some small businesses are born when individuals turn their passion into reality. Chris Emery and Larry Finnson, who have been best friends since grade 10 in Winnipeg, Manitoba, searched for an idea that would allow them to realize their dreams of "going into business together and make a million bucks." When they found that they could not resist Chris's grandmother's delicious graham wafer and fudge crunch, they knew they had found their product. Today their company, Clodhoppers, makes more than 1,000 kilograms an hour of product at the manufacturing facility in Winnipeg.[3]

For those individuals who do not like to "go it alone," a **partnership** is simple to set up and offers a shared form of business ownership. It is a popular choice for professional service firms such as lawyers, accountants, architects, and real estate companies.

The parties agree, *either orally or in writing*, to share in the profits and losses of a joint enterprise. A *written partnership agreement*, spelling out the terms and conditions of the partnership, *is recommended* to prevent later conflicts between the partners. These agreements typically include the name of the partnership, its purpose, and the contributions of each partner (financial, equipment, skill/talent), as well as outline the responsibilities and duties of each partner and their compensation structure (salary, profit sharing, etc.).

It should also contain provisions for the addition of new partners, the sale of partnership interests, and the procedures for resolving conflicts, dissolving the business, and distributing the assets.

There are *three basic types of partnerships: general, limited, and limited liability partnerships.* In a **general partnership,** all partners share in the management and the profits. They co-own the assets, and each can act on behalf of the firm. Each partner also has unlimited liability for all business obligations of the firm. A **limited partnership** has two types of partners: one or more **general partners,**

limited partners
Partners whose liability for the firm's business obligations is limited to the amount of their investment. They help to finance the business but do not participate in the firm's operations.

limited liability partnership (LLP)
In a limited liability partnership, each individual partner is protected from responsibility for the acts of other partners, and each party's liability is limited to harm resulting from that party's own actions.

who have unlimited liability, and one or more **limited partners,** whose liability is limited to the amount of their investment. In return for limited liability, limited partners agree not to take part in the day-to-day management of the firm. They help to finance the business, but the general partners maintain operational control.

In the **limited liability partnership (LLP),** each individual partner is protected from responsibility for the acts of other partners, and each partner's liability is limited to harm resulting from his or her own actions. Ontario was the first province to allow LLPs in 1998, followed by Alberta in 1999. Today most provinces allow LLPs to operate, and they are common in accounting and legal firms.

Advantages of Partnerships

Some advantages of partnerships come quickly to mind:

- *Ease of formation.* Like sole proprietorships, partnerships are easy to form. For most partnerships, applicable laws are not complex. The partners agree to do business together and draw up a *partnership agreement.*

- *Availability of capital.* Because two or more people contribute financial resources, partnerships can raise funds more easily for operating expenses and business expansion. The partners' combined financial strength also increases the firm's ability to raise funds from outside sources.

- *Diversity of skills and expertise.* Partners share the responsibility of managing and operating the business. Ideal partnerships bring together people with complementary backgrounds rather than those with similar experience, skills, and talents. Combining partner skills to set goals, manage the overall direction of the firm, and problem solve increases the chances of the partnership's success. To find the right partner, however, you must examine your own strengths and weaknesses, and know what you need from a partner. In the Perfect Partners section you'll find some advice on choosing a partner.

- *Flexibility.* General partners are actively involved in managing their firm and can respond quickly to changes in the business environment.

- *No corporate taxes.* Partnerships pay no income taxes. Each partner's profit or loss is reported on the partner's personal income tax return, with any profits taxed at personal income tax rates.

- *Relative freedom from government control.* Governments exercise little control over partnership activities.

Disadvantages of Partnerships

Business owners must consider the following disadvantages of setting up their venture as a partnership:

- *Unlimited liability.* All general partners have unlimited liability for the debts of the business. In fact, any one partner can be held personally liable for all partnership debts and legal judgments (such as malpractice)—regardless of who caused them. As with sole proprietorships, business failure can lead to a loss of the general partners' personal assets. To overcome this problem, most provinces now allow the formation of limited liability partnerships, which protect each individual partner from responsibility for the acts of other partners, and limit partners' liability to harm resulting from their own actions.

- *Potential for conflicts between partners.* Partners might have different ideas about how to run the business, which employees to hire, how to allocate responsibilities, and when to expand. Differences in personalities and work styles can cause clashes or breakdowns in communication, sometimes requiring outside intervention to save the business.

- *Sharing of profits.* Dividing the profits is relatively easy if all partners contribute equal amounts of time, expertise, and capital. But if one partner puts in more money and others more time, it might be difficult to arrive at a fair profit-sharing formula.
- *Difficulty exiting or dissolving a partnership.* As a rule, partnerships are easier to form than to leave. When one partner wants to leave, the value of his or her share must be calculated. To whom will that share be sold, and will that person be acceptable to the other partners? To avoid these problems, most partnership agreements include specific guidelines for transfer of partnership interests and buy-sell agreements that make provision for surviving partners to buy a deceased partner's interest. Partners can purchase special life insurance policies on each partner designed to fund such a purchase.

Business partnerships are often compared to marriages. As with a marriage, choosing the right partner is critical, so if you are considering forming a partnership, allow plenty of time to evaluate your and your potential partner's goals, personality, expertise, and working style.

HOT *Links*

In Canada the provinces have jurisdiction with respect to sole proprietorships and partnership. To find out more check your provincial government's Web site.

concept check

How does a partnership differ from a sole proprietorship?

Describe the three main types of partnerships, and explain the difference between a limited partner and a general partner.

What are the main advantages and disadvantages of a partnership?

Perfect Partners

Picking a partner is both an art and a science. Be prepared to talk about everything. On paper someone might have all the right credentials, but does that person share your vision and the ideas you have for the business? Is he or she a straight shooter? Honesty, integrity, and ethics are equally important, as you might be liable for what your partner does. Trust your intuition and "your gut feelings—they're probably right," advises Irwin Gray, author of *The Perils of Partners.* So ask yourself the following questions, and then ask a potential partner and see how well your answers match up:

1. Why do you want a partner?
2. What characteristics, talents, and skills does each person bring to the partnership?
3. How will you divide responsibilities? Consider every aspect of the business, from long-range planning to daily operations. Who will handle marketing, sales, accounting, and customer service?
4. What is your long-term vision for the business (size, life span, financial commitment, etc.)?
5. What are your personal reasons for forming this business: Are you looking for a steady paycheque? For independence? To create a small business? Or to build a large one?
6. Are all parties willing to put in the same amount of time, and, if not, is there an alternative arrangement that is acceptable to everyone?
7. What are your work ethics and values?
8. What requirements should be in the partnership agreement?

SOURCES: Julie Bawden Davis, "Buddy System," *Business Start Ups,* June 1998, http://www.entrepreneurmag.com; Azriela Jaffe, "'Til Death Us Do Part' Is No Way to Start a Business," *Business Week Online,* October 23, 1998, http://www.businessweek.com/smallbiz; Jerry Useem, "Partners on the Edge," *Inc.,* August 1998, 54, 59.

CORPORATIONS: LIMITING YOUR LIABILITY

3 *learning goal*

corporation

A legal entity with an existence and life separate from its owners, who therefore are not personally liable for the entity's debts. A corporation can own property, enter into contracts, sue and be sued, and engage in business operations.

When people think of corporations, they typically think of major, well-known companies like Petro-Canada, TD Canada Trust, Bell Canada Enterprises, and the communications corporation Rogers. But corporations range in size from large multinationals, with thousands of employees and billions of dollars in sales, to midsize or even smaller firms, with few employees and little revenue.

A **corporation** is a legal entity with a life separate from its owners, who therefore are not personally liable for its debts. A corporation is subject to the laws of the jurisdiction in which it is incorporated. A corporation can own property, enter into contracts, sue and be sued, and engage in business operations. Unlike sole proprietorships and partnerships, corporations are taxable entities.

In launching his company eEye Digital Security, 21-year-old Marc Maiffret needed the limited liability protection of the corporate business organization model. Maiffret started hacking at age 15, learning how to mangle Web sites and breach networks. When the authorities suspected him of breaching a military network, Maiffret and Firas Bushnaq, his boss (Maiffret dropped out of school to work for a software firm) decided to capitalize on his expertise. They launched eEye to outsmart the best hackers in the business by designing software to protect corporate network security.

With Maiffret bearing the title "Chief Hacking Officer," the growing company has five offices around the world and includes among its 50 employees a team of engineering hackers whose efforts bring eEye more than $1 million a month. Its unusual background makes eEye an unconventional corporation.[4]

Corporations play an important role in the Canadian economy. A list of the 10 largest Canadian corporations, shown in Exhibit 5.1, is based on after-tax profits, whereas in Exhibit 5.2, size is based on the number of employees. Many of these companies are probably familiar names that affect your daily life.

Public versus Private Corporations

public corporation

A corporation whose shares are widely held and available to the general public.

Corporations can be either public or private. A **public corporation**'s shares are widely held and available to the general public. Once the shares are in the public domain, they are then traded in the secondary markets, either on organized stock

Exhibit 5.1	The 10 Top Publicly Traded Companies According to After-Tax Profits (2004)

	COMPANY	PROFITS ($000)
1	EnCana	3,513,000
2	Bank of Nova Scotia	2,931,000
3	Royal Bank of Canada	2,817,000
4	Manulife Financial	2,564,000
5	Bank of Montreal	2,351,000
6	Toronto-Dominion Bank	2,310,000
7	Canadian Imperial Bank of Commerce	2,199,000
8	Imperial Oil	2,033,000
9	Manufacturers Life Insurance	2,015,000
10	Petro-Canada	1,757,000

SOURCE: Reprinted with permission from *The Globe and Mail.*

COMPANY NAME	NUMBER OF EMPLOYEES
George Weston Ltd.	142,001
Magna International Inc.	75,900
Nortel Networks Corp.	75,000
Hudson's Bay Company	70,678
Bell Canada Enterprises	66,266
Royal Bank of Canada	59,549
Brascan Corporation	50,000
Alcan Inc.	48,000
Canadian Pacific Railway	45,521
Canadian Tire Corporation	45,521

SOURCE: Canadian Business Directory (Version 2) [CD-Rom]. (Mississauga, ON: InfoCanada, 2005).

private corporation

A corporation that does not trade publicly; therefore, the shares are not available to the general public.

markets (e.g., Toronto Stock Exchange) or in the over-the-counter markets (e.g., NASDAQ—see Chapter 17). A **private corporation** does not trade publicly and is not listed in the markets. The shares are not available to the general public. Most corporations begin as a private corporation but, if they choose, may become public corporations as a means of raising extra money. Just as private corporations can become public corporations, public corporations can become private.

The Incorporation Process

Setting up a corporation is more complex than starting a sole proprietorship or partnership. If the business activity is primarily in only one province, it is necessary to incorporate only as a provincial company under that province's Companies Act (or other similarly named act). A corporation can also be set up under the Canada Business Corporations Act if it is to operate in more than one province or across Canada. Either route of incorporation requires more steps than setting up a sole proprietorship or partnership.

Incorporating a company involves five main steps:

1. selecting the company's name (including searching existing company names, to confirm that you can use the name);

2. writing the articles of incorporation (see below) and filing them with the appropriate government office;

3. paying the required fees and taxes;

4. holding an organizational meeting; and

5. adopting bylaws, electing directors, and passing the first operating resolutions.

The province or federal government issues the corporate charter based on the information in the articles of incorporation. Once the corporation has its charter, it holds an organizational meeting to adopt bylaws, elect directors, and pass initial operating resolutions. Bylaws provide the legal and managerial guidelines for operating the firm.

To distinguish a corporation from other forms of ownership, corporations must use Limited (Ltd./Ltée), Incorporated (Inc.), or Corporation (Corp.) at the end of the company name. This tells the customers, suppliers, and other stakeholders that the owners have limited liability for the corporate obligations.

Articles of Incorporation

Articles of incorporation are prepared on a form authorized or supplied by the province or the federal government, if the corporation incorporated federally. Although they may vary slightly from province to province, all articles of incorporation include the following key items:

- the name of the corporation;
- the province in which the registered office is to be situated;
- the classes and any maximum number of shares that the corporation is authorized to issue;
- if the issue, transfer, or ownership of shares is to be restricted, a statement that clearly sets out the restrictions;
- the number of directors, or the minimum and maximum number of directors; and
- any restriction on the business in which the corporation may engage.

The Corporate Structure

As Exhibit 5.3 shows, corporations have their own organizational structure, with three important components: shareholders, directors, and officers.

Shareholders, or stockholders, are the owners of a corporation, holding shares of stock that provide them with certain rights. They may receive a portion of the corporation's profits in the form of dividends, and they can sell or transfer their ownership, their shares of stock in the corporation, at any time. Shareholders can attend annual meetings, elect the board of directors, and vote on matters that affect the corporation, in accordance with its charter and bylaws. Each share of stock generally carries one vote.

It is possible for one person to own all the shares of a corporation. In some cases, when a private corporations first "goes public," it will issue various classes of stock to be able to retain control (the original owners), on the one hand, and attract capital (new investors), on the other, such as Canadian Tire and Magna International Inc. Also, some corporations issue multiple voting shares (more than one vote per share), such as Four Seasons Hotels Inc., to retain control.

The shareholders elect a **board of directors** to govern and handle the overall management of the corporation. The board of directors is responsible for ensuring that the business is managed with the corporation's best interest in mind. The directors set major corporate goals and policies, hire corporate officers, and oversee the firm's operations and finances.

The boards of large corporations typically include both corporate executives (inside directors) and outside directors (not employed by the organization) chosen for their professional and personal expertise. Outside directors often bring fresh viewpoints to the corporation's activities, because they are independent of the firm. See "Making Ethical Choices" (page 147) for an inside look at some of the decisions corporate boards make.

Hired by the board, the *officers* of a corporation are its top management and include the president and chief executive officer (CEO), vice presidents, the treasurer, and the secretary, who are responsible for achieving corporate goals and policies. Besides the CEO, other common titles of officers of a corporation include chief financial officer (CFO), chief information officer (CIO), and chief operating officer (COO). Officers may also be board members (inside directors) and/or shareholders.

shareholders

The owners of a corporation who hold shares of stock that provide certain rights; also known as shareholders.

board of directors

A group of people elected by the shareholders to handle the overall management of a corporation, such as setting major corporate goals and policies, hiring corporate officers, and overseeing the firm's operations and finances.

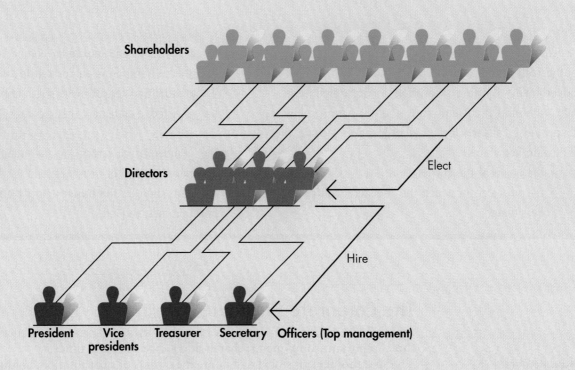

Shareholders

Directors

Elect

Hire

President | Vice presidents | Treasurer | Secretary | Officers (Top management)

Advantages of Corporations

The corporate structure allows companies to merge financial and human resources into enterprises with great potential for growth and profits:

- *Limited liability.* A key advantage of corporations is that they are separate legal entities that exist apart from their owners. An owner's (shareholder's) liability for the debts of the firm is limited to the amount of the stock he or she owns. If the corporation goes bankrupt, creditors can look only to the assets of the corporation for payment. The main exception is when a shareholder personally guarantees a business obligation (most common in corporations with one or only a few owners).

- *Ease of transferring ownership.* Shareholders of public corporations can sell their shares at any time without affecting the status of the corporation.

- *Unlimited life.* The life of a corporation is unlimited. Because the corporation is an entity separate from its owners, the death or withdrawal of an owner does not affect its existence, unlike a sole proprietorship or partnership.

- *Ability to attract financing.* Corporations can raise money by selling new shares of stock. Dividing ownership into smaller units makes it affordable to more investors, who can purchase one or several thousand shares. The large size and stability of corporations also helps them get bank financing. All of these financial resources allow corporations to invest in facilities and human resources, and to expand beyond the scope of sole proprietorships and partnerships. It would be impossible for a sole proprietorship or partnership to make automobiles, provide nationwide telecommunications, or build oil or chemical refineries.

- *Ability to attract potential employees.* Corporations often offer better benefit plans and opportunities, which allows them to attract more potential employees. Larger companies also have the advantage of professional management opportunities (e.g., accounting managers).

Disadvantages of Corporations

Although corporations offer companies many benefits, they have some disadvantages:

- *Double taxation of profits.* Corporations must pay federal and provincial income taxes on their profits. The after-tax profit may then be distributed to the shareholders (dividends), and then the shareholders are taxed on the dividends as investment income.
- *Cost and complexity of formation.* As outlined earlier, forming a corporation involves several steps, and costs can run into thousands of dollars, including filing, registration, and licensing fees, as well as the cost of attorneys and accountants.
- *More government restrictions.* Unlike sole proprietorships and partnerships, corporations are subject to many regulations and reporting requirements.
- Business losses cannot be written off against the other income of the owners (shareholders) of the company.

HOT Links

Find out more about corporations and shareholder rights by searching for "corporations Canada" at http://strategis.gc.ca/engdoc/main.html.

Making Ethical Choices

THE BOARD GAME

After completing your secondary education, you have found your place in the world of business. Everything clicks. You have a knack for seeing the big picture. You excel when working in multifaceted business environments—the more complex, the better. Companies value your fresh approach to structuring businesses for maximum productivity and profitability. Your adeptness has come to the attention of quite a few CEOs from a myriad of companies. In fact, you are one of the youngest people invited to serve on corporate boards of directors.

Wanting to focus most on your career, you accepted a seat on only one board—a young high-technology company, i2T, which has been losing money steadily. You're concerned that decisions about compensation for top executives that come before the board might further erode profitability and shareholder confidence. As a voting member, you must decide whether to approve

awarding a severance package, including a $500,000 consulting fee and a BMW Z-8, to Greg Brady, who was removed as CEO after a year of heavy losses. In addition to your concerns about the company's financial picture and shareholder loyalty, you wonder how your reputation as a young member of the board might be affected if you vote in favour of the award. Many fear boards will continue to play games. How will you play?

ETHICAL DILEMMA

With your expertise in structuring for maximum profitability, would you vote in favour of the severance package and the huge bonus in the face of the company's dismal financial condition?

SOURCES: "Corporate Power, Influence, Money and Interlocking Boards of Directors Page," http://www.verdant.net/corp.htm (accessed February 18, 2003); and Arlene Weintraub and Ronald J. Grover, "Look Who's Still at the Trough," *Business Week*, September 9, 2002, 58.

The One-Person Corporation

one-person corporation

A corporation with only one person as the shareholder; common in professional practices (e.g., medical doctors, accountants, or lawyers) and in trades (e.g., plumbers and electricians).

The **one-person corporation** offers certain personal liability protection to owners of a business. This is common in professional practices such as those of doctors, accountants, and lawyers and in the trades such as plumbers and electricians. Usually the personal assets of the shareholder are not at risk, except when the shareholder has personally guaranteed a business debt (this is quite common in small businesses, because the corporation does not have adequate financing or collateral) or there is professional malpractice. It is important that the corporation have adequate business insurance to protect the company from overwhelming legal liabilities.

A one-person corporation might qualify for small-business tax rates, and the owner might be able to secure a dividend tax credit, which can result in lower corporate and personal taxes than in a sole proprietorship or partnership.

Exhibit 5.4 summarizes the advantages and disadvantages of each form of business ownership.

| Exhibit 5.4 | Advantages and Disadvantages of Major Types of Business Organization |

SOLE PROPRIETORSHIP	PARTNERSHIP	CORPORATION
ADVANTAGES		
Owner receives all profits	More expertise and managerial skill available	Limited liability protects owners from losing more than they invest
Low organizational costs	Relatively low organizational costs	Can achieve large size due to marketability of stock (ownership)
Income taxed as personal income of proprietor	Income taxed as personal income of partners	Ownership is readily transferable
Independence	Fund-raising ability is enhanced by more owners	Long life of firm (not affected by death of owners)
Secrecy		Can attract employees with specialized skills
Ease of dissolution		Greater access to financial resources allows growth
DISADVANTAGES		
Owner receives all losses	Owners have unlimited liability; may have to cover debts of other, less financially sound partners	Double taxation because both corporate profits and dividends paid to owners are taxed although the dividends are taxed at a reduced rate
Owner has unlimited liability; total wealth can be taken to satisfy business debts	Dissolves or must reorganize when partner dies	More expensive and complex to form
Limited fund-raising ability can inhibit growth	Difficult to liquidate or terminate	Subject to more government regulation
Proprietor may have limited skills and management expertise	Potential for conflicts between partners	Financial reporting requirements make operations public
Few long-range opportunities and benefits for employees	Difficult to achieve large-scale operations	
Lacks continuity when owner dies		

Exhibit 5.5 | Some of the Top Crown Corporations Based on Revenues

CROWN CORPORATION	REVENUES (IN THOUSANDS OF DOLLARS)
Bank of Canada, The	1,971,500
British Columbia Lottery Corporation	1,889,637
Manitoba Hydro-Electric Board, The	1,869,000
Export Development Canada	1,365,000
New Brunswick Power Holding Corporation	1,255,000
Saskatchewan Power Corporation	1,217,000
Canadian Commercial Corporation	1,121,831
Canada Mortgage and Housing Corporation	1,069,000
Société de l'assurance automobile du Québec	1,011,121
Saskatchewan Telecommunications Holding Corporation	899,390

concept check

What is a corporation? Describe how corporations are formed and structured.

Summarize the advantages and disadvantages of corporations. Which features contribute to the dominance of corporations in the business world?

A Special Type of Corporation: The Crown Corporation

Crown corporations
Companies that only the provincial and federal governments can set up.

Corporations that are owned by either a provincial or the federal government are called **Crown corporations.** Some of the more recognizable Crown corporations are Canada Post Corporation, the Canadian Broadcasting Corporation (CBC), the Bank of Canada, and the National Museum of Science and Technology. Exhibit 5.5 lists some of the top Crown corporations based on revenues.

SPECIALIZED FORMS OF BUSINESS ORGANIZATION

4 learning goal

In addition to the three main forms, several specialized types of business organization play an important role in our economy. We will look at cooperatives and joint ventures in this section and take a detailed look at franchising in the following section.

Cooperatives

cooperatives
A legal entity typically formed by people with similar interests, such as suppliers or customers, to reduce costs and gain economic power. A cooperative has limited liability, an unlimited life span, an elected board of directors, and an administrative staff; all profits are distributed to the member-owners in proportion to their contributions.

Cooperatives in Canada are a vital component in our economy; there are more than 10,000 cooperatives in Canada, providing goods and services to over 10 million Canadians.[5] Cooperatives are typically formed by people with similar interests, such as customers or suppliers, to reduce costs and gain economic power and are owned by the members who use the services. They exist in almost every sector of the economy and provide goods and services such as business services, childcare, financial services, food, health care, marketing of agricultural and other products, utilities, and housing.

Cooperatives differ from other business in three distinct areas:

1. *Purpose.* The primary focus is to meet the common needs of their members, whereas the primary purpose of investor-owned businesses is to maximize the value of the company.

HOT Links

For more information about cooperatives in Canada, visit the Canadian Co-operative Association's Web site (http://www.coopscanada.coop/). For an alternative source, see http://www.coopcouncil.mb.ca/links.html for the Manitoba Co-operative Association.

2. *Control structure.* Unlike most businesses, with shares that typically give one vote for each share, cooperatives use the one member–one vote system to ensure that people, not capital, control the organization.

3. *Allocation of profit.* This is based on the extent to which members use the cooperative, not the number of shares held.[6]

A cooperative is a legal entity with several corporate features, such as limited liability for the membership, unlimited life span, an elected board of directors, and an administrative staff. Cooperatives distribute all profits to the members in proportion to their contributions. The Calgary Co-operative Association Limited, Credit Union of Central New Brunswick, Ontario Co-operative Association (OnCoop), and Mountain Equipment Co-op are just a few of the cooperatives in Canada.

Joint Ventures

joint venture

Two or more companies that form an alliance to pursue a particular project for a specified time period.

In a **joint venture**, two or more companies form an alliance to pursue a particular project, usually for a specified time period. There are many reasons for joint ventures. The project might be too large for one company to handle on its own, and by forming joint ventures, companies can gain access to new markets, products, or technology. Both large and small companies can benefit from this type of endeavour.

For example, Syncrude Canada Ltd. is a joint venture of oil-producing companies, including Nexen Inc., Imperial Oil Resources, and Petro-Canada. By creating the joint venture, infrastructure costs, production costs, and risks were

Mountain Equipment Co-op provides a wide range of high quality clothing and equipment for their members. Members can shop at one of the 11 stores across Canada, by mail order or online.

COURTESY MOUNTAIN EQUIPMENT CO-OP

Exhibit 5.6 | Ownership of Syncrude Canada Ltd.

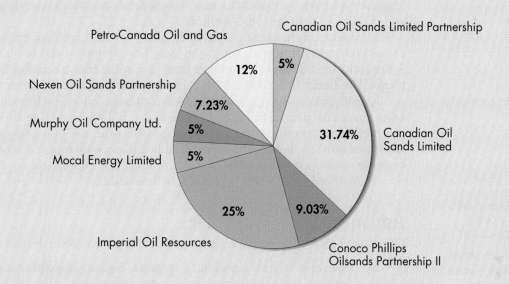

Petro-Canada Oil and Gas

Canadian Oil Sands Limited Partnership 5%

12%

Nexen Oil Sands Partnership 7.23%

Murphy Oil Company Ltd. 5%

Mocal Energy Limited 5%

Canadian Oil Sands Limited 31.74%

Imperial Oil Resources 25%

Conoco Phillips Oilsands Partnership II 9.03%

SOURCE: "Who We Are," ww.syncrude.com/who_we_are/01_01.html. Reprinted with permission.

spread out among the owners. Syncrude is in the midst of a large expansion program called Syncrude 21, which is designed to more than double production after 2015 to reach about 500,000 barrels per day of premium quality, light, sweet oil.[7] Exhibit 5.6 shows the ownership percentages of Syncrude Canada Ltd.

concept check

What is a cooperative, and what are the advantages to the membership?

How do cooperatives differ from other forms of ownership?

What are the benefits of joint ventures?

FRANCHISING: A POPULAR TREND

5 learning goal

Franchises come in all sizes, including McDonald's, the world's largest food service retailer, with 30,000 restaurants in 121 countries (70 percent of which are owned and operated by franchisees). Chances are you deal with one of the more than 2,100 franchise systems in Canada and the United States almost every day. When you have lunch at Tim Hortons or Pizza Pizza, use the services of a UPS store, take your car for servicing at AAMCO, buy candles at Buck or Two, or rent a car from Budget Rent A Car, in each case you are dealing with a franchised business. These and other familiar name brands have come to mean quality, consistency, and value to customers.

franchising

A form of business organization based on a business arrangement between a *franchisor*, which supplies the product concept, and the *franchisee*, which sells the goods or services of the franchisor in a certain geographic area.

franchisor

In a franchising arrangement, the company that supplies the product concept to the *franchisee*.

franchisee

In a franchising arrangement, the individual or company that sells the goods or services of the franchisor in a certain geographic area.

franchise agreement

A contract setting out the terms of a franchising arrangement, including the rules for running the franchise, the services provided by the franchisor, and the financial terms. Under the contract, the franchisee is allowed to use the franchisor's business name, trademark, and logo.

Providing a way to own a business without starting it from scratch, franchising is one of the fastest-growing segments of the economy. **Franchising** is a form of business organization that involves a business arrangement between a **franchisor,** the company supplying the product concept, and the **franchisee,** the individual or company selling those goods or services in a certain geographic area. The franchisee buys a package that includes a proven product, proven operating methods, and training in managing the business.

A **franchise agreement** is a contract allowing the franchisee to use the franchisor's business name, trademark, and logo. The agreement also outlines the rules for running the franchise, the services provided by the franchisor, and the financial terms. The franchisee agrees to keep inventory at certain levels, buy a standard equipment package, keep up sales and service levels, follow the franchisor's operating rules, take part in franchisor promotions, and maintain a relationship with the franchisor. In return, the franchisor provides the use of a proven company name and symbols, help finding a site, building plans, guidance and training, management assistance, managerial and accounting procedures, employee training, wholesale prices for supplies, and financial assistance.

Advantages of Franchises

Like other forms of business organization, franchising offers some distinct advantages:

- *Increased ability for the franchisor to expand.* Because franchisees finance their own units, franchisors can grow without making a major investment. Although franchisors give up a share of profits to their franchisees, they receive ongoing revenues in the form of royalty payments.

- *Recognized name, product, and operating concept.* The franchisee gets a widely known and accepted business with a proven track record, as well as operating procedures, standard goods and services, and national advertising. Consumers know they can depend on products from franchises such as Pizza Hut, Hertz, and Holiday Inn. As a result, the franchisee's risk is reduced and the opportunity for success increased.

- *Management training and assistance.* The franchisor provides a structured training program that gives new franchisees a crash course in how to start and operate their business. Ongoing training programs for managers and employees are another plus. In addition, franchisees have a peer group for support and sharing ideas.

- *Financial assistance.* Being linked to a nationally known company can help a franchisee obtain funds from a lender. The franchisor typically also gives the franchisee advice on financial management, referrals to lenders, and help in preparing loan applications. Many franchisors offer payment plans, short-term credit for buying supplies from the franchise company, and loans to purchase real estate and equipment.

Disadvantages of Franchises

Franchising also has some disadvantages:

- *Loss of control.* The franchisor has to give up some control over operations and has less control over its franchisees than over company employees.

- *Cost of franchising.* Franchising can be a costly form of business. Costs will vary depending on the type of business and might include expensive facilities and equipment. The franchisee also pays fees and/or royalties, which are usually tied to a percentage of sales. Fees for national and local advertising and management advice might also add to a franchisee's ongoing costs.

Franchises offer a recognized name, product, and operating concept, and, in many cases, management training and financial assistance.

COURTESY OF INDU GHUMAN

- *Restricted operating freedom.* The franchisee agrees to conform to the franchisor's operating rules and facilities design, as well as inventory and supply standards. Some franchises require franchisees to purchase from only the franchisor or approved suppliers. The franchisor may restrict the franchisee's territory or site, which could limit growth. Failure to conform to franchisor policies could mean the loss of the franchise.

Franchise Growth

HOT *Links*

Considering buying a franchise? Check out the opportunities and costs at http://canada. franchiseopportunities.com/.

Many of today's major names in franchising, such as McDonald's and Kentucky Fried Chicken, started in the 1950s, but franchising grew rapidly through the 1960s and 1970s, with more types of businesses—clothing, convenience stores, business services, and many others—using franchising to distribute their goods and services. Business owners found franchising a way to expand operations quickly into new geographic areas with limited capital investment, and many are turning to technology to expand their businesses. Exhibit 5.7 shows some of the franchises with a presence in Canada.

International Franchising

Like other forms of business, franchising is part of the global marketplace. As mentioned in Chapter 2, globalization and the elimination of trade barriers have permitted many different types of businesses to operate outside their borders. This is also true for franchise companies; most franchise systems either operate units internationally already or plan to expand overseas as the demand for all types of goods and services grows. "Our research has shown us that this is an ideal time to move into the Korean market," says Doug Dwyer, president of Worldwide Refinishing Systems, a bath and kitchen remodelling franchise. "Because the average living standard now is fairly high in Korea, people not only desire but also can afford a better living environment that refinishing and restoring can provide."[8]

Restaurants, hotels, business services, educational products, car rentals, and non-food retail stores are currently among the most popular types of international franchises. Franchisors in foreign countries face many of the same problems as other firms doing business abroad. In addition to tracking markets and currency changes, franchisors must understand local culture, language differences, and the political environment.

Franchisors in foreign countries also face the challenge of aligning their business operations with the goals of their franchisees, who might be located half a globe away.

concept check

Describe franchising and the main parties to the transaction.

Summarize the major advantages and disadvantages of franchising.

Why has franchising proved so popular?

MERGERS AND ACQUISITIONS

6 *learning goal*

merger

The combination of two or more firms to form a new company, which often takes on a new corporate identity.

acquisition

The purchase of a corporation by another corporation or by an investor group; the identity of the acquired company might be lost.

friendly takeover

A takeover that is supported by the management and board of directors of the targeted company.

A **merger** occurs when two or more firms combine to form one new company, which often takes on a new corporate identity. In an **acquisition,** a corporation or an investor group buys a corporation, and the identity of the acquired company might be lost. (A company can also acquire divisions or subsidiaries of another firm.) Normally, an acquiring company finds a target company and, after analyzing the target carefully, negotiates with its management or shareholders.

When there is a takeover that is supported by the target company's management and board of directors, it is called a **friendly takeover.** On the other hand, if the takeover goes against the wishes of the target company's management and board of directors, it is called a **hostile takeover.** Hostile takeovers are usually accomplished by the acquiring company's buying controlling interest in the targeted company.

The interest of the companies to merge is not the only consideration, however. Some mergers require the approval of the Competition Bureau, which administers and enforces the Competition Act. This is intended to protect not only the general public but also the industry.

Merger Motives

Although the headlines tend to focus on mega-mergers, "merger mania" affects small companies as well. The motives for undertaking mergers and acquisitions are similar regardless of size. Often the goal is strategic: improving the overall performance of the merged firms through cost savings, elimination of overlapping operations, improved purchasing power, increased market share, or reduced competition. Growth, widening of product lines, and the ability to acquire technology or management skill quickly are other motives. Acquiring a company is often faster, less risky, and less costly than developing products internally or expanding internationally.

Another motive for acquisitions is financial restructuring—cutting costs, selling off units, laying off employees, or refinancing—to increase the value of the company to its shareholders. Financially motivated mergers are based not on the potential to achieve economies of scale but, rather, on the acquirer's belief that the target has hidden value that can be unlocked through restructuring. Most financially motivated mergers involve larger companies.

Types of Mergers

The three main types of mergers are horizontal, vertical, and conglomerate. In a **horizontal merger,** companies at the same stage in the same industry merge to reduce costs, expand product offerings, or reduce competition. Many of the large mergers in the late 1990s were horizontal mergers to achieve economies of scale.

In a **vertical merger,** a company buys a firm that is in the same industry but is involved in an earlier or later stage of the production or sales process. Buying a supplier, a distribution company, or a customer gives the acquiring firm more control.

A **conglomerate merger** brings together companies in unrelated businesses to reduce risk. Combining with a company whose products have a different seasonal pattern or that responds differently to the business cycle can result in a more stable sales pattern.

A specialized financially motivated type of merger, the **leveraged buyout (LBO),** became popular in the 1980s but is less common today. LBOs are corporate takeovers financed by large amounts of borrowed money—as much as 90 percent of the purchase price. LBOs can be started by outside investors or the corporation's own management.

Believing that the company is worth more than the value of all the stock, the investors buy the stock and expect to generate cash flow by improving operating efficiency or by selling off some units for cash that can be used to pay the debt. Although some LBOs did improve efficiency, many did not live up to investor expectations or generate enough cash to pay the debt.

concept check

Differentiate between a merger and an acquisition.

What are the most common motives for corporate mergers and acquisitions?

Describe the different types of corporate mergers.

Trends in Business Ownership

7 *learning goal*

As we learned earlier, an awareness of trends in the business environment is critical to business success. Many social, demographic, and technology trends affect how businesses organize. When reviewing options for organizing a business or choosing a career path, consider the following trends in franchising and mergers and acquisitions.

FRANCHISING: CHANGING DEMOGRAPHICS

Although women have been involved in franchising for years, they were usually unseen powers behind the scenes, running the store while their husbands did the business deals. Now franchisors want access to markets they hadn't considered and believe that women can get them there. By making more financing and loan programs available to women, franchisors are creating opportunities for them to become franchisees in their own right. Many of the leading franchisors, such as 7-Eleven, KFC, and Thrifty Car Rental, offer special programs to help women get into the franchise business.

What has prompted this turnaround? Some franchisors made recruiting women a front-burner issue in response to pressure from various groups. One study shows that 22.5 percent of franchisors offer women direct financial assistance, and an additional 50 percent offer indirect help. Industry insiders see this as proof that women are an increasingly valued resource for franchisors—and they are doing what is necessary to get women into their business and keep them there.[9]

FRANCHISE INNOVATIONS

As more franchise systems crowd into growing industry categories, established franchises must find ways to differentiate themselves, such as the following:

- *Multiple-concept franchises.* When franchisors can take the competency they have developed and bridge it over to another franchise (i.e., the skills are transferable), these multi-concept franchises improve efficiencies and save money. For example, combination franchise Molly Maid and Mr. Handyman benefit from shared marketing and promotion, hoping to appeal to a similar customer.[10]

- *Expanded product offerings.* When a company can offer its customers multiple products and services, the customers can enjoy reduced costs and one-stop shopping. An example is a business that will deliver and pick up the dry cleaning, go shopping for gifts and essentials, and so on.

Franchisees enjoy economies of scale and improved efficiency with the multiple-concept franchise by applying expertise learned in one type of franchising to other similar outlets.

© PAUL A. SOUDERS / CORBIS

- *Cross-branding.* Operating two or more franchises in one location generates more customer traffic and maximizes space, personnel, and management utilization. For instance, gas stations frequently offer fast food outlets.
- *New ideas.* Finding new and innovative products and services that can be offered by a franchise helps to expand its target market and provide better service to its customers. For example, a residential cleaning company might offer house and pet-sitting services to it clients when they travel.

MERGERS: EMERGING TRUTHS

Size is definitely an advantage when competing in the global marketplace, but bigger does not always mean better. In a recent cover story, *Business Week* published results of an exclusive new study showing that 17 out of 20 heady mega-merger "winners" were, in fact, a bust for investors who owned their shares. Analysis showed that a full 61 percent of buyers destroyed their own shareholders' wealth. So the merger landscape is changing, with companies considering other options before stuffing their dollars in the biggest merger slot machine they can find.

Why were shareholders hung out to dry in the flood of mergers? In their eagerness to snare a deal, many buyers paid a premium that wiped out the merger's entire potential economic gain. Often managers envisioned grand synergies that proved illusory or unworkable, or bought a pig in a poke—not fully understanding what they were getting. They also underestimated the costs and logistical nightmare of consolidating the operations of merged companies with very different cultures, and failed to keep key employees aboard, sales forces selling, and customers happy.

Companies will continue to seek out acquisition candidates, but the fundamental business case for merging will have to be strong. What should companies look for to identify mergers with a better-than-even chance of turning out well?

- The purchase price should be low enough—a 10 percent premium over the market price as opposed to 50 percent—that the buyer doesn't need heroic synergies to make the deal work.
- The target should be significantly smaller than the buyer—and in a business the buyer understands well. The more "transformational" the deal, such as entering a new business arena, the bigger the risk.
- The buyer should pay in cash and not in over-inflated stock. "Using stock to fund acquisitions has the same effect as using chips in a casino," says Lawrence Cunningham, author of *Outsmarting the Smart Money.* "It's the first emotional step to separating people from their money."
- There should be evidence that the deal isn't purely the brainchild of an egocentric CEO. Mergers are tough—culturally, commercially, and logistically. The most important quality a company can bring to a merger might be humility.[11]

concept check

What incentives are franchisors offering to women to get them involved in the franchise business?
What caused the failure of recent mega-mergers?

Great Ideas to Use Now

It is important to understand the benefits of the different forms of business organization if you start your own company. Even if you decide to work for someone else, this information will help you match a business entity with your goals.

Suppose you are considering two job offers for a computer-programming position: a two-year-old consulting firm with 10 employees owned by a sole proprietor, or a publicly traded software developer with sales of $500 million. In addition to comparing the specific job responsibilities, consider the following:

- Which company offers better training? Do you prefer the on-the-job training you'll get at the small company, or do you want formal training programs as well?
- Which position offers the chance to work on a variety of assignments?
- What are the opportunities for advancement? Employee benefits?
- What happens if the owner of the young company gets sick or decides to sell the company?
- Which company offers a better working environment for you?

Answering these and similar questions will help you decide which job meets your particular needs.

Is Franchising in Your Future?

If the franchise route to business ownership interests you, begin educating yourself on the franchise process by investigating various franchise opportunities. You should research a franchise company thoroughly before making any financial commitment. Once you've narrowed your choices, you must research the franchisor, including its history, operating style, management, and past or pending litigation, the franchisee's financial obligations, and any restrictions on the sale of units. Interviewing current and past franchisees is another essential step.

Would-be franchisees should check recent issues of small-business magazines such as *Franchise Zone, Entrepreneur, Inc., Business Start Ups,* and *Success,* for

Are You Ready to Be a Franchisee?

What can you to do to prepare when considering the purchase of a franchise? Doing your homework can spell the difference between success and failure, and some early preparation can help lay the groundwork for a successful launch of your franchised business.

Getting to know your banker at an early date should speed the loan process if you plan to finance your purchase with a bank loan. Stop by and introduce yourself. The proper real estate is another critical component for a successful retail/food franchise, so establish a relationship with a commercial real estate broker and begin scouting locations.

Professional guidance while evaluating franchise opportunities can prevent expensive mistakes, so interview advisers to find one that is right for you. Selecting an attorney with franchise experience will speed the review of your franchise agreement. Most franchise systems use computers, so if you are not computer literate, take a class in the basics.

Then ask yourself some searching questions:

- Are you willing to work hard and put in long hours?
- Do you have the necessary financial resources?
- Are you excited about a specific franchise concept?
- Do you have prior business experience?
- Do your expectations and personal goals match the franchisor's?

SOURCES: Michael H. Seid and Kay Marie Ainsley, "Are You Ready to be a Franchisee?" *FranchiseZone,* December 9, 2002, http://www.entrepreneur.com; and Thomas Love, "The Perfect Franchisee," *Nation's Business,* April 1, 1998, http://ask. elibrary.com.

industry trends, ideas on promising franchise opportunities, and advice on how to choose and run a franchise. The International Franchise Association Web site, **http://www.franchise.org,** has links to *Franchise World Magazine* and other useful sites.

Is franchising for you? Assertiveness, desire to be your own boss, willingness to make a substantial time commitment, passion about the franchise concept, optimism, patience, and integrity rank high on franchisors' lists. Prior business experience is also a definite plus, and some franchisors prefer or require experience in their field. The information in Are You Ready to Be a Franchisee? can help you make a realistic self-assessment to increase your chances of success.

Mergers and You

Mergers and acquisitions change the business environment for employees, business owners, and customers. A merger announcement increases stress levels for employees, and you might have to live with uncertainty for many months while the companies work out the details of integrating two operations. You might also lose your job when overlapping departments are combined. According to outplacement firm Challenger, Gray and Christmas, mergers have been responsible for huge job losses in past years.

If you work for an acquiring or target company, what does this mean career-wise? It is important to develop a portfolio of transferable skills, and keep the quality and quantity of your work at the highest possible levels. This increases your chance of finding another job, either at the new company or at a new firm. Even if you keep your job, the corporate culture might change, whether the acquirer is a Canadian company or is based overseas.

Customer Satisfaction and Quality

Most companies allocate substantial dollars to winning new business but rarely spend time or money trying to keep the customers they already have. Understanding the importance of satisfying today's demanding consumer can be a matter of business survival. "The fastest, least expensive way to make more money and grow your business is to become a service leader," says John Tschohl, author of *Achieving Excellence through Customer Service*.[12]

An example of this lesson well learned is an auto repair franchise called Caliber Collision Centers. Feeling frazzled after a car accident? Let a Caliber Collision Center take care of you—and your vehicle. Offering the vehicle owner unprecedented customer service and a lifetime warranty on all work done, Caliber's innovative approach to automobile collision repair provides state-of-the-art repair work from highly skilled technical staff using sophisticated equipment.

According to Caliber's chairman, Matthew Ohrnstein, "Unparalleled customer service, superior collision repair expertise, and solid relationships with insurers are some of the factors contributing to the company's remarkable growth." All Caliber Centers are affiliated with rental car networks, ensuring that customers have a car to drive while theirs is being repaired, and long-established relationships with insurers avoid the wait for an adjustor to inspect a vehicle before work can begin. An informative "preaccident" checklist of dos and don'ts posted on its Web site is just another example of how Caliber's management thinks "outside of the box," going the extra mile to take care of their customers—one car at a time.

SOURCES: Justin Martin and David Birch, "Slump? What Slump?" *FSB (Fortune Small Business)*, December 2002/January 2003, http://ask.elibrary.com; company Web site, http://www.caliber.com (accessed December 30, 2002).

If you own a small business, you might become a target, or your customers might disappear as they are acquired by other companies. Should mergers discourage you from starting your own business? Not at all! Even though size is an advantage in many industries, the worldwide economy still needs small, entrepreneurial firms.

Despite consolidation trends, large corporations still prefer to outsource certain projects to companies with specialized expertise in areas such as design and technology. In addition, many niche markets exist where being small provides benefits, such as personal service and quick, creative solutions to customer problems.

SUMMARY OF LEARNING GOALS

1   What are the advantages and disadvantages of the sole proprietorship form of business organization?

The advantages of sole proprietorships include ease and low cost of formation, the owner's rights to all profits, the owner's control of the business, relative freedom from government regulation, absence of special taxes, and ease of dissolution. Disadvantages include owner's unlimited liability for debts, difficulty in raising capital, limited managerial expertise, difficulty in finding qualified employees, large personal time commitment, unstable business life, and the owner's personal absorption of all losses.

2   What are the advantages of operating as a partnership, and what downside risks should partners consider?

Partnerships can be formed as either general or limited partnerships. In a general partnership, the partners co-own the assets and share the profits. Each partner is individually liable for all debts and contracts of the partnership. The operations of a limited partnership are controlled by one or more general partners with unlimited liability. Limited partners are financial partners whose liability is limited to their investment; they do not participate in the firm's operations. The advantages of partnerships include ease of formation, availability of capital, diversity of managerial skills and expertise, flexibility to respond to changing business conditions, no special taxes, and relative freedom from government control. Disadvantages include unlimited liability for general partners, potential for conflict between partners, sharing of profits, and difficulty exiting or dissolving the partnership.

3   How does the corporate structure provide advantages and disadvantages to a company, and what is a special type of corporation?

A corporation is a legal entity chartered by a province. Its organizational structure includes stockholders who own the corporation, a board of directors elected by the stockholders to govern the firm, and officers who carry out the goals and policies set by the board. Stockholders can sell or transfer their shares at any time, and are entitled to receive profits in the form of dividends. Advantages of corporations include limited liability, ease of transferring ownership, and ability to attract financing. Disadvantages include double taxation of profits at a somewhat reduced rate, the cost and complexity of formation, and government restrictions.

A special type of corporation that is owned by either a provincial or the federal government is called a Crown corporation.

4. Does a venture have other business organization options in addition to sole proprietorships, partnerships, and corporations?

Businesses can also organize as cooperatives, joint ventures, and franchises. Cooperatives are collectively owned by individuals or businesses with similar interests that combine to achieve more economic power. Cooperatives distribute profits to their members. Two types of cooperatives are buyer and seller cooperatives.

A joint venture is an alliance of two or more companies formed to undertake a special project. Joint ventures can be set up in various ways, through partnerships or special-purpose corporations. By sharing management expertise, technology, products, and financial and operational resources, companies can reduce the risk of new enterprises.

A franchise is based on a business arrangement between a *franchisor*, which supplies the product concept, and a *franchisee*, who sells the goods or services of the franchisor in a certain geographic area.

5. What makes franchising an appropriate form of organization for some types of business, and why is it growing in importance?

Franchising is one of the fastest-growing forms of business ownership. It involves an agreement between a franchisor, the supplier of goods or services, and a franchisee, an individual or company that buys the right to sell the franchisor's products in a specific area. With a franchise, the business owner does not have to start from scratch but instead buys a business concept with a proven product and operating methods. The franchisor provides management training and assistance; use of a recognized brand name, product, and operating concept; and financial assistance. Franchises can be costly to start and might restrict operating freedom, because the franchisee must conform to the franchisor's standard procedures. The growth in franchising is attributed to its ability to expand business operations quickly into new geographic areas with limited capital investment.

6. Why are mergers and acquisitions important to a company's overall growth?

In a merger, two companies combine to form one. In an acquisition, one company or investor group buys another. Companies merge for strategic reasons, to improve overall performance of the merged firm through cost savings, elimination of overlapping operations, improved purchasing power, increased market share, or reduced competition. Company growth, broadening product lines, and the ability to acquire new markets, technology, or management skills quickly are other motives. Another motive for merging is financial restructuring—cutting costs, selling off units, laying off employees, and refinancing the company to increase its value to stockholders.

There are three types of mergers. In a horizontal merger, companies at the same stage in the same industry combine to gain economic power, to diversify, or to win a greater market share. A vertical merger involves the acquisition of a firm that serves an earlier or later stage of the production or sales process, such as a supplier or sales outlet. In a conglomerate, unrelated businesses come together to reduce risk through diversification.

7. How will current trends affect the business organizations of the future?

Canadians continue to open new businesses, from sole proprietorships to multi-unit franchise operations. The service sector continues to grow to meet the demand for convenience from working women and two-income families. Good franchise opportunities now exist for women and members of minorities, supported by special financial assistance programs. To remain competitive, established franchisors are offering multiple concepts, new types of outlets, and expanded products and services. Key merger trends include a reduction in the number and size of mergers taking place, and more mergers between companies wishing to consolidate to achieve economies of scale.

EXPERIENTIAL EXERCISES

1. **Learn the laws.** Before starting your own company, you should know the legal requirements in your area. Call the appropriate city or provincial departments, such as licensing, health, and zoning, to find out what licences and permits you need, and any other requirements you must meet. Do the requirements vary depending on the type of company? Are there restrictions on starting a home-based business? Then check the Web for information on how to incorporate.

2. **Study franchise opportunities.** Franchising offers an alternative to starting your own business from scratch. Do you have what it takes to be successful? Start by making a list of your interests and skills, and do a self-assessment using some of the suggestions in the last section of this chapter. Next you need to narrow a field of thousands of different franchise systems. At Franchise Handbook Online (**http://www.franchise1.com**), you'll find articles with checklists to help you thoroughly research a franchise and its industry, as well as a directory of franchise opportunities. Armed with this information, you can develop a questionnaire to evaluate a prospective franchise.

3. Bridget Jones wants to open her own business selling her handmade chocolates over the Internet. Although she has some money saved and could start the business on her own, she is concerned about her lack of bookkeeping and management experience. A friend mentions he knows an experienced businessman seeking involvement with a start-up company. As Bridget's business consultant, prepare recommendations for Bridget regarding an appropriate form of business organization, including outlining the issues she should consider and the risks involved, supported by reasons for your suggestions.

4. You and a partner co-own Swim-Clean, a successful pool supply and cleaning service. Because sales have tapered off, you want to expand your operations to another town 100 kilometres away. Given the high costs of expanding, you decide to sell Swim-Clean franchises. The idea takes off, and soon you have 25 units throughout the region. Your success results in an invitation to speak at a local chamber of commerce luncheon. Prepare a brief presentation describing how you evaluated the benefits and risks of becoming a franchisor, the problems you have encountered, and how you've established good working relationships with your franchisees.

5. Find news of a recent merger using an on-line search or in a business periodical such as *Canadian Business* or *The Globe & Mail Report on Business*. Research the merger using a variety of sources including the company's Web site and news articles. Discover the motives behind the merger, the problems facing the new entity, and the company's progress toward achieving its objectives.

REVIEW QUESTIONS

1. What are some of the considerations when choosing a form of business ownership to ensure that it suits your needs?

2. Why are proprietorships the most popular form of business ownership?

3. What should a partnership agreement include?

4. Considering some of the disadvantages of corporations, why do so many choose to use the corporation form?

5. When are joint ventures a good idea?

6. Why are franchise operations popular? What opportunities does it offer to the franchisor and franchisee?

7. What are the various types of mergers? Give examples of each.

CREATIVE THINKING CASE
New Business Takes Shape

Charlie York was trying to read, but the heavy book kept slipping from her lap. She had a vision of a pyramid-shaped book rest and asked her sister, Carolyn Morton, for help in designing it. The result of their collaboration was The Original Peeramid Bookrest, a pyramid-shaped pillow featuring a tasselled cord "bookmark" attached to its peak. York convinced the manager of the bookstore where she worked to display the pillows, and customers bought them and made helpful suggestions for improving the design.

Once the sisters had a final prototype, they needed contract workers to sew them, and months of searching uncovered Hermell Products in Bloomfield, Connecticut, makers of durable medical equipment and pillows for use in homes and hospitals. Hermell agreed to make the pillows, although "it's a very labour-intensive product and the most elaborate pillow we make," says Connie Galli, national sales manager for Hermell.

The company makes two versions of the Peeramid. One features expensive, upscale fabrics provided by Morton and York for sale to their catalogue, bookstore, and gift store customers, with a simpler version made by Hermell for its customers and catalogue, under licence from the sisters, with a royalty paid on every pillow sold.

The sisters incorporated their business, and attorneys helped them obtain a design patent on the Peeramid in 1997. Plans for an inflatable model for poolside use are on the drawing board, as well as a special marketing initiative aimed at the college market—versions of the Peeramid with logos for their bookstores.

Recently obtained permission from the National Institute for Literacy means that each Peeramid's hangtag is printed with the group's hotline number. "One way to sell more book rests is to encourage more people to read," says York, and the newly established Peeramid Book Club on their Web site suggests ways to get involved in reading to others.

The sisters' parents, both entrepreneurs themselves, urge their daughters to keep going and growing. "We feel like we are in the infancy stage of the business," says York. They are learning as they go. "An aspect of our company that has been a godsend has been using Ifulfill.com to handle orders," adds Carolyn Morton. "Not having to set up shop for retail sales distribution has been a lifesaver for us!" With time and money invested and their design patent firmly in place, the sisters are pushing forward in the hopes that their pillow will become a "must have" for book lovers everywhere.[13]

CRITICAL THINKING QUESTIONS

1. Why did Morton and York choose to incorporate instead of organizing as a partnership?

2. As the designers of their product, Morton and York also need general business experience to manage a growing company effectively. Should they consider bringing in additional working shareholders?

3. What other strategies for growth could they pursue?

VIDEO CASE
Mad Science and Franchising

The Mad Science Group is a successful company operating out of Montreal. The founders, Ariel and Ron Shlien, were interested in science as teenagers, with Ariel purchasing his first laser at the age of 12. By their early teens, Ariel and Ron were doing shows at the local YMCA and at birthday parties for children. From such humble beginnings, a multimillion-dollar enterprise has grown. Today the company has more than 150 franchisees in Canada, the United States, and overseas, and boasts sales in excess of $30 million.

On the franchise side of the business, Mad Science provides support, equipment, and training for their franchisees. In return, the franchisees pay 8 percent of their sales to the company. Franchisees are from a variety of backgrounds, such as air force instructors, clerical workers, and those just wanting a change of pace. The success of the individual franchisees depends on their ability to grow their own business. They must seek out business to become profitable. Birthday parties alone won't do it. The franchise costs approximately $55,000. Performing at two parties every day nets the franchisee only $50,000. Not a great return on your investment. Successful franchisees are the ones who have the drive to excel in a competitive environment. After a three-week training period in Montreal, they are provided with additional support and the necessary equipment to begin their business. The Director of Franchise Support feels that the required support had been lacking in the past and plans to increase the level of support to help franchisees grow their businesses. When the franchises make more money, so does Mad Science. Meanwhile, the head office staff continues to experiment with new and exciting shows and products.

Today, Mad Science has grown beyond all expectations and is found in theme parks in the United States, as well as in all major North American markets.

CRITICAL THINKING QUESTIONS

1. Franchising has benefits for the franchisee and for the franchisor. What are the benefits for the Mad Science franchisees and for the company?

2. Why might someone decide to open his or her own entertainment business rather than buy a franchise?

3. What are the advantages and disadvantages opening your own business instead of buying a franchise?

4. What is the status of this company today?

SOURCE: CBC, *Venture*, "Mad Science," July 28, 2002.

E-COMMERCE CASE
In Bed with an Elephant: Molson Coors and Creemore Springs Brewery

In April 2005, Molson Coors bought Creemore Springs Brewery, much to the dismay of Creemore customers. Creemore had been offering its specialty beer in Ontario since 1987, and it focused on providing a quality product with freshness as its hallmark. The capacity of the microbrewery was 80,000 hectolitres of beer a year, whereas Molson Coors produced 48 million hectolitres annually.

On the surface, does this sound like a recipe for success or disaster? When a large corporation takes over the small guy, often the identity of the acquired company is lost. This did not happen with Creemore, however, and it has been able to take advantage of the benefits of a large corporation; for example, the distribution system, the relationships with suppliers, and the employee benefits package, while remaining virtually autonomous. Good luck or good planning?

Before the deal closed, Creemore ensured that some important points were agreed on. There were to be no changes in the product, marketing strategy, or employees. In addition, the company was to remain a stand-alone venture with a single point of contact with Molson Coors. Adherence to these points has allowed Creemore to continue to produce a quality product in the same way it always has while retaining its own profit and loss calculations, its employees, and even its own e-mail system.

Residents of the small community of Creemore Springs get to keep their jobs, Creemore gets many of the benefits of a large corporation while remaining much the same as it has been for almost 20 years, Molson Coors gets a foot in the super-premium beer category, and consumers gets to keep their beer of choice. A win-win-win-win situation!

CRITICAL THINKING QUESTIONS

1. Why did Molson Coors want Creemore?

2. Check the Molson Coors Web site at **http://www.molsoncoors.com,** and examine the annual report. Notice that Creemore beer is not included in the bar scene photo with Canadian, Carling, and Coors. Why is this?

SOURCE: Adapted from Andy Holloway, "Tale of Two Brews," *Canadian Business,* 79 Issue 12, 2006, pg. 79. Reprinted with permission.

Making the Connection

Entrepreneurship: Starting and Managing Your Own Business

This chapter is an extension of Chapter 5, or put more correctly, this chapter involves the decision that comes before deciding on the form of business ownership—the decision to start the business in the first place. What motivates people to start businesses, and what factors shape the business's success?

Individuals with a desire to start a business, whether they are people who simply want to start a small business of their own or entrepreneurs with a grander vision, need to see the big picture. Every business is affected by its external environment, all those environmental factors have an effect on each other, and they also affect whether the business meets its critical success factors. However, the decisions that these individuals make inside their businesses—whether marketing, finance, operations, or human resource decisions—will also affect and be affected by the environment and, in turn, affect the degree to which the business achieves the critical success factors. This is their business—the whole thing, in all its integrative glory! In fact entrepreneurs and small business owners experience the integrative nature of business more than other business people, because, initially at least, they start off handling all aspects of the business. And because it is so all-consuming to start a new business, these individuals have to make sure that they put balance in

their lives—to work hard but to balance that with taking care of their families and their health. This is a critical lesson for entrepreneurs the integrative nature of business extends beyond the business to you personally as well. It creeps into your life outside of work, and therefore the interconnections need to be viewed on a much broader level. You can't get more integrative than that!

This chapter is full of examples of trends in the external environment affecting entrepreneurs and small-business owners. Just look at why people create their own businesses. For example, in the *economic* environment, we see many corporations restructuring and downsizing their staff requirements, and so employees look to creating their own businesses for greater job security. Many of these same corporations have begun to outsource various things they used to do in-house, thus creating an opportunity for small businesses (often the same people that were downsized!) to pick up the slack.

A trend that is both *social* and economic is the fact that there simply aren't as many advancement opportunities for women and minorities as there should be, despite the advancements made in this area, and so many of these people are looking to create their own opportunities in their own businesses. In fact, as you'll read in the chapter, women and minorities are "starting small businesses at rates far above the general population." This, in turn, has led to many *innovations* in the workplace, such as more flexible scheduling, family-like environments, and more socially responsible business practices—changes favoured by women and, therefore, incorporated into their businesses. Furthermore, advancements in the *technological* environment have given small-business people the ability to compete in areas previously inaccessible to them, giving rise to many new small businesses and entrepreneurial ventures. This trend in technology has, in turn, led to a social change in the demographics of small-business owners and entrepreneurs—they are often younger, as most technologically literate people are from the younger generation, which grew up with this technology.

The external environment also presents numerous ideas for new businesses. Often the competition in the economic environment isn't *meeting customer needs* sufficiently, and entrepreneurs see these holes and fill them. There are many examples of this in the chapter. One such example of this is Mike Pratt of OGIO International. Mike was frustrated with "trying to cram his gym bag into a too-small locker" and came up with a solution in The Original Locker Bag. Originally, however, retailers weren't convinced of the products appeal, but because it met the needs of the customer better than other products, the customer ensured its success through demand and forced the retailers' interest. Google is a similar example. The company's founders were not even looking to start a business; they just wanted to find a more efficient way than was currently available to search the infinite amount of information available on the Web. In another arena, Dave Hunegnaw developed GrooveJob.com to fill the void for teens and college students having difficulty finding part-time work using the existing Web-based job boards.

As we state later in the chapter, "Today's global economy rewards innovative, flexible companies that respond quickly to changes in the business environment." Because our economy today is so global, we have much more competition, and we need to be more concerned with meeting customer needs. Smaller, more entrepreneurial firms tend to be more flexible and innovative (one of our critical success factors, remember); therefore, they can respond more quickly as customer needs change in response to the external environment. But larger businesses can also encourage innovation and creativity by simulating this entrepreneurial environment within the organization through "intrapreneurship."

Thus *marketing* decisions made by small business owners and entrepreneurs tend to be innovative and responsive to customer needs; *human resource* decisions are also innovative and are often made to rectify problems these business owners saw in their previous jobs (remember Christopher Halpin of Manna Catering Services in Chapter 5). But *financing* can be difficult for new businesses. However, with good ideas and well-thought-out business plans that see the whole business in an integrative way, funds can be generated to cover *operations* and growth—just as Google was able to get their first $100,000 from a Sun Microsystems founder before Google Inc. even existed as a corporation. Perhaps the biggest challenge though, is for small business owners and entrepreneurs to handle adequately the first of the management functions—*planning*. As discussed in the chapter, economic factors, financial causes, and lack of experience are the most common reasons for business failure. These causes are interrelated and are often directly related to poor management and inadequate planning. It is critical that early on, the new business owner see the integrative nature of all the parts of the business and plan accordingly.

Chapter 6

Entrepreneurship: Starting and Managing Your Own Business

learning goals

1 Why do people become entrepreneurs, and what are the different types of entrepreneurs?
2 Which characteristics do successful entrepreneurs share?
3 How do small businesses contribute to the Canadian economy?
4 What are the advantages and disadvantages facing owners of small businesses?
5 How does the Business Development Bank of Canada help small businesses?
6 What are the first steps to take if you are starting your own business?
7 Why does managing a small business present special challenges for the owner?
8 What trends are shaping entrepreneurship and small-business ownership?

The Excitement and Challenge of Running Your Own Nightclub

In 1979, Gino Panucci was a student in a public relations program at an Alberta college. Little did he realize how his life would change over the next few years. The college program was going well, but Gino's brother, Dominic, had bought a hotel in a small town in southeastern Alberta and needed help running the business. He invited Gino to join him in the venture. Gino agreed, and thus began his life as an entrepreneur. The hotel had a tavern downstairs, as well as 52 rooms that the brothers had to maintain and rent in order to survive. As Gino says,

> It was a struggle, I was a young guy, we stuck it out through thick and thin. It was a seven-day-a-week job, opening at 11:00 a.m. and closing at one or so. Dealing with a combination of the farm community and the oil patch workers was a challenge but business was good until the economy took a dive in the mid-eighties.

The brothers were among the casualties of the economic downturn and were unable to continue. Gino moved to Calgary and worked as a construction worker while helping his wife, Shelley, open two successful hairdressing salons. Dominic moved to Kelowna, British Columbia, and worked in a liquor store while scouting out another business opportunity. The desire to own their own business never left the brothers, even though the previous experience had drained them physically, mentally, and financially. They saw the hotel years as a learning experience and were anxious to leave the past in the past. They worked well together. As Gino says, "Dominic is the back end and I am the front end," meaning Gino is the people person and Dominic is the numbers guy. The brothers observed the "scene" in Kelowna and saw an opportunity to take over a nightclub from a previous owner. They invested every penny they could lay their hands on to start the business and have never looked back.

Today, Gotcha's is one of the most successful nightclubs in the Okanagan Valley. Dominic has left the partnership, but Gino's brother-in-law, Bob, has joined the business. They have recently bought a second club and are continuing on the road to financial success and having fun doing it. Gino says,

> I will never forget the lessons we learned in the hotel business. One of the most important was to put some balance in your life … you can't work all the time and ignore your family and your health. It's just not worth it. And then economic conditions can just come along and take you down anyway! You gotta have fun![1]

Critical Thinking Questions

As you read this chapter, consider the following questions as they relate to the Panucci brothers:

1. What type of entrepreneur is Gino? What were his motives in starting the nightclub Gotcha's?

2. What personal characteristics contributed to Dominic and Gino's success?

3. What opportunities and challenges did Dominic and Gino face as small-business owners, and how did they overcome them?

Typical of many who catch the entrepreneurial bug, Dom and Gino had a vision and pursued it single-mindedly. They are joined by people from all backgrounds and age groups. Teenagers are starting fashion clothing and high-tech companies. Recent college graduates shun the "jacket and tie" corporate world to head out on their own. Downsized employees and mid-career executives form another large group of small-business owners. Retirees who worked for others all their lives might form the company they always wanted to own.

Companies started by entrepreneurs and small-business owners make significant contributions to the Canadian and global economies. Like Gotcha's, they are hotbeds of innovation, taking leadership roles in technological change and the development of new goods and services. Small business is hard to define, because different agencies and researchers use different criteria. For our purposes, we define small businesses as being independently owned and operated, and not dominant in their market. Small businesses make a major contribution to our economy. For example:

- Small businesses account for more than 99 percent of all employers.

- 75.3% of Canadian businesses employ less than five (5) people, 17.6% employ five to nineteen (5–19), 4.5% employ 20 – 49, and 2.4% employ 50 – 500.

- Only .2% off all Canadian businesses have more than 500 employees.

- Approximately 70 percent of all new jobs in the economy were created by the small-business sector.[2]

You might be one of the thousands of Canadians who are considering joining the ranks of business owners. As you read this chapter, you'll get the information and tools you need to help you decide whether owning your own company is the right career path for you. You'll discover why entrepreneurship continues to be one of the hottest areas of business activity, as well as the characteristics you need to become a successful entrepreneur. Then we'll look at the importance of small businesses in the economy, their advantages and disadvantages, and the role of the Business Development Bank of Canada. After that, we will offer guidelines for starting, managing, and growing a small business. Finally, we will explore the trends that are shaping entrepreneurship and small-business ownership.

HOT Links

Check out the Office of the Small and Medium Enterprises on the Canadian government's Web site at http://www.canada.gc.ca.

ENTREPRENEURSHIP TODAY

1 learning goal

From experiments with cardboard and tape, 20-something Mike Pratt pieced together a company that today has revenues of about $50 million. Frustrated with trying to cram his gym bag into a too-small locker, he went home and built a model of his ideal duffel bag. It fit into standard fitness-club lockers and kept all his supplies easily accessible in its rigid-framed interior. Retailers considered The Original Locker Bag too cumbersome. Customers, however, loved the bag that carried like a duffel bag and worked like a locker. In one weekend, they snapped up the 50 bags that Pratt convinced Foot Locker to take on consignment, and soon Pratt's bags were featured at various stores.

Not content to limit OGIO International's fortunes to one bag, Pratt and his employees "geared up" to produce duffels and backpacks with patented design features. His next breakthrough product was the Rig, a protective golf bag designed to go from airport to course that came to market just as golf's popularity began to rise. A complete line of golf bags followed, made in non-traditional colours and fabrics that appealed to younger players. Today OGIO's creative active gear, with aggressive designs, fabrics, and colors, ranges from motocross and golf bags to school packs.[3]

Canada is blessed with a wealth of entrepreneurs like Pratt. And their ranks continue to swell as up-and-coming entrepreneurs aspire to become the next Bill Gates.

Why has entrepreneurship remained a strong part of the foundation of the Canadian business system for so many years? Today's global economy rewards innovative, flexible companies that respond quickly to changes in the business environment. These companies are started by **entrepreneurs**, people with vision, drive, and creativity who are willing to take the risk of starting and managing a business to make a profit.

entrepreneurs
People with vision, drive, and creativity who are willing to take the risk of starting and managing a business to make a profit or of greatly changing the scope and direction of an existing firm.

Entrepreneur or Small-Business Owner?

The term *entrepreneur* is often used in a broad sense to include most small-business owners. But there is a difference between entrepreneurship and small-business management. Entrepreneurship involves taking a risk, either to create a new business or to change significantly the scope and direction of an existing firm. Entrepreneurs typically are innovators who start companies to pursue their ideas for a new product or service. Like Gotcha's founders, they are visionaries who spot trends.

Although entrepreneurs may be small-business owners, not all small-business owners are entrepreneurs. They are managers or people with technical expertise who started a business or bought an existing business and made a conscious decision to stay small. For example, the proprietor of your local independent bookstore is a small-business owner. Jeff Bezos, founder of Amazon.com, also sells books, but Bezos is an entrepreneur. He developed a new model—a Web-based book retailer— that first revolutionized the bookselling world and then moved on to change retailing in general. The two groups share some of the same characteristics, and we'll see that some of the reasons for becoming an entrepreneur or a small-business owner are very similar. However, entrepreneurs are less likely to accept the status quo and generally take a longer term view than the small-business owner does.

Types of Entrepreneurs

Entrepreneurs fall into several categories: classic entrepreneurs, multipreneurs, and intrapreneurs.

Classic Entrepreneurs Classic entrepreneurs are risk takers who start their own companies based on innovative ideas. Some classic entrepreneurs are *micropreneurs*, who start small and plan to stay small. They often start businesses just for personal satisfaction and the lifestyle. Her passion for food led chemistry and psychology major Katrina Markoff to Paris to study at Le Cordon Bleu cooking school. She then took more classes while travelling in Europe, Asia, Australia, and Hawaii, attending cooking schools along the way. Intrigued by the many cultures and tastes she encountered, she returned home and started Vosges Chocolate, a specialty candy company that makes chocolates in unusual flavours, such as curry, spicy wasabi powder from Japan, sweet dulce de leche from Argentina, and a rare white honey from Hawaii. "People are traveling a lot more and wanting more interesting experiences with food," says Markoff. "I want people to take the time to appreciate what's going on in their mouth. What better way to do that than with curry and wasabi?"[4]

In contrast, *growth-oriented entrepreneurs* want their businesses to grow into major corporations. Most high-tech companies are formed by growth-oriented entrepreneurs. Jeff Bezos recognized that with Internet technology, he could compete with large chains of traditional book retailers. Bezos's goal was to build his company into a high-growth enterprise—and he even chose a name that reflected this strategy: Amazon.com. Once his company succeeded in the book sector, Bezos applied his online retailing model to other product lines, from toys and house and garden items to tools, apparel, and services. In partnership with other retailers, Bezos is well on his way to making Amazon's motto—"Earth's Biggest Selection"—a reality.[5]

Multipreneurs Then there are *multipreneurs*, entrepreneurs who start a series of companies. They thrive on the challenge of building a business and watching it grow. In fact, over half of the chief executives at *Inc.* 500 companies say they would start another company if they sold their current one.

Jim Pattison is the Chairman, Chief Executive Officer, and sole owner of The Jim Pattison Group. The Jim Pattison Group started when Mr. Pattison purchased a General Motors automobile dealership. Today the company has more than 28,000 employees with operations in various industries such as food services, packaging, distribution, manufacturing, communications, and entertainment, among others. The Jim Pattison Group is Canada's third largest privately held company and, according to a survey conducted by *The Financial Post*, is the 48th largest company in Canada.[6]

Intrapreneurs Some entrepreneurs don't own their own companies but apply their creativity, vision, and risk taking within a large corporation. Called **intrapreneurs**, these employees enjoy the freedom to nurture their ideas and develop new products, while their employers provide regular salaries and financial backing. Intrapreneurs have a high degree of autonomy to run their own mini-companies within the larger enterprise. They share many of the same personality traits as classic entrepreneurs but take less personal risk. According to Gifford Pinchot, who coined the term *intrapreneur* in his book of the same name in 1985, 30 percent of large companies, including Intel, IBM, Texas Instruments (a pioneering intrapreneurial company), Eastman Kodak, and Xerox, now provide seed funds that finance in-house entrepreneurial efforts.[7]

Whirlpool Corporation's Chairman and Chief Executive David R. Whitwam believes that encouraging employees to think like entrepreneurs is the route to higher revenues and new product offerings. "This is a stalemated industry," he says. "It's not fun slugging it out every day for incremental gains," but if they don't, Whirlpool will be faced with lower sales growth, margins, and share prices. Whitwam promotes brainstorming by reserving a significant chunk of Whirlpool's capital budget for innovations and provides "innovation consultants" and mentors to help Whirlpool employees bring their products to market. The first company-funded venture is off to a good start. Inspired Chef, in-home cooking classes taught by a branded network of chefs, is now nearing the breakeven mark.[8]

Why Become an Entrepreneur?

As the examples in this chapter show, entrepreneurs are found in all industries and have different motives for starting companies. The most common reason cited by CEOs of the *Inc.* 500, the magazine's annual list of fastest-growing private companies, is the challenge of building a business, followed by the desire to control their own destiny. Other reasons, as Exhibit 6.1 shows, include financial independence and frustration at working for someone else. Two other important basic motives mentioned in other surveys are feeling personal satisfaction with your work and creating the lifestyle that you prefer.

Do entrepreneurs feel that going into business for themselves is worth it? The answer is a resounding yes. In one survey, more than 80 percent said that they would do it over again.

intrapreneurs

Entrepreneurs who apply their creativity, vision, and risk taking within a large corporation rather than starting a company of their own.

Exhibit 6.1 | Reasons Entrepreneurs Start Companies

REASON	PERCENTAGE CITING
Wanted the challenge of building a business	31
Wanted to be my own boss, control my own life	26
Believed it was the best route to financial independence	20
Felt frustrated or unhappy working for someone else	11
Other	12

SOURCE: "Are You Building an *Inc.* 500 Company?" *Inc.* 500, October 15, 2002, http://www.inc.com/inc500.

concept check

Describe several types of entrepreneurs.

What differentiates an entrepreneur from a small-business owner?

What are some major factors that motivate entrepreneurs to start businesses?

CHARACTERISTICS OF SUCCESSFUL ENTREPRENEURS

2 *learning goal*

Do you have what it takes to become an entrepreneur? Being an entrepreneur requires special drive, perseverance, passion, and a spirit of adventure in addition to managerial and technical ability. Having a great concept is not enough. An entrepreneur must also be able to develop and manage the company that implements the idea. In addition, entrepreneurs *are* the company; they cannot leave problems at the office at the end of the day. Entrepreneurs tend to work longer hours and take fewer vacations once they have their own company. They also share other common characteristics, as described in the next section.

Mike Becker has built as very successful business on fun and nostalgia. His first effort was bringing back the bobble-headed doll. Many of his Wacky Wobblers have been retired and are now collector's items. He has vowed to keep his company small and fun loving.

COURTESY OF FUNKO INC.

The Entrepreneurial Personality

Studies of the entrepreneurial personality generally find that entrepreneurs share certain key traits. Most entrepreneurs are...

...*ambitious*. Entrepreneurs have a high need for achievement and are competitive.

...*independent*. They are self-starters who prefer to lead rather than follow. They are also individualists.

...*self-confident*. They understand the challenges of starting a business but are decisive and have faith in their abilities to resolve problems.

...*risk taking*. Though they are not averse to risk, most successful entrepreneurs prefer situations with a moderate degree of risk, where they have a chance to control the outcome, over highly risky ventures that depend on luck.

...*visionary*. Entrepreneurs' ability to spot trends and act on them sets entrepreneurs apart from small-business owners and managers.

...*creative*. To compete with larger firms, entrepreneurs need to have creative product designs, marketing strategies, and solutions to managerial problems.

...*energetic*. Starting a business takes long hours. Some entrepreneurs start companies while still employed full-time.

...*passionate*. Entrepreneurs love their work.

...*committed*. They make personal sacrifices to achieve their goals. Because they are so committed to their companies, entrepreneurs are persistent in seeking solutions to problems.

Most entrepreneurs combine many of these characteristics. Tanya York produced her first film at 19 and started York Entertainment, her film production company, two years later. The ambitious and self-confident York was persistent in her efforts to finance her company and produced seven films in just two years. "I like to always have new challenges in front of me," York says. "As soon as we have something under control and are doing well, I'll move on to setting up a new part of the business and expanding it." The strategy is working: Today she is on *The Hollywood Reporter's* list of 100 most powerful women in entertainment, heading a leading independent film company with 2002 sales of about $20 million USD.[9]

Managerial Ability and Technical Knowledge

A person with all the characteristics of an entrepreneur might still lack the business skills to run a successful business. As we'll discuss later in this chapter, entrepreneurs believe they can learn many of these technical skills.

Entrepreneurs need managerial ability to organize a company, develop operating strategies, obtain financing, and manage day-to-day activities. A survey of *Inc.* 500 executives revealed that they spend 39 percent of their time overseeing operations, 35 percent on marketing and sales, and 18 percent on hiring and managing employees.[10] Good interpersonal and communication skills are also essential in dealing with employees, customers, and other businesspeople, such as bankers, accountants, and attorneys. They also need the technical knowledge to carry out their ideas.

Mike Becker learned how to manage Funko, Inc. (**http://www.funko.com**) by trial and error. He started the company to bring back low-tech, nostalgia-based bobble-headed dolls he called Wacky Wobblers. His first character was Bob's Big

Boy, the restaurant chain mascot. Putting his licensing background to work, he began producing cartoon, movie, and advertising character Wobblers—Mr. Magoo, Betty Boop, Charlie Tuna, Count Chocula, Pink Panther, and Austin Powers, for example. "[After my first order,] I still didn't understand what the heck I was doing," Becker says. "I didn't have any distribution networks, sales reps, employees, or even a place of business." He quickly had to become competent in every phase of the business, even tasks he hated, like accounting and paperwork.[11]

Entrepreneurs soon learn that they can't do it all themselves. Often they choose to focus on what they do best and hire others to do the rest. Becker learned to delegate many of the operational responsibilities so he could be "Chairman of Fun" and handle product creation and licensing.

concept check

Describe the personality traits and other skills characteristic of successful entrepreneurs.

What does it mean when we say that an entrepreneur should work on the business, not in it?

SMALL BUSINESS: DRIVING CANADA'S GROWTH

3 *learning goal*

Corporate greed and fraud have given large corporations a bad name. The downsizings that accompanied the recent economic downturn made many more people look toward smaller companies for employment. As stated earlier, 75 percent of Canadian businesses have fewer than 5 employees, and more than 95 percent of all Canadian businesses have fewer than 50 employees.

What Is a Small Business?

How many small businesses are there in the Canada? There are approximately 2.2 million businesses in Canada. About 1.28 million (58 percent) of those 2.2 million businesses represent self-employed individuals, and about 900,000 (41 percent) employ fewer than 50 employees. Businesses with more than 50 employees make up about 1 percent, or 22,000 businesses.[12]

So what makes a business "small"? As we've seen, there are different interpretations, and the range is extremely broad. Statistics Canada defines a small business as having annual revenues between $30,000 and $5,000,000, whereas others define small business by the number of employees, usually ranging somewhere between fewer than 50 to fewer than 100. In addition, a **small business** is

small business

A business that is independently managed, is owned by an individual or a small group of investors, is based locally, and is not a dominant company in its industry.

- independently managed,
- owned by an individual or a small group of investors,
- based locally (although the market it serves might be widespread), and
- not a dominant company (thus, it has little influence in its industry).

Small businesses in Canada can be found in almost every industry group. Services dominate small businesses, accounting for about 75 percent, with the balance of small businesses (25 percent) producing goods.[13] These firms provide everything from health care to computer consulting and food and lodging. Small businesses are found in all of the various sectors, as suggested below.

- *Services.* Service firms are the most popular category of small businesses, because they are easy and inexpensive to start. They are often small; very few service-oriented companies are national in scope. They include repair services, restaurants, specialized software companies, accountants, travel agencies, management consultants, and temporary help agencies.

- *Wholesale and retail trade.* Retailers sell goods or services directly to the end user. Wholesalers link manufacturers and retailers or industrial buyers; they assemble, store, and distribute products ranging from heavy machinery to produce. Most retailers also qualify as small businesses, whether they operate one store or a small chain.

- *Manufacturing.* This category is dominated by large companies, but many small businesses produce goods. Machine shops, printing firms, clothing manufacturers, beverage bottlers, electronic equipment manufacturers, and furniture makers are often small manufacturers. In some industries, small manufacturing businesses have an advantage, because they can focus on customized products that would not be profitable for larger manufacturers.

- *Construction.* Firms employing fewer than 20 people account for many of Canada's construction companies. They include independent builders of industrial and residential properties and thousands of contractors in such trades as plumbing, electrical, roofing, and painting.

- *Agriculture.* Small businesses dominate agriculture-related industry, including forestry and fisheries.

Exhibit 6.2 shows the employment figures by industry.

HOT Links

See http//www.canadaone.ca for information about starting and growing a business.

Exhibit 6.2 | Employment by Industry Sector

INDUSTRY	PERCENTAGE EMPLOYMENT
Services-producing sector	75.25
Manufacturing	13.7
Construction	6.3
Agriculture	2.1
Forestry, fishing, mining, oil, and gas	1.9
Utilities	.8

SOURCE: Adapted from the Statistics Canada website http://www.40.statcan.ca/101/cst01/econ40.htm, accessed June 13, 2006.

Small Business, Large Impact

4 learning goal

As leading small-business researcher David Birch points out,

> We have a vibrant economy in which there are a lot of risk takers, a lot of triers, a lot of testers, a lot of experimenters. It's very different from what you find in Europe or even Japan. And I think we're blessed because of it.[14]

A poll conducted by Léger Marketing shows that two-thirds (2/3) of Canadians believe that small business is making a very positive contribution to our economy.[15] This is not surprising, when you consider the many reasons why small businesses continue to thrive in Canada:

- *Independence and a better lifestyle.* Large corporations no longer represent job security or offer as many fast-track career opportunities. Mid-career employees leave the corporate world—either voluntarily or as the result of downsizing—in search of new opportunities. Many new college and business school graduates shun the corporate world altogether and start their own companies or look for work in small firms.

Brent Lane, an entrepreneurship student, is the force behind the growth of Golden Lane Honey, which now offers a wide range of products. Brent is assisted by his twin brother and marketing student, Bryce Lane.

COURTESY OF SHIRLEY A. ROSE

- *Personal satisfaction from work.* Many small-business owners cite this as one of the primary reasons for starting their companies. They love what they do.
- *Best route to success.* Small businesses offer their owners the potential for profit. Also, business ownership provides greater advancement opportunities for women and minorities, as we discuss later in this chapter.
- *Rapidly changing technology.* Advances in computer and telecommunications technology, as well as the sharp decrease in the cost of this technology, have given individuals and small companies the power to compete in industries that were formerly closed to them. The arrival of the Internet and World Wide Web is responsible for the formation of many small businesses, as we'll discuss in the trends section later in this chapter.
- *Outsourcing.* As a result of downsizing, corporations often contract with outside firms for services they used to provide in-house. This "outsourcing" creates opportunities for smaller companies, many of which offer specialized goods and services.
- *Major corporate restructurings and downsizings.* These force many employees to look for other jobs or careers. They can also provide the opportunity to buy a business unit that a company no longer wants.

HOT *Links*

Check out the Canadian Federation of Independent Business at http://www.cfib.ca.

Why Stay Small?

Owners of small businesses recognize that being small provides special advantages. Their greater flexibility and less complex company structure allow small businesses to react more quickly to changing market forces. They can develop innovative product ideas and bring them to market more quickly, using fewer financial resources and fewer people, than big corporations can. These more efficient operations keep total costs down. Small companies can serve specialized markets that might not be cost-effective for a large company. Another feature is the opportunity to provide a higher level of personal service. Such attention brings many customers back to businesses like gourmet restaurants, health clubs, fashion boutiques, and travel agencies.

Christopher Halpin, the caterer in the opening vignette in Chapter 5, has decided to keep his business small. Christopher believes that to respond to the dynamic tastes of his customers, he can best serve them by not growing too large.

On the other hand, being small is not always an asset. Many small businesses encounter difficulties in obtaining adequate financing. If the founders have limited managerial skills, they might have problems growing the company. As well, complying with regulations is more expensive for small firms. Those with fewer than 20 employees spend about twice as much per employee compared to larger firms. In addition, starting and managing a small business requires a major commitment by the owner. According to Dun & Bradstreet's 21st Annual Small Business Survey, 37 percent of all entrepreneurs work more than 50 hours a week.[16] Long hours, the need for owners to do much of the work themselves, and the stress of being personally responsible for the success of the business can take a toll.

HOT *Links*

Find out more about small business at http://sbinfocanada .about.com/.

concept check

What are the characteristics of a small business?

Why are small businesses becoming so popular?

Discuss the major advantages and disadvantages of small businesses.

THE BUSINESS DEVELOPMENT BANK OF CANADA

 5 *learning goal*

Business Development Bank of Canada (BDC)

Bank that provides small and medium-sized businesses with flexible financing, affordable consulting services, and venture capital.

Many small business owners turn to the **Business Development Bank of Canada (BDC)** for assistance. The BDC is a financial institution that is wholly owned by the Government of Canada. Its mission is to help people start and manage small businesses, help them win federal contracts, and speak on behalf of small business. Through its national network of local offices, the BDC advises and helps small businesses in the areas of finance and management.

BUSINESS SERVICE CENTRES

HOT *Links*

What does it take to start up a business in your province or territory? Go to http://www.cbsc.org, then click on the provincial or territorial flag at the bottom of the page.

Business service centres (a provincial business service) provide services for start-up and growing small businesses. They typically have both print material and databases that provide not only insight into the industry and the competition but also information on start-up regulations for each city and province. An interactive business planner is also available.

In their start-up stages, small business owners have to be masters of multitasking. Companies like business equipment manufacturer Brother target the high-growth small-business market with multifunction machines that appeal to this group.

6 learning goal

Sixteen-year-old Matt Steichen's idea for a half-Titans, half-Rams jersey launched a new business, Torn Apparel. Since rap star Nelly, shown here on the far right, wore the jersey during the halftime show during Super Bowl XXXIV, Torn Apparel has sold more than 3,000 special combo shirts.

READY, SET, START YOUR OWN BUSINESS

You might have decided that you'd like to go into business for yourself. If so, what's the best way to go about it? You have three options: (a) start from scratch, (b) buy an existing business, or (c) buy a franchise. About 75 percent of business start-ups involve brandnew organizations, with the remaining 25 percent representing purchased companies or franchises. We discussed franchising in Chapter 5. We'll cover the other two options in this section.

Getting Started

The first step in starting your own business is a self-assessment to determine whether you have the personal traits you need to succeed and, if so, what type of business would be best for you. The exercise "Your Career," featured on pages 198 and 199, includes a questionnaire and other information to help you make these decisions. Finding the idea and choosing a form of business organization come next.

Finding the Idea Entrepreneurs get ideas for their businesses from many sources. It is not surprising that about 80 percent of *Inc.* 500 executives got the idea for their company while working in the same or a related industry. Starting a firm in a field where you have experience improves your chances of success. Other sources of inspiration are personal experiences as a consumer; hobbies and personal interests; suggestions from customers, family, and friends; and college courses or other education.

A good way to keep up with small-business trends is by reading entrepreneurship and small-business magazines and visiting their Web sites regularly. With articles on everything from idea generation to selling the business, they provide invaluable resources. For example, each year *Entrepreneur* publishes lists of the

fastest-growing young, private companies. Reading about companies that are only a few years old but now have more than $1 million in sales will inspire you.

Ideas are all around you. Do you have a problem that you need to solve or a product that doesn't work as well as you'd like? Maybe one of your coworkers has a complaint. Raising questions about the way things are done is a great way to generate ideas. Many successful businesses get started because someone identifies needs and then finds a way to fill them.

Many business owners have difficulty filling jobs. On the other hand, many students have problems finding jobs. With Web sites such as monster.ca and canadajobs.com, employers and students (as well as others) can connect.

Choosing a Form of Business Organization   A key decision for a person starting a new business is whether it will be a sole proprietorship, partnership, corporation, or limited liability company. As discussed in Chapter 5, each type of business organization has advantages and disadvantages. The choice depends on the type of business, number of employees, capital requirements, tax considerations, and level of risk involved. Most important, though, is the entrepreneurs' tolerance for liability.

Developing the Business Plan

Once you have the basic concept for a product, you must develop a plan to create the business. This planning process is one of the most important steps in starting a business and helps minimize the risks involved. A good **business plan** can be a critical determinant of whether a firm succeeds or fails. "A business plan lets you 'operate' your business on a dry-run basis without financial outlay or risk," say Douglas and Diana Gray, authors of *The Complete Canadian Small Business Guide*. "Many people do not venture out on their own because they become overwhelmed with the 'what if' syndrome." A comprehensive plan lets you run various "what if" analyses and develop strategies to overcome them—well before the business actually opens.[17]

A good business plan can be a critical determinant of whether a firm succeeds or fails. A range of software is available for downloading from both government and industry sites. Here are some examples:

- Business Development Bank of Canada: **http://www.bdc.ca**
- Canada Business Service Centres: **http://www.cbsc.org**
- Nova Scotia Economic Development: **http://www.gov.ns.ca.econ.ced.busplan**

A well-prepared, comprehensive, written business plan helps business owners take an objective and critical look at their business venture and set goals to help them manage the business and monitor its growth and performance. Writing a good business plan can take many months. Many businesspeople, in their eagerness to begin doing business, neglect planning. They immediately get caught up in day-to-day operations and have little time for planning. But taking the time to develop a good business plan pays off. Writing the plan forces them to analyze their concept carefully and make decisions about marketing, production, staffing, and financing. A venture that seems sound at the idea stage might not look so good after closer analysis. The business plan also serves as the first operating plan for the business.

The key features of a business plan are a general description of the company, the qualifications of the owner(s), a description of the product or service, an analysis of the market (demand, customers, competition), and a financial plan. The sections should work together to demonstrate why the business will be successful, focusing on the uniqueness of the business and why it will attract customers. The Outline for a Business Plan section on the next page provides an outline of what to include in each section of a business plan. It is important that the business plan be thorough and contain no mistakes or omissions.

HOT Links

For tips on how to start, grow, or manage your business, check out Entrepreneur magazine's "Smart Tip of the Day" at http://www.entrepreneurmag.com.

HOT Links

Are you looking for work? Search jobs at http://www.monster.ca or http://www.canadajobs.com.

business plan

A formal written statement that describes in detail the idea for a new business and how it will be carried out. It includes a general description of the company, the qualifications of the owner(s), a description of the product or service, an analysis of the market, and a financial plan.

Outline for a Business Plan

Title page. Provides names, addresses, and phone numbers of the venture and its owners and management personnel; date prepared; copy number; and contact person.

Table of contents. Provides page numbers of the key sections of the business plan.

Executive summary. Provides a one- to three-page overview of the total business plan. Written after the other sections are completed, it highlights their significant points and, ideally, creates enough excitement to motivate the reader to continue reading.

Vision and mission statement. Concisely describes the intended strategy and business philosophy for attaining the vision.

Company overview. Explains the type of company, such as manufacturing, retail, or service; provides background information on the company if it already exists; describes the proposed form of organization—sole proprietorship, partnership, or corporation. This section should be organized as follows: company name and location, company objectives, nature and primary product or service of the business, current status (start-up, buyout, or expansion) and history (if applicable), and legal form of organization.

Product and/or service plan. Describes the product and/or service and points out any unique features; explains why people will buy the product or service. This section should offer the following descriptions: product and/or service; features of the product or service providing a competitive advantage; available legal protection—patents, copyrights, trademarks—and dangers of technical or style obsolescence.

Marketing plan. Shows who the firm's customers will be and what type of competition it will face; outlines the marketing strategy and specifies the firm's competitive edge. This section should offer the following descriptions: analysis of target market and profile of target customer; methods of identifying and attracting customers; selling approach, type of sales force, and distribution channels; types of sales promotions and advertising; and credit and pricing policies.

Management plan. Identifies the key players—active investors, management team, and directors—citing the experience and competence they possess. This section should offer the following descriptions: management team, outside investors, and/or directors and their qualifications, outside resource people and their qualifications, and plans for recruiting and training employees.

Operating plan. Explains the type of manufacturing or operating system to be used; describes the facilities, labour, raw materials, and product processing requirements. This section should offer the following descriptions: operating or manufacturing methods, operating facilities (location, space, and equipment), quality control methods, procedures to control inventory and operations, sources of supply, and purchasing procedures.

Financial plan. Specifies financial needs and contemplated sources of financing; presents projections of revenues, costs, and profits. This section should offer the following descriptions: historical financial statements for the past three to five years or as available; pro forma financial statements for three to five years, including income statements, balance sheets, cash flow statements, and cash budgets (monthly for first year and quarterly for second year); break-even analysis of profits and cash flows; and planned sources of financing.

Appendix of supporting documents. Provides materials supplementary to the plan. This section should offer the following descriptions: management team biographies, any other important data that support the information in the business plan, and the firm's ethics code.

SOURCE: From *Small Business Management: An Entrepreneurial Emphasis*, 11th edition by Longenecker / Moore / Petty. © 2000. Reprinted with permission of South-Western, a division of Thomson Learning: www.thomsonrights.com. Fax 800 730-2215.

HOT Links
See the RBC Royal Bank Web site for a template for a business plan at http://www.royalbank.ca.

HOT Links
To look at a business template go to the BDC's Web site at http://www.bdc.ca and click on "business tools."

The most common use of business plans is to persuade lenders and investors to finance the venture. The detailed information in the business plan helps them decide whether to invest. Even though the business plan might have taken months to write, it must capture the potential investor's interest in only a few minutes. For that reason, you should write the basic business plan with a particular reader in mind. Then you can fine-tune and tailor it to fit the type of investor you plan to approach and his or her investment goals.

Don't think you can set aside your business plan once you obtain financing and begin operating the company! Entrepreneurs who think the business plan is only for raising money make a huge mistake. Business plans should be dynamic documents, reviewed and updated on a regular basis—monthly, quarterly, or annually, depending on how fast the particular industry changes.

Owners should adjust their sales and profit projections up or down as they analyze operating results. Reviewing your plan will help you identify strengths and weaknesses in marketing strategies and management and also help you evaluate possible opportunities for expansion in light of current trends and your original mission.

Many resources can help you prepare your business plan. For example, BDC mentioned earlier offers sample business plan templates and online guidance for business plan preparation.

Financing the Business

Once the business plan is complete, the next step is to get the financing to set up the business. The amount required depends on the type of business and the entrepreneur's planned investment. Businesses started by lifestyle entrepreneurs require less financing than growth-oriented businesses. About half the 2002 *Inc.* 500 companies were started with $20,000 or less, with 14 percent requiring no more than $1,000![18] Of course, manufacturing and high-tech companies generally require a larger initial investment.

The two forms of business financing are **debt**, borrowed funds that must be repaid with interest over a stated time period, and **equity**, funds raised through the sale of shares (i.e., ownership) in the business. Those who provide equity funds get a share of the profits. Lenders usually limit debt financing to no more than a quarter to a third of the firm's total needs. Thus, equity financing usually amounts to about 65 to 75 percent of total start-up financing.

Two sources of equity financing for young companies are angel investors and venture-capital firms. **Angel investors** are individual investors or groups of experienced investors who provide funding for start-up businesses. Angels often get involved with companies at a very early stage. **Venture capital** is financing obtained from investment firms that specialize in financing small, high-growth companies and receive an ownership interest and a voice in management in return for their money. They typically invest at a later stage than angel investors.

Who provides the start-up funding, whether debt or equity, for small companies? More than 85 percent of all business owners contribute personal savings to their new companies. Exhibit 6.3 shows how the founders of the *Inc.* 500 companies financed their start-ups. Where personal assets and money from family and friends were most important for new firms, funding from financial institutions became more important as the companies grew.

debt
A form of business financing consisting of borrowed funds that must be repaid with interest over a stated time period.

equity
A form of business financing consisting of funds raised through the sale of stock (i.e., ownership) in a business.

angel investors
Individual investors or groups of experienced investors who provide funding for start-up businesses.

venture capital
Financing obtained from investment firms that specialize in financing small, high-growth companies and receive an ownership interest and a voice in management in return for their money.

Exhibit 6.3 | Sources of Funding of Start-Ups

SOURCE	PERCENTAGE USING*	
	TO START	TO GROW
Owner's personal assets	87	24
Cofounders' personal assets	28	11
Family members or friends	19	23
Commercial bank loans	14	62
Angel investors (private equity)	8	30
Strategic partners and customers	7	12
Other	5	34

*Multiple responses from survey participants mean that results add up to more than 100 percent

SOURCES: "Are You Building an *Inc*. 500 Company?" *Inc*. 500, October 15, 2002, http://www.inc.com/inc500 ; and "The Numbers Game," *Inc*. 500 (October 21, 1997), 62.

Buying a Small Business

HOT *Links*

Check out the listing of venture capital firms at http://www.cvca.ca.

One route to small-business ownership is buying an existing business. Although this approach is less risky that starting a business from scratch, it still requires careful and thorough analysis. The potential buyer must answer several important questions: Why is the owner selling? Does he or she want to retire or move on to another challenge, or are there some problems with the business? Is the business operating at a profit? If not, can the problems be corrected? On what basis has the owner valued the company, and is it a fair price? What are the owner's plans after selling the company? Depending on the type of business, customers might be more loyal to the owner than to the product or service. They could leave the firm if the current owner decides to open a similar business. To protect against this situation, many purchasers include a "non-compete clause" in the contract of sale.

Many of the same steps for starting a business from scratch apply to buying an existing company. You should prepare a business plan that thoroughly analyzes all aspects of the business. Get answers to all your questions, and determine, via the business plan, that the business is a good one. Then you must negotiate the purchase price and other terms and get financing. This can be a difficult process, and it might require the use of a consultant.

Risky Business

Running your own business might not be as easy as it sounds. Despite the many advantages of being your own boss, the risks are great as well. Many businesses fail each year. Businesses close down for many reasons, the most common being

- economic factors—business downturns and high interest rates;
- financial causes—inadequate capital, low cash balances, and high expenses; and
- lack of experience—inadequate business knowledge, management experience, and/or technical expertise.

Many of the causes of business failure are interrelated. For example, low sales and high expenses are often directly related to poor management.

Inadequate planning is often at the core of business problems. As described earlier, a thorough feasibility analysis, from market assessment to financial plan, is critical to business success. And even with the best plans, business conditions change, and unexpected situations arise. An entrepreneur might start a company based on a terrific new product only to find that a large firm with more marketing and distribution clout introduces a similar item.

The stress of managing a business can take its toll. The business can consume your whole life. Owners can find themselves in over their heads and unable to cope with the pressures of business operations, from the long hours to being the main decision maker.

Even successful businesses might have to deal with many of these difficulties. For example, growing too quickly can cause as many problems as sluggish sales. Growth can strain a company's finances. Additional capital is required to fund the expanded operations, from hiring additional staff to purchasing more equipment. Successful business owners must respond quickly as the business changes and develop plans to manage growth.

concept check

How can potential business owners find new business ideas?

Why is it important to develop a business plan? What should such a plan include?

What financing options do small business owners have?

Summarize the risks of small-business ownership.

MANAGING A SMALL BUSINESS

7 learning goal

Whether you start a business from scratch or buy an existing one, you must be able to keep it going. The main job of the small-business owner is to carry out the business plan through all areas of the business—from personnel to production and maintenance. The small-business owner must be ready to solve problems as they arise and move quickly when market conditions change. Hiring, training, and managing employees are other crucial responsibilities. Clearly, managing a small business is quite a challenge.

Over time, the owner's role will change. As the company grows, others will make many of the day-to-day decisions, while the owner focuses on managing employees and making plans for the firm's long-term success. The owner must always watch performance, evaluate company policies in light of changing conditions, and develop new policies as required. She or he must nurture a continual flow of ideas to keep the business growing. The type of employees needed might also change as the firm grows. For example, a firm might need more managerial talent and technical expertise as it grows larger.

Using Outside Consultants

One way to ease the burden of managing a business is to hire outside consultants. Nearly all small businesses need a good accountant (e.g., CA, CMA, or CGA) who can help with financial record keeping, tax planning, and decision making. An accountant who works closely with the owner to help the business grow is a valuable asset. An attorney who knows about small-business law can provide legal advice and draw up essential documents. Consultants in other areas, such as marketing, employee benefits, and insurance, can be hired as needed. Outside directors with business experience are another source of advice for small companies. Resources like these free the small-business owner to concentrate on planning and day-to-day operations.

Some aspects of the business can be outsourced, or contracted out to specialists in that area. Among the departments that most commonly use outsourcing are information technology, customer service, order fulfillment, payroll, and human resources.

Hiring an outside company—in many cases another small business—can save money, because the purchasing firm buys just the services it needs and has no investment in expensive technology. Management should review any outsourced functions as the business grows. At some point, it might be more cost-effective to bring it in-house.

Hiring and Retaining Employees

Small companies might have to be creative to find the right employees and to convince applicants to join their firm. Coremetrics, a Web analytics company that tracks habits of site visitors, ran into problems when founder Brett Hurt hired the wrong person to fill a major role. "A big company won't go under because of one bad hire, but a start-up might," Hurt explains. "If you are starting your own business and you hire someone and they're not ethical, or their heart isn't in it, or they're not of the same frame of mind as you, it can crush your business."[19]

Making the decision to hire the first employee is also a major one. Most realize it is time to hire the first employee when the business owner can no longer do it alone. The business might be held back because the owner is working a very long work week and the owner just cannot keep up. In deciding when to hire an employee it is important to identify all the costs involved in hiring an employee to make sure the business can afford it. Help-wanted ads, extra space, employer responsibilities (e.g., CPP and EI), and employee benefits—these will easily add up to substantial costs of the salary amount. Having an employee might also mean more work for you at first in terms of training and management. It's a catch-22: To grow you need to hire more people, but making the shift from solo worker to boss can be very stressful.[20]

Attracting good employees can be hard for a small firm, which might not be able to match the higher salaries, better benefits, and advancement potential offered by many larger firms. Once they hire employees, small-business owners must promote employee satisfaction to retain them. Comfortable working conditions, flexible hours, employee benefit programs, opportunities to help make decisions, and a share in profits and ownership are some of the ways to do this. The 10 consultants who work at Analytics Operations Engineering, a Boston company, can choose the projects that appeal to them, as well as when, where, and how much they work. "I judge my employees' value by what they create," says CEO Mitchell Burman. This flexibility has helped Analytics build a loyal and dedicated workforce.[21]

Going Global

More and more small businesses are discovering the benefits of looking beyond Canada for markets. As we learned in Chapter 2, the global marketplace represents a huge opportunity for Canadian businesses, both large and small. Small businesses decide to export because of foreign competition in the Canada, new markets in growing economies, economic conditions in Canada, and the need for increased sales and higher profits. When the value of the Canadian dollar declines against other foreign currencies, Canadian goods become less expensive for overseas buyers, and this creates opportunities for Canadian companies to sell globally. Small businesses choosing to do business abroad might also face issues of social responsibility, as "Making Ethical Choices," on page 186, demonstrates.

Like any major business decision, exporting requires careful planning. Many online resources can help you decipher the complexities of preparing to sell in a foreign country and identify potential markets for your goods and services. Export Development Canada (EDC), helps companies grow their export business. Some services that EDC offers are insurance (including political risk insurance) and financing solutions (e.g., foreign customers can access financing through EDC or their partners). EDC recognizes that access to cash is one of the greatest barriers and has developed solutions that can help.

HOT Links

Want to know more about employment? See http://www.employeease.com.

HOT Links

Want a quick course on how to expand into global markets? Check out Deloitte's Web site at http://www.deloitte.com, click on "services," and go to "merger and acquisition services."

"Realize a World of Opportunities" at EDC's Web site, http://www.keys.edc.ca.

Many small businesses hire international-trade specialists to get started selling overseas. They have the time, knowledge, and resources that most small businesses lack. Export trading companies buy goods at a discount from small businesses and resell them abroad. Export management companies (EMCs) act on a company's behalf. For fees of 5 to 15 percent of gross sales and multiyear contracts, they handle all aspects of exporting, including finding customers, billing, shipping, and helping the company comply with foreign regulations.

concept check

How does the small-business owner's role change over time?

What role do technology and the Internet play in creating small businesses and helping them grow?

Making Ethical Choices

MINDING YOUR BUSINESS

http://gitmanxtra.swlearning.com

As the owner of LT Designs, a small South African company, Lisa Taylor loves her work producing competitively priced handcrafted home accessories. She is an advocate for the empowerment of women, recruiting and training workers from nearby towns. These poor rural women are often the sole supporters of their families, and they are grateful for the jobs and eager to learn new skills.

Taylor is thrilled when a Canadian textile wholesaler and distributor, attracted by her unique, well-priced products and socially responsible approach to doing business, starts buying from her. Her business triples, and she hires more workers to handle the extra load. The company is soon Taylor's single largest customer and plans an elaborate and costly marketing campaign to promote her products in Canada. The company assigns you to supervise production and work closely with Taylor on developing appropriate designs for the Canadian market.

At first Taylor welcomes your input, but her receptivity quickly turns into resentment of what she perceives as your company's attempt to "control" her business. Although she has signed an agreement with

your company to approve new designs, her new sample ranges reflect none of the agreed-on design elements. After checking with your boss, you tell Taylor that unless she agrees to follow your design standards, you will have no choice but to terminate the relationship. Taylor insists the new designs fall within agreed design specifications and that you are trying to take advantage of the workers' need for jobs to force her to compromise her artistic integrity.

If your company does not buy the products, she will have to lay off the additional workers she hired, and their families will suffer. Everyone will blame the overbearing Canadian company for ruining the local economy. You are in a bind, because the company will lose its investment in the marketing campaign. It could also get negative publicity, damaging its image as a good corporate citizen.

ETHICAL DILEMMA

The Canadian company can afford to buy LT's products and hold them in inventory, waiting for an appropriate marketing opportunity. Should they absorb the cost of doing this to protect workers' jobs?

SOURCE: Case based on experience of Linda Ravden, former owner of Bellissima Designs, as described in a personal interview, February 24, 2003.

Trends in Entrepreneurship and Small-Business Ownership

8 *learning goal*

HOT Links

What services does the Women Business Owners of Canada Inc. provide? Click over to http://www.wboc.ca.

Entrepreneurship has changed since the heady days of the late 1990s, when the term seemed to imply a quick route to riches and stock options. The days of starting a dot-com while you were still in college and making millions by taking it public in a few years are gone. A new type of entrepreneur is emerging—and we're finding that it isn't really new at all.

Social and demographic trends, combined with the challenges of operating in the fast-paced, technology-dominated business climate of the 1990s and early 21st century, have changed the face of entrepreneurship and small-business ownership. New areas are emerging as entrepreneurial hot spots. Opportunities for women and minority business owners continue to grow. The role of technology in business start-ups has changed, and the Internet is creating numerous opportunities for new types of small businesses.

Over the next few decades, Canada will shift further away from a society dominated by whites and rooted in Western culture toward a society characterized by many racial and ethnic minorities. All minorities will grow in size and in share of the population, while the white majority declines as a percentage of the total. First Nations people and people with roots in Australia, the Middle East, the former Soviet Union, and other parts of the world will further enrich the fabric of Canadian society.

Doug Dokis, a member of the Ojibwe Nation of Ontario, acts as a liaison between a large college and the Native community in the area. According to Doug, the growth rate in the Native population is the largest of any population segment: "This has tremendous implications for business, and to take advantage of the opportunity, businesses must respond to the demands of this sector." Many Native entrepreneurs are emerging to fill the demand for goods and services, for example, Cree-ative Media (1999) Ltd. of Calgary.

Doug Dokis, who works extensively with Native students and entrepreneurs, sees the Native population as an increasingly important group offering a wide range of products and services.

PHOTO COURTESY OF DOUG DOKIS

REDUCED NUMBER OF NEW BUSINESSES

Although the desire to strike out on one's own remains widespread, the number of people actually starting businesses or going solo has slowed down a bit in recent years. Reality has set in. Funding is difficult to obtain. No longer do venture capitalists, burned in the dot-com craze, throw money at all sorts of schemes. They want to see a solid idea and a well-developed business plan. People who were eager to join the ranks of the self-employed are thinking twice before giving up the security of a regular paycheque, corporate benefits like paid vacations, subsidized health insurance, and retirement plans; and workspace and equipment.

Many would-be entrepreneurs are now choosing to get hands-on experience first at larger companies. They recognize that developing their managerial and technical skills improves their chances of successful business ownership. Their employers benefit as well. Applying their entrepreneurial inclinations within existing companies, these employees open up new opportunities by creating new products and identifying new markets.[22]

That's not to say that entrepreneurship is disappearing, however, but those who do take the entrepreneurial route have reasonable expectations about the time and effort it takes to build a company. They are reverting to basic business management principles, core values, and core competencies. They master their primary vision before diverting money and resources into new areas.

OPPORTUNITIES FOR ALL

At one time, most entrepreneurs were career changers starting second or third careers and corporate executives deciding to go out on their own. Today, entrepreneurship cuts across all age and ethnic boundaries. Many young people are choosing entrepreneurship as their first career. For women and minorities, entrepreneurship and small-business ownership are a route to economic independence and personal and professional fulfillment. These groups are starting small businesses at rates far above the general population. According to the Panel Study on

Julz Chavez started her own doll company when none of the major toy companies were interested in her multiracial line of action dolls. Today, Get Real Girl has more than $5 million in sales and boasts a board of advisors including female sports stars such as soccer player Brandi Chastain.

Entrepreneurial Dynamics (PSED), entrepreneurship involves adults at all ages. Exhibit 6.4 shows the likelihood of starting a business depending on your age. For example, for every 1,000 women age 18 to 24, 4 will start a business. Men and women aged 25 to 34 are the most active in forming new businesses, whereas people over 65 are the least.[23]

Women business owners make up one of the most dynamic small-business segments. What motivates women to start their own firms? A study sponsored by three major women's business organizations found that the two leading reasons are the inspiration of an entrepreneurial idea and frustration with their work environment. More women business owners than men report dissatisfaction with their corporate jobs, mentioning inflexibility, lack of promotional opportunities, unpleasant environments, and lack of challenge as reasons for choosing entrepreneurship. The moving company Two Men and a Truck was, in fact, started by a woman, Mary Ellen Sheets, in 1985 after she encountered discrimination from a trade association. Focusing on customers was the key to her success. Today her daughter, Melanie, runs the company, which has grown to 117 franchises and $100 million in sales.[24]

Exhibit 6.4 | At What Age Are You Most Likely to Start a Business?

This table shows the number of people per 1,000 who will start companies.

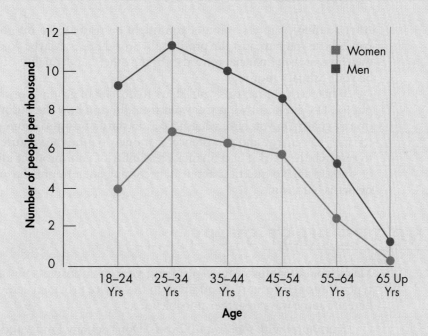

SOURCE: Paul D. Reynolds, Nancy M. Carter, William B. Gartner, Patricia G. Greene, and Larry W. Cox. *The Entrepreneur Next Door: Characteristics of Individuals Starting Companies in America.* (Kansas City, MO: E. M. Kauffman Foundation, 2002).

LOW- OR NO-TECH TAKES OVER

Although high-tech businesses captured the headlines, relatively few start-ups are actually in the technology sector (computers, telecommunications equipment, biotechnology), and very few entrepreneurs have the talents or financial resources to go the high-tech route. They are more likely to come up with better ways to make things or provide services. For example, the manufacturing sector is enjoying a rebirth as small specialty companies fill the holes left by less nimble companies that couldn't respond to changing markets. Steel and textiles are two industries where this is evident.

Technology and the Internet do, however, play a major role in creating small businesses and helping them grow. "The Internet has amazing capacities to do some very unglamorous things like reduce costs and improve customer service," says Burch LaPrade. His firm, brightroom, takes digital photos of participants at large corporate events and sporting activities such as charity runs and marathons. In a few days, the photos are available for viewing and purchase on the brightroom Web site. Using digital photography reduces labour costs and allows the company to photograph more events, and distributing the photos electronically saves mailing costs. "This is just rethinking a business that's been around," says LaPrade.[25]

concept check

What significant trends are occurring in small-business management?

How is the Internet affecting small business?

Great Ideas to Use Now

After reading Chapters 5 and 6, you might be ready to go into business. Perhaps you believe you have just the product the world needs. Maybe you want to be your own boss or seek financial rewards. On the other hand, quality-of-life issues might be your primary motive.

Whatever your reasons, you'll have to do a lot of groundwork before taking the plunge. Do you know what you want from life and how the business fits into your overall goals? Do you have what it takes to start a business, from personal characteristics, like energy and persistence, to money to fund the venture? You'll also have to research the market and financial feasibility of your product idea and develop a business plan. No question about it, becoming an entrepreneur or small-business owner is hard work.

TAKING THE FIRST STEPS

Maybe you know that you want to run your own business but don't know what type of business to start. In addition to the advice provided earlier in the chapter, here are some ways to gather possible ideas:

- *Brainstorm with family and friends.* Don't set any limits, and then investigate the best ideas, no matter how impossible they might seem at first.
- *Be observant.* Look for anything that catches your interest wherever you are, in your hometown or when you travel. What's special about it? Is there a niche market you can fill? Look at products that don't meet your needs and find ways to change them. Pay attention to the latest fads and trends. Amy Wolf remembered how thrilled she was to find a music store at London's Heathrow airport. Six years later, she founded AltiTunes Partners LP, a $15 million chain of music stores for travellers, with outlets in airports and a train station. Wolf knows her idea wasn't new. "I stole the idea, and then did some serious adapting," she says. She saw a need and filled it.[26]

- *Focus on your interests and hobbies.* Opportunities abound, from home-based crafts or consulting businesses to multimillion-dollar companies. Robert Tuchman turned his love of sports into a $10 million company. TSE Sports and Entertainment arranges special travel packages for corporations that want to entertain clients at major sporting and entertainment events.[27]
- *Use your skills in new ways.* Are you computer savvy? You could start a business providing in-home consulting to novices who don't know how to set up or use their computers.

WORKING AT A SMALL BUSINESS

Working for a small company can be a wonderful experience. Many people enjoy the less structured atmosphere and greater flexibility that often characterize the small-business workplace. Several years' experience at a small company can be a good steppingstone to owning your own company. You'll get a better understanding of the realities of running a small business before striking out on your own. There are other potential benefits as well:

- *More diverse job responsibilities.* Small companies might not have formal job descriptions, giving you a chance to learn a wider variety of skills to use later. In a large company, your job might be strictly defined.
- *Less bureaucracy.* Small companies typically have fewer formal rules and procedures. This creates a more relaxed working atmosphere.
- *Greater sense of your contribution to the business.* Your ideas are more likely to count, and you'll see how your work contributes to the firm's success. You'll have greater access to top management and be able to discuss your ideas.

However, you should also be aware of the disadvantages of being a small-business employee:

- *Lower compensation packages.* Although the gap between large and small businesses is narrowing, salaries are likely to be lower at small businesses. In addition, there might be few, if any, employee benefits, such as health insurance and retirement plans.
- *Less job security.* Small businesses might be affected more profoundly by changing economic and competitive conditions. A change in ownership can put jobs at risk as well. However, small businesses run lean to begin with and, as noted earlier, are at the forefront of job creation.
- *Greater potential for personality clashes.* Conflicts between employees are more apparent in a small company and can affect the rest of the staff. In addition, if your boss owns the company, you don't have anyone to go to if you have a problem with him or her.
- *Fewer opportunities for career advancement.* After a few years, you might outgrow a small firm because there are no chances for promotion. As well, with fewer people within the firm with whom to network, you'll have to join outside organizations for these connections.

Evaluating these factors will help you decide whether working at a small business is the right opportunity for you.

CUSTOMER SATISFACTION AND QUALITY

Small can be better when it comes to providing personal and high-quality service. As we've discussed in Chapters 5 and 6, small businesses have an edge in tailoring their products to the customer. A quick response to customer problems is another key component of customer service, and one that can turn a complainer into a customer for life. In the construction company sector, customer satisfaction is the single most important indicator of business success. Income and profits depend on keeping customers happy. It's not enough simply to focus on customer needs. Companies must follow through and develop systems to meet those needs.

Even though customers of Timberlane Woodcrafters might consider its wooden shutters a one-time purchase, the company prides itself on keeping buyers happy. President Rick Skidmore knows that satisfied customers will refer new business his way. Timberlane immediately contacts customers with problems and promises to solve the matter promptly. Skidmore follows up with a special gift: an "Oops Kit" with a flashlight and note thanking the customer for "shedding light on the mistake." Referrals, a very cost-effective way of adding customers, are growing at 5 percent a year and as of 2002 accounted for 25 percent of sales.[28]

SUMMARY OF LEARNING GOALS

1. Why do people become entrepreneurs, and what are the different types of entrepreneurs?

Entrepreneurship involves taking the risk of starting and managing a business to make a profit. Entrepreneurs are innovators who start firms either to have a certain lifestyle or to develop a company that will grow into a major corporation. People become entrepreneurs for four main reasons: the opportunity for profit, independence, personal satisfaction, and lifestyle. Classic entrepreneurs may be micropreneurs, who plan to keep their businesses small, or growth-oriented entrepreneurs. Multipreneurs start multiple companies, whereas intrapreneurs work within large corporations.

2. Which characteristics do successful entrepreneurs share?

Successful entrepreneurs are ambitious, independent, self-confident, creative, energetic, passionate, and committed. They have a high need for achievement and a willingness to take moderate risks. They have good interpersonal and communication skills. Managerial skills and technical knowledge are also important for entrepreneurial success.

3. How do small businesses contribute to the Canadian economy?

A small business is independently owned and operated, has a local base of operations, and is not dominant in its field. Small businesses play an important role in the economy. More than 95 percent of Canadian businesses have fewer than 50 employees. Small businesses are found in every field, but they dominate the construction, wholesale, and retail categories. Most new private sector jobs created in Canada over the past decade were in small firms. Small businesses also create about twice as many new goods and services as larger firms. Approximately 70 percent of all new jobs in the economy were created by the small-business sector

4. What are the advantages and disadvantages facing owners of small businesses?

Small businesses have flexibility to respond to changing market conditions. Because of their streamlined staffing and structure, they can be operated efficiently. Small firms can serve specialized markets more profitably than large firms and provide a higher level of personal service. Disadvantages include limited managerial skill, difficulty in raising the capital needed for start-up and expansion, the burden of complying with increasing levels of government regulation, and the major personal commitment required on the part of the owner.

5 How does the Business Development Bank of Canada help small businesses?

The BDC is the main federal agency serving small businesses. It provides guarantees of private lender loans for small businesses. The BDC also offers a wide range of management assistance services, including courses, publications, and consulting.

6 What are the first steps to take if you are starting your own business?

After finding an idea that satisfies a market need, the small-business owner should choose a form of business organization. The process of developing a formal business plan helps the business owner to analyze the feasibility of his or her idea. This written plan describes in detail the idea for the business and how it will be implemented. The plan also helps the owner obtain both debt and equity financing for the new business.

7 Why does managing a small business present special challenges for the owner?

At first, small-business owners are involved in all aspects of the firm's operations. Wise use of outside consultants can free up the owner's time to focus on planning and strategy in addition to day-to-day operations. Other key management responsibilities are finding and retaining good employees and monitoring market conditions. Expanding into global markets can be a profitable growth strategy for small businesses.

8 What trends are shaping entrepreneurship and small-business ownership?

The tougher business climate has made many people more cautious about starting businesses. Today's entrepreneurs have reasonable expectations about the time and effort it takes to build a company. Funding is harder to secure, and investors want to see a fully developed feasibility plan. Opportunities continue to exist for entrepreneurs of all ages and backgrounds. The numbers of women and minority business owners continue to increase. The number of start-ups in the technology sector has declined, but Internet technology is creating numerous opportunities for new types of small businesses and fuelling small-business growth by making it easier to open Web-based businesses.

EXPERIENTIAL EXERCISES

1. After working in software development with a major food company for 12 years, you are becoming impatient with corporate "red tape" (regulations and routines). You have an idea for a new snack product for nutrition-conscious consumers and are thinking of starting your own company. What are the entrepreneurial characteristics you will need? What other factors should you consider before quitting your job? Working with a partner, choose one to be the entrepreneurial employee and one to play the role of his or her current boss. Develop notes for a script. The employee will focus on why this is a good idea, reasons he or she will succeed, and so on, whereas the employer will play devil's advocate to convince him or her that staying on at the large company is a better idea. Then switch roles and repeat the discussion.

2. What does it really take to become an entrepreneur? Find out by interviewing a local entrepreneur or researching an entrepreneur you've read about in this chapter or in the business press. Get answers to the following questions, as well as any others you'd like to ask:

- How did you develop your vision for the company?

- What are the most important entrepreneurial characteristics that helped you succeed?

- Where did you learn the business skills you needed to run and grow the company?

- How did you research the feasibility of your idea?

- How did you prepare your business plan?

- What were the biggest challenges you had to overcome?

- Where did you obtain financing for the company?

- What are the most important lessons you learned by starting this company?

- What advice do you have for would-be entrepreneurs?

3. A small catering business in your city is for sale for $150,000. The company specializes in business luncheons and smaller social events. The owner has been running the business for four years from her home but is expecting her first child and wants to sell. You will need outside investors to help you purchase the business. Develop questions to ask the owner about the business and its prospects and a list of documents you'd want to see. What other types of information would you need before making a decision to buy this company? Summarize your findings in a memo to a potential investor that explains the appeal of the business for you and how you plan to investigate the feasibility of the purchase.

4. Does it work? Select a type of business that interests you and go through the checklist presented at **http://www.bizmove.com/starting/m1b.htm**, "Starting a Business: Determining the Feasibility of Your Business Idea." Given the results of your feasibility study, should you continue to investigate this opportunity?

5. Do you have what it takes to be an entrepreneur or small-business owner? See **http://www.toolkit.cch.com/text/P01_0001.asp.** To evaluate whether you have the character traits of the entrepreneurial personality, take the quiz **http://www.2h.com/entrepreneur-tests.html.** What did your results tell you, and were you surprised by what you learned?

6. Your class decides to participate in a local business plan competition. Divide the class into small groups and choose one of the following ideas:

- a new computer game based on the stock market,

- a company with an innovative design for a skateboard, or

- travel services for college and high school students.

Prepare a detailed outline for the business plan, including the objectives for the business and the types of information you would need to develop product, marketing, and financing strategies. Each group will then present its outline for the class to critique.

7. Home base. Starting a business from your home is one of the easiest ways to become self-employed. Choose an idea that you feel is suited to this type of business. What other issues do you need to investigate before start-up? How feasible is your idea? Use a variety of research resources to answer these questions.

8. Visit Sample Business Plans at **http://www.bplans.com** to review sample plans for all types of businesses. Select an idea for a company in a field that interests you, and using information from this site, prepare an outline for its business plan.

9. You want to buy a business but don't know much about valuing small companies. Using the "Buy & Sell a Business" column in *Inc.* (also available online at **http://www.inc.com**) and resources on other small-business sites, including advertisements, develop a checklist of questions to ask when buying a business. Also summarize several ways in which businesses arrive at the sale price ("Business for Sale" includes the price rationale for each profiled business).

REVIEW QUESTIONS

1. What is the definition of an entrepreneur? What is the definition of a small business?

2. Why do people become entrepreneurs?

3. What are some of the challenges for entrepreneurs?

4. What impact does small business have on the Canadian economy?

5. Why does small business thrive in Canada?

6. Why would a small business decide to remain small?

7. How does Export Development Canada help small businesses?

8. What needs to be included in a business plan? What is the business plan used for?

9 What are some sources of financing for a small business?

10 What role can outside consultants play in a small business?

11. Why does small business have to be creative in hiring and retaining employees?

12. What are some alternatives to starting your own business?

CREATIVE THINKING CASE
Have you Been Googled Today?

Chances are, you've used Google (**http://www.google.com**) to answer an important research question, or maybe *you* were "googled"—someone entered your name in the world's largest search engine to find information about you. First launched in 1998, Google continues to push the limits of technology, delivering amazingly accurate results to a global audience at blazing speed. Even more remarkable, Google is profitable and growing—setting it apart from most of its dot-com peers.

Cofounders Sergey Brin and Larry Page met in 1995 as Stanford University computer science PhD students. Despite Brin's first reaction to Page—"He was really obnoxious"—the two became friends and collaborators. The result was Google, a play on the word *googol* (which means a huge number—1 followed by 100 zeros), to reflect their desire to find more efficient ways to search the Web's seemingly infinite information sources.

Unlike other classmates, Brin and Page had no desire to start a company and tried unsuccessfully to license their revolutionary search methodology to corporate partners. One company's CEO informed them, "Our users don't really care about search." The pair disagreed and instead followed the advice of fellow Stanford student and Yahoo! founder David Filo, who encouraged them to start Google.

Brin and Page financed the new company with personal credit card advances but soon needed more funds to expand. Postponing their graduate studies, they prepared a business plan and approached potential investors. Their first presentation, to Sun Microsystems founder Andy Bechtolsheim, netted a check for $100,000 made out to Google, *Inc.*—a corporation that did not yet exist. By

September 1998, Brin and Page incorporated Google, *Inc.*, arranged $1 million in start-up capital, and "headquartered" their fledgling company in a friend's garage.

Despite stiff competition, Google quickly became the favourite site for people wanting fast, accurate searches. About 97 percent of Google users found what they needed "every time" or "most of the time." With referrals from devoted Web surfers, not costly advertising campaigns, fuelling Google's growth, the company was able to raise an additional $25 million in venture capital funding in 1999.

Google's informal yet stimulating corporate culture was as unique as its sole focus on solving search problems. When the company moved to larger facilities in Mountain View, California, large exercise balls substituted for desk chairs, pets were welcomed, and staffers were fed by a gourmet chef. Roller hockey games and TGIF parties became hallmarks of Google's employee-friendly work environment, encouraging staffers to share ideas and continually develop technological enhancements.

Google passed the billion-pages-searched mark in 2000, becoming the world's largest search engine. As revenues from advertising and corporate clients climbed steadily, Google's young founders recognized they needed help taking the company to its next level. They recruited Eric E. Schmidt, a former executive at Novell and Sun Microsystems, to be CEO and chairman of the board, and George Reyes, another Sun alumnus, as chief financial officer of their privately held company.

CRITICAL THINKING QUESTIONS

Consider the following questions as they relate to Google, Inc.:

1. Do you think Sergey Brin and Larry Page have entrepreneurial personalities? Explain your answer. What were their motives in starting Google, and what type of entrepreneurial business do you think Google is?

2. Through 2003 the company focused its efforts on becoming the best search engine. Do you think it can continue to be profitable without branching out? Why or why not?

3. What factors should Google's executive team consider in deciding whether to take Google public?

SOURCE: Ben Elgin and Jim Kerstetter, "Why They're Agog over Google," *Business Week*, September 24, 2001, 83, 88; "Google Corporate Information," http://www.google.com (accessed December 16, 2002); Sarah J. Heim, "Vroom Vroom," *Brandweek*, November 27, 2000, http://www.findarticles.com; Jennifer Lee, "Postcards from Planet Google," *The New York Times*, November 28, 2002, http://www.nytimes.com; and Steven Levy, "The World According to Google," *Newsweek*, December 16, 2002, 46–51.

VIDEO CASE

Worm Boy

Tom had his life all laid out for him. He was enrolled in Princeton and with both parents being doctors, there was no problem with tuition and other expenses. So, what did he do? He quit Princeton to start an eco-capitalism company and sell worm droppings. The product involved feeding worms basically garbage so that they would produce twice their body weight daily in fertilizer. With hundreds of thousands of worms doing their thing in the building, it was not an endeavour for everyone. The company, Terra Cycle Inc. used garbage not only to produce the product, but also used garbage, recycled bottles, to package their product.

The composition of the company was rather unusual. Tom was the owner and the boss, his friends were the management team and students from Princeton volunteered as staff. Even with the staff being volunteers, Tom still had monthly expenses of $50,000 and virtually no income. His initial investors contributed $1 million in U.S. dollars. Another $300,000 was needed for factory renovations and more capital was requested to produce enough product to service the big box companies. He was running the business on investors' money and selling potential rather than product.

Many problems occurred for Tom as he tried to develop a viable business. His VP of Sales, Robin, was a good friend but had no experience with the big box companies. While Robin attempted to train the volunteers as sales people, he was missing a very important area of expertise if the company was to crack the big box market. Tom's friend, Alex, who also quit Princeton to be part of the venture, was running the lawn service side of the business. Tom was finding out the difficulties in working with friends. Sometimes Alex's behaviour was inappropriate for a business person representing a company. Tom also had problems with the sloppy work of some of his student volunteers. When people are working for room and board, stock options, and to gain experience, but are not getting paid, it is difficult to motivate them to pay more attention to details.

As Tom continued to invest more time and money into the venture, it became apparent that sales had to be made or they would loose everything.

CRITICAL THINKING QUESTIONS

1. As an entrepreneur, Tom was under a considerable amount of stress. Is this the sort of situation that would suit any eager 20-something person with a good idea?

2. What are the advantages and disadvantages of using friends in your start-up business?

3. Check the status of Tom's business today.

SOURCE: CBC, *Venture*, Worm Boy "The Big Adventures of Wormboy Part A and B," February 6, 2005.

E-COMMERCE CASE
The Ultimate Entrepreneur—K. C. Irving

At the age of 11, Kenneth Colin Irving began a path that would lead him to become one of the richest men in Canada, when he bought a car for eight dollars. His father found out and ordered him to sell it, so K. C. sold the car for $11, a 38 percent profit. The story grows from there. By the age of 25, he opened his first service station in Bouctouche, New Brunswick. The Irving Oil Refinery, built in 1960, is the largest in Canada and produces 300,000 barrels of product per day, an interesting entrepreneurial venture in a province that has no oil wells. The crude oil is brought in and refined into a variety of products, with 175,000 barrels exported daily to the United States. This represents approximately 42 percent of Canadian petroleum exports.

Today Irving Oil serves the Atlantic Provinces, Quebec, and the New England States. In addition to Irving Oil, The Irving Group of companies includes Cavendish Produce, Irving Personal Care, Irving Forest Products, Irving Pulp and Paper, Irving Tissue, Midland Group (transportation services), and ownership of 90 percent of the English language media in New Brunswick. It comprises more than 300 companies worth $4 billion and employs 8 percent of the New Brunswick workforce. The group is managed by K.C.'s three sons, Jack, Arthur, and Jim, and their associates.

K.C.'s early philosophy was to look after customers and they, in turn, would look after you. He believed in hard work and moral behaviour. He worked long hours and expected those around him to do likewise. Today the values of the Irving Group reflect K.C.'s earlier philosophy and include "demonstrating commitment, keeping our word, respecting people as individuals and providing the best for our customers".

K.C. Irving was inducted into the Canadian Business Hall of Fame in 1979, representing one of his few public appearances. The family has always preferred to keep a low profile, and obviously this has done no harm, as the "empire" continues to expand.

CRITICAL THINKING QUESTIONS

1. What is the mission and purpose of Irving Oil? (**http://www.irvingoil.com**) Does it reflect the philosophy of the founder?

2. What is the Irving Group looking for in new employees? Is this somewhere you would want to work? Why or why not? (See **http://www.irvingmoncton.com, http://www.cavendishfarms.com,** or **http://www.jdirving.co**)

SOURCES: http://collections.ic.gc.ca/heirloom_series/volume4/174-177.htm (accessed July 12, 2006); and John Demont, *Citizens Irving, K. C. Irving and His Legacy* (Toronto: McClelland and Stewart Inc., 1992).

your career

as an Entrepreneur

Do you have what it takes to own your own company? Or are you better suited to working for a corporation? To find out, you need to determine whether you have the personal traits for entrepreneurial success. If the answer is yes, you need to identify the type of business that is best for you.

Know Yourself

Owning a business is challenging and requires a great deal of personal sacrifice. You must take a hard and honest look at yourself before you decide to strike out on your own. The quiz in Exhibit YC.1 can help you evaluate whether you have the personality traits to become a successful entrepreneur. Think about yourself and rate yourself—honestly!—on each of these characteristics.

Which Business Is for You?

If you are well suited to owning your own company, the next question is what type of business to start. You need to consider your expertise, interests, and financial resources. Start with a broad field; then choose a specific good or service. The business can involve a new idea or a refinement of an existing idea. It might also bring an existing idea to a new area.

To narrow the field, ask yourself the following questions:

- What do I like to do?
- What am I good at?
- How much can I personally invest in my business?
- Do I have access to other financial resources?
- What is my past business experience?
- What are my personal interests and hobbies?
- How can I use my experience and interests in my own business?
- Do I want or need partners?

Spending time on these and similar questions will help you identify some possible business opportunities and the resources you will need to develop them.

Prior job experience is the number one source of new business ideas. Starting a firm in a field where you have specialized product or service experience improves your chances for success.

Personal interests and hobbies are another major source of ideas. Gourmet food enthusiasts have started many restaurants and specialty food businesses. For example, Eleni Gianopulos transformed the humble cookie into a specialty item, bringing in more than $1 million in sales each year. Eleni's unique, beautifully decorated cookies come in shapes for every season and occasion, such as several series with Academy Award nominees and movie quotes. Customers, who include corporate and celebrity clients, can also place special orders. One customer ordered a cookie model of Elton John's house! Business at Eleni's NYC is growing; the cookies are now sold online (http://www.elenis.com) and featured in many specialty catalogues.

Each January, *Entrepreneur* and *Business Start-Ups* magazines feature lists of top businesses and business trends for the coming year. Check out the current hot lists at http://www.entrepreneur.com/hotcenter.

Exhibit YC.1 | How Do You Rate?

The following quiz will help you to assess your personality and determine if you have what it takes to start your own company. Think about yourself and rate yourself—honestly!—on each of these characteristics.

Personality Trait	High	Above Average	Average	Below Average	Low
Ability to handle uncertainty	○	○	○	○	○
Confidence	○	○	○	○	○
Discipline	○	○	○	○	○
Drive/ambition	○	○	○	○	○
Energy	○	○	○	○	○
Flexibility	○	○	○	○	○
Independence	○	○	○	○	○
Ability to seize opportunity	○	○	○	○	○
Persistence	○	○	○	○	○
Problem solving	○	○	○	○	○
Total	_____	_____	_____	_____	_____

Scoring: Give yourself 5 points for every "high," 4 points for every "above average," 3 points for every "average," 2 points for every "below average," and 1 point, for every "low."

Score results
- 46–50: You are already in business for yourself or should be!
- 40–45: Your entrepreneurial aptitude and desires are high.
- 30–39: A paid staff job and owning your own business rate equally.
- 20–29: Entrepreneurial aptitude is apparently not one of your strong suits.
- 10–19: You might find the going tough and the rewards slim if you owned your own business.

SOURCES: Eleni's NYC Web site, http://www.elenis.com; and "Got ID?" *Entrepreneur*, November 2002, downloaded from http://www.entrepreneur.com.

Making the Connection

Management and Leadership in Today's Organization

In this chapter you will be introduced to management and the first function of a manager in the act of managing a business—*planning*. Management is what managers do to ensure that the organization achieves the critical success factors. As we state later in the chapter, "management is the process of guiding the development, maintenance, and allocation of resources to attain organizational goals." That is why the process of management encircles our model of a successful business. It is the process whereby all of the activities of a business toward achieving the factors critical to its success are implemented. It ties everything together and, when done properly, ensures that activities are integrated.

All of the activities within the process of management—planning, organizing, motivating, and controlling—are highly integrated. As you'll read in this chapter, they form a tightly integrated cycle of thoughts and actions. They are highly interdependent and are performed in such a way that it is difficult, if not impossible, to separate them. Just watch a manager at work. Let's suppose that she has just made a decision to promote a particular individual and leave that person's previous position permanently vacant. You might say that this was a decision made to reward an individual for a job well done and therefore to *motivate* him to continue to work

hard by recognizing his efforts. However, planning would have gone into that decision as well, because managers can't just move people around without looking ahead to the implications of those moves on other employees and the goals of the firm. One of those implications is that a change would have occurred to the structure of the *organization*, as a position was left vacant, perhaps causing that individual's subordinates to change managers and the number of managers to be reduced at that level. It also would require that the performance of that individual had been monitored to determine that he was worthy of this promotion. This is called *control*—results are measured and compared against objectives, and changes are made to keep everything on track or under control.

But remember that managers don't perform this highly integrative process in a vacuum. They make plans contingent on the opportunities and threats they see in the external environment in relation to the strengths and weaknesses the business has internally. What is done to implement the plan, with respect to organizational structure, motivational tactics, and control mechanisms, also depends on the internal and external environments. For example, a company might choose an open, flexible structure with less bureaucracy to encourage employees to be more creative and to seek and pursue opportunities that exist in a rapidly changing and highly competitive *economic* environment. This would, in turn, be dependent on the types of employees the company has, whether they would grow and develop in that type of environment, and whether they would need more direction to be motivated to perform. In other words, the strengths and weaknesses of the employees would need to be considered.

The planning process itself is also highly integrative. As mentioned in the chapter, there are different levels of planning—the main ones being strategic, tactical, and operational—but they must all work together. *Strategic* planning is broad based and determines the goals and plans for the entire organization. Then, at the *tactical* level, each functional area determines its own goals and plans, which enable that area to fulfill its role in achieving the overall strategic plan. Finally, at the operational level, each unit within each functional area determines its goals and plans to implement those at the next higher level.

For example, if a company decided strategically to develop a new product line to compete with another company that is threatening to reduce its market share, then, at the tactical level, *marketing* would need to determine how to promote this new product line, and *operations* would need to determine the most efficient and cost-effective way to produce it. At the operational level, sales quotas, territories, and strategies for salespeople would then be set, and production schedules would be established in the plant. The important factor is that all of these plans are related to each other. They are connected as if by a string to the next higher level; each one helps to achieve the objectives of the next level, so ultimately, the company achieves its overall goals and the critical factors of success.

As we indicate in the chapter, there are many trends in the environment that affect management and leadership today. One of these is empowerment. Employees are being given more freedom to make decisions, which, in turn, *increases employee commitment* to the organization and its goals—our most important critical success factor. But this requires really solid communication and integration, so that when employees make decisions, they are in tune with other decisions that are being made, and everyone is moving in the same direction. This is improved by the impact of *technology*, which wires everyone in the organization together with instant equal access to pertinent information.

This trend toward empowerment is linked to the discussion of leadership. Just as teams need coaches, organizations need leaders to keep everyone moving in the same direction. There are many different leadership styles, but as you'll see in the chapter, the most effective are those that result in individuals' working together as a team. These styles result in the greatest commitment, which is, of course, our primary objective: that employees take ownership of the results of the company as if it were their own, as mentioned by Max Messmer, Chairman and CEO of Robert Half International. "Most people will work harder … [if] they are trusted to be responsible to make their own decisions. Empowering your employees will likely pay off with … loyalty, and the high level of productivity that comes from effective teamwork." The leader and his or her style are critical to developing a vision for the company and inspiring employees to be committed to that vision, so that all the critical success factors can be achieved.

7

SHIRLEY A. ROSE

Management and Leadership in Today's Organizations

learning goals

1   What is the role of management?
2   What are the four types of planning?
3   What are the primary responsibilities of managers in organizing activities?
4   How do leadership styles influence a corporate culture?
5   How do organizations control activities?
6   What roles do managers take on in different organizational settings?
7   What set of managerial skills is necessary for managerial success?
8   What trends will affect management in the future?

middle management
Managers who design and carry out tactical plans in specific areas of the company.

supervisory management
Managers who design and carry out operational plans for the ongoing daily activities of the firm.

The second and third tiers of the hierarchy are called **middle management** and **supervisory management,** respectively. Middle managers (such as division heads, departmental managers, and regional sales managers) are responsible for beginning the implementation of strategic plans. They design and carry out *tactical plans* in specific areas of the company. They begin the process of allocating resources to meet organizational goals, and they oversee supervisory managers throughout the firm. Supervisors, the most numerous of the managers, are at the bottom of the managerial pyramid. These managers design and carry out *operational plans* for the ongoing daily activities of the firm. They spend a great deal of their time guiding and motivating the employees who actually produce the goods and services.

concept check

Explain the managerial function of organizing.

What is the managerial pyramid?

LEADING, GUIDING, AND MOTIVATING OTHERS

4 *learning goal*

Leadership, the third key management function, is the process of guiding and motivating others toward the achievement of organizational goals. Managers are responsible for directing employees on a daily basis as the employees carry out the plans and work within the structure created by management. Organizations need strong, effective leadership at all levels to meet goals and remain competitive.

Exhibit 7.3 | The Managerial Pyramid

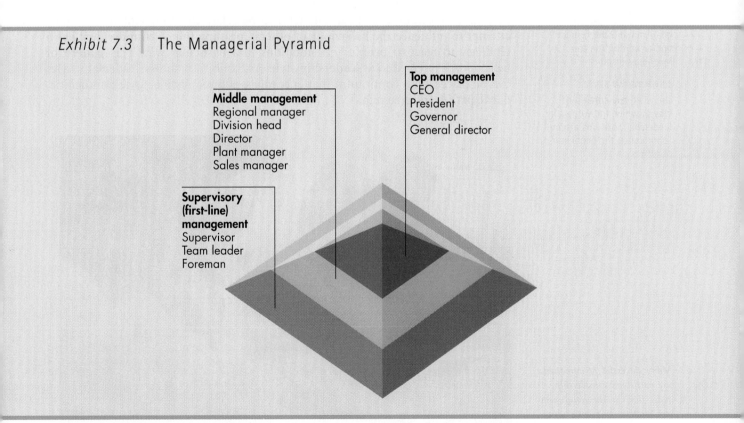

Top management
CEO
President
Governor
General director

Middle management
Regional manager
Division head
Director
Plant manager
Sales manager

Supervisory (first-line) management
Supervisor
Team leader
Foreman

leadership

The process of guiding and motivating others toward the achievement of organizational goals.

power

The ability to influence others to behave in a particular way.

legitimate power

Power that is derived from an individual's position in an organization.

reward power

Power that is derived from an individual's control over rewards.

coercive power

Power that is derived from an individual's ability to threaten negative outcomes.

expert power

Power that is derived from an individual's extensive knowledge in one or more areas.

referent power

Power that is derived from an individual's personal charisma and the respect and/or admiration the individual inspires.

leadership style

The relatively consistent way in which individuals in leadership positions attempt to influence the behaviour of others.

To be effective leaders, managers must be able to influence others' behaviour. This ability to influence others to behave in a particular way is called **power**. Researchers have identified five primary sources, or bases, of power:

- **legitimate power,** which is derived from an individual's position in an organization;
- **reward power,** which is derived from an individual's control over rewards,
- **coercive power,** which is derived from an individual's ability to threaten negative outcomes;
- **expert power,** which is derived from an individual's extensive knowledge in one or more areas; and
- **referent power,** which is derived from an individual's personal charisma and the respect and/or admiration the individual inspires.

Many leaders use a combination of all of these sources of power to influence individuals toward goal achievement. Jim Kilts' legitimate power was a result of his position as CEO of Gillette. His reward power comes from turning the company around and making the stock more valuable. The authority to give raises and bonus to managers who meet their goals is another form of reward power. Jim Kilts was also not hesitant to use his coercive power: He replaced 10 of the top 14 managers in a 2-year span. Kilts was brought to Gillette for his expertise in company turnarounds. He revived the struggling Kool-Aid brand and Kraft cheeses, and also a floundering Nabisco. Kilts is not the "life of the party," but he is highly respected. Investment guru Warren Buffett says, "Everything Jim Kilts says makes sense—and frankly, finding someone like that is a rarity."[5]

Leadership Styles

Individuals in leadership positions tend to be relatively consistent in how they attempt to influence the behaviour of others, meaning that each individual has a tendency to react to people and situations in a particular way. This pattern of behaviour is referred to as **leadership style**. As Exhibit 7.4 shows, leadership styles can be placed on a continuum that encompasses three distinct styles: autocratic, participative, and free rein.

Many successful organizations use participative leadership styles that involve group members in discussing issues and making decisions.

Exhibit 7.4 | Leadership Styles of Managers

Amount of authority held by the leader

AUTOCRATIC STYLE	PARTICIPATIVE STYLE (DEMOCRATIC, CONSENSUAL, CONSULTATIVE)	FREE-REIN (LAISSEZ-FAIRE) STYLE
• Manager makes most decisions and acts in authoritative manner. • Manager is usually unconcerned about subordinates' attitudes toward decisions. • Emphasis is on getting task accomplished. • Approach is used mostly by military officers and some production line supervisors.	• Manager shares decision-making with group members and encourages teamwork. • Manager encourages discussion of issues and alternatives. • Manager is concerned about subordinates' ideas and attitudes • Manager coaches subordinates and helps coodinate efforts. • Approach is found in many successful organizations.	• Manager turns over virtually all authority and control to group. • Members of group are presented with task and given freedom to accomplish it. • Approach works well with highly motivated, experienced, educated personnel. • Approach is found in high-tech firms, labs, and colleges.

Amount of authority held by group members

autocratic leaders

Directive leaders who prefer to make decisions and solve problems on their own with little input from subordinates.

HOT *Links*

Search http://www .canadianbusiness.com for recent articles relating to business leaders that interest you.

participative leadership

A leadership style in which the leader shares decision-making with group members and encourages discussion of issues and alternatives; includes democratic, consensual, and consultative styles.

democratic leaders

Leaders who solicit input from all members of the group and then allow the members to make the final decision through a vote.

Autocratic leaders are directive leaders, allowing for very little input from subordinates. These leaders prefer to make decisions and solve problems on their own and expect subordinates to implement solutions according to very specific and detailed instructions. In this leadership style, information typically flows in one direction, from manager to subordinate. The military, by necessity, is generally autocratic. When autocratic leaders treat employees with fairness and respect, they may be considered knowledgeable and decisive. But often autocrats are perceived as narrow-minded and heavy-handed in their unwillingness to share power, information, and decision-making in the organization. The trend in organizations today is away from the directive, controlling style of the autocratic leader.

A very different management style is when leaders believe in sharing responsibility with employees. For example, they might enlist frontline workers to help design the assembly lines, or involve employees in programs to improve safety, quality, and process efficiency. The goal is to create a business where workers are passionately involved in their work. This type of **participative leadership** has three types: democratic, consensual, and consultative.

Democratic leaders solicit input from all members of the group and then allow the group members to make the final decision through a voting process. This approach works well with highly trained professionals. **Consensual leaders** encourage discussion about issues and then require that all parties involved agree to the final decision. This style is often used when consensus is necessary. **Consultative leaders** confer with subordinates before making a decision but retain the final decision-making authority. This technique has been used in some situations to increase productivity dramatically.

The third leadership style, at the opposite end of the continuum from the autocratic style, is **free-rein**, or **laissez-faire** (French for "leave it alone") **leadership**. Managers who use this style turn over all authority and control to subordinates. Employees are assigned a task and then given free rein to determine the best way to accomplish it. The manager doesn't get involved unless asked and then usually acts only as a facilitator. Under this approach, subordinates have unlimited freedom as long as they do not violate existing company policies. This approach is sometimes used with highly trained professionals, as in a research laboratory.

consensual leaders

Leaders who encourage discussion about issues and then require that all parties involved agree to the final decision.

consultative leaders

Leaders who confer with subordinates before making a decision but who retain the final decision-making authority.

free-rein (laissez-faire) leadership

A leadership style in which the leader turns over all authority and control to subordinates.

empowerment

The process of giving employees increased autonomy and discretion to make decisions, as well as control over the resources needed to implement those decisions.

HOT Links

See "The 7 Traits of Effective Leaders: How Many Do You Share?" at http://www .womentodaymagazine.com/ career/7leader.html.

Although one might at first assume that subordinates would prefer the free-rein style, this approach can have several drawbacks. If free-rein leadership is accompanied by unclear expectations and lack of feedback from the manager, the experience can be frustrating for an employee. Employees might perceive the manager as being uninvolved and indifferent to what is happening or as unwilling or unable to provide the necessary structure, information, and expertise.

concept check

What are the five power bases mentioned? What is the source of each base?

What are the three types of leadership styles mentioned? When is each appropriate?

Explain each: democratic leaders, consensual leaders, and consultative leaders.

Employee Empowerment

Participative and free-rein leaders use a technique called empowerment to share decision-making authority with subordinates. **Empowerment** means giving employees increased autonomy and discretion to make their own decisions, as well as control over the resources needed to implement those decisions. When decision-making power is shared at all levels of the organization, employees feel a greater sense of ownership in, and responsibility for, organizational outcomes.

Max Messmer, Chairman and CEO of Robert Half International, says,

> Most people will work harder and do a better job if they feel their opinions are respected and that they are trusted to be responsible to make their own decisions. Empowering your employees will likely pay off with respect, loyalty, and the high level of productivity that comes from effective teamwork.[6]

There is no one best leadership style. The most effective style for a given situation depends on elements such as the characteristics of the subordinates, the complexity of the task, the source of the leader's power, and the stability of the environment.

Each employee on the Toyota assembly line has been empowered to act as a quality control inspector, stopping the line if necessary to correct a problem.

© MICHAEL S. YAMASHITA / CORBIS

Corporate Culture

The leadership style of managers in an organization is usually indicative of the underlying philosophy, or values, of the organization. The set of *attitudes, values,* and *standards of behaviour* that distinguishes one organization from another is called **corporate culture.** A corporate culture evolves over time and is based on the accumulated history of the organization, including the vision of the founders. It is also influenced by the dominant leadership style within the organization. Evidence of a company's culture is seen in its heroes (e.g., Andy Grove of Intel), myths (stories about the company that are passed from employee to employee), symbols (e.g., the Nike swoosh), and ceremonies.

Although culture is intangible and its rules are often unspoken, it can have a strong impact on a company's success. Therefore, managers must try to influence the corporate culture so that it will contribute to the success of the company. Companies can most often match the competition on the spreadsheet, but they can create a competitive advantage with the corporate culture.

The 2005 Canadian Corporate Culture Study conducted by Canadian Business magazine and Waterstone Human Capital Ltd. over a 6-month period, included comprehensive interviews with Canadian executives at more than 100 companies to determine the value executives place on corporate culture. WestJet was acknowledged as having the most admired corporate culture and was praised for its "entrepreneurial spirit," "delivering what they promise," and its "winning attitude." WestJet's corporate culture is one of its fundamental competitive advantages.[7]

corporate culture
The set of attitudes, values, and standards that distinguishes one organization from another.

HOT Links

See why corporate culture is important to perspective employees at http://www .quintcareers.com/ career_doctor_cures/ corporate_culture.html.

HOT Links

Check out http://www .CEOGO.com for articles about leadership and other related resources.

concept check

How do leaders influence other people's behaviour?

How can managers empower employees?

What is corporate culture?

Innovative organizations empower their employees to present and implement new ideas. WestJet Airlines' corporate culture, for example, encourages employees to solve problems and keep customers happy.

COURTESY WESTJET

Making Ethical Choices

WAITING AND WAITING AND WAITING

You've always been in a hurry, whether it's to get to a party or to find a job. You were in a hurry to land a supervisory position immediately on college graduation and looked for an organization that satisfied your goals of providing community service and moving up quickly. As an adept organizer with an innate sense of the right number of people and amount of money necessary to complete a task, you wanted your ability to plan and stay focused on goals to be recognized.

Your search led you to the police department of a major metropolitan city, as the supervisor of 911—the perfect job for someone in a hurry. On taking over, you analyzed the department's requirements and determined you needed more operators to service the growing call volume. You shared your findings with the chief of police, who had to approve all staffing allocations, and he agreed with your evaluation. Human resources, however, repeatedly denied your requests for more operators, even though your department received numerous complaints from callers who were left waiting and waiting. Even more serious,

you knew people were dying because of missed calls and delayed responses.

Investigating further, you discovered that although he told you otherwise, the chief of police never, in fact, approved your proposal, which would have permitted human resources to hire the additional staff. When the mayor called to discuss complaints his office had received about poor 911 service, the chief told the mayor the call centre was fully staffed and placed the blame on your department's inefficiency. Based on current call volume, your department is short approximately 25 percent of the operators needed to service the 911 calls it receives efficiently.

ETHICAL DILEMMA

Once you realize your staffing proposal has been ignored and take into account the serious ramifications that result from this, do you report this to the mayor and the city's board of elected officials?

SOURCES: Mike Fitzgerald, "911 Problem Began Months Ago," *Belleville News-Democrat*, October 13, 2002, http://www.belleville.com; and Phil Mendelson, "Want an Explanation of D.C.'s 911 Deficiencies? Hold, Please," *The Washington Post*, March 9, 2003, B8.

CONTROLLING

5 learning goal

controlling

The process of assessing the organization's progress toward accomplishing its goals; includes monitoring the implementation of a plan and correcting deviations from it.

The fourth key function that managers perform is **controlling.** Controlling is the process of assessing the organization's progress toward accomplishing its goals. It includes monitoring the implementation of a plan and correcting deviations from that plan. As Exhibit 7.5 shows, controlling can be visualized as a cyclical process made up of five stages:

1. setting performance standards (goals),

2. measuring performance,

3. comparing actual performance to established performance standards,

4. taking corrective action (if necessary), and

5. using information gained from the process to set future performance standards.

Performance standards are the levels of performance the company wants to attain. These goals are based on its strategic, tactical, and operational plans. The most effective performance standards state a measurable behavioural objective that can be achieved in a specified time frame. For example, the performance objective for the sales division of a company could be stated as "$100,000 in gross sales for the month of January." Each individual employee in that division would also have a specified performance goal. Actual firm, division, or individual performance can be measured against desired performance standards to see if a gap exists between the desired level of performance and the actual level of performance. If a performance gap does exist, the reason for it must be determined and corrective action taken.

Feedback is essential to the process of control. Most companies have a reporting system that identifies areas where performance standards are not being met. A feedback system helps managers detect problems before they get out of hand. If a problem exists, the managers take corrective action. Toyota uses a simple but effective control system on its automobile assembly lines. Each worker serves as the "customer" for the process just before his or hers and is empowered to act as a quality control inspector. If a part is defective or not installed properly, the next worker won't accept it. Any worker can alert the supervisor to a problem by tugging on a rope that turns on a warning light (i.e., feedback). If the problem isn't corrected, the worker can stop the entire assembly line.

Exhibit 7.5 | The Control Process

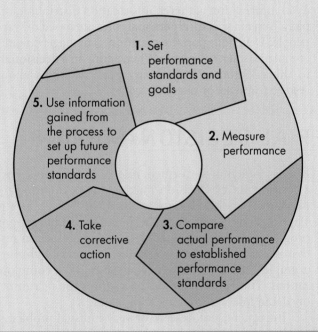

1. Set performance standards and goals

2. Measure performance

3. Compare actual performance to established performance standards

4. Take corrective action

5. Use information gained from the process to set up future performance standards

---

Supervisory managers need to be knowledgeable about the specific production and operation tools, techniques, and methods relevant to their specific area of the organization.

© AP / WORLD WIDE PHOTOS

Why is controlling such an important part of a manager's job? First, it helps managers to determine the success of the other three functions: planning, organizing, and leading. Second, control systems direct employee behaviour toward achieving organizational goals. Third, control systems provide a means of coordinating employee activities and integrating resources throughout the organization.

concept check

Describe the control process.

Why is the control process important to the success of the organization?

MANAGERIAL ROLES

 6 *learning goal*

informational roles

A manager's activities as an information gatherer, information disseminator, or spokesperson for the company.

In carrying out the responsibilities of planning, organizing, leading, and controlling, managers take on many roles. A role is a set of behavioural expectations, or a set of activities that a person is expected to perform. Managers' roles fall into three basic categories: *informational roles, interpersonal roles,* and *decisional roles.* These roles are summarized in Exhibit 7.6. In an **informational role,** the manager may act as an information gatherer, information distributor, or spokesperson for the company. A manager's **interpersonal roles** are based on various interactions with other people. Depending on the situation, a manager might need to act as a figurehead, company leader, or liaison. When acting in a **decisional role,** a manager might have to think like an entrepreneur, make decisions about resource allocation, help resolve conflicts, or negotiate compromises.

MANAGERIAL DECISION-MAKING

interpersonal roles

A manager's activities as a figurehead, company leader, or liaison.

decisional roles

A manager's activities as an entrepreneur, resource allocator, conflict resolver, or negotiator.

programmed decisions

Decisions made in response to frequently occurring routine situations.

non-programmed decisions

Responses to infrequent, unforeseen, or very unusual problems and opportunities, where the manager does not have a precedent to follow in decision-making.

In every function performed, role taken on, and set of skills applied, a manager is a decision maker. Decision-making means choosing among alternatives. Decision-making occurs in response to the identification of a problem or an opportunity. The decisions managers make fall into two basic categories: programmed and non-programmed. **Programmed decisions** are made in response to routine situations that occur frequently in a variety of settings throughout an organization. For example, the need to hire new personnel is a common situation for most organizations. Therefore, standard procedures for recruitment and selection are developed and followed in most companies.

Infrequent, unforeseen, or very unusual problems and opportunities require **non-programmed decisions** by managers. Because these situations are unique and complex, the manager rarely has a precedent to follow. For example, after Hurricane Katrina in New Orleans, many non-programmed decisions were needed. The overwhelming magnitude of the disaster was unforeseen, and rescue and emergency workers responded to the disaster to the best of their ability but were unable to keep up with the needs. Had this situation been anticipated, more and better planning would have resulted.

Managers typically follow five steps in the decision-making process, as illustrated in Exhibit 7.7:

1. Recognize or define the problem or opportunity. Although it is more common to focus on problems because of their obvious negative effects, managers who do not take advantage of new opportunities might lose the company's competitive advantage over other firms.

2. Gather information so as to identify alternative solutions or actions.

Exhibit 7.6 | The Many Roles That Managers Play in an Organization

ROLE	DESCRIPTION	EXAMPLE
Informational		
Monitor	Seeks out and gathers information relevant to the organization.	Finding out about legal restrictions on new product technology.
Disseminator	Provides information where it is needed in the organization.	Providing current production figures to workers on the assembly line.
Spokesperson	Transmits information to people outside the organization.	Representing the company at a shareholders' meeting.
Interpersonal		
Figurehead	Represents the company in a symbolic way.	Cutting the ribbon at a ceremony for the opening of a new building.
Leader	Guides and motivates employees to achieve organizational goals.	Helping subordinates to set monthly performance goals.
Liaison	Acts as a go-between among individuals inside and outside the organization.	Representing the retail sales division of the company at a regional sales meeting.
Decisional		
Entrepreneur	Searches out new opportunities and initiates change.	Implementing a new production process using new technology.
Disturbance handler	Handles unexpected events and crises.	Handling a crisis situation such as a fire.
Resource allocator	Designates the use of financial, human, and other organizational resources.	Approving the funds necessary to purchase computer equipment and hire personnel.
Negotiator	Represents the company at negotiating processes.	Participating in salary negotiations with union representatives.

Exhibit 7.7 | The Decision-Making Process

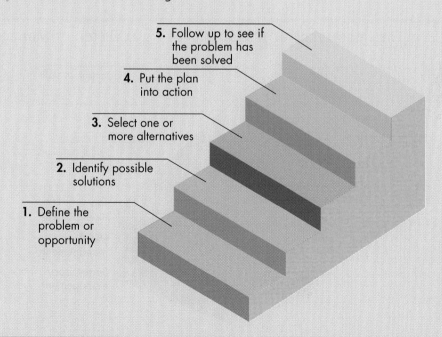

5. Follow up to see if the problem has been solved

4. Put the plan into action

3. Select one or more alternatives

2. Identify possible solutions

1. Define the problem or opportunity

3. Select one or more alternatives after evaluating the strengths and weaknesses of each possibility. This must be based not only on the ability to solve the problem or take advantage of the opportunity but also on the available resources.

4. Put the chosen alternative into action.

5. Gather information to obtain feedback on the effectiveness of the chosen plan.

concept check

What are the three types of managerial roles?

Give examples of things managers might do when acting in each of the different types of roles.

List the five steps in the decision-making process.

MANAGERIAL SKILLS

learning goal

To be successful in planning, organizing, leading, and controlling, managers must use a wide variety of skills. A *skill* is the ability to do something proficiently. Managerial skills fall into three basic categories: conceptual, human relations, and technical skills. The degree to which each type of skill is used depends on the level of the manager's position, as seen in Exhibit 7.8. Additionally, in an increasingly global marketplace, it pays for managers to develop a special set of skills to deal with global management issues.

Technical Skills

technical skills

A manager's specialized areas of knowledge and expertise, as well as the ability to apply that knowledge

Specialized areas of knowledge and expertise and the ability to apply that knowledge make up a manager's **technical skills**. Preparing a financial statement, programming a computer, designing an office building, and analyzing market research are all examples of technical skills. These types of skills are especially important for supervisory managers, because they work closely with employees who are producing the goods and/or services of the firm.

Exhibit 7.8 The Importance of Managerial Skills at Different Management Levels

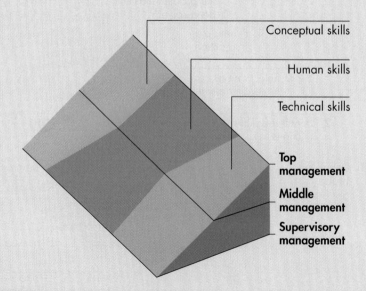

Human Relations Skills

human relations skills
A manager's interpersonal skills that are used to accomplish goals through the use of human resources.

Human relations skills are the interpersonal skills managers use to accomplish goals through the use of human resources. This set of skills includes the ability to understand human behaviour, to communicate effectively with others, and to motivate individuals to accomplish their objectives. Giving positive feedback to employees, being sensitive to their individual needs, and showing a willingness to empower subordinates are all examples of good human relations skills.

At many service companies, one of the keys to success is genuinely friendly service. Achieving their service standards requires genuinely enthusiastic staff. The capacity for such enthusiasm must be determined before the employee is hired. Prospective employees might be asked to take a written test that measures skills and gives personality insights. Once an applicant is hired, the coaching process should begin almost immediately.

Conceptual Skills

conceptual skills
A manager's ability to view the organization as a whole, understand how the various parts are interdependent, and assess how the organization relates to its external environment.

Conceptual skills include the ability to view the organization as a whole, understand how the various parts are interdependent, and assess how the organization relates to its external environment. These skills allow managers to evaluate situations and develop alternative courses of action. Good conceptual skills are especially necessary for managers at the top of the management pyramid, where strategic planning takes place.

Global Management Skills

global management skills
A manager's ability to operate in diverse cultural environments.

The increasing globalization of the world market, as discussed in Chapter 2, has created a need for managers who have **global management skills,** that is, the ability to operate in diverse cultural environments. With more and more companies choosing to do business in multiple locations around the world, employees are often required to learn the geography, language, and social customs of other cultures. It is expensive to train employees for foreign assignments and pay their relocation costs; therefore, choosing the right person for the job is especially important. Individuals who are open-minded, flexible, willing to try new things, and comfortable in a multicultural setting are good candidates for international management positions.

For many managers, accepting an international position might mean helping their spouses and children adapt to the new environment.

© AP / WORLD WIDE PHOTOS

Although a single manager might possess some or most of the skills described above, rarely does one person excel in all types of managerial skills. Every business needs a leader, but in today's marketplace things move too fast, the need for specialization is too great, and competition is too fierce for a one-man or one-woman show to survive.

concept check

Define the basic managerial skills.

How important is each of these skill sets at the different levels of the management pyramid?

What new challenges do managers face due to increasing globalization?

Trends in Management and Leadership

8 *learning goal*

Four important trends in management today are increasing employee empowerment, the growing use of information technology, the increasing need for global management skills, and the need to prepare for crises management.

MANAGERS EMPOWERING EMPLOYEES

Today many firms are including more employees in the decision-making process than ever before. This increased level of employee involvement comes from the realization that people at all levels in the organization possess unique knowledge, skills, and abilities that can be of great value to the company. With empowerment, managers share information and responsibility with employees at all levels in the organization. Along with the authority to make decisions, empowerment gives employees the control over resources needed to implement those decisions. Empowering employees enhances their commitment to the organization by giving them a feeling of ownership in the firm and an increased sense of competency.

For empowerment to work, managers have to facilitate employee decision-making by providing access to necessary information, clear expectations for results, behavioural boundaries, and the resources employees need to carry out their decisions. Empowered employees are also guided by the use of a strategic principle. A company's strategy is expressed in its strategic principle.[8] It gives immediate guidance to make decisions that advance the company's position, not undermine it. Companies like General Electric, Dell, Wal-Mart, and WestJet Airlines have successfully used this concept. When employees understand Wal-Mart's "Low Prices, Every Day," decision-making gets easier.

MANAGERS AND INFORMATION TECHNOLOGY

The second trend having a major impact on managers is the proliferation of information technology. An increasing number of organizations are selling technology, and an increasing number are looking for cutting-edge technology to make and market the products and services they sell. A brief look at companies such as PeopleSoft (now integrated with Oracle), a rapidly growing provider of automated human resource functions, provides some insight into the crucial role information technology can play in today's organizations. Plenty of new technology is being used at PeopleSoft, but it is "people-oriented" technology, and it starts with a backpack. Every new employee is issued a backpack filled with a laptop, pager, cell phone, and digital assistant. Steve Zarate,

HOT Links

For more information about the merger of Oracle and PeopleSoft see: http://www.oracle.com/peoplesoft/index.html.

former chief information officer at PeopleSoft, calls it "information-to-go." Every employee has access to PeopleSoft's "massive information infrastructure that spans continents and time zones"

MANAGING MULTINATIONAL CULTURES

As companies expand around the globe, managers will face the challenges of directing the behaviour of employees around the world. They must recognize that because of cultural differences, people respond to similar situations in very different ways. Managers must decide how they are going to accomplish managing employee behaviour consistently, given such diverse cultural employee backgrounds. The best way to meet this challenge of managing international employees is to develop an individual-level program that is based on values and principles.

Managers should apply three specific principles to this process: example, involvement, and trust. *Example* means that managers should set and live out the standard for others to follow. They must act as role models for all employees of the organization. Leaders must also create personal *involvement* in the organization for all members. Involvement brings the whole person into the company's operations. People are treated like valuable partners, not just as an expense to the company. Leaders must develop a culture of *trust*. This is essential to getting people to invest themselves for the mutual benefit of everyone. When these principles are applied, people are able to manage themselves, and they can release incredible talent and energy.[9]

CRISIS MANAGEMENT

Crises can occur in even the best-managed organizations. For example, there have been power grid meltdowns where the supply of electricity was suspended because of a system overload. No manager or executive can be completely prepared for these types of unexpected crises. However, how a manager handles the situation could mean the difference between disaster, survival, or even financial gain.

No matter what the crisis, there are some basic guidelines that managers should follow to minimize negative outcomes. Managers should not become immobilized by a problem, nor should they ignore it. Managers should face the problem head on. They should always tell the truth about the situation and then put the best people on the job to correct the problem. They should ask for help if they need it, and, finally, managers must learn from the experience to avoid the same problem in the future.[10]

concept check

How can information technology aid in decision-making?

What are three principles of managing multinational cultures?

Describe several guidelines for crisis management.

Great Ideas to Use Now

Many of the skills managers use to accomplish organizational goals can be applied outside the organizational setting. You could be using these skills in your life right now to accomplish your personal goals.

Management and Leadership in Today's Organizations **Chapter 7** | 221

EFFECTIVE TIME MANAGEMENT

Successful managers use their time wisely. Adopting the following time management techniques will help you become a more successful student now and will help prepare you for the demands of your future workplace:

- *Plan ahead.* This is first and most obvious. Set both long- and short-term goals. Review your list often, and revise it when your situation changes.
- *Establish priorities.* Decide what is most important and what is most urgent. Sometimes they are not the same thing. Keep in mind the 80–20 rule: 20 percent of one's effort delivers 80 percent of the results.
- *Delegate.* Ask yourself if the task can be accomplished as effectively by someone else. Empower other people, and you might be surprised by the quality of the outcome.
- *Learn to say no.* Be stingy with your time. Be realistic about how long tasks will take. Don't feel guilty when you don't have the time, ability, or inclination to take on an additional task.
- *Batch.* Group activities together so they take up less of your day. For example, set aside a certain time to return phone calls, answer e-mail, and do any necessary written correspondence.
- *Stay on task.* Learn how to handle diversions. For example, let your answering machine take messages until you finish a particular task.
- *Set deadlines.* Don't let projects drag on. Reward yourself each time you cross a certain number of items off your "to do" list.

Customer Satisfaction and Quality

If managers are going to succeed in business, they must make certain that their companies have a laser-like focus on customer satisfaction and quality. A satisfied customer is a firm's best guarantee of reaching profit goals and gaining repeat business.

Frederick Smith, founder of FedEx, has always done everything possible to give the customer what he or she wants. Acquisitions like RPS in 1998 and American Freightways in 2001 have rounded out FedEx's offerings to include ground and freight delivery, a wise move given the corporate cost cutting that followed. "Having the ground network in place has been particularly important as the economy has slowed," says Jim Winchester, transportation analyst at Lazard Freres. "It allowed us to walk and chew gum at the same time," quips founder and CEO Fred Smith. One of FedEx's customers agrees: George Kurth, director of supply chain and logistics at Hyundai Motor America, consolidated his $450,000 monthly shipping business from a hodgepodge of companies into FedEx. "We wanted the best," he says.[11]

STRESS MANAGEMENT

One of the things that can stop any career in its tracks is burnout. One way to prevent burnout is to examine how well you are dealing with the current stress you are experiencing and learn how to develop coping mechanisms. To start this process, look to see if you are exhibiting any of the warning signs of being overstressed. Students under stress can have a wide range of symptoms, including headaches, asthma attacks, nail biting, and sleep problems.[12] More serious symptoms can include stomach problems and even depression.

If you feel that you are not coping with the stress in your life, now is the time to learn some stress management skills. Here are some helpful ideas:

- Make sure to include physical exercise in your schedule. Try some mind/body work, such as yoga or stretching.
- Find someone you trust and can confide in. Talking out your problems can help a lot.
- If there is no one you feel comfortable talking to, try keeping a diary to work out your stressful situations.
- For more information, visit the Canadian Institute of Stress Web site: **http://www.stresscanada.org**.

SUMMARY OF LEARNING GOALS

1   What is the role of management?

Management is the process of guiding the development, maintenance, and allocation of resources to attain organizational goals. Managers are the people in the organization responsible for developing and carrying out this management process. The four primary functions of managers are planning, organizing, leading, and controlling.

2   What are the four types of planning?

Planning is deciding what needs to be done, identifying when and how it will be done, and determining by whom it should be done. Managers use four types of planning: strategic, tactical, operational, and contingency planning. Strategic planning involves creating long-range (one to five years), broad goals and determining the necessary resources to accomplish those goals. Tactical planning has a shorter time frame (less than one year) and more specific objectives that support the broader strategic goals. Operational planning creates specific standards, methods, policies, and procedures that are used in specific functional areas of the organization. Contingency plans identify alternative courses of action for very unusual or crisis situations.

3   What are the primary responsibilities of managers in organizing activities?

Organizing involves coordinating and allocating a firm's resources to carry out its plans. It includes developing a structure for the people, positions, departments, and activities within the firm. This is accomplished by dividing up tasks (division of labour), grouping jobs and employees (departmentalization), and assigning authority and responsibilities (delegation).

4   How do leadership styles influence a corporate culture?

Leading is the process of guiding and motivating others toward the achievement of organizational goals. Managers have unique leadership styles that range from autocratic to free rein. The set of attitudes, values, and standards of behaviour that distinguishes one organization from another is called corporate culture. A corporate culture evolves over time and is based on the accumulated history of the organization, including the vision of the founders.

5 How do organizations control activities?

Controlling is the process of assessing the organization's progress toward accomplishing its goals. The control process is as follows: set performance standards (goals), measure performance, compare actual performance to established performance standards, take corrective action (if necessary), and use information gained from the process to set future performance standards.

6 What roles do managers take on in different organizational settings?

In an informational role, the manager may act as an information gatherer, an information distributor, or a spokesperson for the company. A manager's interpersonal roles are based on various interactions with other people. Depending on the situation, a manager might need to act as a figurehead, company leader, or liaison.

7 What set of managerial skills is necessary for managerial success?

Managerial skills fall into three basic categories: technical, human relations, and conceptual skills. Specialized areas of knowledge and expertise and the ability to apply that knowledge make up a manager's technical skills. Human relations skills include the ability to understand human behaviour, to communicate effectively with others, and to motivate individuals to accomplish their objectives. Conceptual skills include the ability to view the organization as a whole, understand how the various parts are interdependent, and assess how the organization relates to its external environment.

8 What trends will affect management in the future?

Four important trends in management today are increasing employee empowerment, the increasing use of information technology, the need to manage multinational cultures, and the need to prepare for crisis management. Empowerment means giving employees increased autonomy and discretion to make their own decisions. Using the latest information technology, managers can make quicker, better informed decisions. As more companies "go global," the need for multinational cultural management skills is growing. Managers must set a good example, create personal involvement for all employees, and develop a culture of trust. Crisis management requires quick action, telling the truth about the situation, and putting the best people on the task to correct the situation. Finally, management must learn from the crisis to prevent it from happening again.

EXPERIENTIAL EXERCISES

1. **Would you be a good manager?** Do a self-assessment that includes your current technical, human relations, and conceptual skills. What skills do you already possess, and which do you need to add? Where do your strengths lie? Based on this exercise, develop a description of an effective manager.

2. You are planning to start one of the following companies. Develop a mission statement that defines its vision and give examples of how you would apply each of the four types of planning (strategic, tactical, operational, and contingency) in building the business.

   - Ethnic restaurant near your campus

   - Custom skateboard manufacturer

   - Computer training firm

   - Boutique specializing in Latin American clothing and jewellery

3. Focusing on either your educational institution or a place where you have worked, prepare a brief report on its unique culture. How would you describe it? What has shaped it? What changes do you see occurring over time?

4. Strategic Advantage, **http://www.strategy4u.com,** offers many reasons why companies should develop strategic plans, as well as a strategy tip of the month, assessment tools, planning exercises, and resource links. Explore the site to learn the effect of strategic planning on financial performance, and present your evidence to the class. Then select a planning exercise and, with a group of classmates, perform it as it applies to your school.

5. Are you leadership material? Go to the Leadership section at About.com, **http://management.about.com/cs/leadership/.** Read several articles that interest you to develop a list of characteristics of effective leaders. How do you measure up?

6. How do entrepreneurs develop corporate culture in their companies? Do a search on the term "corporate culture" in *Inc.* (**http://www.inc.com**), *Entrepreneur* (**http://www.entrepreneur.com**), or Fast Company (**http://www.fastcompany.com**). Prepare a short presentation for your class that explains the importance of corporate culture and how it's developed in young firms.

REVIEW QUESTIONS

1. Briefly describe the four primary management functions.

2. How does proper planning help the organization to achieve its mission statement?

3. What are the impacts on a company that does not allocate its resources properly? (Relate this to their stakeholders.)

4. What are the various power bases? What determines the power in each of these?

5. How do the various leadership styles impact a corporate culture?

6. In what situation would each of the three leadership styles be appropriate?

7. Why is it important for leaders to set performance standards? After the performance standards have been set, what actions should follow?

8. As a manager what are the roles you have to play?

9. What skills are necessary to be an effective manger? How does the focus change between the various levels of management?

10. What are the trends that are becoming more important in leadership?

CREATIVE THINKING CASE
A Ford Takes on Ford

If Bill Ford started out as a reluctant CEO, there was a good reason. He hadn't really wanted the job. His first day, he says, "was not a joyful day in my life, particularly given the ages of my [four school-age] children." He didn't want to sacrifice evenings at home with his family and time helping to manage his beloved Detroit Lions, which his family owns (and which were performing almost as badly as Ford Motor). "But," he adds, "I felt I had no choice."

The situation would be a nail-biter for any CEO. But consider this: Bill Ford was only 45 years old. Yes, he had spent 23 years at the company his great-grandfather had founded, toiling away at 18 jobs, proving himself. Yes, he had gotten high marks for his smarts and his humility. But he was still so green. His résumé didn't look anything like that of a Big Three CEO. Though he had been the chairman of Ford Switzerland and the head of the company's climate control division—and chairman of Ford Motor since January 1999—he had never held a top operating or finance position at the company. But he didn't come bulldozing into the job. He reluctantly led a coup when he and the board lost confidence in the former CEO, Jacques Nasser, in part because quality problems were soaring and morale was plummeting.

Ford learned that his job required him to be as much shrink as businessman—something every decent manager quickly realizes. He told some of his executives that he occasionally wondered if he should have gotten a psychology degree instead of a business degree. For instance, he found himself having to manage tension between the laid-back Nick Scheele, the former chairman of Ford Europe whom he'd tapped to be his president and COO (chief operating officer), and the more combative David Thursfield, the former CEO of Ford Europe, whom he'd made group VP (vice president) of international and global purchasing. Ford also had to fend off Wolfgang Reitzle, the head of Ford's premier automotive luxury group, who was pushing Ford for more power. Reitzle left in April 2002 with a fat consulting contract to keep him out of the arms of GM.

For now Ford plans to stay his course. In 2004, his mandate was to get his team to deliver the extra $1 billion in cuts he's promised investors. He must see to it that the problems with Jaguar are fixed and that launches of the Jaguar XJ sedan and the new F-Series pickup truck go smoothly. He must continue to boost quality and slash costs even as new contract talks loom with the United Auto Workers (UAW). A crucial part of Ford's turnaround calls for the closing of five plants by mid-decade, and Ford has said he will work with the union to get that done.[13]

CRITICAL THINKING QUESTIONS

1. How would you describe Bill Ford's leadership style?
2. Do you think Bill Ford's job entails more strategic planning than tactical planning? Why?
3. Is corporate culture important at Ford?

SOURCE: Adapted from Betsy Morris, "Can Ford Save Ford," FORTUNE, November 18, 2002. © 2002 Time Inc. All rights reserved. Reprinted with permission.

VIDEO CASE
SAS Knows How to Keep Employees. . . .

Insanity Inc.? "It's been called worse," says James H. Goodnight, CEO, of the company he helped cofound, SAS Institute, Inc. "If you treat people right they will make a difference. What we do here makes good business sense." The $50 to $70 million SAS saves annually, thanks to an employee defection rate of less than 4 percent, proves him right. And what does SAS do with the dollars its saves? It rewards its employees by creating a work environment that no one wants to leave.

What would keep you happy on the job? A 35-hour workweek? A health-and-recreational centre with Olympic-sized pool, gym, and basketball court? How about an on-site massage therapist and free daily laundering of your workout clothes? Or unlimited sick days, with free comprehensive health insurance and access to on-site health care at a company-run clinic? And of course there are the usual financial rewards: a competitive salary, bonuses, and a profit-sharing plan.

Impossible you say? Welcome to SAS (**http://www.sas.com**), the world's largest privately held software company and leader in e-business solutions, where every day is a dress-down day for the 4,000 people working at the company's 200-acre campus in North Carolina.

Goodnight's free-rein leadership and belief in employee empowerment reflects a corporate culture that supports employees' independent working styles. SAS "hires hard and manages easy." It makes sure employees have the technical and intellectual skills for the job, then lets them get on with it. "We are not into 'face time' here," says Goodnight. "If you need to leave at 4 p.m. on a Wednesday to go watch your child's soccer game, we trust that you will get your work done."

SAS also offers employees unlimited opportunity for growth. Many staffers come as students and stay because they are able to leapfrog around the organization, learning new skills and tackling fresh challenges. Says Goodnight,

> SAS is in the intellectual-property business and our employees work on cutting-edge products. Developing employees' intellectual prowess makes them increasingly valuable to the company. It is not a disgrace to fail, as long as they learn something from it and share the information so we can all learn. Our people are our assets and we believe in taking good care of our assets.

CRITICAL THINKING QUESTIONS

1. Using McGregor's Theory X/Y, explain the relationship between the management and the employees of SAS.

2. Examine the workplace environment and the job itself in light of Herzberg's motivation-hygiene theory.

3. Given your personal experinces in the workplace, compare the SAS environment with what you have experienced.

SOURCE: Adapted from material in the video "Work Hard, Play Hard, and Have a Nice Lunch: Corporate Culture at SAS"; SAS Web site, http://www.sas.com (accessed March 16, 2003).

E-COMMERCE CASE
Stapling Together an E-Commerce Strategy

Wander into one of Staples's more than 240 stores, and you will soon reach an Access Point. These on-line kiosks link you to Staples.ca or Staples.com, where you can order products, build PCs to order, and tap into an on-line library with product and service information.

Why have on-line kiosks in the regular stores? "We're letting customers do business the way they want to do business, not the way we want them to," says Paul Gaffney, executive vice president and chief information officer (CIO) of the Framingham, Massachusetts–based office supplies superstore chain. The Access Point system increases the available products from about 7,500 stocked in the typical store to 45,000 products and dozens of business services. The build-to-order PC feature is so popular that about 35 percent of Staples stores no longer carry computers on-site.

Access Point is just one of Staples's many e-commerce initiatives. The Staples.com Web site focuses on small-business users, whereas 20,000 medium- to large-size companies use StaplesLink.com, their own specialized business-to-business (B2B) e-commerce site. About 70 percent of Staples Contract Division customers place orders through StaplesLink, where users can pull up real-time inventory availability, company-specific contract pricing, and order status. Corporate purchasing managers like the site, which lets them decentralize office supply purchasing while centralizing and controlling costs.

E-commerce is an integral part of Staples's long-term strategy to redefine the customer experience. The company's slogan—"Staples: That was easy"—is now guiding its business decisions. Making sure the firm's customer-focused e-commerce technology does, indeed, simplify purchasing for customers falls to CIO Gaffney. The behind-the-scenes integration work so that Staples shoppers can buy on-line or in-store calls for a big-picture, comprehensive strategy. "To best serve our customers, we follow a disciplined approach to our technology and process integration initiatives," he explains. "That approach aligns our portfolio of projects to our overall business goals."

Gaffney has appointed several groups to help him implement his strategies. An e-commerce steering committee composed of both IT and business managers from these areas has become a primary forum for sharing technology across units and creating a common technology infrastructure. As a result, Staples.com and StaplesLink.com now share applications like order processing. Another team with people from all business areas is examining Staples's business processes and looking at how people, process, and technology relate. The goal is to identify projects that will have the greatest impact.

CRITICAL THINKING QUESTIONS

1. What special challenges does the CIO face in developing and implementing a firm's e-commerce strategy? Discuss and evaluate Gaffney's approach at Staples.

2. What managerial roles does Gaffney take? How would you describe his leadership style and the corporate culture he is promoting?

3. According to a recent article in CIO magazine, the CIO's role in e-commerce has passed through three stages. In the early years of e-commerce (1996–2000), the CIO took a back seat to the dedicated e-commerce business unit managers. From 2000 to 2002, as the dot-com bubble burst, the CIO moved into a major role in overall e-commerce management, focusing on execution, cost control, and consolidation. Now that e-commerce is considered an essential part of corporate strategy, many industry experts expect business unit leaders to want more control. How should the CIO's role shift to accommodate the maturing of e-commerce? What has Gaffney done to adapt his management approach to this third stage?

SOURCES: Todd Datz, "Strategic Alignment," *CIO,* August 15, 2002, http://www.cio.com; "Staples Inc. Corporate Overview," Staples corporate Web site, http://www.staples.com (accessed April 20, 2003); "Staples Launches National Advertising Campaign to Introduce New Brand Promise," *Business Wire,* February 27, 2003, http://www.staples.com; "Staples Launches New Version of StaplesLink.com B-to-B Procurement Web Site," *Business Wire,* February 18, 2003, http://www.staples.com; "Staples Inc. Receives CIO Magazine's CIO-100 Award for Technology and Process Integration," *Business Wire,* August 15, 2002, http://www.staples.com; Elana Varon, "The New Lords of E-Biz," *CIO,* March 15, 2003, http://www.cio.com.

8

Making the Connection

Designing Organizational Structures

We saw in the previous chapter how all of the functions of a manager are highly integrated. They are done almost simultaneously, and they affect and are affected by one another. They are the glue that binds the organization together, because it is the process of management that guides the internal organization to achieve its critical success factors, within the external environment that it is faced with, and to the satisfaction of its stakeholders. Sounds complicated, doesn't it? Well, management isn't easy. The rewards of a successful business don't come without effort, but they are definitely worth it. To make it easier, we will examine each of the functions of a manager separately. Just remember that they are connected.

In this chapter, we will examine the design of organizational structures suitable for achieving the goals of the company. Take the example of BMG, discussed in this chapter. The company's goal was improved *financial performance* through greater efficiency and competitiveness to become the "world's largest and most efficient music company." To achieve this goal, it centralized its structure, cut jobs, and realigned or eliminated less profitable markets. It also created BMG Strategic Marketing Group to guide its international marketing. Centralizing operations is often done, as it was in this case, to reduce the duplication of effort that can occur in a looser, decentralized structure

but brings with it its own problems. Procter & Gamble (P&G) (discussed in Chapter 7) also made changes to its organizational structure in 2005. Its goal was faster product *innovation* and increased flexibility and response time. This goal came in response to today's rapidly changing business environment, which demands that businesses respond more quickly to meet both competitive threats and changing customer needs. Innovation, we know, is a critical success factor, and P&G needed to be a step ahead of the competition. To achieve this goal, it shifted from a geographically based structure to a structure based on products. It also introduced a new compensation system to encourage innovation. This is a very integrative example. We can see that the strategic plan fits with the environment, that the organizational structure fits with the strategic plan, and that the tactical plan for compensation was changed to fit with the strategic plan as well.

In fact, you'll see that when organizations change their structures, they are attempting to increase their ability to *satisfy the customer*, the central ingredient to organizational success—whether through centralizing some operations to improve customer service, reduce costs, and ultimately reduce price; decentralizing to be more responsive to customer needs; or using information technology to get closer to the customer.

One of the structural building blocks of the organization is the managerial hierarchy. The traditional configuration is a pyramid structure with employees at the bottom and top management at the top. However, some companies alter this to *improve employee commitment*. Once such company is Halsall Associates. As discussed in the chapter, it is one of Canada's leading engineering firms and is considered one of the best places to work in Canada. Halsall has followed the trend that some companies have followed—inverting the pyramid and putting employees at the top. This demonstrates graphically that "employees are the priority within the company," in the same way that we understand how important a factor employee commitment is to a company's success.

As discussed in the chapter, the organizing or structuring process is accomplished by dividing the work to be done, grouping the parts together, and assigning authority and responsibility. A formal organizational structure is the result of this design process. In this chapter, we describe this formal organization as "human, material, financial, and information resources deliberately connected to form the business organization." In other words, the resources of each functional area are structured in such a way that even though they are in separate areas—human resources, operations, finance, and marketing—they are linked together so that the organization can achieve its goals. If the organization is not structured in this way, with all the parts working together in an integrative way, success is not possible. We know from our discussion in the introduction to the model that all of the critical success factors are connected. They are also connected to each of the functional areas. The most obvious connections are

- achieving financial performance (*finance*);
- meeting and exceeding customer needs (*marketing*);
- providing value—quality products at a reasonable price (*operations* and *marketing*);
- encouraging creativity and innovation (all areas); and
- gaining employee commitment (*human resources*).

However the parts of the business can't work independently and achieve these success factors. It all starts, as we've said, with the customer. As you'll see in the chapter, every organization is structured with the customer as the central thread. With this in mind, operations and marketing must work together. Marketing determines the needs of the customer and works with operations to design a product to meet those needs. Operations provides it in a quality manner, and marketing prices it to reflect the level of quality and provide something of value to the customer. They can't do this without people committed to making it work, and they can't keep doing it without fresh ideas that keep the organization providing something that distinguishes it from the competition. All of these areas provide the income for the business, but that money must flow back to each of the areas as needed to fuel the plans. It is therefore necessary that whatever structure is designed should take into consideration the inseparable connections among the different areas of the business.

Certain structures specifically integrate the different functional areas intentionally, so that they are working together on specific projects. A matrix structure is one such example. All areas are represented, so that conflicting objectives can be balanced, and overall goals, rather than individual ones, become the priority. This structure also allows for other factors that contribute to success—different minds working together increases creativity and innovation, for example.

Another type of structure takes the topic of integration beyond the borders of the business, as in the case with most successful businesses today. As we describe in the chapter, the virtual corporation is a "network of independent companies linked by information technology," which allows them to take advantages of opportunities they couldn't act on alone and share each other's key competencies to become a truly integrative organization. Cisco is one such company that is at the forefront of this new type of structure. Cisco CEO John Chambers's beliefs reflect the essence of this integrative structure—organizations should be built on change, organized as networks, and based on interdependencies.

Chapter 8

© AP/WORLD WIDE PHOTOS

Designing Organizational Structures

learning goals

1 What are the five structural building blocks that managers use to design organizations?

2 What are the five types of departmentalization?

3 How can the degree of centralization/decentralization be altered to make an organization more successful?

4 How do mechanistic and organic organizations differ?

5 What is the difference between line positions and staff positions?

6 What is the goal of re-engineering?

7 How does the informal organization affect the performance of the company?

8 What trends are influencing the way businesses organize?

The Restructuring of BMG

Finding the appropriate corporate structure for a multinational organization is never an easy task. However, when you're the music arm of one of the largest conglomerates in the world bent on becoming the leader in the music industry, the task is even greater. BMG's music-publishing operations are the third largest in the world and include more than 200 record labels in 41 countries, including Sony BMG in Canada. The careers of hundreds of artists have been launched and nurtured under BMG, including Avril Lavigne, INXS, Kalan Porter, and Santana. Reorganizing for growth is the goal of BMG (**http://www.sonybmg.ca**), the music and entertainment division of German media giant Bertelsmann. This objective has consumed much of the time of BMG's top managers in the past few years.

In 2001, Rolf Schmidt-Holtz was appointed CEO of BMG. At that time, BMG was loosely organized and very decentralized. Many managers and workers were duplicating one another's tasks, resulting in wasted time and energy. Each of BMG's record labels, including RCA, Arista, J Records, and others, had its own management team. BMG also had regional management teams overseeing the activities of each division. One of Schmidt-Holtz's earliest objectives was to restructure BMG management units to make the company more efficient, competitive, and profitable and to create a more centralized structure.

Schmidt-Holtz restructured the organization with the intent of becoming the world's largest and most efficient music company. He cut more than 1,300 jobs and realigned or eliminated less profitable BMG markets. In Europe, Schmidt-Holtz combined some markets, and in others he entered into joint ventures with other large music companies such as EMI's Capital Records. In Greece, BMG is closing shop and outsourcing its dealings to EMI's Virgin Records. In the profitable American market, BMG North America was eliminated, and RCA Records executives took over management duties. Schmidt-Holtz also created BMG Strategic Marketing Group to guide the international marketing campaigns of BMG worldwide.[1]

Critical Thinking Questions

1. How will the return to centralized decision-making affect BMG?
2. Will the restructure succeed in making BMG more efficient?
3. How will the development of the specialized Strategic Marketing division affect marketing decisions within each individual unit?

Principles of Organizational Structures

In today's dynamic business environment, organizational structures need to be designed so that the organization can respond quickly to new competitive threats and changing customer needs. Future success for companies such as BMG will depend on the company's ability to be flexible and respond to the needs of customers. In this chapter, we'll present the five structural building blocks of organizations and look at how each can be used to build unique organizational structures. We'll explore how communication, authority, and job specialization are combined to create both formal and informal organizational structures. Finally, we'll consider how re-engineering and new business trends are changing the way businesses organize.

STRUCTURAL BUILDING BLOCKS

1 learning goal

As you learned in Chapter 7, the key functions that managers perform include planning, organizing, leading, and controlling. In this chapter, we focus specifically on the organizing function. *Organizing* involves coordinating and allocating a firm's resources so that the firm can carry out its plans and achieve its goals. This organizing, or structuring, process is accomplished by

- determining work activities and dividing tasks (*division of labour*),
- grouping jobs and employees (*departmentalization*), and
- assigning authority and responsibilities (*delegation*).

The result of the organizing process is a formal organizational structure. A **formal organization** is the order and design of relationships within the firm. It consists of two or more people working together with a common objective and clarity of purpose. Formal organizations also have well-defined lines of authority, channels for information flow, and means of control. Human, material, financial, and information resources are deliberately connected to form the business organization. Some connections are long lasting, such as the links among people in the finance or marketing department. Others can be changed at almost any time, as when a committee is formed to study a problem.

Five structural building blocks are used in designing an efficient and effective organizational structure. They are division of labour, departmentalization, managerial hierarchy, span of control, and centralization of decision-making (the last three relating to delegation).

Division of Labour

The process of dividing work into separate jobs and assigning tasks to workers is called **division of labour.** In a fast-food restaurant, for example, some employees take or fill orders, others prepare food, a few clean and maintain equipment, and at least one supervises all the others. In an auto assembly plant, some workers install rearview mirrors, while others mount bumpers on bumper brackets. The degree to which the tasks are subdivided into smaller jobs is called **specialization.** Employees who work at highly specialized jobs, such as assembly line workers, perform a limited number and variety of tasks. Employees who become specialists at one task, or a small number of tasks, develop greater skill in doing that particular job. This can lead to greater efficiency and consistency in production and other work activities. However, a high degree of specialization can also result in employees who are uninterested or bored due to the lack of variety and challenge.

formal organization
The order and design of relationships within a firm; consists of two or more people working together with a common objective and clarity of purpose.

division of labour
The process of dividing work into separate jobs and assigning tasks to workers.

specialization
The degree to which tasks are subdivided into smaller jobs.

Specialization can have a greater downside than lack of interest if employees do not work in an environment of empowerment and trust. When workers are specialists at their particular jobs, they can become extremely productive by creating innovative techniques for high-quality and high-quantity output. This process can give invaluable knowledge that can be used to the workers' advantage. However, in some cases, it can spell trouble for the company. Manufacturing company Boeing uses giant cutting machines run by highly specialized workers who cut metal shafts for its aircraft. The slightest deviation in accuracy can ruin the cut and create a defective product.

Some employees can outperform others hands down using innovative techniques. Management would love to have these tricks and techniques shared among all employees. Unfortunately, the star performers sometimes refuse regardless of how much coaxing management does. These top performers cite job security, bargaining power, and insurance against reassignment as their reasons for non-compliance.[2]

Departmentalization

The second building block used to create a strong organizational structure is called **departmentalization.** After the work is divided into jobs, jobs are then grouped together so that similar or associated tasks and activities can be coordinated. This grouping of people, tasks, and resources into organizational units facilitates the planning, leading, and control processes. An **organization chart** is a visual representation of the structured relationships among tasks and the people given the authority to do those tasks. In the organization chart in Exhibit 8.1, each figure represents a job, and each job includes several tasks. The sales manager, for instance, must hire salespeople, establish sales territories, motivate and train the salespeople, and control sales operations. The chart also indicates the general type of work done in each position.

2 *learning goal*

departmentalization

The process of grouping jobs together so that similar or associated tasks and activities can be coordinated.

organization chart

A visual representation of the structured relationships among tasks and the people given the authority to do those tasks.

HOT Links

What benefits can a company gain by using Web-based organizational charting software? Find out the features Peopleboard.com offers companies at http://www.peopleboard.com.

Motorola sells more cell phones in China, the world's largest market with 200 million subscribers, than anyone. Motorola, therefore, has a geographic departmentalization and has invested significantly in manufacturing and research and development facilities in China.

© PHOTODISC RED / GETTY IMAGES

Exhibit 8.1 | Organizational Chart for a Typical Appliance Manufacturer

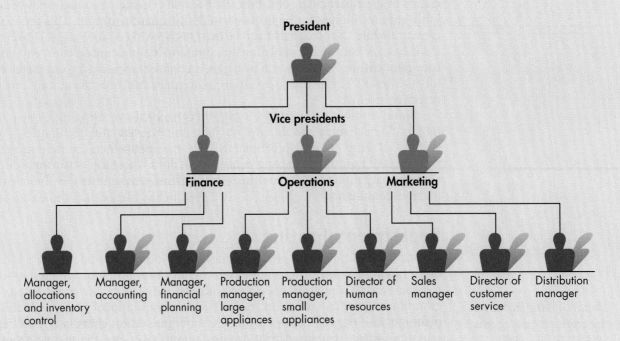

As Exhibit 8.2 (page 238) shows, five basic types of departmentalization are commonly used in organizations:

1. *functional departmentalization*, which is based on the primary functions performed within an organizational unit (marketing, finance, production, sales, and so on);

2. *product departmentalization*, which is based on the goods or services produced or sold by the organizational unit (such as outpatient/emergency services, pediatrics, cardiology, and orthopedics);

3. *process departmentalization*, which is based on the production process used by the organizational unit (such as lumber cutting and treatment, furniture finishing, shipping);

4. *customer departmentalization*, which is based on the primary type of customer served by the organizational unit (such as wholesale or retail purchasers); and

5. *geographic departmentalization*, which is based on the geographic segmentation of organizational units (such as Canadian and U.S. marketing, European marketing, South American marketing).

People are assigned to a particular organizational unit because they perform similar or related tasks, or because they are jointly responsible for a product, client, or market. Decisions about how to departmentalize affect the way in which management assigns authority, distributes resources, rewards performance, and sets up lines of communication. Many large organizations use several types of departmentalization. For example, a global company might be departmentalized first geographically (North American, European, and Asian units), then by product line (foods/beverages and health care), and finally by functional area (marketing, operations, finance, and so on).

---

functional departmentalization

Departmentalization that is based on the primary functions performed within an organizational unit.

product departmentalization

Departmentalization that is based on the goods or services produced or sold by the organizational unit.

process departmentalization

Departmentalization that is based on the production process used by the organizational unit.

customer departmentalization

Departmentalization that is based on the primary type of customer served by the organizational unit.

geographic departmentalization

Departmentalization that is based on the geographic segmentation of the organizational units.

Managerial Hierarchy

managerial hierarchy
The levels of management within an organization; typically, includes top, middle, and supervisory management.

The third building block used to create effective organizational structure is the **managerial hierarchy** (also called the *management pyramid*), or the levels of management within the organization. Generally, the management structure has three levels: top, middle, and supervisory management. These three levels were introduced in Chapter 7.

In a managerial hierarchy, each organizational unit is controlled and supervised by a manager in a higher unit. The person with the most formal authority is at the top of the hierarchy. The higher a manager, the more power he or she has. Thus, the amount of power decreases as you move down the management pyramid. At the same time, the number of employees increases as you move down the hierarchy.

Not all companies today are using this traditional configuration. An interesting trend in designing a company's management structure is the inverted pyramid. For instance, Toronto-based Halsall Associates Ltd., an engineering firm, describes itself just that way.[3] When the president of the company, Peter Halsall, discusses his management structure, he draws an upside-down pyramid. At the bottom of the pyramid, he puts himself. Above him, he lists the layers of management and, finally, the frontline employees. The reason he does this is to show graphically that the employees are the priority within the company. He explains, "Decisions are made so these people maximize their opportunities." This unusual view must pay off: Halsall Associates is one of Canada's leading engineering firms and is considered one of the best places to work.

chain of command
The line of authority that extends from one level of an organization's hierarchy to the next, from top to bottom, and makes clear who reports to whom.

An organization with a well-defined hierarchy has a clear **chain of command,** which is the line of authority that extends from one level of the organization to the next, from top to bottom, and makes clear who reports to whom. The chain of command is shown in the organization chart and can be traced from the CEO all the way down to the employees producing goods and services. Under the *unity of command* principle, everyone reports to and gets instructions from only one boss. Unity of command guarantees that everyone will have a direct supervisor and will not be taking orders from a number of supervisors. Unity of command and chain of command give everyone in the organization clear directions and help coordinate people doing different jobs.

The growth of the global marketplace has led some companies to examine the traditional principle of unity of command with a single person at the top of the organization. These organizations are finding the need for quick decision-making and flexibility around the world too difficult for any one individual to handle. Many companies are moving to alternative management models, including co-CEOs or even a committee model of leadership. American Eagle Outfitters, the retailer of cool specialty apparel for men and women ages 16 to 34, has opted for dual CEOs. Roger Markfield and James O'Donnell work together as a team to build the brand. The company now has more than 900 stores in Canada and the United States. Recently, it repositioned its Canadian Bluenotes brand stores from traditional jeans stores to "lifestyle stores" with more fashion-driven merchandise.

authority
Legitimate power, granted by the organization and acknowledged by employees, that allows an individual to request action and expect compliance.

delegation of authority
The assignment of some degree of authority and responsibility to persons lower in the chain of command.

Individuals who are part of the chain of command have authority over other persons in the organization. **Authority** is legitimate power, granted by the organization and acknowledged by employees, that allows an individual to request action and expect compliance. Exercising authority means making decisions and seeing that they are carried out. Most managers delegate, or assign, some degree of authority and responsibility to others below them in the chain of command. The **delegation of authority** makes the employees accountable to their supervisor. *Accountability* means responsibility for outcomes. Typically, authority and responsibility move downward through the organization as managers assign activities to, and share decision-making with, their subordinates. Accountability moves upward in the organization as managers in each successively higher level are held accountable for the actions of their subordinates.

Exhibit 8.2 | Five Ways to Organize

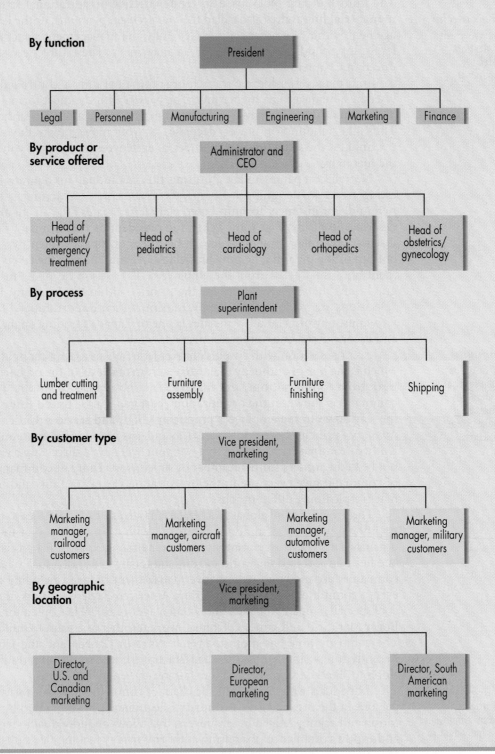

By function

President

Legal | Personnel | Manufacturing | Engineering | Marketing | Finance

By product or service offered

Administrator and CEO

Head of outpatient/ emergency treatment | Head of pediatrics | Head of cardiology | Head of orthopedics | Head of obstetrics/ gynecology

By process

Plant superintendent

Lumber cutting and treatment | Furniture assembly | Furniture finishing | Shipping

By customer type

Vice president, marketing

Marketing manager, railroad customers | Marketing manager, aircraft customers | Marketing manager, automotive customers | Marketing manager, military customers

By geographic location

Vice president, marketing

Director, U.S. and Canadian marketing | Director, European marketing | Director, South American marketing

Span of Control

span of control
The number of employees a manager directly supervises; also called span of management.

The fourth structural building block is the managerial span of control. Each firm must decide how many managers are needed at each level of the management hierarchy to effectively supervise the work performed within organizational units. A manager's **span of control** (sometimes called *span of management*) is the number of employees the manager directly supervises. It can be as narrow as 2 or 3 employees or as wide as 50 or more. In general, the larger the span of control, the more efficient the organization. As Exhibit 8.3 shows, however, both narrow and wide spans of control have benefits and drawbacks.

If hundreds of employees perform the same job, one supervisor might be able to manage a very large number of employees. Such might be the case at a clothing plant, where hundreds of sewing machine operators work from identical patterns. But if employees perform complex and dissimilar tasks, a manager can effectively supervise only a much smaller number. For instance, a supervisor in the research and development area of a pharmaceutical company might oversee just a few research chemists because of the highly complex nature of their jobs.

The optimal span of control is determined by the following five factors:

1. *Nature of the task.* The more complex the task, the narrower the span of control.

2. *Location of the workers.* The more locations, the narrower the span of control.

3. *Ability of the manager to delegate responsibility.* The greater the ability to delegate, the wider the span of control.

4. *Amount of interaction and feedback between the workers and the manager.* The more feedback and interaction required, the narrower the span of control.

5. *Level of skill and motivation of the workers.* The higher the skill level and motivation, the wider the span of control.

Exhibit 8.3	Narrow and Wide Spans of Control	
	ADVANTAGES	**DISADVANTAGES**
Narrow span of control	• High degree of control. • Fewer subordinates may mean manager is more familiar with each individual. • Close supervision can provide immediate feedback.	• More levels of management, therefore more expensive. • Slower decision-making due to vertical layers. • Isolation of top management. • Discourages employee autonomy.
Wide span of control	• Fewer levels of management means increased efficiency and reduced costs. • Increased subordinate autonomy leads to quicker decision-making. • Greater organizational flexibility. • Higher levels of job satisfaction due to employee empowerment.	• Less control. • Possible lack of familiarity due to large number of subordinates. • Managers spread so thin that they can't provide necessary leadership or support. • Lack of coordination or synchronization.

Centralization of Decision-Making

3 learning goal

centralization
The degree to which formal authority is concentrated in one area or level of an organization.

The final component in building an effective organizational structure is deciding at what level in the organizational decisions should be made. **Centralization** is the degree to which formal authority is concentrated in one area or level of the organization. In a highly centralized structure, top management makes most of the key decisions in the organization, with very little input from lower level employees. Centralization lets top managers develop a broad view of operations and exercise tight financial controls. It can also help to reduce costs by eliminating redundancy in the organization. But centralization can also mean that lower-level personnel don't get a chance to develop their decision-making and leadership skills and that the organization is less able to respond quickly to customer demands.

The span of control is wide for employees who have highly specialized and similar skills like these memory chip technicians. A wide span of control means that managers can supervise more employees.

© CHARLES O'REAR / CORBIS

decentralization

The process of pushing decision-making authority down the organizational hierarchy.

Decentralization is the process of pushing decision-making authority down the organizational hierarchy, giving lower-level personnel more responsibility and power to make and implement decisions. Benefits of decentralization can include quicker decision-making, increased levels of innovation and creativity, greater organizational flexibility, faster development of lower-level managers, and increased levels of job satisfaction and employee commitment. But decentralization can also be risky. If lower-level personnel don't have the necessary skills and training to perform effectively, they might make costly mistakes. Additionally, decentralization can increase the likelihood of inefficient lines of communication, incongruent or competing objectives, and duplication of effort.

Several factors must be considered when deciding how much decision-making authority to delegate throughout the organization. These factors include the size of the organization, the speed of change in its environment, managers' willingness to give up authority, employees' willingness to accept more authority, and the organization's geographic dispersion.

Decentralization is usually desirable when the following conditions are met:

- The organization is very large, such as Magna, Petro-Canada, or Ford.
- The firm is in a dynamic environment where quick, local decisions must be made, as in many high-tech industries.
- Managers are willing to share power with their subordinates.
- Employees are willing and able to take more responsibility.
- The company is spread out geographically, such as The Bay, Parmalat Canada, and Prudential Financial.

As organizations grow and change, they continually re-evaluate their structure to determine whether it is helping the company to achieve their goals.

concept check

What are the five building blocks of organizational structure?

What are the basic types of departmentalization?

What factors determine the optimal span of control?

What are the primary characteristics of a decentralized organization?

MECHANISTIC VERSUS ORGANIC STRUCTURES

mechanistic organization

An organizational structure that is characterized by a relatively high degree of job specialization, rigid departmentalization, many layers of management, narrow spans of control, centralized decision-making, and a long chain of command.

organic organization

An organizational structure that is characterized by a relatively low degree of job specialization, loose departmentalization, few levels of management, wide spans of control, decentralized decision-making, and a short chain of command.

Using different combinations of the building blocks described, organizations can build a wide variety of organizational structures. Nevertheless, structural design generally follows one of the two basic models described in Exhibit 8.4: mechanistic or organic. A **mechanistic organization** is characterized by a relatively high degree of job specialization, rigid departmentalization, many layers of management (particularly middle management), narrow spans of control, centralized decision-making, and a long chain of command. This combination of elements results in what is called a tall organizational structure. The Canadian Armed Forces and the United Nations are typical mechanistic organizations.

In contrast, an **organic organization** is characterized by a relatively low degree of job specialization, loose departmentalization, few levels of management, wide spans of control, decentralized decision-making, and a short chain of command. This combination of elements results in what is called a flat organizational structure. Colleges and universities tend to have flat organizational structures, with only two or three levels of administration between the faculty and the president. Exhibit 8.5 shows examples of flat and tall organizational structures.

concept check

Compare and contrast mechanistic and organic organizations.
What factors determine whether an organization should be mechanistic or organic?

Although few organizations are purely mechanistic or purely organic, most tend more toward one type or the other. The decision to create a more mechanistic or a more organic structural design is based on factors such as the firm's overall strategy, the size of the organization, the types of technologies used in the organization, and the stability of its external environment. Many e-commerce software companies and research labs are more organic than mechanistic. A few examples are Priceline.com, PetFoodDirect.com, Intel, Expedia.com, Logitech, Activision, Bio-Rad Laboratories, and RAND Corporation, the internationally known think tank.

COMMON ORGANIZATIONAL STRUCTURES

There is no single best way to design an organization. Within the basic mechanistic and organic models and the hybrids that contain elements of both, an almost infinite variety of organizational structures can be developed. Many organizations

---

Exhibit 8.4 | Mechanistic versus Organic

STRUCTURAL CHARACTERISTIC	MECHANISTIC	ORGANIC
Job specialization	High	Low
Departmentalization	Rigid	Loose
Management hierarchy (levels of management)	Tall (many levels)	Flat (few levels)
Span of control	Narrow	Wide
Decision-making authority	Centralized	Decentralized
Chain of command	Long	Short

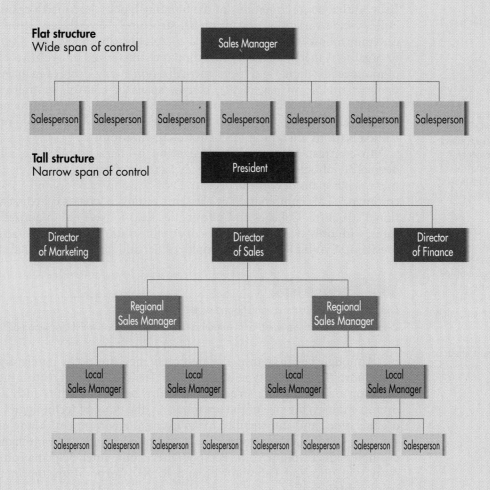

Exhibit 8.5 | Flat versus Tall Organizational Structures

Flat structure
Wide span of control

Sales Manager

Salesperson | Salesperson | Salesperson | Salesperson | Salesperson | Salesperson | Salesperson

Tall structure
Narrow span of control

President

Director of Marketing | Director of Sales | Director of Finance

Regional Sales Manager | Regional Sales Manager

Local Sales Manager | Local Sales Manager | Local Sales Manager | Local Sales Manager

Salesperson | Salesperson | Salesperson | Salesperson | Salesperson | Salesperson | Salesperson | Salesperson

use a combination of elements from different structural types to meet their unique organizational needs. Some of the most common structural designs are discussed in this section.

In addition, some companies are creating "virtual structures" for tax benefits. It is called the offshore virtual corporation and it offers advantages to the small-business owner as well as some large corporations. The way it works is that Internet-based companies are setting up shop outside Canada in places such as Bermuda. What makes this possible is new telecommunication links to these remote locations that allow small local companies to operate like much larger international corporations.

Line Organization

The **line organization** is designed with direct, clear lines of authority and communication flowing from the top managers downward. Managers have direct control over all activities, including administrative duties. An organization chart for this

line organization

An organizational structure with direct, clear lines of authority and communication flowing from the top managers downward.

Apple Computer's CEO Steve Jobs uses an organic structure to develop new products like the iMac computer. Organic structures allow firms like Apple to succeed in rapidly changing environments.

line-and-staff organization

An organizational structure that includes both line and staff positions.

line positions

All positions in the organization directly concerned with producing goods and services and that are directly connected from top to bottom.

staff positions

Positions in an organization held by individuals who provide the administrative and support services that line employees need to achieve the firm's goals.

committee structure

An organizational structure in which authority and responsibility are held by a group rather than an individual.

type of structure would show that all positions in the firm are directly connected via an imaginary line extending from the highest position in the organization to the lowest (where production of goods and services takes place). This structure, with its simple design, clear chain of command, and broad managerial control, is often well suited to small, entrepreneurial firms.

Line-and-Staff Organization

As an organization grows and becomes more complex, the line organization can be enhanced by adding staff positions to the design. Staff positions provide specialized advisory and support services to line managers in the **line-and-staff organization**, shown in Exhibit 8.6. In daily operations, those individuals in **line positions** are directly involved in the processes used to create goods and services. Those individuals in **staff positions** provide the administrative and support services that line employees need to achieve the firm's goals. Line positions in organizations are typically in areas such as production, marketing, and finance. Staff positions are found in areas such as legal counselling, managerial consulting, public relations, and human resource management.

Committee Structure

In **committee structure,** authority and responsibility are held by a group rather than an individual. Committees are typically part of a larger line-and-staff organization. Often the committee's role is only advisory, but in some situations the committee has the power to make and implement decisions. Committees can make the coordination of tasks in the organization much easier. For example, Novartis, the huge Swiss pharmaceutical company, revamped its committee structure, which reports to its board of directors. The company hopes "to reflect best practices" in global corporate governance. Novartis will have four permanent committees reporting to the board: the chairman's committee, the compensation committee, the audit and compliance committee, and a newly created corporate governance committee. The chairman's committee will deal with business matters arising between board meetings and will be responsible for high-level appointments and acquisitions. The compensation committee looks at the remuneration of board members, whereas the audit and compliance committee oversees accounting and financial reporting practices. The newly created corporate governance committee's duties include focusing on board nominations, board performance evaluations, and possible conflicts of interest.

Committees bring diverse viewpoints to a problem and expand the range of possible solutions, but there are some drawbacks. Committees can be slow to reach a decision and are sometimes dominated by a single individual. It is also more difficult to hold any one individual accountable for a decision made by a group. Committee meetings can sometimes go on for long periods of time with little seemingly being accomplished.

Exhibit 8.6 | Line-and-Staff Organization

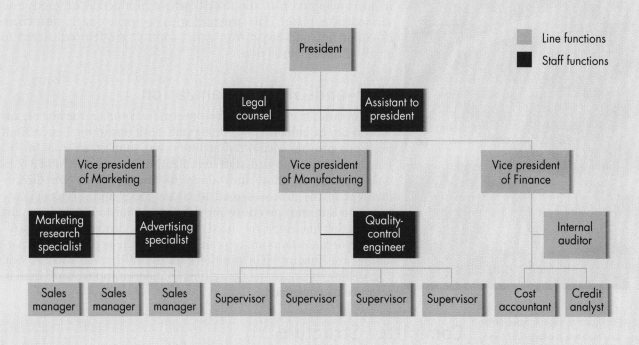

Matrix Structure

**matrix structure
(project management)**
An organizational structure
that combines functional
and product
departmentalization by
bringing together people
from different functional
areas of the organization to
work on a special project.

The **matrix structure** (also called the *project management* approach) is sometimes used in conjunction with the traditional line-and-staff structure in an organization. Essentially, this structure combines two different forms of departmentalization, functional and product, that have complementary strengths and weaknesses. The matrix structure brings together people from different functional areas of the organization (such as manufacturing, finance, and marketing) to work on a special project. Each employee has two direct supervisors: the line manager from her or his specific functional area and the project manager. Exhibit 8.7 shows a matrix organization with four special project groups (A, B, C, D), each with its own project manager. Because of the dual chain of command, the matrix structure presents some unique challenges for both managers and subordinates.

Advantages of the matrix structure include the following.

- *Teamwork.* By pooling the skills and abilities of various specialists, the company can increase creativity and innovation and tackle more complex tasks.

- *Efficient use of resources.* Project managers use only the specialized staff they need to get the job done, instead of building large groups of underused personnel.

- *Flexibility.* The project structure is flexible and can adapt quickly to changes in the environment; the group can be disbanded quickly when it is no longer needed.

- *Ability to balance conflicting objectives.* The customer wants a quality product and predictable costs. The organization wants high profits and the development of technical capability for the future. These competing goals serve as a focal point for directing activities and overcoming conflict. The marketing representative can represent the customer, the finance representative can advocate high profits, and the engineers can push for technical capabilities.

Exhibit 8.7 | Matrix Organization

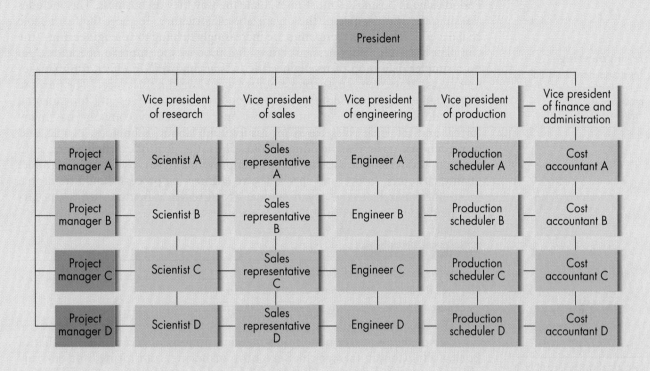

- *Higher performance.* Employees working on special project teams may experience increased feelings of ownership, commitment, and motivation.
- *Opportunities for personal and professional development.* The project structure gives individuals the opportunity to develop and strengthen technical and interpersonal skills.

Disadvantages of the matrix structure include the following.

- *Power struggles.* Functional and product managers might have differing goals and management styles.
- *Confusion among team members.* Reporting relationships and job responsibilities might be unclear.
- *Lack of cohesiveness.* Team members from different functional areas might have difficulty communicating effectively and working together as a team.

HOT *Links*

How is Ford Motor Credit Company's matrix structure working? Get the latest performance statistics by clicking on "investors" at http://www.fordcredit.com.

What benefits does a matrix structure offer a company? According to Jim Cain of the Ford Motor Company, you get the ability to leverage expertise in transactions, management, and execution.[4] To accomplish this goal, Ford decided to create a matrix organizational structure by integrating its treasury and finance groups with those of the Ford Motor Credit Company. The idea was to simplify access for investment bankers, commercial bankers, brokers, analysts, and others to the company's treasury. This was accomplished by creating three assistant treasurers to oversee a team of directors with responsibility for specific areas such as asset management, credit, pension administration, trading, short-term funding, and risk management. Another benefit was increased responsibility in each of these areas. Through this change, the company expected great improvements in both internal and external communication.

RE-ENGINEERING ORGANIZATIONAL STRUCTURE

6 *learning goal*

re-engineering
The complete redesign of business structures and processes to improve operations.

Periodically, all businesses must re-evaluate the way they do business. This includes assessing the effectiveness of the organizational structure. To meet the formidable challenges of the future, companies are increasingly turning to **re-engineering**—the complete redesign of business structures and processes to improve operations. An even simpler definition of re-engineering is "starting over." In effect, top management asks, "If we were a new company, how would we run this place?" The purpose of re-engineering is to identify and abandon the outdated rules and fundamental assumptions that guide current business operations. Every company has many formal and informal rules based on assumptions about technology, people, and organizational goals that no longer hold. Thus, the goal of re-engineering is to redesign business processes to achieve improvements in cost control, product quality, customer service, and speed. The re-engineering process should result in a more efficient and effective organizational structure that is better suited to the current (and future) competitive climate of the industry.

concept check

How do line and staff positions differ?

Why does the matrix structure have a dual chain of command?

What are advantages of a matrix structure? Disadvantages?

HOT *Links*

An excellent source of links and information about the ins and outs of the re-engineering process is the Business Process Reengineering Advisory Group at http://www.eil.utoronto.ca/tool/BPR.html.

One of the most dramatic re-engineering projects of recent times is that of Boeing. Phil Condit, former chief executive of Boeing, transformed the 86-year-old defence contractor. Condit's vision is to reshape Boeing into an organization that is not only a manufacturer but also a service provider. After taking office in 1996, Condit spent $16 billion to purchase McDonnell Douglas and $7 billion to buy a large portion of Rockwell International and Hughes Electronics to expand Boeing's involvement in the aerospace sector. In addition, Boeing is using this newly acquired technology to offer services in other industries as well. One example of this expansion is the movie industry. Boeing is using its satellite system to offer delivery of newly released movies. Instead of physically transporting canisters of celluloid, Boeing will deliver the movie digitally. The cost of digital satellite delivery of the movie runs approximately $500 compared to $2,500 per movie-viewing screen for shipping traditional canisters.[5]

concept check

What is meant by re-engineering?

What is the purpose of re-engineering?

THE INFORMAL ORGANIZATION

7 *learning goal*

informal organization
The network of connections and channels of communication based on the informal relationships of individuals inside an organization.

Up to this point in the chapter, we have focused on formal organizational structures that can be seen in the boxes and lines of the organization chart. Yet many important relationships within an organization do not show up on an organization chart. Nevertheless, these relationships can affect the decisions and performance of employees at all levels of the organization.

The network of connections and channels of communication based on the informal relationships of individuals inside the organization is known as the **informal organization.** Informal relationships can be between people at the same hierarchical level or between people at different levels and in different departments. Some connections are work related, such as those formed among people who car-pool or ride the same train to work. Others are based on non-work commonalties, such as belonging to the same church or health club, or having children who attend the same school. The informal channels of communication of the informal organization are often referred to as the *grapevine*, the *rumour mill*, or the *intelligence network*.

Functions of the Informal Organization

The informal organization has several important functions. First, it provides a source of friendships and social contact for organization members. Second, the interpersonal relationships and informal groups help employees feel better informed about and connected with what is going on in their firm, thus giving them some sense of control over their work environment. Third, the informal organization can provide status and recognition that the formal organization cannot or will not provide employees. Fourth, the network of relationships can aid the socialization of new employees by informally passing along rules, responsibilities, basic objectives, and job expectations. Finally, the organizational grapevine helps employees to be more aware of what is happening in their workplace by transmitting information quickly and conveying it to places that the formal system does not reach.

Although the informal organization can help the formal organization to achieve its goals, it can also create problems if not managed well. *Group norms* (commonly accepted standards of behaviour) might conflict with the company's standards and cause problems. For instance, during a merger or acquisition, informal groups might strongly resist change (especially structural change), spread incorrect information through the grapevine, and foster fear and low morale among employees. With this in mind, managers need to learn to use the existing informal organization as a tool that can potentially benefit the formal organization. An excellent way of putting the informal organization to work for the good of the company is to bring informal leaders into the decision-making process.

The grapevine is a source of information that travels informally among employees. Although it usually carries accurate information, most employees prefer to receive work-related information from their managers.

© PHOTODISC GREEN / GETTY IMAGES

Trends in Organizational Structures

To achieve long-term objectives, organizations constantly evaluate and alter their organizational structures. The increased use of information technology and globalization are creating new options for organizing a business.

THE VIRTUAL CORPORATION

virtual corporation

A network of independent companies linked by information technology to share skills, costs, and access to one another's markets; allows the companies to come together quickly to exploit rapidly changing opportunities.

One of the biggest challenges for companies today is adapting to the technological changes that are affecting all industries. Organizations are struggling to find new organizational structures that will help them transform information technology into a competitive advantage. One alternative that is becoming increasingly prevalent is the **virtual corporation,** which is a network of independent companies (suppliers, customers, even competitors) linked by information technology to share skills, costs, and access to one another's markets. This network structure allows companies to come together quickly to exploit rapidly changing opportunities. These are the key attributes of a virtual corporation:

- *Technology.* Information technology helps geographically distant companies form alliances and work together.
- *Opportunism.* Alliances are less permanent, less formal, and more opportunistic than in traditional partnerships.
- *Excellence.* Each partner brings its core competencies to the alliance, so it is possible to create an organization with higher quality in every functional area and to increase competitive advantage.
- *Trust.* The network structure makes companies more reliant on one another and forces them to strengthen relationships with partners.
- *No borders.* This structure expands the traditional boundaries of an organization.

In the concept's purest form, each company that links with others to create a virtual corporation is stripped to its essence. Ideally, the virtual corporation has neither central office nor organization chart, no hierarchy, and no vertical integration. It contributes to an alliance only its core competencies, or key capabilities. It mixes and matches what it does best with the core competencies of other companies and entrepreneurs. For example, a manufacturer would only manufacture, while relying on a product design firm to decide what to make and a marketing company to sell the products.

Although firms that are purely virtual organizations are still relatively scarce, many companies are embracing several of the characteristics of the virtual structure. One great example is Cisco Systems. Cisco has 34 plants that produce its products, but the company only owns 2 of them. Human hands touch only 10 percent of customer orders. Less than half of all orders are processed by Cisco employees. To the average customer, the interdependency of Cisco's suppliers and inventory systems makes it look like one huge, seamless company.

HOT Links

Go to www.google.ca and, using the search words "virtual corporation concepts," read about new approaches by Canadian companies.

VIRTUAL TEAMS

Technology is also enabling corporations to create virtual work teams. Geography is no longer a limitation when employees are considered for a work team. Virtual teams mean reduced travel time and costs, reduced relocation expenses, and utilization of specialized talent regardless of employee's location. Sabre, Incorporated, which processes more than 400 million travel bookings each year, has created 65 permanent virtual teams with members in Canada and the United States and several other foreign countries. Teams average eight members.[6]

When managers need to staff a project, all they need to do is make a list of required skills and a general list of employees who possess those skills. When the pool of employees is known, the manager simply chooses the best mix of people and creates the virtual team. Special challenges of virtual teams include keeping team members focused, motivated, and communicating positively despite their location. If feasible, at least one face-to-face meeting during the early stages of team formation will help with these potential problems.

Dale Pratt doesn't share an office with her team members. She's not even in the same building or postal code. Pratt, director of Human Resources for Nortel Networks Corporation, works at company headquarters in Ontario. But as a member of a virtual team, she has colleagues as far away as Europe and China. The company creates Internet technologies and has 80,000 employees located in 150 countries.

"We have to work in real time across the globe, really fast, and our employees have to be where our customers are," Pratt says. "For us, working with our virtual team is the same as other companies where people might sit together under a centralized roof. We simply use different tools to do our job every day." Virtual teams might be composed of full- or part-time employees. They might have a global reach, or involve combinations of local telecommuting members and more traditional in-house workers. A senior executive might be on one planning committee for a product release, for example, another for identifying minority vendors, another to study relocating a plant, and another to evaluate software tracking. He might deal with key players who not only are out of the country but also are working for another company, or perhaps are suppliers, who are on the virtual team to add information and technical support.[7]

Making Ethical Choices

SLIPPING UP

While many of your friends like exploring boutiques, you always preferred shopping at chain stores. Walking into a Best Buy or Staples, you know exactly where to look for the items you want. You are curious about how chain stores are structured to provide uniform customer service.

After college graduation you gain firsthand knowledge about division of labour and centralized decision-making as manager of a family-owned hardware business with three local stores. After a few years in this position, a major nationwide pharmacy chain offers you a job as an Ontario regional manager, which you accept. You learn that the tasks required to manage regional operations differ in some ways from those for the local stores you managed. One difference is responsibility for maintaining the exterior as well as the interior, to ensure that customers can move inside and outside safely.

In reviewing corporate policies, you discover that decisions about maintaining the exterior are the same, regardless of the stores' locations. Some stores are located in areas that seldom experience heavy snowfall and are not equipped with shovels for snow removal. This became troublesome one winter, as areas that rarely get snow spent much of the winter repeatedly digging out. After the first major snowstorm, customers complained to local store managers about difficulty traversing the sidewalk in front of the store. Knowing they didn't have resources for snow removal, the managers shared their concerns with you. Your request to upper management for resources was denied, even after you explained the local legal requirement. After the second big snowstorm, several customers slip on the ice trying to enter the store.

ETHICAL DILEMMA

As a regional manager intent on providing a high level of customer service and safety, should you override upper management's decision to comply with local laws and hire a snow removal company?

SOURCES: "D.C. Snow Removal Regulations," ChevyChaseCommunity Listserv@yahoogroups.com, February 21, 2003; District of Columbia Official Code 2001 Edition Division I. Government of District. Title 9. Transportation Systems. Subtitle I. Highways, Bridges, Streets, and Alleys. Chapter 6. Removal of Snow and Ice from Streets and Sidewalks; DC ST 1981 § 7-901; "Snow Shoveling," ChevyChaseCommunity Listserv@yahoogroups.com, February 11, 2003.

STRUCTURING FOR GLOBAL MERGERS

HOT Links

What organizational changes were required when Hewlett-Packard merged with Compaq? Uncover the details at http://www.hp.com.

Recent mergers (such as that of Hewlett Packard and Compaq) creating mega firms raise some important questions regarding corporate structure. How can managers hope to organize the global pieces of these huge, complex new firms into a cohesive, successful whole? Should decision-making be centralized or decentralized? Should the firm be organized around geographic markets or product lines? And how can managers consolidate distinctly different corporate cultures? These issues and many more must be resolved if mergers of global companies are to succeed.

Beyond designing a new organizational structure, one of the most difficult challenges when merging two large companies is uniting the cultures and creating a single business. The recent merger between Pfizer and Pharmacia, makers of Dramamine and Rogaine, is no exception. Failure to effectively merge cultures can have serious effects on organizational efficiency.

In a plan scheduled to last three years, Pfizer put together 14 groups that would make recommendations concerning finances, human resources, operation support, capital improvements, warehousing, logistics, quality control, and information technology. An outside consultant was hired to facilitate the process. One of the first tasks for the groups was to deal with the conqueror (Pfizer) versus conquered (Pharmacia) attitudes. Company executives wanted to make sure all employees knew that their ideas were valuable and they were listening.

concept check

How does technology enable firms to organize as virtual corporations?

What are some organizational issues that must be addressed when two large firms merge?

When Hewlett Packard and Compaq merged, its management teams had to develop a new organizational structure for the newly formed single business while carefully blending two unique corporation cultures.

© AP/WORLD WIDE PHOTOS

Great Ideas to Use Now

How is organizational structure relevant to you? A common thread linking all of the companies profiled in this chapter is you, the consumer. Companies structure their organizations to facilitate achieving their overall organizational goals. To be profitable, companies must have a competitive advantage, and competition is based on meeting customer expectations. The company that best satisfies customer wants and demands is the company that will lead the competition.

When companies make changes to their organizational structures, they are attempting to increase in some way their ability to satisfy the customer. For example, several of the companies profiled in this chapter were consolidating or centralizing parts of their operation. Why? Those companies hope to become more efficient and reduce costs, which should translate into better customer service and more reasonable prices. Some companies are decentralizing operations, giving departments or divisions more autonomy to respond quickly to changes in the market or to be more flexible in their response to customer demands. Many companies are embracing new information technology, because it brings them closer to their customers faster than was previously possible. Internet commerce is benefiting consumers in a number of ways. When you buy books at **http://www.amazon.ca** or use **http://www.ebay.ca** to sell a used bicycle, you are sending the message that the virtual company is a structure you will patronize and support. Increasing globalization and use of information technology will continue to alter the competitive landscape, and the big winner should be the consumer, in terms of increased choice, increased access, and reduced price!

There was a time when large organizations needed only open their doors and customers were waiting to do business. They didn't need to worry about being responsible to customers or having a structure flexible enough to respond to customer needs. Today, no company can afford to take its customers for granted. To keep a strong and loyal customer base, an organization structure must be created to constantly monitor the level of satisfaction the customer is experiencing and then be able to address any problems. One recent example of just how far a company is willing to go to keep its customers happy is Enterprise Rent-A-Car.

After the attacks of September 11, 2001, Enterprise found itself faced with many stranded customers. With all airports shut down, stranded travellers found themselves with no way to get home other than by car. In an unprecedented move, Andy Taylor, Chairman and CEO, told the 4,300 U.S. neighbourhood locations to permit out-of-state one-way rentals for stranded travellers and waive or reimburse drop-off fees. In an e-mail message to the employees, Taylor said, "Right now, we're just concerned about taking care of our customers."[8] As a result of this decision, thousands of Enterprise's cars were displaced in other cities without any means of return. Some cars were sold, employees retrieved others, and still others were shipped back on flatbed trucks. By putting customers' needs first during this national emergency, Enterprise incurred significant costs but maintained its firm policy on customer satisfaction.

SUMMARY OF LEARNING GOALS

1 What are the five structural building blocks that managers use to design organizations?

The five structural building blocks that are used in designing an efficient and effective organizational structure are

- division of labour, which is the process of dividing work into separate jobs and assigning tasks to workers;
- departmentalization;
- the managerial hierarchy (or the *management pyramid*), which is the levels of management within the organization;
- the managerial span of control, which is the number of employees the manager directly supervises; and
- the amount of centralization or decentralization in the organization, which entails deciding at what level in the organizational decisions should be made.

2 What are the five types of departmentalization?

The five basic types of departmentalization (see Exhibit 8.2) commonly used in organizations are

- *functional*—based on the primary functions performed within an organizational unit;

- *product*—based on the goods or services produced or sold by the organizational unit;

- *process*—based on the production process used by the organizational unit;

- *customer*—based on the primary type of customer served by the organizational unit; and

- *geographic*—based on the geographic segmentation of organizational units.

3 How can the degree of centralization/decentralization be altered to make an organization more successful?

In a highly centralized structure, top management makes most of the key decisions in the organization with very little input from lower-level employees. Centralization lets top managers develop a broad view of operations and exercise tight financial controls. In a highly decentralized organization, decision-making authority is pushed down the organizational hierarchy, giving lower-level personnel more responsibility and power to make and implement decisions. Decentralization can result in faster decision-making and increased innovation and responsiveness to customer preferences. It should be noted, however, that the success of centralized versus decentralized organization depends on many factors.

4 How do mechanistic and organic organizations differ?

A mechanistic organization is characterized by a relatively high degree of work specialization, rigid departmentalization, many layers of management (particularly middle management), narrow spans of control, centralized decision-making, and a long chain of command. This combination of elements results in a tall organizational structure. In contrast, an organic organization is characterized by a relatively low degree of work specialization, loose departmentalization, few levels of management, wide spans of control, decentralized decision-making, and a short chain of command. This combination of elements results in a flat organizational structure.

5 What is the difference between line positions and staff positions?

In daily operations, those individuals in line positions are directly involved in the processes used to create goods and services. Those individuals in staff positions provide the administrative and support services that line employees need to achieve the firm's goals. Line positions in organizations are typically in areas such as production, marketing, and finance. Staff positions are found in areas such as legal counselling, managerial consulting, public relations, and human resource management.

6 What is the goal of re-engineering?

Re-engineering is a complete redesign of business structures and processes to improve operations. The goal of re-engineering is to redesign business processes to achieve improvements in cost control, product quality, customer service, and speed.

7 How does the informal organization affect the performance of a company?

The informal organization is the network of connections and channels of communication based on the informal relationships of individuals inside the organization. Informal relationships can be between people at the same hierarchical level or between people at different levels and in different departments. Informal organizations give employees more control over their work environment by delivering a continuous stream of company information throughout the organization, thereby helping employees stay informed.

Also, it should be noted that the informal organization is not just simply the grapevine; it is also the informal relationships that play a role in shaping corporate culture.

8 What trends are influencing how businesses organize?

The virtual corporation is a network of independent companies (suppliers, customers, even competitors) linked by information technology to share skills, costs, and access to one another's markets. This network structure allows companies to come together quickly to exploit rapidly changing opportunities.

Many companies are now using technology to create virtual teams. Team members may be down the hall or across the ocean. Virtual teams mean that travel time and expenses are eliminated and the best people can be placed on the team regardless of where they live. Sometimes, however, it might be difficult to keep virtual team members focused and motivated.

Large global mergers, such as DaimlerChrysler, which was created from the merger of America's Chrysler Corporation and Germany's Daimler Benz, raise important issues in organizational structure. The ultimate question is, How does management take two huge global organizations and create a single, successful, cohesive organization? Should it be centralized or decentralized? Should it be organized along product or geographic lines? These are some of the questions management must answer.

EXPERIENTIAL EXERCISES

1. Evaluate your leadership skills. If you want to evaluate your own leadership skills, go to **http://www.humanlinks.com/skilhome.htm** and scroll down to "Managerial Skills." By taking the self-assessment quizzes offered here, you will gain insight into your ability to manage virtual teams, test your ability to think logically and analogically, and even your perceptions about management. Companies are seeking managerial leaders who have leadership traits that will guide employees through the competitive business landscape.

2. Draw an organization chart of the firm you work for, your college, or a campus student organization. Show the lines of authority and formal communication. Describe the informal relationships that you think are important for the success of the organization.

3. How would you restructure a large mechanistic organization to be more customer-friendly and to increase customer satisfaction? Choose a specific organization and give a detailed plan to accomplish your organizational goals.

4. Using a search engine such as Google or Yahoo! to search for the term "company organizational charts," find at least three examples of organizational charts for corporations, nonprofits, or government agencies. Analyze each entity's organizational structure. Is it organized by function, product/service, process, customer type, or geographic location?

5. At either the *Business Week* (**http://www.businessweek.com**), *Fortune* (**http://www.fortune.com**), or Forbes (**http://www.forbes.com**) Web site, search the archives for stories about companies that have re-engineered. Find an example of a re-engineering effort that succeeded and one that failed and discuss why. Also visit the BPR Online Learning Center at **http://www.prosci.com** to answer the following questions: What is benchmarking and how can it help companies with business process re-engineering (BPR)? What were the key findings of the best-practices surveys for change management and benchmarking?

6. Visit the *Inc.* magazine Web site (**http://www.inc.com**) and use the search engine to find articles about virtual corporation. Using a search engine, find the Web site of at least one virtual corporation and look for information about how the company uses span of control, informal organization, and other concepts from this chapter.

7. Managing change in an organization is no easy task, as you've discovered in your new job with a consulting firm that specializes in change management. To get up to speed, go to Bpubs.com, the Business Publications Search Engine, **http://www.bpubs.com,** and navigate to the Change Management section of the Management Science category. Select three articles that discuss how companies approached the change process and summarize their experiences.

8. After managing your first project team, you think you might enjoy a career in project management. The Project Management Institute is a professional organization for project managers. Its Web site, **http://www.pmi.org,** has many resources about this field. Start at the Professional Practices section to learn what project management is; then go to the professional Development and Careers pages. What are the requirements to earn the Project Management Professional designation? Explore other free areas of the site to learn more about the job of project manager. Prepare a brief report on the career and its opportunities. Does what you've learned make you want to follow this career path?

REVIEW QUESTIONS

1. What is division of labour? Specialization?

2. What does the organizational chart show?

3. What are the five (5) basic types of departmentalization that are commonly found in organizations?

4. What is managerial hierarchy? Span of control (span of management)?

5. What is the difference between a centralized and decentralized organization?

6. What are a line organization, line-and-staff organization, committee structure, and matrix structure?

7. What is the informal organization? What are its functions?

8. What is a virtual corporation? What are virtual teams?

CREATIVE THINKING CASE

Can you imagine an organization with 6,000 employees, $1.4 billion in sales, and no hierarchy structure? Then take a look at W. L. Gore & Associates. Wilbert Gore, who left DuPont to explore new uses for Teflon, started the company in 1958. Best known for its breathable, weatherproof Gore-Tex fabric, the company is a model of unusual business practices. For instance, there is no managerial hierarchy at Gore. Employees, called associates, are treated as peers by top management. The concept fosters the idea that there are no bosses, no titles, and no formal job descriptions.

Committees, composed of employees, are charged with making major decisions such as hiring, firing, and compensation. Even top executives' compensation is set by committee. To get a new idea implemented, all an employee needs to do is gain enough acceptance among fellow employees. In fact, all employees are expected to make minor decisions instead of relying on the "boss" to make them.

The company tries to maintain a family-like atmosphere by dispersing the 6,000 employees into 60 buildings, with no more than 200 employees in any one place. As no formal lines of authority exist, employees can speak to anyone in the company at any time. This arrangement also forces employees to spend considerable time developing relationships. As one employee described it, instead of trying to please just one "boss," you have to please everyone.[9]

CRITICAL THINKING QUESTIONS

1. Given the lack of formal structure, how important do you think the informal structure becomes?

2. Do you think that Gore's reliance on committee work slows processes down?

3. How do you think this structure would affect the division of labour?

VIDEO CASE
Do You Yahoo!

Every day thousands of people do. What began as a hobby for Stanford engineering doctoral students Jerry Yang and David Filo in 1994—as a way to organize and classify Web sites they often visited—evolved into a business and quickly became the Internet's largest on-line navigational service.

Yahoo! was free to the consumer, attracting advertising revenues by emphasizing product innovation and the creation of new services. The company used more than 1,000 daily e-mails it received as valuable feedback for product development. It also catered to what it identified as "defined user groups," with Beatrice's Web Guide targeted to a female audience and Yahooligans specially designed for kids.

As one of the few profitable Internet companies, Yahoo! was riding the crest of the dot-com wave when dramatic changes in the industry caused its revenues to fall precipitously. The flexible organizational structure designed by Yang and Filo needed an overhaul, and Terry Semel, a former Hollywood executive, was hired for the job. As Yahoo!'s new chief executive officer, Semel streamlined the business and restored its profitability through significant restructuring of the company.

He reduced the number of Yahoo!'s businesses from more than 40 to just 6, cutting costs and sharpening the company's focus. It meant abandoning properties that had little chance of making money, like on-line invitations, and meant major staff changes. Nearly half of Yahoo!'s sales force and 44 percent of its top management were replaced with seasoned veterans.

To diversify its revenue streams, Yahoo! devised strategies to turn users into paying subscribers, tapping non-advertising sources, such as job listings, for additional revenue. The company's acquisition of HotJobs, and a paid-search partnership with Overture, will add more than $100 million to its bottom line.

A new alliance with SBC Communications Inc. to sell broadband access is projected to generate an additional $70 million in 2003. Additionally, Yahoo! will roll out its own competitively priced gateway for broadband users, charging subscribers only $5 per month compared with the $10 or $15 monthly fee charged by Microsoft Network (MSN) and America Online (AOL), respectively.

With a focus on exciting new products, supported by a corporate culture that values product integrity and customer satisfaction, Yahoo! has been able to maintain its position as one of the most recognized brand names in the world today.

CRITICAL THINKING QUESTIONS

1. How is Yahoo!'s organizational structure contributing to its ongoing success?

2. What is the company doing to ensure continued revenue growth? Explain.

3. Is Yahoo! a mechanistic or organic organization?

SOURCES: Adapted from material in the video: "Yahoo! A Case Study in Entrepreneurship"; and from the Yahoo! Corporate Web site, http://www.yahoo.com; Ben Elgin, "Terry Semel: Rebuilding a Portal," *Business Week Online*, October 1, 2002; Ben Elgin, "Can Yahoo! Make the Bounce Last?" *Business Week*, February 17, 2003; Mylene Mangalindan, "Yahoo Breaks Dot-Com Mold, Sees a Rebound," *Wall Street Journal*, January 13, 2003, B1, B12.

E-COMMERCE CASE

In Charge at Oracle

Oracle is one of the world's largest software firms, second only to Microsoft in size. Selling $9.6 billion of business software a year, Oracle has more than 42,000 employees and operates around the world. The Internet has long been an integral part of founder and CEO Larry Ellison's vision for the company. Oracle introduced a line of e-business software applications several years ago that allow businesses to manage all of their computers and databases through the Internet. Since then, Ellison has constantly pushed the benefits of using the Web as a business tool. He claims Oracle saved $1 billion in operating costs in the first year after the firm began using its own Web-based software.

Before 2000, Ellison shared leadership of Oracle with company president Ray Lane and chief financial officer Jeff Henley. Each ran their own area—technology, sales, and finances, respectively—relatively independently. Lane was credited with helping to streamline Oracle's bloated organizational structure, opening the door for the company to compete more effectively in the e-commerce marketplace.

In 2000, however, after a power struggle with Ellison, Ray Lane abruptly resigned. Since then, Ellison has refused to name a new president. "The problem I found is that it's hard to have two leaders," Ellison says. "What happened with Oracle was we had two separate visions of where the company should go. The company was divided into two factions. It's not a healthy thing."

Many analysts, however, think Ellison needs a counterbalance, especially since Oracle's sales started to slip after Lane's departure. "When Ray Lane was there, he was a good complement to Larry," explains one analyst. "When he left, some of the things weren't managed quite as effectively. You don't need to have Ray Lane, but you do need that skill set."

Oracle's most pressing problem is that many customers complain that the firm's sales force has been overly aggressive and made false claims about the performance of the company's e-commerce software products. Several customers—including the state of California—have actually filed lawsuits against Oracle because of its sales practices.

Ellison says a recent company restructuring will solve the problem. Before, each salesperson was responsible for selling all of Oracle's products to customers. Now, salespeople will specialize in selling just a few particular products. Ellison says this new structure will allow salespeople to understand and serve customer needs better. "We can't possibly have salespeople who are experts in everything," Ellison says. "That's simply impossible."

CRITICAL THINKING QUESTIONS

1. Do you agree or disagree with Ellison's decision not to name a new company president? Discuss the benefits and disadvantages of centralizing company control in Ellison's hands.

2. How effective do you think Ellison's new sales force structure will be? How can the Internet help implement and support Ellison's plan?

3. What organizational structure do you think is most appropriate for Oracle? Why?

SOURCES: David Futrelle, "Jumping Ship at Oracle and Sun," *Fortune*, May 2, 2002, http://www.business2.com; Eric Hellweg, "Oracle's Larry Ellison, a Solitary Man," *Business 2.0*, July 15, 2002, http://www.business2.com (accessed DATE); G. Christian Hill, "Updates: Trouble with Larry," *eCompany*, May 2001, http://www.ecompany.com; Ian Mount, "Out of Control," *Business 2.0*, August 2002, http://www.business2.com.

Making the Connection

Managing Human Resources and Labour Relations

In this chapter we'll take a look at our last critical success factor. The old adage "last but not least" certainly applies here. As we discussed earlier, *gaining the commitment of employees* is the most critical factor, because all of the other four critical success factors are achieved through the people in the company. Without a strong human resource area and the strong commitment of the employees toward organizational goals, the company simply cannot be successful in any functional area or overall.

The business environment today provides many challenges for the human resource manager. In the *political* environment, regulations govern many aspects of the human resource function, such as how workers can be selected (e.g., drug testing, human rights legislations governing the application and interview process). The mix of people hired is also regulated for some companies through employment equity legislation. Issues relating to diversity are critically important, because without a diverse workforce companies will have a difficult time understanding the diverse global marketplace and designing products and marketing plans to appeal to our diverse society. Therefore companies must consider this trend toward greater diversity in the make-up of society very seriously and take proactive steps rather than just reacting to government legislation. The importance of diversity to a company's success can be seen in the example of PepsiCo in the

opening vignette to this chapter. PepsiCo has a long-standing commitment to diversity within its marketing and human resources that has made it both more responsive to the marketplace and a better place to work, giving it a competitive advantage. In the *economic* environment, organizations are competing not only for customers but also for a shrinking pool of qualified job applicants, and they must also pay attention to the salaries of the competition to remain competitive. In the *social* environment, workers are seeking to better balance their home and work lives, making it more critical and more difficult to gain commitment in the traditional ways, and the aging workforce is also creating difficulties. The *technological* environment is reshaping how work is done, offering options to human labour and changing the nature of many jobs and the skills required to do them. Technology also affects how the human resource department does its job. You'll find many examples both in the chapter and in trying to find a job yourself, such as using the Internet to recruit workers and using specially designed software to pick out key phrases from résumés to sort through them more quickly.

An environmental factor that has a dramatic impact on how a company operates is the presence of unions. This is a very integrative factor as it has implications for all the environmental factors and all the areas of the business. It is *political*, because legislation governs how unions become involved with a group of workers and how the union-management relationship works; it is social, because the culture and attitude of the workers affect how they view unions and whether they would want to work in a unionized environment; it is technological, because the union contract could impact the rights of management to use technology if it replaces workers; and it is economic, because a unionized workplace often has less flexibility and higher compensation costs than a non-unionized environment, and that can impact a company's competitiveness. Unions can therefore affect the financial success of the company, and they can definitely signal an issue with respect to worker commitment when the workers feel compelled to have a third party represent them with management. This point stresses the importance of management's operating with the commitment of the workers foremost in its mind if it wishes to operate without a union. It is management's job to create a work environment that gains commitment and loyalty, where the human resource policies are so worker focused that unions are the last thought on the workers' minds.

As with the other functional areas, the main basis for all decisions in the human resource area is the company's goals and *strategy*. The role of the human resource area is to provide the right numbers of the right kinds of people in the right places at the right times to assist the other functional areas to help the organization achieve its objectives. To do this, the human resource area must work very closely with *marketing*, *operations*, and *finance* to understand their objectives and thus their human resource requirements. It must also understand the jobs that need to be done to determine the skills that it must recruit and train for.

One area in which human resources must work especially closely with finance is in the area of employee compensation and benefits. Because of the relative size of this expense, it has a tremendous impact on the bottom line on the one hand, but on the other it also affects the level of commitment from employees, and therefore an integrative approach must be taken in determining compensation. This matter is becoming more important as workers are changing jobs more often.

Compensation is just one decision area in which the human resource manager must develop and implement policies in an integrative way to create a more committed workforce. For example, one common approach in recruitment and selection is to promote first from within. This practice shows employees that the organization is committed to them, which is an essential ingredient in gaining commitment from employees. An example of a human resource approach that is a particularly integrative example is telecommuting. The technological environment has made telecommuting possible, thus improving the productivity of workers, saving companies money, and helping firms retain key people who would otherwise have to leave. In training and development as well, the organization can show its commitment to the employees by helping them to achieve their potential. Again, employees will be more committed to an organization that shows commitment to them in its human resource policies. This effort to train and develop employees makes them both better at their jobs and more loyal, which translates into being more *innovative*, providing greater *quality*, and working harder to meet and exceed *customer needs*, thereby allowing the organization to *achieve financial performance* both through lower turnover and through greater customer satisfaction.

© DIGITAL VISION / GETTY IMAGES

Chapter

9

Managing Human Resources and Labour Relations

learning goals

1 What is the human resource management process, and how are human resource needs determined?

2 How do human resource managers recruit and select qualified applicants?

3 What types of training and development do organizations offer their employees?

4 How are performance appraisals used to evaluate employees' performance?

5 What are the different methods for compensating employees?

6 What is organizational career management?

7 Why does a diverse workforce lead to stronger performance in the marketplace?

8 What are the key pieces of legislation affecting human resource management?

9 How are labour-management relations different in a unionized environment?

10 What trends are affecting human resource management?

NEL

PepsiCo Is Committed to Diversity

PepsiCo (http://www.pepsico.com) is the parent company of some of Canada's best-known brands, including Pepsi, Frito-Lay, Tropicana, and Quaker Oats. With more than 140,000 employees around the world, PepsiCo employees share a common set of values and goals. Top executives and human resource managers know that success takes the work of talented and dedicated people who are committed to making an impact every day. Their ability to grow year after year is driven by their ability to attract, develop, and retain world-class people who will thrive in a dynamic environment. To achieve this, PepsiCo recognizes that they need employees who are anxious to be part of a dynamic, results-oriented company, with powerful brands and top-notch people.

Early in the firm's history—as far back as the 1940s—Pepsi-Cola acknowledged the importance of diversity within its workplaces and in the marketplace. Recognizing the importance of tailoring its marketing to minority groups, Pepsi pioneered advertising specifically to minority groups. These ads featured minority actors and actresses and focused on minority lifestyles. The company also developed education and sports programs spotlighting minorities, and sponsored major musical tours by entertainers such as Michael Jackson and Tina Turner. The firm also spends millions of dollars advertising in minority media such as *Ebony* and *Black Enterprise.*

PepsiCo has been nationally recognized as one of the top places for women and minorities to work. The firm has been hiring minorities in professional positions for more than 65 years. Pepsi was the first Fortune 500 Company to have an African American vice president. PepsiCo has developed a number of diversity initiatives to ensure that the firm's core value of diversity is a competitive advantage. These initiatives include the following:

- Within Pepsi-Cola, Frito-Lay, and Tropicana operating divisions, executives are completely dedicated to managing diversity in the workplace.

- Multiyear strategic plans for diversity are developed with the same vigour and goal-setting process as other business issues. Goals include turnover reduction, increased diversity hiring, and creation of an "inclusion" culture.

- An External Diversity Advisory Board consisting of educators, politicians, practitioners, and customers advises PepsiCo senior management on how to leverage diversity in the marketplace.

- Annual employee reviews incorporate the need to "Act with Integrity," "Create a Positive Work Environment," and "Align and Motivate Teams."

- A mandatory annual Affirmative Action Planning process is in place.

- An annual organizational health survey incorporates diversity questions and requires analysis at the minority and female level. Senior management is held accountable for results.

- A corporate program is dedicated to training employees on how to work and manage in an inclusive environment.

- Employee networks mentor and support minority and female employees.

Critical Thinking Questions

As you read this chapter, consider these questions as they relate to PepsiCo:

1. How can diversity in the workplace be an advantage to PepsiCo?

2. What role does the federal government play in ensuring that diversity exists at PepsiCo and all other companies?

Principles of Human Resource Management

Human resource management in today's organization is instrumental in driving an organization toward its objectives. Successful human resource management hinges on a company's ability to attract and hire the best employees, equip them with the skills they need to excel, compensate them fairly, and motivate them to reach their full potential. Achieving these objectives in today's business environment is made more difficult because of these challenges:

- A shortage of employees for many knowledge and highly-skilled occupations is forcing organizations to compete for a limited number of employees.
- Employees are placing priority on their families and struggling to balance their home and work lives.
- Because of the worldwide expansion of business, managers are challenged to manage and communicate with employees around the globe.
- A diverse and multicultural workforce requires better workplace communication and training to maximize teamwork.
- Technology is impacting the way managers and employees make decisions, communicate with each other, and operate their business.
- Human resource laws are dictating many aspects of the employee-employer relationship.

Each day, human resource experts and frontline supervisors deal with these challenges while sharing responsibility for attracting and retaining skilled, motivated employees. Whether faced with a large or small human resource problem, supervisors need some understanding of difficult employee relations issues, especially if there are legal implications.

In this chapter, you will learn about the role of human resource management in building and maintaining an exceptional workforce. We will explore human resource planning, recruiting and selection, training, and motivating employees toward reaching organizational objectives. The chapter will also cover employee job changes within an organization, managing a diverse workforce, and the laws

As business expands around the globe, human resource managers need to develop communication systems and training strategies that build teamwork among diverse employees who may be located around the world.

© PHOTODISC RED / GETTY IMAGES

guiding human resource decisions. Labour-management relations are also discussed. Finally, we will look at important trends influencing human resource management and labour-management relations.

DEVELOPING PEOPLE TO HELP REACH ORGANIZATIONAL GOALS

1 *learning goal*

human resource management
The process of hiring, developing, motivating, and evaluating employees to achieve organizational goals.

HOT Links

Does TeamStaff, a professional employer organization, live up to its motto "Simply a better way to employ people"? Find out at http://www .teamstaff.com.

Human resource management is the process of hiring, developing, motivating, and evaluating employees to achieve organizational goals. Organizational strategies and objectives form the basis for making all human resource management decisions. All companies strive to hire and develop well-trained, motivated employees. The human resources management process includes these steps, illustrated in Exhibit 9.1:

- job analysis and design,
- human resource planning and forecasting,
- employee recruitment,
- employee selection,
- training and development,
- performance planning and evaluation,
- compensation and benefits, and
- organizational career management, including employee job changes and disengagement.

Exhibit 9.1 | Human Resource Management Process

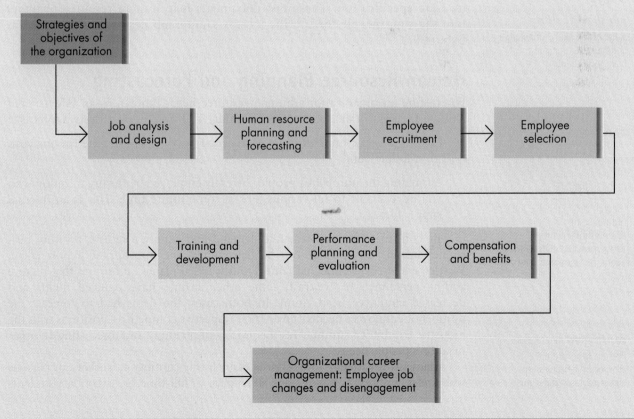

Define human resource management.

Describe the human resource management process.

In the following sections, you will learn more about each of these important functions.

HUMAN RESOURCE PLANNING

Firms need to have the right number of people, with the right training, in the right jobs, to do the organization's work when it needs to be done. Human resource specialists are the ones who must determine future human resource needs. Then they assess the skills of the firm's existing employees to see if new people must be hired or existing ones retrained.

human resource (HR) planning

Creating a strategy for meeting future human resource needs.

Creating a strategy for meeting future human resource needs is called **human resource (HR) planning.** Two important aspects of HR planning are job analysis and forecasting the firm's people needs. The HR planning process begins with a review of corporate strategy and policy. By understanding the mission of the organization, planners can understand its human resource needs.

Job Analysis and Design

job analysis

A study of the tasks required to do a particular job well.

job description

The tasks and responsibilities of a job.

job specification

A list of the skills, knowledge, and abilities a person must have to fill a job.

Human resource planners must know what skills different jobs require. Information about a specific job is typically assembled through a **job analysis,** a study of the tasks required to do a job well. This information is used to specify the essential skills, knowledge, and abilities.

The tasks and responsibilities of a job are listed in a **job description.** The skills, knowledge, and abilities a person must have to fill a job are spelled out in a **job specification.** These two documents help human resource planners find the right people for specific jobs. A sample job description is shown in Exhibit 9.2.

Human Resource Planning and Forecasting

Forecasting an organization's human resource needs, known as an HR *demand forecast,* is an essential aspect of HR planning. This process involves two forecasts:

1. determining the number of people needed by some future time (in one year, for example), and

2. estimating the number of people currently employed by the organization who will be available to fill various jobs at some future time. This is an *internal* supply forecast.

HOT *Links*

Search the extensive job database of CareerBuilder.com, http://www.careerbuilder .com, for a job in a new city.

By comparing human resource demand and supply forecasts, a future personnel surplus or shortage can be determined and appropriate action taken. WestJet, a low-cost airline, has continuously added planes and routes that require adding personnel. In contrast, some other airlines have reduced flights and decreased employee head count. In both cases, the firms had to forecast the number of employees needed, given their respective competitive positions with the industry. Exhibit 9.3 summarizes the process of planning and forecasting an organization's people needs.

contingent workers

Persons who prefer temporary employment, either part- or full-time.

Many firms with employee shortages are hiring **contingent workers,** or persons who prefer temporary employment, either part- or full-time. Postsecondary students

Exhibit 9.2 | Job Description

Position: College Recruiter   **Location:** Corporate Offices

Reports to: Vice President of Human Resources   **Classification:** Salaried/Exempt

Job Summary: Member of HR corporate team. Interacts with managers and department heads to determine hiring needs for college graduates. Visits 20 to 30 college and university campuses each year to conduct preliminary interviews of graduating students in all academic disciplines. Following initial interviews, works with corporate staffing specialists to determine persons who will be interviewed a second time. Makes recommendations to hiring managers concerning best-qualified applicants.

Job Duties and Responsibilities:

Estimated time spent and importance

15 percent	Working with managers and department heads, determines college recruiting needs.
10 percent	Determines colleges and universities with degree programs appropriate to hiring needs to be visited.
15 percent	Performs college relations activities with numerous colleges and universities.
25 percent	Visits campuses to conduct interviews of graduating seniors.
15 percent	Develops applicant files and performs initial applicant evaluations.
10 percent	Assists staffing specialists and line managers in determining who to schedule for second interviews.
5 percent	Prepares annual college recruiting report containing information and data about campuses, number interviewed, number hired, and related information.
5 percent	Participates in tracking college graduates who are hired to aid in determining campuses that provide the most outstanding employees.

Job Specification (Qualifications):

Bachelor's degree in human resource management or a related field. Minimum of two years of work experience with the firm in HR or department that annually hires college graduates. Ability to perform in a team environment, especially with line managers and department heads. Very effective oral and written communication skills. Reasonably proficient in Excel, Word, and Windows computer environment and familiar with PeopleSoft.

and retired persons make up a large portion of Canada's contingent workforce. Other people who want to work but don't want to be permanent employees can join a temporary employment agency. A temporary employment agency performs staffing, training, and compensation functions by contracting with a business to provide employees for a specified period. A firm with a shortage of accountants can rent or lease an accountant from the temporary employment agency for the expected duration of the shortage.

concept check

Describe the job analysis and design process.

What is the process for human resource forecasting?

EMPLOYEE RECRUITMENT

2 learning goal

When a firm creates a new position or an existing one becomes vacant, it starts looking for people with qualifications that meet the requirements of the job. Two sources of job applicants are the internal and external labour markets. The internal labour market consists of employees currently employed by the firm; the external labour market is the pool of potential applicants outside the firm.

Exhibit 9.3 | Human Resource Planning Process

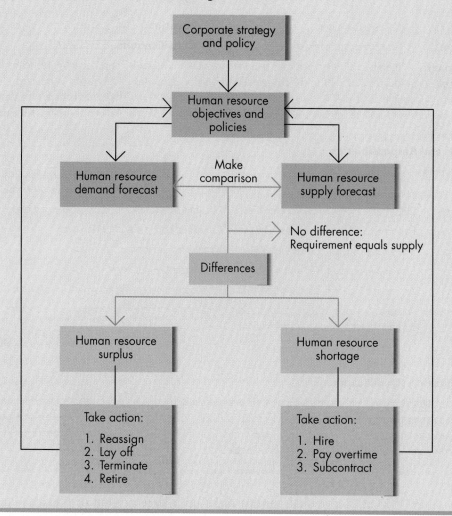

Recruiting from the Internal Labour Market

Most companies, including UPS, WestJet Airlines, and Wal-Mart, follow a policy of promotion from within and try to fill positions with their existing employees. The internal search for job applicants usually means that a person must change his or her job. People are typically either promoted or transferred. A firm's skills inventory can help find the right person for a job opening. A skills inventory is a computerized employee database containing information on each employee's previous work experience, educational background, performance records, career objectives, and job location preferences. General Electric has used a skills inventory for many years as a means of determining promotions and transfers.

Recruiting from the External Labour Market

If qualified job candidates cannot be found inside the firm, the external labour market must be tapped. **Recruitment** is the attempt to find and attract qualified applicants in the external labour market. The type of position determines which recruitment method will be used and which segment of the labour market will be searched. Boeing will not recruit an experienced engineer in the same way that it would recruit a secretary or clerk typist.

recruitment

The attempt to find and attract qualified applicants in the external labour market.

Non-technical, unskilled, and other non-supervisory workers are recruited through newspaper, radio, and sometimes even television help-wanted ads in local media. Starbucks placed ads in the *Beijing Youth Daily* to attract workers for its Beijing coffee shops. Entry-level accountants, engineers, and systems analysts are commonly hired through postsecondary campus recruitment efforts. Each year the Canadian financial institutions send recruiters across Canada to campuses that have a business program.

A firm that needs executives and other experienced professional, technical, and managerial employees may employ the services of an executive search firm. The hiring firm pays the search firm a fee equivalent to one to four months of the employee's first-year salary. Many search firms specialize in a particular occupation, industry, or geographic location.

Many firms participate in local job fairs. A **job fair** is typically a one-day event held at a convention center to bring together thousands of job seekers and hundreds of firms searching for employees. Some firms conduct a **corporate open house.** Persons attend the open house, are briefed about various job opportunities, and are encouraged to submit a job application on the spot or before leaving the employer's premises.

Using Technology to Recruit Applicants

An increasingly common and popular recruiting method involves using the Internet. Nearly all large and most medium-sized business firms now use on-line recruiting by either drawing applicants to their own Web site or utilizing the services of a job board, such as Monster.ca, CareerMosaic.com, Hotjobs.ca, or CareerPath.ca. A firm can be assisted in these efforts by consulting an Internet recruitment directory such s the Riley Guide. Some large firms, such as General Electric, receive more than 200,000 Web site visitors each month and receive as many as 10,000 résumés per month.[1]

job fair
An event, typically one day, held at a convention centre to bring together thousands of job seekers and hundreds of firms searching for employees.

corporate open house
Persons are invited to an open house on the premises of the corporation. Qualified applicants are encouraged to complete an application before leaving.

Job fairs bring together hundreds of employers and thousands of job seekers. Job fairs are one of the ways human resource managers identify employees from the external job market.

Managing Human Resources and Labour Relations **Chapter 9** | 267

Other firms, including Coca-Cola, use artificial intelligence software to scan and track résumés. Motive Communications uses Hire.com's e-Recruiter software because of its profiling capabilities. Applicant résumé information can be matched with current and future job openings. Motive Communications' applicant pool becomes a dynamic database that is constantly churning as new applicants are added. The e-Recruiter system can search and scan thousands of résumés in minutes. With such systems the words and phrases used to describe one's background and experience become very important.

concept check

What are the two labour markets?

Describe different ways that employees are recruited.

How is technology helping firms find the right recruits?

EMPLOYEE SELECTION

selection

The process of determining which persons in the applicant pool possess the qualifications necessary to be successful on the job.

After a firm has attracted enough job applicants, employment specialists begin the selection process. **Selection** is the process of determining which persons in the applicant pool possess the qualifications necessary to be successful on the job. The steps in the employee selection process are shown in Exhibit 9.4 and are described below:

1. *Initial screening.* During the initial screening, an applicant usually completes an application form and has a brief interview of 30 minutes or less. The application form includes questions about education, work experience, and previous job duties. A personal résumé may be substituted for the application form. If the potential employer believes that the potential employee is suitable, then the next step is the interview. The interview is normally structured and consists of a short list of specific questions. For example: Are you familiar with any accounting software packages? Did you supervise anyone in your last job? Did you use a company car when making sales calls?

2. *Employment testing.* Following the initial screening, an applicant may be asked to take one or more employment tests, such as the Minnesota Clerical Test or the Wonderlic Personnel Test, a mental-ability test. Some tests are designed to measure special job skills, others measure aptitudes, and some are intended to capture characteristics of one's personality. The Myers-Briggs Type Indicator is a personality and motivational instrument widely used on college campuses as an aid in providing job and career counselling as well as assisting a student in selecting his or her major. In recent years some firms have begun to use a test that assesses one's emotional intelligence. Frequently called the e-quotient, the emotional intelligence quotient reveals how well a person understands his or her own emotions and the emotions of others, and how he or she behaves based on this understanding.

3. *Selection interview.* The tool most widely used in making hiring decisions by Intel, Merck, and other firms is the **selection interview,** an in-depth discussion of an applicant's work experience, skills and abilities, education, and career

selection interview

An in-depth discussion of an applicant's work experience, skills and abilities, education, and career interests.

Exhibit 9.4 | Steps of the Employee Selection Process

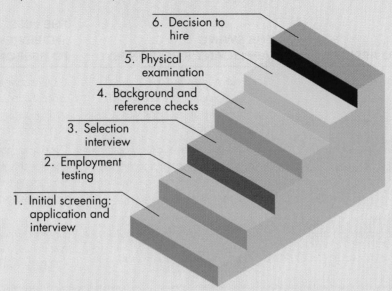

6. Decision to hire

5. Physical examination

4. Background and reference checks

3. Selection interview

2. Employment testing

1. Initial screening: application and interview

interests. For managerial and professional positions, an applicant may be interviewed by several persons, including the line manager for the position to be filled. This interview is designed to determine an applicant's communication ability and motivation. It is also a means for gathering additional factual information from the applicant such as college major, years of part-time work experience, computer equipment used, and reason for leaving the last job. The applicant may be asked to explain how to solve a particular management problem or how she or he provided leadership to a group in a previous work situation when an important problem had to be solved quickly. United Airlines asks prospective flight attendants how they handled a conflict with a customer or coworker in a previous job.

Carolyn Murray, a recruiter for W. C. Gore and Associates, makers of Gore-Tex, says she pays little attention to a candidate's carefully scripted responses to her admittedly easy questions. Instead, she listens for a casual remark that reveals the reality behind an otherwise thought-out reply. Using a baseball analogy, Carolyn's examples of how three job candidates struck out are presented in Exhibit 9.5.[2]

4. *Background and reference check.* If applicants pass the selection interview, most firms examine their background and check their references. In recent years an increasing number of employers are carefully researching applicants' backgrounds, particularly their legal history, reasons for leaving previous jobs, and even creditworthiness. Retail firms, where employees have extensive contact with customers, tend to be very careful about checking applicant backgrounds. Some checking can be done easily using the Internet. In fact, many retired law enforcement officers have started their own firms that specialize in these investigations.

Exhibit 9.5 | Striking Out with Gore-Tex

THE PITCH (QUESTION TO APPLICANT)	THE SWING (APPLICANT'S RESPONSE)	THE MISS (INTERVIEWER'S REACTION TO RESPONSE)
"Give me an example of a time when you had a conflict with a team member."	"Our leader asked me to handle all of the FedExing for our team. I did it, but I thought that FedExing was a waste of my time."	"At Gore, we work from a team concept. Her answer shows that she won't exactly jump when one of her teammates needs help."
"Tell me how you solved a problem that was impeding your project."	"One of the engineers on my team wasn't pulling his weight, and we were closing in on a deadline. So I took on some of his work."	"The candidate may have resolved the issue for this particular deadline, but he did nothing to prevent the problem from happening again."
"What's the one thing that you would change about your current position?"	"My job as a salesman has become boring. Now I want the responsibility of managing people."	"He's probably not maximizing his current territory, *and* he is complaining. Will he find his next role 'boring' and complain about that role, too?"

5. *Physical exams.* Companies frequently require job candidates to have a medical checkup to ensure they are physically able to perform a job. In Canada drug testing can be conducted only after a conditional offer of employment has been extended. If the new employee tests positive, he or she will probably still be hired unless there is undue hardship to the firm as a result. If the condition turns out to be an addiction, the employee will be treated under the new employer's benefit plan, and any issues as a result of the addiction become performance management issues.[3]

6. *Decision to hire.* If an applicant progresses satisfactorily through all the selection steps, a decision to hire the individual is made. The decision to hire is nearly always made by the manager of the new employee.

concept check

What are the steps in the employee selection process?

Describe some ways in which applicants are tested.

3 learning goal

training and development

Activities that provide learning situations in which an employee acquires additional knowledge or skills to increase job performance.

Employee Training and Development

To ensure that both new and experienced employees have the knowledge and skills to perform their jobs successfully, organizations invest in training and development activities. **Training and development** involves learning situations in which the employee acquires additional knowledge or skills to increase job performance. Training objectives specify performance improvements, reductions in errors, job knowledge to be gained, and/or other positive organizational results. The design of training programs at General Electric, for example, includes determining instructional methods, number of trainees per class, printed materials (cases, notebooks, manuals, and the like) to be used, location of training, use of audiovisual equipment and software, and many other matters. The process of creating and implementing training and development activities is shown in Exhibit 9.6.

Training for new employees is instrumental in getting them up to speed and familiar with their job responsibilities. The first type of training that new employees experience is **employee orientation,** which entails getting the new employee ready to perform on the job. Formal orientation (a half-day classroom program) provides

Exhibit 9.6 | Employee Training and Development Process

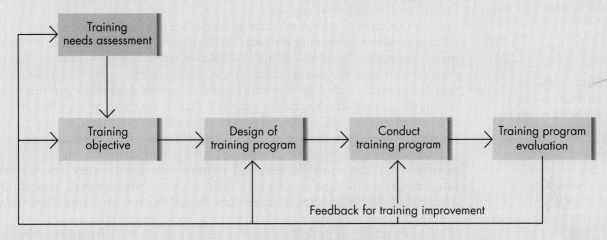

Training needs assessment → Training objective → Design of training program → Conduct training program → Training program evaluation

Feedback for training improvement

---

employee orientation

Training that prepares a new employee to perform on the job; includes information about job assignments, work rules, equipment, and performance expectations, as well as about company policies, salary and benefits, and parking.

HOT Links

For the latest news in the human resources field, visit the Web site of the Society for Human Resource Management at http://www.shrm.org.

on-the-job training

Training in which the employee learns the job by doing it with guidance from a supervisor or experienced coworker.

job rotation

Reassignment of workers to several different jobs over time so that they can learn the basics of each job.

apprenticeship

A form of on-the-job training that combines specific job instruction with classroom instruction.

information about company policies, salary and benefits, and parking. Although this information is very helpful, the more important orientation is about job assignments, work rules, equipment, and performance expectations provided by the new employee's supervisor and coworkers. This second briefing tends to be more informal and can last for several days or even weeks. Many firms use video for employee orientation, because they want a standardized message and delivery tone expressed to new employees. DSM Chemicals North America shows a video to employees about safety procedures when entering a chemical-manufacturing area. Professional videos can be expensive, costing $1,000 to $3,000 per finished minute.[4]

On-the-Job Training

Continuous training for both new and experienced employees is important to keep job skills fresh. Job-specific training, designed to enhance a new employee's ability to perform a job, includes **on-the-job training,** during which the employee learns the job by doing it with guidance from a supervisor or experienced coworker.

On-the-job training takes place at the job site or workstation and tends to be directly related to the job. This training involves specific job instructions, coaching (guidance given to new employees by experienced ones), special project assignments, or job rotation. **Job rotation** is the reassignment of workers to several different jobs over time. It is not uncommon for management trainees to work sequentially in two or three departments, such as customer service, credit, and human resources, during their first year on the job.

An **apprenticeship** usually combines specific on-the-job instruction with classroom training. It might last as long as four years and can be found in the skilled trades of carpentry, plumbing, and electrical work.

With **mentoring,** another form of on-the-job training, a senior manager or other experienced employee provides job- and career-related information to a protégé. Inexpensive and providing instantaneous feedback, mentoring is becoming increasingly popular with many firms.

Off-the-Job Training

Even with the advantages of on-the-job training, many firms recognize that it is often necessary to train employees away from the workplace. With off-the-job training, employees learn the job away from the job. There are numerous popular

mentoring
A form of on-the-job training in which a senior manager or other experienced employee provides job- and career-related information to a protégé.

vestibule training
A form of off-the-job training in which trainees learn in a scaled-down version or simulated work environment.

programmed instruction
A form of computer-assisted off-the-job training.

methods of off-the-job training. Frequently, it takes place in a classroom, where cases, role-play exercises, films, videos, lectures, and computer demonstrations are utilized to develop workplace skills.

Another form of off-the-job training takes place in a facility called a vestibule, or training simulator. In **vestibule training,** used by Honda, trainees learn about products, manufacturing processes, and selling in a scaled-down version of an assembly line or retail outlet. When mistakes are made, no customers are lost or products damaged. A training simulator, such as Air Canada's flight simulator for pilot training, is much like a vestibule facility. Pilots can practice hazardous flight manoeuvres or learn the controls of a new aircraft in a safe, controlled environment with no passengers.

In a very rapidly developing trend that will undoubtedly accelerate in the 21st century, many companies, including Compaq and Microsoft, are using computer-assisted, electronically delivered training and development courses and programs. Many of these courses have their origins in **programmed instruction,** a self-paced, highly structured training method that presents trainees with concepts and problems using a modular format.

Usually, off-the-job training is more expensive than on-the-job training, its impact is less direct, and the transfer of learning to the job is less immediate. Nevertheless, despite these shortcomings, some training can be done only away from the job.

concept check

Describe several types of on-the-job training.

Explain vestibule training and programmed instruction.

PERFORMANCE PLANNING AND EVALUATION

4 *learning goal*

performance appraisal
A comparison of actual performance with expected performance to assess an employee's contributions to the organization.

Along with employee orientation and training, new employees learn about performance expectations through performance planning and evaluation. Managers provide employees with expectations about the job. These are communicated as job objectives, schedules, deadlines, and product and/or service quality requirements. As an employee performs job tasks, the supervisor periodically evaluates the employee's efforts. A **performance appraisal** is a comparison of actual performance with expected performance to assess an employee's contributions to the organization and to make decisions about training, compensation, promotion, and other job changes. The performance planning and appraisal process is shown in Exhibit 9.7 and is described below:

Exhibit 9.7 | Performance Planning and Evaluation

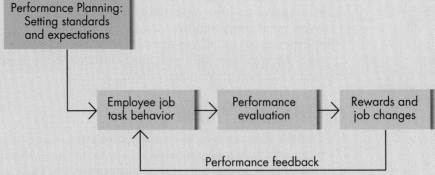

During a performance appraisal, a manager evaluates an employee's performance, comparing actual performance to expected performance goals. At General Electric, employees receive feedback from work teams, peers, and customers to develop perspective on their management style and skills.

1. The manager establishes performance standards.

2. The employee works to meet the standards and expectations.

3. The employee's supervisor evaluates the employee's work in terms of quality and quantity of output and various characteristics such as job knowledge, initiative, relationships with others, and attendance and punctuality.

4. Following the performance evaluation, reward (pay raise) and job change (promotion) decisions can be made.

5. Rewards are positive feedback and provide reinforcement, or encouragement, for the employee to work harder in the future.

Performance appraisals serve a number of purposes, but they are most often used to make decisions about pay raises, training needs, advancement opportunities, and employee terminations.

concept check

What are the steps in the performance planning and appraisal process?

What purposes do performance appraisals serve?

EMPLOYEE COMPENSATION AND BENEFITS

5 *learning goal*

Compensation, which includes both pay and benefits, is closely connected to performance appraisal. Employees who perform better tend to get bigger pay raises. Several factors affect an employee's pay:

1. *Pay structure and internal influences.* Wages, salaries, and benefits usually reflect the importance of the job. The jobs that management considers more important are compensated at a higher rate; president, chief engineer, and chief financial officer are high-paying jobs. Likewise, different jobs of equal importance to the firm are compensated at the same rate. For instance, if a drill-press operator and a lathe operator are considered of equal importance, they might both be paid $21 per hour.

2. *Pay level and external influences.* In deciding how much to pay workers, the firm must also be concerned with the salaries paid by competitors. If competitors are paying much higher wages, a firm might lose its best employees. Larger firms conduct salary surveys to see what other firms are paying. Wage and salary surveys conducted by Statistics Canada, for example, can also be useful.

An employer can decide to pay at, above, or below the going rate. Most firms try to offer competitive wages and salaries within a geographic area or an industry. If a company pays below-market wages, it might not be able to hire skilled people. The level, or competitiveness, of a firm's compensation is determined by the firm's financial condition (or profitability), efficiency, and employee productivity, as well as the going rates paid by competitors.

Types of Compensation or Pay

There are two basic types of compensation: direct and indirect. Direct pay is the wage or salary received by the employee; indirect pay consists of various employee benefits and services. Employees are usually paid directly on the basis of the amount of time they work, the amount they produce, or some combination of time and output. The following are the most common types of compensation:

- *Hourly wages.* According to Statistics Canada, the average hourly wage for those over 15 years of age was $19.56 in June 2006. For full-time workers, the average hourly wage was $20.74, and for part-time workers, it was $13.71.[5]
- *Salaries.* Managerial and professional employees are usually paid an annual salary on either a biweekly or a monthly basis.
- *Piecework and commission.* Some employees are paid according to how much they produce or sell. A car salesperson might be paid $500 for each car sold or a 3 percent commission on the car's sale price. Thus, a salesperson who sold four cars in one week at $500 per car would earn $2,000 in pay for that week. Alternatively, a 3 percent commission on four cars sold with total sales revenue of $70,000 would yield $2,100 in pay.

Increasingly, business firms are paying employees using a base wage or salary and an incentive. The incentive feature is designed to increase individual employee, work group, and/or organizational performance. Incentive pay plans are commonly referred to as variable or contingent pay arrangements.

- *Accelerated commission schedule.* A salesperson could be paid a commission rate of 3 percent on the first $50,000 of sales per month, 4 percent on the next $30,000, and 5 percent on any sales beyond $80,000. For a salesperson who made $90,000 of sales in one month, the monthly pay would be as follows:

  3 percent × $50,000 = $1,500

  4 percent × $30,000 = $1,200

  5 percent × $10,000 = $ 500

  $90,000 → $3,200

- *Bonus.* A bonus is a payment for reaching a specific goal; it may be paid on a monthly, quarterly, or annual basis. A bank with several offices or branches might set monthly goals for opening new accounts, making loans, and customer service. Each employee of a branch that meets all goals would be paid a monthly bonus of $100. Although the bonuses are paid to the employees individually, the employees must function as an effective, high-performing group to reach the monthly goals.

- *Profit sharing.* A firm that offers profit sharing pays employees a portion of the profits over a preset level. For example, profits beyond 10 percent of gross sales might be shared at a 50 percent rate with employees. The company retains the remaining profits. All employees might receive the same profit shares, or the shares might vary according to base pay.

Making Ethical Choices

KEEPING SECRETS

Working on national security issues for a consulting firm with the Canadian Security Intelligence Service contracts has been both exciting and increasingly stressful. The excitement comes from the actual work of investigating and evaluating potential terrorist threats to Canada. The stress is a result of a greatly increased workload and much closer scrutiny of your work. When you started your job in June 2000, 40- to 45-hour weeks were common. Since the September 11, 2001, terrorist attacks in the United States, your workload has increased dramatically, and you now must work 55 to 65 hours per week. Managers appear to be monitoring employees' activities and paying closer attention to their mental state for evidence of instability. Along with your fellow workers, you are concerned that the heightened security measures might change the policies with regard to confidentiality of medical records.

Because the consulting firm's culture doesn't support open discussion, you don't feel comfortable talking with your colleagues or your supervisor about the stress you are experiencing. Instead, you seek counsel from HR and are given names of several psychotherapists who participate in the company's employee assistance plan. You assume that your visit to HR and the subject of that visit are as secret as the nature of your work. Your psychotherapist has advised you that your visits and the content of all sessions are confidential.

You begin to sense that your supervisor is aware of your 90-minute absences, even though you made sure to schedule visits to the therapist on a different day and different time each week. The idea that your supervisor might know you are seeking psychological counselling only increases your stress level.

ETHICAL DILEMMA
Does your employer have the right to know about your visits to a psychotherapist?

SOURCES: Tybe Diamond, "American Psychoanalytic Association Files a Lawsuit to Challenge the Bush Administration HIPPA Abuses," e-mail, April 14, 2003; "Protecting Privacy and Personal Security—Our World's Need for a Careful Balance and the 10 Commandments of Ethical Surveillance," *PRNewsire*, September 13, 2001, http://www.findarticles.com; and Jonathan A. Segal, "Security vs. Privacy: To Ensure a Secure Environment for All Workers Avoid Violating the Privacy of Any One Individual," *HR Magazine*, February 2002, http://www.findarticles.com.

fringe benefits
Indirect compensation, such as pensions, health insurance, and vacations.

- *Fringe benefits.* **Fringe benefits** are indirect compensation and include pensions, health insurance, vacations, and many others. Some fringe benefits are required by law (e.g., paid vacations and holidays, employment insurance [EI] and Canada or Quebec Pension Plan [CPP or QPP]), the EI and CPP/QPP are paid at least in part by the employer).

Many employers also offer fringe benefits not required by law. Among these are paid time off (e.g., extra vacations, and sick days), insurance (health care, disability, life, dental, vision, and accidental death and dismemberment), pensions and retirement savings accounts, and stock purchase options.

Some firms with numerous fringe benefits allow employees to mix and match benefit items or select items based on individual needs. This is a flexible, or cafeteria-style, benefit plan. A younger employee with a family might desire to purchase medical, disability, and life insurance, whereas an older employee might want to put more benefit dollars into a retirement savings plan. All employees are allocated the same number of benefit dollars but can spend these dollars on different items and in different amounts.

Executive Compensation

Employees are paid different amounts according to the value of the job to the firm and the performance of the job incumbent (or employee). Persons at higher levels of the firm are paid more, and generally employees with greater experience, seniority, and education are paid more than newer, inexperienced employees. Executives are the highest paid of various groups of employees. The average chief executive officer (CEO) is compensated 500 times the amount paid to the lowest paid worker.[6] This is up from 42 times in 1980. Additionally, executives are given a greater variety of fringe benefits (country club membership, car allowance, and annual physical exam with physical fitness prescription) and frequently are paid various incentives, such as bonuses, profit shares, and other benefits. Although these incentives are intended to stimulate executive and firm performance as measured by increased sales, profits, market share, and stock price, there have been many examples in recent years where a CEO's pay has been significantly increased even when the firm's profits declined or the firm even lost money.

Of the executive incentives mentioned above, stock options are the most controversial. A *stock option* is the right to buy company stock at a set price at a later date. An executive can be given options to buy shares of the firm's stock at a reduced price and then be allowed to sell the shares, after being held for a specified time, for a profit. In some cases the executive is given a low-interest loan by the firm to exercise the options and purchase the shares of stock. The stock option functions as an incentive, because the executive is expected to manage the firm so that the stock price increases and shareholder value is enhanced. Although the executive can be successful in the short run (a few months to two or three years) in raising the stock price, some short-term executive decisions can become long-term problems. But in the short term, the executive has prospered significantly through exercising stock options for thousands of shares of stock and making profits on stock sales.

Determining a CEO's fair salary isn't easy. CEOs are responsible for making decisions that can impact tens of thousands of employees and dramatically increase or decrease the value of a company. Indigo CEO Heather Reisman's compensation package would have to reflect her 25 years of extensive business experience.

CP PHOTO/FRANK GUNN

Another controversial element of an executive compensation package is the *golden parachute,* a very lucrative severance or retirement deal that an executive might receive even when firm performance has suffered.

concept check

How does a firm establish a pay scale for its employees?

What is the difference between direct and indirect pay?

What makes executive compensation controversial?

ORGANIZATIONAL CAREER MANAGEMENT

 6 *learning goal*

An important aspect of the human resource management process is organizational career management, or facilitating employee job changes, including promotions, transfers, demotions, layoffs, terminations, and retirements.

Job Changes within the Organization

A **promotion** is an upward move in an organization to a position with more authority, responsibility, and pay. Promotion decisions are usually based on merit (ability and performance) and seniority (length of service). Union employees usually prefer a strict seniority system for employee advancement. Managers and technical employees strongly prefer promotions based on merit.

A **transfer** is a horizontal move in an organization to a position with about the same salary and at about the same organizational level. An employee might seek a transfer for personal growth, for a more interesting job, for convenience (better work hours, work location, or training opportunity), or for a job that offers more potential for advancement. Employers might transfer workers from positions where they are no longer needed to ones where they are needed. Or the goal might be to find a better fit for the employee within the firm. Sometimes transfers are made to give employees a different perspective or to reenergize them.

When a person is downgraded or reassigned to a position with less responsibility, it is called a **demotion.** This usually occurs when an employee isn't performing satisfactorily. In most companies, a person is given several warnings before a demotion takes place.

Separations

A **separation** occurs when an employee leaves the company. Layoffs, terminations, resignations, and retirements are all types of separations. Sometimes separations occur because companies are trying to remain competitive in the global marketplace. In November of 2005, General Motors, the world's largest manufacturing company, announced that it would lay off 3,600 of its Canadian workers, 20 percent of its Canadian workforce.[7]

A **layoff** is a temporary separation arranged by the employer, usually because business is slow. Layoffs can be planned, such as seasonal reductions of employees (e.g., road construction in Canada), or unplanned, as when sales unexpectedly decline. Generally, employees with the least seniority are laid off first.

There are several alternatives to a layoff. With a *voluntary reduction in pay,* all employees agree to take less pay so that everyone can keep working. Other firms arrange to have all or most of their employees take vacation time during slow periods. Major league baseball teams, for example, encourage their full-time year-round employees to take vacations during the off-season from November through April. Other employees agree to take *voluntary time off* or to work fewer hours, which, again, has the effect of reducing the employer's payroll and avoiding the

promotion

An upward move in an organization to a position with more authority, responsibility, and pay.

transfer

A horizontal move in an organization to a position with about the same salary and at about the same organizational level.

demotion

The downgrading or reassignment of an employee to a position with less responsibility.

separation

The departure of an employee from the organization; can be a layoff, termination, resignation, or retirement.

layoff

A temporary separation of an employee from the organization; arranged by the employer, usually because business is slow.

termination

A permanent separation of an employee from the organization, arranged by the employer.

resignation

A permanent separation of an employee from the organization, done voluntarily by the employee.

retirement

The separation of an employee from the organization at the end of his or her career.

need for a layoff. It is common practice in Canada's road construction industry to hire temporary workers for the warmer months with the clear understanding that they will be laid off after the construction season has ended.

A **termination** is a permanent separation arranged by the employer. Reasons for terminations include failure to perform as expected, violation of work rules, downsizing (terminating workers to lower costs and become more competitive in the marketplace), dishonesty, theft, sexual harassment, excessive absenteeism, or insubordination (disobedience).

Most companies follow a series of steps before terminating an employee for poor performance or violations of company rules. First, the employee is given an oral warning. The second step is a written statement that the employee's actions are not acceptable. If the employee fails to improve, he or she is suspended from work for a time. If the employee persists in wrongdoing after suspension, his or her employment is terminated.

Resignation is a permanent form of separation that is undertaken voluntarily by the employee, whereas layoff and termination are involuntary. An employee may resign for almost any reason: to seek a new career, move to a different part of the country, accept an employment offer with a significant pay raise, or join a fast-growing firm with numerous advancement opportunities.

For companies in high-growth industries, keeping employees from resigning and moving to "greener pastures" is a number one priority. This is particularly true in smaller entrepreneurial firms, where losing a key employee can be disastrous.

Retirement usually ends one's career. Common retirement age is between 55 and 70. Under the Canadian Human Rights Act, at the federal level it is not considered discrimination to terminate an employee that has reached the normal age of retirement. Normal retirement age is determined as the retirement age of others working in similar positions.

Workers in companies with too many employees might be offered early-retirement incentives. This option offers retirement benefits to younger employees or adds extra retirement benefits or both. Employees can thus retire more comfortably without working longer. Many companies in Canada have used early-retirement plans to reduce their workforces when economic conditions have caused declines in product demand and production schedules must be reduced.

concept check

What is organizational career management?

Define promotion, transfer, termination, and retirement.

MANAGING DIVERSITY WITHIN THE ORGANIZATION

7 *learning goal*

managing diversity
Fully utilizing the potential of all employees in a work environment.

As explained in Chapter 3, diversity refers to the blend of people with differences in ages, gender, origin, ethnicity, physical abilities, and sexual orientation. **Managing diversity** means fully utilizing the potential of all employees in a work environment that is free of diversity-related problems such as bigotry, all forms of harassment, employee turnover, absenteeism, low productivity, and poor work quality. A broad objective of managing diversity is the creation of a multicultural organization with a culture that values diversity. To achieve this, the organizational culture and its systems might need to be adapted to improve employee relationships and equip all employees to be fully productive. Companies that excel in managing diversity have found that it can add up to stronger performance in the marketplace by offering it a competitive advantage.

Diversity as a Competitive Advantage

HOT Links

Interested in a career in human resources? The Student Center in the HR Resources area of the International Public Management Association-Human Resources Web site, http://www.ipma-hr.org, has valuable tips to point you in the right direction.

A **competitive advantage**, also called a *differential advantage,* is a set of unique features of a company and its products that are perceived by the target market (the people or companies that the firm wishes to serve) as significant and superior to those of the competition. As Andrew Grove, former CEO of Intel, says, "You have to understand what it is you are better at than anybody else and mercilessly focus your efforts on it." Competitive advantage is the factor or factors that cause customers to patronize a firm and not the competition. Many things can be sources of a competitive advantage. Intel's better use of technology, Procter & Gamble's more efficient distribution, Wal-Mart's lower prices, or even Coca-Cola's well-known brand name can be a competitive advantage.

Many organizations now recognize diversity as a means of obtaining a competitive advantage. In Exhibit 9.8, we describe six ways in which diversity can help create a competitive advantage.

To achieve these sources of competitive advantage, top management must support and be fully committed to diversity. Top managers must be champions of diversity and take a strong stand on the need to improve relationships among people who are different. Managers must put policies in place to keep the organization moving forward. Arthur Martinez, former CEO of Sears, was very aggressive about managing diversity. He had the chief diversity executive reporting directly to him. Sears even has a Chairman's Diversity Advisement Council that meets quarterly to work on diversity strategies.

Exhibit 9.8	Managing Cultural Diversity Can Provide Competitive Advantage	
1.	Lower costs	As organizations become more diverse, the cost of doing a poor job in integrating workers will increase. Those who handle this well will thus create cost advantages over those who don't.
2.	Better hiring	Companies develop reputations on favorability as prospective employers of women and ethnic minorities. Those with the best reputation for managing diversity will win the competition for the best personnel. As the labour pool shrinks and changes in composition, this edge will become increasingly important.
3.	More effective marketing	For multinational organizations, the insight and cultural sensitivity that members with roots in other countries bring to the marketing effort should improve these efforts in important ways. The same rationale applies to marketing to subpopulations within domestic operations.
4.	Greater employee creativity	Diversity of perspectives and less emphasis on conformity to norms of the past (which characterize the modern approach to management of diversity) should improve the level of creativity.
5.	More effective problem solving	Heterogeneity in decision- and problem-solving groups potentially produces better decisions through a wider range of perspectives and more thorough critical analysis of issues.
6.	Quicker adaptation to change	An implication of the multicultural model for managing diversity is that the system will become less determinant, less standardized, and therefore more fluid. The increased fluidity should create greater flexibility to react to environmental changes (i.e., reactions should be faster and at less cost).

SOURCE: "Managing Cultural Diversity: Implications for Organizational Competitiveness" ACADEMY OF MANAGEMENT EXECUTIVE: THE THINKING MANAGER'S SOURCE by Cox, Taylor and Stacy Blake. Copyright 1991 by ACADEMY OF MANAGEMENT (NY). Reproduced with permission of ACADEMY OF MANAGEMENT (NY) in the format Textbook via Copyright Clearance Center.

The Best Companies for Managing Diversity

The growing recognition of the importance of diversity in the workforce is exemplified by *Fortune*'s annual list of the "Best Companies for Minorities." To compile the list, company editors examine a variety of factors. They wanted to know not just how diverse their workforce is as a whole but also whether that diversity extends to the executive suite: How many directors and officers are of a visible minority? What portion of management? They also looked at compensation: Are bonuses tied to progress on diversity? How many of the 50 highest-paid employees represent a visible minority? And they checked how a company spends its money: Does it use a minority-owned investment firm for financing? Finally, they crunched the numbers and gave each company an overall grade. (For more details, go to **http://www.fortune.com/diversity**.)

concept check

What is involved in managing diversity?

How does a diverse workplace create a competitive advantage?

LAWS AFFECTING HUMAN RESOURCE MANAGEMENT

8 learning goal

HOT Links

Learn more about the Employment Equity Act by searching The Department of Justice Canada at http://www.justice.gc.ca.

HOT Links

Check out the Canadian Human Rights Commission Web site at http://www.chrc-ccdp.ca.

HOT Links

Look through a variety of interesting information on the HRDC Web site at http://www.hrdc-drhc.gc.ca.

Federal laws help ensure that job applicants and employees are treated fairly and not discriminated against. Hiring, training, and job placement must be unbiased. Promotion and compensation decisions must be based on performance. These laws help all Canadians who have talent, training, and the desire to get ahead.

New legislation and the continual interpretation and reinterpretation of existing laws will continue to make the jobs of human resource managers challenging and complicated. The key laws that currently affect human resource management are shown in Exhibit 9.9.

Employers may not discriminate against persons with disability. They must make "reasonable accommodations," so that qualified employees can perform the job, unless doing so would cause "undue hardship" for the business. Altering work schedules, modifying equipment so a wheelchair-bound person can use it, and making buildings accessible by ramps and elevators are considered reasonable. Two companies often praised for their efforts to hire people with disabilities are McDonald's and IBM Canada.

Canada's overall employment equity record of the past decade has been mixed. The employment of women in professional occupations continues to grow, but minority representation among professionals has not significantly increased, even though professional jobs have been among the fastest-growing areas. Technical jobs have the most equitable utilization rates of minorities. Almost 400 federal and federally regulated organizations submit annual reports to Human Resources Development Canada (HRDC) under the Employment Equity Act. The organizations are then graded on an alphabetical scale.

concept check

What are the key laws affecting employment?

What is employment equity?

Exhibit 9.9 | Laws Impacting Human Resource Management

LAW	PURPOSE	APPLICABILITY
Charter of Rights and Freedoms (contained in the Constitution Act of 1982)	Provides the right to live and seek employment anywhere in Canada	Takes precedence over all other laws
Human rights legislation	Provides equal opportunity for members of protected groups in areas such as accommodation, contracts, provision of goods and services, and employment	Comprised of federal, provincial, and territorial laws with a common objective
Canadian Human Rights Act (1977)	Prohibits discrimination on a number of grounds	Applies to federal government agencies, Crown corporations, and businesses under federal jurisdiction
Employment Equity Act (amended in 1996)	Attempts to remove employment barriers and promote equality for the members of four designated groups: women, visible minorities, Aboriginal people, and persons with disabilities	Every employer must implement the Act and make every reasonable accommodation to ensure that people in the designated groups are represented in their organization. The degree of representation in each occupational group should reflect the Canadian workforce and be consistent with their ability to meet reasonable occupational requirements
Occupational Health and Safety Act	Designed to protect the health and safety of workers by minimizing work-related accidents and illness	All provinces, territories, and the federal jurisdiction have occupational health and safety legislation
WHMIS (Workplace Hazardous Materials Information System)	Designed to protect workers by providing information about hazardous materials in the workplace	Canada-wide legally mandated system

UNDERSTANDING LABOUR RELATIONS IN A UNIONIZED ENVIRONMENT

learning goal

labour union

An organization that represents workers in dealing with management over issues involving wages, hours, and working conditions.

collective bargaining

The process of negotiating labour agreements that provide for compensation and working arrangements mutually acceptable to the union and to management.

A **labour union** is an organization that represents workers in dealing with management over issues involving wages, hours, and working conditions. The labour relations process that produces a union-management relationship consists of three phases: union organizing, negotiating a labour agreement, and the day-to-day administering of the agreement. In Phase 1, a group of employees within a firm might form a union on their own, or an established union may target an employer and organize many of the firm's workers into a local labour union. The second phase constitutes **collective bargaining,** which is the process of negotiating labour agreements that provide for compensation and working arrangements mutually acceptable to the union and to management.

The third phase of the labour relations process involves the daily administering of the labour agreement primarily through the handling of worker grievances and other workforce management problems that require interaction between managers and labour union officials.

Local Unions

local union

A branch or unit of a national union that represents workers at a specific plant or in a specific geographic area.

national union

A union that consists of many local unions in a particular industry, skilled trade, or geographic area and thus represents workers throughout an entire country.

shop steward

An elected union official who represents union members to management when workers have issues.

A **local union** is a branch or unit of a **national union** that represents workers at a specific plant or over a specific geographic area. In conformance to national union rules, local unions determine the number of local union officers, procedures for electing officers, the schedule of local meetings, financial arrangements with the national organization, and the local's role in negotiating labour agreements.

The largest national union is the Canadian Union of Public Employees (CUPE) with more than half a million members across Canada. The CUPE represents workers in airlines, education, emergency services, health care, libraries, municipalities, public utilities, social services, transportation, and universities. Under the CUPE national union are the various local unions (e.g. CUPE local 774 in Abbotsford, British Columbia).

The three main functions of the local union are collective bargaining, worker relations and membership services, and community and political activities. Collective bargaining generally takes place every two or three years. Local union officers and shop stewards oversee worker-management relations on a day-to-day basis. A **shop steward** is an elected union official who represents union members to management when workers have issues. For most union members, his or her primary contact with the union is through union officials at the local level.

Negotiating Union Contracts

A union contract is created through collective bargaining. Typically, both management and union negotiating teams are made up of a few persons. One person on each side is the chief spokesperson.

Bargaining begins with union and management negotiators setting a bargaining agenda, a list of contract issues that will be discussed. Much of the bargaining over the specific details takes place through face-to-face meetings and the exchange of written proposals. Demands, proposals, and counterproposals are exchanged during several rounds of bargaining. The resulting contract must then be approved by top management and by union members. The collective bargaining process is shown in Exhibit 9.10.

Late in 2002 the Canadian Auto Workers Union reached a contract settlement with the Ford Motor Company. Along with wage increases of 3 percent each of the first two years and 2 percent for the third contract year, provisions included a cost-of-living allowance, a contract-signing bonus of $1,000 Canadian, and a pledge from the company to provide new jobs for 900 of 1,400 employees at a pickup assembly plant in Oakville, Ontario. With the early-retirement package and the provision for new jobs, no layoffs will happen when the plant closes, according to the local union president.[8]

The union contract is a legally binding agreement that typically covers such issues as union security, management rights, wages, job benefits, and job security. Each of these is discussed in this section.

Union Security

closed shop

A company where only union members can be hired.

union shop

A company where non-union workers can be hired but must then join the union.

agency shop

A company where employees are not required to join the union but must pay it a fee to cover its expenses in representing them.

One of the key issues in a contract is union security. From the union's perspective, the most secure arrangement is the **closed shop,** a company where only union members can be hired. The union serves, in effect, as an employment agency for the firm. Today, the most common form of union security is the **union shop.** Non-union workers can be hired, but then they must join the union, normally within 30 or 60 days.

An **agency shop** does not require employees to join the union, but to keep working at the company, employees must pay the union a fee to cover its expenses in representing them. The union must fairly represent all workers, including those who do not become members.

Exhibit 9.10 | The Process of Negotiating Labour Agreements

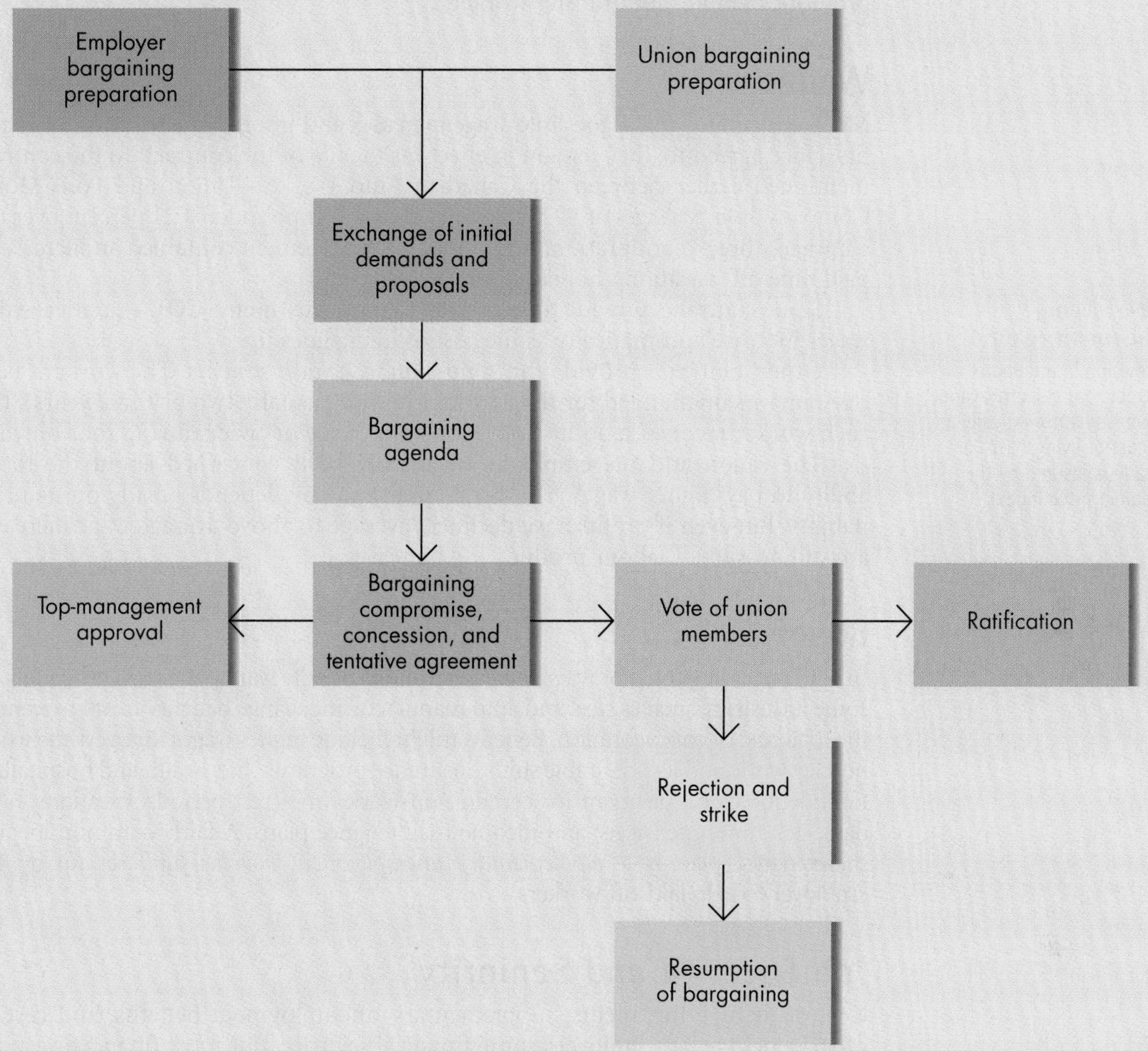

```
┌─────────────────┐                    ┌─────────────────┐
│    Employer     │                    │      Union       │
│   bargaining    │────────┬───────────│   bargaining     │
│   preparation   │        │           │   preparation    │
└─────────────────┘        │           └─────────────────┘
                           ▼
                 ┌─────────────────┐
                 │  Exchange of     │
                 │  initial         │
                 │  demands and     │
                 │  proposals       │
                 └─────────────────┘
                           │
                           ▼
                 ┌─────────────────┐
                 │   Bargaining     │
                 │    agenda        │
                 └─────────────────┘
                           │
                           ▼
┌──────────────┐   ┌─────────────────┐   ┌──────────────┐   ┌──────────────┐
│     Top-     │◄──│   Bargaining     │──►│ Vote of union│──►│ Ratification │
│ management   │   │  compromise,     │   │   members    │   │              │
│  approval    │   │  concession, and │   └──────────────┘   └──────────────┘
└──────────────┘   │ tentative        │           │
                   │ agreement        │           ▼
                   └─────────────────┘   ┌──────────────┐
                                         │ Rejection and│
                                         │    strike    │
                                         └──────────────┘
                                                 │
                                                 ▼
                                         ┌──────────────┐
                                         │  Resumption  │
                                         │ of bargaining│
                                         └──────────────┘
```

open shop

A company where employees do not have to join the union or pay dues or fees to the union; established under right-to-work laws.

When employees can work at a unionized company without having to join the union, this arrangement is commonly known as an **open shop.** Workers don't have to join the union or pay dues or fees to the union.

Management Rights

When a company becomes unionized, management loses some of its decision-making abilities. But management still has certain rights that can be negotiated in collective bargaining.

One way to lessen a union's influence in the management of an organization is by having a *management rights clause* in the labour agreement. Most union contracts have one. A typical clause gives the employer all rights to manage the business except as specified in the contract. For instance, if the contract does not specify the criteria for promotions, with a management rights clause managers will have the right to use any criteria they wish. Another way to preserve management rights is to list areas that are not subject to collective bargaining. This list might secure management's right to schedule work hours, hire and fire workers, set production standards, determine the number of supervisors in each department, and promote, demote, and transfer workers.

Wages

Much bargaining effort goes into wage increases and improvements in fringe benefits. Once agreed to, they remain in effect for the life of the contract. In the contract mentioned earlier between the Canadian Auto Workers Union and Ford Motor Company, hourly wages of $27.70 increased by a compounded 8.21 percent over the contract's three-year duration. Additionally, the agreement contained an increase in paid time off (vacations, holidays, and personal days).

Some contracts provide for a **cost-of-living adjustment (COLA)**, under which wages increase automatically as the cost of living goes up.

Other contracts provide for *lump-sum wage adjustments*. The workers' base pay remains unchanged for the contract period (usually two or three years), but each worker receives a bonus (or lump sum) once or twice during the contract.

The union and the employer are usually both concerned about the firm's ability to pay higher wages. The firm's ability to pay depends greatly on its profitability. But even if profits have declined, average to above-average wage increases are still possible if labour productivity increases.

cost-of-living adjustment (COLA)

A provision in a labour contract that calls for wages to increase automatically as the cost of living rises (usually measured by the consumer price index).

Benefits

In addition to requests for wage increases, unions usually want better fringe benefits. In some industries, such as steel and auto manufacturing, fringe benefits are 40 percent of the total cost of compensation. Benefits might include higher wages for overtime work, holiday work, and less desirable shifts; insurance programs (life, health and hospitalization, dental care); payment for certain non-work time (rest periods, vacations, holidays, sick time); pensions; and income maintenance plans. A fairly common income maintenance plan is a *supplementary unemployment benefits fund* set up by the employer to help laid-off workers.

Job Security and Seniority

Cost-of-living adjustments, supplementary unemployment benefits, and certain other benefits give employees some financial security. But most financial security is directly related to job security—the assurance, to some degree, that workers will keep their jobs. Of course, job security depends primarily on the continued success and financial well-being of the company.

Seniority, the length of an employee's continuous service with a firm, is discussed in about 90 percent of all labour contracts. Seniority is a factor in job security; usually, unions want the workers with the most seniority to have the most job security.

concept check

Explain the collective bargaining process.

Explain each of the following: closed shop, union shop, agency shop, and open shop.

Grievance and Arbitration

grievance

A formal complaint, filed by an employee or by the union, charging that management has violated the contract.

The union's main way of policing the contract is the grievance procedure. A **grievance** is a formal complaint, by an employee or by the union, that management has violated some part of the contract. Under a typical contract, the employee starts by presenting the grievance to the supervisor, either in person or in writing. The typical grievance procedure is illustrated in Exhibit 9.11.

If the problem isn't solved, the grievance is put in writing. The employee, one or more union officials, the supervisor, and perhaps the plant manager then discuss the grievance. If the matter still can't be resolved, another meeting takes place with higher level representatives of both parties present. If top management and the local union president can't resolve the grievance, it goes to arbitration.

Arbitration is the process of settling a labour-management dispute by having a third party—a single arbitrator or a panel—make a decision. The decision is final and binding on the union and the employer. The arbitrator reviews the grievance at a hearing and then makes the decision, which is presented in a document called the award.

Similar to arbitration is **mediation,** the process of settling issues in which the parties present their case to a neutral mediator. The mediator (the specialist) holds talks with union and management negotiators at separate meetings and at joint sessions. The mediator also suggests compromises. Mediators cannot issue binding decisions or impose a settlement on the disputing parties. Their only tools are communication and persuasion. Mediation almost always produces a settlement between the union and a firm, but sometimes the process takes months or even a year, and either or both sides can reject the mediator's assistance.

Exhibit 9.11 | Typical Grievance Procedure

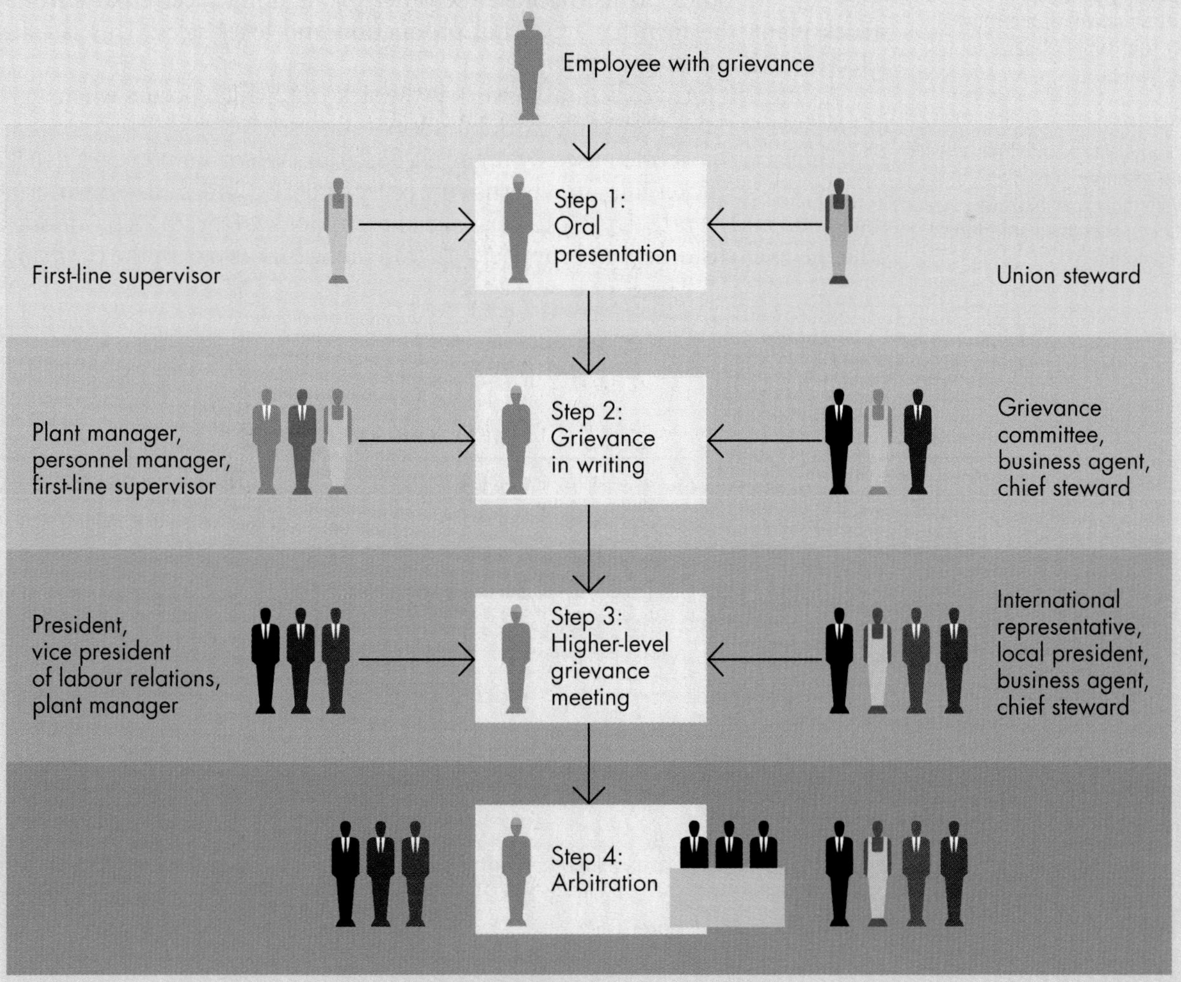

- Employee with grievance
- First-line supervisor → **Step 1: Oral presentation** ← Union steward
- Plant manager, personnel manager, first-line supervisor → **Step 2: Grievance in writing** ← Grievance committee, business agent, chief steward
- President, vice president of labour relations, plant manager → **Step 3: Higher-level grievance meeting** ← International representative, local president, business agent, chief steward
- **Step 4: Arbitration**

Describe the grievance procedure.

In what ways do arbitrators act like judges?

Managing Labour–Management Conflict

Both sides to labour-management conflicts have powerful tools for exerting economic (or financial) pressure. Unions can fight with strikes, product boycotts, picketing, and corporate campaigns. Employers can fight with lockouts, strike replacements, and mutual-aid pacts and can also shift production to non-union plants or out of the country. Exhibit 9.12 lists the methods used by both sides.

Union Strategies

wildcat strike

A strike by a group of union members or an entire local union without the approval of the national union while the contract is still in effect.

selective strike strategy

A union strategy of conducting a strike (shutting down) at a critical plant that supplies parts to other plants.

sick-out

A union strategy in which a group of employees claim they cannot work because of illness, thereby disrupting the company.

The strike is the most powerful union tool, but it is usually the means of last resort. Although a strike might hurt the employer, it also means loss of pay to employees. Strikes occur most often over economic issues, such as wages, pensions, vacation time, and other benefits. A strike normally starts immediately after the old union contract has expired, if management and labour can't agree on new contract terms. Sometimes a group of union members or an entire local union will strike without the approval of the national union, while the contract is still in effect. This action, which is often illegal because it violates the contract, is called a **wildcat strike.**

Another union strike strategy is to shut down (strike) a critical plant that supplies parts to other plants. Because the other plants don't receive parts from the struck plant, the firm has to curtail production and loses sales. This is called a **selective strike strategy.**

A different form of refusal to work is the **sick-out,** which occurs when a group of employees claim they can't work because of illness.

The tactic most often used by unions is **picketing.** When a union calls a strike, it usually sets up picket lines to advertise the strike and discourage the employer from staying open. The picketers try to persuade non-striking workers to stop working and other people (customers and suppliers) to stop doing business with the company.

Exhibit 9.12 | Strategies of Unions and Employers

UNION STRATEGIES		EMPLOYER STRATEGIES	
Strike:	Employees refuse to work.	**Lockout:**	Employer refuses to let employees enter plant to work.
Boycott:	Employees try to keep customers and others from doing business with employer.	**Strike replacements:**	Employer uses non-union employees to do jobs of striking union employees.
Picketing:	Employees march near entrance of firm to publicize their view of dispute and discourage customers.	**Mutual-aid pact:**	Employer receives money from other companies in industry to cover some of income lost because of strikes.
Corporate campaign:	Union disrupts stockholder meetings or buys company stock to have more influence over management.	**Shift production:**	Employer moves production to non-union plant or out of country.

Strikes are powerful union tools, usually used as a last resort when labour and management cannot reach agreement on issues such as wages, pensions, vacation time, and other benefits.

CP/BRENT REANEY

picketing
Union members parade in front of the employer's plant carrying signs and trying to persuade non-striking workers to stop working and customers and suppliers to stop doing business with the company.

corporate campaign
A union strategy in which a union disrupts a corporation's relations with its shareholders or investors as a means of attacking the company.

lockout
An employer tactic in a labour dispute in which the employer refuses to allow workers to enter a plant or building to work, which means that the workers do not get paid.

strike replacements
Non-union employees hired to replace striking union members; also known as *scabs*.

mutual-aid pact
An agreement by companies in an industry to create a fund that can be used to help cover fixed costs of any member company whose workers go on strike.

Another union weapon is the consumer and product boycott. If a union has a dispute with a firm that produces a consumer product, it asks its own and other union members to stop purchasing the product. Product sales drop, and the company suffers financially.

The **corporate campaign** is a fairly new union strategy. With this strategy, a union might try to disrupt the stockholder meetings of a company it wants to pressure. Sometimes the union buys stock in the company so it can have more influence. The union might also threaten to withdraw great sums of money from banks that do business with the firm.

Employer Strategies

Employers have their own strategies in labour issues. One of the most effective is the **lockout,** in which the company refuses to let workers enter a plant or building to work. If the workers can't perform their jobs, they don't get paid. Management can also hire temporary workers during a lockout. Sometimes, however, a lockout can benefit the union. Overhead costs (costs for lease payments, insurance premiums, and management salaries) continue whether a plant is open or closed, putting pressure on management to end the lockout.

Strike replacements (or "scabs") are non-union employees hired to replace striking union members. If suitable replacements can be found, the company can stay open and keep making sales and earning profits. The problem with strike replacements is finding qualified people.

Another strategy used by employers in some industries is the **mutual-aid pact.** Companies in an industry pool some of their financial resources in a fund that can be used to help cover costs of any member company whose workers go on strike. These pacts have been used with some success in the airline, tire, and newspaper industries.

10 *learning goal*

Protecting whistle blowers, growing minority recruiting, proactively managing diversity, advancing technology, and globally competing are driving the trends in human resource management in the 21st century.

PROTECTING WHISTLE BLOWERS

An employee "blows the whistle" when he or she discloses some wrongdoing and/or illegal behaviour or practice committed by another person in the firm. Some companies have an "ethics" hotline that can be used to make this disclosure, or someone can report misconduct to legal authorities, or even the news media. If the reported wrongdoing is investigated and corrective action taken, the whistle blower has benefited the organization. On the other hand, the whistle blower could suffer if a higher authority in the organization retaliates against him or her for reporting the improper behaviour.

In recent years whistle blowers, such as Sherron Watkins at Enron and Cynthia Cooper at Worldcom, have received national attention for their reports of illegal executive behaviour. Although these whistle blowers did the correct thing, they brought considerable attention, some of it negative, to themselves. Some jurisdictions have passed laws in recent years that protect whistle blowers from employer retaliation. Recently many firms have developed a whistle blower policy that provides encouragement and protection to an employee who reveals misconduct.

HOT Links

"CIBC Sets up Ethics Hotline for Staff"—see http://www .tnwinc.com/news/ newsarchive/TNW_ RLTORONTOSTAR_CM.asp.

THE GROWTH IN MINORITY RECRUITING

Progressive firms today have moved far beyond government mandates for hiring minorities. These organizations recognize that diversity is necessary to understand and meet the needs of their customers, and diversity is an important source of competitive advantage. Nowhere is this truer than in the field of retailing.

At one Home Depot store the general store manager, Tony Gonzalez, discusses a popular "langosta" (lobster) dish with a customer perusing food processors. Gonzalez and his customer are natives of Latin American culture and both prepare and enjoy the culture's popular foods. Gonzalez thinks a certain model would be best for the job; a passing associate, one of many bilingual employees, agrees. The customer leaves the store with the appliance and a seafood recipe.

Such in-store interactions are becoming more commonplace throughout the retail industry as companies realize they need to establish and exploit the cultural and lingual bonds between their store associates and shoppers. What's more, an increasing number of retailers are adding diversity to their corporate ranks, from buyers to the corner office in an effort to understand more fully the needs of the fastest-growing segment of their customer base—the ethnic shopper.

PROACTIVE MANAGEMENT OF DIVERSITY

In the past, most companies responded to government legislation related to diversity, such as employment equity, in order to fall in line with federal guidelines. Organizations were reactive rather than proactive. Today there is a decided trend toward proactive management of diversity. Companies are creating initiatives to build effective multicultural organizations. This requires construction of an environment and culture in which all members can excel. Companies accomplish this by hiring and promoting people who truly believe in the firm's diversity values, reinforcing these values in performance and evaluation systems, and educating all employees about diversity issues.

Being proactive also means blending the community with the organization. This involves incorporating diversity into major committees and implementing employment equity, education, and targeted career-development programs. A proactive company must also minimize interpersonal and intergroup conflicts related to group identity and must promote understanding of cultural differences.

ADVANCING TECHNOLOGY

outsourcing
The assignment of various functions, such as human resources, accounting, or legal work, to outside organizations.

Advances in information technology have greatly improved the efficiency of handling many transaction-based aspects (payroll and expense reimbursement) of employee services. Technology enables instant communication of human resource data from far-flung branches to the home office. Ease of communication has also led many companies to outsource some or all of their human resource functions. **Outsourcing** is the assignment of various functions, such as human resources, accounting, or legal work, to outside organizations. The National Geographic Society outsourced all of its employee benefits programs to Workforce Solutions. Without computer databases and networks, such outsourcing would be impossible.

telecommuting
An arrangement in which employees work at home and are linked to the office by phone, fax, and computer.

Technology has also made telecommuting a reality for millions of workers. **Telecommuting** is now commonplace. In this arrangement, employees work at home and are linked to the office by phone, fax, and computer. At Cisco Systems, a computer-networking firm, telecommuters have improved their productivity by up to 25 percent, while the company has saved about $1 million (USD) on overhead and retained key employees who might otherwise have left. What's more, those who have traded suits for sweats say they love setting their own schedules, skipping rush hour, spending more time with their kids, and working at least part-time in comfortable surroundings. Telecommuting grows when the economy is strong because employers must do what they can to attract the best and brightest workers.

GLOBAL COMPETITION

As more firms "go global," they are sending an increasing number of employees overseas. Magna, ScotiaBank, RIM, Microsoft, Federal Express, and many others have tens of thousands of employees abroad. Such companies face somewhat different human resource management issues than do firms that operate only within North America. For example, criteria for selecting employees include not only technical skills and knowledge of the business but also the ability to adapt to a local culture and to learn a foreign language.

Once an individual is selected for an overseas assignment, language training and cultural orientation become important. Salary and benefits, relocation expenses, and special allowances (housing, transportation, and education) can increase human resource costs by as much as three times normal annual costs. After an overseas assignment of one year or more, the firm must repatriate the employee, or bring the individual back home. Job placement and career progression frequently become issues during repatriation because the firm has changed, and the employee's old job might no longer exist.

concept check

Why are companies spending resources on minority recruiting?

Describe how advances in communication technology make outsourcing and telecommuting possible.

What issues does "going global" present for human resource management?

Great Ideas to Use Now

PLANNING YOUR CAREER

It's never too early to start thinking about your career in business. No, you don't have to decide today, but it's important to decide fairly soon how you will spend your life's work. A very practical reason for doing so is that it will save you a lot of time and money. We have seen too many students who aren't really sure what they want to do after graduation. The longer you wait to choose a profession, the more credit hours you might have to take in your new field, and the longer it will be before you start earning real money.

A second reason to choose a career field early is that you can get a part-time or summer job and "test-drive" the profession. If it's not for you, you will find out very quickly.

Your school career centre can give you plenty of information about various careers in business. We also describe many career opportunities at the end of each part of this text. Another source of career information is the Internet. Go to any search engine, such as Excite or Lycos, and enter "careers in business," or narrow your search to a specific area such as management or marketing.

Career planning will not end when you find your first professional job. It is a lifelong process that ends only with retirement. Your career planning will include conducting a periodic self-assessment of your strengths and weaknesses, gathering information about other jobs both within the firm and externally, learning about other industries, and setting career goals for yourself. You must always think about your future in business.

HUMAN RESOURCES DECISION-MAKING

During your professional career in business, you will likely have the opportunity to become a manager. As a manager, you will have to make many human resource decisions, including hiring, firing, promoting, giving a pay raise, sending an employee to a training program, disciplining a worker, approving a college tuition reimbursement request, and reassigning an employee to a different job. In short, you will be involved in virtually every human resource decision or activity affecting the employees you manage. Always treat people as you wish to be treated when making human resource decisions. Be fair, be honest, offer your experience and advice, and communicate frequently with your employees. If you follow this simple advice, you will be richly rewarded in your career.

Employees provide most, if not all, of a firm's customer service. Usually, employees who are more experienced can provide better customer service and solve more difficult customer service problems. More experienced employees are normally persons who have worked for a firm for an extended period. Accordingly, employee retention is important in support of high-quality products and customer service. If an organization experiences high employee retention, or low employee turnover, it also minimizes its staffing and training costs, because it doesn't need to hire as many people each year.

Nursing is a profession for which retention is a huge factor because of acute nursing shortages that have been forecast for the next 15 to 20 years. In a survey by the University of Washington School of Nursing, it was determined that retention of nurses increased with greater employee teamwork, lowering of patient-nurse ratios, and rewarding nurses with more decision-making authority. Higher pay also had a positive impact on retention.[9] Would you prefer to receive care from an experienced nurse who had worked for several years at the hospital where you might be a patient, or from an inexperienced nurse who is completing his or her first week of work?

SUMMARY OF LEARNING GOALS

1 What is the human resource management process, and how are human resource needs determined?

The human resource management process consists of a sequence of activities that begins with job analysis and HR planning; progresses to employee recruitment and selection; then focuses on employee training, performance appraisal, and compensation; and ends when the employee leaves the organization.

Creating a strategy for meeting human resource needs is called human resource planning, which begins with job analysis. Job analysis is the process of studying a job to determine its tasks and duties for setting pay, determining employee job performance, specifying hiring requirements, and designing training programs. Information from the job analysis is used to prepare a job description, which lists the tasks and responsibilities of the job. A job specification describes the skills, knowledge, and abilities a person needs to fill the job described in the job description. By examining the human resource demand forecast and the internal supply forecast, human resource professionals can determine if the company faces a personnel surplus or shortage.

2 How do human resource managers recruit and select qualified applicants?

When a job vacancy occurs, most firms begin by trying to fill the job from within. If a suitable internal candidate is not available, the firm begins an external search. Firms use local media to recruit non-technical, unskilled, and non-supervisory workers. To locate highly trained recruits, employers use college recruiters, executive search firms, job fairs, and company Web sites to promote job openings.

Typically, an applicant submits an application or résumé and then receives a short, structured interview. If an applicant makes it past the initial screening, he or she might be asked to take an aptitude, personality, or skills test. The next step is the selection interview, which is an in-depth discussion of the applicant's work experience, skills and abilities, education, and career interests.

3 What types of training and development do organizations offer their employees?

Training and development programs are designed to increase employees' knowledge, skills, and abilities to foster job performance improvements. Formal training (usually classroom in nature and off the job) takes place shortly after being hired. Development programs prepare employees to assume positions of increasing authority and responsibility. Job rotation, executive education programs, mentoring, and special-project assignments are examples of employee development programs.

4 How are performance appraisals used to evaluate employees' performance?

A performance appraisal compares an employee's actual performance with the expected performance. Performance appraisals serve several purposes but are typically used to determine an employee's compensation, training needs, and advancement opportunities.

5 What are the different methods for compensating employees?

Direct pay is the hourly wage or monthly salary paid to an employee. In addition to the base wage or salary, direct pay may include bonuses and profit shares. Indirect pay consists of various benefits and services. Some benefits are required by law: unemployment compensation, worker's compensation, Canada or Quebec Pension Plan, and paid vacations and holidays. Others are voluntarily made available by employers to employees. These include pensions, health and other insurance products, employee wellness programs, and college tuition reimbursement.

6 What is organizational career management?

Organizational career management is the facilitation of employee job changes, including promotions, transfers, layoffs, and retirements. A promotion is an upward move with more authority, responsibility, and pay. A transfer is a horizontal move in the organization. When a person is downgraded to a position with less responsibility, it is a demotion. A layoff is a temporary separation arranged by the employer, usually when business is slow. A termination is a permanent separation arranged by the employer. A resignation is a voluntary separation by the employee. Retirement is a permanent separation that ends one's career.

7 Why does a diverse workforce lead to stronger performance in the marketplace?

Human resource managers should strive to create a culture that values diversity. Managing diversity means using the full potential of all of the employees in the workforce. The benefits of a diverse workforce include lower costs, better hiring, more effective marketing, greater creativity, more effective problem solving, and quicker adaptation to change. These factors can give the organization a competitive advantage, a unique set of features considered superior to those of the competition.

8 What are the key pieces of legislation affecting human resource management?

A number of federal, provincial, and territorial laws affect human resource management. These include the Charter of Rights and Freedoms (contained in the Constitution Act of 1982), the Canadian Human Rights Act (1977), the Employment Equity Act (amended in 1995), the Occupational Health and Safety Act, and the Workplace Hazardous Materials Information System.

9 How are labour-management relations different in a unionized environment?

Many organizations have unionized employees. A labour union is organized to represent workers in dealing with management over issues involving wages, hours, and working conditions. Contracts are negotiated that set out the responsibilities of management and the workers through collective bargaining.

10 What trends are affecting human resource management?

Whistle blowers report wrongdoing or illegal behaviour in organizations. The actions of these people have brought down companies. New laws have been passed to protect whistle blowers from retaliation.

Today more and more companies are actively recruiting minorities. A diverse workforce often leads to increased market share and profits. Organizations are becoming proactive in their management of diversity. Companies are creating initiatives to build effective multicultural organizations.

Technology continues to improve the efficiency of human resource management. It also enables firms to outsource many functions done internally in the past. Telecommuting is becoming increasingly popular among employers and employees. As more firms enter the international market, they are sending an increasing number of employees overseas. In addition to normal job requirements, selected workers must have the ability to adapt to a local culture and perhaps to learn a foreign language.

EXPERIENTIAL EXERCISES

1. Make telecommuting work for you. Maybe a part-time job requires too much driving time. Perhaps there are simply no jobs in the immediate area that suit you. Try telecommuting right now. Is telecommuting for you? Many people are more satisfied with their personal and family lives than before they started working at home. But telecommuting is not for every person or every job, and you'll need plenty of self-discipline to make it work for you. Ask yourself if you can perform your duties without close supervision. Think also about whether you would miss your coworkers. If you decide to give telecommuting a try, consider these suggestions to maintain your productivity:

- *Set ground rules with your family.* Spouses and small children have to understand that even though you're in the house, you are busy earning a living. It's fine to throw in a few loads of laundry or answer the door when the plumber comes. It's another thing to take the kids to the mall or let them play games on your office PC.

- *Clearly demarcate your work space by using a separate room with a door you can shut.* Let your family know that, emergencies excepted, the space is off-limits during working hours.

- *If you have small children, you might want to arrange for childcare during your working hours.*

- *Stay in touch with your coworkers and professional colleagues.* Go into the office from time to time for meetings to stay connected.

Above all, you can make telecommuting work for you by being productive. Doing your job well, whether on-site or telecommuting, will help assure you of a bright future.

2. The fringe benefit package of many employers includes numerous voluntarily provided items such as health care insurance, life insurance, a pension plan, tuition reimbursement, employee price discounts on products of the firm, and paid sick leave. At your age, what are the three or four most important benefits? Why? Twenty years from now, what do you think will be your three or four most important benefits? Why?

3. As a corporate recruiter, you must know how to screen prospective employees. The Integrity Center Web site, at **http://www.integctr.com,** offers a brief tutorial on pre-employment screening, a glossary of key words and phrases, and related information. Prepare a short report that tells your assistant how to go about this process.

4. Go to the Monster Board at **http://resume.monster.ca** to learn how to prepare an electronic résumé that will get results. Develop a list of rules for creating effective electronic résumés, and revise your own résumé into electronic format.

5. Working as a contingent employee can help you explore your career options. Visit the Manpower Web site at **http://www.manpower.com,** and search for several types of jobs that interest you. What are the advantages of being a temporary worker? What other services does Manpower offer job seekers?

6. Web-based training is becoming popular at many companies as a way of bringing a wider variety of courses to more people at lower costs. The Web-Based Training Information Center site, at **http://www.webbasedtraining.com,** provides a good introduction. Learn about the basics of on-line training at its Primer page. Then link to the Resources section, try a demo, and explore other areas that interest you. Prepare a brief report on your findings, including the pros and cons of using the Web for training, to present to your class.

7. Your 250-employee company is considering outsourcing some of its HR functions because it wants to offer a wider range of services. You've been asked to prepare a report on whether it should proceed and if so, how. Visit BuyerZone.com, **http://www.buyerzone.com,** click on HR Outsourcing and then HR Outsourcing Buyer's Guide, to learn more about why companies are going outside for this important function and the advantages and disadvantages of doing so. Summarize your finding and make a recommendation. Then use a search engine to locate two to three firms that offer HR outsourcing services. Compare them and recommend one, explaining the reasons for your choice.

REVIEW QUESTIONS

1. Why is human resource management in today's organization instrumental in driving an organization toward its goals?

2. What is the human resource management process?

3. Why is human resource planning and forecasting so important?

4. What is recruitment? What are some recruitment methods?

5. What are the steps in employee selection?

6. Differentiate between training and development.

7. What are the steps in performance evaluation?

8. What is compensation? How is it determined?

9. Discuss the types of compensation.

10. What are some of the career management steps?

11. Explain managing diversity. How can diversity create a competitive advantage?

12. What are the primary laws that affect human resource management?

13. What is a labour union?

14. How are labour agreements negotiated?

15. What are the management and union strategies for dealing with conflict?

16. Discuss the trends in HRM.

CREATIVE THINKING CASE
"People First" at FedEx

FedEx founder and CEO Frederick Smith wants employees to be an integral part of the decision-making process at FedEx. He believes that putting the people first leads to better service for the customer and this leads, ultimately, to higher profits for the company. The People-Service-Profit (P-S-P) focus ensures that employee satisfaction, empowerment, risk taking, and innovation are encouraged, leading to 100 percent customer satisfaction, 100 percent of the time, and resulting in corporate profits.

FedEx Canada employs more than 5,000 people in 63 locations, with more 1,000 drop-off locations, and three call centres dealing with more than 35,000 calls per day. To emphasize the "people first" approach, the president traded jobs with one of his couriers for a week, and had the experience televised. An unusual exercise such as this sent a clear message to customers and employees alike. "We are serious about putting people first."

To help employees with the P-S-P focus, the following processes are in place at FedEx:

- an annual employee satisfaction survey;

- a promotion-from-within policy;

- employee recognition and reward programs;

- leadership evaluation;

- open communication including e-mail, print, broadcast and face-to-face;

- pay-for-performance remuneration; and

- an employee appeal procedure and guaranteed fair treatment policies.

The P-S-P philosophy, supported by the appropriate policies, leads to motivated employees who go beyond what might be delineated in the usual job description. Corporate legend reports a story of an employee who looked after a customer's cat after the cat was inadvertently wrapped into a package by the customer. Another story describes how a FedEx manager personally flew to Ottawa to hand-deliver lifesaving medication to a customer. These examples illustrate the service commitment FedEx has encouraged and obtained from their employees. Many companies profess that "people are our greatest asset," but FedEx has managed actually to live this philosophy through their "people first" focus.

CRITICAL THINKING QUESTIONS

1. To maintain the culture FedEx has developed, it is important to hire employees who "fit." How might FedEx do this?

2. Look at the compensation and evaluation aspects of HR. Suggest strategies for FedEx in keeping with their P-S-P focus.

SOURCES: Brenda McWillams and Gary Burkett, "Empowered Employees," *Marketing*, 3 no. 22 (June 19, 2006), 40; FedEx Canada History, http://www.fedex.com/ca (accessed July 10, 2006); FedEx Philosophy, http://www.fedex.com/ca (accessed July 10, 2006).

VIDEO CASE
Nurturing Individuality at Valassis

Who doesn't love a freebie? And your Sunday paper often includes one—a sachet of free shampoo, a miniature box of washing powder, a new kind of toothpaste to try—all brought to you by Valassis Communications, Inc. (**http://www.valassis.com**), a leader in marketing services for more than a quarter of a century.

This publicly held company headquartered in Livonia, Michigan, employs 1,300 people across the United States and Canada, and boasts annual sales in excess of $740 million. The company's flagship product is the Free-Standing Insert (FSI), distributed through newspapers to more than 57 million households every Sunday.

The FSI booklet contains coupons, refunds, and other promotional items from America's largest packaged-goods companies. Among other Valassis products are the delivery of manufacturers' product samples through Sunday newspapers and the oversight of clients' games and sweepstakes promotions. To expand its existing product base, Valassis recently acquired Illinois-based NCH Marketing Services, the premier coupon-processing and promotion information management company in the United States and worldwide.

Valassis sets the standard in its industry for quality, service, reliability, and expertise with its unique corporate philosophy, titled "Change to Grow," which is based on eight fundamental principles:

- Change is good.

- Don't point fingers—solve problems.

- Go—with speed.

- Create positive energy.

- Set the bar high—don't fear failure.

- Be empowered, and be accountable.

- Communicate clearly and openly.

- Stick to fundamentals.

Executives at Valassis believe it is the company's capable and highly motivated employees who are responsible for its competitive advantage in the marketplace. With more than 14,000 applicants for approximately 100 annual job openings, Valassis makes sure it hires the right people through a rigorous screening and interview process. Only those applicants most likely to embody and adhere to the principles of the company's "Change to Grow" culture are considered for a position.

Those fortunate enough to be hired embark on career paths geared to their unique strengths, talents, and career goals. The company also prefers to promote from within, so it invests heavily in employee training, supporting independent continuing education for employees through an educational assistance reimbursement program.

There is also company-run Valassis University, offering a broad spectrum of professional and personal development courses, as well as those covering specific business functions. Employees can work toward a variety of Valassis "degrees," including a Bachelor or Master of Leadership. When it comes to managing its people, there is no doubt that Valassis means business.

CRITICAL THINKING QUESTIONS

1. Why is it advantageous for Valassis Communications to hire employees with abilities and motivation that match the company's Change to Grow culture?

2. How does the Valassis approach to training and development help reinforce the company's culture?

3. Would you like to work for a company like Valassis Communications given its Change to Grow culture? Why or why not?

SOURCE: Adapted from material in the video *Employee Recruitment and Selection: A Study of Valassis Communications;* "The 100 Best Companies to Work for in America," *Fortune,* January 20, 2003, http://www.fortune.com; and Valassis Communications corporate Web site, http://www.valassis.com (accessed March 17, 2003).

E-COMMERCE CASE
Is Trust in the Workplace *Really* Important?

According to the Great Place to Work Institute in San Francisco, which spent two and a half decades researching workplace culture, the answer is a resounding "YES." But does this finding hold true in Canada? "YES" again. The Great Place to Work Institute Canada conducted an analysis of almost 10,000 employee surveys in the fall of 2005. The Great Place to Work Model focuses on workplace trust as opposed to the usual attention-getters, such as compensation, benefits, and other perks. The Trust Index comprises 57 questions in the areas of credibility, respect, fairness, pride, and camaraderie.

The number one company in Canada, according to the fall 2005 survey, was Vancity, Canada's largest credit union, with 46 branches, 2000 employees, and assets of $11.8 billion. Dave Mowat, the CEO, believes that simple gestures, if sincere, can help build respect and enhance credibility. The Vancity managers show appreciation to their employees by gestures such as Starbucks gift cards. It's not the action but the sentiment, the "thank you," that has the most meaning for employees.

TD Bank Financial Group also ranked high in the survey. With 55,000 employees, the merger of TD Bank and Canada Trust was the largest bank merger in Canadian history. Merging two different cultures could have been a huge problem, but obviously, management handled it well, with Ed Clark, of the acquired company, Canada Trust, becoming the new CEO. TD tends to focus on instilling pride in its employees as one aspect of its trust-based culture. Volunteerism is important in the company, and employees can access paid time off for volunteer activities.

Graham Lowe, one of the founding partners of the Great Place to Work Institute Canada provides a number of principles to help managers move toward a "great" workplace. These include talking about employee trust openly, being aware of trust-building and -breaking actions, focusing on a few trust-building changes and pursuing them, focusing on the *process* rather than the end result of these changes, and celebrating what already works well. By creating a high-trust culture, management can increase the company's competitive advantage, which benefits employees, management, shareholders, and customers.

CRITICAL THINKING QUESTIONS

1. What sort of corporate culture would you, as an employee, prefer?

2. Focus on a potential employer, and investigate the culture through secondary research.

3. Look at http://www.greatplacetowork.ca and determine how this company would rank using the criteria discussed on the Web site.

SOURCES: Andrew Wahl "Best Workplaces," *Canadian Business,* April 10–23, 2006, 64–66; Andrew Wahl, "On the Money," *Canadian Business,* April 10–23, 2006, 68–69; and Peter Evans, "TD Bank Financial Group," *Canadian Business,* April 10–23, 2006, 77–79.

10

Making the Connection

Motivating Employees and Creating Self-Managed Teams

In this chapter we'll look at the third step in the process of management—*motivating* employees toward the accomplishment of organizational goals. As we saw in Chapter 9, organizational structures are designed to support the accomplishment of the overall plans of the company. But these plans cannot be accomplished, appropriate structure or not, if the individuals responsible for their implementation are not committed to the outcome. As we've said numerous times, without the final critical success factor—*gaining employee commitment*—none of the critical success factors can be accomplished. This is, therefore, perhaps our most important management function but, unfortunately, also one of the most difficult. We're dealing with human beings, not push-button machines, and, therefore, it is extremely important that managers understand what makes people tick.

For example, have you ever walked into a restaurant, gone up to a service counter in a store, or called a company's customer service department on the phone and been served by an employee that didn't appear to be overjoyed to answer your questions? Most of us have. The important question here is— did you just assume that the employee was having a bad day and not let it affect your perception of the company, or did it enter your mental database and register as a less-than-pleasurable experience with

that company as a whole? Probably the latter. We all see our contact with employees in different companies as a contact with the company, and one employee's attitude as the company's attitude— consciously or not. As customers we see it in a very integrative way—we see it as the whole company. As managers in that company, we need to recognize that and focus on understanding our employees' needs to gain their commitment. Recent research, discussed in this chapter, demonstrates that employee turnover has a significant impact on customer satisfaction. Employee turnover results when employee commitment is low; therefore, the higher the commitment, the greater the likelihood that customer needs will be met.

In this chapter we discuss different motivation theories that will help you understand what motivates individuals to work harder to please the customer. But everyone is different. Therefore, a manager must play a truly integrative role here. He or she must see each employee as an individual but also in the context of how that person fits into the larger organization. Managers must integrate the different theories to find a style that works both for them and for their employees. Just as Jennifer Shroeger, a district manager for UPS, does in the opening vignette. Faced with a 50 percent turnover rate for part-time employees, one of things she did was identify different groups of employees and tailor her communication to each group to address the areas of concerns that affected each employee. It is essential that managers understand how to gain the commitment of all of the different individuals that make up their team, as many different personalities are needed to make a successful business work, but people with different skills and motivations must work together as one.

You'll see how different techniques are used to integrate employees in the organization to get them working together toward goals. Cross-functional teams are one example, made up of employees from different functional areas working together on a common task. This is essential, as we have seen in our discussion of the functional areas. Without this integration and commitment of the employees toward integration, the areas can't work together to achieve the overall goals of the company. We've also seen this through our discussion of *planning*. Different departments or areas within the organization have different roles to play in the overall plan, but they must work together in an integrative fashion to achieve these overall goals.

You'll also learn that when a company shows commitment to its employees it gets commitment in return—something discovered initially through the Hawthorne experiments, when researchers saw that employees performed better when they felt that management was concerned for their welfare. A commitment to education and training— one of the trends in employee motivation discussed in the chapter—goes a long way toward showing employees that they are valued and that the organization is a place where they can grow to their full potential. The trends of employee ownership and work-life benefits are other examples.

Remember as you learn the different theories of motivation to keep in mind that the manager's job here is to gain employee commitment to achieve the other factors critical to a successful business. Each of the success factors is achieved through people, and thus the people at all levels in the organization must be motivated to achieve these success factors. They must be committed to the organization's success for it to happen.

One factor not discussed so far but integral to achieving this success is the external environment. The external environment can and does have concrete implications on the work environment, as well as affecting the mind-set that people bring to work every day, thereby affecting their levels of motivation. Managers must therefore take into consideration the elements in the external environment that might affect employee motivation. Examples are the political environment and its effect on legislation pertaining to employment standards, the economy and its effect on job security and levels of pay, the *social* environment and the resulting expectations that people have regarding the work environment, and the *technological* environment and how it changes the demands of different jobs. One obvious instance of the effect of the environment that is discussed in the chapter is the effect of culture on motivation. The *societal* culture of different countries makes certain motivation theories inapplicable. As a company hires a more diverse workforce, it gains the benefit of a better understanding of its diverse customers, especially if it competes in the global marketplace, but it also becomes even more necessary to understand workers' individuality to gain their commitment to work toward the goals of the organization.

© WALTER HODGES / STONE / GETTY IMAGES

Motivating Employees and Creating Self-Managed Teams

learning goals

1 What are the basic principles of Frederick Taylor's concept of scientific management?

2 What did Elton Mayo's Hawthorne studies reveal about worker motivation?

3 What is Maslow's hierarchy of needs, and how do these needs relate to employee motivation?

4 How are McGregor's Theories X and Y, and Ouchi's Theory Z used to explain worker motivation?

5 What are the basic components of Herzberg's motivator-hygiene theory?

6 What three contemporary theories on employee motivation offer insights into improving employee performance?

7 How can managers redesign existing jobs to increase employee motivation and performance?

8 What different types of teams are being used in organizations today?

9 What initiatives are organizations using today to motivate and retain employees?

Getting the Lead out at UPS

United Parcel Service (UPS) has more than 400,000 employees worldwide, and provides service to every address in Canada, the United States, and more than 200 countries and territories. Suppose your job at UPS consisted of unloading packages from a truck and placing them on a conveyor belt. After unloading the first package, you unload another and then another. You unload one box every three seconds, 1,200 every hour. This might not sound like a very exciting job, but it is a job that is essential to UPS (**http://www.ups.com**), which hires thousands of part-time workers to move millions of packages daily. However, keeping a well-trained workforce motivated was a major problem for UPS.

In an article in "Fast Forward," Keith Hammond described the efforts of Jennifer Shroeger when she became a district manager for UPS. Her region was experiencing a 50 percent turnover rate among its part-time employees. This was both costly and disruptive, as part-time employees made up half of the workforce. Shroeger made attracting, retaining, and motivating a part-time workforce her immediate priority. She addressed the problem by focusing on better hiring and more effective communication and by giving frontline supervisors more responsibility for keeping employees motivated.

Specifically, Shroeger changed the "first applicant through the door" hiring practice to targeting people whose need for a part-time job matched the company's need. Then she identified different groups of employees by age and career stage. By tailoring her communication to each group, she was able to address those areas of concern that really affected each employee. Another initiative was to provide a positive work environment by upgrading the facilities. Employee retention committees were installed to mentor new employees through their initial hiring phase, when fears and frustration were at their highest levels. Finally, to increase effectiveness, frontline supervisors were given additional training on how to communicate, listen, and solve problems facing the large and diverse workforce.[1]

Critical Thinking Questions

1. Do the new initiatives at UPS help employees feel more empowered?

2. How do you think these efforts will affect turnover?

3. Do you think that matching the needs of the employee's with the company's needs will increase an employee's motivation?

Principles of Employee Motivation

HOT Links

Want to find out more about organizational efficiency at United Parcel Service? Visit http://www.ups.com.

People can be a firm's most important resource. They can also be the most challenging resource to manage well. Employees who are motivated and work hard to achieve personal and organizational goals can become a crucial competitive advantage for a firm. The key, then, is to understand the process of motivation, *what* motivates individuals, and *how* an organization like UPS can create a workplace that allows people to perform to the best of their abilities. Motivation is basically a need-satisfying process. A need is the lack of something, the gap between what is and what one desires. An unsatisfied need pushes (motivates) the individual to pursue behaviour that will result in the need being met.

Successful managers help employees to achieve organizational goals and guide workers through the motivation process using the leadership skills discussed in Chapter 7. To succeed, managers must understand human relations, how employees interact with one another, and how managers interact with employees to improve effectiveness. Human relations skills include the ability to motivate, lead, communicate, build morale, and teach others. In this chapter, we present the traditional theories on human motivation and the modern application of these theories. We also explore the use of teams in creating and maintaining a motivated workforce.

THE EVOLUTION OF MOTIVATION THEORY

How can managers and organizations promote enthusiastic job performance, high productivity, and job satisfaction? Many studies of human behaviour in organizations have contributed to our current understanding of these issues. A look at the evolution of management theory and research shows how managers have arrived at the practices used today to manage human behaviour in the workplace. We will discuss a sampling of the most influential of these theorists and research studies in this section.

Frederick Taylor's Scientific Management

1 *learning goal*

scientific management

A system of management developed by Frederick W. Taylor and based on four principles: developing a scientific approach for each element of a job, scientifically selecting and training workers, encouraging cooperation between workers and managers, and dividing work and responsibility between management and workers according to who can better perform a particular task.

One of the most influential figures of the classical era of management, which lasted from about 1900 to the mid-1930s, was Frederick W. Taylor, a mechanical engineer sometimes called the "father of **scientific management**." Taylor's approach to improved performance was based on economic incentives and the premise that there is "one best way" to perform any job. As a manager at the Midvale and Bethlehem Steel companies in Philadelphia in the early 1900s, Taylor was frustrated at the inefficiency of the labourers working in the mills.

Convinced that productivity could be improved, Taylor studied the individual jobs in the mill and redesigned the equipment and the methods used by workers. Taylor timed each job with a stopwatch and broke down every task into separate movements. He then prepared an instruction sheet telling exactly how each job should be done, how much time it should take, and what motions and tools should be used. Taylor's ideas led to dramatic increases in productivity in the steel mills and resulted in the development of four basic principles of scientific management:

1. Develop a scientific approach for each element of a person's job.

2. Scientifically select, train, teach, and develop workers.

3. Encourage cooperation between workers and managers, so that each job can be accomplished in a standard, scientifically determined way.

4. Divide work and responsibility between management and workers according to who is better suited to each task.

Employers of factory workers in the early 1900s applied scientific methods to improve productivity. During this classical era of management, employers believed performance was motivated only by economic incentives.

© MINNESOTA HISTORICAL SOCIETY / CORBIS

Taylor published his ideas in *The Principles of Scientific Management*. His pioneering work vastly increased production efficiency and contributed to the specialization of labour and the assembly line method of production. Taylor's approach is still being used nearly a century later in companies such as United Parcel Service (UPS), where industrial engineers maximize efficiency by carefully studying every step of the delivery process, looking for the quickest possible way to deliver packages to customers. Though Taylor's work was a giant step forward in the evolution of management, however, it had a fundamental flaw in that it assumed that all people are motivated primarily by economic factors. Taylor's successors in the study of management found that motivation is much more complex than he envisioned.

The Hawthorne Studies

2 learning goal

The classical era of management was followed by the *human relations era*, which began in the 1930s and focused primarily on how human behaviour and relations affect organizational performance. The new era was ushered in by the Hawthorne studies, which changed the way many managers thought about motivation, job productivity, and employee satisfaction. The studies began when engineers at the Hawthorne Western Electric plant decided to examine the effects of varying levels of light on worker productivity—an experiment that might have interested Frederick Taylor. The engineers expected brighter light to lead to increased productivity, but the results showed that varying the level of light in either direction (brighter or dimmer) led to increased output from the experimental group. In 1927, the Hawthorne engineers asked Harvard professor Elton Mayo and a team of researchers to join them in their investigation.

From 1927 to 1932, Mayo and his colleagues conducted experiments on job redesign, length of workday and workweek, length of break times, and incentive plans. The results of the studies indicated that improvements in performance were tied to a complex set of employee attitudes. Mayo claimed that both experimental and control groups from the plant had developed a sense of group pride because they had been selected to participate in the studies. The pride that came from this special attention motivated the workers to increase their productivity. Supervisors who allowed the employees to have some control over their situation appeared to increase the workers' motivation further. These findings gave rise to what is now known as the **Hawthorne effect**, which suggests that employees will perform better when they feel singled out for special attention or feel that management is concerned about employee welfare. The studies also provided evidence that informal work groups (the social relationships of employees) and the resulting group pressures have positive effects on group productivity. The results of the Hawthorne studies enhanced our understanding of what motivates individuals in the workplace. They indicate that in addition to the personal economic needs emphasized in the classical era, social needs play an important role in influencing work-related attitudes and behaviours.

Hawthorne effect
The phenomenon that employees perform better when they feel singled out for attention or feel that management is concerned about their welfare.

Maslow's Hierarchy of Needs

3   learning goal

Another well-known theorist from the behavioural era of management history, psychologist Abraham Maslow, proposed a theory of motivation based on universal human needs. Maslow believed that each individual has a hierarchy of needs, consisting of physiological, safety, social, esteem, and self-actualization needs, as shown in Exhibit 10.1.

Exhibit 10.1 | Maslow's Hierarchy of Needs

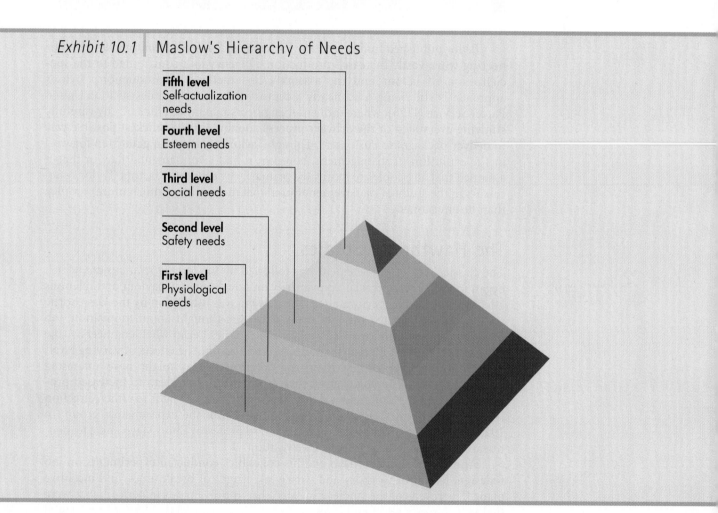

Fifth level
Self-actualization needs

Fourth level
Esteem needs

Third level
Social needs

Second level
Safety needs

First level
Physiological needs

Maslow's theory of motivation contends that people act to satisfy their unmet needs. When you're hungry, for instance, you look for and eat food, thus satisfying a basic physiological need. Once a need is satisfied, its importance to the individual diminishes, and a higher level need is more likely to motivate the person.

According to **Maslow's hierarchy of needs**, the most basic human needs are physiological needs, that is, the needs for food, shelter, and clothing. In large part, it is the physiological needs that motivate a person to find a job. People need to earn money to provide food, shelter, and clothing for themselves and their families. Once people have met these basic needs, they reach the second level in Maslow's hierarchy, which is safety needs. People need to feel secure, to be protected from physical harm, and to avoid the unexpected. In work terms, they need job security and protection from work hazards. Many companies provide their permanent employees with the job security they need by having no-layoff policies.[2] When times are good, these companies are careful about bloating the workforce; and when times are bad, they use creative ways to keep the staff working until business improves.

Physiological needs and safety are physical needs. Once these are satisfied, individuals focus on needs that involve relationships with other people. At Maslow's third level are social needs, or needs for belonging (acceptance by others) and for giving and receiving friendship and love. Informal social groups on and off the job help people satisfy these needs. At the fourth level in Maslow's hierarchy are esteem needs, which are needs for the respect of others and for a sense of accomplishment and achievement. Satisfaction of these needs is reflected in feelings of self-worth. Praise and recognition from managers and others in the firm contribute to the sense of self-worth.

Finally, at the highest level in Maslow's hierarchy are self-actualization needs, or needs for fulfillment, for living up to one's potential, and for using one's abilities to the utmost. Many mid- and upper-level managers, who have satisfied all of the lower order needs, are driven by very personal self-actualization goals. For instance, look at Paul Allen, one of the founders of the Microsoft Corporation. Along with the other founders of Microsoft, Allen is a billionaire several times over. Although he has no financial need to work, Allen felt he had more to give professionally to the community, so he maintains a Senior Strategy Advisor position at Microsoft. He also owns a venture capital firm, an NFL football franchise, and an NBA basketball team. Given these diverse holdings, what would motivate Allen to invest in The Experience Music Project? Allen's motivation was his love of music and desire to share this love and his financial good fortune with others.[3] To do this, Allen invested millions to create the interactive music museum. The museum not only houses Allen's extensive personal collection of Jimi Hendrix memorabilia but also provides visitors with a way to experience, appreciate, and develop their own love of music.

Managers who accept Maslow's ideas attempt to improve employee motivation by modifying organizational and managerial practices to increase the likelihood that employees will meet all levels of needs. Maslow's theory has also helped managers understand that it is hard to motivate people by appealing to already satisfied needs. For instance, overtime pay might not motivate employees who earn a high wage and value their leisure time.

Maslow's theory is not without criticism, however. Maslow claimed that a higher level need was not activated until a lower level

Maslow's hierarchy of needs

A theory of motivation developed by Abraham Maslow; holds that humans have five levels of needs and act to satisfy their unmet needs. At the base of the hierarchy are fundamental physiological needs, followed in order by safety, social, esteem, and self-actualization needs.

© TERRY MCCORMICK/TAXI / GETTY IMAGES

TELUS, a telecommunications company, created a program called Team Machine to recognize and reward performance. The company makes everyone aware of employees who have outstanding performance and who support the company's values and strategies.

Theory X

A management style, formulated by Douglas McGregor, that is based on a pessimistic view of human nature and assumes that the average person dislikes work, will avoid it if possible, prefers to be directed, avoids responsibility, and wants security above all.

Theory Y

A management style, formulated by Douglas McGregor, that is based on a relatively optimistic view of human nature; assumes that the average person wants to work, accepts responsibility, is willing to help solve problems, and can be self-directed and self-controlled.

need was met. He also claimed that a satisfied need is not a motivator. A farmer who has plenty to eat is not motivated by more food (the physiological hunger need). Research has not verified these principles in any strict sense. The theory also concentrates on moving up the hierarchy without fully addressing moving back down it. Despite these limitations, Maslow's ideas are very helpful for understanding the needs of people at work and for determining what can be done to satisfy them.

McGregor's Theories X and Y

Douglas McGregor, one of Maslow's students, influenced the study of motivation with his formulation of two contrasting sets of assumptions about human nature—Theory X and Theory Y.

The **Theory X** management style is based on a pessimistic view of human nature and assumes the following:

- The average person dislikes work and will avoid it if possible.
- Because people don't like to work, they must be controlled, directed, or threatened with punishment to get them to make an effort.
- The average person prefers to be directed, avoids responsibility, is relatively lacking in ambition and wants security above all else.

This view of people suggests that managers must constantly prod workers to perform and must closely control their on-the-job behaviour. Theory X managers tell people what to do, are very directive, like to be in control, and show little confidence in employees. They often foster dependent, passive, and resentful subordinates.

In contrast, a **Theory Y** management style is based on a more optimistic view of human nature and assumes the following:

- Work is as natural as play or rest. People want to and can be self-directed and self-controlled and will try to achieve organizational goals they believe in.
- Workers can be motivated using positive incentives and will try hard to accomplish organizational goals if they believe they will be rewarded for doing so.
- Under proper conditions, the average person not only accepts responsibility but seeks it out. Most workers have a relatively high degree of imagination and creativity and are willing to help solve problems.

Managers who operate on Theory Y assumptions recognize individual differences and encourage workers to learn and develop their skills. An administrative assistant might be given the responsibility for generating a monthly report. The reward for doing so might be recognition at a meeting, a special training class to enhance computer skills, or a pay increase. In short, the Theory Y approach builds on the idea that worker and organizational interests are the same. The SAS Institute, a leader in business intelligence and analytics, has successfully created a corporate culture based on Theory Y assumptions. With a 4 percent turnover rate and a recruitment ratio of 200 applicants for each open position, the success of this culture is evident. VP Human Resources Jeff Chambers claims that employee retention has more to do with the company's environment than any other factor:

> The two key concepts are flexibility and trust. We have a flat organizational structure so usually an employee is no more than four to five levels away from the CEO. And we treat people like adults and allow them to do their jobs. We hire hard and then manage easy. Just leave them alone and trust them to do the right thing for the company.[4]

Theory Z

William Ouchi (pronounced O Chee), a management scholar at the University of California, Los Angeles, has proposed a theory that combines North American and Japanese business practices. He calls it **Theory Z**. Exhibit 10.2 compares the traditional North American and Japanese management styles with the Theory Z approach. Theory Z emphasizes long-term employment, slow career development, moderate specialization, group decision-making, individual responsibility, relatively informal control over the employee, and concern for workers. Theory Z has many Japanese elements but reflects North American cultural values.

In the past decade, admiration for Japanese management philosophy, which centres on creating long-term relationships, has declined. The cultural beliefs of groupthink, of not taking risks, and of employees' not thinking for themselves are passé. Such conformity has limited Japanese competitiveness in the global marketplace. Today there is a realization that Japanese firms need to be more proactive and nimble to prosper.

The average profitability of a Japanese company on the Tokyo Stock Exchange declined from about 9 to 1 percent in the past decade. This is often attributed partially to Japanese management philosophy. Sony, Hitachi, and other big companies are moving away from lifetime employment and now emphasize information disclosure, profitability, and management accountability.

Theory Z
A theory developed by William Ouchi that combines U.S. and Japanese business practices by emphasizing long-term employment, slow career development, moderate specialization, group decision-making, individual responsibility, relatively informal control over the employee, and concern for workers.

Exhibit 10.2 | Differences in Management Approaches

FACTOR	TRADITIONAL NORTH AMERICAN MANAGEMENT	JAPANESE MANAGEMENT	THEORY Z (COMBINATION OF NORTH AMERICAN AND JAPANESE MANAGEMENT)
Length of employment	Relatively short term; worker subject to layoffs if business is bad	Lifetime; layoffs never used to reduce costs	Long term but not necessarily lifetime; layoffs "inappropriate"; stable, loyal workforce; improved business conditions don't require new hiring and training
Rate of evaluation and promotion	Relatively rapid	Relatively slow	Slow by design; manager thoroughly trained and evaluated
Specialization in a functional area	Considerable; worker acquires expertise in single functional area	Minimal; worker acquires expertise in organization instead of functional areas	Moderate; all experience various functions of the organization and have a sense of what's good for the firm rather than for a single area
Decision-making	On individual basis	Input from all concerned parties	Group decision-making for better decisions and easier implementation
Responsibility for success or failure	Assigned to individual	Shared by group	Assigned to individual
Control by manager	Very explicit and formal	More implicit and informal	Relatively informal but with explicit performance measures
Concern for workers	Focuses on work-related aspects of worker's life	Extends to whole life of worker	Is relatively concerned with worker's whole life, including the family

SOURCE: Based on information from Jerry D. Johnson, Austin College. Dr. Johnson was a research assistant for William Ouchi.

HOT Links

What are ways to motivate your employees without raising their pay? Visit http://www.biztrain.com/motivation/stories/20ways.htm.

motivating factors

Intrinsic job elements that lead to worker satisfaction.

hygiene factors

Extrinsic elements of the work environment that do not serve as a source of employee satisfaction or motivation.

Herzberg's Motivator–Hygiene Theory

Another important contribution to our understanding of individual motivation came from Frederick Herzberg's studies, which addressed the question "What do people really want from their work experience?" In the late 1950s, Herzberg surveyed numerous employees to find out what particular work elements made them feel exceptionally good or bad about their jobs. The results indicated that certain job factors are consistently related to employee job satisfaction, whereas others can create job dissatisfaction. According to Herzberg, **motivating factors** (also called *job satisfiers*) are primarily intrinsic job elements that lead to satisfaction. **Hygiene factors** (also called *job dissatisfiers*) are extrinsic elements of the work environment. A summary of motivating and hygiene factors appears in Exhibit 10.3.

One of the most interesting results of Herzberg's studies was the implication that the opposite of satisfaction is not dissatisfaction. Herzberg believed that proper management of hygiene factors could prevent employee dissatisfaction but that these factors could not serve as a source of satisfaction or motivation. Good working conditions, for instance, will keep employees at a job but won't make them work harder. Poor working conditions, which are job dissatisfiers, on the other hand, might make employees quit. According to Herzberg, a manager who wants to increase employee satisfaction needs to focus on the motivating factors, or satisfiers.

Exhibit 10.3 | Herzberg's Motivating and Hygiene Factors

MOTIVATING FACTORS	HYGIENE FACTORS
Achievement	Company policy
Recognition	Supervision
Work itself	Working conditions
Responsibility	Interpersonal relationships at work
Advancement	Salary and benefits
Growth	Job security

According to Herzberg's motivation theory, the job factors that motivate employees, such as this Starbuck's employee, are the work itself, achievement, recognition, responsibility, advancement, and growth.

© AP / WIDE WORLD PHOTOS

A job with many satisfiers will usually motivate workers, provide job satisfaction, and prompt effective performance, but a lack of job satisfiers doesn't always lead to dissatisfaction and poor performance. Instead, a lack of job satisfiers might merely lead to workers' doing an adequate job rather than their best.

Although Herzberg's ideas have been widely read and his recommendations implemented at numerous companies over the years, there are some very legitimate concerns about them. Although his findings have been used to explain employee motivation, his studies actually focused on job satisfaction, a different concept from motivation, though related to it. Other criticisms focus on the unreliability of Herzberg's method, the fact that the theory ignores the impact of situational variables, and the assumed relationship between satisfaction and productivity. Nevertheless, the questions raised by Herzberg about the nature of job satisfaction and the effects of intrinsic and extrinsic factors on employee behaviour have proved a valuable contribution to the evolution of theories of motivation and job satisfaction.

concept check

What did Elton Mayo's studies reveal about employee productivity?

How can a manager use an understanding of Maslow's hierarchy to motivate employees?

How do the Theory X, Theory Y, and Theory Z management styles differ?

What is the difference between Herzberg's hygiene factors and motivating factors?

CONTEMPORARY VIEWS ON MOTIVATION

6   *learning goal*

The early management scholars laid a foundation that enabled managers to understand their workers better and how best to motivate them. Since then, new theories have given us an even deeper understanding of worker motivation. Three of these theories are explained in this section: the expectancy theory, the equity theory, and the goal-setting theory.

Expectancy Theory

One of the best-supported and most widely accepted theories of motivation is expectancy theory, which focuses on the link between motivation and behaviour. According to **expectancy theory**, the probability that an individual will act in a particular way depends on the strength of that individual's belief that the act will have a particular outcome and on whether the individual values that outcome. The degree to which an employee is motivated depends on three important relationships, shown in Exhibit 10.4:

1. the link between *effort and performance*, or the strength of the individual's expectation that a certain amount of effort will lead to a certain level of performance;

2. the link between *performance and outcome*, or the strength of the expectation that a certain level of performance will lead to a particular outcome; and

3. the link between *outcomes and individual needs*, or the degree to which the individual expects the anticipated outcome to satisfy personal needs. Some outcomes have more valence, or value, for individuals than others do.

Based on the expectancy theory, managers should do the following to motivate employees:

- determine the rewards valued by each employee,

- determine the desired performance level and then communicate it clearly to employees,

expectancy theory
A theory of motivation that holds that the probability of an individual's acting in a particular way depends on the strength of that individual's belief that the act will have a particular outcome and on whether the individual values that outcome.

Exhibit 10.4 | How Expectations Can Lead to Motivation

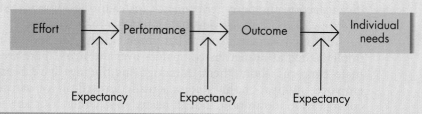

- make the performance level attainable,
- link rewards to performance,
- determine what factors might counteract the effectiveness of an award, and
- make sure the reward is adequate for the level of performance.

Equity Theory

equity theory

A theory of motivation that holds that worker satisfaction is influenced by employees' perceptions about how fairly they are treated compared to their coworkers.

Another contemporary explanation of motivation, **equity theory** is based on individuals' perceptions about how fairly they are treated compared to their coworkers. Equity means justice or fairness, and in the workplace it refers to employees' perceived fairness of the way they are treated and the rewards they earn. Employees evaluate their own *outcomes* (e.g., salary, benefits) in relation to their *inputs* (e.g., number of hours worked, education, and training) and then compare the outcomes-to-inputs ratio to one of the following:

1. the employee's past experience in a different position in the current organization,
2. the employee's past experience in a different organization,
3. another employee's experience inside the current organization, or
4. another employee's experience outside the organization.

According to equity theory, if employees perceive that an inequity exists, they will make one of the following choices:

- *change their work habits* (exert less effort on the job),
- *change their job benefits and income* (ask for a raise, steal from the employer),
- *distort their perception of themselves* ("I always thought I was smart, but now I realize I'm a lot smarter than my coworkers"),
- *distort their perceptions of others* ("Joe's position is really much less flexible than mine"),
- *look at the situation from a different perspective* ("I don't make as much as the other department heads, but I make a lot more than most graphic artists"), or
- *leave the situation* (quit the job).

Managers can use equity theory to improve worker satisfaction. Knowing that every employee seeks equitable and fair treatment, managers can make an effort to understand an employee's perceptions of fairness and take steps to reduce concerns about inequity.

Goal-Setting Theory

goal-setting theory

A theory of motivation based on the premise that an individual's intention to work toward a goal is a primary source of motivation.

Goal-setting theory is based on the premise that an individual's intention to work toward a goal is a primary source of motivation. Once set, the goal clarifies for the employee what needs to be accomplished and how much effort will be required for completion. The theory has three main components:

1. specific goals lead to a higher level of performance than do more generalized goals ("do your best"),

2. more difficult goals lead to better performance than do easy goals (provided the individual accepts the goal), and

3. feedback on progress toward the goal enhances performance.

Feedback is particularly important, because it helps the individual identify the gap between the *real* (the actual performance) and the *ideal* (the desired outcome defined by the goal). Given the trend toward employee empowerment in the workplace, more and more employees are participating in the goal-setting process.

HOT *Links*

ASTD is a professional association and leading resource on workplace learning and performance issues. Visit its site, http://www.astd.org, to learn more about these topics.

Motivation Is Culture Bound

Most motivation theories in use today were developed in the United States.[5] Of those that were not, many have been strongly influenced by the U.S. theories. In Canada, although to a lesser extent than in the United States, there is a relatively strong emphasis on individualism. This has led to expectancy and equity theories of motivation: theories that emphasize rational, individual thought as the primary basis of human behaviour. The emphasis placed on achievement is not surprising, given a willingness to accept risk and high concern for performance, but several motivation theories do not apply to all cultures.

Maslow's theory does not often hold outside of Canada and the United States. For instance, in countries whose citizens on average rate higher on uncertainty avoidance (such as Greece and Japan) as compared to those lower on uncertainty avoidance (such as Canada), security motivates employees more strongly than does self-actualization. Employees in high–uncertainty-avoidance countries often consider job security and lifetime employment more important than holding a more interesting or challenging job. Also contrasting with the U.S. and, to a lesser extent, the Canadian pattern, social needs often dominate the motivation of workers in countries such as Denmark, Norway, and Sweden, whose residents stress the quality of life over materialism and productivity.

When researchers tested Herzberg's theory outside the United States, they encountered varied results. In New Zealand, for example, supervision and interpersonal relationships appear to contribute significantly to satisfaction and not merely to reducing dissatisfaction. Similarly, researchers found that citizens of Canada, Asia, Europe, Latin America, the Republic of Panama, and the West Indies cited certain extrinsic factors as satisfiers with greater frequency than did their American counterparts. The factors that motivate U. S. employees, summarized in Exhibit 10.3, might not spark the same motivation in employees in other cultures.

Even the expectancy theory, considered a well-accepted contemporary motivation theory, does not always hold up in other cultures. Some of the major differences among the cultural groups include the following:

1. Citizens of English-speaking countries rank higher than average on individual achievement and lower on the desire for security.

2. Citizens of French-speaking countries, although similar to those of English-speaking countries, give greater importance to security and somewhat less to challenging work.

3. Northern Europeans have less interest in "getting ahead" and work recognition goals and place more emphasis on job accomplishment. In addition, they have more concern for people and less for the organization as a whole (it is important that their jobs not interfere with their personal lives).

4. Latin Americans and Southern Europeans find individual achievement somewhat less important; Southern Europeans place the highest emphasis on job security, whereas citizens of both groups of countries emphasize fringe benefits.

5. Germans ranks high on security and fringe benefits and among the highest on "getting ahead."

6. The Japanese, although placing a low priority on advancement, also rank second highest on challenge and lowest on autonomy, with a strong emphasis on good working conditions and a friendly working environment.

Expectancy theories are universal to the extent that they do not specify the types of reward that motivate a given group of workers. Managers themselves must determine the level and type of reward most sought after by a particular group.[6]

concept check

Discuss the three relationships central to expectancy theory.

Explain the comparison process that is a part of equity theory.

How does goal-setting theory contribute to our understanding of motivation?

FROM MOTIVATION THEORY TO APPLICATION

7 learning goal

The material presented thus far in this chapter demonstrates the wide variety of theorists and research studies that have contributed to our current understanding of employee motivation. Now we turn our attention to more practical matters: to ways in which these concepts can be applied in the workplace to meet organizational goals and improve individual performance.

Reinforcing Behaviour

Reinforcement is described as the application of consequences in response to behaviour. According to B. F. Skinner's operant learning theory, the premise behind reinforcement is that consequences *influence* behaviour. The rules of consequences describe the outcomes that typically occur.

1. Introducing a positive consequence increases or maintains desired behaviours.

2. Removing a negative consequence increases or maintains desired behaviours.

3. Introducing a negative consequence (punishment) decreases behaviours.

4. Activities that do not give positive or negative consequences decrease behaviours.

Say, for example, that you have an employee who is consistently meeting or exceeding his or her sales targets. You might consider giving that person a bonus (positive reinforcement), but when this person no longer meets the targets, you remove the bonus (extinction). On the other hand you might have other employees who are not meeting their sales targets, and so you give them warnings whenever they don't meet their targets (punishment). When the employees meet the targets, you no longer give the warnings (negative reinforcement).

Several factors are important with respect to using reinforcement strategies. Positive reinforcement must be clearly contingent on specific behaviour, diversity must be considered with respect to the choice of reinforcer, and other sources of reinforcement within the workforce must be taken into consideration (e.g., peer pressure).

Motivational Job Design

How might managers redesign or modify existing jobs to increase employee motivation and performance? The following three options have been used extensively in the workplace:

job enlargement

The horizontal expansion of a job based on an increase in the number and variety of tasks that a person performs.

job enrichment

The vertical expansion of a job based on an increase in the employee's autonomy, responsibility, and decision-making authority.

job rotation

The shifting of workers from one job to another; also called cross-training.

- *Job enlargement.* The horizontal expansion of a job, through an increase in the number and variety of tasks that a person performs, is called **job enlargement**. Increasing task diversity can enhance job satisfaction, particularly when the job is mundane and repetitive in nature. A potential drawback to job enlargement is that employees might perceive that they are being asked to work harder and do more with no change in their level of responsibility or compensation. This can cause resentment and lead to dissatisfaction.
- *Job enrichment.* **Job enrichment** is the vertical expansion of an employee's job. Whereas job enlargement addresses the breadth or scope of a job, enrichment is an attempt to increase job depth by providing the employee with more autonomy, responsibility, and decision-making authority. In an enriched job, the employee can use a variety of talents and skills and has more control over the planning, execution, and evaluation of the required tasks. In general, job enrichment has been found to increase job satisfaction and reduce absenteeism and turnover.
- *Job rotation.* Also called *cross-training*, **job rotation** is the shifting of workers from one job to another. This might be done to broaden an employee's skill base or because an employee has ceased to be interested in or challenged by a particular job. The organization might benefit from job rotation, because it increases flexibility in scheduling and production, as employees can be shifted to cover for absent workers or changes in production or operations. It is also a valuable tool for training lower level managers in a variety of functional areas. Drawbacks of job rotation include an increase in training costs and decreased productivity while employees are getting "up to speed" in new task areas.

Work-Scheduling Options

As companies try to meet the needs of a diverse workforce and retain quality employees, while remaining competitive and financially prosperous, managers are challenged to find new ways of keeping workers motivated and satisfied. Increasingly popular are alternatives to the traditional work schedule, such as the compressed workweek, flextime, job sharing, and telecommuting.

One option for employees who want to maximize their leisure hours, indulge in three-day weekends, and avoid commuting during morning and evening rush hours is the *compressed* workweek. Employees work the traditional 40 hours but fit those hours into a shorter workweek. Most common is the 4-40 schedule, whereby employees work four 10-hour days a week. Organizations that offer this option claim benefits ranging from increased motivation and productivity to reduced absenteeism and turnover.

Another scheduling option, called *flextime*, allows employees to decide what their work hours will be. Employees are generally expected to work a certain number of hours per week but have some discretion as to when they arrive at work and when they leave for the day.

job sharing

A scheduling option that allows two individuals to split the tasks, responsibilities, and work hours of one 40-hour-per-week job.

Job sharing is a scheduling option that allows two individuals to split the tasks, responsibilities, and work hours of one 40-hour-per-week job. Though used less frequently than flextime and the compressed workweek, this option can also provide employees with job flexibility. The primary benefit to the company is that it gets "two for the price of one"—the company can draw on two sets of skills and abilities to accomplish one set of job objectives.

Most countries have a mandatory minimum of time off per year given to a worker. In Canada the legal minimum is two weeks.

Telecommuting, described in Chapter 9, is a work-scheduling option that allows employees to work from home via a computer that is linked with their office, headquarters, or colleagues. It is the fastest growing of the four scheduling options.

HSBC Canada, like many Canadian companies, recognized that its policies and practices around work-life balance were important for competing for talent. They now offer flextime and job sharing to assist employees in meeting both their professional and their personal responsibilities.

Many companies have found themselves in a similar position to that of HSBC Bank Canada: recognizing that their policies and practices around work-life balance—important for an employer competing for talent in a small pool—could be enhanced and improved. And although some employers might not have accepted this challenge, HSBC took it as an opportunity to improve its policies related to work-life and change its culture to be more supportive and flexible.

Although each of these work-scheduling options might have some drawbacks for the sponsoring organizations, the benefits far outweigh the problems. For this reason, not only is the number of companies offering compressed work increasing, so is the number of companies offering other options.

Recognition, Empowerment, and Economic Incentives

All employees have unique needs that they seek to fulfill through their jobs. Organizations must devise a wide array of incentives to ensure that a broad spectrum of employee needs can be addressed in the work environment, thus increasing the likelihood of motivated employees. A sampling of these motivational tools is discussed here.

Formal recognition of superior effort by individuals or groups in the workplace is one way of enhancing employee motivation. Recognition serves as positive feedback and reinforcement, letting employees know what they have done well and that their contribution is valued by the organization. Recognition can take many forms, both formal and informal. Some companies use formal awards ceremonies to acknowledge and celebrate their employees' accomplishments. Others take advantage of informal interactions to congratulate employees on a job well done and offer encouragement for the future. Recognition can take the form of an employee-of-the-month plaque, a monetary reward, a day off, a congratulatory e-mail, or a verbal "pat on the back."

As described in Chapter 7, employee empowerment, sometimes called employee involvement or participative leadership, involves delegating decision-making authority to employees at all levels of the organization. Employees are given greater responsibility for planning, implementing, and evaluating the results of decisions. Empowerment is based on the premise that human resources, especially at lower levels in the firm, are an underutilized asset. Employees are capable of contributing much more of their skills and abilities to organizational success if they are allowed to participate in the decision-making process and are given access to the resources needed to implement their decisions.

Any discussion of motivation has to include the use of monetary incentives to enhance performance. Currently, companies are using a variety of variable-pay programs, such as piece-rate plans, profit sharing, gain sharing, and bonuses, to encourage employees to be more productive. Unlike the standard salary or hourly

HOT Links

What are the best companies to work for in Canada? Check out http://www.theglobeandmail.com/special/robmagazinecover/; then click on "The Top 1000."

wage, variable pay means that a portion of an employee's pay is linked directly to an individual or organizational performance measure. In *piece-rate pay plans*, for example, employees are paid a given amount for each unit they produce, directly linking the amount they earn to their productivity. *Profit-sharing plans* are based on overall company profitability. Using an established formula, management distributes some portion of company profits to all employees. *Gain-sharing* plans are incentive programs based on group productivity. Employees share in the financial gains attributed to the increased productivity of their group. This encourages them to increase productivity within their specific work area regardless of the overall profit picture for the organization as a whole. A *bonus* is simply a one-time lump-sum monetary reward.

concept check

Explain the difference between job enlargement and job enrichment.

What are the four work-scheduling options that can enhance employee performance?

Are all employees motivated by the same economic incentives? Explain.

USING TEAMS TO ENHANCE MOTIVATION AND PERFORMANCE

8 *learning goal*

One of the most apparent trends in business today is the use of teams to accomplish organizational goals. The use of a team-based structure can increase individual and group motivation and performance. In this section, we give a brief overview of group behaviour, define work teams as specific types of groups, and provide suggestions for creating high-performing teams.

Understanding Group Behaviour

Teams are a specific type of organizational group. Every organization contains groups, social units of two or more people who share the same goals and cooperate to achieve those goals. Understanding some fundamental concepts related to group behaviour and group processes provides a good foundation for understanding concepts about work teams. Groups can be formal or informal in nature. Formal groups are designated and sanctioned by the organization; their behaviour is directed toward accomplishing organizational goals. Informal groups are based on social relationships and are not determined or sanctioned by the organization.

Formal organizational groups, like the sales department at Dell Computers, must operate within the larger organizational system. To some degree, elements of the larger Dell system, such as organizational strategy, Dell's company policies and procedures, available resources, and the highly motivated employee corporate culture of Dell, determine the behaviour of smaller groups within Dell, such as the sales department.

Other factors that affect the behaviour of organizational groups are individual member characteristics (e.g., ability, training, and personality), the roles and norms of group members, and the size and cohesiveness of the group. Norms are the implicit behavioural guidelines of the group, or the standards for acceptable and unacceptable behaviour. For example, a sales manager might be expected to work at least two Saturdays per month without extra pay. Although this isn't written anywhere, it is the expected norm.

COURTESY HOME DEPOT

Members of formal work groups share the same organizational goals and work together to achieve these goals. Group members are guided by norms that dictate acceptable behaviour to accomplish effective group performance.

group cohesiveness
The degree to which group members want to stay in the group and tend to resist outside influences.

Group cohesiveness refers to the degree to which group members want to stay in the group and tend to resist outside influences (such as a change in company policies). When group performance norms are high, group cohesiveness will have a positive impact on productivity. Cohesiveness tends to increase when the size of the group is small, individual and group goals are congruent, the group has high status in the organization, rewards are group rather than individual based, and the group competes with other groups within the organization. Work group cohesiveness can benefit the organization in several ways, including increased productivity, enhanced worker self-image because of group success, increased company loyalty, reduced employee turnover, and reduced absenteeism. WestJet Airlines is known for its work group cohesiveness. On the other hand, cohesiveness can also lead to restricted output, resistance to change, and conflict with other work groups in the organization.

The opportunity to turn the decision-making process over to a group with diverse skills and abilities is one of the arguments for using work groups (and teams) in organizational settings. For group decision-making to be most effective, however, both managers and group members must acknowledge its strengths and weaknesses (see Exhibit 10.5).

Work Groups versus Work Teams

work groups
Groups of employees who share resources and coordinate efforts so as to help members perform their individual duties and responsibilities better. The performance of the group can be evaluated by adding up the contributions of the individual group members.

We have already noted that teams are a special type of organizational group, but we also need to differentiate between work groups and work teams. **Work groups** share resources and coordinate efforts to help members perform their individual duties and responsibilities better. The performance of the group can be evaluated by adding up the contributions of the individual group members. **Work teams** require not only coordination but also *collaboration*, the pooling of knowledge, skills, abilities, and resources in a collective effort to attain a common goal. A work team creates *synergy*, causing the performance of the team as a whole to be greater than the sum of team members' individual contributions. Simply assigning employees to groups and labelling them a team does not guarantee a positive outcome. Managers and team members must be committed to creating, developing, and maintaining high-performance work teams. Factors that contribute to their success are discussed later in this section.

work teams
Groups of employees who not only coordinate their efforts but also collaborate by pooling their knowledge, skills, abilities, and resources in a collective effort to attain a common goal; causing the performance of the team to be greater than the sum of the members' individual efforts.

Types of Teams

problem-solving teams
Teams of employees from the same department or area of expertise and from the same level of the organizational hierarchy who meet regularly to share information and discuss ways to improve processes and procedures in specific functional areas.

The evolution of the team concept in organizations can be seen in three basic types of work teams: problem solving, self-managed, and cross-functional. **Problem-solving teams** are typically made up of employees from the same department or area of

---

Exhibit 10.5 | Strengths and Weaknesses of Group Decision-Making

STRENGTHS	WEAKNESSES
• Groups bring more information and knowledge to the decision process	• Groups typically take a longer time to reach a solution to than an individual takes
• Groups offer a diversity of perspectives and, therefore, generate a greater number of alternatives	• Group members might pressure others to conform, reducing the likelihood of disagreement
• Group decision-making results in a higher-quality decision than individual decision-making does	• The process might be dominated by one or a small number of participants
• Participation of group members increases the likelihood that a decision will be accepted	• Groups lack accountability, because it is difficult to assign responsibility for outcomes to any one individual

expertise and from the same level of the organizational hierarchy. They meet on a regular basis to share information and discuss ways to improve processes and procedures in specific functional areas. Problem-solving teams generate ideas and alternatives and might recommend a specific course of action, but they typically do not make final decisions, allocate resources, or implement change.

Every day select DaimlerChrysler dealers ship every part they replace on warranty to the company's quality engineering centre. The parts are then given to the centre's problem-solving teams to examine. One team, for example, might examine parts from a Jeep Wrangler that was brought to the dealer with only 8,000 kilometres on it. Warranty repairs on that vehicle cost more than $4,000.[7] Often the problem-solving team will call in the suppliers to help them understand what went wrong. By using problem-solving teams, costs can be reduced considerably.

Many organizations that have experienced success using problem-solving teams were willing to expand the team concept to allow team members greater responsibility in making decisions, implementing solutions, and monitoring outcomes. These highly autonomous groups are called **self-managed work teams**. They manage themselves without any formal supervision, taking responsibility for setting goals, planning and scheduling work activities, selecting team members, and evaluating team performance. PepsiCo, Hewlett-Packard, and Xerox are just a few of the well-known, highly successful companies using self-managed work teams.

self-managed work teams
Highly autonomous teams of employees who manage themselves without any formal supervision and take responsibility for setting goals, planning and scheduling work activities, selecting team members, and evaluating team performance.

Making Ethical Choices

TEAM SPIRIT—OH REALLY

You work in the HR department of a corporation that focuses on training and organizational development. Over the next year, you will be creating a division devoted to managing virtual teams that are responsible for developing new training materials or updating existing ones. The job is organized so that you are spending your first year being mentored by your boss, the vice president of HR.

With full understanding of the benefits technology brings to virtual teams, you are also aware of the need for trust among members of virtual teams. The first project you are following is a virtual team tasked with updating one of the corporation's most sought-after guides. The HR vice president appointed all team members and assigned one person as the team leader. None of the team members knows the others, and the team leader is the only team member who has direct contact with your boss. In following the team's work, you realize that no one knows exactly what each member has contributed, because members are not in contact with each other. Their only contact is with the team leader.

Your sense is that the team leader is taking full credit for all the work. Not only is she the only one with direct contact to your boss, she lives in the same area as the corporation's headquarters. The other team members are located across the country. Your sense is confirmed when only the team leader is invited to the annual awards dinner and at the dinner receives singular acknowledgment for her work on updating the guide.

ETHICAL DILEMMA

How can the vice president of HR, and eventually you, determine whether each team member pulled his or her weight or the team lead had to step in to complete or redo the guide?

SOURCES: Sirkka L. Jarvenpaa and Dorothy E. Leidner, "Communication and Trust in Global Virtual Teams," *Journal of Computer-Mediated Communication*, June 1998, http://www.ascusc.org; Carla Joinson, "Managing Virtual Teams: Keeping Members on the Same Page without Being in the Same Place Poses Challenges for Managers," *HR Magazine*, June 2002, http://www.findarticles.com; and Charlene Marmer Solomon, "Managing Virtual Teams," *Workforce*, June 1, 2001, http://www.findarticles.com.

An adaptation of the team concept is called a **cross-functional team**. These teams are made up of employees from about the same hierarchical level but different functional areas of the organization. Many task forces, organizational committees, and project teams are cross-functional. Often the team members work together only until they solve a given problem or complete a specific project. Cross-functional teams allow people with various levels and areas of expertise to pool their resources, develop new ideas, solve problems, and coordinate complex projects. Both problem-solving teams and self-managed teams may also be cross-functional teams. Many companies use both types of teams to increase their efficiency.

Building High-Performance Teams

When teams are formed to address issues or solve complex problems, they often are under tight deadlines to provide effective solutions. Rarely do they spend time properly setting up the team for maximum effectiveness. Frequently, much time is lost resolving conflicts before the team returns to its primary focus. Here are some tips for setting teams up properly to deliver the expected results:

1. *Create and share the team's purpose.* Discuss why the team exists.

2. *Create specific and challenging goals.* Discuss measurable results and expectations.

3. *Create a collaborative approach.* Discuss the methods and strategies for working together.

4. *Define clear roles.* Discuss everyone's role on the team. Resolve conflicts early.

5. *Define complementary skills.* Discuss what skills are present within the team. Discuss how each member can use his or her skills to ensure the team's success. Reorganize any skill gaps within the team and discuss how to resolve them.[8]

In addition to getting the team off on the right foot, there are also some pitfalls to avoid. According to team-building expert Margrit Harris, President of Strata Team–Team Strategist Group, here are some sure-fire team destroyers:

1. *No common objective.* If you don't have a vision, you certainly won't get there.

2. *Clashing personalities.* When people are in conflict, cooperation and creativity are lost. This doesn't mean everyone needs to have the same personality, but everyone needs to be able to resolve conflict quickly and build a spirit of harmony.

3. *Too similar expertise.* When there is no diversity of skills among the team members, the team can suffer. Complementary skill sets add strength to the overall effectiveness.

4. *Questionable ethical standards.* Questions regarding ethical standards can destroy teams quickly. Suspicions can undo even the best of teams.

5. *Different operating styles.* Complementary operating styles are usually best. Clashing styles can create frustration and conflict among the team members.[9]

HOT Links
Find team-building resources galore at Teambuilding, Inc.'s super site, http://www.teambuildinginc.com.

concept check

What is the difference between a work team and a work group?

Identify and describe three types of work teams.

What are some ways of building a high-performance team?

9 *learning goal*

So far, we have focused in this chapter on understanding what motivates people and how employee motivation and satisfaction affect productivity and organizational performance. Organizations can improve performance by investing in people. In reviewing the ways in which companies are currently choosing to invest in their human resources, we can spot four positive trends:

1. education and training,

2. employee ownership,

3. work-life benefits, and

4. nurturing knowledge workers.

All of the companies making the *Report on Business Magazine*'s "Best Employers in Canada" list know the importance of treating employees properly. They all have programs that allow them to invest in their employees through programs such as these and many more.[10] Today's businesses also face the challenge of increased costs of absenteeism. In the next section, we discuss each of these trends in motivating employees.

EDUCATION AND TRAINING

Companies that provide educational and training opportunities for their employees reap the benefits of a more motivated, as well as a more skilled, workforce. Employees who are properly trained in new technologies are more productive and less resistant to job change. Education and training provide additional benefits by increasing employees' feelings of competence and self-worth. When companies spend money to upgrade employee knowledge and skills, they convey the message "we value you and are committed to your growth and development as an employee."

EMPLOYEE OWNERSHIP

Behind employee ownership programs is the belief that they cause workers to act more like partners than clock watchers. The theory is that employees who think like owners are better motivated to take care of customers' needs, reduce unnecessary expenses, make operations smoother, and stay around longer. According to economist Douglas Kruse, "On average, worker-owned companies survive longer, lose fewer workers, enjoy bigger profits, and are more productive than their non–employee-owned competitors."[11] Most companies that have employee ownership programs have achieved positive results. In fact, for the past decade these companies have, on average, outperformed the general stock market.[12]

WORK-LIFE BENEFITS

In another growing trend in the workplace, companies are helping their employees to manage the numerous and sometimes competing demands in their lives. Organizations are taking a more active role in helping employees achieve a balance between their work responsibilities and their personal obligations. The desired result is employees who are less stressed, better able to focus on their jobs, and, therefore, more productive. Ford Motor Company is a leader in providing work-life benefits for employees. The company offers telecommuting, part-time positions, job sharing, subsidized childcare, eldercare referral, and on-site fitness centres.

NURTURING KNOWLEDGE WORKERS

Most organizations have specialized workers, and managing them all effectively is a big challenge. In many companies, knowledge workers (now two-fifths of the workforce) might have a supervisor, but they are not "subordinates." They are "associates." Within their area of knowledge, they are supposed to do the telling. As knowledge is effective only if specialized, knowledge workers are not homogeneous, particularly the fast-growing group of knowledge technologists, such as computer systems specialists, lawyers, programmers, and others. And because knowledge work is specialized, it is deeply splintered.

Many businesses, such as hospitals, have many knowledge specialists. In financial services, too, there is increasing specialization and need for concentration on one specialty!

It is important today to pay close attention to the health and well-being of all workers. A knowledge-based workforce is qualitatively different from one that is less skilled. True, knowledge workers are still in the minority, but they are fast becoming the largest single group, and they have already become the major creator of wealth. Increasingly the success, indeed the survival, of every business will depend on the performance of its knowledge workforce. The most effective way an organization in a knowledge-based economy and society can excel is managing its knowledge workers for greater productivity and "by creating a work environment that encourages and rewards ordinary people for doing extraordinary things."

Knowledge-based businesses need to concentrate on the productivity of their capital, that is, of the knowledge worker. Managers need to focus on the business rather than on employment-related rules, regulations, and paperwork. To spend one-quarter of one's time on job-related paperwork is, indeed, a waste of precious, expensive, scarce resources. It is also boring.

The only way to achieve leadership in a knowledge-based business is to spend time with the company's promising knowledge professionals: to get to know them and to be known by them, to mentor them and to listen to them, to challenge them and to encourage them.[13]

COPING WITH THE RISING COSTS OF ABSENTEEISM

The rate of employee absenteeism is very consistent from year to year, but the costs continue to rise very rapidly. Short-term absence costs have doubled in the past decade. Much of this is due to the cost of health-related absences.

As Canadian workers age, they will experience more responsibilities for caring for elderly parents. An older workforce also means more health-related time off. Experts speak about the "entitlement mentality" of many workers; that is, "I am entitled to take off when I want or need to." Stress-related absenteeism is also on the rise.

Companies are trying to lower absenteeism in the following ways:

• allowing employees who arrive late or miss a day to do "make-up time," usually the same day or within the same week;

- establishing a grace period of a certain number of minutes for late arrivals that won't count as tardiness;
- eliminating advance-notice requirements for tardiness, which lets employees call at the last minute and be excused for a late arrival if operations won't be disrupted;
- allowing employees to refuse mandatory overtime occasionally—for example, for 25 percent of the time;
- eliminating formal attendance policies altogether. Instead, they treat poor attendance as they do performance problems. Employees who slip receive feedback and counselling, followed by a performance or development plan. The employee is discharged if the behaviour doesn't improve;[14]
- providing on-site day care for employees' children; and/or
- contracting with a firm specializing in eldercare to make on-site visits to employees' older relatives.

concept check

What benefits can an organization derive from training and educational opportunities, stock ownership programs, and work-life benefits?

How are knowledge workers different from traditional employees?

Why is the cost of absenteeism rising, and what can be done about it?

Great Ideas to Use Now

HOT *Links*

Expand your knowledge about motivation in the workplace at Accel-Team's site, http://www .accel-team.com/motivation/ index.html

We've come a long way from the days of Taylor's scientific management. Organizations now offer a wide variety of incentives to attract and retain high-quality employees. A knowledgeable, creative, committed, and highly skilled workforce provides a company with a source of sustainable advantage in an increasingly competitive business environment. What does that mean to you? It means that companies are working harder than ever to meet employee needs. It means that when you graduate from college or university, you may choose a prospective employer on the basis of its daycare facilities and fitness programs as well as its salaries. It means that you need to think about what motivates you. Would you forgo a big salary to work for a smaller company that gives you lots of freedom to be creative and make your own decisions? Would you trade extensive health coverage for a share of ownership in the company? Most organizations try to offer a broad spectrum of incentives to meet a variety of needs, but each company makes trade-offs, and so will you in choosing an employer. Do a little research on a company you are interested in working for (paying particular attention to its corporate culture); then use the first exercise in the "Experiential Exercises" to help you determine how well your values fit with the company's values.

So often we think of employee motivation as a purely internal process. However, recent research shows that happy, satisfied employees who stay in jobs can affect an organization's level of customer satisfaction. Unifi, a division of PricewaterhouseCoopers, and Roper Starch Worldwide, recently conducted a survey of customers of businesses in six industries. Across all six, the survey results showed that employee turnover has a significant impact on customer satisfaction. Customers felt that employee retention affected the quality of the service they received from the organization.

Gary Wallace, the CEO of a credit union, recognized this connection between motivated employees and happy customers some time back. With customer satisfaction as his primary goal, Wallace first went about implementing programs to find new and better ways to serve his employees. The credit union redecorated the employee lounge in the colours of the local football teams and offered employees an enjoyable place to relax. It also installed multimedia stations at each branch to offer motivational messages and information about employee benefits and upcoming company and community events. The company also built larger employee cubicles and constructed an outdoor patio with umbrella tables.[16]

How has all of this worked? Quite well for Mr. Wallace and the credit union. The company has expanded its market share, and its assets have passed the $500 million mark. Service has improved, employee turnover is down, and customer satisfaction has never been higher.

SUMMARY OF LEARNING GOALS

1 What are the basic principles of Frederick Taylor's concept of scientific management?

Scientific management is based on the belief that employees are motivated by economic incentives and that there is "one best way" to perform any job. The four basic principles of scientific management developed by Taylor are as follows:

1. Develop a scientific approach for each element of a person's job.
2. Scientifically select, train, teach, and develop workers.
3. Encourage cooperation between workers and managers, so that each job can be accomplished in a standard, scientifically determined way.
4. Divide work and responsibility between management and workers according to who is better suited to each task.

2 What did Elton Mayo's Hawthorne studies reveal about worker motivation?

The pride that comes from special attention motivates workers to increase their productivity. Supervisors who allow employees to have some control over their situation appeared to increase the workers' motivation further. The Hawthorne effect suggests that employees will perform better when they feel singled out for special attention or feel that management is concerned about their welfare.

3 What is Maslow's hierarchy of needs, and how do these needs relate to motivation?

Maslow believed that each individual has a hierarchy of needs, consisting of physiological, safety, social, esteem, and self-actualization needs. Managers who accept Maslow's ideas attempt to increase employee motivation by modifying organizational and managerial practices to increase the likelihood that employees will meet all levels of needs. Maslow's theory has also helped managers understand that it is hard to motivate people by appealing to already satisfied needs.

4 How are McGregor's Theories X and Y and Ouchi's Theory Z used to explain worker motivation?

Douglas McGregor influenced the study of motivation with his formulation of two contrasting sets of assumptions about human nature—designated Theory X and Theory Y. Theory X says people don't like to work and will avoid it if they can. Because people don't like to work, they must be controlled, directed, or threatened to get them to make an effort. Theory Y says that people want to be self-directed and will try to accomplish goals that they believe in. Workers can be motivated with positive incentives. McGregor personally believed that Theory Y assumptions describe most employees and that managers seeking to motivate subordinates should develop management practices based on those assumptions.

William Ouchi's Theory Z combines North American and Japanese business practices. Theory Z emphasizes long-term employment, slow career development, and group decision-making. The long-term decline of the Japanese economy has resulted in most North American firms' moving away from Japanese management practices.

5 What are the basic components of Herzberg's motivator–hygiene theory?

Frederick Herzberg's studies indicated that certain job factors are consistently related to employee job satisfaction, whereas others can create job dissatisfaction. According to Herzberg, motivating factors (also called satisfiers) are primarily intrinsic job elements that lead to satisfaction, such as achievement, recognition, the (nature of) work itself, responsibility, advancement, and growth. What Herzberg termed hygiene factors (also called dissatisfiers) are extrinsic elements of the work environment, such as company policy, relationships with supervisors, working conditions, relationships with peers and subordinates, salary and benefits, and job security. These are factors that can result in job dissatisfaction if not managed well. One of the most interesting findings of Herzberg's studies was the implication that the opposite of satisfaction is not dissatisfaction. Herzberg believed that proper management of hygiene factors could prevent employee dissatisfaction but that these factors could not serve as a source of satisfaction or motivation.

6 What three contemporary theories on employee motivation offer insights into improving employee performance?

According to expectancy theory, the probability that an individual will act in a particular way depends on the strength of that individual's belief that the act will have a particular outcome and on whether the individual values that outcome. Equity theory is based on individuals' perceptions about how fairly they are treated compared to their coworkers. Goal-setting theory states that employees are highly motivated to perform when specific goals are established and feedback on progress is offered.

7 How can managers redesign existing jobs to increase employee motivation and performance?

The horizontal expansion of a job by increasing the number and variety of tasks that a person performs is called job enlargement. Increasing task diversity can enhance job satisfaction, particularly when the job is mundane and repetitive in nature. Job enrichment is the vertical expansion of an employee's job to provide the employee with more autonomy, responsibility, and decision-making authority. Other popular motivational tools include work-scheduling options, employee recognition programs, empowerment, and variable-pay programs.

8   What different types of teams are being used in organizations today?

Work groups share resources and coordinate efforts to help members perform their individual duties and responsibilities more effectively. The performance of the group can be evaluated by adding up the contributions of the individual group members. Work teams require not only coordination but also *collaboration*, the pooling of knowledge, skills, abilities, and resources in a collective effort to attain a common goal. Four types of work teams are used: problem solving, self-managed, cross-functional, and virtual teams.

9   What initiatives are organizations using today to motivate and retain employees?

Today, firms are using several key tactics to motivate and retain workers. First, companies are investing more in employee education and training, which make workers more productive and less resistant to job change. Second, managers are offering employees a chance for ownership in the company. This can strongly increase employee commitment. Enlightened employers are providing work-life benefits to help employees achieve a better balance between work and personal responsibilities. Businesses are also recognizing the importance of managing knowledge workers and reducing the growing cost of employee absenteeism.

EXPERIENTIAL EXERCISES

1. The accompanying table lists 17 personal characteristics and 13 institutional values you might encounter at a company. Select and rank-order the 10 personal characteristics that best describe you; do the same for the 10 institutional values that would be most evident in your ideal workplace. Test your fit at a firm by seeing whether the characteristics of the company's environment match your top 10 personal characteristics.

THE CHOICE MENU

RANK ORDER (1–17) YOU ARE	RANK ORDER (1–13) YOUR IDEAL COMPANY OFFERS
_____ 1. Flexible	_____ 1. Stability
_____ 2. Innovative	_____ 2. High expectations of performance
_____ 3. Willing to experiment	_____ 3. Opportunities for professional growth
_____ 4. Risk taking	_____ 4. High pay for good performance
_____ 5. Careful	_____ 5. Job security
_____ 6. Autonomy seeking	_____ 6. A clear guiding philosophy
_____ 7. Comfortable with rules	_____ 7. A low level of conflict
_____ 8. Analytical	_____ 8. Respect for the individual's rights
_____ 9. Team oriented	_____ 9. Informality
_____ 10. Easygoing	_____ 10. Fairness
_____ 11. Supportive	_____ 11. Long hours
_____ 12. Aggressive	_____ 12. Relative freedom from rules
_____ 13. Decisive	_____ 13. The opportunity to be distinctive, or different from others
_____ 14. Achievement oriented	
_____ 15. Comfortable with individual responsibility	
_____ 16. Competitive	
_____ 17. Interested in making friends at work	

2. How are job satisfaction and employee morale linked to job performance? Do you work harder when you are satisfied with your job? Explain your answer.

3. Review the assumptions of Theories X, Y, and Z. Under which set of assumptions would you prefer to work? Is your current or former supervisor a Theory X, Theory Y, or Theory Z manager? Explain by describing the person's behaviour.

4. Think about several of your friends who seem to be highly self-motivated. Talk with each of them and ask them what factors contribute the most to their motivation. Make a list of their responses and compare them to the factors that motivate you.

5. Both individual motivation and group participation are needed to accomplish certain goals. Describe a situation you're familiar with in which cooperation achieved a goal that individual action could not. Describe one in which group action slowed progress and individual action would have been better.

6. Using expectancy theory, analyze how you have made and will make personal choices, such as a major area of study, a career to pursue, or job interviews to seek.

7. Looking for 1,001 ways to motivate or reward your employees? Bob Nelson can help. Visit the "Recognition" resources section of his Nelson Motivation site at **http://www.nelson-motivation.com** to get some ideas you can put to use to help you do a better job, either as a manager or as an employee.

8. More companies are offering their employees stock ownership plans. To learn the differences between an employee stock ownership plan (ESOP) and stock options, visit the National Center for Employee Ownership (NCEO), at **http:/www.nceo.org**, and the Foundation for Enterprise Development (FED), at **http:/www.fed.org**. Which stock plan would you rather have? Why? Also visit the "Ownership Culture" area of the NCEO site. What does research on employee ownership indicate? Cite specific examples.

9. Open-book management is one of the better known ways to create a participatory work environment. More than 2,000 companies have adopted this practice, which involves sharing financial information with non-management employees and training them to understand financial information. Does it really motivate employees and improve productivity? Do a search for this topic at the NCEO site, **http:/www.nceo.org**. You'll find survey results, case studies, related activities, and links that will help you answer this question.

10. Use a search engine to find companies that offer "work-life benefits." Link to several companies and review their employee programs in this area. How do they compare? Which benefits would be most important to you if you were job hunting, and why?

REVIEW QUESTIONS

1. Summarize the following:

- Frederick Taylor's scientific management,

- Hawthorne studies,

- Maslow's hierarchy of needs,

- McGregor's Theories X and Y,

- Ouchi's Theory Z, and

- Herzberg's motivator-hygiene theory.

2. Explain E > P > O of expectancy theory. How does this explain employee behaviour?

3. What are the choices available when an employee feels that there is unfairness on the job?

4. How can the use of goal-setting theory lead to motivation?

5. How does culture affect motivation and its theories?

6. Explain

   • job enlargement, job enrichment, and job rotation;

   • work-scheduling options and how they can be a motivator; and

   • how motivation is affected by recognition, empowerment, and economic incentives.

7. How can managers use teams to enhance motivation and performance?

8. What are some of the fundamental concepts related to group behaviours and group processes, and how do they affect the effectiveness of groups/teams?

9. What are the general rules for developing high-performance teams?

10. Explain how the following affect employee motivation:

    • education and training opportunities,

    • employee ownership,

    • work-life benefits, and

    • the nurturing of knowledge workers.

CREATIVE THINKING CASE
De-Motivating Your Top Producer

The Max Call Centre had been home to Sandy Rolf for many years. She had a good salary, excellent bonus system (cash and other incentives), and a reasonable benefits package and pension plan. Sandy's job was outbound cold calls to bring customers back to the company. Many of us would cringe at the thought of spending eight hours a day doing this. Sandy loved it, as she said, "my two favourite things, talking on the phone and making money." As a top producer in the area, she received gift certificates in the hundreds of dollars for various local merchants, as well as her base salary and commissions. She was celebrated at company functions by upper management, received congratulatory e-mails and plaques, and was honoured at departmental meetings. Her managers could not say enough positive things about her.

So what did the company ultimately do to reward this loyal and valued employee? They outsourced her job. As a result of an executive decision, the department no longer existed. Sandy was told not to worry, she still had a job. The job turned out to be fielding inbound calls, most of which were complaints against the company for perceived wrongs against the customer.

Sandy's health began to deteriorate because of extreme stress, and the once happy, outgoing, fun-loving woman now spent most of her leisure time sleeping, watching TV, and avoiding her friends and family.

Research suggests that small pleasures (e.g., a job you enjoy) are more likely to yield long-term joy than high-profile positive events. "It's the frequency and not the intensity of the positive events in your life that leads to happiness, like comfortable shoes or a single malt scotch," according to Daniel Gilbert, a Harvard University psychology professor. By going to a job she loved, Sandy experienced happiness and job satisfaction on a daily basis. Now that this situation had changed, her happiness and motivation levels dropped, leaving Sandy in a depressed state, struggling for the energy and interest even to access the on-line job search sites.

CRITICAL THINKING QUESTIONS

1. Using the motivation theories in the chapter, explain why Sandy was so motivated in a job such as cold calling.

2. Given that she still had a salary, benefits, and a pension plan, why did she become so extremely unmotivated after the change?

SOURCE: July Stoffman, "You're Happy. Imagine That!: Why People Are So Bad at Predicting What Will Make Them Feel Good," *Toronto Star*, May 21, 2006, D4.

VIDEO CASE
Teamwork Matters At Hill, Holiday

"Teamwork helps foster the creative spirit," say Tim Jones and Marty Smith, the creative directors responsible for the coveted Dunkin' Donut account at 32-year-old advertising agency Hill, Holiday Creative, located in Boston.

"Advertising by committee doesn't work," says Jones. "Too many opinions water down the essence and energy of the work." They prefer working with autonomous creative teams, who are given their own space to work on a project. In Smith and Jones's experience this encourages "ownership" of the work, causing people to work harder and produce better results.

They review team output at the end of the workday. "People can be defensive when they've spent all day on an idea and we tell them they're heading down the wrong path," says Smith. "They may need time to think things over and regroup, so they go home and get it out of their system. Usually they are already working on new stuff by the next morning."

One exercise they found helpful was having their people review all 60 Dunkin' Donut advertising spots, which they mounted, gallery-style, on an office wall. The two creative directors "graded" each one, highlighting its strengths and weaknesses, including some they themselves had created—which received Ds and Fs. "It makes people feel better if they know you have made mistakes along the way too," says Smith.

They encourage people to be forthcoming with all their ideas, no matter how bad they think they are, because sometimes a brilliant idea comes out of a really bad one. "It doesn't matter where ideas come from," says Jones. "Sometimes writers come up with visual ideas and art directors with text suggestions." It can be tempting to put another team on a project if the ideas aren't flowing well, but competition seems to work against the creative process.

Dunkin' Donuts's TV spots air 52 weeks a year, in addition to print ads and holiday and seasonal promotions. So one team may be working on a coffee campaign, while another focuses on summer beverages, and still another on donuts. With plenty of work to go around, Smith and Jones are happy to give others the chance to work on a major account. "We bring a palpable enthusiasm to everything we do—it motivates others and helps us gel as a team," says Jones.

CRITICAL THINKING QUESTIONS

1. Distinguish between two major types of teams in the workplace. Which type does Hill, Holiday utilize?
2. Does Hill, Holiday utilize contemporary theories on employee motivation? Explain.
3. What else could Hill, Holiday do to increase employee motivation?

SOURCE: Adapted from material in the video: "Coffee Talk: Teamwork at Hill," Holiday Creative; Hill, Holiday Creative Web site, http://www.hhcc.com, accessed March 17, 2003.

E-COMMERCE CASE
Virtual Assistants Can Take Care of Your Business

Neal Lekwa, owner of the Calbert Group, prefers to hire multiple virtual assistants to avoid the "agony" of running a traditional office. His virtual company, which employs teams of subcontractors and virtual assistants scattered between Maine and India, provides e-commerce, Web construction, program design, photography, and consulting services to companies in the lodging and airline industries. "It is a very efficient way of delegating work," he says. "Everything is pure business."

Virtual assistants are highly motivated team players. They understand that their clients' success ultimately means their success. Calbert's Web site (**http://www.calbertgroup.com**), states that team building "is always a matter of chance—searching in the right places, and luck." Clearly Lekwa knew where to search for his highly qualified virtual teams, who use results as their benchmark for success. State-of-the-art Web sites, insightful intuitive design, navigational efficiency, and superb software delivery systems mean good results.

Using virtual assistants is one way small businesses can operate and compete by containing costs. Dan Stafford, owner of PS Associates based on Vashon Island, Washington, couldn't manage without his virtual assistant, Terri Vincent of Cody, Wyoming, who takes care of his mass mailings, travel arrangements, and other daily office operations. Vincent, a self-employed administrative professional, works from her downtown Cody office for a dozen regular clients each month, charging by the hour or by the project.

But managing a virtual workforce can present unique challenges. None of the virtual employees knows the others—their only connection is through the contractor they work for. Keeping far-flung assistants in different time zones in the communication loop can be a major challenge, so superior project management skills are important to the success of operating a virtual business.

Cheryl Allin, 33, a working mother from Tacoma, Washington, signed her first client just six weeks after opening her virtual-assistant business. "I wanted to use my experience in Internet businesses and still be available for my four children," she says. Now, thanks to technology and the growing acceptance of virtual business arrangements, a valuable and previously underutilized segment of the workforce can reap the benefits of doing useful and rewarding work, while their clients benefit from what they bring to the (virtual) table.

CRITICAL THINKING QUESTIONS

1. What are some of the benefits virtual assistants and their clients derive from this unique way of doing business?

2. What are some of the challenges of motivating and retaining a team of virtual employees?

SOURCES: Jenny Lynn Zappala, "Virtual Assistants Enjoy Flexibility, Independence," Puget Sound Business Journal, January 18, 2002, http://www.bizjournals.com (accessed April 7, 2003); International Virtual Assistants Association Web site, http://www.ivaa.org (accessed April 7, 2003); Staffcentrix Web site, http://www.msvas.com/ (accessed April 7, 2003); and Calbert Group Web site, http://www.calbertgroup.com (accessed April 7, 2003).

Making the Connection

Achieving World-Class Operations Management

In this section of the text we will take a look at the internal environment of a business, or, more simply, the functional areas of a business. These areas are what most people think of when they think of a business or a career in business—marketing, operations, finance and accounting, and human resources. We have looked at human resources earlier in the Management section of the text. Although this is typically considered a functional area, because it deals with the management of human resources, and human resources are used in every area of a business, it is inextricably linked to management in general. We will, however, continue to refer to the connections between human resource management and the other functional areas throughout this section.

Before we take a look inside each of the functional areas in detail in separate chapters, one very important message must be communicated clearly at the outset. Even though each of these areas is discussed separately in different chapters in introductory textbooks and later in separate courses in business schools, they cannot act separately if the business is to be successful. They are all part of the integrated business model that has been the central theme of this text. Each of these areas must work together to make the business successful overall. For example, a company cannot design and market a product for which it does not have the human, operational, and financial resources. Just imagine The Bay attempting to produce a new all-terrain

vehicle and introduce it to the market. It could perhaps alter its store setup to sell the vehicle, but does it have the facilities and people skills to produce it? Would it even have the financial resources to put toward this type of endeavour, considering the tight budgets most businesses are working with today to keep their core business alive?

It was clear from Chapter 7, which deals with management and planning, that all decisions made at the tactical level in the functional areas come from decisions made at a higher *strategic* level that affect the whole company. Top management first scans the external environment (PEST model) to look for opportunities and threats and matches those with the strengths and weaknesses of the company in the different functional areas to decide the direction for the company. It is therefore unlikely that a decision like this one would ever be made by The Bay. Even if there were opportunities in the market for ATVs, it would not match with the strengths of the company. Financial resources would therefore not be released for this type of project to begin with.

This particular chapter, on the management of the operations area of a business, starts with a discussion of Harley-Davidson's operations. This example is very appropriate to the title of the chapter, as Harley definitely epitomizes world-class operations and offers many lessons for companies struggling to get there. For years Harley tried to sell freedom and adventure but with a poor-quality product sold at a high price because of outdated and inefficient facilities. Its *financial performance* was extremely poor, because it simply did not *meet customer needs*—poor *quality* at a high price did not provide the customer with anything of value. Once it stopped trying to produce quantity and focused instead on quality, Harley turned it all around. Today the company is a leader in quality management. But it required a view of the business as a whole—meeting the needs of the customer (*marketing*) through *committed employees* (*human resources*) and providing quality (*operations*) at the lowest cost to improve the bottom line (*finance*) while uniting all the *stakeholders* in the "Harley-Davidson family."

As explained in the chapter, sound operations management is vital to the financial success of the company, because this area accounts for as much as three-quarters of the company's costs. It is a wonderful example of the integrative nature of business, as it must work very closely with the other functional areas to achieve maximum financial performance. Most obviously, operations must develop processes to provide for the demand created and forecasted by marketing, but it must also work with marketing to develop and design products so that the operations processes used to provide them are the most efficient and effective and the distribution of those products—both an operations and a marketing issue—is done efficiently, cost-effectively, and in a manner that meets the customers' needs. Similarly, operations must work with human resources to have the right numbers of the best-qualified people available to produce products and service customers, as well as deciding whether to replace this human effort with robots or other computerized techniques. In fact, most of the decisions made in the operations area have wider functional implications. For example, the choice of location can affect transportation costs and thus the final cost of the product as well as the availability and cost of labour, whereas implementing a flexible manufacturing system is expensive but needs little labour to operate and provides consistent quality products that meet individual customer specifications.

A terrific example in the chapter of the need for a successful business to integrate operations with the other functional areas is that of DaimlerChrysler and its computerized design system, "FastCar." FastCar links the design process with operations, finance, and marketing so that as the cars are designed all of the areas can see the implications in terms of costs, manufacturing requirements and specifications, demand, and so on.

Another area where we can see the integration of operations with the other facets of our business model is in the external environment. Many businesses today are faced with environmental challenges in an effort to meet their operational goals. For example, in the *social* environment, consumers are expecting customized products of greater quality delivered in a timely manner at a reasonable price. This requires using whatever *technology* is available to allow the company to stay ahead of the competition and improving relationships with suppliers and vendors (both important stakeholder groups), so that there is a smooth flow from provider to consumer. If consumers don't get what they want, they will simply go to the increasing number of competitors in the global *economic* environment who can often produce at a lower cost, and they will often do this at breakneck speed using technology to shop over the Internet, switching their loyalties at the click of a mouse!

The technology that is available to the operations area of a business has improved tremendously. In this chapter we outline many of these *innovations*. One of the most integrative examples of technology is manufacturing resource planning (MRPII). It uses a complex computerized system to integrate data from the different departments of the company, so that they are all working as one to meet customer needs. Enterprise resource planning (ERP) takes this a step further by going outside the business and integrating information about suppliers and customers into the system. These technologies and others help to manage the supply chain so that the entire sequence, from securing inputs into the process to delivering goods to the consumer, is done in a manner that meets the needs of the customer at the highest possible level.

Operations management is also an excellent example of the management process at work. You will read in the chapter about production *planning* and *control*, and the specific tools and techniques that are used to plan and control the production process. Quality control is a particularly important issue for management in meeting the customers' needs for a quality product. Part of the process is also deciding on the layout for the production or service facility, which involves *organizing* the company's resources in the most appropriate way to produce goods or provide services to the customer efficiently. The final management function is pivotal—*motivating*—as we know that workers must be committed to the task for it all to come together. Operations managers working directly with the workers that produce the goods or services for the customers have the ultimate responsibility to gain that commitment.

In this chapter, you'll learn about many trends in operations that allow companies to both enhance innovation to meet changing customer needs in a timely manner and adapt to changes in technology, while improving quality, keeping costs down, and gaining employee commitment by involving teams of employees throughout the process. And isn't that what it's all about—meeting the critical success factors by integrating the functional areas in the context of the dynamic business environment?

11

© AP / WORLD WIDE PHOTOS

Achieving World-Class Operations Management

learning goals

1 Why are production and operations management important in both manufacturing and service firms?

2 What types of production processes are used by manufacturers and service firms?

3 How do organizations decide where to put their production facilities? What choices must be made in designing the facility?

4 Why are resource-planning tasks like inventory management and supplier relations critical to production?

5 How do operations managers schedule and control production?

6 How can quality management and lean-manufacturing techniques help firms improve production and operations management?

7 What roles do technology and automation play in manufacturing and service industry operations management?

8 What key trends are affecting the way companies manage production and operations?

Building on Success at Harley-Davidson

Harley-Davidsons aren't just motorcycles. They're an American legend, known for their unique style, sound, and power ever since the first one was assembled in a backyard workshop in 1903. "People want more than two wheels and a motor," explains former Harley-Davidson CEO Jeffrey Bleustein. "Harleys represent something very basic—a desire for freedom, adventure, and individualism."

Twenty years ago, Harley also represented everything that was wrong with American manufacturing. The company's production facilities were outdated and inefficient, keeping prices high. Quality was so poor that owners sometimes joked they needed two Harleys—one to ride and one for parts. As fed-up consumers turned to motorcycles made by Japanese and German manufacturers, Harley-Davidson's sales plummeted, and the company teetered on bankruptcy.

Today, however, Harley-Davidson (**http://www.harley-davidson.com**) is a company reborn. The company posted its 17th consecutive year of profits in 2002. With retail sales growing at 19 percent a year, Harley-Davidson has roared off with 50 percent of the motorcycle market. How did this turnaround happen? With single-minded focus on just one thing: turning cost-effective manufacturing excellence into a company-wide passion.

The quest for excellence begins with product design. Every component in a Harley bike is put through a rigorous design process that examines its manufacturability according to quality standards. Special software estimates the cost of each design proposal, so that expenses can be carefully controlled. Vendors hoping to supply various components to Harley-Davidson automatically receive this same information electronically, integrating them into the product development cycle.

Lasers and robots automate many production tasks. Components ready for assembly are loaded onto specially designed carts that swivel 360 degrees and can be lowered or raised to suit different workers or tasks. The carts then move into workstations where groups of employees assemble them into motorcycle frames. No motorcycle leaves a Harley-Davidson plant without a final quality inspection. A team of test drivers revs up and rides each motorcycle, checking operating quality and listening for the classic Harley sound.

Employees play a critical role in Harley's production facilities. Working in teams, many employees are cross-trained to perform a variety of production tasks. Each work team is asked to look constantly for ways to build better motorcycles. The company has implemented many employee-generated ideas for improving equipment, factory layout, and production processes.

Industry analysts say Harley-Davidson's rebirth and continued growth is intimately tied to its dedication to quality and efficiency in its operations and production processes. "Harley-Davidson succeeded because they aligned all stakeholders—from customers to shareholders to employees and suppliers," says consultant Stephen Shapiro. "They created the Harley-Davidson family, where everyone, including unions, are united in a common purpose."[1]

Critical Thinking Questions

As you read this chapter, consider the following questions as they relate to Harley-Davidson:

1. How has focusing on quality in its operations and production supported Harley-Davidson's growth?
2. What external factors have led to this focus?
3. What future production decisions will Harley need to make if it is to continue to grow?

Finding the most efficient and effective methods of producing the goods or services it sells to customers is an ongoing focus of nearly every type of business organization. Today more than ever, changing consumer expectations, technological advances, and increased competition are all forcing business organizations to rethink where, when, and how they will produce products or services.

Like Harley-Davidson, manufacturers have discovered that it is no longer enough simply to push products through the factory and onto the market. Consumers demand high quality at reasonable prices. They also expect manufacturers to deliver products in a timely manner. Firms that can't meet these expectations often face strong competition from businesses that can. To compete, many manufacturers are reinventing how they make their products by automating their factories, developing new production processes, using quality control techniques, and tightening their relationships with suppliers.

Service organizations are also facing challenges. Their customers are demanding better service, shorter waits, and more individualized attention. Just like manufacturers, service organizations are using new methods to deliver what customers need and want. Banks, for example, are using technology such as ATMs and the Internet to make their services more easily accessible to customers. Many colleges now offer weekend and even on-line courses for working students. Tax services are filing tax returns via computer.

In this chapter, we examine how manufacturers and service firms manage and control the creation of products and services. We'll discuss production planning, including the choices firms must make concerning the type of production process they will use, the location where production will occur, the design of the facility, and the management of resources needed in production. Next, we'll explain routing and scheduling, two critical tasks for controlling production and operations efficiency. Many businesses are improving productivity by employing quality control methods and automation. We'll discuss these methods before summarizing some of the trends affecting production and operations management.

PRODUCTION AND OPERATIONS MANAGEMENT— AN OVERVIEW

1 *learning goal*

production
The creation of products and services by turning inputs, such as natural resources, raw materials, human resources, and capital, into outputs, which are products and services.

operations management
Management of the production process.

Production, the creation of products and services, is an essential function in every firm. Production turns inputs, such as natural resources, raw materials, human resources, and capital, into outputs, which are products and services. This process is shown in Exhibit 11.1. Managing this conversion process is the role of **operations management**.

In the 1980s, many Canadian industries, such as automotive and steel, lost customers to foreign competitors because their production systems could not provide the quality customers demanded. As a result, most Canadian companies, both large and small, now consider a focus on quality to be a central component of effective operations management.

The goal of customer satisfaction, closely linked to quality, is also an important part of effective production and operations. In the past, the manufacturing function in most companies was focused inward. Manufacturing had little contact with customers and didn't always understand their needs and desires. Today, however, stronger links between marketing and manufacturing have encouraged production

Exhibit 11.1 Production Process for Products and Services

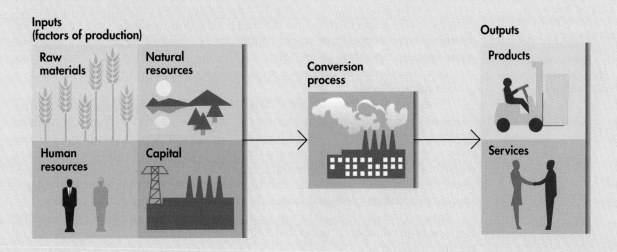

managers to be more outwardly focused and to consider decisions in light of their effect on customer satisfaction. Service companies have also found that making operating decisions with customer satisfaction in mind can be a competitive advantage.

Operations managers, the personnel charged with managing and supervising the conversion process, play a vital role in today's firm. They often control about three-fourths of a firm's assets, including inventories, wages, and benefits. They work closely with other major functions of the firm, such as marketing, finance, accounting, and human resources, to help ensure that the firm produces its goods profitably and continually satisfies customers. They face the challenge of combining people and other resources to produce high-quality goods on time and at a reasonable cost. Working with marketing, they help to decide which products to make or which services to offer. They become involved with the development and design of goods and determine what production processes will be most effective.

Production and operations management involves three main types of decisions that are made at three different stages:

1. *Production planning.* The first decisions facing operations managers come at the *planning stage*. At this stage, managers decide where, when, and how production will occur. They obtain resources and determine site locations.

2. *Production control.* At this stage, the decision-making process focuses on scheduling, controlling quality and costs, and the day-to-day operations of running a factory or service facility.

3. *Improving production and operations.* The final stage of operations management focuses on developing more efficient methods of producing the firm's goods or services.

These three types of decisions are ongoing and often occur simultaneously.

In the following sections, we will take a closer look at the decisions and considerations firms face in each of these stages of production and operations management.

GEARING UP: PRODUCTION PLANNING

production planning
The aspect of operations management in which the firm considers the competitive environment and its own strategic goals in an effort to find the best production methods.

An important part of operations management is **production planning**. During production planning, the firm considers the competitive environment and its own strategic goals in an effort to find the best production methods. Good production planning balances goals that might conflict, such as providing high-quality service while keeping operating costs down, or keeping profits high while maintaining adequate inventories of finished products. Sometimes accomplishing all of these goals is quite difficult.

Production planning involves three phases. Long-term planning has a time frame of three to five years. It focuses on which goods to produce, how many to produce, and where they should be produced. Medium-term planning decisions cover about two years. They concern the layout of the factory or service facilities, where and how to obtain the resources needed for production, and labour issues. Short-term planning, with a one-year time frame, converts these broader goals into specific production plans and materials management strategies.

Four important decisions must be made in production planning. They involve the type of production process that will be used, site selection, facility layout, and resource planning.

concept check

Define production.

What is production planning? Production control?

The Production Process: How Do We Make It?

production process
The way in which a good is made.

In production planning, the first decision involves which type of **production process**—the way in which a good is made—best fits with the company's goals and customer demands. Another important consideration is the type of good or service being produced, as different goods might require different production processes. In general, there are three types of production: mass production, mass customization, and customization. In addition to production type, operations managers also classify production processes in two ways: by how inputs are converted into outputs and by the timing of the process.

mass production
The ability to manufacture many identical goods at once.

One For All: Mass Production **Mass production**, manufacturing many identical goods at once, was a product of the Industrial Revolution. Henry Ford's Model T automobile is a good example of mass production. Each car turned out by Ford's factory was identical, right down to its colour. If you wanted a car in any colour except black, you were out of luck. Canned goods, over-the-counter drugs, and household appliances are examples of goods that are still mass produced. The emphasis in mass production is on keeping manufacturing costs low by producing highly uniform products using repetitive and standardized processes. Mass production, therefore, relies heavily on standardization, mechanization, and specialization. As many products become more complicated to produce, however, mass production is becoming more complex. Automobile manufacturers, for example, must now incorporate more sophisticated electronics into their car designs. As a result, the number of assembly stations in most automobile manufacturing plants has increased.

mass customization
A manufacturing process in which goods are mass produced up to a point and then custom tailored to the needs or desires of individual customers.

Just For You: Customizing Goods In **mass customization**, goods are produced using mass production techniques but only up to a point. At that point, the product or service is custom tailored to the needs or desires of individual customers. Many Canadian furniture manufacturers use mass customization to produce couches and chairs to customer specifications, usually within 30 days. The basic frames used to make the furniture are the same, but automated machinery precuts the colour and type of leather or fabric ordered by each customer. These coverings are then added to the frame through mass production techniques.

Customization is the opposite of mass production. In customization, the firm produces goods or services one at a time according to the specific needs or wants of individual customers. Unlike mass customization, each product or service produced is unique. For example, a print shop might handle a variety of projects, including newsletters, brochures, stationery, and reports. Each print job varies in quantity, type of printing process, binding, colour of ink, and type of paper. A manufacturing firm that produces goods in response to customer orders is called a **job shop**.

Some types of service businesses also deliver customized services. Doctors, for instance, usually must consider the individual illnesses and circumstances of each patient before developing a customized treatment plan. Real estate agents also develop a customized service plan for each customer based on the type of house the person is selling or wants to buy. The differences between mass production, mass customization, and customization are summarized in Exhibit 11.2.

customization

The production of goods or services one at a time according to the specific needs or wants of individual customers.

job shop

A manufacturing firm that produces goods in response to customer orders.

concept check

What is mass production?

Differentiate mass customization from customization.

Converting Inputs to Outputs Production involves converting *inputs* (raw materials, parts, human resources) into *outputs* (products or services). In a manufacturing company, the inputs, the production process, and the final outputs are usually obvious. Harley-Davidson, for instance, converts steel, rubber, paint, and other inputs into motorcycles. The production process in a service company involves a less obvious conversion. For example, a hospital converts the knowledge and skills of its medical personnel, along with equipment and supplies from a variety of sources, into health care services for patients. Exhibit 11.3 provides examples of the inputs and outputs used by several other types of businesses.

Exhibit 11.2 | Classification of Production Types

MASS PRODUCTION	MASS CUSTOMIZATION	CUSTOMIZATION
Highly uniform products or services. Many products made sequentially.	Uniform and standardized production to a point, then unique features added to each product.	Each product or service produced according to individual customer requirements.
Examples: Breakfast cereals, soft drinks and computer keyboards.	Examples: Dell computers, tract homes, and Taylor Made Golf clubs.	Examples: Custom homes, legal services, and haircuts.

process manufacturing

A production process in which the basic input is *broken down* into one or more outputs (products).

assembly process

A production process in which the basic inputs are either *combined* to create the output or *transformed* into the output.

continuous process

A production process that uses long production runs lasting days, weeks, or months without equipment shutdowns; generally used for high-volume, low-variety products with standardized parts.

intermittent process

A production process that uses short production runs to make batches of different products; generally used for low-volume, high-variety products.

There are two basic processes for converting inputs into outputs. In **process manufacturing**, the basic input (raw materials, parts) is *broken down* into one or more outputs (products). For instance, bauxite (the input) is processed to extract aluminium (the output). The **assembly process** is just the opposite. The basic inputs, like parts, raw materials, or human resources, are either *combined* to create the output or *transformed* into the output. An airplane, for example, is created by assembling thousands of parts. Steel manufacturers use heat to transform iron and other materials into steel. In services, customers may play a role in the transformation process. For example, a tax preparation service combines the knowledge of the tax preparer with the client's information about personal finances to complete tax returns.

Production Timing A second consideration in choosing a production process is timing. A **continuous process** uses long production runs that can last days, weeks, or months without equipment shutdowns. It is best for high-volume, low-variety products with standardized parts, such as nails, glass, and paper. Some services also use a continuous process. Your local electric company is one example. Per-unit costs are low, and production is easy to schedule.

In an **intermittent process**, short production runs are used to make batches of different products. Machines are shut down to change them to make different products at different times. This process is best for low-volume, high-variety products, such as those produced by mass customization or customization. Job shops are examples of firms using an intermittent process.

Although some service companies use continuous processes, most rely on intermittent processes. For instance, a restaurant preparing gourmet meals, a physician performing physical examinations or surgical operations, and an advertising agency developing ad campaigns for business clients all customize their services to suit each customer. They use the intermittent process. Note that their "production runs" might be very short—one grilled salmon or one eye exam at a time.

concept check

Define process manufacturing and the assembly process.

What is the difference between continuous and intermittent processes?

Exhibit 11.3 | Converting Inputs to Outputs

TYPE OF ORGANIZATION	INPUT	OUTPUT
Airline	Pilots, crew, flight attendants, reservations system, ticketing agents, customers, airplanes, fuel, maintenance crews, ground facilities	Movement of customers and freight
Grocery store	Merchandise, building, clerks, supervisors, store fixtures, shopping carts, customers	Groceries for customers
High school	Faculty, curriculum, buildings, classrooms, library, auditorium, gymnasium, students, staff, supplies	Graduates, public service
Manufacturer	Machinery, raw materials, plant, workers, managers	Finished products for consumers and other firms
Restaurant	Food, cooking equipment, serving personnel, chefs, dishwashers, host, patrons, furniture, fixtures	Meals for patrons

General Motors operates a 111,500-square-metre plant in Silao, Mexico. The plant employs 3,000 workers and builds Chevy Suburbans. Access to low-cost labour was a major factor in GM's choice of Mexico for its plant location.

© DANNY LEHMAN / CORBIS

3 *learning goal*

Location, Location, Location: Where Do We Make It?

A big decision that managers must make early in production and operations planning is where to put the facility, be it a factory or a service office. The facility's location affects operating and shipping costs and, ultimately, the price of the product or service and the company's ability to compete. Mistakes made at this stage can be expensive, because moving a factory or service facility once production begins is difficult and costly. Firms must weigh a number of factors to make the right decision.

Making Ethical Choices

SWEATING IT OUT AT NEW ERA CAP

As production manager for New Era Cap, the largest North American manufacturer of ball caps, you supervise operations at three factories. The oldest plant, in Derby, New York, has 600 workers and produces 120,000 caps a week, the lowest production rate of the three plants. The Derby factory also has the highest worker absentee rate of any plant, with as many as 13 percent of workers calling in sick on any given day.

In an attempt to bring the Derby plant up to the same level of efficiency as the other two, you've implemented several changes in the past few years. You've introduced new production schedules, made staff cuts, and tried to reduce absentee rates.

Unhappy with the changes you've made, Derby workers went on strike 10 months ago. After New Era executives refused to settle with the striking workers' demands for reduced hours and pay raises, their union, the Communications Workers of America (CWA), issued public statements accusing the Derby plant of "sweatshop" working conditions. At the CWA's urging, the United Students Against Sweatshops (USAS) started a campaign to get colleges and universities to boycott New Era caps. Several universities have already joined the boycott.

You are convinced that the Derby plant is not a sweatshop. You've shifted most of Derby's production to New Era's other two factories with minimal problems. The union now says it will end the strike and call off the boycott if the company grants immediate pay raises and health benefit increases to all Derby workers. You feel this is blackmail.

ETHICAL DILEMMA

Should you recommend that New Era's president agree to the union's demands?

SOURCES: "New Era Union Plans Boycott," *Buffalo Business First*, July 20, 2001; "Cap Maker Shifts Production after Walkout," *Buffalo Business First*, July 16, 2001; "New Era Says 'Sweatshop' Label Is False," *Buffalo Business First*, June 4, 2002; "New Era Cap Makes New Offer to CWA Strikers," *Buffalo Business First*, February 26, 2002; all sources downloaded from http://buffalo.bizjournals.com.

Availability of Production Inputs As we discussed earlier, organizations need certain resources to produce products and services for sale. Access to these resources, or inputs, is a huge consideration in site selection. Executives must assess the availability of raw materials, parts, and equipment for each production site under consideration. The costs of shipping raw materials and finished goods can be as much as 25 percent of a manufacturer's total cost, so locating a factory where these and other costs are as low as possible can make a major contribution to a firm's success. Companies that use heavy or bulky raw materials, for example, might choose to be located near suppliers. Metal refiners want to be near ore deposits, oil refiners near oil fields, paper mills near forests, and food processors near farms.

The availability and cost of labour are also very important to both manufacturing and service businesses. Payroll costs can vary widely from one location to another because of differences in the cost of living, the number of jobs available, and the skills and productivity of the local workforce. The unionization of the local labour force is another point to consider in many industries.

Low labour costs were one reason why Globe Motors, a manufacturer of motors and power steering systems for automotive, aerospace, and defence applications, chose Portugal as the site for its production facility. In addition to low labour costs, Portugal offers manufacturers the lowest operating costs in the European Union.[2]

Marketing Factors Businesses must also evaluate how their facility location will affect their ability to serve their customers. For some firms, it might not be necessary to be located near customers. Instead, the firm will need to assess the difficulty and costs of distributing its goods to customers from the chosen location.

Other firms might find that locating near customers can provide marketing advantages. When a factory or service centre is close to customers, the firm can often offer better service at a lower cost. Other firms might gain a competitive advantage by locating their facilities so that customers can easily buy their products or services. The location of competitors might also be a factor. Businesses with more than one facility might also need to consider how far to spread their locations to maximize market coverage. Globe Motors decided to build its new production facility in Europe because the continent is a major market for Globe's products. By building its motors closer to this large customer base, rather than exporting them to Europe after producing them elsewhere, Globe believes it will be able to improve customer service and response time.[3]

HOT Links

Learn more about the products Globe Motors manufactures at http://www.globe-motors.com.

Manufacturing Environment Another factor to consider is the manufacturing environment in a potential location. Some localities have a strong existing manufacturing base. When a large number of manufacturers, perhaps in a certain industry, are already located in an area, that area is likely to offer greater availability of resources, such as manufacturing workers, better accessibility to suppliers and transportation, and other factors that can increase a plant's operating efficiency.

Industry Week magazine conducts a regular survey of the manufacturing climate offered by metropolitan areas around the world. Each metropolitan area is rated on the productivity of its manufacturing sector, the percentage of the local workforce employed in manufacturing, the contribution of manufacturing to the area's overall economy, and several other factors. Though not necessarily the largest manufacturing cities in the world, the top-rated cities are considered "world-class" manufacturing cities by *Industry Week*. Past cities have included Barcelona, Spain; Houston, Texas; Milan/Turin, Italy; Osaka, Japan; Portland, Oregon; San José, California; and Singapore.[4]

HOT Links

What characteristics contribute to a city's manufacturing climate? Find out by reading more at Industry Week's Web site:

http://www.industryweek.com.

Local Incentives Incentives offered by countries, states, or cities might also influence site selection. Tax breaks are a common incentive. A locality might reduce the amount of taxes the firm will pay on income, real estate, utilities, or payroll. Local governments also sometimes offer exemption from certain regulations or financial assistance to attract or keep production facilities in their area. For example, Portugal helped entice Globe Motors by offering $7.6 million USD in financial incentives, as well as tax breaks and assistance with employee-training programs.[5]

International Location Considerations Like Globe Motors, many manufacturers have chosen to move much of their production to international locations in recent years. There are often sound financial reasons for considering this step. Labour costs are considerably lower in countries like Singapore, China, and Mexico. Foreign countries might also have fewer regulations governing how factories operate. A foreign location might place production closer to new markets. As we've seen, all of these considerations motivated Globe Motors to build a new production facility in Portugal.

Consulting firm KPMG LLP, Canada, recently conducted a study that examined the cost of doing business in nine industrial countries. The study measured 27 factors, including labour, taxes, government regulatory costs, and utilities. Canada was found to be the least expensive country overall, especially for the manufacturing of electronics and specialty chemicals. Germany and Japan were ranked as the most expensive, followed by the United States. Exhibit 11.4 summarizes the study's results.

Exhibit 11.4 | Cost of Doing Business: Least to Most Expensive Countries

1. Singapore
2. Canada
3. France
4. Netherlands
5. Italy
6. UK
7. United States
8. Japan
9. Germany

SOURCE: KPMG "2006 Competitive Alternatives Study." http://www.kpmg.ca/en/news/pr20060321.html (accessed Nov 20, 2006).

Discuss how each of the following impacts the location of production:

- *Availability of production inputs*
- *Marketing factors*
- *Manufacturing environment*
- *Local incentives*
- *International location considerations*

Designing the Facility

After the site location decision has been made, the next focus in production planning is the facility's layout. Here, the goal is to determine the most efficient and effective design for the particular production process. A manufacturer might opt for a U-shaped production line, for example, rather than a long, straight one to allow products and workers to move more quickly from one area to another.

Service organizations must also consider layout, but they are more concerned with how it affects customer behaviour. It might be more convenient for a hospital to place its freight elevators in the centre of the building, for example, but doing so might block the flow of patients, visitors, and medical personnel between floors and departments.

There are three main types of facility layouts: process, product, and fixed-position layouts. All three are illustrated in Exhibit 11.5. Cellular manufacturing is another type of facility layout.

Process Layout: All Welders Stand Here The **process layout** arranges workflow around the production process. All workers performing similar tasks are grouped together. Products pass from one workstation to another (but not necessarily to every workstation). For example, all grinding would be done in one area, all assembling in another, and all inspection in yet another. The process layout is best for firms that produce small numbers of a wide variety of products, typically using general-purpose machines that can be changed rapidly to new operations for different product designs. For example, a manufacturer of custom machinery would use a process layout.

process layout

A facility arrangement in which work flows according to the production process. All workers performing similar tasks are grouped together, and products pass from one workstation to another.

A product or assembly line layout, described on page 344.

Exhibit 11.5 | Facility Layouts

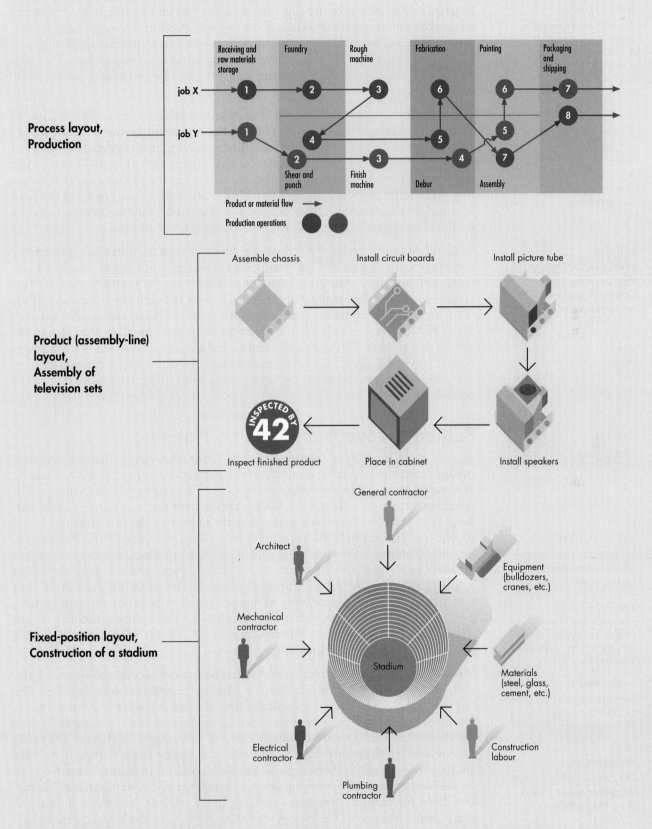

Process layout, Production

Receiving and raw materials storage — Foundry — Rough machine — Fabrication — Painting — Packaging and shipping

Shear and punch — Finish machine — Debur — Assembly

job X
job Y

Product or material flow →
Production operations ⬤ ⬤

Product (assembly-line) layout, Assembly of television sets

Assemble chassis → Install circuit boards → Install picture tube

Inspect finished product ← Place in cabinet ← Install speakers

INSPECTED BY 42

Fixed-position layout, Construction of a stadium

General contractor
Architect
Mechanical contractor
Electrical contractor
Plumbing contractor
Stadium
Equipment (bulldozers, cranes, etc.)
Materials (steel, glass, cement, etc.)
Construction labour

SOURCE: From *Production and Operations Management* (Text Only) 9th edition by GAITHER/FRAZIER. 2002. Reprinted with permission of South-Western, a division of Thomson Learning: www.thomsonrights.com. Fax 800 730-2215.

product (assembly line) layout

A facility arrangement in which workstations or departments are arranged in a line with products moving along the line.

Product Layout: Moving Down the Line Products that require a continuous or repetitive production process use the **product** (or **assembly line**) **layout**. When large quantities of a product must be processed on an ongoing basis, the workstations or departments are arranged in a line with products moving along the line. Automobile and appliance manufacturers, as well as food-processing plants, usually use a product layout. Service companies may also use a product layout for routine processing operations. For example, overnight film processors use assembly line techniques.

fixed-position layout

A facility arrangement in which the product stays in one place and workers and machinery move to it as needed.

Fixed-Position Layout: Staying Put Some products cannot be put on an assembly line or moved about in a plant. A **fixed-position layout** lets the product stay in one place while workers and machinery move to it as needed. Products that are impossible to move—ships, airplanes, and construction projects—are typically produced using a fixed-position layout. Limited space at a project site often means that parts of the product must be assembled at other sites, transported to the fixed site, and then assembled. Other examples of the fixed-position layout are on-site services like housecleaning services, pest control, and landscaping.

cellular manufacturing

Production technique that uses small, self-contained production units, each performing all or most of the tasks necessary to complete a manufacturing order.

Cellular Manufacturing: A Start-to-finish Focus **Cellular manufacturing** combines some aspects of both product and fixed-position layout. Work cells are small, self-contained production units that include several machines and workers arranged in a compact, sequential order. Each work cell performs all or most of the tasks necessary to complete a manufacturing order. There are usually between 5 and 10 workers in a cell, and they are trained to perform all of the steps in the production process. The goal is to create a team environment where team members are involved in production from beginning to end. Clothing manufacturing can use cellular manufacturing by having small work cells completing all the work of each order.

4 learning goal

Pulling It Together: Resource Planning

As part of the production-planning process, firms must ensure that the resources needed for production, such as raw materials, parts, and equipment, will be available at strategic moments in the production process. This can be a huge challenge. The components used to build just one Boeing airplane, for instance, number in the millions. Cost is also an important factor. In many industries, the cost of materials and supplies used in the production process amounts to as much as half of sales revenues. Resource planning is therefore a big part of any firm's production strategy. Resource planners begin by specifying which raw materials, parts, and components will be required, and when, to produce finished goods. To determine the amount of each item needed, the expected quantity of finished goods to be produced must be forecast. A **bill of material** is then drawn up that lists the items and the number of each required to make the product. **Purchasing**, or *procurement*, is the process of buying production inputs from various sources.

bill of material

A list of the items and the number of each required to make a given product.

purchasing

The process of buying production inputs from various sources; also called *procurement*.

make-or-buy decision

The determination by a firm of whether to make its production materials or buy them from outside sources.

outsourcing

The purchase of items from an outside source rather than making them internally.

Make or Buy? Next, the firm must decide whether to make its production materials or buy them from outside sources. This is the **make-or-buy decision**. The quantity of items needed is one consideration. If a part is used in only one of many products, buying the part might be more cost-effective than making it. Buying standard items, such as screws, bolts, rivets, and nails, is usually cheaper and easier than producing them internally. Sometimes purchasing larger components from another manufacturing firm is cost-effective as well. Purchasing items from an outside source instead of making them internally is called **outsourcing**. Harley-Davidson, for example, purchases its tires, brake systems, and other motorcycle components from other businesses that make them to Harley's specifications. If a

inventory

The supply of goods that a firm holds for use in production or for sale to customers.

inventory management

The determination of how much of each type of inventory a firm will keep on hand and the ordering, receiving, storing, and tracking of inventory.

perpetual inventory

A continuously updated list of inventory levels, orders, sales, and receipts.

product has special design features that need to be kept secret to protect a competitive advantage, however, a firm might decide to produce all parts internally.

In deciding whether to make or buy, a firm must also consider whether outside sources can provide high-quality supplies in a reliable manner. Having to shut down production because vital parts weren't delivered on time can be a costly disaster. Just as bad are inferior parts or materials, which can damage a firm's reputation for producing high-quality goods. Therefore, firms that buy some or all of their production materials from outside sources should pay close attention to building strong relationships with quality suppliers.

Inventory Management: Not Just Parts A firm's **inventory** is the supply of goods it holds for use in production or for sale to customers. Deciding how much inventory to keep on hand is one of the biggest challenges facing operations managers. With large inventories, the firm can meet most production and customer demands. Buying in large quantities can also allow a company to take advantage of quantity discounts. On the other hand, large inventories can tie up the firm's money, are expensive to store, and can become obsolete.

Inventory management involves deciding how much of each type of inventory to keep on hand and the ordering, receiving, storing, and tracking of it. The goal of inventory management is to keep down the costs of ordering and holding inventories while maintaining enough on hand for production and sales. Good inventory management enhances product quality, makes operations more efficient, and increases profits. Poor inventory management can result in dissatisfied customers, financial difficulties, and even bankruptcy.

One way to determine the best inventory levels is to look at three costs: the cost of holding inventory, the cost of reordering frequently, and the cost of not keeping enough inventory on hand. Managers must measure all three costs and try to minimize them.

To control inventory levels, managers often track the use of certain inventory items. Most companies keep a **perpetual inventory**, a continuously updated list of inventory levels, orders, sales, and receipts, for all major items. Today, companies

Because millions of parts are required to build a jet, inventory management is critical for aerospace manufacturers like Boeing. Computerized resource planning systems are used to help track and schedule the flow of parts, raw materials, and equipment so they are available to production workers at the correct time.

© ED KASHI / CORBIS

often use computers to track inventory levels, calculate order quantities, and issue purchase orders at the right times.

Computerized Resource Planning Many manufacturing companies have adopted computerized systems to control the flow of resources and inventory. **Materials requirement planning (MRP)** is one such system. MRP uses a master schedule to ensure that the materials, labour, and equipment needed for production are at the right places in the right amounts at the right times. The schedule is based on forecasts of demand for the company's products. It says exactly what will be manufactured during the next few weeks or months and when the work will take place. Sophisticated computer programs coordinate all the elements of MRP. The computer comes up with materials requirements by comparing production needs to the materials the company already has on hand. Orders are placed so that items will be on hand when they are needed for production. MRP helps ensure a smooth flow of finished products.

Manufacturing resource planning II (MRPII) was developed in the late 1980s to expand on MRP. It uses a complex computerized system to integrate data from many departments, including finance, marketing, accounting, engineering, and manufacturing. MRPII can generate a production plan for the firm, as well as management reports, forecasts, and financial statements. The system lets managers make more accurate forecasts and assess the impact of production plans on profitability. If one department's plans change, the effects of these changes on other departments are transmitted throughout the company.

Whereas MRP and MRPII systems are focused internally, **enterprise resource planning (ERP)** systems go a step further and incorporate information about the firm's suppliers and customers into the flow of data. ERP unites all of a firm's major departments into a single software program. For instance, production can call up sales information and know immediately how many units must be produced to meet customer orders. By providing information about the availability of resources, including both human resources and materials needed for production, the system allows for better cost control and eliminates production delays. The system automatically notes any changes, such as the closure of a plant for maintenance and repairs on a certain date or a supplier's inability to meet a delivery date, so that all functions can adjust accordingly. Both large and small organizations use ERP to improve operations.

Keeping the Goods Flowing: Supply Chain Management

In the past, the relationship between purchasers and suppliers was often competitive and antagonistic. Businesses used many suppliers and switched among them frequently. During contract negotiations, each side would try to get better terms at the expense of the other. Communication between purchasers and suppliers was often limited to purchase orders and billing statements.

Today, however, many firms are moving toward a new concept in supplier relationships. The emphasis is increasingly on developing a strong **supply chain**. The supply chain can be thought of as the entire sequence of securing inputs, producing goods, and delivering goods to customers. If any links in this process are weak, chances are that customers—the end point of the supply chain—will end up dissatisfied.

Strategies for Supply Chain Management Ensuring a strong supply chain requires that firms implement supply chain management strategies. **Supply chain management** focuses on smoothing transitions along the supply chain, with the ultimate goal of satisfying customers with quality products and services. A critical element of effective supply chain management is to develop tighter bonds with suppliers. In many cases, this means reducing the number of suppliers used and

---

materials requirement planning (MRP)
A computerized system of controlling the flow of resources and inventory. A master schedule is used to ensure that the materials, labour, and equipment needed for production are at the right places in the right amounts at the right times.

manufacturing resource planning II (MRPII)
A complex computerized system that integrates data from many departments to allow managers to forecast and assess the impact of production plans on profitability more accurately.

enterprise resource planning (ERP)
A computerized resource-planning system that incorporates information about the firm's suppliers and customers with its internally generated data.

supply chain
The entire sequence of securing inputs, producing goods, and delivering goods to customers.

supply chain management
The process of smoothing transitions along the supply chain, so that the firm can satisfy its customers with quality products and services; focuses on developing tighter bonds with suppliers.

asking those suppliers to offer more services or better prices in return for an ongoing relationship. Instead of being viewed as "outsiders" in the production process, many suppliers are now playing an important role in supporting the operations of their customers. They are expected to meet higher quality standards, offer suggestions that can help reduce production costs, and even contribute to the design of new products.

Talk to Us: Improving Supplier Communications Effective supply chain management requires the development of strong communications with suppliers. Technology, particularly the Internet, is providing new ways to do this. **E-procurement**, the process of purchasing supplies and materials on-line, is booming. Some manufacturing firms use the Internet to keep key suppliers informed about their requirements. Intel, for example, has set up a special Web site for its suppliers and potential suppliers. Would-be suppliers can visit the site to get information about doing business with Intel; once they are approved, they can access a secure area to make bids on Intel's current and future resource needs.

The Internet also streamlines purchasing by providing firms with quick access to a huge database of information about the products and services of hundreds of potential suppliers. Many large manufacturers now participate in *reverse auctions* on-line, whereby the manufacturer posts its specifications for the materials it requires. Potential suppliers then bid against each other to get the job. Reverse auctions can slash procurement costs. Owens Corning, for example, has cut materials costs by 10 percent through on-line auction procurement.

However, there are risks with reverse auctions. For example, it can be difficult to establish and build ongoing relationships with specific suppliers using reverse auctions, because the job ultimately goes to the lowest bidder. Therefore, reverse auctions might not be an effective procurement process for critical production materials.[6]

Another communications tool is **electronic data interchange (EDI)**, in which two trading partners exchange information electronically. EDI can be conducted via a linked computer system or over the Internet. The advantages of exchanging information with suppliers electronically include speed, accuracy, and lowered communication costs.

Dana Corporation, a manufacturer of auto and truck frames, has only one customer, New United Motor Manufacturing Inc. (NUMMI), a joint venture between Toyota and General Motors. In the past, NUMMI could give Dana only a six-week production forecast. A fax was sent to Dana each day updating NUMMI's needs. Dana and NUMMI then installed an EDI system that continually alerts Dana about NUMMI's purchasing requirements on an hourly basis. As a result, Dana has been able to cut its inventory, smooth its production scheduling, and meet NUMMI's needs more efficiently and rapidly.[7]

e-procurement
The process of purchasing supplies and materials on-line using the Internet.

electronic data interchange (EDI)
The electronic exchange of information between two trading partners.

concept check

What are the four types of decisions that must be made in production planning?
How is technology being used in resource planning?

PRODUCTION AND OPERATIONS CONTROL

5   learning goal

routing
The aspect of production control that involves setting out the workflow, the sequence of machines and operations through which the product or service progresses from start to finish.

Every company needs to have systems in place to see that production and operations are carried out as planned and to correct errors when they are not. The coordination of materials, equipment, and human resources to achieve production and operating efficiencies is called *production control*. Two of its key aspects are **routing** and scheduling.

Routing: Where to Next?

Routing is the first step in production control. It sets out a workflow, that is, the sequence of machines and operations through which a product or service progresses from start to finish. Routing depends on the type of goods being produced and the facility layout. Good routing procedures increase productivity and cut unnecessary costs.

One useful tool for routing is **value-stream mapping**, where production managers "map" the flow from suppliers through the factory to customers. Simple icons represent the materials and information needed at various points in the flow. Value-stream mapping can help identify where bottlenecks might occur in the production process and is a valuable tool for visualizing how to improve production routing.

Medical manufacturer Medtronic, Inc., used value-stream mapping to understand more fully how materials and information were routed through its production plant. The company identified 48 streams for the various products the plant produced. From the map, Medtronic was able to determine where waste and slowdowns were most likely to occur and to develop an improvement plan that reduced standard production cycle time, cut inventory levels, and improved overall productivity.[8]

Scheduling: When Do We Do It?

Closely related to routing is **scheduling**. Scheduling involves specifying and controlling the time required for each step in the production process. The operations manager prepares timetables showing the most efficient sequence of production and then tries to ensure that the necessary materials and labour are in the right place at the right time.

Scheduling is important to both manufacturing and service firms. The production manager in a factory schedules material deliveries, work shifts, and production processes. Trucking companies schedule drivers, clerks, truck maintenance, and repair with customer transportation needs. Scheduling at a college entails deciding when to offer which courses, in which classrooms, with which instructors. A museum must schedule its special exhibits, ship the works to be displayed, market its services, and conduct educational programs and tours.

Scheduling can range from simple to complex. Giving numbers to customers waiting to be served in a bakery and making interview appointments with job applicants are examples of simple scheduling. Organizations that must produce large quantities of products or services, or service a diverse customer base, face more complex scheduling problems.

Three common scheduling tools used for complex situations are Gantt charts, the critical path method, and PERT.

Tracking Progress with Gantt Charts Named after their originator, Henry Gantt, **Gantt charts** are bar graphs plotted on a timeline that show the relationship between scheduled and actual production. Exhibit 11.6 is an example. On the left, the chart lists the activities required to complete the job or project. Both the scheduled time and the actual time required for each activity are shown, so the manager can easily judge progress.

Gantt charts are most helpful when only a few tasks are involved, when task times are relatively long (days or weeks rather than hours), and when job routes are short and simple. One of the biggest shortcomings of Gantt charts is that they are static. They also fail to show how tasks are related. These problems can be

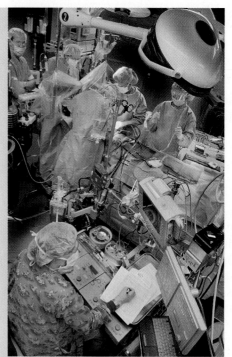

Routing and scheduling are just as important to service organizations as they are to manufacturing firms. Hospitals, for instance, must carefully schedule the equipment, personnel, and facilities needed to conduct patient surgeries and other treatments.

value-stream mapping
Routing technique that uses simple icons to visually represent the flow of materials and information from suppliers through the factory and to customers.

scheduling
The aspect of production control that involves specifying and controlling the time required for each step in the production process.

Gantt charts
Bar graphs plotted on a timeline that show the relationship between scheduled and actual production.

HOT Links

Learn how to build your own Gantt chart at http://www.mindtools.com/pages/article/newPPM_03.htm.

Exhibit 11.6 | A Typical Gantt Chart

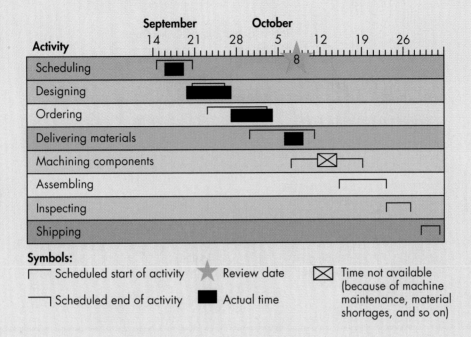

Symbols:

⌐ Scheduled start of activity	★ Review date
⌐ Scheduled end of activity	■ Actual time
⊠ Time not available (because of machine maintenance, material shortages, and so on)	

solved, however, by using two other scheduling techniques, the critical path method and PERT.

The Big Picture: Critical Path Method and PERT To control large projects, operations managers need to closely monitor resources, costs, quality, and budgets. They also must be able to see the "big picture"—the interrelationships of the many tasks necessary to complete the project. Finally, they must be able to revise scheduling and divert resources quickly if any tasks fall behind schedule. The critical path method (CPM) and the program evaluation and review technique (PERT) are related project management tools that were developed in the 1950s to help managers accomplish this.

In the **critical path method (CPM)**, the manager identifies all of the activities required to complete the project, the relationships between these activities, and the order in which they need to be completed. Then, he or she develops a diagram that uses arrows to show how the tasks are dependent on each other. The longest path through these linked activities is called the **critical path**. If the tasks on the critical path are not completed on time, the entire project will fall behind schedule.

To understand better how CPM works, look at Exhibit 11.7, which shows a CPM diagram for constructing a house. All of the tasks required to finish the house and an estimated time for each have been identified. The arrows indicate the links between the various steps and their required sequence. As you can see, most of the jobs to be done can't be started until the house's foundation and frame are completed. It will take five days to finish the foundation and an additional seven days to erect the house frame. The activities linked by red arrows form the critical path for this project. It tells us that the fastest possible time the house can be built is 38 days, the total time needed for all of the critical path tasks. The non-critical path jobs, those connected with black arrows, can be delayed a bit or done early. Short delays in installing appliances or roofing won't delay construction of the house, for example, because these activities don't lie on the critical path.

critical path method (CPM)

A scheduling tool that enables a manager to determine the critical path of activities for a project—the activities that will cause the entire project to fall behind schedule if they are not completed on time.

critical path

In a critical path method network, the longest path through the linked activities.

Exhibit 11.7 A CPM Network for Building a House

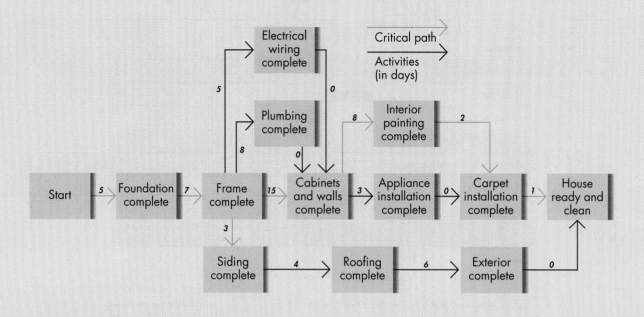

program evaluation and review technique (PERT)

A scheduling tool that is similar to the CPM method but assigns three time estimates for each activity (optimistic, most probable, and pessimistic); allows managers to anticipate delays and potential problems and schedule accordingly.

Like CPM, **program evaluation and review technique (PERT)** helps managers identify critical tasks and assess how delays in certain activities will affect operations or production. In both methods, managers use diagrams to see how operations and production will flow. PERT differs from CPM in one important respect, however. CPM assumes that the amount of time needed to finish a task is known with certainty; therefore, the CPM diagram shows only one number for the time needed to complete each activity. In contrast, PERT assigns three time estimates for each activity: an optimistic time for completion, the most probable time, and a pessimistic time. These estimates allow managers to anticipate delays and potential problems and schedule accordingly.

What is production control, and what are its key aspects?

Identify and describe three commonly used scheduling tools.

LOOKING FOR A BETTER WAY: IMPROVING PRODUCTION AND OPERATIONS

6 *learning goal*

Competing in today's business world is challenging. To compete effectively, firms must keep production costs down. At the same time, however, it's becoming increasingly complex to produce and deliver the high-quality goods and services customers demand. Methods to help meet these challenges include quality management techniques, lean manufacturing, and automation.

Putting Quality First

Successful businesses recognize that quality and productivity must go hand in hand. **Quality** goods and services meet customer expectations by providing reliable performance. Defective products waste materials and time, increasing costs. Worse, poor quality causes customer dissatisfaction, which usually means lost sales.

A consumer measures quality by how well a good serves its purpose. From the company's point of view, quality is the degree to which a good conforms to a set of predetermined standards. **Quality control** involves creating those quality standards, producing goods that meet them, and measuring finished products and services against them. It takes more than just inspecting goods at the end of the assembly line to ensure quality control, however. Quality control requires a company-wide dedication to managing and working in a way that builds excellence into every facet of operations.

Dr. W. Edwards Deming, an American management consultant, was the first to say that quality control should be a company-wide goal. His ideas were adopted by the Japanese in the 1950s but were largely ignored in the United States until the 1970s. Deming believed that quality control must start with top management, who must foster a culture dedicated to producing quality.

Deming's concept of **Total Quality Management (TQM)** emphasizes the use of quality principles in all aspects of a company's production and operations. It recognizes that all employees involved with bringing a product or service to customers—marketing, purchasing, accounting, shipping, manufacturing—contribute to its quality. TQM focuses on **continuous improvement**, a constant commitment to seeking better ways of doing things to achieve greater efficiency and improve quality. Company-wide teams work together to prevent problems and systematically improve key processes instead of troubleshooting problems only as they arise. Continuous improvement continually measures performance using statistical techniques and looks for ways to apply new technologies and innovative production methods.

Another quality control method is the **Six Sigma** quality program. Six Sigma is a company-wide process that focuses on measuring the number of defects that occur and systematically eliminating them to get as close to "zero defects" as possible. In

quality
Goods and services that meet customer expectations by providing reliable performance.

quality control
The process of creating standards for quality, producing goods that meet them, and measuring finished products and services against them.

total quality management (TQM)
The use of quality principles in all aspects of a company's production and operations.

continuous improvement
A constant commitment to seeking better ways of doing things to achieve greater efficiency and improve quality.

Six Sigma
A quality control process that relies on defining what needs to be done to ensure quality, measuring and analyzing production results statistically, and finding ways of improving and controlling quality.

The Six Sigma quality program directly involves production employees in setting quality standards and in measuring and analyzing finished goods to ensure that quality has been achieved. Here, a worker in an electronics factory inspects a finished circuit board, looking for any defects.

© AP / WORLD WIDE PHOTOS

fact, Six Sigma quality aims to have every process produce no more than 3.4 defects per million. Six Sigma focuses on designing products that not only have fewer defects but also satisfy customer needs. A key process of Six Sigma is called *DMAIC*. This stands for Define, Measure, Analyze, Improve, and Control. Employees at all levels define what needs to be done to ensure quality, then measure and analyze production results using statistics to see if the standards are met. They are also charged with finding ways of improving and controlling quality.

General Electric was one of the first companies to institute Six Sigma throughout the organization. All GE employees are trained in Six Sigma concepts, and many analysts believe this has given GE a competitive manufacturing advantage. Service firms have applied Six Sigma to their quality initiatives as well.

Worldwide Excellence: International Quality Standards

The International Organization for Standardization (ISO), located in Belgium, is an industry organization that has developed standards of quality that are used by businesses around the world. **ISO 9000**, introduced in the 1980s, is a set of five technical standards designed to offer a uniform way of determining whether manufacturing plants and service organizations conform to sound quality procedures. To register, a company must go through an audit of its manufacturing and customer service processes, covering everything from how it designs, produces, and installs its goods to how it inspects, packages, and markets them. More than 500,000 organizations worldwide have met ISO 9000 standards.

ISO 14000, launched after ISO 9000, is designed to promote clean production processes in response to environmental issues such as global warming and water pollution. To meet ISO 14000 standards, a company must commit to improving environmental management continually and reducing pollution resulting from its production processes. Some accredited ISO 14000 organizations include ASQR Canada, Intertek Testing Services NA Limited, and KPMG Performance Registrar Inc.

Lean Manufacturing Trims the Fat

Manufacturers are discovering that they can respond better to rapidly changing customer demands, while keeping inventory and production costs down, by adopting lean manufacturing techniques. **Lean manufacturing** streamlines production by eliminating steps in the production process that do not add benefits that customers are willing to pay for. In other words, *non–value-added production processes* are cut, so that the company can concentrate its production and operations resources on items essential to satisfying customers. Toyota was a pioneer in developing these techniques, but today manufacturers in many industries subscribe to the lean-manufacturing philosophy.

Another Japanese concept, **just-in-time (JIT)**, goes hand in hand with lean manufacturing. JIT is based on the belief that materials should arrive exactly when they are needed for production rather than being stored on-site. Relying closely on computerized systems such as MRP, MRPII, and ERP, manufacturers determine what parts will be needed and when, and then order them from suppliers, so they arrive "just in time." Under the JIT system, inventory and products are "pulled" through the production process in response to customer demand. JIT requires close teamwork between vendors and purchasing and production personnel, because any delay in deliveries of supplies could bring JIT production to a halt.

HOT Links

Learn more about Six Sigma at the Knowledge Management Group's Web site, http://www.tkmg.org/services.html.

ISO 9000

A set of five technical standards of quality management created by the International Organization for Standardization to provide a uniform way of determining whether manufacturing plants and service organizations conform to sound quality procedures.

ISO 14000

A set of technical standards designed by the International Organization for Standardization to promote clean production processes to protect the environment.

lean manufacturing

Streamlining production by eliminating steps in the production process that do not add benefits that customers are willing to pay for.

just-in-time (JIT)

A system in which materials arrive exactly when they are needed for production rather than being stored on-site.

HOT Links

Quality Management Products of Oakville, Ontario, helps its customers to improve their organization with a comprehensive line of quality software products and services. Visit their Web site at http://www.qmproducts.com.

Transforming the Factory Floor with Technology

Technology is helping many firms improve their operating efficiency and ability to compete. Computer systems, in particular, are enabling manufacturers to automate factories in ways never before possible.

Among the technologies helping to automate manufacturing are computer-aided design and manufacturing systems, robotics, flexible manufacturing systems, and computer-integrated manufacturing.

Computer-Aided Design and Manufacturing Systems Computers have transformed the design and manufacturing processes in many industries. In **computer-aided design (CAD)**, computers are used to design and test new products and modify existing ones. Engineers use these systems to draw products and look at them from different angles. They can analyze the products, make changes, and test prototypes before making even one item. **Computer-aided manufacturing (CAM)** uses computers to develop and control the production process. The systems analyze the steps required to make the product. They then automatically send instructions to the machines that do the work. **CAD/CAM systems** combine the advantages of CAD and CAM by integrating design, testing, and manufacturing control into one linked computer system. The system helps design the product, control the flow of resources needed to produce the product, and operate the production process.

Cardianove Inc., a Montreal-based manufacturer of medical and surgical equipment, used CAD software to develop the world's smallest heart pump. The company says using computer-aided design shaved two years off the normal design time for cardiac devices. The company's CAD program ran complex three-dimensional simulations to confirm that the design would function properly inside the human body. Cardionove tested more than 100 virtual prototypes using the software before the top three designs were actually produced for real-life testing.[9]

Robotics *Robots* are computer-controlled machines that can perform tasks independently. **Robotics** is the technology involved in designing, constructing, and operating robots. The first robot, or "steel-collar worker," was used by General Motors in 1961. Today the company has more than 25,000 robots at work in its plants.[10]

Robots can be mobile or fixed in one place. Fixed robots have an arm that moves and does what the computer instructs. Some robots are quite simple, with limited movement for a few tasks such as cutting sheet metal and spot welding. Others are complex, with hands or grippers that can be programmed to perform a series of movements. Some robots are even equipped with sensing devices for sight and touch.

Robots usually operate with little or no human intervention. Replacing human effort with robots is most effective for tasks requiring accuracy, speed, or strength. Although manufacturers such as Harley-Davidson, as described at the beginning of this chapter, are most likely to use robots, some service firms are also finding them useful. Some hospitals, for example, use robots to sort and process blood samples, freeing medical personnel from a tedious, sometimes hazardous, repetitive task.

Adaptable Factories: Flexible Manufacturing Systems A **flexible manufacturing system (FMS)** automates a factory by blending computers, robots, machine tools, and materials-and-parts-handling machinery into an integrated system. These systems combine automated workstations with computer-controlled transportation devices. Automatic guided vehicles (AGVs) move materials between workstations and into and out of the system.

Flexible manufacturing systems are expensive. Once in place, however, a system requires little labour to operate and provides consistent product quality. The system can be changed easily and inexpensively. FMS equipment can be programmed to perform one job and then quickly be reprogrammed to perform another. These systems work well when small batches of a variety of products are required or when each product is made to individual customer specifications.

---

7 *learning goal*

computer-aided design (CAD)

The use of computers to design and test new products and modify existing ones.

computer-aided manufacturing (CAM)

The use of computers to develop and control the production process.

CAD/CAM systems

Linked computer systems that combine the advantages of *computer-aided design* and *computer-aided manufacturing*. The system helps design the product, control the flow of resources, and operate the production process.

robotics

The technology involved in designing, constructing, and operating computer-controlled machines that can perform tasks independently.

HOT *Links*

Want to know more about how robots work? Find out at http://electronics .howstuffworks.com/robot .htm.

flexible manufacturing system (FMS)

A system that combines automated workstations with computer-controlled transportation devices—automatic guided vehicles (AGVs)—that move materials between workstations and into and out of the system.

---

computer-integrated manufacturing (CIM)

The combination of computerized manufacturing processes (such as robots and flexible manufacturing systems) with other computerized systems that control design, inventory, production, and purchasing.

Quick Change With Computer-Integrated Manufacturing **Computer-integrated manufacturing (CIM)** combines computerized manufacturing processes (like robots and FMS) with other computerized systems that control design, inventory, production, and purchasing. With CIM, when a part is redesigned in the CAD system, the changes are quickly transmitted both to the machines producing the part and to all other departments that need to know about and plan for the change.

Technology and Automation at Your Service

Manufacturers are not the only businesses benefiting from technology. Non-manufacturing firms are also using automation to improve customer service and productivity. Banks now offer services to customers through automated teller machines (ATMs), via automated telephone systems, and even over the Internet. Retail stores of all kinds use point-of-sale (POS) terminals that track inventories, identify items that need to be reordered, and tell which products are selling well. Wal-Mart, the leader in retailing automation, has its own satellite system connecting POS terminals directly to its distribution centres and headquarters.

concept check

Define total quality management, lean manufacturing, and just-in-time, and explain how each can help a firm improve its production and operations.

How are both manufacturing and non-manufacturing firms using technology and automation to improve operations?

Trends in Production and Operations Management

8 *learning goal*

Some manufacturing employment has been eliminated as manufacturers attempt to cut operating costs. Many of these jobs have been moved overseas, where manufacturers have opened new production facilities or contracted out production to foreign firms with lower operating and labour costs. Continued growth in global competition, increasingly complex products, and more demanding consumers continue to force manufacturers to plan carefully how, when, and where they produce the goods they sell. New production techniques and manufacturing technologies are vital to keeping production costs as low as possible and productivity levels high. At the same time, many firms are re-evaluating the productivity of their production facilities and, in some cases, are deciding to close underperforming factories.

Non-manufacturing firms must carefully manage how they use and deploy their resources, while keeping up with the constant pace of technological change. Non-manufacturing firms must be ever vigilant in their search for new ways of streamlining service production and operation to keep their overall costs down.

ASSET MANAGEMENT

In a tight economy, businesses must be careful about how their operating assets are used. From raw materials to inventories and manufacturing equipment, wasted, malfunctioning, or misused assets are costly. For example, one telephone company reported it had lost track of $5 billion worth of communications equipment. "I would say that every big company I have worked with has lost track of many major assets and a plethora of minor ones," said one executive. In fact, when chief financial officers of large companies were surveyed by *CFO Magazine*, 70 percent reported that asset management in their firms was "inefficient" or "erratic."[11]

Asset management software systems, many of which are Internet based, are beginning to help fix this problem. These programs automatically track materials, equipment, and inventory. They also automate inventory management, and maintenance and repairs scheduling.

ChevronTexaco has successfully implemented this type of system in its enormous production facility in Bakersfield, California. The facility is one of the largest outdoor factories in the world, stretching 160 kilometres from north to south, and containing a maze of storage tanks, filtering installations, and pipelines. In all, there are 230,000 separate pieces of equipment and machinery in hundreds of categories in the facility. To manage all of these assets, ChevronTexaco has installed an automated asset management system that schedules preventive maintenance for all equipment and tracks where surplus equipment and supplies are stored. ChevronTexaco estimates it is saving millions of dollars a year in the facility because of more effective asset management.[12]

MODULAR PRODUCTION

Increasingly, manufacturers are relying on *modular production* to speed up and simplify production. Modular production involves breaking a complex product, service, or process into smaller pieces that can be created independently and then combined quickly to make a whole. Modular production not only cuts the cost of developing innovative products but also gives businesses a tool for meeting rapidly changing conditions. It also makes implementation of mass or pure customization strategies easier.

Johnson Controls Inc. (JCI), a manufacturer, works closely with its suppliers to build automotive interiors modularly. JCI uses 11 major components from 35 suppliers to build Jeep Liberty cockpits. The parts, designed to fit and function together, are then assembled in JCI's factory. "Our product development strategy is to build from the best capabilities and technologies in the world, but that doesn't mean they have to be owned and operated by us," says JCI vice president Jeff Edwards.[13]

Toyota focuses design and engineering on "crossover vehicles"—car model designs that appeal to different consumer segments yet are built using many of the same components and parts. This has allowed Toyota's factories to become flexible and modular.

© MICHAEL S. YAMASHITA / CORBIS

DESIGNING PRODUCTS FOR PRODUCTION EFFICIENCY

Today's operations managers recognize that production efficiency must begin *before* the first part reaches the factory floor. As a result, many manufacturers are investing in new methods of integrating product design and engineering with the manufacturing supply chain.

DaimlerChrysler, for example, has instituted a computerized design system dubbed FastCar. FastCar links the computer-aided design process to internal business functions such as production, finance, procurement, and marketing. As cars are designed, all of these groups are immediately able to see how proposed designs will affect production costs, manufacturability, and other factors. The system also alerts suppliers to engineering and production specifications to guarantee receipt of quality parts for new components. FastCar has cut the time required to roll out new products from design to production by 70 percent.[14]

Another developing trend is the use of factory simulation tools for product design. These tools allow product designers to see the effects their designs will have on production equipment. For example, if a design calls for a specific size of drilled hole on a product, factory simulation tools will specify which particular drill bit and machine will be necessary for the task.

concept check

Explain modular production.

Why does production efficiency have to begin before the first part reaches the factory floor?

Great Ideas to Use Now

As we've seen throughout this chapter, every organization produces something. Cereal manufacturers turn grains into breakfast foods. Law firms turn the skills and knowledge of attorneys into legal services. Retailers provide a convenient way for consumers to purchase a variety of goods. Colleges and universities convert students into educated individuals. Therefore, no matter what type of organization you end up working for in the future, you will be involved, to one degree or another, with your employer's production and operations processes.

Some employees, such as plant managers and quality control managers, will have a direct role in the production process. However, employees of manufacturing firms are not the only ones involved with production. Software developers, bank tellers, medical personnel, magazine writers, and a host of other employees are also actively involved in turning inputs into outputs. If you manage people in these types of jobs, you'll need insight into the tools used to plan, schedule, and control production processes. Understanding production processes, resource management, and techniques for increasing productivity is vital to becoming a more valuable employee, who sees how his or her job fits into "the big picture" of the firm's operating goals.

If you plan to start your own business, you'll also face many production and operations decisions. You can use the information from this chapter to help you find suppliers, design an operating facility (no matter how small), and put customer-satisfying processes in place. This information can also help you make decisions about whether to manufacture goods or rely on outside contractors to handle production.

CUSTOMER SATISFACTION AND QUALITY

Although we have talked a great deal in this chapter about methods for producing products faster and less expensively, it is important to remember that the most efficient factory in the world would be deemed a failure if the products it made broke soon after customers purchased them. Underlying every production and operations management decision is a very simple question: How will this affect our customers' satisfaction? To compete in today's marketplace, businesses must make sure they have the right answer.

The Honeywell Control Products plant realized it didn't have the right answer. The plant makes electromechanical snap-action switches that are used in machines such as icemakers and washing machines. In the face of foreign competition in the early 1990s, the plant had developed a successful strategy to improve productivity and reduce manufacturing costs. By 1998, however, it was clear that customers weren't happy. Complaints and returns were constantly rising.

The problem? "We were driving the wrong behaviours," says Cynthia Knautz, manufacturing engineer at the plant. "All of our employee goals were set on output. Our production employees could build 36,000 bad switches in a day and still get rewarded." The plant set up new processes to help track and control quality and tied employee incentives to quality and customer satisfaction. As a result, customer reject rates have dropped dramatically, while production rates have actually increased.

SOURCE: Best Plant Winners 2002: Honeywell Control Products, Industry Week Online, 2002. Reprinted with permission of Penton Media.

Reprinted with the permission of The Calgary Herald.

SUMMARY OF LEARNING GOALS

1 Why are production and operations management important in both manufacturing and service firms?

In the 1980s, many manufacturers lost customers to foreign competitors because their production and operations management systems did not support the high-quality, reasonably priced products consumers demanded. Service organizations also rely on effective operations management to satisfy consumers. Operations managers, the personnel charged with managing and supervising the conversion of inputs into outputs, work closely with other functions in organizations to help ensure quality, customer satisfaction, and financial success.

2 What types of production processes are used by manufacturers and service firms?

Products are made using one of three types of production processes. In mass production, many identical goods are produced at once, keeping production costs low. Mass production, therefore, relies heavily on standardization, mechanization, and specialization. When mass customization is used, goods are produced using mass production techniques up to a point, after which the product or service is custom tailored to individual customers by adding special features. When a firm's production process is built around customization, the firm makes many products one at a time according to the very specific needs or wants of individual customers.

3 How do organizations decide where to put their production facilities? What choices must be made in designing the facility?

Site selection affects operating costs, the price of the product or service, and the company's ability to compete. In choosing a production site, firms must weigh the availability of resources—raw materials, human resources, and even capital—needed for production, as well as the ability to serve customers and take advantage of marketing opportunities. Other factors include the availability of local incentives and the manufacturing environment. Once a site is selected, the firm must choose an appropriate design for the facility. The three main production facility designs are process, product, and fixed-position layouts. Cellular manufacturing is another type of facility layout.

4 Why are resource-planning tasks like inventory management and supplier relations critical to production?

Production converts input resources, such as raw materials and labour, into outputs, finished products, and services. Firms must ensure that the resources needed for production will be available at strategic moments in the production process. If they are not, productivity, customer satisfaction, and quality might suffer. Carefully managing inventory can help cut production costs while maintaining enough supply for production and sales. Through good relationships with suppliers, firms can get better prices, reliable resources, and support services that can improve production efficiency.

5 How do operations managers schedule and control production?

Routing is the first step in scheduling and controlling production. Routing involves analyzing the steps needed in production and setting out a workflow, the sequence of machines and operations through which a product or service progresses from start to finish. Good routing increases productivity and can eliminate unnecessary costs. Scheduling involves specifying and controlling the time and resources required for each step in the production process. Operations managers use three methods to schedule production: Gantt charts, the critical path method, and program evaluation and review techniques.

6 How can quality management and lean-manufacturing techniques help firms improve production and operations management?

Quality and productivity go hand in hand. Defective products waste materials and time, increasing costs. Poor quality also leads to dissatisfied customers. By implementing quality control methods, firms often reduce these problems and streamline production. Lean manufacturing also helps streamline production by eliminating unnecessary steps in the production process. When activities that don't add value for customers are eliminated, manufacturers can respond to changing market conditions with greater flexibility and ease.

7 What roles do technology and automation play in manufacturing and service industry operations management?

Many firms are improving their operational efficiency by using technology to automate parts of production. Computer-aided design and manufacturing systems, for example, help design new products, control the flow of resources needed for production, and even operate much of the production process. By using robotics, human time and effort can be minimized. Factories are being automated by blending computers, robots, and machinery into flexible manufacturing systems that require less labour to operate. Service firms are automating operations too, using technology to cut labour costs and control quality.

8 What key trends are affecting the way in which companies manage production and operations?

The manufacturing sector has been faced with growing global competition, increased product complexity, and more demanding customers, so manufacturers must carefully plan how, when, and where they produce the goods they sell. New production techniques and manufacturing technologies can help keep costs as low as possible. Managing assets like inventory, raw materials, and production equipment is increasingly important. Asset management software systems automatically track materials and inventory to help reduce waste, misuse, and malfunctions. Modular production allows manufacturers to produce products using high-quality parts without investments in expensive technology. Production efficiency must begin before the factory floor. Many firms are using tools that integrate product design and engineering with the manufacturing supply chain to understand the cost and quality implications of producing new products.

EXPERIENTIAL EXERCISES

1. Track a project with a Gantt chart. Your instructor has just announced a huge assignment, due in three weeks. Where do you start? How can you best organize your time? A Gantt chart can help you plan and schedule more effectively. You'll be able to see exactly what you should be doing on a particular day.

   - First, break the assignment down into smaller tasks: pick a topic, conduct research at the library or on the Internet, organize your notes, develop an outline, and write, type, and proofread the paper.

   - Next, estimate how much time each task will take. Be realistic. If you've spent a week or more writing similar papers in the past, don't expect to finish this paper in a day.

   - At the top of a piece of paper, list all of the days until the assignment is due. Along the side of the paper, list all of the tasks you've identified in the order in which they need to be done.

   - Starting with the first task, block out the number of days you estimate each task will take. If you run out of days, you'll know you need to adjust how you've scheduled your time. If you know that you will not be able to work on some days, note them on the chart as well.

   - Hang the chart where you can see it.

2. Look for ways in which technology and automation are used at your school, in the local supermarket, and at your doctor's office. As a class, discuss how automation affects the service you receive from each of these organizations. Does one organization use any types of automation that might be effectively used by one of the others? Explain.

3. Pick a small business in your community. Make a list of the resources critical to the firm's production and operations. What would happen if the business suddenly couldn't acquire any of these resources? Discuss strategies that small businesses can use to manage their supply chain.

4. Today's Fashions is a manufacturer of women's dresses. The company's factory has 50 employees. Production begins when the fabric is cut according to specified patterns. After being cut, the pieces for each dress style are placed into bundles, which then move through the factory from worker to worker. Each

worker opens each bundle and does one assembly task, such as sewing on collars, hemming dresses, or adding decorative items such as appliqués. Then, the worker puts the bundle back together and passes it on to the next person in the production process. Finished dresses are pressed and packaged for shipment. Draw a diagram showing the production process layout in the Today's Fashions factory. What type of factory layout and process is Today's Fashions using? Discuss the pros and cons of this choice. Could Today's Fashions improve the production efficiency by using a different production process or factory layout? How? Draw a diagram to explain how this might look.

5. As discussed in this chapter, many firms have moved their manufacturing operations to overseas locations in the past decade. Although there can be sound financial benefits to this choice, moving production overseas can also raise new challenges for operations managers. Identify several of these challenges, and offer suggestions for how operations managers can use the concepts in this chapter to minimize or solve them.

6. Reliance Systems is a manufacturer of computer keyboards. The company plans to build a new factory and hopes to find a location with access to low-cost but skilled workers, national and international transportation, and favourable government incentives. As a team, use the Internet and your school library to research possible site locations, both domestic and international. Choose a location you feel would best meet the company's needs. Make a group presentation to the class explaining why you have chosen this location. Include information about the location's labour force, similar manufacturing facilities already located there, availability of resources and materials, possible local incentives, the political and economic environments, and any other factors you feel make this an attractive location. After all teams have presented their proposed locations, as a class rank all of the locations and decide the top two that Reliance should investigate further.

7. Find the supplier information Web sites of several firms by using the Google search engine, **http://www.google.ca**, to conduct a search for "supplier information." Visit two or three of these sites. Compare the requirements the companies set for their suppliers. How do the requirements differ? How are they similar?

8. Find out about the manufacturing environment in Canada by using **http://www.google.ca** and searching for manufacturing in Canada. You will have many options for learning more about the manufacturing opportunities.

9. Using a search engine such as Excite (**http://www.excite.com**) or Info Seek (**http://www.infoseek.com**), search for information about technologies like robotics, CAD/CAM systems, or ERP. Find at least three suppliers for one of these technologies. Visit their Web sites and discuss how their clients are using their products to automate production.

REVIEW QUESTIONS

1. Define *production* and *operations management*.

2. What is production planning? What is the production process, and what options are available to manufacturers?

3. What are some of the considerations when determining the location of production facilities?

4. After management has decided on a location for the facilities, they need to design the facilities' layout. What are some options in the design?

5. What are the considerations when we are formulating our resource planning?

6. What are supply chain and supply chain management?
7. What is scheduling? What are the three (3) common scheduling tools available to management?
8. Discuss some ways of improving production and operations.
9. How can technology be used to improve operating efficiencies and the ability for companies to compete?
10. Discuss the importance of asset management.
11. What is modular production?

CREATIVE THINKING CASE
Shipshape Quality at Bombardier

Bombardier, a Montreal-based manufacturer of jets, railcars, and snowmobiles with revenues of $14 billion a year, knew it was taking on a big risk when it bought the manufacturing operations of Outboard Marine Corporation (OMC) for $55 million in 2001. OMC, maker of Evinrude and Johnson outboard boat engines, was in a tailspin. Product quality had declined so severely that the company's share of the $2-billion-a-year outboard engine market had plummeted from 55 percent in 1995 to just 23 percent in 2000.

OMC manufactured its components and parts at nine production facilities scattered around the United States, Mexico, and China. Engine transmission housings die-cast in Waukegan, Illinois, were shipped to Andrews, North Carolina, for machining and subassembly and then sent to the Calhoun, Georgia, plant for final assembly. It often took three weeks or more for component parts to move between plants, boosting production costs and delaying production.

Bombardier did not want to wait for OMC to turn around on its own. It sent a cross-functional team of specialists from its plant maintenance, operations, marketing, finance, and quality control departments to determine how to improve OMC's quality and operations. The first recommendation? Shut down two plants, and reduce production in a third to consolidate operations and drastically shorten parts supply routes. OMC would now concentrate final assembly at its four-year-old Sturtevant, Wisconsin, plant. Bombardier would spend $50 million upgrading the plant with new technology and equipment. The team next hired a new workforce, carefully selecting workers who were team players with problem-solving skills.

The Bombardier team studied all of OMC's engineering drawings and recommended that OMC redesign many parts to improve quality control. Defective parts stored in inventory were identified and eliminated. Bombardier now requires that all assembly workers spend as much as 20 percent of their time inspecting engines for quality defects. Bombardier also set what it calls DQR—durability, quality, and reliability—standards for each unit produced.

Bombardier implemented these and other changes within 78 days of acquiring OMC. The results have been dramatic. Quality has improved enough that Bombardier offers a three-year warranty on its engines, the longest in the industry. Market share is almost back to previous levels. Bombardier plans to expand the Sturtevant plant to boost production to 60,000 engines a year, including many new models—9 times the current rate.

CRITICAL THINKING QUESTIONS

1. Could Bombardier have achieved the same results without closing any plants? How?
2. What technologies would you recommend Bombardier invest in at its Sturtevant plant? Describe what each technology could do to help meet Bombardier's goals.

3. What new challenges do you think Bombardier will face as it boosts production to nine times the current rate? How should Bombardier prepare for those challenges?

SOURCES: Gene Bylinsky, "Elite Factories: They're Setting Lofty Standards in Quality Control, Preventive Maintenance, and Automation," *Fortune*, September 2, 2002, 172B; "Bombardier First-Built Outboard Engines Delivered to Worldwide Market," Bombardier company press release, October 17, 2001.

VIDEO CASE
Big Blue Turns Small Businesses into Large Competitors

"It is like music, once it is in place and working," says Susan Jain, a marketing executive with IBM Global Services. She is talking about Enterprise Resource Planning, or ERP, complex software modules that do just about everything to help companies run more efficiently and competitively.

"The old systems couldn't relate one piece of information to another," she says. Separate databases meant information systems weren't integrated, so day-to-day operations were cumbersome and management reporting often inaccurate. With ERP, information is accessible immediately, greatly improving overall operating efficiency and speeding up and shortening internal reporting procedures, and even reducing the time it takes to bring new products to market.

ERP is a "relational database" that ties all aspects of information gathering and dissemination together in a tidy package. For example, ERP software modules can receive an order, check raw material stocks to make sure the order can be produced, order any additional materials that might be needed, place the order in the production schedule, and send it to shipping and invoicing. Its human resources module will even help hire and train the staff needed to produce and fulfill the order.

Companies no longer need to predict what products customers might want, or keep tons of product on warehouse shelves gathering dust. ERP literally allows companies to "build to order"—in fact, IBM has an automobile customer that does just that. It builds to order, one car at a time, eliminating the customary guessing games of what colours or styles might be popular at a given time.

Even small companies are investing in ERP systems to enable them to grow and compete, despite the substantial investment in time and dollars that is required. Jain is candid about the costs involved. The software costs about $1 million dollars, with an equal expenditure required for new hardware. Implementation, training, and education can cost two to three times that amount and take years in the case of very large companies.

IBM Global Financing supports all elements of an ERP acquisition with a broad array of financing offerings with flexible payment options. But after all that expense, return on investment is difficult to measure. With so many variables driving business success, good results could be due to other factors, such as changes in working styles or a general upswing in the current business environment. IBM's promotional material asks "Are You Ready for IBM?" It's a big decision for small companies to make.

CRITICAL THINKING QUESTIONS

1. As the production manager for a large manufacturing company, you recommend the acquisition of ERP software to your bosses. Be specific in describing how such a system would help your company be more competitive.

2. What kind of information would you want such a system to integrate for your company?

3. Explain how you would propose to track performance to justify the cost of installing such a system.

SOURCE: Adapted from material in the video "Are You Ready for IBM?" Information Management Systems at IBM, http://www.ibm.com (accessed April 8, 2003).

E-COMMERCE CASE
GM Goes Digital

Six years ago, General Motors was an e-commerce dinosaur. The giant automaker was bogged down with 7,000 different information technology (IT) systems spread across the company. Communications with suppliers, dealers, and customers—as well as between the company's own divisions—often stumbled, resulting in long product development delays and an inefficient supply chain.

To solve these problems, GM had to go digital. It started by consolidating the company's telecommunications infrastructure to increase Internet bandwidth. This allowed GM to support connectivity between the company and its business partners. The next step was to reduce the number of company IT systems by nearly half, so that communications could flow freely from computer to computer via the Internet.

GM chose a single CAD program that allows 3-D design documents to be shared on-line by the company's 18,000 designers and engineers at its 14 global design labs. GM also hooked more than 1,000 of its key suppliers' engineers into the same system. Now, all parties involved in the design and development process are able to view and discuss design plans on-line in real time. The time required to bring a new vehicle to market has been cut to just 18 months. GM purchases many of its raw materials and parts through the Internet as well, through an on-line joint procurement effort formed with other automakers, further streamlining production and operations.

GM also launched a consumer on-line shopping and buying site in 40 countries, **http://www.GMBuyPower.com**. U.S. consumers can visit the site, choose which options they want their car to have, find a dealer that has it in inventory, and shop for the best price.

Brazilian consumers can actually complete their entire sales transaction on-line through **http://www.GMBuyPower.com**. GM worked with its Brazilian dealers to develop a special Chevrolet model, the Celta, specifically for Internet sales. Since GM began selling the Celta on-line in Brazil, more than 80,000 of the cars have been sold entirely over the Internet. GM hopes to expand on-line sales to other countries within the next few years.

CRITICAL THINKING QUESTIONS

1. What are the benefits and disadvantages for suppliers who are connected to GM's Internet-based CAD system? How do you think GM decides which suppliers should be included?

2. If you were GM's information technology manager, what other uses of the Internet would you recommend the company pursue? Why?

3. What challenges might GM face in attempting to expand on-line sales globally? How can the Internet be used to overcome these challenges in various countries? Do you think GM will ever offer complete on-line sales transactions for car purchases in the United States? Why or why not?

SOURCES: John Teresko, "Technology Leader of the Year—Transforming GM," *Industry Week*, December 1, 2001; Missy Sullivan, Constance Gustke, and Nikhil Hutheesing, "Case Studies: Digital Do-Overs," Forbes, October 7, 2002, http://www.forbes.com; and "Brazil: Internet Car Sales Grow," *South American Business Information*, March 9, 2001.

12

Making the Connection

Understanding the Customer and Creating Marketing Strategy

In the next few chapters we will continue to look at the functional areas of the company by examining the area of marketing. Marketers make decisions about what products to bring to market in conjunction with the overall strategic direction of the company, and then work with *operations* to design those products and allocate the resources needed to provide them—whether that be production facilities or alliances with other firms if it is a good that is being produced, or layouts and procedures to be followed if it is a service. And, of course, both marketing and operations need to work with *human resources* to make sure people with the needed skills are in place in all areas, as well as with *finance* to make sure the product is financially worthwhile for the company to pursue and that funds will be available to pursue it. It is an integrated effort. This is evident from the example of Lexus in the chapter. The company "adopted a customer-driven approach with particular emphasis on service" by stressing "product *quality* with a standard of zero defects in manufacturing" and a service goal to "treat each customer as a guest in one's home." Marketing couldn't do this alone. It would have to work with operations to provide this level of product quality as well as human resources to provide this level of customer service. And it

would also need an investment of funds to pull it all together.

But just think for a minute what would happen if there were no customer demand for the quality cars sold by Lexus? Obviously, just as the decisions that are made in the functional areas to bring a product to market are integrated, the decisions about which products to bring to market obviously have to be integrated with the outside environment—they must come ultimately from the customer. The customer is the central focal point of any successful business. Look at the critical success factors. As we've said many times, you can't *achieve financial success* if you aren't earning revenue, and you can't earn revenue if customers aren't buying your products. And they won't buy your products if they don't at least *meet and at best exceed* their needs. That is what this chapter is all about—understanding your customer and creating a marketing strategy that satisfy his or her needs.

This requires that the company keep an eye on all areas of the external environment that may affect marketing decisions, as discussed in the chapter, but particularly on the *social* environment, including demographic changes, to understand the trends that affect customer needs, as well as to better understand the different factors that influence consumer decision-making. As the chapter explains, it is important to do market research to understand the customer, and advances in *technology* have made that easier. Technology has also made it possible to create a unique marketing mix for each customer, discussed in the chapter as "one-to-one marketing," based on information kept on customers in the marketing database. The company also has to keep an eye on the *economic* environment to make sure it keeps ahead of the competition and that it takes into consideration the effect of changing incomes and interest rates, etc., as well as the *political* environment to make sure it is meeting all the requirements in its package labeling, etc.

Many concepts in this chapter are important for understanding marketing and its integrative nature. For example, in this chapter you'll discuss the marketing concept—focusing on customer wants and needs, and integrating the organization's activities in the functional areas to satisfy the customer, but doing so with a responsibility toward the *stakeholders*—profitably for the owners, ethically for the customer, and fairly for the employee. The marketing concept is an important integrative concept as it is the thread that ties all the marketing activities, functional areas, and the business as a whole together to stay focused on the customer and make decisions responsibly so that success is achieved with all the stakeholders in mind and all critical success factors met.

You'll also discuss relationship marketing. This is critical to the long-term success of the company—meeting the critical success factors over time by establishing long-term relationships with customers. This can be done through loyalty programs as one example, but also requires *commitment* from your employees to be customer oriented. As discussed in the chapter, employee attitudes and actions are critical to building relationships. A good example of this is WestJet airlines. Just give them a call and chat with one of their reps, and then call another airline, and you'll see the difference in attitude toward the customer.

Target marketing is another important concept. Identifying a target market helps a company focus marketing efforts on those customers most likely to buy its products. The unique features of the product that appeal to the target group and are seen by the target group as superior to competitive offerings are the company's competitive advantage. If that competitive advantage is cost—operating at a lower cost than competitors and passing this saving on to the customer (as in Wal-Mart)—we see another integration of marketing with the other functional areas. As the chapter explains, this cost advantage is gained through using less expensive raw materials and/or controlling overhead costs (finance), and making plant operations more efficient and/or designing products that are easier to manufacture (operations), and so on. This is done by these areas through people committed to this goal and often with the help of technology.

And finally, the target market of consumers whose needs the company is focusing on is determined after segmenting the market. Though it seems like a purely marketing exercise—dividing up the market of consumers into different groups based on some common characteristics—it has some very definite integrative implications. Take Avon's foray into a new customer segment—teenagers and young women, as discussed in the opening vignette—with a new cosmetics line called "mark." The social environment would have influenced the move, with demographic variables and buying behaviour making the 15- to 24-year-old age group particularly appealing. This in turn caused changes in the functional areas to accommodate the new line, particularly the move to recruit teens as sales representatives, a very innovative move on the part of Avon. Marketing is without a doubt a very central integrative function within a successful business.

© AP/WORLD WIDE PHOTOS

Understanding the Customer and Creating Marketing Strategy

learning goals

1 What is the marketing concept, and what is relationship building?

2 How do managers create a marketing strategy?

3 What is the marketing mix?

4 How do consumers and organizations make buying decisions?

5 What are the five basic forms of market segmentation?

6 How is marketing research used in marketing decision-making?

7 What are the trends in understanding the consumer?

Avon Goes for the Younger Set

Avon Products, Inc. (**http://www.avon.com**) is ringing the doorbells of a new customer generation: teenagers and young women. And teens are doing some of the ringing. The big direct seller of beauty products, eager to reach 16- to 24-year-old shoppers, who mostly associate the Avon name with their mothers, launched a cosmetics line called mark. The hip packaging is distinctly more upscale than other teen-focused brands, including Procter & Gamble's Cover Girl or mass market brands such as Bonne Bell. It is also trendier than Avon's traditional look, which is aimed squarely at 25- to 55-year-old women.

Avon is recruiting teens as sales representatives, even as it pushes ahead on efforts to boost its main North American sales ranks. Although the company expects some door-to-door selling by its new recruits, it envisions youth sales mostly taking place among groups of friends at slumber parties and other informal gatherings. Avon hopes the opportunity to sell cosmetics to peers will prove more alluring than toiling behind the counter in fast-food restaurants.

About 2.2 million young women in Canada are in the 15- to 24-year-old age group,[1] and many of them spend money on beauty and beauty-related products. "It's not just lip gloss," says Deborah I. Fine, the former publisher of *Glamour* magazine tapped by Avon to lead the youth charge. "It's lip gloss with an earnings opportunity."

Avon executives say research shows that young women have a "neutral to positive" image of the company. But when mark made its debut, its own name was in lights. The name Avon appears but only in tiny letters.[2]

Critical Thinking Questions

1. Why do companies identify target customers for their products?
2. Why is it important to differentiate a product?
3. How does a company like Avon find out what customers and potential customers want in the way of cosmetics?

SOURCE: Adapted from Sally Beatty, "Avon is Set to Call on Teens," Wall Street Journal (October 17, 2002), pp. B1, B7. Reprinted by permission of the Wall Street Journal, Copyright (c) 2002 Dow Jones & Company, Inc. All Rights Reserved Worldwide.

marketing

The process of discovering the needs and wants of potential buyers and customers and then providing goods and services that meet or exceed their expectations.

exchange

The process in which two parties give something of value to each other to satisfy their respective needs.

HOT Links

What's new at Avon since it launched its mark line? Browse the company's Web site, at http://www.avoncompany.com, to find out how the teen products are doing.

Marketing played an important role in Avon's successful launch of mark. Marketing is the process of getting the right goods or services to the right people at the right place, time, and price, using the right promotion techniques. This concept is referred to as the *"right" principle*. We can say that **marketing** is finding out the needs and wants of potential buyers and customers and then providing goods and services that meet or exceed their expectations. Marketing is about creating exchanges. An **exchange** takes place when two parties give something of value to each other to satisfy their respective needs. In a typical exchange, a consumer trades money for a good or service.

To encourage exchanges, marketers follow the "right" principle. If your local Avon rep doesn't have the right lipstick for you when you want it, at the right price, you will not exchange money for a new lipstick from Avon. Think about the last exchange (purchase) you made: What if the price had been 30 percent higher? What if the store or other source had been less accessible? Would you have bought anything? The "right" principle tells us that marketers control many factors that determine marketing success. In this chapter, you will learn about the marketing concept and how organizations create a marketing strategy. You will learn how the marketing mix is used to create sales opportunities. Next, we examine how and why consumers and organizations make purchase decisions. Then, we will discuss the important concept of market segmentation, which helps marketing managers focus on the most likely purchasers of their wares. We conclude the chapter by examining how marketing research and decision support systems help guide marketing decision-making.

THE MARKETING CONCEPT

1 *learning goal*

marketing concept

Identifying consumer needs and then producing the goods or services that will satisfy them while making a profit for the organization.

If you study today's best organizations, you'll see that they have adopted the **marketing concept**, which involves identifying consumer needs and then producing the goods or services that will satisfy them while making a profit. The marketing concept is oriented toward pleasing consumers by offering value. Specifically, the marketing concept involves

- focusing on customer wants, so the organization can distinguish its product(s) from competitors' offerings;
- integrating all of the organization's activities, including production, to satisfy these wants; and
- achieving long-term goals for the organization by satisfying customer wants and needs legally and responsibly.

Today, companies of every size in all industries are applying the marketing concept. McDonald's, for example, found that burger eaters like to determine what's on their burger rather than buying a hamburger that is already dressed in a heated bin. Now, its restaurants can deliver fresh sandwiches made to order.

production orientation

An approach in which a firm works to lower production costs without a strong desire to satisfy the needs of customers.

Firms have not always followed the marketing concept. Around the time of the Industrial Revolution in North America (1860–1910), firms had a **production orientation**, which meant that they worked to lower production costs without a strong desire to satisfy the needs of their customers. To do this, organizations concentrated on mass production, focusing internally on maximizing the efficiency of operations, increasing output, and ensuring uniform quality. They also asked such questions as What can we do best? What can our engineers design? What is economical and easy to produce with our equipment?

There is nothing wrong with assessing a firm's capabilities. In fact, such assessments are necessary in planning. But the production orientation does not consider whether what the firm produces most efficiently also meets the needs of the marketplace. By implementing the marketing concept, an organization looks externally to the consumers in the marketplace and commits to customer value, customer satisfaction, and relationship marketing, as explained in this section.

Customer Value

customer value

The ratio of benefits to the sacrifice necessary to obtain those benefits, as determined by the customer; reflects the willingness of customers to buy a product.

Customer value is the ratio of benefits to the sacrifice necessary to obtain those benefits. The customer determines the value of both the benefits and the sacrifices. Creating customer value is a core business strategy of many successful firms. Customer value is rooted in the belief that price is not the only thing that matters. A business that focuses on the cost of production and price to the customer will be managed as though it were providing a commodity differentiated only by price. In contrast, businesses that provide customer value believe that many customers will pay a premium for superior customer service. Sir Colin Marshall, chairman of the board of British Airways (BA), is explicit about his commitment to superior customer service, insisting that BA can succeed only by meeting all of its customers' value-driven needs, not just price.

The automobile industry also illustrates the importance of creating customer value. To penetrate the fiercely competitive luxury automobile market, Lexus adopted a customer-driven approach, with particular emphasis on service. Lexus stresses product quality with a standard of zero defects in manufacturing. The service quality goal is to treat each customer as one would treat a guest in one's home, to pursue the perfect person-to-person relationship, and to strive to improve continually. This strategy has enabled Lexus to establish a clear quality image and capture a significant share of the luxury car market.

Customer Satisfaction

customer satisfaction

The customer's feeling that a product has met or exceeded expectations.

Customer satisfaction is a theme that we have stressed throughout the text. **Customer satisfaction** is the customer's feeling that a product has met or exceeded expectations. Lexus consistently wins awards for its outstanding customer satisfaction. J. D. Power and Associates surveys car owners two years after they make their purchase. The Customer Satisfaction Survey is made up of four measures that each describe an element of overall ownership satisfaction at two years: vehicle quality/reliability, vehicle appeal, ownership costs, and service satisfaction from a dealer. Lexus continues to lead the industry. Lexus manager Stuart McCullough comments, "In close collaboration with our dealers we aim to provide the best customer service, not only in the car industry, but in any industry. The J. D. Power surveys are a testament to our success in making our customers happy."[3]

At Doubletree Hotels, guests are asked to fill out a CARE card several times during their stay to let staff know how they are doing. Managers check the cards daily to solve guests' problems before they check out. Guests can also use a CARE phone line to call in their complaints at the hotel. A CARE committee continually seeks ways to improve guest services. The goal is to offer a solution to a CARE call in 15 minutes. Embassy Suites goes one step further by offering a full refund to guests who are not satisfied with their stay.

See Exhibit 12.1 to see Sony Canada's Customer Satisfaction Survey.

Building Relationships

Relationship marketing is a strategy that focuses on forging long-term partnerships with customers. Companies build relationships with customers by offering value and providing customer satisfaction. Companies benefit from repeat sales and referrals that lead to increases in sales, market share, and profits. Costs fall because it is less expensive to serve existing customers than to attract new ones. Keeping a customer's costs about one-fourth of what it costs to attract a new one, and the probability of retaining a customer is more than 60 percent, whereas the probability of landing a new customer is less than 30 percent.[4]

Exhibit 12.1 | Sony Style Customer Satisfaction Survey

Sony Style Customer Satisfaction Survey

Sony Style is constantly finding ways to improve your on-line shopping experience, and we'd like to hear from you, our valued customer. Please take just a few minutes to complete our customer satisfaction survey.

Please tell us your age group   [Click here to select ▼]

What is your gender?

○ Male

○ Female

How did you hear about our website? (please select all that apply)

☐ Sony Style Magazine

☐ Friends/family

What are your reasons for visiting our site today?

☐ To find Sony product information

☐ To locate technical support information

☐ To purchase a Sony product

☐ To check out status of your order

☐ To register your Sony product

☐ To find Sony contact information

☐ To find a dealer or repair centre for your product

☐ To find other promotions

How often have you visited Sonystyle.ca?

[Click here to select ▼]

Please rate our site for the following

	Excellent	Better than average	Average	Poor
Navigation	○	○	○	○
Design and Presentation	○	○	○	○
Product Information	○	○	○	○
Support and Policies Information	○	○	○	○
Membership Benefits	○	○	○	○
Overall	○	○	○	○

If you have any further questions or comments, please contact Sony at customersupport@sonystyle.ca and you will receive a response shortly.

HOT Links

Visit Sony Style Canada at http://www.SonyStyle.ca.

Customers also benefit from stable relationships with suppliers. Business buyers have found that partnerships with their suppliers are essential to producing high-quality products while cutting costs. Customers remain loyal to firms that provide them greater value and satisfaction than they expect from competing firms.

Loyalty programs, sometimes referred to as frequent-buyer clubs, are an excellent way to build long-term relationships. All major airlines have frequent-flyer programs. After you fly a certain number of miles, you become eligible for a free ticket. Now, cruise lines, hotels, car rental agencies, credit card companies, and even mortgage companies give away "airline miles" with purchases. Consumers patronize the airline and its partners, because they want the free tickets. Thus, the program helps to create a long-term relationship with the customer.

If an organization is to build relationships with customers, its employees' attitudes and actions must be customer oriented. Any person, department, or division that is not customer oriented weakens the positive image of the entire organization. An employee might be the only contact a potential customer has with the firm. In that person's eyes, the employee is the firm. If greeted discourteously, the potential customer might well assume that the employee's attitude represents the whole firm.

Building long-term relationships with customers is an excellent way for small businesses to compete against the big chains. Sometimes small firms, with few employees, are in a better position to focus on a tiny segment of the market.

concept check

Explain the marketing concept.

Explain the difference between customer value and customer satisfaction.

What is meant by relationship marketing?

As a "guest" on WestJet, you can expect friendly, casual, yet competent service from everyone you encounter, from captain to customer service representative.

PHOTO COURTESY OF WESTJET

CREATING A MARKETING STRATEGY

2   *learning goal*

There is no secret formula for creating goods and services that provide customer value and customer satisfaction. An organization that is committed to providing superior customer satisfaction puts customers at the very centre of its marketing strategy. Creating a customer-focused *marketing strategy* involves four main steps: understanding the external environment, defining the target market, creating a competitive advantage, and developing a marketing mix. In this section, we will examine the first three steps, and in the next section, we will discuss how a company develops a marketing mix.

Understanding the External Environment

Unless marketing managers understand the external environment, a firm cannot plan for the future intelligently. Thus, many organizations assemble a team of specialists who continually collect and evaluate environmental information, a process called **environmental scanning**. The goal in gathering the environmental data is to identify future market opportunities and threats.

For example, as technology continues to blur the lines between personal computers, television, and other electronic devices, a company like Sony might find itself competing against a company like Hewlett-Packard. Research shows that children would like more games bundled with computer software, whereas adults desire various types of word-processing and business-related software. Is this information an opportunity or a threat to Hewlett-Packard marketing managers?

In general, six categories of environmental data shape marketing decisions:

- *social forces*, such as the values of potential customers and the changing roles of families and women working outside the home;
- *demographic forces*, such as the ages, birth and death rates, and locations of various groups of people;
- *economic forces*, such as changing incomes, inflation, and recession;
- *technological forces*, such as advances in communications and data retrieval capabilities;
- *political and legal forces*, such as changes in laws and regulatory agency activities; and
- *competitive forces* from domestic and foreign-based firms.

environmental scanning

The process by which a firm continually collects and evaluates information about its external environment.

The "milk moustache" ads target different market segments to promote the consumption of milk. This one targets the youth market with an ad featuring actress Neve Campbell.

COURTESY OF THE NATIONAL FLUID MILK PROCESSOR PROMOTION BOARD

Defining the Target Market

target market

The specific group of consumers toward which a firm directs its marketing efforts.

Managers and employees focus on providing value for a well-defined target market. The **target market** is the specific group of consumers toward which a firm directs its marketing efforts. It is selected from the larger overall market. For instance, Carnival Cruise Lines says its main target market is "blue-collar entrepreneurs," people with an income of $25,000 to $50,000 a year who own auto supply shops, dry cleaners, and the like. Unlike other cruise lines, it does not seek affluent retirees. Quaker Oats targets its grits to blue-collar consumers in the Southern United States. Kodak targets Ektar colour print film, designed for use only in rather sophisticated cameras, to advanced amateur photographers. Laura's Shoppe Canada Limited has several different types of stores, each for a distinct target market: Laura's for average-size women, Laura Petites for petite women, Laura II for plus-size women, and Melanie Lyne for upscale women's apparel featuring designer labels.

Identifying a target market helps a company focus its marketing efforts on those who are most likely to buy its products or services. Concentrating on potential customers lets the firm use its resources efficiently. The target markets for Marriott International's lodging alternatives are shown in Exhibit 12.2. The latest in the Marriott family is SpringHill Suites. The SpringHill idea came from another Marriott chain, Fairfield Suites, an offshoot of Marriott's Fairfield Inns. The suites, opened in 1997, were roomy but devoid of most frills: The closets didn't have doors, and the lobby floors were covered with linoleum. Some franchisees complained to Marriott that the suites were *under*priced: Fairfield Suites guests were saying they would pay a little more for a few more frills, so Marriott began planning an upgrade. To create each of the first 20 or so SpringHill locations, Marriott spent $200,000 renovating an existing Fairfield Suites unit, adding ergonomic chairs, ironing boards, and other amenities. Lobbies at SpringHill hotels are fancier than the rooms themselves: The lobbies have fireplaces, breakfast rooms, crown moldings at the ceiling, and granite or ceramic tile floors.

Creating a Competitive Advantage

competitive advantage

A set of unique features of a company and its products that are perceived by the target market as significant and superior to those of the competition; also called *differential advantage*.

cost competitive advantage

A firm's ability to produce a product or service at a lower cost than all other competitors in an industry while maintaining satisfactory profit margins.

A competitive advantage, also called a differential advantage, is a set of unique features of a company and its products that are perceived by the target market as significant and superior to those of the competition. As Andrew Grove, CEO of Intel, says, "You have to understand what it is you are better at than anybody else and mercilessly focus your efforts on it." **Competitive advantage** is the factor or factors that cause customers to patronize a firm and not the competition. There are three types of competitive advantage: cost, product/service differential, and niche.

Cost competitive advantage   A firm that has a **cost competitive advantage** can produce a product or service at a lower cost than all its competitors while maintaining satisfactory profit margins. Firms become cost leaders by obtaining inexpensive raw materials, making plant operations more efficient, designing products for ease of manufacture, controlling overhead costs, and avoiding marginal customers.

Over time, the cost competitive advantage might fail. Typically, if one firm is using an innovative technology to reduce its costs, then others in the industry will adopt this technology and reduce their costs as well. For example, Bell Labs invented fibre optic cables, which reduced the cost of voice and data transmission by dramatically increasing the number of calls that could be transmitted simultaneously through a 5 cm cable. Within five years, however, fibre optic technology had spread through the industry, and Bell Labs lost its cost competitive advantage. Firms might also lose their cost competitive advantage if competing firms match their low costs by using the same lower cost suppliers. Therefore, a cost competitive advantage might not offer a long-term competitive advantage.

Exhibit 12.2 | The Target Markets for Marriott International

	PRICE RANGE	TARGET MARKET
Fairfield Inn	$45–65	Economizing business and leisure travellers
TownePlace Suites	$55–70	Moderate-tier travellers who stay three to four weeks
SpringHill Suites	$75–95	Business and leisure travellers looking for more space and amenities
Courtyard	$75–105	Travellers seeking quality and affordable accommodations designed for the road warrior
Residence Inn	$85–110	Travellers seeking a residential-style hotel
Marriott Hotels, Resorts, and Suites	$90–235	Grounded achievers who desire consistent quality
Renaissance Hotels and Resorts	$90–235	Discerning business and leisure travellers who seek creative attention to detail
Ritz-Carlton	$175–300	Senior executives and entrepreneurs looking for a unique, luxurious, personalized experience

differential competitive advantage

A firm's ability to provide a unique product or service with a set of features that the target market perceives as important and better than the competitor's.

niche competitive advantage

A firm's ability to target and effectively serve a single segment of the market within a limited geographic area.

A differential competitive advantage offers a unique value to consumers. Keebler promises chocolate lovers that their Fudge Shoppe Clusters "don't fudge on the fudge."

Differential competitive advantage A product/service **differential competitive advantage** exists when a firm provides something unique that is valuable to buyers beyond simply offering a low price. Differential competitive advantages tend to be longer lasting than cost competitive advantages, because cost advantages are subject to continual erosion as competitors catch up.

The durability of a differential competitive advantage tends to make this strategy more attractive to many top managers. Common differential advantages are brand names (Lexus), a strong dealer network (Caterpillar Tractor for construction equipment), product reliability (Maytag washers), image (Holt Renfrew in retailing), and service (Federal Express). Brand names such as Coca-Cola, BMW, and Cartier stand for quality the world over. Through continual product and marketing innovations and attention to quality and value, managers at these organizations have created enduring competitive advantages. Arthur Doppelmayr, an Austrian manufacturer of aerial transport systems, believes his main differential advantage, besides innovative equipment design, is his service system, which allows the company to come to the assistance of users anywhere in the world within 24 hours. Doppelmayr uses a worldwide system of warehouses and skilled personnel prepared to move immediately in emergency cases.

Niche competitive advantage A company with a **niche competitive advantage** targets and effectively serves a single segment of the market within a limited geographic area. For small companies with limited resources that potentially face giant competitors, "niche-ing" might be the only viable option. A market segment that has good growth potential but is not crucial to the success of major competitors is a good candidate for a niche strategy. Once a potential segment has been identified, the firm needs to make certain it can defend against challengers through its superior ability to serve buyers in the segment. For example, STI Music Private Banking Group follows a niche strategy with its concentration on country music stars and entertainment industry professionals in Nashville. Its office is in the heart of Nashville's music district. STI has decided to expand its niche strategy to Miami, the "epicentre" of Latin music, and Atlanta. The latter is a longtime rhythm-and-blues capital and now is the centre of contemporary "urban" music. Both new markets have the kinds of music professionals—entertainers, record executives, producers, agents, and others—that have made STI so successful in Nashville.

DEVELOPING A MARKETING MIX

3 *learning goal*

marketing mix

The blend of product offering, pricing, promotional methods, and distribution system that brings a specific group of consumers superior value.

four Ps (4Ps)

Product, price, promotion, and place (distribution), which together make up the marketing mix.

Once a firm has defined its target market and identified its competitive advantage, it can create the **marketing mix**, that is, the blend of product offering, pricing, promotional methods, and distribution system that brings a specific group of consumers superior value. Distribution is sometimes referred to as place, so the marketing mix is based on the **four Ps (4Ps)**: product, price, promotion, and place. Every target market requires a unique marketing mix to satisfy the needs of the target consumers and meet the firm's goals. A strategy must be constructed for each of the 4Ps and blended with the strategies for the other elements. Thus, the marketing mix is only as good as its weakest part. An excellent product with a poor distribution system could be doomed to failure. A successful marketing mix requires careful tailoring. For instance, at first glance you might think that McDonald's and Wendy's have roughly the same marketing mix. After all, they are both in the fast-food business. But McDonald's targets parents with young children through Ronald McDonald, heavily promoted children's Happy Meals, and playgrounds. Wendy's is targeted to a more adult crowd. Wendy's has no playgrounds, but it does have carpeting (a more adult atmosphere) and has expanded its menu to include items for adult tastes.

Product Strategy

product strategy

Taking the good or service and selecting a brand name, packaging, colours, a warranty, accessories, and a service program.

Marketing strategy typically starts with the product. You can't plan a distribution system or set a price if you don't know what you're going to market. Marketers use the term *product* to refer to both *goods*, such as tires, stereos, and clothing, and *services*, such as hotels, hair salons, and restaurants. Thus, the heart of the marketing mix is the good or service. Creating a **product strategy** involves choosing a brand name, packaging, colours, a warranty, accessories, and a service program.

Marketers view products in a much larger context than you might imagine. They include not only the item itself but also the brand name and the company image. The names Ralph Lauren and Gucci, for instance, create extra value for everything from cosmetics to bath towels. That is, products with those names sell at higher prices than identical products without the names. We buy things not only for what they do but also for what they mean. Product strategies are discussed further in Chapter 13.

Pricing Strategy

pricing strategy

Setting a price based on the demand and cost for a good or service.

Pricing strategy is based on demand for the product and the cost of producing it. Some special considerations can also influence the price. Sometimes, for instance, a special introductory price is used to get people to try a new product. Some firms enter the market with low prices and keep them low, such as Carnival Cruise Lines and Suzuki cars. Others enter a market with very high prices and then lower them over time, such as producers of high-definition televisions and personal computers. You can learn more about pricing strategies in Chapter 13.

Distribution Strategy

distribution strategy
Creating the means by which products flow from the producer to the consumer.

Distribution strategy is creating the means (the channel) by which a product flows from the producer to the consumer. One aspect of distribution strategy is deciding how many stores and which specific wholesalers and retailers will handle the product in a geographic area. Cosmetics, for instance, are distributed in many different ways. Avon has a sales force of several hundred thousand representatives who call directly on consumers. Clinique and Estee Lauder are distributed through selected department stores. Cover Girl and Del Laboratories use mostly chain drugstores and other mass merchandisers. Redken sells through beauticians. Revlon uses several of these distribution channels. Distribution is examined in detail in Chapter 14.

Promotion Strategy

promotion strategy
The unique combination of personal selling, advertising, publicity, and sales promotion to stimulate the target market to buy a product or service.

Many people feel that promotion is the most exciting part of the marketing mix. **Promotion strategy** covers personal selling, advertising, public relations, and sales promotion. Each element is coordinated with the others to create a promotional blend. An advertisement, for instance, helps a buyer get to know the company and paves the way for a sales call. A good promotion strategy can dramatically increase a firm's sales. Promotion is the topic of Chapter 15.

Public relations plays a special role in promotion. It is used to create a good image of the company and its products. Bad publicity costs nothing to send out, but it can cost a firm a great deal in lost business. Good publicity, such as a television or magazine story about a firm's new product, can be the result of much time, money, and effort spent by a public relations department.

Sales promotion directly stimulates sales. It includes trade shows, catalogues, contests, games, premiums, coupons, and special offers. Tim Hortons' discount coupons and "Roll up the rim to win" contests offering money and food prizes are examples of sales promotions.

The Canadian Red Cross, a not-for-profit organization, uses social marketing to remind families to prepare their homes and families for emergencies and disasters.

CANADIAN PRESS

Not-for-Profit Marketing

HOT *Links*

Visit the Web site for the Canadian Museum of Civilization at http://www.civilization.ca.

Profit-oriented companies are not the only ones that analyze the marketing environment, find a competitive advantage, and create a marketing mix. The application of marketing principles and techniques is also vital to not-for-profit organizations. Marketing helps not-for-profit groups identify target markets and develop effective marketing mixes. In some cases, marketing has kept symphonies, museums, and other cultural groups from having to close their doors. In other organizations, marketing ideas and techniques have helped managers do their jobs better. In the private sector, the profit motive is both an objective for guiding decisions and a criterion for evaluating results. Not-for-profit organizations do not seek to make a profit for redistribution to owners or shareholders. Rather, their focus is often on generating enough funds to cover expenses. For example, organized religions do not gauge their success by the amount of money left in offering plates. The Canadian Museum of Civilization does not base its performance evaluations on the dollar value of tokens put into the turnstile.

social marketing

The application of marketing techniques to social issues and causes.

Not-for-profit marketing is also concerned with social marketing, that is, the application of marketing to social issues and causes. The goals of **social marketing** are to effect social change (for instance, by creating racial harmony), further social causes (for instance, by helping the homeless), and evaluate the relationship between marketing and society (for instance, by asking whether society should allow advertising on television shows for young children). Individual organizations also engage in social marketing. Mothers Against Drunk Driving (MADD) counsels against drunk driving, and the Canadian Wildlife Federation asks your help in protecting endangered animals and birds and their spaces.

HOT *Links*

Considering a career in marketing? See various options in marketing (or any other field) at http://www.workopolis.ca.

concept check

What is meant by the marketing mix?

What are the components of the marketing mix?

How can marketing techniques help not-for-profit organizations?

Define social marketing.

BUYER BEHAVIOUR

4 learning goal

buyer behaviour

The actions people take in buying and using goods and services.

An organization cannot reach its goals without understanding buyer behaviour. **Buyer behaviour** is the actions people take in buying and using goods and services. Marketers who understand buyer behaviour, such as how a price increase will affect a product's sales, can create a more effective marketing mix.

To understand buyer behaviour, marketers must understand how consumers make buying decisions. The consumer decision-making process has several steps, which are shown in Exhibit 12.3. The entire process is affected by cultural, social, individual, and psychological factors. The buying process starts with need recognition. This might be as simple as running out of coffee. Yes, I need to purchase more coffee. Or perhaps you recently got married and recognize that you need to start building equity instead of paying rent. Perhaps you are also considering starting a family. Therefore, you decide to buy your first home (Step 1 in Exhibit 12.3).

Next, you begin to gather information about financing, available homes, styles, locations, and so forth (Step 2). After you feel that you have gathered enough information, you begin to evaluate alternatives (Step 3). For example, you might eliminate all homes that cost more than $250,000 or are more than a 30-minute drive to your work. Then an offer is made and, if it is accepted, a purchase is made (Step 4). Finally, you assess the experience and your level of satisfaction with your new home (Step 5).

Influences on Consumer Decision-Making

Cultural, social, individual, and psychological factors have an impact on consumer decision-making from the time a person recognizes a need through post-purchase behaviour. We will examine each of these in more detail.

Culture   Purchase roles within the family are influenced by culture. **Culture** is the set of values, ideas, attitudes, and symbols created to shape human behaviour. Culture is environmentally oriented. The nomads of Finland have developed a culture for Arctic survival. Similarly, the natives of the Brazilian jungle have created a culture suitable for jungle living.

Culture, by definition, is social in nature. It is human interaction that creates values and prescribes acceptable behaviour. Thus culture gives order to society by creating common expectations. Sometimes these expectations are codified into law; for example, if you come to a red light, you stop the car. As long as a value or belief meets the needs of society, it will remain part of the culture; if it is no longer functional, the value or belief recedes. The value that very large families are "good" is no longer held by a majority of Canadians. As Canadians live in an urban rather than a rural environment, children are no longer needed to perform farm chores.

Culture is not static. It adapts to changing societal needs and evolving environmental factors. The rapid growth of technology has accelerated the rate of cultural change. Inventions such as the elevator made possible modern high-rise cities. Television changed entertainment patterns and

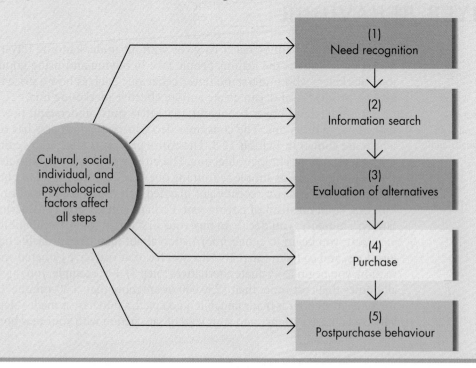

Merrill Lynch targets consumers reaching retirement age with advertisements promoting its financial services. Demographic segmentation is the most common form of market segmentation.

© THINKSTOCK / GETTY IMAGES

Exhibit 12.3 | Consumer Decision-Making Process

Cultural, social, individual, and psychological factors affect all steps

(1) Need recognition

(2) Information search

(3) Evaluation of alternatives

(4) Purchase

(5) Postpurchase behaviour

culture
The set of values, ideas, attitudes, and other symbols created to shape human behaviour.

reference groups
Formal and informal groups that influence buyer behaviour.

opinion leaders
Those who influence others.

socialization process
The passing down of cultural norms and values to children.

family communication flows, and heightened public awareness of political and other news events. The Internet has changed how we communicate and how many of us work.

Social factors Most consumers are likely to seek out the opinions of others to reduce their search and evaluation effort or uncertainty, especially as the perceived risk of the decision increases. Consumers might also seek out others' opinions for guidance on new products or services, products with image-related attributes, or products where attribute information is lacking or uninformative. Specifically, consumers interact socially with reference groups, opinion leaders, and family members to obtain product information and decision approval. All the formal and informal groups that influence the buying behaviour of an individual are that person's **reference groups**. Consumers might use products or brands to identify with or become a member of a group. They learn from observing how members of their reference groups consume, and they use the same criteria to make their own consumer decisions. A reference group might be a fraternity or sorority, a group you work with, or a club to which you belong.

Reference groups frequently include individuals known as group leaders, or **opinion leaders**—those who influence others. Obviously, it is important for marketing managers to persuade such people to purchase their goods or services. Many products and services that are integral parts of Canadians' lives today got their initial boost from opinion leaders. For example, DVDs and sport utility vehicles were embraced by opinion leaders well ahead of the general public. Opinion leaders are often the first to try new products and services out of pure curiosity. They are typically self-indulgent, making them more likely to explore unproven but intriguing products and services.

The family is the most important social institution for many consumers, strongly influencing values, attitudes, and self-concept—and buying behaviour. For example, a family that strongly values good health will have a grocery list distinctly different from that of a family that views every dinner as a gourmet event. Moreover, the family is responsible for the **socialization process**, the passing down of cultural values and norms to children. Children learn by observing their parents' consumption patterns, and so they will tend to shop in a similar pattern.

Marketers should consider family purchase situations along with the distribution of consumer and decision maker roles among family members. Ordinary marketing views the individual as both decision maker and consumer. Family marketing adds several other possibilities: Sometimes more than one family member or all family members are involved in the decision; sometimes only children are involved in the decision; sometimes more than one consumer is involved; and sometimes the decision maker and the consumer are different people. For example, a parent will select a dentist for a child to visit.

Individual influences on consumer buying decisions A person's buying decisions are also influenced by personal characteristics that are unique to each individual, such as gender, personality, and self-concept. Individual characteristics are generally stable over the course of one's life. For instance, most people do not change their gender, and the act of changing personality requires a complete reorientation of one's life.

Physiological differences between men and women result in different needs, such as health and beauty products. Just as important are the distinct cultural, social, and economic roles played by men and women and the effects that these have on their decision-making processes. Men and women also shop differently. Studies show that men and women share similar motivations in terms of where to shop—that is, seeking reasonable prices, merchandise quality, and a friendly, low-pressure environment—but they don't necessarily feel the same about shopping in general. Most women enjoy shopping; their male counterparts claim to dislike the experience and shop only out of necessity. Furthermore, men desire simple shopping experiences, stores with less variety, and convenience.

Each consumer has a unique personality. **Personality** is a broad concept that can be thought of as a way of organizing and grouping how an individual typically reacts to situations. Thus, personality combines psychological make-up and environmental forces. It includes people's underlying dispositions, especially their most dominant characteristics. Although personality is one of the least useful concepts in the study of consumer behaviour, some marketers believe that personality influences the types and brands of products purchased. For instance, the type of car, clothes, or jewellery a consumer buys can reflect one or more personality traits.

Self-concept, or self-perception, is how consumers perceive themselves. Self-concept includes attitudes, perceptions, beliefs, and self-evaluations. Although self-concept can change, the change is often gradual. Through self-concept, people define their identity, which, in turn, provides for consistent and coherent behaviour.

Self-concept combines the **ideal self-image** (the way an individual would like to be) and the **real self-image** (how an individual actually perceives him or herself). Generally, we try to raise our real self-image toward our ideal (or at least narrow the gap). Consumers seldom buy products that jeopardize their self-image. For example, someone who sees herself as a trendsetter wouldn't buy clothing that doesn't project a contemporary image.

Psychological influences on consumer buying decisions An individual's buying decisions are further influenced by psychological factors such as perception and beliefs and attitudes. These factors are what consumers use to interact with their world. They are the tools consumers use to recognize their feelings, gather and analyze information, formulate thoughts and opinions, and take action. Unlike the other three influences on consumer behaviour, psychological influences can be affected by a person's environment because they are applied on specific occasions. For example, you will perceive different stimuli and process these stimuli in different ways depending on whether you are sitting in class concentrating on the instructor, sitting outside of class talking to friends, or sitting in your dorm room watching television.

The world is full of stimuli. A stimulus is any unit of input affecting one or more of the five senses: sight, smell, taste, touch, and hearing. The process by which we select, organize, and interpret these stimuli into a meaningful and coherent picture is called **perception**. In essence, perception is how we see the world around us and how we recognize that we need some help in making a purchasing decision. People cannot perceive every stimulus in their environment. Therefore, they use **selective exposure** to decide which stimuli to notice and which to ignore. A typical consumer is exposed to more than 250 advertising messages a day but notices only between 11 and 20.

A **belief** is an organized pattern of knowledge that an individual holds as true about his or her world. A consumer might believe that Sony's camcorder makes the best home videos, tolerates hard use, and is reasonably priced. These beliefs might be based on knowledge, faith, or hearsay. Consumers tend to develop a set of beliefs about a product's attributes and then, through these beliefs, a *brand image*—a set of beliefs about a particular brand. In turn, the brand image shapes consumers' attitudes toward the product.

An **attitude** is a learned tendency to respond consistently toward a given object, idea, or concept, such as a brand. Attitudes rest on an individual's value system, which represents personal standards of good and bad, right and wrong,

personality
A way of organizing and grouping how an individual reacts to situations.

self-concept
How people perceive themselves.

ideal self-image
The way an individual would like to be.

real self-image
How an individual actually perceives him- or herself.

perception
The process by which we select, organize, and interpret stimuli into a meaningful and coherent picture.

selective exposure
The process of deciding which stimuli to notice and which to ignore.

belief
An organized pattern of knowledge that an individual holds as true about the world.

attitude
Learned tendency to respond consistently toward a given object, idea, or concept.

and so forth; therefore, attitudes tend to be more enduring and complex than beliefs. For an example of the nature of attitudes, consider the differing attitudes of consumers around the world toward the practice of purchasing on credit. Americans have long been enthusiastic about charging goods and services and are willing to pay high interest rates for the privilege of postponing payment. To many European consumers, doing what amounts to taking out a loan—even a small one—to pay for anything seems absurd.

Types of Consumer Buying Decisions

All consumer buying decisions generally fall along a continuum of three broad categories: routine response behaviour, limited decision-making, and extensive decision-making (see Exhibit 12.4). Goods and services in these three categories can best be described in terms of five factors: level of consumer involvement, length of time to make a decision, cost of the good or service, degree of information search, and the number of alternatives considered. The level of consumer involvement is perhaps the most significant determinant in classifying buying decisions. **Involvement** is the amount of time and effort a buyer invests in the search, evaluation, and decision processes of consumer behaviour.

Frequently purchased, low-cost goods and services are generally associated with **routine response behaviour**. These goods and services can also be called low-involvement products, because consumers spend little time on searching and decision-making before making the purchase. Usually, buyers are familiar with several different brands in the product category but stick with one brand. Consumers engaged in routine response behaviour normally don't experience need recognition until they are exposed to advertising or see the product displayed on a store shelf.

Limited decision-making typically occurs when a consumer has previous product experience but is unfamiliar with the current brands available. Limited decision-making is also associated with lower levels of involvement (although higher than routine decisions), because consumers do expend moderate effort in searching for information or in considering various alternatives. Suppose the children's usual brand of cereal, Kellogg's Corn Flakes, is unavailable in the grocery store. Completely out of cereal at home, the parent now must select another brand. Before making a final selection, he or she might pull from the shelf several brands similar to Kellogg's Corn Flakes, such as Cheerios, to compare their nutritional value and calories and to decide whether the children will like the new cereal.

involvement

The amount of time and effort a buyer invests in the searches, evaluations, and decision processes of consumer behaviour.

routine response behaviour

Purchase of low-cost, frequently bought items with little search or decision-making.

limited decision-making

Situation in which a consumer has previous product experience but is unfamiliar with the current brands available.

Exhibit 12.4 Continuum of Consumer Buying Decisions

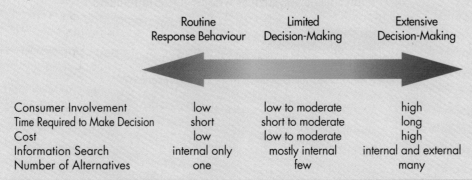

	Routine Response Behaviour	Limited Decision-Making	Extensive Decision-Making
Consumer Involvement	low	low to moderate	high
Time Required to Make Decision	short	short to moderate	long
Cost	low	low to moderate	high
Information Search	internal only	mostly internal	internal and external
Number of Alternatives	one	few	many

extensive decision-making

Purchasing an unfamiliar, expensive, infrequently bought item.

Consumers practice **extensive decision-making** when buying an unfamiliar, expensive product or an infrequently bought item. This process is the most complex type of consumer buying decision and is associated with high involvement on the part of the consumer. This process resembles the model outlined in Exhibit 12.3. These consumers want to make the right decision, so they want to know as much as they can about the product category and available brands. Buyers use several criteria for evaluating their options and spend much time seeking information. Buying a home or a car, for example, requires extensive decision-making.

Business-to-Business Purchase Decision-Making

Business buyer behaviour and business markets are different from consumer markets. Business markets include institutions such as hospitals and schools, manufacturers, wholesalers and retailers, and various branches of government. The key difference between a consumer product and a business product is the intended use. If you purchase a certain model of Dell computer for your home so you can surf the Internet, it is a consumer good. If a purchasing agent for MuchMusic buys exactly the same computer for a MuchMusic scriptwriter, it is a business good. Why? The reason is that MuchMusic is a business, so the computer will be used in a business environment.

Characteristics of the Business-to-Business Market

The main differences between consumer markets and business markets are as follows:

1. *Purchase volume.* Business customers buy in much larger quantities than consumers. Think how many truckloads of sugar M&M/Mars must purchase to make one day's output of M&Ms. Imagine the number of batteries Sears buys each day for resale to consumers. Think of the number of pens the federal government must use each day.

2. *Number of customers.* Business marketers usually have far fewer customers than consumer marketers. As a result, it is much easier to identify prospective buyers and monitor current needs. Think about how few customers for airplanes or industrial cranes there are compared to the more than 4 million consumer households in the Canada.

3. *Location of buyers.* Business customers tend to be much more geographically concentrated than consumers. For example, the automobile industry is concentrated in Ontario, and the oil industry is concentrated in Alberta. Suppliers to these industries often locate close to the industries to lower distribution costs and facilitate communication.

4. *Direct distribution.* Business sales tend to be made directly to the buyer, because such sales frequently involve large quantities or custom-made items like heavy machinery. Consumer goods are more likely to be sold through intermediaries, such as wholesalers and retailers.

concept check

Explain the consumer decision-making process.

How do business markets differ from consumer markets?

MARKET SEGMENTATION

 learning goal

market segmentation
The process of separating, identifying, and evaluating the layers of a market to identify a target market.

The study of buyer behaviour helps marketing managers better understand why people make purchases. To identify the target markets that might be most profitable for the firm, managers use **market segmentation**, which is the process of separating, identifying, and evaluating the layers of a market to identify a target market. For instance, a target market might be segmented into two groups: families with children and those without children. Families with young children are likely to buy hot cereals and pre-sweetened cereals. Families with no children are more likely to buy health-oriented cereals. You can be sure that cereal companies plan their marketing mixes with this difference in mind. A business market, on the other hand, might be segmented by large customers and small customers or by geographic area.

The five basic forms of consumer market segmentation are demographic, geographic, psychographic, benefit, and volume. Their characteristics are summarized in Exhibit 12.5 and are discussed in the following sections.

Demographic Segmentation

demographic segmentation
The differentiation of markets through the use of categories such as age, education, gender, income, and household size.

Demographic segmentation uses categories such as age, education, gender, income, and household size to differentiate among markets. This form of market segmentation is the most common. Statistics Canada provides a great deal of demographic data. For example, marketing researchers can use census data to find areas within cities that contain high concentrations of high-income consumers, singles, blue-collar workers, and so forth.

Many products are targeted to various age groups. Most music CDs, Pepsi, Coke, many movies, and thousands of other products are targeted toward teenagers and persons under 25 years old. In contrast, most cruises, medical products, fine jewellery, vacation homes, Buicks, and denture products are targeted toward people 50 years old and up. An example of how Frito Lay targets various age groups for three of its most popular products is shown is Exhibit 12.6.

Certain markets are segmented by gender. These include clothing, cosmetics, personal care items, magazines, jewellery, and footwear. Gillette, for example, is one of the world's best-known marketers of personal care products and has historically targeted men for the most part. Yet women's products have generated most of Gillette's growth since 1992. Gillette's shaving line for women has expanded into a $400 million global business, growing nearly 20 percent annually. Gillette has increased its advertising budget to help it reach a goal of more than $1 billion in revenues from women's shaving products worldwide.

Exhibit 12.5 | Forms of Consumer Market

FORM	GENERAL CHARACTERISTICS
Demographic segmentation	Age, education, gender, income, race, social class, household size
Geographic segmentation	Regional location (e.g., Maritimes and Newfoundland and Labrador, Central Canada, Western Canada, Northern Canada); population density (urban, suburban, rural); city or county size; climate
Psychographic segmentation	Lifestyle, personality, interests, values, attitudes
Benefit segmentation	Benefits provided by the good or service
Volume segmentation	Amount of use (light versus heavy)

Exhibit 12.6 | Age Segmentation for Fritos, Doritos, and Tostitos

	NAME DERIVATION	YEAR INTRODUCED	MAIN INGREDIENTS	DEMOGRAPHIC	SNACK NICHE, ACCORDING TO FRITO-LAY
Frito	"Little fried bits" (Spanish)	1932	Corn, vegetable oil, salt	33- to 51-year-old males	"Hunger satisfaction"
Doritos	"Little bits of gold"	1964	Corn, vegetable oil, cheddar cheese, salt	Teens, mostly male	"Bold and daring snacking"
Tostitos	"Little toasted bits" (Spanish)	1981	White corn, vegetable oil, salt	Upscale consumers born between 1946 and 1964	"Casual interaction through friends and family . . . a social food that brings people together"

SOURCE: Frito-Lay.

Income is another popular way of segmenting markets. Income level influences consumers' wants and determines their buying power. Housing, clothing, automobiles, and alcoholic beverages are among the many markets segmented by income. Michelina's frozen dinners are targeted to lower income groups, whereas Stouffer's Lean Cuisine line is aimed at higher income consumers.

Geographic Segmentation

geographic segmentation

The differentiation of markets by region of the country, city or county size, market density, or climate.

Geographic segmentation means segmenting markets by region of the country, city or county size, market density, or climate. *Market density* is the number of people or businesses within a certain area. Many companies segment their markets geographically to meet regional preferences and buying habits. Both Ford and Chevrolet, for instance, sell more pickup trucks and truck parts in the middle of the country than on either coast.

Psychographic Segmentation

psychographic segmentation

The differentiation of markets by personality or lifestyle.

Race, income, occupation, and other demographic variables help in developing strategies but often do not paint the entire picture of consumer needs. Demographics provide the skeleton, but psychographics add meat to the bones. **Psychographic segmentation** is market segmentation by personality or lifestyle. People with common activities, interests, and opinions are grouped together and given a "lifestyle name." For example, Harley-Davidson divides its customers into seven lifestyle segments, from "cocky misfits," who are most likely to be arrogant troublemakers, to "laid-back camper types" committed to cycling and nature, to "classy capitalists," who have wealth and privilege.

L. L. Bean is a world-renowned outfitter serving people who love the outdoors. Psychographic segmentation is market segmentation by personality or lifestyle.

Benefit Segmentation

benefit segmentation
The differentiation of markets based on what a product will do rather than on customer characteristics.

Benefit segmentation is based on what a product will do rather than on consumer characteristics. For years Crest toothpaste was targeted toward consumers concerned with preventing cavities. Recently, Crest subdivided its market. It now offers regular Crest; Crest Tartar Control, for people who want to prevent cavities and tartar buildup; Crest for kids, with sparkles that taste like bubble gum; another Crest that prevents gum disease, and Crest Vivid White, for people wanting whiter teeth. Sensodyne toothpaste is aimed at people with highly sensitive teeth.

Volume Segmentation

volume segmentation
The differentiation of markets based on the amount of the product purchased.

The fifth main type of segmentation is **volume segmentation**, which is based on the amount of the product purchased. Just about every product has heavy, moderate, and light users, as well as non-users. Heavy users often account for a very large portion of a product's sales. Thus, a firm might want to target its marketing mix to the heavy user segment.

concept check

Define market segmentation.

List and discuss the five basic forms of market segmentation.

USING MARKETING RESEARCH TO SERVE EXISTING CUSTOMERS AND FIND NEW CUSTOMERS

6 *learning goal*

How do successful companies learn what their customers value? Through marketing research, companies can be sure they are listening to the voice of the customer. **Marketing research** is the process of planning, collecting, and analyzing

marketing research
The process of planning, collecting, and analyzing data relevant to a marketing decision.

HOT Links

A good place to learn more about marketing research is Quirks Marketing research review, http://www.quirks.com. In addition to articles, you can link to major marketing research firms.

data relevant to a marketing decision. The results of this analysis are then communicated to management. The information collected through marketing research includes the preferences of customers, the perceived benefits of products, and consumer lifestyles. Research helps companies make better use of their marketing budgets. Marketing research has a range of uses from fine-tuning existing products to discovering whole new marketing concepts.

For example, everything at the Olive Garden restaurant chain, from the décor to the wine list, is based on marketing research. Each new menu item is put through a series of consumer taste tests before being added to the menu. Hallmark Cards uses marketing research to test messages, cover designs, and even the size of the cards. Hallmark's experts know which kinds of cards will sell best in which places. For instance, in geographic regions where engagement parties are popular, engagement cards sell best.

In this section, we examine the marketing research process, which consists of the following steps:

1. Define the marketing problem.
2. Choose a method of research.
3. Collect the data.
4. Analyze the research data.
5. Make recommendations to management.

Define the Marketing Problem

The most critical step in the marketing research process is defining the marketing problem. This involves writing either a problem statement or a list of research objectives. If the problem is not defined properly, the remainder of the research will be a waste of time and money. Two key questions can help in defining the marketing problem correctly:

1. Why is the information being sought? By discussing with managers what the information is going to be used for and what decisions might be made as a result, the researcher can get a clearer grasp of the problem.

2. Does the information already exist? If so, money and time can be saved, and a quick decision can be made.

Choose a Method of Research

survey research
A marketing research method in which data are gathered from respondents in person, by telephone, by mail, at a mall, or through the Internet to obtain facts, opinions, and attitudes.

After the problem is correctly defined, a research method is chosen. There are three basic research methods: survey, observation, and experiment.

With **survey research**, data are gathered from respondents in person, at a mall, or through the Internet, by telephone, or mail to obtain facts, opinions, and attitudes. A questionnaire is used to provide an orderly and structured approach to data gathering. Face-to-face interviews might take place at the respondent's home, in a shopping mall, or at a place of business.

observation research
A marketing research method in which the investigator monitors respondents' actions without interacting directly with the respondents; for example, by using cash registers with scanners.

Observation research is research that monitors respondents' actions without direct interaction. In the fastest-growing form of observation research, researchers use cash registers with scanners that read tags with bar codes to identify the item being purchased. Technological advances are rapidly expanding the future of observation research. For example, ACNielsen has been using black boxes for years on television sets to obtain information on a family's viewing habits silently. But what if the set is on but no one is in the room? To overcome that problem, researchers will soon rely on infrared passive "people meters," which will identify the faces of family members watching the television program. Thus, the meter can duly record when the set is on and no one is watching.

In the third research method, **experiment**, the investigator changes one or more variables—price, package, design, shelf space, advertising theme, or advertising expenditures—while observing the effects of those changes on another variable (usually sales). The objective of experiments is to measure causality. For example, an experiment might reveal the impact that a change in package design has on sales.

Collect the Data

Two types of data are used in marketing research: **primary data**, which are collected directly from the original source to solve a problem; and **secondary data**, information that has already been collected for a project other than the current one but can be used to help solve it. Secondary data can come from a number of sources, among them government agencies, trade associations, research bureaus, universities, the Internet, commercial publications, and internal company records. Company records include sales invoices, accounting records, data from previous research studies, and historical sales data.

Primary data are usually gathered through some form of survey research. As described earlier, survey research often relies on interviews. See Exhibit 12.7 for the different types of surveys. Today, conducting surveys over the Internet is the fastest-growing form of survey research.

Analyze the Data

After the data have been collected, the next step in the research process is data analysis. The purpose of this analysis is to interpret and draw conclusions from the mass of collected data. Many software statistical programs, such as SAS and SPSS, are available to make this task easier for the researcher.

Make Recommendations to Management

After completing the data analysis, the researcher must prepare the report and communicate the conclusions and recommendations to management. This is a key step in the process, because marketing researchers who want their conclusions acted on must convince the manager that the results are credible and justified by the data collected. Today, presentation software like PowerPoint and Astound provides easy-to-use tools for creating reports and presentations that are more interesting, compelling, and effective than was possible just a few years ago.

concept check

Define marketing research.

Explain the marketing research process.

What are the three basic marketing research methods?

Exhibit 12.7 | Common Types of Survey Research

Internet surveys
Conducted on the Internet, often using respondents from huge Internet panels (persons agreeing to participate in a series of surveys).

Executive surveys
Interviews of professionals (e.g., engineers, architects, doctors, executives) or decision makers that are conducted at their place of business.

Mall-intercept surveys
Interviews with consumers that are conducted in a shopping mall or other high-traffic location. Interviews may be done in a public area of the mall, or respondents might be taken to a private test area.

Central location telephone surveys
Interviews are conducted from a telephone facility set up for that purpose. These facilities typically have equipment that permits supervisors to monitor the interviewing unobtrusively while it is taking place. Many of these facilities do national sampling from a single location. An increasing number have computer-assisted interviewing capabilities. At these locations, the interviewer sits in front of a computer terminal attached to a mainframe or personal computer. The questionnaire is programmed into the computer, and the interviewer uses the keyboard to enter responses directly.

Self-administered questionnaires
Self-administered questionnaires are most frequently employed at high-traffic locations, such as shopping malls, or in captive audience situations, such as classrooms and airplanes. Respondents are given general information on how to fill out the questionnaire and are expected to fill it out on their own. Kiosk-based point-of-service touch screens provide a way of capturing information from individuals in stores, health clinics, and other shopping or service environments. Sometimes software-driven questionnaires on diskettes are sent to individuals who have personal computers.

Ad hoc (one-shot) mail surveys
Questionnaires are mailed to a sample of consumers or industrial users, without prior contact by the researcher. Instructions are included, and respondents are asked to fill out the questionnaire and return it via mail. Sometimes a gift or monetary incentive is provided.

Mail panels
Questionnaires are mailed to a sample of individuals who have been pre-contacted. The panel concept has been explained to them, and they have agreed to participate for some period of time in exchange for gratuities. Mail panels typically generate much higher response rates than do ad hoc mail surveys.

Trends in Marketing

 learning goal

To discover exactly what customers value most, organizations are using innovative techniques for collecting customer information. Some of the more sophisticated marketing research techniques that are growing in popularity are scanner-based research, capitalizing on loyalty cards, and one-to-one marketing.

SCANNER-BASED RESEARCH

scanner-based research
System for gathering information from a single group of respondents by continuously monitoring the advertising, promotion, and pricing they are exposed to and the things that they buy.

Scanner-based research is a system for gathering information from a single group of respondents by continuously monitoring the advertising, promotion, and pricing they are exposed to and the things they buy. The variables measured are advertising campaigns, coupons, displays, and product prices. The result is a huge database of marketing efforts and consumer behaviour. Scanner-based research is bringing ever closer the Holy Grail of marketing research: an accurate, objective picture of the direct causal relationship between different kinds of marketing efforts and actual sales.

The two major scanner-based suppliers are Information Resources, Inc. (IRI), and the ACNielsen Company. Each has about half the market. However, IRI is the founder of scanner-based research.

4 How do consumers and organizations make buying decisions?

Buyer behaviour is what people and businesses do in buying and using goods and services. The consumer decision-making process consists of the following steps: recognizing a need, seeking information, evaluating alternatives, purchasing the product, judging the purchase outcome, and engaging in post-purchase behaviour. A number of factors influence the process. Cultural, social, individual, and psychological factors have an impact on consumer decision-making. The main differences between consumer and business markets are purchase volume, number of customers, location of buyers, direct distribution, and rational purchase decisions.

5 What are the five basic forms of market segmentation?

Success in marketing depends on understanding the target market. One technique used to identify a target market is market segmentation. The five basic forms of segmentation are demographic (population statistics), geographic (location), psychographic (personality or lifestyle), benefit (product features), and volume (amount purchased).

6 How is marketing research used in marketing decision–making?

Much can be learned about consumers through marketing research, which involves collecting, recording, and analyzing data important in marketing goods and services, and communicating the results to management. Marketing researchers can use primary data, which are gathered through door-to-door, mall-intercept, telephone, the Internet, and mail interviews. The Internet is becoming a quick, cheap, and efficient way of gathering primary data. Secondary data are available from a variety of sources including government, trade, and commercial associations. Secondary data save time and money, but they might not meet researchers' needs. A huge amount of secondary data is available on the Internet. Both primary and secondary data give researchers a better idea of how the market will respond to the product. Thus, they reduce the risk of producing something the market doesn't want.

7 What are the trends in understanding the consumer?

BehaviorScan uses scanners and television meters to measure the impact of marketing on sales of specific products. BehaviorScan panels can also measure the impact of coupons, free samples, store displays, new packaging, and pricing. A second trend is retailers capitalizing on shopper loyalty cards. These enable managers to make customer shopping patterns. A third trend is the growing use of one-to-one marketing by using databases to target the needs of customers and non-customers more accurately.

KEY TERMS

attitude 378
belief 378
benefit
  segmentation 383
buyer behaviour 375
cognitive
  dissonance 389

EXPERIENTIAL EXERCISES

1. Can the marketing concept be applied effectively by a sole proprietorship, or is it more appropriate for larger businesses with more managers? Explain.

2. Before starting your own business, you should develop a marketing strategy to guide your efforts. Choose one of the business ideas listed, and develop a marketing strategy for the business. Include the type of market research (both

primary and secondary) you will perform and how you will define your target market.

   a. Crafts store to capitalize on the renewed interest in knitting and other crafts

   b. On-line corporate-training company

   c. Ethnic restaurant near your campus

   d. Another business opportunity that interests you

3. "Market segmentation is the most important concept in marketing." Why do you think some marketing professionals make this statement? Give an example of each form of segmentation.

4. Pick a specific product that you use frequently, such as a cosmetic or toiletry item, a snack food, article of clothing, book, computer program, or music CD. What is the target market for this product, and does the company's marketing strategy reflect this? Now consider the broader category of your product. How can this product be changed and/or the marketing strategy adjusted to appeal to other market segments?

5. Can marketing research be carried out in the same manner all over the world? Why or why not?

6. Visit the SRI Consulting site, **http://www.sric-bi.com**, and click on the VALS Survey link. First read about the VALS survey and how marketers can use it. Describe its value. Then take the survey to find out which psychographic segment you're in. Do you agree or disagree with the results? Why or why not?

7. How good was the marketing strategy you developed in Question 2? Using advice from the marketing section of *Entrepreneur* (**http://www.entrepreneur.com**) or other resources, revisit your marketing strategy for the business you selected and revise the plan accordingly. (*Entrepreneur*'s article "Write a Simple Marketing Plan" is a good place to start.) What did you overlook? (If you didn't do this exercise, pick one of the businesses and draft a marketing strategy using on-line resources to guide you.)

8. As the number of people on-line continues to grow, more of the Web surfers are also buying products on-line. What do researchers say about the characteristics of the on-line market? What market segments are appearing? Visit several sites to research this topic, and then prepare a report on the demographics of on-line markets and other key considerations for marketers. NUA Internet Surveys is a good place to start: **http://www.gdsourcing.ca/**. You'll find summaries of the latest research studies and can search for others by category. From there, you can link to the sites of market research companies. (Many research company sites require registration or subscriptions; however, you can check press releases for summaries of research findings.) Also search for "Internet marketing" or "on-line marketing" using search engines and business publication sites such as *Business Week*, *Entrepreneur*, and *Inc.*

REVIEW QUESTIONS

1. What is marketing? What is an exchange in marketing?

2. What does the marketing concept involve?

3. What is the difference between customer value and customer satisfaction? How are these related to building relationships?

4. Why is it important for marketers to understand the external environment? What are the six general categories of the environment that marketers must evaluate?

5. What is a target market?

6. What are the various competitive advantages that a company can create?

7. What are the four variables in the marketing mix?

8. What influences consumers in their decision-making?

9. What are the characteristics of the business-to-business market?

10. What is market segmentation? What are the five basic forms of consumer market segmentation?

11. What is market research, and what are the steps in the market research process?

CREATIVE THINKING CASE
Icebergs Are Hot

Scott Lundquist has a rather unusual company. His firm harvests and sells icebergs. Listen to what he says about such an unusual occupation.

I'm the only person in Alaska with a "glacier ice harvesting" permit. You need one. They don't want you screwing around with baby seals. My ice costs $1.56 a pound. It isn't 7-Eleven ice. I'm trying to reach the 1 or 2 percent of the population who want premium ice. In my sales pitch, I stress that my ice is 8,000 to 10,000 years old, the remnants of the last Ice Age. Glacier ice is dense, so it melts slower, chilling your beverage without diluting it. That point works. Everything cold is cool now, so I'm sure ice is going to be the next fad. Right now, I've got six customers. Lufthansa buys it for cocktail parties. One day they called up the state and asked, "Is there any way we can get some glacier ice? Some German clients want it for their drinks." I sold them a 5,600-pound piece. I've also sold ice to Johnnie Walker for the same thing, and I just sent a company down in Santa Barbara [California] a 25-pound sample,—by FedEx. I'm also talking with Princess Cruises, trying to get 1,000-pound pieces on their cruise ships. They could put them right on their decks. It will last five days before melting. People could reach out and touch one. Being in front of a glacier is like being in God's country. Selling isn't all I do. I have to go get the ice, and that is the hard work. We'll board a 51-foot fishing boat and steam for Blackstone Glacier. The best ice is closest to the face where it's just dropped into the water. We only take ones that are clear and pure. We wrap a chain around it and hoist it into the boat. Then it's two hours back to Whittier, where we load the ice with a forklift, onto a flatbed truck or into my one-ton pickup before driving back to my freezer in Anchorage. You gotta get back fast. You hope for cold, cloudy days and you dread the sun. You lose some. You always lose some.[7]

SOURCE: "The Persuaders," Business 2.0, November 2002. © 2002 Time Inc. All Rights Reserved.

CRITICAL THINKING QUESTIONS

1. Is Scott following the marketing concept?

2. Is he segmenting the market?

3. Who might be some other customers for his product?

4. Can you think of any way that Scott might expand his product line?

VIDEO CASE
Building Customer Relationships—One Kid at a Time

If giving consumers what they want is an excellent way to ensure loyalty and build long-term customer relationships, Fisher-Price has the right idea. Inviting its customers to participate in product design and development studies is an integral part of its marketing research programs. It is also one way Fisher-Price makes sure that products will achieve high levels of customer acceptance and success when they finally do reach the marketplace.

Founded in 1930, Fisher-Price is the most widely recognized brand of infant and preschool toys in the industry, and a trusted name in early childhood development. The company has earned a reputation for designing and producing high-quality toys that provide both developmental benefits and fun for children from birth to age 5.

Shelly Glick Gryfe, Director of Marketing Research at Fisher-Price, is proud of its Play Lab and Mom Talks, which are conducted in-house. Drawing from a list of several thousand volunteers, Gryfe and her team invite mothers with children who meet a specific demographic requirement to spend the day at their facility. In the Play Lab children do arts and crafts, read stories, and are encouraged to interact with a selection of toys. Some of the toys are still in development, whereas others, including those from competing companies, are already on the market.

These sessions are designed to provide the marketing research team with "directional information." Their designers, who observe the children from behind a one-way mirror, are looking for feedback on how they can make Fisher-Price products even better. It was this level of detailed observation that was responsible for the large feet on the company's preschool-age action figures called Rescue Heroes. The designers noted how frustrated the children became when a competitor's action figures kept toppling over.

Mothers are also an important part of the process. After viewing models, videos, and photo boards, and observing children's interactions with the toys, they are consulted on such topics as ranking products in order of desirability and giving opinions on age appropriateness and product pricing. Gryfe says parents participate because they "want to have good toys coming out for their children."

There is no doubt that kids and moms know what they like. Mothers loved the "good guy" theme of the Rescue Heroes line when it was first introduced in 1998 and declared it a winner. CBS television agreed, creating a Rescue Heroes TV series for young viewers, which has helped boost ongoing demand for the products. At Fisher-Price, giving the customer a voice means everyone wins.

CRITICAL THINKING QUESTIONS

1. How does Fisher-Price's marketing research strategy help build customer loyalty?

2. What other "spin-off" benefits does it produce for the company? For the consumer?

3. Is there a downside to having customers involved in the product development process? Explain.

SOURCES: Adapted from the video "Fisher-Price: The Pre-School Boy;" and information on Fisher-Price brands from the Mattel corporate Web site, http://www.mattel.com (accessed April 22, 2003).

E-Commerce Case
Sunworks Organic Farm: For profit or health?

In the case of Sunworks Farm, the original idea was to produce organic products to help Sheila, one of the owners, battle fibromyalgia, which had been plaguing her for four years. A naturopath had suggested that Sheila use organic food, and within six weeks, she recovered, marking the beginning of great things for the family. The Hamilton farm has been certified organic since 1997. They started with 80 chickens, and they now raise 55,000 chickens. Sunworks Farm provides 550 dozen eggs every week, and they always sell out early in the weekend. The farm also produces whole chickens, roasts, sausages, and other products.

The Hamiltons have a strong family orientation as well, with Sheila's sister raising pigs and lambs, which the Hamiltons then market. Sheila's daughters and their families also work in the business. Sunworks' philosophy is heavily influenced by their ethics. As Ron Hamilton says, "When our 2,000 customers buy our food, they buy our ethics package." This package includes a concern for the health of the earth as well as people and animals. They use only one 27 horsepower tractor for the entire outdoor aspect of their farm. The animals are raised outdoors when weather permits and graze naturally, supplemented only by organic feed.

By offering a choice to consumers, the Hamiltons are living their values. There are no chemicals, medications, or other toxins applied to their land or fed to their animals. In addition, products such as sausage, wieners, and bacon contain no fillers, nitrates, sulphites, or MSG. The philosophy, as stated on their Web site (**http://www.sunworksfarm.com**), is as follows:
We believe that:

1. It is our privilege to be stewards of the land and that we should leave it in a better state than when we got it. We do our best to work with nature and not against it.

2. Our children should be raised in a healthy mental and physical environment.

3. Animals should be treated kindly, humanely, ethically and have access to fresh air, clean water, green grass and sunshine.

4. A healthy environment and gentle handling grows healthy animals, which reduces disease and the need for medication.

5. We want to grow good healthy food for our customers. We guarantee that you will not taste better meat than our pasture-raised products.

Under this philosophy, based on the ancient Haida saying "We do not inherit the land from our ancestors, we borrow it from our children," Sunworks Farms has continued to prosper, with many customers reaping the benefits of the superior product produced with care and concern for the animals and the earth.

CRITICAL THINKING QUESTIONS

1. As a consumer, you might have noticed that organic products are generally more expensive than traditionally mass-produced products. Why are these products more expensive? Are you willing to pay the extra cost? Why or why not?

2. Suggest a marketing strategy for a company such as Sunworks Farm.

SOURCES: Pamela Irving, "Farming for the Love of It: Organic Food," Edmonton Journal, March 22, 2006; and Sunworks Farms Web site, http://www.sunworksfarm.com (accessed July 17, 2006).

Making the Connection

Developing Quality Products at the Right Price

In this chapter we will continue to look at the functional area of marketing but more specifically at two of the four Ps of the marketing mix—product and price. One of our critical success factors is to *provide value through offering quality products at a reasonable price.* That is what this chapter is all about. One of the keys to success in marketing, therefore, is to provide something of unique value to the customer. Understanding our customers and what their needs are was the focus of the previous chapter. With this understanding of what will *meet the customers' needs,* the second key to success in marketing is to market the product in such a way that you convince customers of its benefit. They must believe that it will satisfy their needs, or they won't buy it. This is where the four Ps come in. Not only does marketing have to work with the other functional areas in an integrative fashion, as we discussed in Chapter 12, the marketing functions must also work together in an integrative way to convince the customer of the unique benefit of the product. For example, if a company wants to promote a product that is of better quality than the competition and therefore designs it to have the features as well as the look of higher quality, promotes it in high-end publications, distributes it in high-end stores, but prices it below the competition, consumers will be confused about its quality.

All four of the elements must give a consistent message—they must form an integrative whole.

This integrative nature of marketing is quite evident when you consider that consumers make purchase decisions after considering many attributes of the product, including price. They consider the total value package—the combination of all the features that they receive at the price they have to pay. In this chapter, we discuss how consumers buy packages of benefits that include both the tangible and intangible attributes of the product and often require a combination of both the good itself and the service provided; for example, Burger King sells burgers and fries but also, along with that, quick food preparation and cleanliness. Therefore, product design is a very integrative concept in itself as well as involving other function areas, as in this example, the company must take into consideration *human resource* and *operational* issues to deliver these attributes to the customer.

One of the attributes that is considered in the purchase decision is packaging. In the chapter, we describe how packaging integrates both marketing and operational issues. From an operations perspective, packaging must protect the product's contents and make it convenient for the customer. Technology has influenced packaging to develop methods that keep products fresher, more convenient to use, and so on. However packaging is also important in brand identification and providing information on the product's features to appeal to the customer from a marketing perspective. From an external perspective, companies must consider the *political* environment and the impact of regulations on packaging design and on labelling in particular.

Another very integrative product concept is the product life cycle. It sounds like just a product concept, but the implications of what stage in the life cycle a product is at go far beyond the product itself into how it is priced, promoted, and distributed. At the new product stage, there are also obvious connections to the other parts of our business model. New product goals are usually stated in financial terms, and ideas are rejected if they don't meet financial goals. The firm must also consider whether it has the operational facilities to produce the product, as well as access to the necessary technology and human and *financial* resources. New product ideas need to be checked against long-range strategies as well, to ensure that plans at all levels relate back to the overall corporate *strategy*.

Whether a product is in the introductory or more mature stage, the price that is set for the product has obvious marketing implications but also has obvious connections to finance. The company must set a price that will earn a fair return but also provide value to the consumer. This connection with finance is no more obvious than in the discussion of the breakeven point. If the costs from operations, human resources, and marketing cannot be covered from the revenue generated by the product, then financially it is not feasible and can't be done within the current cost structure, regardless of its marketing appeal. Many students decide they like marketing because of the creative nature of it, and they think that if they pursue a career in marketing they can stay away from the numbers and let the finance people handle them. Try bringing a product to market without considering its price! Like it or not, all areas of the business are connected.

The external environment also has implications on both products and pricing. We've already discussed regulations on packaging emanating from the political environment, but the most obvious impact is in idea generation—the wants and needs of the *social* environment are the basis for new product ideas and improvements on existing merchandise. As both the expectations of this environment and competition from the *economic* environment increase and change at a rapid rate, understanding this environment is critical. Being *innovative* to stay ahead of the competition is very critical to success. *Technology* has had a great impact on developing products and pricing. In the chapter, we discuss using the Internet for new product development research, as well as using software models for adjusting pricing to maximize revenue.

An example of the impact of the external environment can be seen in the opening vignette describing the Crest SpinBrush, a spinning toothbrush that has helped Crest and Procter & Gamble "reclaim the title as the No. 1 oral care brand in the United States." The key to the success of the SpinBrush has undoubtedly been seeing a hole in the marketplace—between $50 electric toothbrushes and inexpensive manual ones—where customer needs were not met. However, pricing the SpinBrush just slightly higher than manual toothbrushes, at $5, was critical to meeting this need with a product that provided value to the customer. P&G's usual strategy was to price goods at a premium, based on the cost of the technology. Because of the speed of market entry in today's competitive environment, the company started with a more aggressive price, and sales growth was quite rapid as a result.

Chapter 13

© AP/WORLD WIDE PHOTOS

Developing Quality Products at the Right Price

learning goals

P&G's Positive Spin on Sales

The only time he loses sleep, says A. G. Lafley, is when he thinks a competitor might beat him to a hot new product. And Lafley is sleeping pretty well these days. The soft-spoken, silver-thatched CEO is leading consumer products giant Procter & Gamble (**http://www.pg.com**) from one hit to another. Crest's battery-powered SpinBrush for dental care and its Whitestrips for tooth brightening have helped Crest global sales grow 50 percent in the past two years—a surge unheard of for such a big, mature brand. That kind of innovation has sent P&G's profits into double-digit growth.

With the SpinBrush, P&G showed that it no longer suffers from the Not-Invented-Here syndrome. Making a bet on a small Cleveland, Ohio, start-up called Dr. John's and its invention of an ingenious battery-powered toothbrush that could be sold at a profit for roughly $6, Crest bought the firm at the beginning of last year and, by applying its marketing and distribution muscle, has turned it into a $200 million category killer. Lafley hopes it can be a model for the future. "I'd love to see a third to half of 'discovery' come from outside," he says. "I really want the doors open."

Davin Yates, team leader on the new toothbrush, never imagined how successful the Crest SpinBrush would be. Although most electric brushes cost more than $50, SpinBrush works on batteries and sells for just $5. Since receiving positive feedback in a focus group in October 2000, it has become the nation's best-selling toothbrush, manual or electric. In P&G's most recent fiscal year, it posted more than $200 million in global sales, helping Crest become the consumer product maker's twelfth billion-dollar brand. It has also helped Crest reclaim the title as number one oral care brand in the United States, a position it had lost to Colgate Palmolive's Colgate brand in 1998. "It's hard for P&G's business models to conceive of a business growing as quickly as SpinBrush," Yates says.

Perhaps the biggest change for P&G was in SpinBrush's pricing. P&G usually prices its goods at a premium based on the cost of technology. But competitors now follow new products more quickly, eroding P&G's pricing power. With SpinBrush, P&G reversed its usual thinking. It started with an aggressive price and then found a way to make a profit. If P&G had conceived of SpinBrush, admits Yates, "my gut tells me we would not have priced it where we did."

That's just the opportunity John Osher and his three colleagues saw when they had the SpinBrush brainstorm session back in 1998. Osher, then 55, had spent most of his career inventing things and selling them to big companies. His latest creation had been the Spin Pop, a lollipop attached to a battery-powered plastic handle, in which the candy spun at the press of a button. He had teamed up on the Spin Pop with John R. Nottingham and John W. Spirk, the principals of a Cleveland industrial design firm, and their in-house patent lawyer, Lawrence A. Blaustein. The Spin Pop had recently sold to Hasbro for millions, and the men were looking for another way to utilize the technology.

They can't remember who came up with the concept, but they know it came from their group walks through the aisles of their local Wal-Mart, where they went for inspiration. They saw that electric toothbrushes, from Sonicare to Interplak, cost more than $50 and for that reason held a fraction of the overall toothbrush market. They reasoned, Why not create a $5 electric brush using the Spin Pop technology? At just $1 more than the most expensive manual brushes, they figured many consumers would trade up. They spent 18 months designing and sourcing a high-quality brush that wouldn't cost more than $5, batteries included. "If it had cost $7.99, we wouldn't have gone forward," Osher says.[1]

Critical Thinking Questions

1. How are new products usually developed?
2. Where is the SpinBrush in the product life cycle?
3. What price strategy is being used for the SpinBrush?

The creation of a marketing mix normally begins with the first of the four Ps, product. Only when there is something to sell can marketers create a promotional theme, set a price, and establish a distribution channel (place). Organizations prepare for long-term success by creating and packaging products that add value and pricing them to meet the organization's financial objectives. In addition, organizations respond to changing customer needs by creating new products. We will now examine products, brands, and the importance of packaging. We will also discuss how new products are created and how they go through periods of sales growth and then decline. First, you will discover how managers set prices to reach pricing goals. Alternative pricing strategies used to reach specific target markets are then discussed. We conclude with a look at trends in products and pricing.

WHAT IS A PRODUCT?

1 learning goal

product
In marketing, any good or service, along with its perceived attributes and benefits, that creates value for the customer.

In marketing, a **product** is any good or service, along with its perceived attributes and benefits, that creates value for the customer. Attributes can be tangible or intangible. Among the tangible attributes are packaging and warranties, as illustrated in Exhibit 13.1. Intangible attributes are symbolic, such as brand image. People make decisions about which products to buy after considering both tangible and intangible attributes of a product. For example, when you buy a pair of jeans, you consider price, brand, store image, and style before you buy. These factors are all part of the marketing mix.

Exhibit 13.1 | Tangible and Intangible Attributes of a Product Create Value for the Buyer

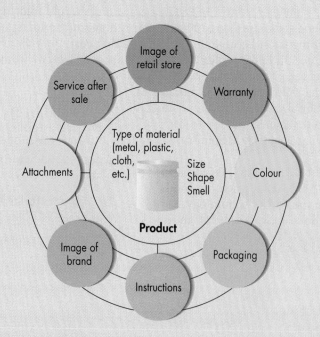

Exhibit 13.2 | Products Are Typically a Blend of Goods and Services

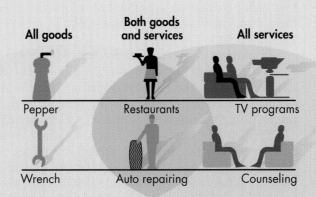

Products are often a blend of goods and services, as shown in Exhibit 13.2. For example, a Honda Accord (a good) would have less value without Honda's maintenance agreement (a service). Although Burger King sells such goods as sandwiches and French fries, customers expect quality service as well, including quick food preparation and cleanliness. When developing a product, an organization must consider how the combination of goods and services will provide value to the customer.

Classifying Consumer Products

Because most things sold are a blend of goods and services, the term *product* can be used to refer to both. After all, consumers are really buying packages of benefits that deliver value. The person who buys a plane ride on Air Canada is looking for a quick way to get from one city to another (the benefit). Providing this benefit requires goods (a plane, food) and services (ticketing, maintenance, piloting).

Marketers must know how consumers view the types of product their companies sell, so that they can design the marketing mix to appeal to the selected target market. To help them define target markets, marketers have devised product categories. Products that are bought by the end user are called *consumer products.* They include electric razors, sandwiches, cars, stereos, magazines, and houses. Consumer products that get used up, such as Breck hair mousse and Lay's potato chips, are called *consumer non-durables.* Those that last for a long time, such as Whirlpool washing machines and computers, are *consumer durables.*

Another way to classify consumer products is by the amount of effort consumers are willing to make to acquire them. The four major categories of consumer products are unsought products, convenience products, shopping products, and specialty products, as summarized in Exhibit 13.3.

Unsought products are products unknown to the potential buyer or known products that the buyer does not actively seek. New products fall into this category until advertising and distribution increase consumer awareness of them. Some goods are always marketed as unsought items, especially products we do not like to think about or care to spend money on. Life insurance, cemetery plots, medical services, and similar items require aggressive personal selling and highly persuasive advertising. Salespeople actively seek leads to potential buyers. Because consumers usually do not seek out this type of product, the company must go directly to them through a salesperson, direct mail, telemarketing, or direct-response advertising.

unsought products
Products that either are unknown to the potential buyer or are known but not actively sought by the buyer.

convenience products

Relatively inexpensive items that require little shopping effort and are purchased routinely without planning.

shopping products

Items that are bought after considerable planning, including brand-to-brand and store-to-store comparisons of price, suitability, and style.

specialty products

Items for which consumers search long and hard and for which they refuse to accept substitutes.

capital products

Large, expensive items with a long life span that are purchased by businesses for use in making other products or providing a service.

expense items

Items, purchased by businesses, that are smaller and less expensive than capital products and usually have a life span of less than one year.

Convenience products are relatively inexpensive items that require little shopping effort. Soft drinks, candy bars, milk, bread, and small hardware items are examples. We buy them routinely without much planning. This does not mean that such products are unimportant or obscure. Many, in fact, are well known by their brand names—such as Pepsi-Cola, Domino's pizza, Secret deodorant, and UPS shipping.

In contrast to convenience products, **shopping products** are bought only after a brand-to-brand and store-to-store comparison of price, suitability, and style. Examples are furniture, automobiles, a vacation in Europe, and some items of clothing. Convenience products are bought with little planning, but shopping products might be chosen months or even years before their actual purchase.

Specialty products are products for which consumers search long and hard and for which they refuse to accept substitutes. Expensive jewellery, designer clothing, state-of-the-art stereo equipment, limited-production automobiles, and gourmet dinners fall into this category. Because consumers are willing to spend much time and effort to find specialty products, distribution is often limited to one or two sellers in a given region, such as Holt Renfrew, Gucci, or the Porsche dealer.

Classifying Business Products

Products bought by businesses or institutions for use in making other products or in providing services are called *business* or *industrial products.* They are classified as either capital products or expense items. **Capital products** are usually large, expensive items with a long life span. Examples are buildings, large machines, and airplanes. **Expense items** are typically smaller, less expensive items that usually have a life span of less than a year. Examples are printer cartridges and paper. Industrial products are sometimes further classified in the following categories:

1. *Installations.* These are large, expensive capital items that determine the nature, scope, and efficiency of a company. Capital products like the General Motors Saturn assembly plant represent a big commitment against future earnings and profitability. Buying an installation requires longer negotiations, more planning, and the judgments of more people than buying any other type of product.

Exhibit 13.3 | Classification of Consumer Products by the Effort Expended to Buy Them

CONSUMER PRODUCT	EXAMPLES	DEGREE OF EFFORT EXPENDED BY CONSUMER
Unsought products	Life insurance Burial plots New products	No effort
Convenience products	Soft drinks Bread Milk Coffee	Very little or minimum effort
Shopping products	Automobiles Homes Vacations	Considerable effort
Specialty products	Expensive jewellery Gourmet dinners Limited-production automobiles	Maximum effort

2. *Accessories.* Accessories do not have the same long-run impact on the firm as installations, and they are less expensive and more standardized, but they are still capital products. Xerox copy machines, IBM personal computers (PCs), and smaller machines such as Black & Decker table drills and saws are typical accessories. Marketers of accessories often rely on well-known brand names and extensive advertising as well as personal selling.

3. *Component parts and materials.* These are expense items that are built into the end product. Some component parts are custom-made, such as a drive shaft for an automobile, a case for a computer, or a special pigment for painting harbour buoys; others are standardized for sale to many industrial users. Intel's Pentium chip for PCs and cement for the construction trade are examples of standardized component parts and materials.

4. *Raw materials.* Raw materials are expense items that have undergone little or no processing and are used to create a final product. Examples include lumber, copper, and zinc.

5. *Supplies.* Supplies do not become part of the final product. They are bought routinely and in fairly large quantities. Supply items run the gamut from pencils and paper to paint and machine oil. They have little impact on the firm's long-run profits. Bic pens, Unisource copier paper, and Pennzoil machine oil are typical supply items.

6. *Services.* These are expense items used to plan or support company operations; for example janitorial cleaning and management consulting.

HOT *Links*

See how one consulting firm helps clients pick the right name by pointing your Web browser to
http://www.namebase.com.

concept check

What is a product?

What are the classes of consumer goods?

Explain how business products are classified

Component parts need to be assembled to create the finished product for the consumer. Ground beef, hamburger buns, ketchup, mustard, and pickles are all component parts for Burger King hamburgers.

© ALYX KELLINGTON / INDEX STOCK IMAGERY

BUILDING BRAND EQUITY AND MASTER BRANDS

2   *learning goal*

brand

A company's product identifier that distinguishes the company's products from those of its competitors.

trademark

The legally exclusive design, name, or other identifying mark associated with a company's brand.

brand equity

The value of company and brand names.

master brand

A brand so dominant that consumers think of it immediately when a product category, use, attribute, or customer benefit is mentioned.

Most industrial and consumer products have a brand name. If everything came in a plain brown wrapper, life would be less colourful, and competition would decrease. Companies would also have less incentive to put out better products, because consumers would be unable to tell one company's products from those of another.

The product identifier for a company is its **brand.** Brands appear in the form of words, names, symbols, or designs. They are used to distinguish a company's products from those of its competitors. Examples of well-known brands are Kleenex tissues, Jeep automobiles, and IBM computers. A **trademark** is the legally exclusive design, name, or other identifying mark associated with a company's brand. No other company can use that same trademark.

Benefits of Branding

Branding has three main purposes: product identification, repeat sales, and new-product sales. The most important purpose is *product identification*. Branding allows marketers to distinguish their products from all others. In Exhibit 13.4, we identify the characteristics of an effective brand name. Many brand names are familiar to consumers and indicate quality. The term **brand equity** refers to the value of company and brand names. A brand that has high awareness, perceived quality, and brand loyalty among customers has high brand equity. Brand equity is more than awareness of a brand—it is the personality, soul, and emotion associated with the brand. Think of the feelings you have when you see the brand name Harley-Davidson, Nike, or even Microsoft. A brand with strong brand equity is a valuable asset. Some brands, such as Coke, Kodak, Marlboro, and Chevrolet, are worth hundreds of millions of dollars.

A brand so dominant in consumers' minds that they think of it immediately when a product category, use, attribute, or customer benefit is mentioned is a **master brand.** Scotch tape and Kleenex tissues are examples of master brands. Exhibit 13.5 lists some of North America's master brands in several product categories.

North American master brands command substantial premiums in many places around the world. Band-Aids command a 500 percent premium in China.

The MINI Cooper reflects the characteristics of an effective brand name. It's short, distinctive, and easy to remember, and describes the product's benefits.

Exhibit 13.4 | Characteristics of Effective Brand

- Easy to pronounce (by both domestic and foreign buyers)
- Easy to recognize
- Easy to remember
- Short
- Distinctive, unique
- Describes the product
- Describes the product's use
- Describes the product's benefits
- Has a positive connotation
- Reinforces the desired product image
- Is legally protectable in home and foreign markets of interest

Exhibit 13.5 | Master Brands of North America

PRODUCT CATEGORY	MASTER BRAND
Adhesive bandages	Band-Aid
Antacids	Alka-Seltzer
Baking soda	Arm & Hammer
Cellophane tape	Scotch Tape
Fast food	McDonald's
Gelatin	Jell-O
Rum	Bacardi
Salt	Morton
Soft drinks	Coca-Cola
Soup	Campbell's

Building Repeat Sales with Brand Loyalty

brand loyalty

A consumer's preference for a particular brand.

A consumer who tries one or more brands may decide to buy a certain brand regularly. The preference for a particular brand is **brand loyalty.** It lets consumers buy with less time, thought, and risk. Brand loyalty ensures future sales for the firm. It can also help protect a firm's share of the market, discourage new competitors, and thus prolong the brand's life. Brand loyalty can even allow companies to raise prices.

What makes people loyal to a brand? Though pricing, promotion, and product quality are important, customer interaction with the company might be most important in service businesses. A recent study found that consumers have little brand loyalty when shopping for themselves and their children, with fewer than a quarter having favourite brands in most grocery categories and just 27 percent being brand loyal for baby food and baby items. On the other hand, 53 percent stick to one brand of pet food. Nearly four in five consumers (78 percent) switch brands for price, 66 percent for product quality, 40 percent lured by promotional offers or coupons, and 33 percent just because of the availability of products or brands. Weekly store sale flyers generate the most consumer awareness among various promotions studies and are responsible for the most sales. Although 86 percent of grocery shoppers prepare a list, just 28 percent adhere to it after reaching the store.[2]

Brand loyalty typically builds over time. The first level is *brand recognition,* in which consumers recall having seen or heard of the brand. Companies often spend millions on promotion for new products to achieve brand recognition. A product might then achieve *brand preference,* where a consumer prefers a certain brand, such as the SpinBrush, but might buy an alternative because of lack of availability of the SpinBrush, price, or effective promotion by a competing product. The ultimate for any product manager is *brand insistence,* whereby consumers will buy only that brand. Lexus, for example, has reached this level among some car purchasers.

Facilitating New-Product Sales

The third main purpose of branding is to facilitate *new-product sales.* Let's assume that your class forms a company to market frozen tarts and pies under the name University Frozen Desserts. Now, assume that Pepperidge Farm develops a new line of identical frozen tarts and pies. Which ones will consumers try? The Pepperidge Farm products, without doubt. Pepperidge Farm is known for its quality frozen bakery products. Consumers assume that its new tarts and pies will be of high quality and therefore will be willing to give them a try. The well-known Pepperidge Farm brand is facilitating new-product introduction.

Types of Brands

manufacturer brands
Brands that are owned by national or regional manufacturers and widely distributed; also called national brands.

Brands owned by national or regional manufacturers and widely distributed are **manufacturer brands.** (These brands are sometimes called national brands, but because some of the brands are not owned by nationwide or international manufacturers, *manufacturer brand* is a more accurate term.) A few well-known manufacturer brands are Ford, Maytag, Nike, and Sony.

Manufacturer brands can bring new customers and new prestige to small retailers. For instance, a small bicycle repair shop in an Atlantic university town got the franchise to sell and repair Trek bicycles. The shop's profits grew quickly, and it became one of the most successful retail businesses in the university area. Because manufacturer brands are widely promoted, sales are often high. As well, most manufacturers of these brands offer frequent deliveries to their retailers. Thus, retailers can carry less stock and have less money tied up in inventory.

dealer brands
Brands that are owned by the wholesaler or retailer rather than the manufacturer.

Brands that are owned by the wholesaler or retailer, rather than the manufacturer, are **dealer brands.** Sears has several well-known dealer (or private) brands, including Craftsman, Diehard, and Kenmore. Dealer brands tie consumers to particular wholesalers or retailers. If you want a Kenmore washing machine, you must go to Sears.

Although profit margins are usually higher on dealer brands than on manufacturer brands, dealers must still stimulate demand for their products. Sears's promotion of its products has made the company one of the largest advertisers in North America. But promotion costs can cut heavily into profit margins, and if a dealer brand item is of poor quality, the dealer must assume responsibility for it. Sellers of manufacturer brands can refer a disgruntled customer to the manufacturer.

generic products
Products that carry no brand name, come in plain containers, and sell for much less than brand name products.

Many consumers don't want to pay the costs of manufacturer or dealer brands. One popular way to save money is to buy **generic products.** These products carry no brand name, come in plain containers, and sell for much less than brand name products. They are typically sold in simple packages with such simple labels as "liquid bleach" or "spaghetti." Sometimes manufacturers simply stop the production line and substitute a generic package for a brand package, though the product is exactly the same. The most popular generic products are garbage bags, jelly, paper towels, coffee cream substitutes, and paper napkins.

3 *learning goal*

THE IMPORTANCE OF PACKAGING IN A SELF-SERVICE ECONOMY

Just as a brand gives a product identity, its packaging also distinguishes it from competitors' products and increases its customer value. When you go to the store and reach for a bottle of dishwashing detergent, the package is the last chance a manufacturer has to convince you to buy its brand over a competitor's. A good package might cause you to reach for Joy rather than Palmolive.

The Functions of a Package

A basic function of packaging is to protect the product from breaking or spoiling and thus extend its life. A package should be easy to ship, store, and stack on a shelf and convenient for the consumer to buy. Many new packaging methods have been developed recently. Aseptic packages keep foods fresh for months without refrigeration. Examples are McCain's drinking boxes for juices, the Olinda Tetra Prisms for olive oil, and Hunt's/Del Monte's aseptic boxes for tomato sauce. Some package developers are creating "micro-atmospheres," which allow meat to stay fresh in the refrigerator for weeks.

A second basic function of packaging is to help promote the product by providing clear brand identification and information about the product's features. For example, Purina's Dog Chow brand, the leading dog food, was losing market share. The company decided that the pictures of dog breeds on the package were too old-fashioned and rural. With a new package featuring a photo of a dog and a child, sales have increased.

International Delight introduced a sleek, new package that offers consumers the convenience of opening, pouring, and closing using one hand. The flip-top spout increases the customer value.

HOT Links

Curious about how generic and private label products are manufactured? Visit the Private Label Manufacturers Association at http://www.plma.com.

HOT Links

For the latest trends in packaging, visit the Packaging Digest site, http://www.packagingdigest.com.

persuasive labelling

A type of product label that reinforces or repeats a promotional theme or logo.

informational labelling

A type of product label that provides product information to aid consumers in making product selections and minimize cognitive dissonance after the purchase.

Labelling

An integral part of any package is its label. Labelling generally takes one of two forms: persuasive or informational. **Persuasive labelling** focuses on a promotional theme or logo, and consumer information is secondary. Cheetos Crunchy, for example, features Chester Cheetah throwing a switch from "cheesy" to "dangerously cheesy." As Frito-Lay notes, "it's the taste against which all other crunchy cheese-flavoured snacks are measured by." Note that the standard promotional claims—such as "new," "improved," and "super"—are no longer very persuasive. Consumers have been saturated with "newness" and thus discount these claims.

Informational labelling, in contrast, is designed to help consumers make proper product selections and lower their cognitive dissonance after the purchase. Sears attaches a "label of confidence" to all its floor coverings. This label gives such product information as durability, colour, features, cleanability, care instructions, and construction standards. Most major furniture manufacturers affix labels to their wares that explain the products' construction features, such as type of frame, number of coils, and fabric characteristics.

Informational labelling might give consumers easy-to-understand instructions, explain how to use a product, or warn about potential misuse. The labels on vitamins, for example, include a list of ingredients, supplement facts, directions for use, and consumer warnings.

HOT Links

For more information about labelling requirements in Canada, search at http://afi.mytradeassociation.org.

warranty
A guarantee of the quality of a good or service.

implied warranty
An unwritten guarantee that a product is fit for the purpose for which it is sold.

express warranty
A written guarantee about a product, such as that it contains certain materials, will perform a certain way, or is otherwise fit for the purpose for which it was sold.

full warranty
The manufacturer's guarantee to meet certain minimum standards, including repair or replacement of the product or refunding the customer if the product does not work.

© DON MASON / CORBIS

Adding Value through Warranties

A **warranty** guarantees the quality of a good or service. An **implied warranty** is an unwritten guarantee that the product is fit for the purpose for which it was sold. An **express warranty** is made in writing. Express warranties range from simple statements, such as "100 percent cotton" (a guarantee of raw materials) and "complete satisfaction guaranteed" (a statement of performance), to extensive documentation that accompanies a product.

A **full warranty** means the manufacturer must meet certain minimum standards, including repair of any defects "within a reasonable time and without charge" and replacement of the merchandise or a full refund if the product does not work "after a reasonable number of attempts" at repair. Under the law, any warranty that does not live up to this tough standard must be "conspicuously" promoted as a limited warranty.

concept check

What are the functions of packaging?

Explain the differences between an implied warranty, an express warranty, and a full warranty.

CREATING PRODUCTS THAT DELIVER VALUE

4 learning goal

New products pump life into company sales, enabling the firm not only to survive but also to grow. Companies like Stelco (steel), Dow (chemicals), Hewlett-Packard (computers), Campbell Soup (foods), and Stryker (medical products) get most of their profits from new products. Companies that lead their industries in profitability and sales growth generate approximately half of their revenues from products developed within the previous five years.

Marketers have several different terms for new products, depending on how the product fits into a company's existing product line. When a firm introduces a product that has a new brand name and is in a product category new to the organization, it is classified as a new product.

A new flavour, size, or model using an existing brand name in an existing category is called a **line extension.** Diet Cherry Coke and caffeine-free Coke are line extensions. The strategy of expanding the line by adding new models has enabled companies like Seiko (watches), Kraft (cheeses), Oscar Mayer (lunch meats), and Sony (consumer electronics) to tie up a large amount of shelf space and brand recognition in a product category.

Organizing the New-Product Effort

In large organizations, such as Procter & Gamble and Kraft General Foods, new-product departments are responsible for generating new products. The department typically includes people from production, finance, marketing, and engineering. In smaller firms, committees perform the same functions as a new-product department.

For major new-product development tasks, companies sometimes form venture teams. IBM, for example, formed a venture group to create the first PC. Like a new-product department, a venture team includes members from most departments of the company. The idea, however, is to isolate the team members from the organization's day-to-day activities so that they can think and be creative. IBM is headquartered in New York, but the PC venture team was located in Florida.

How New Products Are Developed

Developing new products is both costly and risky. New-product failure rates for household and grocery products approach 80 percent.[3] The overall failure rate is approximately 60 percent. Industrial goods failure rates tend to be lower than those for consumer goods. To increase their chances for success, most firms use the following product development process, which is also summarized in Exhibit 13.6.

1. *Set new-product goals.* New-product goals are usually stated as financial objectives. For example, a company may want to recover its investment in three years or less. Or it may want to earn at least a 15 percent return on the investment. Non-financial goals might include using existing equipment or facilities.

2. *Develop new-product ideas.* Smaller firms usually depend on employees, customers, investors, and distributors for new ideas. Larger companies use these sources and more structured marketing research techniques, such as focus groups and brainstorming. A **focus group** consists of 8 to 12 participants led by a moderator in an in-depth discussion on one particular topic or concept. The goal of focus group research is to learn and understand what people have to say and why. The emphasis is on getting people talking at length and in detail about the subject at hand. The intent is to find out how they feel about a product, concept, idea, or organization, how it fits into their lives, and their emotional involvement with it. Focus groups often generate excellent product ideas. A few examples of focus group–influenced products are the interior design of the Toyota RAV4, Stick-Up room deodorizers, the Swiffer, and Wendy's Salad Sensations. In the industrial market, machine tools, keyboard designs, aircraft interiors, and backhoe accessories evolved from ideas generated in focus groups.

   Brainstorming is also used to generate new-product ideas. With **brainstorming,** the members of a group think of as many ways to vary a product or solve a problem as possible. Criticism is avoided, no matter how ridiculous an idea seems at the time. The emphasis is on sheer numbers of ideas. Evaluation of these ideas is postponed to later steps of development.

Exhibit 13.6 | Steps to Develop New Products That Satisfy Customers

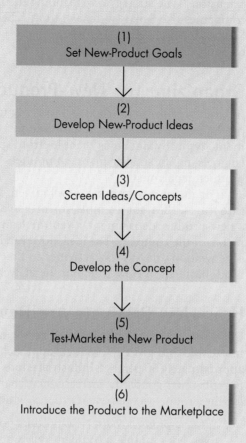

3. *Screen ideas and concepts.* As ideas emerge, they are checked against the firm's new-product goals and long-range strategies. Many product concepts are rejected because they don't fit well with existing products, needed technology is not available, the company doesn't have enough resources, or the sales potential is low.

4. *Develop the concept.* Developing the new-product concept involves creating a prototype of the product, testing the prototype, and building the marketing strategy. The type and amount of product testing vary, depending on such factors as the company's experience with similar products, how easy it is to make the item, and how easy it will be for consumers to use it. Suppose that Kraft is developing a new salad dressing flavour. The company already has a lot of experience in this area, so the new dressing will go directly into advanced taste tests and, perhaps, home use tests. To develop a new line of soft drinks, however, Kraft would most likely do a great deal of testing. It would study many aspects of the new product before actually making it.

While the product is being tested, the marketing strategy is refined. Channels of distribution are selected, pricing policies are developed and tested, the target market is further defined, and demand for the product is estimated. Management also continually updates the profit plan.

As the marketing strategy and prototype tests mature, a communication strategy is developed. A logo and package wording are created. As part of the communication strategy, promotion themes are developed, and the product is introduced to the sales force.

The HUMMER H2 is designed for serious off-roading. With 89 centimetre tires and steep approach angles, the H2 can cross streams and power through 60 centimetres of snow. This new product was developed for consumers who want both interior comfort and off-road capabilities.

© AP/WORLD WIDE PHOTOS

test-marketing

The process of testing a new product among potential users.

5. *Test-market the new product.* **Test-marketing** is testing the product among potential users. It allows management to evaluate various strategies and to see how well the parts of the marketing mix fit together. Few new-product concepts reach this stage. For those that pass this stage, the firm must decide whether to introduce the product on a regional or national basis.

   Companies that don't test-market their products run a strong risk of product failure. In essence, test-marketing is the "acid test" of new-product development. The product is put into the marketplace, and then the manufacturer can see how it performs against the competition.

6. *Introduce the product.* A product that passes test-marketing is ready for market introduction, called *rollout,* which requires a lot of logistical coordination. Various divisions of the company must be encouraged to give the new item the attention it deserves. Packaging and labelling in a different language might be required. Sales training sessions must be scheduled, spare parts inventoried, service personnel trained, advertising and promotion campaigns readied, and wholesalers and retailers informed about the new item. If the new product is to be sold internationally, it might have to be altered to meet the requirements of the target countries. For instance, electrical products might have to run on different electrical currents.

concept check

How do companies organize for new-product development?

What are the steps in the new-product development process?

Explain the role of the product manager.

product manager

The person who develops and implements a complete strategy and marketing program for a specific product or brand.

The Role of the Product Manager

When a new product enters the marketplace in large organizations, it is often placed under the control of a product or brand manager. A **product manager** develops and implements a complete strategy and marketing program for a specific product or brand. Product management first appeared at Procter & Gamble in 1929. A new company soap, Camay, was not doing well, so a young Procter & Gamble executive was assigned to devote his exclusive attention to developing and promoting this product. He was successful, and the company soon added other product managers. Since then, many firms, especially consumer products companies, have set up product management organizations.

THE PRODUCT LIFE CYCLE

product life cycle
The pattern of sales and profits over time for a product or product category; consists of an introductory stage, growth stage, maturity, and decline (and death).

Product managers create marketing mixes for their products as they move through the life cycle. The **product life cycle** is a pattern of sales and profits over time for a product (Ivory dishwashing liquid) or a product category (liquid detergents). As the product moves through the stages of the life cycle, the firm must keep revising the marketing mix to stay competitive and meet the needs of target customers.

Stages of the Life Cycle

As illustrated in Exhibit 13.7, the product life cycle consists of the following stages.

1. *Introduction.* When a product enters the life cycle, it faces many obstacles. Although competition might be light, the *introductory stage* usually features frequent product modifications, limited distribution, and heavy promotion. The failure rate is high. Production and marketing costs are also high, and sales volume is low. Hence profits are usually small or negative.

2. *Growth stage.* If a product survives the introductory stage, it advances to the *growth stage* of the life cycle. In this stage, sales grow at an increasing rate, profits are healthy, and many competitors enter the market. Large companies might start to acquire small pioneering firms that have reached this stage.

Exhibit 13.7 | Sales and Profits during the Product Life Cycle

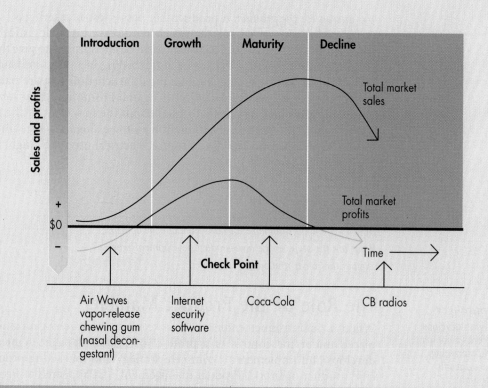

Emphasis switches from primary demand promotion to aggressive brand advertising and communicating the differences between brands. For example, the goal changes from convincing people to buy compact DVD players to convincing them to buy Sony versus Panasonic or Sharp.

Distribution becomes a major key to success during the growth stage, as well as in later stages. Manufacturers scramble to acquire dealers and distributors and to build long-term relationships. Without adequate distribution, it is impossible to establish a strong market position.

Toward the end of the growth phase, prices normally begin falling and profits peak. Price reductions result from increased competition and from cost reductions from producing larger quantities of items (economies of scale). As well, most firms have recovered their development costs by now, and their priority is in increasing or retaining market share and enhancing profits.

3. *Maturity.* After the growth stage, sales continue to mount—but at a decreasing rate. This is the *maturity stage.* Most products that have been on the market for a long time are in this stage. Thus, most marketing strategies are designed for mature products. One such strategy is to bring out several variations of a basic product (line extension). Kool-Aid, for instance, was originally offered in six flavours. Today there are many flavours, as well as sweetened and unsweetened varieties.

   Products that are in the maturity stage in Canada might be at the introduction or growth phase in other countries. A good example is dishwashers in Japan, where as of 2000, approximately 7% of households had one.[4]

4. *Decline (and death).* When sales and profits fall, the product has reached the decline stage. The rate of decline is governed by two factors: the rate of change in consumer tastes and the rate at which new products enter the market. Sony VCRs are an example of a product in the death stage. The demand for VCRs is virtually nil (except those that have tapes that have not been converted to DVD).

THE PRODUCT LIFE CYCLE AS A MANAGEMENT TOOL

The product life cycle can be used in planning. Marketers who understand the cycle concept are better able to forecast future sales and plan new marketing strategies. Exhibit 13.8 is a brief summary of strategic needs at various stages of the product life cycle. Marketers must be sure that a product has moved from one stage to the next before changing the company's marketing strategy. A temporary sales decline should not be interpreted as a sign that the product is dying. Pulling back marketing support can become a self-fulfilling prophecy that brings about the early death of a healthy product.

concept check

What is the product life cycle?

Describe each stage of the product life cycle.

What are the marketing strategies for each stage of the product life cycle?

PRICING PRODUCTS RIGHT

6 *learning goal*

An important part of the product development process is setting the right price. Price is the perceived value that is exchanged for something else. Value in our society is most commonly expressed in dollars and cents. Thus, price is typically the amount of money exchanged for a good or service. Note that *perceived value* refers to the time of the transaction. After you've used a product you've bought, you might decide that its actual value was less than its perceived value at the time you bought it. The price you pay for a product is based on the *expected satisfaction* you will receive and not necessarily the *actual satisfaction* you will receive.

Although price is usually a dollar amount, it can be anything with perceived value. When goods and services are exchanged for each other, the trade is called *barter*. If you exchange this book for a math book at the end of the term, you have engaged in barter.

Pricing Objectives

Price is important in determining how much a firm earns. The prices charged customers times the number of units sold equals the *gross revenue* for the firm. Revenue is what pays for every activity of the company (production, finance, sales, distribution, and so forth). What's left over (if anything) is profit. Managers strive to charge a price that will allow the firm to earn a fair return on its investment.

The chosen price must be neither too high nor too low. And the price must equal the perceived value to target consumers. If consumers think the price is too high, sales opportunities will be lost. Lost sales mean lost revenue. If the price is too low, consumers might view the product as a great value, but the company may not meet its profit goals. Three common pricing objectives are maximizing profits, achieving a target return on the investment, and offering good value at a fair price.

Maximizing Profits

profit maximization

A pricing objective that entails getting the largest possible profit from a product by producing the product as long as the revenue from selling it exceeds the cost of producing it.

Profit maximization means producing a product as long as the revenue from selling it exceeds the cost of producing it. In other words, the goal is to get the largest possible profit from the product. For example, suppose Carl Morgan, a builder of houses, sells each house for $200,000. His revenue and cost projections are shown in Exhibit 13.9. Notice in column 3 that the cost of building each house

---

Exhibit 13.8 | Strategies for Success at Each Stage of the Product Life Cycle

CATEGORY	INTRODUCTION	GROWTH	MATURITY	DECLINE
Marketing objectives	Encourage trial, establish distribution	Get triers to re-purchase, attract new users	Seek new users or uses	Reduce marketing expenses, keep loyal users
Product	Establish competitive advantage	Maintain product quality	Modify product	Maintain product
Distribution	Establish distribution network	Solidify distribution relationships	Provide additional incentives to ensure support	Eliminate trade allowances
Promotion	Build brand awareness	Provide information	Reposition product	Eliminate most advertising and sales promotions
Pricing	Set introductory price (skimming or penetration pricing)	Maintain prices	Reduce prices to meet competition	Maintain prices

drops for the second through the fifth house. The lower cost per house results from two things: First, by having several houses under construction at the same time, Morgan can afford to hire a full-time crew. The crew is more economical than the independent contractors to whom he would otherwise subcontract each task. Second, Morgan can order materials in greater quantities than usual and thus get quantity discounts on his orders.

Morgan decides that he could sell 15 houses a year at the $200,000 price. But he knows he cannot maximize profits at more than seven houses a year. Inefficiencies begin to creep in at the sixth house. (Notice in column 3 that the sixth house costs more to build than any of the first five houses.) Morgan can't supervise more than seven construction jobs at once, and his full-time crew can't handle even those seven. Thus, Morgan has to subcontract some of the work on the sixth and seventh houses. To build more than seven houses, he would need a second full-time crew.

The exhibit also shows why Morgan should construct seven houses a year. Even though the profit per house is falling for the sixth and seventh houses (column 4), the total profit is still rising (column 5). But at the eighth house, Morgan would go beyond profit maximization. That is, the eighth unit would cost more than its selling price. He would lose $15,000 on the house, and total profit would fall to $154,000 from $169,000 after the seventh house.

Achieving a Target Return on Investment

target return on investment

A pricing objective where the price of a product is set so as to give the company the desired profitability in terms of return on its money.

Another pricing objective used by many companies is **target return on investment**, whereby a price is set to give the company the desired profitability in terms of return on its money. Among the companies that use target return on investment as their main pricing objective are 3M, Procter & Gamble, General Electric, and DuPont.

To get an idea of how target return works, imagine that you are a marketing manager for a cereal company. You estimate that developing, launching, and marketing a new hot cereal will cost $2 million. If the net profit for the first year is $200,000, the return on investment will be $200,000 ÷ $2,000,000, or 10 percent. Let's say that top management sets a 15 percent target return on investment. (The average target return on investment for large corporations is now about 14 percent.) As a net profit of $200,000 will yield only a 10 percent return, one of two things will happen: Either the cereal won't be produced, or the price and marketing mix will be changed to yield the 15 percent target return.

Exhibit 13.9 | Revenue, Cost, and Profit Projections for Morgan's Houses

(1) UNIT OF OUTPUT (HOUSE)	(2) SELLING PRICE (REVENUE)	(3) COST OF BUILDING HOUSE	(4) PROFIT ON HOUSE	(5) TOTAL PROFIT
1st	$ 200,000	$ 176,000	$ 24,000	$ 24,000
2nd	200,000	175,000	25,000	49,000
3rd	200,000	173,000	27,000	76,000
4th	200,000	170,000	30,000	106,000
5th	200,000	170,000	30,000	136,000
6th	200,000	177,000	23,000	159,000
7th	**200,000**	**190,000**	**10,000**	**169,000**
8th	200,000	215,000	(15,000)	154,000

Value Pricing

value pricing
A pricing strategy in which the target market is offered a high-quality product at a fair price and with good service.

Value pricing has become a popular pricing strategy. **Value pricing** means offering the target market a high-quality product at a fair price and with good service. It is the notion of offering the customer a good value. Value pricing doesn't mean high quality that's available only at high prices, nor does it mean bare-bones service or low-quality products. Value pricing can be used to sell a variety of products, from a $50,000 Jeep Grand Cherokee to a $1.99 package of food napkins.

A value marketer does the following.

- *Offers products that perform.* This is the price of entry because consumers have lost patience with shoddy merchandise.
- *Gives consumers more than they expect.* Soon after Toyota launched Lexus, the company had to order a recall. The weekend before the recall, dealers phoned all Lexus owner that were affected and arranged to pick up their cars and provide replacement vehicles.
- *Gives meaningful guarantees.* DaimlerChrysler offers a 70,000-mile power train warranty. Michelin recently introduced a tire warranted to last 140,000 kilometres.
- *Gives the buyer facts.* Today's sophisticated consumer wants informative advertising and knowledgeable salespeople.
- *Builds long-term relationships.* Air Canada's Aeroplan program, Hyatt's Passport Club, and Moen's 800-number hotline all help build good customer relations.

concept check

Explain the concept of price.

What is meant by target return on investment, and how does it differ from profit maximization?

What is value pricing?

HOW MANAGERS SET PRICES

 learning goal

After establishing a pricing objective, managers must set a specific price for the product. Two techniques that are often used to set a price are mark-up pricing and breakeven analysis.

Markup Pricing

markup pricing
A method of pricing in which a certain percentage (the markup) is added to the product's cost to arrive at the price.

One of the most common forms of pricing is **markup pricing.** In this method, a certain dollar amount is added to a product's cost to arrive at the retail price. (The retail price is thus *cost plus markup.*) The cost is the expense of manufacturing the product or acquiring it for resale. The markup is the amount added to the cost to cover expenses and leave a profit. For example, if Banana Boat suntan cream costs Shoppers Drug Mart $8 and sells for $11, it carries a markup of 37.5 percent:

Cost	$8	Cost to Shoppers
Markup	+ 3	Shoppers markup to cover expenses (utilities, wages, etc.)
Retail price	$11	Banana Boat suntan cream price paid by the consumer

Shoppers' markup percentage = Markup / Retail price × 100%
= $3 / $8 × 100%
= 37.5%

Several elements influence markups. Among them are tradition, the competition, store image, and stock turnover. Traditionally, department stores used a 40 percent markup. But today competition has forced retailers to respond to consumer demand and meet competitors' prices. A department store that tried to sell household appliances at a 40 percent markup would lose customers to discounters such as Wal-Mart. However, a retailer trying to develop a prestige image will use markups that are much higher than those used by a retailer trying to develop an image as a discounter.

Breakeven Analysis

Manufacturers, wholesalers (companies that buy from manufacturers and sell to retailers and institutions), and retailers (firms that sell to end users) need to know how much of a product must be sold at a certain price to cover all costs. The point at which the costs are covered and additional sales result in profit is the **breakeven point**.

To find the breakeven point, the firm measures the various costs associated with the product:

- **Fixed costs** do not vary with different levels of output. The rent on a manufacturing facility is a fixed cost. It must be paid whether production is one unit or a million.

- **Variable costs** change with different levels of output. Wages and expenses of raw materials are considered variable costs.

- The **fixed-cost contribution** is the selling price per unit (revenue) minus the variable costs per unit.

- **Total revenue** is the selling price per unit times the number of units sold.

- **Total cost** is the total of the fixed costs and the variable costs.

- **Total profit** is total revenue minus total cost.

Knowing these amounts, the firm can calculate the breakeven point:

Breakeven point in units = Total fixed cost ÷ Fixed cost contribution

Let's see how this works: Gray Corporation, a manufacturer of aftershave lotion, has variable costs of $3 per bottle and fixed costs of $50,000. Gray's management believes the company can sell up to 100,000 bottles of aftershave at $5 a bottle without having to lower its price. Gray's fixed-cost contribution is $2 ($5 selling price per bottle minus $3 variable costs per bottle). Therefore, $2 per bottle is the amount that can be used to cover the company's fixed costs of $50,000.

To determine its breakeven point, Gray applies the previous equation:

Breakeven point in bottles = $50,000 fixed cost ÷ $2 fixed-cost contribution
= 25,000 bottles

Gray Corporation will, therefore, break even when it sells 25,000 bottles of aftershave lotion. After that point, at which the fixed costs are met, the $2 per bottle becomes profit. If Gray's forecasts are correct and it can sell 100,000 bottles at $5 a bottle, its total profit will be $150,000 ($2 per bottle × 75,000 bottles).

By using the equation, Gray Corp. can quickly find out how much it needs to sell to break even. It can then calculate how much profit it will earn if it sells more units. A firm that is operating close to the breakeven point might change the profit picture in two ways. Reducing costs will lower the breakeven point and expand profits. Increasing sales will not change the breakeven point, but it will provide more profits.

---

breakeven point

The price at which a product's costs are covered, so additional sales result in profit.

fixed costs

Costs that do not vary with different levels of output; for example, rent.

variable costs

Costs that change with different levels of output; for example, wages and cost of raw materials.

fixed-cost contribution

The selling price per unit (revenue) minus the variable costs per unit.

total revenue

The selling price per unit times the number of units sold.

total cost

The sum of the fixed costs and the variable costs.

total profit

Total revenue minus total cost.

concept check

Explain how markups are calculated.

Describe breakeven analysis.

What does it mean to "break even"?

PRODUCT PRICING STRATEGIES

8 *learning goal*

Managers use various pricing strategies when determining the price of a product, as we explain in this section. Price skimming and penetration pricing are strategies used in pricing new products; other strategies, such as leader pricing and bundling, might be used for established products as well.

Price Skimming

price skimming

The strategy of introducing a product with a high initial price and lowering the price over time as the product moves through its life cycle.

The practice of introducing a new product on the market with a high price and then lowering the price over time is called **price skimming.** As the product moves through its life cycle, the price usually is lowered because competitors are entering the market. As the price falls, more and more consumers can buy the product.

Price skimming has four important advantages. First, a high initial price can be a way to find out what buyers are willing to pay. Second, if consumers find the introductory price too high, it can be lowered. Third, a high introductory price can create an image of quality and prestige. Fourth, when the price is lowered later, consumers might think they are getting a bargain. The disadvantage is that high prices attract competition.

Price skimming can be used to price virtually any new product, such as high-definition televisions, PCs, and colour computer printers. For example, the Republic of Tea has launched new Imperial Republic White Tea, which it says is among the rarest of teas. Because it is minimally processed, white tea is said to retain the highest level of antioxidants and has less caffeine than black and green teas. The company says the tea is picked only a few days each year, right before the leaves open, yielding a small harvest. The product retails for $14 per tin of 50 bags. Products don't have to be expensive to use a skimming strategy.

Penetration Pricing

penetration pricing

The strategy of selling new products at low prices in the hope of achieving a large sales volume.

A company that doesn't use price skimming will probably use **penetration pricing.** With this strategy, the company offers new products at low prices in the hope of achieving a large sales volume. Procter & Gamble did this with SpinBrush. Penetration pricing requires more extensive planning than skimming does, because the company must gear up for mass production and marketing. When Texas Instruments entered the digital watch market, its facilities in Lubbock, Texas, could produce 6 million watches a year, enough to meet the entire world demand for low-priced watches. If the company had been wrong about demand, its losses would have been huge.

Penetration pricing has two advantages. First, the low initial price might induce consumers to switch brands or companies. Using penetration pricing on its jug wines, Gallo has lured customers away from Taylor California Cellars and Inglenook. Second, penetration pricing might discourage competitors from entering the market. Their costs would tend to be higher, so they would need to sell more at the same price to break even.

Dell offers new products at low prices to achieve a high sales volume. In a successful strategy to increase market share, Dell slashed prices of personal computers, requiring competitors Gateway, HP, and Compaq to do the same.

Leader Pricing

leader pricing
The strategy of pricing products below the normal markup or even below cost to attract customers to a store where they would not otherwise shop.

loss leader
A product priced below cost as part of a leader pricing strategy.

Pricing products below the normal markup or even below cost to attract customers to a store where they wouldn't otherwise shop is **leader pricing.** A product priced below cost is referred to as a **loss leader.** The customers go to the retailer and will often purchase many other products that are competitively priced, not just the loss leader. Retailers hope that this type of pricing will increase their overall sales volume and thus their profit.

Items that are leader priced are usually well known and priced low enough to appeal to many customers. They also are items that consumers will buy at a lower price, even if they have to switch brands. Supermarkets often feature coffee and bacon in their leader pricing. Department stores and specialty stores also rely heavily on leader pricing.

Bundling

bundling
The strategy of grouping two or more related products together and pricing them as a single product.

Bundling means grouping two or more related products together and pricing them as a single product. Weston Hotels' special weekend rates often include the room, breakfast, and one night's dinner. Department stores might offer a washer and dryer together for a price lower than if the units were bought separately. Rogers Communications and Shaw Cable bundle services such as telephone, Internet, and television into one package. This is not only convenient for the customer but, as the next paragraph highlights, allows the companies to sell more products.

The idea behind bundling is to reach a segment of the market that the products sold separately would not reach as effectively. Some buyers are more than willing to buy one product but have much less use for the second. Bundling the second product to the first at a slightly reduced price thus creates some sales that otherwise would not be made. Aussie 3 Minute Miracle Shampoo is typically bundled with its conditioner, because many people use shampoo more than conditioner, so they don't need a new bottle of conditioner.

Odd-Even Pricing

odd-even (psychological) pricing
The strategy of setting a price at an odd number to connote a bargain and at an even number to suggest quality.

Psychology often plays a big role in how consumers view prices and what prices they will pay. **Odd-even pricing** (or **psychological pricing**) is the strategy of setting a price at an odd number to connote a bargain and at an even number to imply quality. For years, many retailers have priced their products in odd numbers—for example, $99.95 or $49.95—to make consumers feel that they are paying a lower price for the product.

Some retailers favour odd-numbered prices because they believe that $9.99 sounds much less imposing to customers than $10.00. Other retailers believe that an odd-numbered price signals to consumers that the price is at the lowest level possible, thereby encouraging them to buy more units. Neither theory has ever been proved conclusively, although one study found that consumers perceive odd-priced products as being on sale. Even-numbered pricing is sometimes used to denote quality. Examples include a fine perfume at $100 a bottle, a good watch at $500, or a Holt Renfrew coat at $3,000.

Prestige Pricing

prestige pricing
The strategy of increasing the price of a product so that consumers will perceive it as being of higher quality, status, or value.

The strategy of raising the price of a product so consumers will perceive it as being of higher quality, status, or value is called **prestige pricing.** This type of pricing is common where high prices indicate high status. In the specialty shops on Rodeo Drive in Beverly Hills, which cater to the super-rich of Hollywood, shirts that would sell for $40 elsewhere sell for at least $150. If the price were lower, customers would perceive them as being of low quality.

concept check

What is the difference between penetration pricing and price skimming?

Explain the concept of price bundling.

Describe odd-even pricing and prestige pricing.

Trends in Developing Products and Pricing

9 *learning goal*

As customer expectations rise and competition becomes fiercer, perceptive managers will find innovative strategies to satisfy demanding consumers and establish unique products in the market. Management is under pressure to develop new products more quickly and move them to the marketplace—thus the trend toward using the Internet for new-product development. Two other significant trends are the use of yield management systems to maximize revenues and the growing importance of colour in packaging and product design.

NEW-PRODUCT DEVELOPMENT MOVES TO THE INTERNET

In the recent past, big companies like Kraft, General Motors, and Colgate Palmolive would spend five years or longer in developing a new product. Today, competitive pressures are bringing the time frame down to months instead of years.

A few cutting-edge marketing research companies are now offering new-product research on the Internet to make the new-product development process even faster. Decision Analyst, a global leader in Internet marketing research, offers "Conceptor," an Internet-based new-product concept-testing system. First, a sample of 250 is drawn from Decision Analyst's 3.5 million consumers in their Internet panel. Then the respondents visit a special Web site to view a new-product concept and a complete battery of questions and diagnostic ratings. Finally, a sophisticated mathematical model is used to predict the concept's chances for success. The entire process can be completed in a couple of days.

If a product concept looks promising, then the prototype can be evaluated on Decision Analyst's Optima Internet-based product-testing system. Households are given a test product to try in their home for a few days or weeks depending on frequency of use. The consumers go to the Internet and answer a series of questions about the product, including overall rating, likes, dislikes, feelings about specific product features, and purchase interest. A sophisticated mathematical model then tells the company if the product is optimal or not, and indicates what features need to be changed to improve the product. Decision Analyst has used this new Internet research system to test many products, including soups, beer, coffee, salad dressings, restaurant entrées, breads, snacks, wine, and processed meats.[5]

YIELD MANAGEMENT SYSTEMS HELP COMPANIES MAXIMIZE THEIR REVENUES

yield management systems (YMS)

Mathematical software that helps companies adjust prices to maximize revenue

When competitive pressures are high, a company must know when it can raise prices to maximize its revenues. More and more companies are turning to yield management systems to help adjust prices. First developed in the airline industry, **yield management systems (YMS)** use complex mathematical software to fill unused capacity profitably. The software employs techniques such as discounting early purchases, limiting early sales at these discounted prices, and overbooking capacity. YMS now are appearing in other services, such as lodging, other transportation forms, rental firms, and even hospitals.

Yield management systems are spreading beyond service industries as their popularity increases. The lessons of airlines and hotels aren't entirely applicable to other industries, however, because plane seats and hotel beds are perishable—if they go empty, the revenue opportunity is lost forever. For that reason, it makes sense to slash prices to move toward capacity if it's possible to do so without reducing the prices that other customers pay. Cars and steel aren't so perishable. Still, the capacity to make these goods is perishable. An underused factory or mill is a lost revenue opportunity, so it makes sense to cut prices to use up capacity if it's possible to do so while getting other customers to pay full price.

ProfitLogic has helped customers such as The Gap determine the best markdown price. The software has boosted profit margins from 5 to 18 percent. KhiMetrics, used by Buy.com and others, analyzes dozens of factors such as a product's life cycle, competitors' prices, and past sales data at various price points before churning out a list of possible prices and calculating the best ones. New sales data are fed back into the formulas daily to refine the process. Systems such as this aren't cheap, however, costing between $200,000 and $500,000.[6]

COLOUR MOVES TO THE FOREFRONT

In the past, colour was viewed as just another design element in a package or a product. Today marketers know that colours have the power to create brand imagery and convey moods. They also know it's essential to take demographic differences into account when selecting a brand's plumage, because colours are accepted by different ages, genders, and ethnic groups in different ways.

Traditionally, men and women have had different tastes in colour, with women drawn to brighter tones and more sensitive to subtle shadings and patterns. The differences are attributed in part to biology, as women see colour better than men do (colour blindness is 16 times more prevalent in men), and in part to socialization, with girls more likely to be steered toward colouring books and art supplies. North American men—compared to Europeans—have traditionally avoided brighter, more complex, and warmer hues in favour of darker, richer neutrals and blues, says Kathy LaManchusa, a colour trend strategist for companies such as Kmart, Motorola, and Philip Morris.[7]

Young people are typically more open than their elders to experimenting with colour, and kids today are exposed to an even wider palette from an early age than their parents were. Crayola crayons come in 120 hues, and advanced computer graphics offer a remarkably extensive selection. That makes preteen and teen preferences unusually sophisticated (in colour theory, "sophisticated" describes a colour created by a complex mixture of pigments, e.g., deep maroon). Preferences run to offbeat combinations and colour effects such as glitter, translucence, pearlescence, and metallics.

Making Ethical Choices

PRICING MISDIAGNOSIS

Your 80-year-old grandmother takes many different medicines and pays close attention to their prices. For the past year, she has been feeling overwhelmed by the detailed medical literature she receives and about the steadily increasing costs of her medicines.

When you last visited, she asked you, an interning pharmacist at an independent drugstore, to review the material she received. In her medical file are letters from drugstore chains. One letter promotes an alternative treatment for her diabetes. Another letter from a different chain announces an important change for people with osteoporosis who take Fosamax daily and encourages switching to the new Fosamax weekly. Your grandmother wasn't clear about the reason for doing so and was afraid she might forget to take the medicine if she took it only once a week. Neither letter mentions that the new drugs cost significantly more than the ones she is taking.

Your inquiry leads to the reason: In small print at the bottom of the letters are disclaimers from Merck, Fosamax's maker, and Eli Lilly, developer of both her current and the alternative diabetes medicine. Both companies paid the drug chains to send the letter to customers who take the particular medicine. Drugstores participate with drug manufacturers in this target marketing effort by compiling lists of names, addresses, and phone numbers with prescriptions for a specific drug. Further exploration reveals that drug companies consider such letters patient education.

When you return to your job, you receive a memo from the association of independent pharmacies to which your store belongs. The memo asks you to join drug company marketing programs that would send your customers letters similar to what your grandmother received.

ETHICAL DILEMMA

Your store manager (not a pharmacist) wants to join the program, because it would generate significant additional revenue. What would you tell him or her to do in response to the memo?

SOURCES: Scott Hensley, "Drug Makers Are Boosting Prices on Key Medicines," *Wall Street Journal Online*, April 13, 2003; Denise Myshko, "Pricing—The Cost of Doing Business," PharmaVOICE, March 1, 2002, http://www.websterconsultinggroup,com/pharmapricing; and Ann Zimmerman and David Armstrong, "How Drug Makers Use Pharmacies to Push Pricey Pills," *Wall Street Journal*, May 1, 2002.

The trend toward brighter and more complex colours (i.e., created through a mixture of multiple tones, often with special effects such as translucence or metallic sheen) also reflects the increasingly multicultural makeup of the country. Ethnic differences arising from cultural, religious, and historical experiences are also a major influence on colour preferences.

Exhibit 13.10 depicts how managers can interpret and use colours in their marketing strategies.

concept check

How can the Internet be used in new-product development?

What is the main advantage of a yield management system?

How can colour impact a consumer's desire for a product?

Exhibit 13.10 | The Power of Colours

COLOUR	ATTRIBUTES	ASSOCIATED WITH	THE EFFECT	PREFERRED BY	USED FOR	BRANDS
Red	exciting, daring, dynamic, sexy, intense, impulsive, active, aggressive, passionate	blood, fire, competition, heat, emotion, optimism, life, Valentine's Day, violence, communism	arousal, stimulation, increases heart and rate respiration	achievers, high-powered, active women, most economically stable, most secure	cars, lingerie, cosmetics, bridalwear (among Asian Americans; red is popular in Chinese and in Korean cultures, too)	Coca-Cola, Red Cross, Revlon
Orange	in your face, vibrant, warm	extroversion, adventure, celebration	stimulating but less than red, triggers alert	influentials, adolescents, bright orange is second least favourite colour overall	safety colour—to alert our attention; not for full-blown danger but potential danger	Cingular, Home Depot, Sanka coffee
Yellow	the warmest colour, cheerful, happy	sunshine, creativity, imagination, optimism, futuristic, spirituality, newness, low prices	warming, cheering	the first colour kids reach for, yet the least preferred colour overall	the lead colour projected for women's, men's, children's and home use through 2004	Kodak, Juicy Fruit, National Geographic
Green	fresh, clean, restful	economy, nature, balance, envy, fertility, spring	stabilizing, nurturing, healing, revitalizing	popular among influentials, opinion leaders, trendsetters; "slime green" preferred by youths; no. 2 favourite	higher-end vehicles (rich, dark hunter green); in interiors popular for for lack of natural light/outdoors), natural foods	John Deere, Starbucks, British Petroleum
Blue	calm, tranquil, holy	constancy, dependability, water, sky, holiness, protection, purity, peace, trust, loyalty, patience, hope, perseverance, sadness and depression, the future	calming, cleansing, cooling	No. 1 favourite in America	No. 1 for casual clothing; No. 2 for business clothing, not for most rooms, especially not dining room	Microsoft, American Express, Jet Blue
Purple/ Violet	exciting, mysterious, complex, intriguing	passion, spirituality, art, creativity, wit, sensitivity, vanity, moodiness, royalty, superiority, homosexuality, richness	inspiring, thought provoking, polarizing	No. 3 favourite, popular among 18- to 29-year-olds, artists; more androgynous than other colours; loved or hated more than any other colour	not used much in interiors or for clothing; Americans have gone back to purple in times of war	Sun, Yahoo, Barney

Continued

Pink	warm, cheerful, simple, uncomplicated emotions femininity, innocence	romance, sweetness, delicacy, tenderness, refinement, sentimentality	Subduing, flattering	soft pink preferred overall to bright pink; preferred by women	mainstream traditional pink is still the colour for little girls	Mary Kay, Barbie, Pepto Bismol
Brown	comfortable, reliable, steady, simple	earth, substance, stability, harmony, hearth, home, neutrality	comforting, soothing	practical people; down-to-earth people; Midwesterners; noncoastals	rich earth tones and neutrals preferred for the home	UPS, Aveda shampoo
Black	mysterious, elegant, sophisticated, worldly, sexy, powerful	sophistication, simplicity, death and mourning, bad luck, night, power, evil	empowering	intellectuals, rebels, fashion industry, increasingly broad in appeal	No. 1 for business clothing; No. 2 for casual clothing	Frexinet Champagne
Gray	safe, secure, practical, dependable, elegant	neutrality, boredom, coolness, safety, conservatism, ashes	reassuring, dulling	not generally chosen as a favourite; usually not a big seller, though fashionable for past few years among creative people, visual artists	men's business attire, growing popularity with women	Brite Nails, Black Pearl Resort
White	clean, fresh, pure, modern, neat	purity, sterility, calm, mourning (China and India), brides (West)	eyestrain, headaches, attention getting	intellectuals, modern types, limited appeal overall	summer attire, bridal fashion though not in some parts of the world; low-fat and diet foods	Ivory Soap, Dove soap

SOURCE: Roper/Pantone, Colour Matters, C.A.U.S., Supermarketguru.com.interviews; "Would You Trust IBM If It Were Big Orange?" *Business 2.0* (November 22, 2003), p. 52; "Why Does Orange Signify Decaf?" *Fortune*, May 17, 2002, 30; and the author's research.

Great Ideas to Use Now

Chances are that someday you will be a buyer or seller on eBay. The auction site has more than 46 million users with more than 18,000 categories of items on the auction block. Yet, finding what you want or getting the best deal can be tough. Here are a few helpful tips.

A BUYER'S GUIDE

Browsing/searching

- Before diving in, get a solid sense of what the items you're interested in are worth. Use the "completed items" advanced search to see the prices that similar items actually sold for, or check eBay's library for the category-specific "inside scoop," which generally features a useful page titled "Factors Influencing Value."
- Search in both related and general categories, as sellers often classify their wares differently. For example, if you're looking for a CD by Elvis Costello, check classic rock, pop, and punk in addition to alternative rock.

- Be descriptive when searching. Specify dates, colours, brands, sizes, and model numbers. Try variations—if a model number has a hyphen, search both with and without it.
- Conduct searches often, as items are constantly added and removed. Save yourself from having to monitor the site on a daily basis by using the "favourite searches" service, which will notify you by e-mail when items matching your search criteria are put up for sale.
- Think eBay for retail too. Many companies, such as Dell and Handspring, off-load surplus inventory at deep discounts, so check here before you try standard retail outlets.

Bidding

- Don't bid if you don't intend to buy, as bids are binding contracts. Bids can be retracted only under exceptional circumstances (e.g., the seller changes the product description after you've placed your bid).
- Don't bid in the first days of an auction. Doing so merely reveals your interest and increases the likelihood of other bidders joining the fray, causing the price to rise quickly. Instead, wait until the auction is near its close (10 to 30 seconds before, depending on the speed of your Internet connection), and then bid the maximum amount you are willing to pay, regardless of any previous bids—a strategy known as sniping. To do this, open a second browser window and fill in all the relevant information, stopping just short of submitting your bid. Watch the auction wind down in the first window, and when the time is right, place your bid in the second. Don't fret—you can always use a professional sniper service to handle this for you automatically (see "Resources").
- Factor in shipping costs, which typically fall on the buyer. If the item is bulky or the seller lives overseas, your "bargain" might end up costing more than you bargained for.
- Try adding a penny or two to your bid. Since many bids are placed in round-number increments, this little extra something can mean the difference between winning by a nose and coming up short.

A SELLER'S GUIDE

Listing

On-line auctions bring out the competitive nature in bidders, especially as the clock runs out. Bidding wars are a seller's dream; to make sure your auction gets significant play, follow these steps:

- Include specifics, such as manufacturer or product name, in both the title and description.
- Be honest in describing imperfections. This gives buyers comfort that you're being honest and could head off conflicts later.
- Set a low initial bid amount to attract more bidders. The mere *possibility* of getting a great deal on that rare Tony Gwynn rookie card encourages competition and increases the likelihood of rival bidders' driving up the price. This can also save you money, as eBay's listing fees are based on the minimum bid you set.
- Include a picture, as most buyers are reluctant to make a big purchase sight unseen. But don't overdo it: Including too many photos, or big ones with large file sizes, slows download times and tends to frustrate buyers with dial-up connections.

- Set a "buy it now" price, which allows buyers to subvert the bidding process and nab an item outright for a predetermined amount.
- Don't set a "reserve" price, which requires bidders to meet or exceed a certain minimum. As bidders can't see this minimum price, many avoid such auctions altogether out of fear that they'll be wasting their time.
- Accept multiple forms of payment, which increases the likelihood that interested buyers will place bids.
- Pay attention to when your auction is scheduled to end. eBay auctions run 3, 5, 7, or 10 days; to get the most traffic, make sure that yours includes a full weekend and ends at a time when people will be around to bid up the price.

Closing the Deal

- Congratulate the winner by e-mail. Include the auction number, a description of the item, the amount of the winning bid, and estimated shipping charges.
- Send the item as soon as the buyer's payment clears, and alert the buyer by e-mail (be sure to include the tracking number).
- Include links to your other auctions in all e-mail correspondence with buyers; if they are satisfied with their experience, they might want to check out what else you have.[8]

CUSTOMER SATISFACTION AND QUALITY

Creating new products demands that quality be built into those items from the beginning. If a new product is of poor quality, consumers might buy it once but never a second time. Moreover, a dissatisfied customer will tell others of his or her bad experiences, which will further reduce demand. Building quality into products not only helps keep customers but also cuts down on the expense of servicing warranty repairs and attracts new customers.

The French automaker Renault sold cars in North America in the 1960s and 1970s. Yet, the quality was not there, and sales suffered. Renault found that poor quality would not let them earn a profit in the North American market. Renault withdrew and has not since attempted to re-enter the North American market.

SUMMARY OF LEARNING GOALS

1 ### What is a product, and how is it classified?

A product is any good or service, along with its perceived attributes and benefits, that creates customer value. Tangible attributes include the good itself, packaging, and warranties. Intangible attributes are symbolic, such as a brand's image. Products are categorized as either consumer products or industrial products. Consumer products are goods and services that are bought and used by the end users. They can be classified as unsought products, convenience products, shopping products, or specialty products, depending on how much effort consumers are willing to exert to get them. Industrial products are those bought by organizations for use in making other products or in rendering services and include capital products and expense items.

2   How does branding distinguish a product from its competitors?

Products usually have brand names. Brands identify products by words, names, symbols, designs, or a combination of these things. The two major types of brands are manufacturer (national) brands and dealer (private) brands. Generic products carry no brand name. Branding has three main purposes: product identification, repeat sales, and new-product sales.

3   What are the functions of packaging?

Often the promotional claims of well-known brands are reinforced in the printing on the package. Packaging is an important way to promote sales and protect the product. A package should be easy to ship, store, and stack on a store shelf. Companies can add value to products by giving warranties. A warranty guarantees the quality of a good or service.

4   How do organizations create new products?

To succeed, most firms must continue to design new products to satisfy changing customer demands. But new-product development can be risky. Many new products fail. To be successful, new-product development requires input from production, finance, marketing, and engineering personnel. In large organizations, these people work in a separate department. The steps in new-product development are setting new-product goals, exploring ideas, screening ideas, developing the concept (creating a prototype and building the marketing strategy), test-marketing, and introducing the product. When the product enters the marketplace, it is often managed by a product manager.

5   What are the stages of the product life cycle?

After a product reaches the marketplace, it enters the product life cycle. This cycle typically has four stages: introduction, growth, maturity, and decline (and possibly death). Profits usually are small in the introductory phase, reach a peak at the end of the growth phase, and then decline. Marketing strategies for each stage are listed in Exhibit 13.8.

6   What is the role of pricing in marketing?

Price indicates value, helps position a product in the marketplace, and is the means for earning a fair return on investment. If a price is too high, the product won't sell well, and the firm will lose money. If the price is too low, the firm might lose money, even if the product sells well. Prices are set according to pricing objectives. Among the most common objectives are profit maximization, target return on investment, and value pricing.

7   How are product prices determined?

A cost-based method for determining price is markup pricing. A certain percentage is added to the product's cost to arrive at the retail price. The markup is the amount added to the cost to cover expenses and earn a profit. Breakeven analysis determines the level of sales that must be reached before total cost equals total revenue. Breakeven analysis provides a quick look at how many units the firm must sell before it starts earning a profit. The technique also reveals how much profit can be earned with higher sales volumes.

8 What strategies are used for pricing products?

The two main strategies for pricing a new product are price skimming and penetration pricing. Price skimming involves charging a high introductory price and then, usually, lowering the price as the product moves through its life cycle. Penetration pricing involves selling a new product at a low price in the hope of achieving a large sales volume.

Pricing tactics are used to fine-tune the base prices of products. Sellers that use leader pricing set the prices of some of their products below the normal markup or even below cost to attract customers who might otherwise not shop at those stores. Bundling is grouping two or more products together and pricing them as one. Psychology often plays a role in how consumers view products and in determining what they will pay. Setting a price at an odd number tends to create a perception that the item is cheaper than the actual price. Prices in even numbers denote quality or status. Raising the price so an item will be perceived as having high quality and status is called prestige pricing.

9 What trends are occurring in products and pricing?

Because of competitive pressures to develop new products more quickly, many companies are now using the Internet for new-product development. A second trend is that many service businesses and other companies have turned to yield management systems to maximize their revenues. Finally, colour is playing a key role in packaging and product design strategies.

EXPERIENTIAL EXERCISES

1. Your company plans to start selling gourmet frozen foods through the Internet. You are chairing a team to name this new service. Write an e-mail to team members suggesting things that they should consider in creating a brand name.

2. Under what circumstances would a jeans maker market the product as a convenience product? A shopping product? A specialty product?

3. Go to the library and look through magazines and newspapers to find examples of price skimming, penetration pricing, and value pricing. Make copies and show them to the class.

4. Write down the names of two brands to which you are loyal. Indicate the reasons for your loyalty.

5. Thousands of new products are introduced each year, but many don't stay on store shelves for long. NewProductWorks, a new-product development consulting firm, uses its collection of more than 70,000 new and once-new products as the foundation for its services. The site also has an on-line poll that gives you a chance to vote on proposed new products. Go to http://www.newproductworks.com and click on "Poll: Hits or Misses?" Read the descriptions of new products, rate them, and then see how your view compares to the composite rating of the product so far. Summarize your experience. Then click on "Hits & Misses." In this section you'll find products that the NPW experts expect to succeed and those that won't. Pick a product from the "We Expect Them to be Successes" or "Jury Is Out," category and find out where it currently stands.

6. You're working for a company that plans to introduce gourmet treats for pets. Your job is to determine the market for this new product and the marketing issues that might need to be addressed. Do a search on-line for articles on pet

ownership, pet food, and pet products. In addition to search engines, include marketing magazine sites such as *Adweek* and *Brandweek* (http://www .adweek.com and http://www.brandweek.com) and an on-line database such as InfoTrak. Write a short report to your manager based on your research.

7. Visit an on-line retailer such as Amazon.ca (http://www.amazon.ca), PCConnection.com (http://www.pcconnection.com), or Drugstore.com (http://www.drugstore.com). At the site, try to identify examples of leader pricing, bundling, odd-even pricing, and other pricing strategies. Do on-line retailers have different pricing considerations from "real-world" retailers? Explain.

8. Do a search on Yahoo (http://www.yahoo.ca) for on-line auctions for a product you are interested in buying. Visit several auctions to get an idea of how the product is priced. How do these prices compare with the price you might find in a local store? What pricing advantages or disadvantages do companies face in selling their products through on-line auctions? How do on-line auctions affect the pricing strategies of other companies? Why?

9. Learn more about branding strategies at the *Brandweek* magazine site, http://www.brandweek.com. Pick two companies featured in recent articles and search the site for more articles about them. Summarize their approach to branding their products. Do you think they have been effective in strengthening the brand? Explain.

REVIEW QUESTIONS

1. What is a product? How do products create value for the buyer?

2. What are the four (4) classifications of consumer products?

3. How are business products classified?

4. What is a brand? What are the benefits of branding?

5. What are the characteristics of effective brand names?

6. Discuss the various types of brands.

7. List the functions of a package. What are the two (2) forms of labelling?

8. Describe the steps in new product development.

9. Discuss the strategies for success at each stage of the product life cycle.

10. What is the role of pricing in marketing?

11. How are product prices determined?

12. What are the various pricing strategies available to managers?

CREATIVE THINKING CASE
How About a Peppermint Three-Piece Suit?

Not everyone would buy underwear that's coated with soil, but Chang Seong Ho is particular about his health. The 26-year-old Korean university student recently paid $12 for a pair of "yellow earth" boxer shorts made from a fabric infused with microgranules of a yellow soil purported to emit far-infrared rays. Those rays, the low-energy waves farthest in the spectrum from visible light, cut odour and improve circulation, the maker of his shorts says. "I'm always interested in anything concerning health," says Mr. Chang.

Mr. Chang's soiled underwear isn't an outlandish wardrobe choice here. Textile innovation is a big and growing business around the world, and Asia, where consumers love both New World gadgets and Old World naturopathy, is leading the way with some of the most unusual fabrics. In a land of conservatively dressed business professionals, South Korea's Kolon Corp. has been boosting its sales with a line of "fragrant suits," available in stress-busting lavender or peppermint. Cheil Industries Inc. is doing a brisk business with its new Rogatis brand "Ki" business suits, which have sachets of a charcoal-and-jade powder sewn into the armpits and crotch. The mixture, according to the company, blocks electromagnetic radiation emitted by computer and television screens and also gives the wearer an energy boost.

Dupont has teamed up with Levi's to product Lycra-blend jeans. Recently it launched Kevlar jeans with Polo Ralph Lauren Corp. Dupont is now making clothes that can be detected by global positioning satellites.

Asia has been leading the charge with some of the most bizarre inventions. In January, the Hong Kong unit of the United Kingdom lingerie maker Triumph International Ltd. launched in Asia the aloe vera bra and underwear set, which promises to lubricate the wearer's skin for up to 40 washes.[9]

CREATIVE THINKING QUESTIONS

1. Do you think that these products would sell well in America? Why or why not?
2. Should market research be done prior to launching such products?
3. What pricing strategy should be used for "fragrant suits"?

SOURCE: Adapted from Cris Prystay and Meeyong Song, "Fragrant Fabrics: Peppermint 3-Piece is Hot in Hong Kong," Wall Street Journal (October 21, 2002), pp. A1, A8. Reprinted by permission of the Wall Street Journal, Copyright © 2002 Dow Jones & Company, Inc. All Rights Reserved Worldwide.

VIDEO CASE
The Toronto Blue Jays Hit a Home Run with Pricing

Can doubling the number of ticket categories bring more fans out to the ball game? For the Toronto Blue Jays, an improved pricing strategy and additional promotional strategies helped the team raise its profile in its hometown.

Prior to the 1999 baseball season, the Toronto Blue Jays (http://www.bluejays.ca) had just five ticket-pricing categories. After thorough study of their ticket prices, the Blue Jays established a new pricing structure with 10 levels to provide fans different product value. From single-ticket $7 seats to season tickets costing more than $13,000 ($165 per game) for the "In the Action" seats, fans can pick the ticket program that suits them best. In-between seats range from $24 to $49, depending on location. In addition to individual seats and season passes, Blue Jays fans can buy Flex-Packs with 5, 20, or 40 tickets to the games they choose. These packages sell at a discount from the single-ticket price. Group ticket sales, an important component of the Blue Jays product mix, are targeted toward the seats priced at about $40 and under.

As part of the Toronto team's effort to provide a high-quality product at a fair price, the Blue Jays added several regularly occurring special promotions during many home games. For example, every Tuesday home game is a TIM-BR Mart Tuesday. The building supplies chain collaborates with the Blue Jays in a three-part promotion. When a Toronto player hits the official TIM-BR Mart target, a fan chosen at random wins a cottage supplied and built by TIM-BR Mart. Another fan chosen at random gets to watch the game from a custom-built wood deck in the Toronto SkyDome. This fan is also provided food and beverage service. A third lucky fan wins a custom-built deck for his or her home by TIM-BR Mart.

Saturday home games have special promotions for children. On Junior Jays Saturdays, sponsored by *The Toronto Star*, children 14 and under are admitted at discounted prices. The gates open early, so fans can watch batting practice, and kids can participate in many activities and contests, win prizes, and get player autographs. Children can enter a drawing to throw out the ceremonial first pitch at the next Junior Jays Saturday game; nine youngsters get to take the field along with the Blue Jays starting lineup, and a child is selected to announce the Blue Jays batters for one inning. Children can also run the bases following the game. Each child 14 and under also receives Blue Jays souvenir giveaways.

The Blue Jays' marketing staff continue to add special promotions to please their fans. For example, they asked fans what they enjoy the most about attending a Blue Jays game and combined many of these elements to create Premium Games. Tickets for these games cost a few dollars more but include a pre-game party, early admission to watch batting practice, autograph signing, giveaway items, and post-game entertainment. Staples Business Depot "Deal of the Game," the FedEx Home Run Club, and Schneider's Juicy Jumbo Toss are among the team's recent promotions.

This well-planned package of special promotions, along with different ticket prices for seats providing different amenities, has increased the Toronto Blue Jays' popularity. As a result, attendance at games is up and the fan base is growing.

CRITICAL THINKING QUESTIONS

1. How would you describe the Toronto Blue Jays' baseball franchise as a product?
2. What decision criteria do you think the Blue Jays used in establishing their new ticket price structure? Do you agree with this pricing strategy?

SOURCE: Toronto Blue Jays Web site, http://toronto.bluejays.mlb.com.

E-COMMERCE CASE
A Perfect Fit for Lands' End

How do you like your chinos? That's the question Lands' End asked its customers when it began offering customized pants on its Web site about two years ago (http://www.landsend.com). Customers simply sign on, choose their preferred style and fit from millions of choices, and enter a few details about their body shape, and in a few weeks a custom-made pair of pants is delivered to their doorstep. The customized chinos proved so successful that Lands End has since started offering made-to-order jeans, dress shirts, and twill pants on its Web site as well. About 40 percent of the firm's Web sales are now made to order.

Ironing out the details took some effort. Lands' End teamed with Archetype, a California technology firm specializing in mass-customization ordering systems. At the end of every day, Lands' End electronically sends customer orders to Archetype's California offices, where Archetype's software compares body measurements, factors in individual fit preferences, and adjusts the base pattern designs accordingly. The patterns are then electronically transmitted to a contract manufacturer in Mexico for production.

At the factory, each unique pattern is entered into automated equipment that cuts the fabric according to customer specifications. To control quality, Lands' End worked closely with its Mexican partner, which had to install new machinery to meet Lands' End specifications. Quality inspections are also critical. "The last person in the mod setup measures the pants. If they miss on any of five critical points, the pants are scrapped and remade," says Ron James, Lands' End customer project manager. After passing the final quality check, the clothes are bulk-shipped to a distribution centre in the United States, where they are packaged and mailed directly to customers.

Lands' End was an "early adopter" of the Internet, launching its Web site in 1995. Initially, the site featured 100 products as well as stories, essays, and travelogues. Today, landsend.com is the world's largest apparel Web site based on business volume. The company has also been a leader in using the Web to enhance the shopping experience and to foster one-on-one relationships with its customers.

Customer satisfaction with the custom-made clothes is high, even though they cost as much as 40 percent more than regular Lands' End products. Returns are far below those of non-customized Lands' End products. Lands' End has also been able to reduce its inventory levels dramatically. "What we've done is solve a consumer problem, which is getting a garment I want in a style that fits," says Robert Holloway, CEO of Archetype.

CRITICAL THINKING QUESTIONS

1. Evaluate Lands' End's product and pricing strategy. Do you think the custom-made clothes justify a 40 percent pricing premium? Why or why not?

2. Visit the Lands' End site and briefly discuss how the company uses the Internet for the custom clothing line and its other products. What innovative features does it offer? (Also check the landsend.com description in the "General Information" section.) Does it add value, and if so, how?

3. What role, if any, does the Lands' End brand play in this product line?

SOURCES: Anne D'Innocenzio, "Lands' End Expands Custom Clothes," *AP Online Wire,* September 4, 2002; David Drickhammer; "A Leg Up on Mass Customization," *Industry Week,* September 9, 2002, http://www.industryweek.com; Jon Swartz, "Have It Your Way," *USA Today,* October 30, 2002, 3B; and "Custom Pants in a Click; Lands' End Custom Gives Shoppers More Choices than Ever Before," Lands' End company press release, November 1, 2001.

14

Making the Connection

Distributing Products in a Timely and Efficient Manner

In this chapter we cover a very integrative topic, as we look at one of the 4Ps of marketing—distribution (or place)—which is itself a cross between a *marketing* and an *operations* topic. Primarily because of the importance placed on managing the supply chain in today's businesses (that is, the route the product takes from provider to consumer), these two areas are inseparable.

From a marketing perspective, the distribution system is critical, as it enhances the value of the product to the consumer (helping to *meet customer needs*) by communicating the benefit of the product through the choice of distribution channel (quality product in an exclusive retail location, for example) and by getting the product to the customer how, where, and when he or she wants it. From an operations perspective, this supply chain must be managed efficiently and effectively for the transfer of the product from producer to consumer to occur. Marketing relies on its relationship with operations for this critical aspect of the 4Ps. If the product is not where customers want it when they want it, they can't and won't buy it!

The other functional areas also affect and are affected by distribution. If the distribution system is not managed efficiently, it becomes a *finance* issue, as the supply chain is one that is difficult and expensive to set up and very difficult and costly to change; decisions affect inventory levels, transportation

costs, and so on, as well as customer demand—all very expensive items that affect *financial performance*. From a *human resource* perspective, the decisions are so critical to the success of the business that supply chain management has become a highly specialized field with very highly trained professionals, and distribution alone is a huge industry. A good example of this is in this chapter's discussion on the "Components of a Successful Retailing Strategy." All retail operations are businesses themselves, and the same topics we've covered for all businesses in general obviously apply: determining a target market, developing the product offering, creating a promotional strategy, setting prices, and so on. And remember: The decisions made by these organizations affect the image the customer has of your company's products if they are sold in these locations—a very highly integrative system indeed!

Integration is evident not only within the functional areas; it can be seen in the distribution system itself. All the channel members must work together as one large organization to distribute the product to the customer efficiently, each one relying on the other, as explained in the chapter. Sometimes companies integrate forward or backward, taking over the roles of different channel members ahead or behind them in the chain, and at other times there are many different companies whose activities must be coordinated.

The external environment affects distribution as well. The *technological* environment plays a large role. We also discuss in the chapter applications of technology in retailing, such as "efficient consumer response" operated with the aid of "electronic data interchange." Systems that automatically manage inventory levels are at the heart of the success of companies such as Wal-Mart. The *social* environment, on the other hand, drives all the activities in the supply chain. In today's marketplace, as we've discussed, products are driven by customers—customer wants and needs drive what is produced and how it is distributed. An excellent example of this is Dell—building computers according to customer specifications. Nothing is produced until ordered by the customer. The beauty of today's supply chain is that because it is so carefully integrated, information on customer demand is communicated through the supply chain back to the producer, just as goods flow forward to the customer. Efficient and effective management of a company's distribution system is essential to success in today's highly competitive *economic* environment.

© JB REED/BLOOMBERG NEWS/LANDOV

Distributing Products in a Timely and Efficient Manner

learning goals

Home Depot Builds a (Data) Warehouse

Home Depot Inc. (**http://www.homedepot.com**), once the high-growth leader among home improvement retailers, is in the midst of its own major remodelling project. The company was losing ground to its major competitor, as sales and profits dropped steadily. With both companies opening new big-box stores at a fast clip, the market was approaching the saturation point.

A key element in the plan to spruce up the country's second largest retailer is a heavy investment in information technology (IT). Ranging from new self-service checkout terminals for its customers—the first in a home improvement store chain—to new IT infrastructure, the company hopes to use technology to position itself for future success.

Although Home Depot was ahead of other retailers in some IT areas, such as using wireless applications in stores, it lagged in developing a *data* warehouse, that is, a collection of data that supports management decision making. In late 2002, Home Depot partnered with IBM to build a new Web-accessible data warehouse to give it state-of-the-art information management technology.

"We know that more timely analysis of customers' buying patterns will help us better anticipate their needs," said Bob DeRodes, Home Depot's executive vice president and chief information officer (CIO). "Now, we will be able to do a better job of predicting these needs and providing the right assortment of goods and services for each set of customers, whether they are do-it-yourself enthusiasts or professionals. This is an important component of our ongoing business strategy."

Even though the company is late in adopting data-warehousing technology, DeRodes considers it a plus. "Because of the rate of [technical] change, the last guy in has the advantage. That's us," he says. The company doesn't have to worry about integrating old systems with the newest technology. "As we begin this initiative, we know more about how to do this than anyone who previously built an enterprise-wide data warehouse, and we can do it much faster," he continues. He believes that Home Depot will be able to get better information, much faster and in much more useable fashion.

Home Depot's first purely analytical database is an expensive project, costing tens of millions of dollars and the addition of 25 new people to its 25-member database administration department. An important consideration was future growth, so the data warehouse is designed for virtually unlimited expansion. Ease of use is another factor; managers access the data warehouse through a specialized "dashboard" interface. The answers they get when they make queries result in better forecasting and planning.

The company is rolling out the new data warehouse project in stages. The initial phase focuses on human resources functions. For example, the new system will automate performance measurement of Home Depot's 300,000 employees, making it easier to retain and reward its personnel. Then the system will expand to include the Atlanta-based retailer's supply chain, inventory management, and replenishment operations. DeRodes expects the data warehouse eventually to process sales data almost in real time and use it for pricing decisions, inventory forecasting, and in-store space management.[1]

Critical Thinking Questions

1. How will managing information give a company a competitive advantage?
2. Do you agree with Bob DeRodes that implementing technology later than sooner (i.e., when technology is not as advanced) is, in fact, an advantage?
3. What problems might a company have while implementing a data warehouse?

In this chapter, we explore how organizations use a distribution (logistics) system to enhance the value of a product and examine the methods they use to move products to locations where consumers wish to buy them. First, we'll discuss the functions and members of a distribution system. Then we'll explore the role of wholesalers and retailers in delivering products to customers. We'll also discuss how supply chain management increases efficiency and customer satisfaction. Finally, we'll look at trends in distribution.

THE ROLE OF DISTRIBUTION

1 learning goal

physical distribution (logistics)
Efficiently managing the acquisition of raw materials to the factory and the movement of products from the producer to industrial users and consumers.

manufacturer
A producer; an organization that converts raw materials to finished products.

Physical distribution is efficiently managing the acquisition of raw materials to the factory and the movement of products from the producer, or **manufacturer,** to industrial users and consumers. Physical distribution activities are usually the responsibility of the marketing department and are part of the large series of activities included in the supply chain. As discussed in Chapter 11, a supply chain is the system through which an organization acquires raw material, produces products, and delivers the products and services to its customers. Exhibit 14.1 illustrates a supply chain. Supply chain management helps increase the efficiency of logistics service by minimizing inventory and moving goods efficiently from producers to the ultimate users.

concept check

Define physical distribution.

Physical distribution is usually the responsibility of which department?

THE NATURE AND FUNCTIONS OF DISTRIBUTION CHANNELS

2 learning goal

distribution channel
The series of marketing entities through which goods and services pass on their way from producers to end users.

marketing intermediaries
Organizations that assist in moving goods and services from producers to end users.

agents
Sales representatives of manufacturers and wholesalers.

brokers
Go-betweens that bring buyers and sellers together.

On their way from producers to end users and consumers, goods and services pass through a series of marketing entities known as a distribution channel. In this section we will look first at the entities that make up a **distribution channel** and then at the functions that channels serve.

Marketing Intermediaries in the Distribution Channel

A distribution channel is made up of **marketing intermediaries,** or organizations that assist in moving goods and services from producers to end users and consumers. Marketing intermediaries are in the middle of the distribution process between the producer and the end user. The following marketing intermediaries most often appear in the distribution channel.

- *Agents and brokers.* **Agents** are sales representatives of manufacturers and wholesalers, and **brokers** are entities that bring buyers and sellers together. Both agents and brokers are usually hired on commission basis by either a buyer or a seller. Agents and brokers are go-betweens whose job is to make deals. They do not own or take possession of goods.

industrial distributors

Independent wholesalers that buy related product lines from many manufacturers and sell them to industrial users.

wholesalers

Firms that sell finished goods to retailers, manufacturers, and institutions.

retailers

Firms that sell goods to consumers and to industrial users for their own consumption.

HOT Links

See http://www.awmanet .org to browse the latest issue of *Distribution Channels* magazine and learn more about this field.

- *Industrial distributors.* **Industrial distributors** are independent wholesalers that buy related product lines from many manufacturers and sell them to industrial users. They often have a sales force to call on purchasing agents, make deliveries, extend credit, and provide information. Industrial distributors are used in such industries as aircraft manufacturing, mining, and petroleum.
- *Wholesalers.* **Wholesalers** are firms that sell finished goods to retailers, manufacturers, and institutions (such as schools and hospitals). Historically, their function has been to buy from manufacturers and sell to retailers.
- *Retailers.* **Retailers** are firms that sell goods to consumers and to industrial users for their own consumption.

At the end of the distribution channel are final consumers, like you and me, and industrial users. Industrial users are firms that buy products for internal use or for producing other products or services. They include manufacturers, utilities, airlines, railroads, and service institutions, such as hotels, hospitals, and schools.

Exhibit 14.2 shows various ways marketing intermediaries can be linked. For instance, a manufacturer may sell to a wholesaler, who sells to a retailer, who, in turn, sells to a customer. In any of these distribution systems, goods and services are physically transferred from one organization to the next. As each takes possession of the products, it might take legal ownership of them. As the exhibit indicates, distribution channels can handle either consumer products or industrial products.

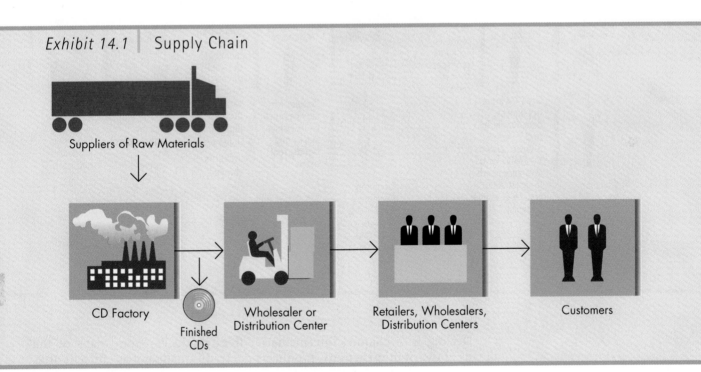

Exhibit 14.1 | Supply Chain

Suppliers of Raw Materials

CD Factory

Finished CDs

Wholesaler or Distribution Center

Retailers, Wholesalers, Distribution Centers

Customers

The Functions of Distribution Channels

Why do distribution channels exist? Why can't every firm sell its products directly to the end user or consumer? Why are go-betweens needed? Channels serve a number of functions.

Channels reduce the number of transactions Channels make distribution simpler by reducing the number of transactions required to get a product from the manufacturer to the consumer. Assume for the moment that only four students are in your class. Also assume that your professor requires five textbooks, each from a different publisher. If there were no bookstore, 20 transactions would be necessary for all students in the class to buy the books, as shown in Exhibit 14.3. If the bookstore serves as a go-between, the number of transactions is reduced to nine. Each publisher sells to one bookstore rather than to four students. Each student buys from one bookstore instead of from five publishers.

Exhibit 14.2 | Channels of Distribution for Industrial and Consumer Products

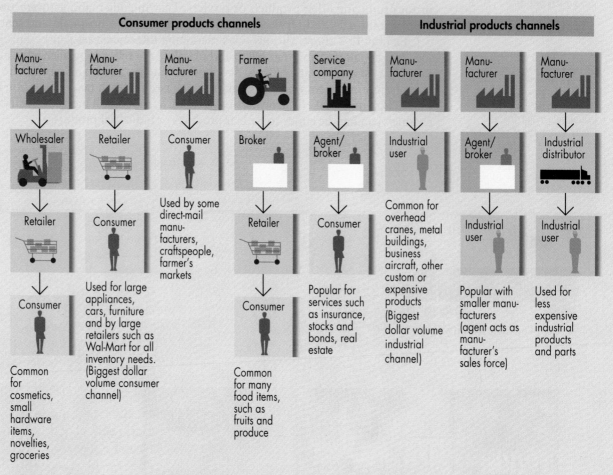

Dealing with channel intermediaries frees producers from many of the details of distribution activity. Producers are traditionally not as efficient or as enthusiastic about selling products directly to end users as channel members are. First, producers might wish to focus on production. They might feel that they cannot both produce and distribute in a competitive way. On the other hand, manufacturers are eager to deal directly with larger retailers, such as HBC and Sport Chek. The larger retailers offer huge sales opportunities to producers.

An efficient distribution system allows Home Depot to offer customers a vast assortment of building materials, appliances, and tools economically.

© MICHAEL NEWMAN / PHOTOEDIT INC.

Exhibit 14.3 | How Distribution Channels Reduce the Number of Transactions

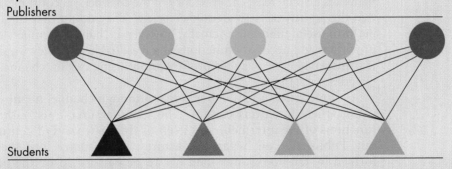

Without a marketing intermediary:
5 publishers × 4 students = 20 transactions

Publishers

Students

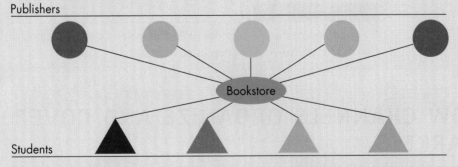

With a marketing intermediary:
5 publishers + 4 students = 9 transactions

Publishers

Bookstore

Students

Channels ease the flow of goods Channels make distribution easier in several ways. The first is by *sorting,* which consists of the following:

- *Sorting out.* Breaking many different items into separate stocks that are similar. Eggs, for instance, are sorted by grade and size.
- *Accumulating.* Bringing similar stocks together into a larger quantity. Twelve large Grade A eggs could be placed in some cartons and 12 medium grade B eggs in other cartons.

breaking bulk

The process of breaking large shipments of similar products into smaller, more usable lots.

• *Allocating.* Breaking similar products into smaller and smaller lots. (Allocating at the wholesale level is called **breaking bulk.**) For instance, a tank car load of milk could be broken down into gallon jugs. The process of allocating generally is done when the goods are dispersed by region and as ownership of the goods changes.

Without the sorting, accumulating, and allocating processes, modern society would not exist. We would have home-based industries providing custom or semi-custom products to local markets. In short, we would return to a much lower level of consumption.

A second way in which channels ease the flow of goods is by locating buyers for merchandise. A wholesaler must find the right retailers to sell a profitable volume of merchandise. A sporting goods wholesaler, for instance, must find the retailers who are most likely to reach sporting goods consumers. Retailers have to understand the buying habits of consumers and put stores where consumers want and expect to find the merchandise. Every member of a distribution channel must locate buyers for the products it is trying to sell.

Channel members also store merchandise so that goods are available when consumers want to buy them. The high cost of retail space often means that goods are stored by the wholesaler or the manufacturer.

Channels perform needed functions The functions performed by channel members help increase the efficiency of the channel, yet consumers sometimes feel that the go-betweens create higher prices. They doubt that these intermediaries perform useful functions. Actually, however, if channel members did not perform important and necessary functions at a reasonable cost, they would cease to exist. If firms could earn a higher profit without using certain channel members, they would not use them.

A useful rule to remember is that although channel members can be eliminated, their functions cannot. The manufacturer must either perform the functions of the intermediaries itself or find new ways of getting them carried out. Publishers can bypass bookstores, for instance, but the function performed by the bookstores then has to be performed by the publishers or by someone else.

HOT Links

To do business with Wal-Mart, you'll have to meet the retailer's tough supplier requirements. Go to http://www.walmartstores .com and click on the "Suppliers" tab to learn more.

concept check

List and define the marketing intermediaries that make up a distribution channel.

How do channels reduce the number of transactions?

Define breaking bulk.

HOW CHANNELS ORGANIZE AND COVER MARKETS

3 learning goal

In an efficient distribution channel, all the channel members work smoothly together and do what they're expected to do. A manufacturer expects wholesalers to promote its products to retailers and to perform several other functions as well. Not all channels have a leader or a single firm that sets channel policies, but all channels have members who rely on one another.

vertical marketing system

An organized, formal distribution channel in which firms are aligned in a hierarchy such as from manufacturer to wholesaler to retailer.

Vertical Marketing Systems

To increase the efficiency of distribution channels, many firms have turned to vertical marketing systems. In a **vertical marketing system,** firms are aligned in a hierarchy (such as manufacturer to wholesaler to retailer). Such systems are planned, organized,

corporate distribution system

A vertical marketing system in which one firm owns the entire distribution channel.

forward integration

The acquisition by a market intermediary of another marketing intermediary closer to the customer.

backward integration

The acquisition of the production process by a wholesaler or retailer.

administrative distribution system

A vertical marketing system in which a strong organization takes over as leader and sets policies for the distribution channel.

contractual distribution system

A vertical marketing system in which a network of independent firms at different levels (manufacturer, wholesaler, retailer) coordinate their distribution activities through a written contract.

formalized versions of distribution channels. The three basic types of vertical marketing systems are corporate, administrative, and contractual.

Corporate distribution systems In a **corporate distribution system**, one firm owns the entire channel of distribution. Corporate systems are tops in channel control. A single firm that owns the whole channel has no need to worry about channel members. The channel owner will always have supplies of raw materials and long-term contact with customers. It will have good distribution and product exposure in the marketplace.

Examples of corporate distribution systems abound. Evans Forest Products Ltd. (a manufacturer of plywood), for instance, bought wholesale lumber distributors to market its products to retail dealers more effectively. This move was an example of forward integration. **Forward integration** occurs when a manufacturer acquires a marketing intermediary closer to the customer, such as a wholesaler or retailer. A wholesaler could integrate forward by buying a retailer. An example of forward integration is Sherwin-Williams, a paint maker that operates more than 2,000 paint stores. On the other hand, a manufacturer might integrate forward by buying a wholesaler. For decades, Pepsi-Cola focused on supplying syrup and concentrate to independent bottlers, but in the 1980s, it decided it could best satisfy retailers' demands by serving them itself. After spending several billion dollars to buy out independent bottlers, Pepsi-Cola today owns bottling and distributing operations that account for half the soda in its system. This strategy created many opportunities for supply chain improvement through a reorganization of its bottling and distribution network. To guide those decisions, Pepsi analyzed demographic trends to identify locations that would yield long-term growth and warrant future expansion. It coupled this information with soft drink consumption trends and marketing forecasts, thus determining when and where new plants should be located. But none of this would have been possible without the purchase of its bottling and distribution outlets.

Backward integration is just the reverse of forward integration. It occurs when a wholesaler or retailer gains control over the production process. Many large retail organizations have integrated backward. Sears has part ownership of production facilities that supply more than 30 percent of its inventory and therefore can avoid outside distributors and can lower overall costs.

Administrative distribution systems In an **administrative distribution system**, a strong organization takes over as leader and sets channel policies. The leadership role is informal; it is not written into a contract. Companies such as Gillette, Campbell's, and Westinghouse are administrative system leaders. They can often influence or control the policies of other channel members without the costs and expertise required to set up a corporate distribution system. They might be able to dictate how many wholesalers will be in the channel or, for example, require that the wholesalers offer 60-day credit to retail customers, among other things.

Contractual distribution systems The third form of vertical marketing is a **contractual distribution system**. It is a network of independent firms at different levels (manufacturer, wholesaler, retailer) that coordinate their distribution activities through a written contract. Franchises (described in Chapter 5) are a common form of the contractual system. The parent company of McDonald's, for instance, controls distribution of its products through the franchise agreement that each franchisee signs.

The Intensity of Market Coverage

4 *learning goal*

All types of distribution systems must be concerned with market coverage. How many dealers will be used to distribute the product in a particular area? As Exhibit 14.4 shows, the three degrees of coverage are exclusive, selective, and intensive. The type of product determines the intensity of the market coverage.

exclusive distribution

A distribution system in which a manufacturer selects only one or two dealers in an area to market its products.

selective distribution

A distribution system in which a manufacturer selects a limited number of dealers in an area (but more than one or two) to market its products.

When a manufacturer selects one or two dealers in an area to market its products, it is using **exclusive distribution**. Only items that are in strong demand can be distributed exclusively, because consumers must be willing to travel some distance to buy them. If Wrigley's chewing gum were sold in only one drugstore per city, Wrigley's would soon be out of business. However, Bang and Olufsen audio components, Jaguar automobiles, and Adrienne Vittadini designer clothing are distributed exclusively with great success.

A manufacturer that chooses a limited number of dealers in an area (but more than one or two) is using **selective distribution**. Because the number of retailers handling the product is limited, consumers must be willing to seek it out. Timberland boots, a high-quality line of footwear, are distributed selectively. So are Sony televisions, Maytag washers, Waterford crystal, and Tommy Hilfiger clothing. When choosing dealers, manufacturers look for certain qualities. Sony might seek retailers that can offer high-quality customer service. Tommy Hilfiger might look for retailers with high-traffic locations in regional shopping malls. All manufacturers try to exclude retailers that are a poor credit risk or that have a weak or negative image.

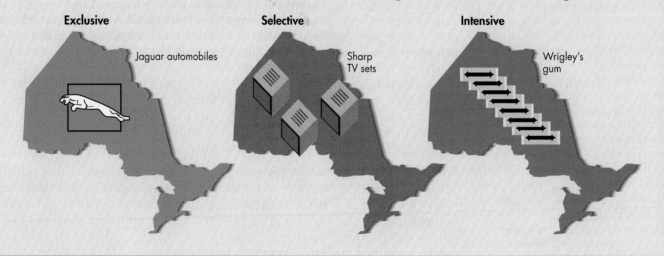

Exhibit 14.4 | Different Products Require Different Degrees of Market Coverage

Exclusive — Jaguar automobiles

Selective — Sharp TV sets

Intensive — Wrigley's gum

intensive distribution

A distribution system in which a manufacturer tries to sell its products wherever there are potential customers.

A manufacturer that wants to sell its products everywhere there are potential customers is using **intensive distribution**. Consumer goods such as bread, tape, and light bulbs are often distributed intensively. Usually, these products cost little and are bought frequently, which means that complex distribution channels are necessary. Coca-Cola is sold in just about every type of retail business, from gas stations to supermarkets.

concept check

What is meant by an efficient channel of distribution?

Name the three degrees of market coverage.

Describe the types of products that are distributed using intensive distribution.

WHOLESALING

5 learning goal

Wholesalers are channel members that buy finished products from manufacturers and sell them to retailers. Retailers, in turn, sell the products to consumers. Manufacturers that use selective or exclusive distribution normally sell directly to retailers. Manufacturers that use intensive distribution often rely on wholesalers.

Wholesalers also sell products to institutions, such as manufacturers, schools, and hospitals, for use in performing their own missions. A manufacturer, for instance, might buy computer paper from Xerox Canada Ltd. A hospital might buy its cleaning supplies from a large wholesaler of janitorial supplies.

Sometimes wholesalers sell products to manufacturers for use in the manufacturing process. A builder of custom boats, for instance, might buy batteries from a battery wholesaler and switches from an electrical wholesaler. Some wholesalers even sell to other wholesalers, creating yet another stage in the distribution channel.

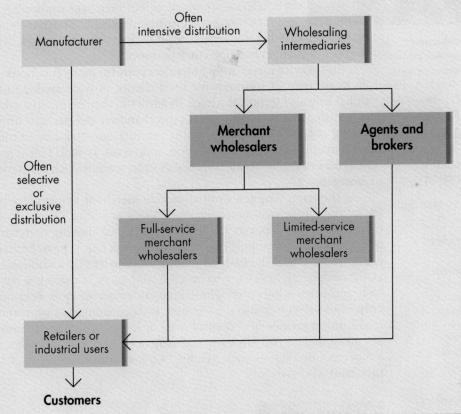

Exhibit 14.5 | The Two Categories of Wholesalers

About half of all wholesalers offer financing for their clients. They sell products on credit and expect to be paid within a certain time, usually 60 days. Other wholesalers operate like retail stores. The retailer goes to the wholesaler, selects the merchandise, pays cash for it, and transports it to the retail outlet.

Because wholesalers usually serve limited areas, they are often located closer to retailers than the manufacturers are. Retailers can thus get faster delivery at

Business and retail customers pay cash for and carry their purchases from Costco, a limited-service wholesaler that doesn't offer credit or delivery service (although they accept some credit cards).

merchant wholesaler

An institution that buys goods from manufacturers (takes ownership) and resells them to businesses, government agencies, other wholesalers, or retailers.

full-service merchant wholesalers

Wholesalers that provide many services for their clients, such as providing credit, offering promotional and technical advice, storing and delivering merchandise, or providing installation and repairs.

limited-service merchant wholesalers

Wholesalers that typically carry a limited line of fast-moving merchandise and do not offer many services to their clients.

cash-and-carry wholesaler

A limited-service merchant wholesaler that does not offer credit or delivery services.

lower cost from wholesalers. A retailer who knows that a wholesaler can restock store shelves within a day can keep a low level of inventory on hand. More money is then available for other things, because less cash is tied up in items sitting on the shelves or in storerooms.

Types of Wholesalers

The two main types of wholesalers are merchant wholesalers and agents and brokers, as shown in Exhibit 14.5. Merchant wholesalers take title to the product (ownership rights); agents and brokers simply facilitate the sale of a product from producer to end user.

Merchant wholesalers Merchant wholesalers make up 80 percent of all wholesaling establishments and conduct slightly less than 60 percent of all wholesale sales. A **merchant wholesaler** is an institution that buys goods from manufacturers and resells them to businesses, government agencies, other wholesalers, or retailers. All merchant wholesalers take title to the goods they sell. Most merchant wholesalers operate one or more warehouses where they receive goods, store them, and later reship them. Customers are mostly small or moderate-size retailers, but merchant wholesalers also market to manufacturers and institutional clients. Merchant wholesalers can be categorized as either full-service or limited-service wholesalers, depending on the number of channel functions they perform.

Full-service merchant wholesalers perform many functions. They assemble an assortment of products for their clients, provide credit, and offer promotional help and technical advice. In addition, they maintain a sales force to contact customers, store and deliver merchandise, and perhaps offer research and planning support. Depending on the product line, full-service merchant wholesalers sometimes provide installation and repair as well. Full service also means "going the extra mile" to meet special customer needs, such as offering fast delivery in emergencies.

As the name implies, **limited-service merchant wholesalers** perform only a few of the full-service merchant wholesaler's activities. Generally, limited-service merchant wholesalers carry a limited line of fast-moving merchandise. They do not extend credit or supply market information. One type of limited-service merchant wholesaler is the **cash-and-carry wholesaler.** This wholesaler doesn't offer credit or delivery, hence the term "cash-and-carry." Costco is a nationally known cash-and-carry wholesaler. These companies are unique, because they are not only wholesalers but also do business with consumers. Government employees, credit union members, and employees of large corporations, among others, can pay an annual fee (usually $50) and shop at Costco. Retail customers typically pay a 5 percent markup as well. Exhibit 14.6 lists additional types of limited-service merchant wholesalers.

concept check

Define wholesaling, and describe what wholesalers do.

Describe merchant wholesalers and the categories of merchant wholesalers.

Explain the difference between agents and brokers.

Agents and brokers As mentioned earlier, agents represent manufacturers and wholesalers. **Manufacturers' representatives** (also called **manufacturers' agents**) represent non-competing manufacturers. These salespeople function as independent agents rather than as salaried employees of manufacturers. They do not take title to or possession of merchandise. They get commissions if they make

© MARK RICHARDS / PHOTOEDIT

manufacturers' representatives
Salespeople who represent non-competing manufacturers; function as independent agents rather than as salaried employees of the manufacturers.

sales—and nothing if they don't. They are found in a variety of industries, including electronics, clothing, hardware, furniture, and toys.

Brokers bring buyers and sellers together. Like agents, brokers do not take title to merchandise, they receive commissions on sales, and they have little say over company sales policies. They are found in markets where the information that would join buyers and sellers is scarce. These markets include real estate, agriculture, insurance, and commodities.

Exhibit 14.6	Limited-Service Merchant Wholesalers
Cash-and-carry wholesalers	Have a limited line of fast-moving goods and sell to small retailers for cash. Normally do not deliver.
Truck wholesalers	Perform primarily a selling and delivery function. Carry a limited line of semi-perishable merchandise (such as milk, bread, snack foods), which they sell for cash as they make their rounds of supermarkets, small groceries, hospitals, restaurants, factory cafeterias, and hotels.
Drop shippers	Operate in bulk industries, such as coal, lumber, and heavy equipment. Do not carry inventory or handle the product. On receiving an order, they select a manufacturer, who ships the merchandise directly to the customer on the agreed-upon terms and time of delivery. The drop shipper assumes title and risk from the time the order is accepted to its delivery to the customer.
Rack jobbers	Serve grocery and drug retailers, mostly in the area of non-food items. They send delivery trucks to stores, and the delivery people set up toys, paperbacks, hardware items, health and beauty aids, and so on. They price the goods, keep them fresh, set up point-of-purchase displays, and keep inventory records. Rack jobbers retain title to the goods and bill the retailers only for the goods sold to consumers. They do little promotion, because they carry many branded items that are highly advertised.
Producers' cooperatives	Owned by farmer members, they assemble farm produce to sell in local markets. The co-op's profits are distributed to members at the end of the year. Co-ops often attempt to improve product quality and promote a co-op brand name, such as Sun Maid raisins or Sunkist oranges.

THE COMPETITIVE WORLD OF RETAILING

6 learning goal

Approximately 220,000 Canadians are engaged in retailing. Of this number, 39 percent are male and 61 percent are female, with 58 percent working full time and 42 percent part time. The main industries of employment are clothing and clothing accessories (17 percent), general merchandise (14 percent), food and beverage (8 percent), and sporting goods, hobby, book, and music stores (6 percent).[1]

Types of Retail Operations

HOT Links

Visit the Retail Council of Canada at http://www.retailcouncil.org—the voice of retail in Canada.

There is a great deal of variety in retail operations. The major types of retailers are described in Exhibit 14.7, where they are divided into two main categories: in-store and non-store retailing. Examples of *in-store retailing* include The Bay, Sears, and Wal-Mart. These retailers get most of their revenue from people who come to the store to buy what they want. Many in-store retailers also do some catalogue and telephone sales.

Non-store retailing includes vending, direct selling, direct-response marketing, home shopping networks, and Internet retailing. Vending uses machines to sell food and other items, usually as a convenience in institutions such as schools and hospitals.

Direct selling involves face-to-face contact between the buyer and seller, but not in a retail store. Usually, the seller goes to the consumer's home. Sometimes

HOT Links

Want to learn more about direct selling? Learn how people become Amway representatives and find out more about the company by visiting http://www.amway.com.

contacts are made at the place of work. Mary Kay Cosmetics, Avon, Herbalife, and Amway each employ direct salespeople. Some companies, such as Tupperware and Weekender Clothing, specialize in parties in a person's home. Most parties are a combination social affair and sales demonstration. The person hosting the party usually gets a discount and a special gift for rounding up a group of friends. Such parties seem to be replacing door-to-door canvassing. The sales of many direct-sales companies have suffered as women continue to enter the workforce on a full-time basis.

Exhibit 14.7 | Retailing Takes Many Forms

TYPES OF IN-STORE RETAILING	DESCRIPTION	EXAMPLES
Department store	Houses many departments under one roof, with each treated as a separate buying centre to achieve economies of buying, promotion, and control	The Bay, Zellers, Sears
Specialty store	Specializes in a category of merchandise and carries a complete assortment	Toys "R" Us, Radio Shack, Mappins Jewellers
Convenience store	Offers convenience goods with long store hours and quick checkout	7-Eleven, Mac's
Supermarket	Specializes in a wide assortment of food, with self-service	Safeway, Sobeys, IGA
Discount store	Competes on the basis of low prices and high turnover; offers few services	Wal-Mart
Off-price retailer	Sells at prices 25 percent or more below traditional department store prices in Spartan environment	Winners
Factory outlet	Owned by manufacturer; sells close-outs, factory seconds, and cancelled orders	Gap, Cotton Ginny, Levi Strauss
Catalogue store	Sends catalogues to customers and displays merchandise in showrooms where customers can order from attached warehouse	IKEA and Sears

TYPES OF NON-STORE RETAILING	DESCRIPTION	EXAMPLES
Direct selling	Sells face-to-face, usually in the person's home	Fuller Brush, Avon, Amway
Direct-response marketing	Attempts to get immediate consumer sale through media advertising, catalogues, or direct mail	K-Tel and L.L. Bean
Home shopping networks	Selling via cable television	Home Shopping Network
Internet retailing (e-commerce)	Selling over the Internet	Bluefly.com, landsend.com, gap.com, Amazon.com, Cheapstuff.com, Dell.com

Direct-response marketing is conducted through media that encourage a consumer to reply. Popular direct-response media are catalogues, direct mail, television, newspapers, and radio. The ads invite a person to "call the toll-free number now" or to fill out an order blank. Direct-response marketing includes K-Tel selling "golden oldies" and a former race car driver touting herbal baldness remedies. It also includes the catalogues sent out by numerous retailers.

Internet retailing, also called e-commerce, is the selling of merchandise over the Internet. E-commerce sales are exploding and will have a profound impact on retailers around the world. It is also going to change how you shop. Strategies for on-line shopping are covered later in this chapter.

Components of a Successful Retailing Strategy

Retailing is a very competitive business. Managers have to develop an effective strategy to survive. The key tasks in building a retail strategy are defining a target market, developing a product offering, creating an image and a promotional strategy, choosing a location, and setting prices.

Defining a target market The first and foremost task in developing a retail strategy is to define the target market. This process begins with market segmentation, the topic of an earlier chapter, and the determination of a target market. For example, Sport Chek's merchandising approach for sporting goods is to match its product assortment to the demographics of the local store and region. Sport Chek stores in the areas where skiing is popular stock a variety of ski equipment to satisfy the local interest in down-hill and cross-country skiing. The amount of space devoted to sporting goods, as well as in-store promotions, also varies according to each store's target market.

Target markets in retailing are often defined by demographics. The popular dollar store concept stores target households earning less than $25,000 per year. Eddie Bauer targets suburban 25- to 45-year-olds. Claire's, a retailer selling inexpensive costume jewellery, such as Y-shaped necklaces, wire triceps bracelets, and headbands, targets 12- to 14-year-old girls.

Developing the product offering The second element in determining a retail strategy is the product offering, also called the product assortment or merchandise mix. Retailers decide what to sell on the basis of what their target market wants to buy. They can base their decision on market research, past sales, fashion trends, customer requests, and other sources. For example, after more companies began promoting office casual days, Brooks Brothers, the upscale retailer of men's and women's conservative business wear, updated its product line with khaki pants, casual shirts, and a selection of brightly coloured shirts and ties.

After determining what products will satisfy target customers' desires, retailers must find sources of supply and evaluate the products. When the right products are located, the retail buyer negotiates a purchase contract. The buying function can be performed in-house or delegated to an outside firm. The goods must then be moved from the seller to the retailer, which means shipping, storing, and stocking the inventory. The trick is to manage the inventory by cutting prices to move slow goods and by keeping adequate supplies of hot-selling items in stock.

One of the more efficient new methods of managing inventory and streamlining the way products are moved from supplier to distributor to retailer is called **efficient consumer response (ECR)**. At the heart of ECR is **electronic data interchange (EDI)**, the computer-to-computer exchange of information, including automatic shipping notifications, invoices, inventory data, and forecasts. In a full implementation of ECR, products are scanned at the retail store when purchased, which updates the store's inventory lists. Headquarters then polls the stores to retrieve the data needed to produce an order. The vendor confirms the order, shipping date, and delivery time, then ships the order and transmits the invoice electronically. The item is received at the warehouse, scanned into inventory, and then sent to the store. The invoice and receiving data are reconciled, and payment via an electronic transfer of funds completes the process. Many retailers are experimenting with or have successfully implemented ECR and EDI. The pioneer and market leader in ECR systems is Wal-Mart.

HOT Links

Find out about the more than 100 stores that Sport Chek has in Canada at http://www.sportcheck.ca.

efficient consumer response (ECR)
A method of managing inventory and streamlining the movement of products from supplier to distributor to retailer; relies on electronic data interchange to communicate information such as automatic shipping notifications, invoices, inventory data, and forecasts.

electronic data interchange (EDI)
Computer-to-computer exchange of information, including automatic shipping notifications, invoices, inventory data, and forecasts; used in efficient consumer response systems.

A retailer's image is made up of the store's merchandise mix, service level, and atmosphere. Williams-Sonoma's store image includes knowledgeable salespeople, elegant merchandise displays, and specialty bake ware.

© TERRI L. MILLER / E-VISUAL COMMUNICATIONS, INC.

Creating an image and promotional strategy The third task in developing a retail strategy is to create an image and a promotional strategy. Promotion combines with the store's merchandise mix, service level, and atmosphere to make up a retail image. We will discuss promotion in more detail in the next chapter. *Atmosphere* refers to the physical layout and décor of the store. Retailers can create a relaxed or busy feeling, a sense of luxury, a friendly or cold attitude, and a sense of organization or clutter.

These are the most influential factors in creating a store's atmosphere:

- *Employee type and density.* Employee type refers to an employee's general characteristics—for instance, neat, friendly, knowledgeable, or service oriented. Density is the number of employees per 1,000 square metres of selling space. A company that has a low employee density creates a "do-it-yourself," casual atmosphere.

- *Merchandise type and density.* The type of merchandise carried and how it is displayed add to the atmosphere the retailer is trying to create. A prestigious retailer such as Holt Renfrew carries the best brand names and displays them in a neat, uncluttered arrangement.

- *Fixture type and density.* Fixtures can be elegant (rich woods), trendy (chrome and smoked glass), or old, beat-up tables, as in an antique store. They should, however, be consistent with the general atmosphere the store is trying to create. By displaying its merchandise on tables and shelves rather than on traditional pipe racks, the Gap creates a relaxed and uncluttered atmosphere that enables customers to see and touch the merchandise more easily.

- *Sound.* Sound can be pleasant or unpleasant for a customer. Classical music at a nice Italian restaurant helps create ambiance, just as country and western music does at a truck stop. Music can also entice customers to stay in the store longer and buy more or encourage them to eat quickly and leave a table for others.

- *Odours.* Smell can either stimulate or detract from sales. The wonderful smell of pastries and breads entices bakery customers. Conversely, customers can be repulsed by bad odours, such as cigarette smoke, musty smells, antiseptic odours, and overly powerful room deodorizers.

Choosing a location The next task in creating a retail strategy is figuring out where to put the store. First, a community must be chosen. This decision depends on the strength of the local economy, the nature of the competition, the political climate, and so forth. Then a specific site must be selected. One important decision is whether to locate in a shopping centre. Large retailers and sellers of shopping goods such as furniture and cars can use a free-standing store, because customers will seek them out. Such a location also has the advantages of low-cost land or rent and no direct competitors close by. It might be harder to attract customers to a free-standing location, however. Another disadvantage is that the retailer can't share costs for promotion, maintenance, and holiday decorating, as do stores in a mall.

Setting prices Another strategic task of the retail manager is to set prices. The strategy of pricing was presented in Chapter 13. Retailing's goal is to sell products, and the price is critical in ensuring that sales take place.

Price is also one of the three key elements in the store's image and positioning strategy. Higher prices often imply quality and help support the prestige image of such retailers as Holt Renfrew. On the other hand, discounters and off-price retailers offer good value for the money.

concept check

Describe at least five (5) types of in-store retailing and four (4) forms of non-store retailing. Discuss the components of a successful retail strategy.

USING SUPPLY CHAIN MANAGEMENT TO INCREASE EFFICIENCY AND CUSTOMER SATISFACTION

7 *learning goal*

Distribution is an important part of the marketing mix. Retailers don't sell products they can't deliver, and salespeople don't (or shouldn't) promise deliveries they can't make. Late deliveries and broken promises might mean the loss of a customer. Accurate order filling and billing, timely delivery, and arrival in good condition are important to the success of the product.

The goal of supply chain management is to create a satisfied customer by coordinating all of the activities of the supply chain members into a seamless process. Therefore, an important element of supply chain management is that it is completely customer driven. In the mass production era, manufacturers produced standardized products that were "pushed" down through the supply channel to the consumer. In contrast, in today's marketplace, products are being driven by customers, who expect to receive product configurations and services matched to their unique needs. For example, Dell builds computers only according to its customers' precise specifications, such as the amount of RAM memory; type of monitor, modem, or CD drive; and amount of hard disk space.[2]

Through the channel partnership of suppliers, manufacturers, wholesalers, and retailers along the entire supply chain who work together toward the common goal of creating customer value, supply chain management allows companies to respond with the unique product configuration and mix of services demanded by the customer. Today, supply chain management plays a dual role: first, as a *communicator* of customer demand that extends from the point of sale all the way back to the supplier, and second, as a *physical flow process* that engineers the timely and cost-effective movement of goods through the entire supply pipeline.

Accordingly, supply chain managers are responsible for making channel strategy decisions, coordinating the sourcing and procurement of raw materials, scheduling production, processing orders, managing inventory, transporting and storing supplies and finished goods, and coordinating customer service activities. Supply chain managers are also responsible for the management of information that flows through the supply chain. Coordinating the relationships between the company and its external partners, such as vendors, carriers, and third-party companies, is also a critical function of supply chain management. Because supply chain managers play such a major role in both cost control and customer satisfaction, they are more valuable than ever.

Making Ethical Choices

CUTTING THE MUSTARD

Although you have always wanted to own a restaurant, the price is beyond your reach at the moment. You decide to learn about the food industry by becoming a sales representative for a small regional gourmet mustard manufacturer. In addition to basic varieties, such as Dijon, you are introducing a new line of gourmet flavours, such as raspberry, balsamic, horseradish, and curry.

You sell to a variety of food outlets: restaurants, gourmet food stores, upscale markets, and major grocery chains, such as Safeway and any of the many Loblaw outlets (e.g., Dominion, Real Canadian Superstore, or Atlantic Superstore). One of your biggest challenges is getting the chains to give you decent shelf space for your products. Your company must compete with large food manufacturers like French's and Kraft, whose Nabisco division makes the popular Grey Poupon line. Kraft's large product line and huge promotional budget give it incredible marketing clout with retailers.

Although your products are well received by consumers in smaller retail outlets, getting the chains to carry them isn't easy. It's standard practice for food manufacturers and distributors to pay retailers "slotting

fees" for premium shelf position in their stores and even to limit shelf space for competing products.

Until now, your CEO has refused to pay slotting fees and considers them unethical, believing that they ultimately raise prices for consumers and curtail competition. Retailers, on the other hand, consider the fees a legitimate promotional expense and compensation for the risk of selling new products—not to mention a revenue source that can range from $5,000 to more than $50,000. Your fellow specialty food manufacturers have been hesitant to speak up in government hearings about these fees for fear of being blacklisted by supermarkets.

ETHICAL DILEMMA

Your company's three-year sales plan—and your success in meeting your sales quota—depends on getting larger distribution for your new product line. Should you recommend that your company begin to pay slotting fees to get better and more shelf space?

SOURCES: Chris Baker, "It's Yellow, but Not French," *The Washington Times*, March 19, 2003, http://www.washingtontimes.com; Brandon Copple, "Shelf-Determination," *Forbes*, April 14, 2002, http://www.Forbes.com; "Controversial 'Slotting Fees' More Common, Costly," *Silicon Valley/San Jose Business Journal*, December 12, 2002, http://sanjose.bizjournals.com; and Eric Wieffering, "Grocery Shelves: Stock Strategies," *Minneapolis Star Tribune*, March 7, 2003.

Managing the Logistical Components of the Supply Chain

Logistics, discussed earlier, is a term borrowed from the armed forces that describes the process of strategically managing the efficient flow and storage of raw materials, in-process inventory, and finished goods from the point of origin to point of consumption. The supply chain team manages the logistical flow. Key decisions in managing the logistical flow are finding and procuring raw materials and supplies, production scheduling, choosing a warehouse location and type, setting up a materials-handling system, and making transportation decisions.

Sourcing and Procurement

One of the most important links in the supply chain is that between the manufacturer and the supplier. Purchasing professionals are on the front lines of supply chain management. Purchasing departments plan purchasing strategies, develop specifications, select suppliers, and negotiate price and service levels.

The goal of most sourcing and procurement activities is to reduce the costs of raw materials and supplies and to have the items available when they are needed for production or for the office but not before (see just-in-time manufacturing in Chapter 11).

Production Scheduling

In traditional mass market manufacturing, production begins when forecasts call for additional products to be made or inventory control systems signal low inventory levels. The firm then makes a product and transports the finished goods to its own warehouses or those of intermediaries, where the goods wait to be ordered by retailers or customers. Production scheduling based on pushing a product down to the consumer obviously has its disadvantages, the most notable being that companies risk making products that become obsolete or that consumers don't want in the first place.

In a customer "pull" manufacturing environment, which is growing in popularity, production of goods or services is not scheduled until an order is placed by the customer specifying the desired configuration. This process, known as *mass customization,* or *build-to-order,* uniquely tailors mass market goods and services to the needs of the individuals who buy them. Mass customization was explained in Chapter 11. Companies as diverse as BMW, Dell Computer, Levi Strauss, Mattel, and a slew of Web-based businesses are adopting mass customization to maintain or obtain a competitive edge.

Choosing a Warehouse Location and Type

Deciding where to put a warehouse is mostly a matter of deciding which markets will be served and where production facilities will be located. A *storage warehouse* is used to hold goods for a long time. For instance, Jantzen makes bathing suits at an even rate throughout the year to provide steady employment and hold down costs. It then stores them in a warehouse until the selling season.

Reliable and inexpensive water transportation is one of the five major modes of transportation that distribution managers can choose from to move products from the producer to the buyer.

© AP/WORLD WIDE PHOTOS

distribution centres

Warehouses that specialize in changing shipment sizes rather than in storing goods.

Distribution centres are a special form of warehouse. They specialize in changing shipment sizes rather than storing goods. Such centres make bulk (put shipments together) or break bulk. They strive for rapid inventory turnover. When shipments arrive, the merchandise is quickly sorted into orders for various retail stores. As soon as the order is complete, it is delivered. Distribution centres are the wave of the future, replacing traditional warehouses. Companies simply can't afford to have a lot of money tied up in idle inventory.

Setting Up a Materials-Handling System

A materials-handling system moves and handles inventory. The goal of such a system is to move items as quickly as possible while handling them as little as possible. Rite Aid, the huge U.S. drugstore chain, uses Universal Product Codes (bar codes), moving carousels, and eight miles of conveyors to process 60,000 cartons a day in its California distribution centre. Its sophisticated materials-handling system provides 99.6 percent accuracy and a 99 percent on-time delivery to its retail drugstores.[3]

Making Transportation Decisions

HOT Links

Freightworld, http://www.freightworld.com offers detailed information on various modes of transportation and links to transportation companies.

Transportation typically accounts for between 5 and 10 percent of the price of goods. Physical-distribution managers must decide which mode of transportation to use to move products from producer to buyer. This decision is, of course, related to all other physical-distribution decisions. The five major modes of transportation are railroads, motor carriers, pipelines, water transportation, and airways. Distribution managers generally choose a mode of transportation on the basis of several criteria:

- *cost*—the total amount a specific carrier charges to move the product from the point of origin to the destination;
- *transit time*—the total time a carrier has possession of goods, including the time required for pickup and delivery, handling, and movement between the point of origin and the destination;
- *reliability*—the consistency with which the carrier delivers goods on time and in acceptable condition;
- *capability*—the carrier's ability to provide the appropriate equipment and conditions for moving specific kinds of goods, such as those that must be transported in a controlled environment (for example, under refrigeration);
- *accessibility*—the carrier's ability to move goods over a specific route or network; and
- *traceability*—the relative ease with which a shipment can be located and transferred.

HOT Links

The Logistics Institute is an organization focused on building logistical skills and provides information on a logistics-related designation. See its Web site at http://www.loginstitute.ca.

Using these six criteria, a shipper selects the mode of transportation that will best meet its needs. Exhibit 14.8 shows how the basic modes of transportation rank in terms of these criteria.

concept check

Discuss the components of a successful retail strategy.

What is the goal of supply chain management?

Describe the key decisions in managing the logistical flow.

What factors are considered when selecting a mode of transportation?

Exhibit 14.8 | Criteria for Ranking Modes of Transportation

	HIGHEST				LOWEST
Relative cost	Air	Truck	Rail	Pipe	Water
Transit time	Water	Rail	Pipe	Truck	Air
Reliability	Pipe	Truck	Rail	Air	Water
Capability	Water	Rail	Truck	Air	Pipe
Accessibility	Truck	Rail	Air	Water	Pipe
Traceability	Air	Truck	Rail	Water	Pipe

Trends in Distribution

8 *learning goal*

Companies are using new distribution strategies to boost their profits and gain a competitive edge. The Internet is spurring many of these new strategies by opening up a whole new avenue for buying goods and services. In this section, we'll discuss two emerging trends in distribution, category management and information sharing.

CATEGORY MANAGEMENT

category management
Suppliers manage the inventory of a category of products for a retailer.

Borders Books used to carry more than 10 titles about sushi in its cooking section. It later cut the number to three, because HarperCollins, the publishing house, told Borders to do so. This is the mushrooming trend toward category management. **Category management** is where the nation's largest retailers ask one supplier in a category to determine how the retailer should best stock its shelves. Thus, HarperCollins tells Borders which cookbooks to carry from all cookbook publishers! Category management is becoming standard practice at nearly every supermarket, convenience store, mass merchant, and drug chain. The reason is that it works. Retailers attribute 14 percent sales growth to category management.

A retailer can increase profits by managing itself not as a collection of products but as product categories. People don't shop for soft drinks the way that they shop for meat. With soft drinks, it might be more effective to group brands (Pepsi, Coke, store brand) together; in another category, freshness is most important. Sophisticated computer programs and marketing research help decide which products and how much should be carried. Manufacturers that supply most of the category management are called captains. Category captains include soft drinks—Coca-Cola; wine—E&J Gallo; shaving—Gillette; pet food—Purina; and detergent—Procter & Gamble.

The best retailers are far from passive when it comes to accepting category captains' recommendations. Wal-Mart runs the captain's plan by a "validator," which is a second supplier, so Dole, for example, runs a check on what Del Monte proposes.[4]

HOT *Links*

Stores magazine, http://www.stores.org, offers hundreds of ideas for putting together a successful retail strategy.

SHARING INFORMATION AND THE LOAD

General Mills had a problem that plagues most companies that use trucks to ship products: trucks that ship only air. Drivers carrying loads of Betty Crocker cake mixes, Cheerios, or Yoplait yogurt were hauling an empty trailer as often as 15 percent of the time. Once a load was delivered, the trucks had to return empty if the driver couldn't find a load. Therefore, the return trip was wasted by empty trucks.

General Mills found a solution. The company teamed with other manufacturers, such as a paper products maker, to use new logistics software to find loads for otherwise empty trucks. If General Mills has a truckload of Wheaties to send to Vancouver but no load to fill the truck as it returns to its Mississauga, Ontario, location, the software examines the other companies' shipping schedules and finds that the paper products maker has a load of paper towels and paper cups that needs to go from Vancouver to Mississauga. The software alerts both companies, who have agreed in advance on terms. General Mills and the paper products maker pay less per mile, and General Mills does not have to find a load to haul back.[5]

concept check

Explain category management and why it is popular.
How does information sharing save shippers money?

Great Ideas to Use Now

This chapter covers retailing, so we decided to offer you a few shopping tips to make your life easier. It might also put a few extra dollars in your wallet!

FLYING IN EUROPE? GO CHEAP

It used to be that flying 200 miles in Europe cost you as much or more than flying across the Atlantic. With Europe's discount airlines, that has changed. Check out these Web sites:

Ryanair: http://www.ryanair.com

Easy Jet: http://www.easyjet.com

Virgin Express: http://www.virgin-express.com

Customer Satisfaction and Quality

Distribution is all about getting the right product to the right person, at the right place, at the right time. Even if only one of these things does not occur, then the firm will have a dissatisfied customer. Sophisticated supply chain management programs, using the latest software, have dramatically reduced distribution errors in addition to lowering costs for the firm.

Oracle, the giant software company, has switched from an overly aggressive sales force to making customer service its top priority. "It's more than just the sale," said Paul Ciandrini, former Oracle senior vice

president who headed up the company's commercial sales in the western region of North America. "I can make the sale and be a hero, but I can't go back in and expand that sale if it's of no value to the customer."[6]

Even the smallest details have been reconsidered. Oracle used to offer slick presentations on its products and the features that distinguished them from those of SAP AG of Germany. Now, it uses demonstrations that map its customers' specific technology environment, so it can put itself in its customers' shoes by focusing on problems as they see them.

THE POINT OF NO RETURN

Many companies are tightening their returns policies and the "no" word is cropping up more often. The latest policies from some of Canada's largest retailers are shown in Exhibit 14.9. It is always better to know the return policy before you buy.

Exhibit 14.9	Return Policies of Selected Retailers

CRACKING DOWN:

COMPANY	RETURN POLICY
Home Depot	New 90-day window on returns, and store credit given if you don't have a receipt.
Best Buy	Electronics buyers beware: 15 percent restocking fees on some items and short return windows of 14–30 days.
Gap	Hurry. 14-day window on returns for any reason with the receipt. After that, items must have tags and look new.

BETTER DEALS:

COMPANY	RETURN POLICY
Circuit City	A good spot for electronics—no restocking fees.
Radio Shack	Again, no restocking fees. But make returns within 30 days.
	"Guaranteed Period." Returns or refunds at any time, for any reason.

SOURCE: Adapted from Jane Spencer, "The Point of No Return," Wall Street Journal (May 14, 2002), p. D2. Reprinted by permission of the Wall Street Journal, Copyright © 2002 Dow Jones & Company, Inc. All Rights Reserved Worldwide.

SUMMARY OF LEARNING GOALS

1   What is physical distribution?

Physical distribution is efficiently managing the acquisition of raw materials to the factory and the movement of products from the producer or manufacturer to industrial users and consumers. Physical distribution activities are usually the responsibility of the marketing department and are part of the large series of activities included in the supply chain.

2   What are distribution channels and their functions?

Distribution channels are the series of marketing entities through which goods and services pass on their way from producers to end users. Distribution systems focus on the physical transfer of goods and services and on their legal ownership at each stage of the distribution process. Channels (a) reduce the number of transactions, (b) ease the flow of goods, and (c) increase channel efficiency.

3 How are channels organized?

A vertical marketing system is a planned, hierarchical, organized distribution channel. There are three types of vertical marketing systems: corporate, administrative, and contractual. In a corporate system, one firm owns the entire channel. In an administrative system, a strong organization takes over as leader and sets channel policies. In a contractual distribution system, the independent firms coordinate their distribution activities by written contract. Forward integration occurs in a distribution channel when a marketing intermediary acquires another marketing intermediary closer to the customer, such as a retailer. Backward integration occurs when a wholesaler or retailer gains control over the production process.

4 When would a marketer use exclusive, selective, or intensive distribution?

The degree of intensity depends in part on the type of product being distributed. Exclusive distribution (one or two dealers in an area) is used when products are in high demand in the target market. Selective distribution has a limited number of dealers per area, but more than one or two. This form of distribution is used for consumer shopping goods, some specialty goods, and some industrial accessories. Intensive distribution occurs when the manufacturer sells its products in virtually every store willing to carry them. It is used mainly for consumer convenience goods.

5 What is wholesaling, and what are the types of wholesalers?

Wholesalers typically sell finished products to retailers and to other institutions, such as manufacturers, schools, and hospitals. They also provide a wide variety of services, among them storing merchandise, financing inventory, breaking bulk, providing rapid delivery to retailers, and supplying market information. The two main types of wholesalers are merchant wholesalers, and agents and brokers. Merchant wholesalers buy from manufacturers and sell to other businesses. Full-service merchant wholesalers offer a complete array of services to their customers, who are retailers. Limited-service merchant wholesalers typically carry a limited line of fast-moving merchandise and offer few services to their customers. Agents and brokers are essentially independents who provide buying and selling services. They receive commissions according to their sales.

6 What are the different kinds of retail operations and the components of a successful retailing strategy?

Retailing can be either in-store or non-store. In-store retail operations include department stores, specialty stores, discount stores, off-price retailers, factory outlets, and catalogue showrooms. Non-store retailing includes vending machines, direct sales, direct-response marketing, and Internet retailing (e-commerce).

Creating a retail strategy is important in all kinds of retailing and involves defining a target market, developing a product offering, creating an image and a promotional strategy, choosing a location, and setting prices. The most important factors in creating a store's atmosphere are employee type and density, merchandise type and density, fixture type and density, sound, and odours.

7 How can supply chain management increase efficiency and customer satisfaction?

The goal of supply chain management is to coordinate all of the activities of the supply chain members into a seamless process, thereby increasing customer satisfaction. The logistical components of the supply chain include sourcing and procurement, production scheduling, choosing a warehouse location and type, setting up a materials-handling system, and making transportation decisions.

8 What are the trends in distribution?

Two emerging trends in distribution are category management and information sharing. The former is where large retailers ask one supplier in a category of products to determine how the retailer should best stock its shelves. Nearly every supermarket chain, convenience store chain, mass merchant, and drugstore chain uses category management. Vendors use sophisticated computer programs and marketing research to determine which products and how much should be carried. The result is greater sales and higher profits.

Information sharing among shippers by truck is resulting in fewer empty loads to haul back. By sharing their shipping needs, manufacturers have found that they can use each other's trucks to avoid making a shipment and then having to return empty. Sophisticated software helps members of the shipping alliance find loads for the return haul home. The greater the number of manufacturers in the alliance, the lower the chance that a return trip will be empty.

EXPERIENTIAL EXERCISES

1. Do some comparison shopping. A beauty of the Internet is the ability to comparison shop like never before. Tour and Internet travel companies offer many last-minute specials where travellers can save on their trips. To compare brands, features, and prices of products, go to one of these sites: **http://www .airtransat.com, http://www.aircanadavacations.com, http://www.expedia .com, http://www.itravel2000.com,** and any others that you have researched.

2. Kick the tires before you buy. At some point you are going to buy a car. The Web can simplify the process, help you make an intelligent decision, and save you money. Start at **http://www.edmunds.com.** The on-line version of the respected car buying guide is crammed with information about new and used cars. The site offers thousands of car reviews and current loan rates.

3. Trace the distribution channel for some familiar product. Compose an e-mail explaining why the channel has evolved as it has and how it is likely to change in the future.

4. You work for a small chain of department stores (six stores total) located within a single province. Write a memo to the president explaining how e-commerce might affect the chain's business.

5. Go to a successful, independent specialty store in your area that has been in business for quite a while. Interview the manager and try to determine how the store successfully competes with the national chains.

6. Visit a local manufacturer. Interview managers to determine how its supply chain functions. Make a report to the class.

7. Visit *Industry Week*'s Web site at **http://www.industryweek.com.** Under "Archive," do a search using the search term "supply chain management." Choose an article from the results that describes how a company has used supply chain management

to improve customer satisfaction, performance, or profitability. Give a brief presentation to your class on your findings.

8. What are some of the logistics problems facing firms that operate internationally? Visit the *Logistics Management* magazine Web site at **http://www.manufacturing.net/lm/,** and see if you can find information about how firms manage global logistics. Summarize the results.

9. Search for information on retail careers at the About.com's retail industry information site, **http://www.retailindustry.about.com.** What types of careers are available in retailing? What skills are needed? Does a career in retailing appeal to you? Why or why not?

10. How does category management help companies? For one view, visit the InfoCenter's Category Management pages of Hershey's Vending division at **http://www.hersheysvending.com/infocenter/category.shtml.** What benefits does this system claim to offer to owners of vending machines? What are the advantages for Hershey's? Browse the rest of the Web site. What other helpful information does it provide?

11. One of the biggest challenges for retailers is integrating their various channels to provide a seamless experience for customers, regardless of the channel. Pick two of the following companies, explore their Web sites, and compare the channel integration strategies: Staples (**http://www.staples.com**), Gap (**http://www.gap.com**), or Borders (**http://www.borders.com**). In addition to looking at the Web sites from a channel perspective, you might want to look at the company information and news sites.

REVIEW QUESTIONS

1. What is physical distribution?

2. Define *marketing intermediaries.* What are four common marketing intermediaries?

3. What is the distribution channel? What are the functions of distribution channels?

4. Define the following:
   a. Vertical marketing system
   b. Corporate distribution system
   c. Forward integration
   d. Backward integration
   e. Administrative distribution system
   f. Contractual distribution system

5. Discuss the various intensity of market coverage.

6. What are wholesalers? What are the two main types of wholesalers? Describe each.

7. What forms can retailing take?

8. Describe the components of a successful retailing strategy.

9. What is the goal of supply chain management? What are the logistical components of the supply chain?

10. What new distribution strategies are companies using to boost their profits and gain a competitive edge?

CREATIVE THINKING CASE

Peanuts and Cheesecake: Facing a common challenge

John Picard of Waterford, Ontario, grows 400,000 pounds of peanuts each year. John started in 1979 roasting Valencia peanuts and now sells more than 150 different flavours. He imports another million pounds from the Southern United States. These products are sold in his six Picard Peanut Shoppe outlets in southern Ontario. John's distribution system consists of two delivery vehicles to service his 750,000 customers.

Darlene Landino produces 1,500 cheesecakes per month from her Winnipeg plant, and after unsuccessfully partnering with a distributor, Darlene does her own deliveries. The cakes must be stored at −25° C and remain frozen until ready for serving. Darlene cannot afford the high transportation fees of the large distributors, and she feels this severely limits her ability to grow the business.

Due to the increase in the offerings of niche products, the old way of distributing the same things to the same places at the same times is changing. With today's consumers, the products must be available whenever the customer wants them. Baby boomers make up a large percentage of the population and often have a great deal of disposable income, demanding premium products at premium prices, available on demand. For example, fresh herbs to enhance the cooking experience would be a premium product. How would Randie, from the Sunshine Coast of British Columbia, get her fabulous fresh herbs to the Saskatoon market?

The challenge of product delivery can be very daunting, but the use of new technology can help some producers. There is software available that can track an item from the taking of an order to the shipping, delivery, and payment. RFID (Radio Frequency Identification) is a technological innovation that can track and trace products to ensure safety and security. Other strategies include radio frequency bar code scanners, computer-controlled temperature monitoring, temperature controlled trucks, and voice-directed workplace technology, as well as the use of the Internet.

Some retailers have moved forward by engaging in self-distributing, which offers the producers the advantage of selling and shipping to fewer centres, thus cutting distribution costs. Does all this techno-tracking help the little guy? John of Picard's Peanuts thinks not. He prefers "taking orders on Mondays, packing on Tuesdays, and shipping and delivery the rest of the week."

CRITICAL THINKING QUESTIONS

1. Given the many advances in distribution of food products, is there a way to deal with the challenges facing John, Darlene, or Randie?

2. What overall retailing strategy would you suggest for small operations such as those mentioned in the case?

SOURCE: Peanuts and Cheesecake: Facing a Common Challenge Adapted from Jack Kohane, "Delivering the Goods," from Food in Canada, 2006, pp. 57–59. Used by permission.

VIDEO CASE

Ping-Karsten Hits the Sweet Spot

Inventor Karsten Solheim was having trouble with his golf game, so he decided to build a better golf club. Named for the sound it makes when it strikes the ball, his PING Putter, introduced in 1959, revolutionized golf club design. Seven years later, his Anser putter clocked more than 500 wins and changed putting forever.

From humble beginnings working out of his garage, Solheim, a former engineer with General Electric, stayed ahead of the pack with his pioneering product designs. His company, Karsten Manufacturing, now employs 900 people and has a

Canadian distributor, PING Canada, in Oakville, Ontario (carolb@karsten.com). Karsten's belief that properly fitted clubs are critical to a golfer's performance has been responsible for the company's specialization in manufacturing custom-fitted clubs. A custom set of clubs can incorporate the small modifications that make all the difference to a player's game.

Today, more than 2,200 club fitters, who have completed an intensive three-day club-fitting seminar at the company's headquarters, help customers choose the right PING clubs designed to fit their own personal specifications. After being measured by a trained professional, the customer's specifications are sent to the Karsten plant, where a set of custom clubs is made on-site in just two days. Each set of clubs has a unique serial number, and the company's revolutionary tracking system keeps tabs on all club specifications. It is a key strategy in making and keeping customers happy. If a customer loses a club, it can be quickly and easily replaced.

In late 2002, Karsten Manufacturing became the first golf equipment company to allow golfers to design clubs on-line. By visiting **http://www.pinggolf.com/Specify/**, customers can select the look, style, feel, and weight of their own custom-designed PING SPECIFY putter. "This new on-line program will not only help the consumer understand the concept and options available with the SPECIFY putter, it is another example of how our company supports its retailers with innovation and service," said John Solheim, PING Chairman and CEO.

Karsten Manufacturing's commitment to quality innovative products, an efficient supply and delivery system, and a uniquely personal approach to customer service, can only mean more winners for the country's 25 million golfers and the next generation of PING products.

CRITICAL THINKING QUESTIONS

1. How has PING set itself apart in the highly competitive arena of golf equipment design and manufacturing? Explain.

2. Describe the benefits of the company's unique golf club–tracking system in the context of timely and efficient distribution of products.

3. How do PING's innovative marketing concepts benefit retailers?

SOURCES: Adapted from material in the video "PING-Karsten"; PING-Karsten corporate Web site http://www.pinggolf.com (accessed May 7, 2003); "PING Introduces Web Site for Golfers to Create Their Own Specify Putter," *PRNewswire*, December 9, 2002, http://www.findarticles.com; and "PING Named Top Custom-Fitting Golf Equipment Company by National Survey of Golfers," *PRNewswire*, October 24, 2001, http://www.findarticles.com.

E-COMMERCE CASE
A Blockbuster Idea

Movies delivered right to your door? What could be more convenient? Select from 13,500 movies at the company's easy-to-use Web site. List favourites in your "movie rental queue," then sit back until the letter carrier arrives. Within 48 hours, your DVD movies are delivered in a prepaid return envelope. View as many movies as you like in a month, keeping them as long as you wish—no more late fees!—a maximum of three at a time. When you return a movie, your next selection is automatically plucked from your rental queue and mailed to you. And you can have all this at a cost of just $19.95 per month.

Reed Hastings, CEO of the Los Gatos, California–based company Netflix (**http://www.netflix.com**), confidently projects continued rapid growth. American ownership of DVD players stands at 35 million, up from zero in 1997. "Over the next four years we will grow our subscriber base to 5 million," predicts Hastings. "With a billion in revenue, we'll be a 'real' media company. At $150 million in annual revenues we are still just a promising niche."

One of the few successful e-commerce public stock offerings of 2002, Netflix's second-quarter revenues doubled to $36.4 million from $18.4 million one year earlier. Its earnings of $6.5 million in the second quarter compared to losses of $100,000 of the previous year.

The company is an interesting marriage of high and low tech. It uses the Internet as a cost-effective way to reach its customers. DVD delivery is by mail, however, because it costs only 37 cents to send a DVD by mail—well below the $3.50 or so that Hastings estimates it would cost to send movies over the Internet.

Now Hollywood has come calling. The studios are eager to sign deals with Netflix to counter the growing power of Blockbuster, which has launched a copycat subscription service in four metropolitan markets and plans to go national in 2004. Wal-Mart, the largest U.S. retailer of DVDs, also plans to roll out a competitive service by year-end.

Although both announcements knocked down Netflix stock, Hastings isn't worried. "We've been doing this for four years and know how to do it well," he says. His plan to stay ahead of the competition is to excel at what made the company a hit—delivering an amazing assortment of movies quickly by mail. And with 10 new distribution centres on the drawing board, the company aims to deliver its DVDs in 24 hours, which should keep its 670,000 subscribers very happy.

CRITICAL THINKING QUESTIONS

1. Describe Netflix's distribution strategy and its role in the company's huge success as an e-commerce company. What function does the Netflix Web site serve in its distribution channel?

2. How will an alliance with the Hollywood studios benefit the company? Explain.

3. How can Netflix counter the impact on its business from growing competition? Do you think Blockbuster's and Wal-Mart's network of stores will give them an advantage? Explain.

SOURCES: Jane Black, "Movies by Mail," *Business Week Online,* October 1, 2002, http://www.businessweek.com (accessed April 14, 2003); Netflix Web site, http://www.netflix.com (accessed April 27, 2003); and Bob Tedeschi, "As Blockbuster Moseys Online, Two Competitors Are Already Running Hard: But Will That Matter?" *New York Times,* April 28, 2003.

15

Making the Connection

Using Integrated Marketing Communications to Promote Products

The last of the 4Ps of marketing is promotion. Promotion is the most direct method that a company can use to convince the consumer that its product provides the benefit(s) the consumer is seeking—that is, *meets the customer's needs*. Promotion offers an excellent example of how all the 4Ps are integrated. In this chapter, we discuss the promotional strategies of "push" and "pull." The type of strategy used depends on the type of distribution the company uses—thus promotional decisions are related to place or distribution decisions.

It is not only necessary for promotion to be integrated with the other elements of the marketing mix or 4Ps to convince the customer of the benefit(s) that the product provides; the elements of the promotional mix must be integrated as well. This is the concept of "integrated marketing communications," as discussed in the chapter. Just as all of the 4Ps must project the same message, so must all elements of the promotional mix. If this is not done, the company risks confusing the consumer, who will simply buy a different product. The area where there is the least control is in personal selling. Your salespeople are your message, and therefore, the message might not be the same every

time. This creates obvious human resource issues that must be handled very carefully to ensure consistency.

As with all aspects of a company's operations, promotional decisions affect and are affected by other areas of the business. For example, one of the elements of a promotional mix is personal selling. This has definite *human resource* implications. The sales force must be managed to communicate the intended message. And how much is spent on personal selling as opposed to other forms of promotion depends to a great extent on the financial situation of the company, as personal selling, although more effective, is also more expensive than other forms of promotion per contact. This same logic extends, of course, to other types of promotion, such as expensive TV advertising campaigns; the financial situation of the company will in part determine the promotional budget. The obvious reason for promotion is to influence demand for the product. An indirect effect of this is on the *operations* area of the business to meet the increased demand.

In fact, it is very critical that the other areas of the business be considered before promotional decisions are made. As discussed in the chapter, "if you are going to claim something about your product, then you had better deliver"—operations must be capable of *providing the quality* that the customer expects at the level of demand that is created. "Advertising is the last thing you bring into the mix. You start by getting the product right (product decisions), getting your employee attitude right (*gaining employee commitment*), [and] getting everyone internally understanding the mission (your strategy)."

The external environment affects promotion as well. The government (*political* environment) sets guidelines on what can and cannot be done in advertising; the competition (*economic* environment) has to be monitored carefully, so that you are aware of what message they are projecting versus your company's message, as the consumer hears and sees them all and is affected by the comparison; *social* trends will influence your advertising design and what will appeal to the customer; and, of course, *technology* is always changing and expanding the limits of what can be done. For example, the Internet cannot be ignored as a potential vehicle for building a brand presence (in fact, more quickly than traditional methods), nor can it be ignored as a powerful tool for tailoring the message to meet the needs of specific consumers. Just go visit Amazon.ca. Other trends, as discussed in the text, are posters that emit smells or make noises, and electronic billboards that profile drivers as they go by to personalize ads. There really is no limit.

© AP/WORLD WIDE PHOTOS

Using Integrated Marketing Communications to Promote Products

learning goals

1 What are the goals of promotional strategy?
2 What are the elements of the promotional mix, and what is integrated marketing communications?
3 What is advertising, and what are the different types of advertising?
4 What are the advertising media, and how are they selected?
5 What is personal selling?
6 What are the goals of sales promotion, and what are several types of sales promotion?
7 How does public relations fit into the promotional mix?
8 What factors affect the promotional mix?
9 What are three important trends in promotion?

New Beetle Fights Bug Problem

Volkswagen (http://www.vw.ca) is hoping its Beetle convertible will turn its frown upside down. Europe's biggest carmaker recently began promoting its Beetle convertible in North America with a 60-second commercial featuring a sombre young man experiencing the banalities of daily life. He finally cracks a smile after seeing the Beetle convertible. The ad was shown in movie theatres nationwide and during popular television shows on various stations.

Volkswagen has a lot riding on the car, which has a starting price of approximately $25,000. The car maker needs the new convertible to stimulate Beetle sales, which were down about 25 percent in 2002 and 2003. Still, the company has high hopes. "We think this is going to re-energize the Beetle brand overall," says Karen Marderosian, director of marketing for Volkswagen. The company spends about $500 million on advertising each year in North America. "It is a tough market," says Ms. Marderosian. "We haven't had a lot of new products in the past couple of years. We are hoping that this is the thing that will bring Volkswagen more to the forefront."

To help get noticed, Volkswagen dispatched "street teams" that went to cities and fed parking meters and handed out coffee coupons, newspapers, and subway tokens—all in the name of advertising.

They also held car-washing events, and gave out driver "wanted" posters.

Magazine ads, running in publications such as *Vanity Fair* and *InStyle*, featured just a single word, such as "Grass" or "Beach," and offered consumers a whiff of fresh-cut grass and ocean breezes through the use of scent strips.

Volkswagen also placed classified ads in daily newspapers that included this memorable copy: "Passing smiles for sale. Ear to ear, some with dimples, most with teeth. Finger pointing included as well as prolonged stares."[1]

Critical Thinking Questions

As you read this chapter, consider the following questions as they relate to the new Volkswagen convertible:

1. Was it necessary to use any type of promotion other than advertising to launch the new Beetle convertible?
2. What other means could be used to promote the new vehicle?
3. Could the Internet play a role in promoting the new convertible?

SOURCE: Adapted from Suzanne Vranica, "New Beetle Takes on Bug Problem," Wall Street Journal (October 31, 2002). Reprinted by permission of the Wall Street Journal, Copyright © 2002 Dow Jones & Company, Inc. All Rights Reserved Worldwide.

promotion

The attempt by marketers to inform, persuade, or remind consumers and industrial users to engage in the exchange process.

Very few goods or services can survive in the marketplace without good promotion. Marketers, such as those touting the Volkswagen convertible, promote their products to build demand. **Promotion** is an attempt by marketers to inform, persuade, or remind consumers and industrial users to engage in the exchange process. Once the product has been created, promotion is often used to convince target customers that it has a differential advantage over the competition. A *differential advantage*, or competitive advantage, as explained in Chapter 12, is a set of unique features that the target market perceives as both important and better than the competition's features and might result in purchase of the brand. Such features might include high quality, fast delivery, low price, good service, and the like. Lexus, for example, is seen as having a quality differential advantage over other luxury cars. Therefore, promotion for Lexus stresses the quality of the vehicle.

In this chapter, we present the goals of promotion, the last element of the marketing mix, and explore the elements of the promotional mix. You will also learn about advertising and how personal selling and public relations fit into the promotional mix.

PROMOTIONAL GOALS

1 learning goal

Most firms use some form of promotion. The meaning of the Latin root word is "to move forward." Hence actions that move a company toward its goals are promotional in nature. Because company goals vary widely, so do promotional strategies. The goal is to stimulate action. In a profit-oriented firm, the desired action is for the consumer to buy the promoted item. McCain's, for instance, wants people to buy more frozen pies. Not-for-profit organizations seek a variety of actions with their promotions. They tell us not to litter, to buckle up, to help the food bank, and to attend the ballet.

Promotional goals include creating awareness, getting people to try products, providing information, retaining loyal customers, increasing the use of products, and identifying potential customers. Any promotional campaign might seek to achieve one or more of these goals:

1. *Creating awareness.* All too often, firms go out of business because people don't know they exist or what they do. Small restaurants often have this problem. Simply putting up a sign and opening the door is rarely enough. Promotion through ads on local radio or television, coupons in local papers, flyers, and so forth can create awareness of a new business or product.

2. *Getting consumers to try products.* Promotion is almost always used to get people to try a new product or to get non-users to try an existing product. Sometimes free samples are given away. Lever, for instance, mailed more than 2 million free samples of its Lever 2000 soap to target households. Coupons and trial-size containers of products are also common tactics used to tempt people to try a product. Volkswagen spent more than $200 million (USD) trying to get consumers to consider the new convertible when shopping for a car.

3. *Providing information.* Informative promotion is more common in the early stages of the product life cycle. An informative promotion might explain what ingredients (like fibre) will do for your health, tell you why the product is better (high-definition television versus regular television), inform you of a new low price, or explain where the item may be bought.

People typically will not buy a product or support a not-for-profit organization until they know what it will do and how it might benefit them. Thus, an informative ad might stimulate interest in a product. Consumer watchdogs and social critics applaud the informative function of promotion, because it helps consumers make more intelligent purchase decisions. Star-Kist, for instance, lets customers know that its tuna are caught in dolphin-safe nets.

4. *Keeping loyal customers.* Promotion is also used to keep people from switching brands. Slogans such as "Campbell's Soups are 'M'm! M'm! Good!'" and "Intel Inside" remind consumers about the brand. Marketers also remind users that the brand is better than the competition. Dodge Ram trucks claim that they have superior safety features. For years, Pepsi has claimed it has the taste that consumers prefer. Such advertising reminds customers about the quality of the product.

   Firms can also help keep customers loyal by telling them when a product or service is improved. Blockbuster has used the guarantee that the hit movie you want to rent is in stock or it's free.

5. *Increasing the amount and frequency of use.* Promotion is often used to get people use more of a product and to use it more often. When smoking was banned on domestic flights, Wrigley's began promoting its chewing gum as a good alternative to smoking. The most popular promotion to increase the use of a product might be frequent-flyer or -user programs. The Marriott Rewards program awards points for each dollar spent at a Marriott property. At the Platinum level, members receive a guaranteed room, an upgrade to their finest available accommodations, access to the concierge lounge, a free breakfast, free local phone calls, and a variety of other goodies.

6. *Identifying target customers.* Promotion helps find customers. One way to do this is to list a Web site. For instance, the *Wall Street Journal* and *Business Week* include Web addresses for more information on computer systems, corporate jets, colour copiers, and other types of business equipment, to help target those who are truly interested. Fidelity Mutual Funds ads trumpet, "Solid investment opportunities are out there," and then direct customers to go to **http://www.fidelity.com**.

The Promotional Mix and Integrated Marketing Communications

promotional mix
The combination of advertising, personal selling, sales promotion, and public relations used to promote a product.

The combination of advertising, personal selling, sales promotion, and public relations used to promote a product is called the **promotional mix**. Each firm creates a unique mix for each product, but the goal is always to deliver the firm's message efficiently and effectively to the target audience. These are the elements of the promotional mix:

- *advertising*—any paid form of non-personal promotion by an identified sponsor;
- *personal selling*—a face-to-face presentation to a prospective buyer;
- *sales promotion*—marketing activities (other than personal selling, advertising, and public relations) that stimulate consumer buying, including coupons and samples, displays, shows and exhibitions, demonstrations, and other types of selling efforts; and
- *public relations*—the linking of organizational goals with key aspects of the public interest and the development of programs designed to earn public understanding and acceptance.

To convey a message of action and highlight the unique features of Heelys, the company carefully chooses photo shots that portray the feeling of the product—in this case, freedom.

integrated marketing communications (IMC)

The careful coordination of all promotional activities—media advertising, sales promotion, personal selling, and public relations, as well as direct marketing, packaging, and other forms of promotion—to produce a consistent, unified message that is customer focused.

Ideally, marketing communications from each promotional mix element (personal selling, advertising, sales promotion, and public relations) should be integrated. That is, the message reaching the consumer should be the same regardless of whether it comes from an advertisement, a salesperson in the field, a magazine article, or a coupon in a newspaper insert.

An un-integrated, disjointed approach to promotion has propelled many companies to adopt the concept of **integrated marketing communications (IMC)**. IMC involves carefully coordinating all promotional activities—media advertising, sales promotion, personal selling, and public relations, as well as direct marketing, packaging, and other forms of promotion—to produce a consistent, unified message that is customer focused. Following the concept of IMC, marketing managers carefully work out the roles the various promotional elements will play in the marketing mix. Timing of promotional activities is coordinated, and the results of each campaign are carefully monitored to improve future use of the promotional mix tools. Typically, a marketing communications director is appointed who has overall responsibility for integrating the company's marketing communications.

Pepsi relied on IMC to launch Pepsi One. The $100 million program relied on personal selling in the distribution channels, a public-relations campaign with press releases to announce the product, and heavy doses of advertising and sales promotion. The company toured the country's shopping malls setting up Pepsi One "lounges"—inflatable couches with plastic carpeting—for random taste tests. It also produced 11,000 end-cap displays for supermarket aisles and created stand-up displays for 12-packs to spark impulse purchases. It also secured Oscar-winning actor Cuba Gooding, Jr., as spokesperson for the ad campaign, which made its debut during the World Series. The tagline for the ad campaign was "Only One has it all."

In the sections that follow, we examine the elements of the promotional mix in more detail.

concept check

List and discuss the goals of promotion.

What is the promotional mix?

What are the features of an integrated marketing communications campaign?

Power Bar's Protein Plus bars target health-conscious consumers who want a tasty source of protein without a lot of sugar. This advertisement provides information to explain the benefits of Protein Plus.

ADVERTISING BUILDS BRAND RECOGNITION

advertising
Any paid form of non-personal presentation by an identified sponsor.

Most Canadians are bombarded daily with advertisements to buy things. **Advertising** is any paid form of non-personal presentation by an identified sponsor. It may appear on television or radio; in newspapers, magazines, books, or direct mail; or on billboards or transit cards.

The money that big corporations spend on advertising is mind-boggling. Total advertising expenses in this country are estimated at more than $8 billion a year, with the top two media being television and newspaper, with radio a distant third.[2] Global advertising expenditures are approximately $321 billion annually.[3] General Motors is North America's largest advertiser, spending more than $3.4 billion (USD) annually. This is slightly under $400,000 per hour, seven days a week, 24 hours per day. The top five advertising spending categories are automotive; retail, department, and discount stores; movies and media; food and beverages; and medicines.[4]

In this section, you will learn about the different types of advertising, the strengths and weaknesses of advertising media, the functions of an advertising agency, and how advertising is regulated.

Types of Advertising

3 learning goal

product advertising
Advertising that features a specific good or service.

comparative advertising
Advertising that compares the company's product with competing, named products.

reminder advertising
Advertising that is used to keep a product's name in the public's mind.

The form of advertising most people know is **product advertising**, which features a specific good or service. It can take many different forms. One special form is **comparative advertising**, in which the company's product is compared with competing, named products. Coca-Cola and Pepsi often use comparative advertising. Does comparative advertising work? Recent research says that comparative ads grab your attention and increase your purchase intention. Some comparative ads, however, lack believability and are not effective.[5] Another special form is **reminder advertising**, which is used to keep the product name in the public's mind. It is used most often during the maturity stage of the product life cycle. Reminder advertising assumes that the target market has already been persuaded of the product's merits and just needs a memory boost. V8 vegetable juice and the FTD florist association use reminder promotion.

institutional advertising
Advertising that creates a positive picture of a company and its ideals, services, and roles in the community.

advocacy advertising
Advertising that takes a stand on a social or economic issue; also called *grassroots lobbying*.

In addition to product advertising, many companies use **institutional advertising**. This type of advertising creates a positive picture of a company and its ideals, services, and roles in the community. Instead of trying to sell specific products, it builds a desired image and goodwill for the company. For example, Weyerhaeuser ran a full-page ad in a number of publications that said, "There's a reason we'll never run out of trees. We put them back after we use them." The ad goes on to say that Weyerhaeuser plants more than 100 million seedlings every year to replenish the forests. Some institutional advertising supports product advertising that targets consumers. Other ads are aimed at stockholders or the public. **Advocacy advertising** takes a stand on a social or economic issue. It is sometimes called *grassroots lobbying*. Energy companies often use this type of advertising to influence public opinion about regulation of their industry.

Choosing Advertising Media

4 learning goal

advertising media
The channels through which advertising is carried to prospective customers; include newspapers, magazines, radio, television, outdoor advertising, direct mail, and the Internet.

The channels through which advertising is carried to prospective customers are the **advertising media**. Both product and institutional ads appear in all the major advertising media. Exhibit 15.1 indicates where all of the money spent on advertising goes. Exhibit 15.2 summarizes the advantages and disadvantages of these media. Each company must decide which media are best for its products. Two of the main factors in making that choice are the cost of the medium and the audience reached by it.

The Zoom-Zoom tagline, used to promote Mazda's line of high performance cars like this Mazda RX-8, is familiar to many customers because of Mazda's integrated marketing communications campaign.

cost per thousand (CPM)
Cost per thousand contacts is a term used in expressing advertising costs; refers to the cost of reaching 1,000 members of the target market.

reach
The number of different target consumers who are exposed to a commercial at least once during a specific period, usually four weeks.

frequency
The number of times an individual is exposed to an advertising message.

audience selectivity
An advertising medium's ability to reach a precisely defined market.

Advertising Costs and Market Penetration Cost per contact is the cost of reaching one member of the target market. Naturally, as the size of the audience increases, so does the total cost. Cost per contact enables an advertiser to compare media vehicles, such as television versus radio, magazine versus newspaper, or, more specifically, Macleans versus Time. An advertiser debating whether to spend local advertising dollars for TV spots or radio spots could consider the cost per contact of each. The advertiser might then pick the vehicle with the lowest cost per contact to maximize advertising punch for the money spent. Often costs are expressed on a **cost per thousand (CPM)** contacts basis.

Reach is the number of different target consumers who are exposed to a commercial at least once during a specific period, usually four weeks. Media plans for product introductions and attempts at increasing brand awareness usually emphasize reach. For example, an advertiser might try to reach 70 percent of the target audience during the first three months of the campaign. Because the typical ad is short-lived, and often only a small portion of an ad might be perceived at one time, advertisers repeat their ads, so that consumers will remember the message. **Frequency** is the number of times an individual is exposed to a message. Average frequency is used by advertisers to measure the intensity of a specific medium's coverage.

Media selection is also a matter of matching the advertising medium with the product's target market. If marketers are trying to reach teenage girls, they might select *Seventeen* magazine. If they are trying to reach consumers over 50 years old, they might choose *Modern Maturity*. A medium's ability to reach a precisely defined market is its **audience selectivity**. Some media vehicles, like general newspapers and network television, appeal to a wide cross-section of the population. Others—such as *Brides*, *Popular Mechanics*, *Architectural Digest*, MuchMusic, and ESPN—appeal to very specific groups.

Exhibit 15.1 | Total Canadian Advertising Expenditures by Media Categories

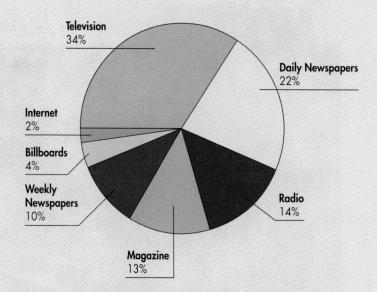

SOURCE: The Consumer Trends Report—Industry Research Paper. http://strategis.ic.gc.ca/epic/internet/inoca-bc.nsf/en/ca02088e.html. Strategis © 2006. Reproduced with the permission of the Minister of Public Works and Government Services Canada, 2006.

Advertising Agencies

advertising agencies

Companies that help create ads and place them in the proper media.

Advertising agencies are companies that help create ads and place them in the proper media. Many firms rely on agencies to both create and monitor their ad campaigns.

Full-service advertising agencies offer the five services shown in Exhibit 15.3. Members of the creative-services group develop promotional themes and messages, write copy, design layouts, take photos, and draw illustrations. The media services group selects the media mix and schedules advertising. Researchers might conduct market research studies for clients, help develop new products, or gauge the firm's or product's image. Merchandising advice might include developing contests and brochures for the sales force. Campaign design and planning are often wholly in the hands of the agency, although some firms prefer to do much of the work in-house, relying on the agency only for scheduling media and evaluating the campaign.

Advertising Regulation

In addition to planning advertising campaigns and scheduling media, advertising agencies must also cope with the growing role and scope of advertising regulation.

Advertising Standards Canada

The Canadian advertising industry's self-regulatory body.

Self-Regulation in the Advertising Industry To avoid increasing government regulation, **Advertising Standards Canada** (**ASC**) serves as the Canadian advertising industry's self-regulatory body. Its mission is to "ensure the integrity and viability of advertising." The ASC is responsible for the administration of the Canadian Code of Advertising Standards, the industry's principal instrument of self-regulation. As well, the ASC provides consumers with a mechanism to submit complaints about an advertisement.

HOT *Links*

To find out more about Advertising Standards Canada and to view complaint reports, see http://www.adstandards.com.

After receiving a complaint about an advertisement, the ASC investigates. It collects and evaluates information and then decides whether the ad's claims are substantiated. If the ad is deemed unsatisfactory, the ASC negotiates with the advertiser to obtain a change in the ad or its discontinuation.

Exhibit 15.2 | Strengths and Weaknesses of Major Media

MEDIUM	STRENGTHS	WEAKNESSES
Newspapers	Geographic selectivity and flexibility Short-term advertiser commitments News value and immediacy Constant readership High individual market coverage Low cost	Little demographic selectivity Limited colour facilities Short-lived
Magazines	Good reproduction, especially colour Message permanence Demographic selectivity (can reach affluent audience) Regionality Local-market selectivity Special-interest possibilities Relatively long advertising life	Long-term advertiser commitments Slow audience buildup Limited demonstration capacities Lack of urgency Long lead time for ad placement Can be expensive for national coverage
Radio	Low and negotiable costs High frequency Immediacy of message Relatively little seasonal change in audience Highly portable Short scheduling notice Short-term advertiser commitments Entertainment carryover	No visuals Advertising message short-lived Background sound Commercial clutter (a large number of ads in a short time)
Television	Widely diversified audience Creative visual and audio opportunities for demonstration Immediacy of message Entertainment carryover	High cost Limited demographic selectivity Advertising message short-lived Consumer skepticism about advertising claims
Network	Association with programming prestige	Long-term advertiser commitments
Local	Geographic selectivity Associated with programs of local origin and appeal Short lead time	Narrow audience on independent stations High cost for broad geographic coverage
Outdoor advertising	Repetition possibilities Moderate cost Flexibility	Short messages Lack of demographic selectivity Many distractions when observing the message
Direct mail	Very efficient with good mailing list Can be personalized by computer Can reach very specific demographic market Lengthy message with photos and testimony	Very costly with poor mailing list Might never be opened
Internet	Inexpensive global coverage Available at any time Interactive personalized message via e-mail	Not everyone has access Difficult to measure ad effectiveness Pop-up clutter

Exhibit 15.3 | Functions of an Advertising Agency

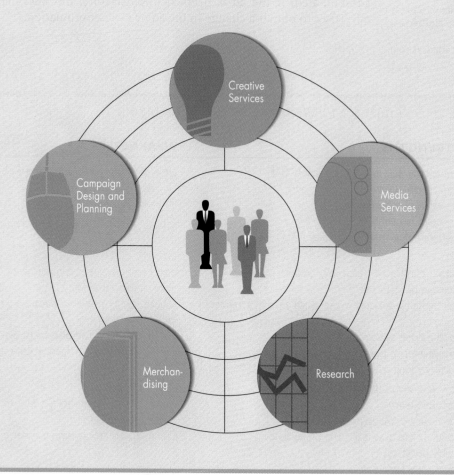

Advertising managers want to avoid having to drop or modify advertisements or commercials. Not only does the controversy create ill will for the company, the ad must also be remade, which can be expensive. In addition, if a substitute commercial is unavailable, the timing of the campaign might be destroyed.

Government Regulation of Advertising Self-regulation doesn't always work. In Canada there are various authorities that are concerned with deception and misrepresentation in advertising. Under the Canadian Constitution, the federal and provincial/territorial governments share the responsibility for protecting consumers. The federal government has exclusive authority with regard to the banking and the telecommunications industry, but generally speaking, most consumer services are regulated by the provinces and territories.

Under the Federal Competition Act, administered by the Competition Bureau of Industry Canada, it is a criminal offence to use misleading advertising.

corrective advertising
An advertisement run to correct false impressions left by previous ads.

HOT Links
See what is new at the Competition Bureau at http://www.strategis.ic.gc.ca.

concept check

Define five different types of advertising, and give examples.

Indicate some of the strengths and weaknesses of the seven main advertising media.

Name the groups that regulate advertising, and explain what remedies they might prescribe.

THE IMPORTANCE OF PERSONAL SELLING

learning goal

personal selling
A face-to-face sales presentation to a prospective customer.

Advertising acquaints potential customers with a product and thereby makes personal selling easier. **Personal selling** is a face-to-face sales presentation to a prospective customer. Sales jobs range from salesclerks at clothing stores to engineers with MBAs who design large, complex systems for manufacturers. Personal selling offers several advantages over other forms of promotion:

- It allows the company to provide a detailed explanation or demonstration of the product. This capability is especially desirable for complex or new goods and services.
- The sales message can be varied according to the motivations and interests of each prospective customer. Moreover, when the prospect has questions or raises objections, the salesperson is there to provide explanations. In contrast, advertising and sales promotion can respond only to the objections the copywriter thinks are important to customers.
- Personal selling can be directed only to qualified prospects. Other forms of promotion include some unavoidable waste, because many people in the audience are not prospective customers.
- Companies can control personal selling costs by adjusting the size of the sales force (and resulting expenses) in one-person increments. In contrast, advertising and sales promotion must often be purchased in fairly large amounts.
- Perhaps the most important advantage is that personal selling is considerably more effective than other forms of promotion in obtaining a sale and gaining a satisfied customer.[6]

The Professional Salesperson

Companies that recruit university or college graduates to enter the field of selling want to develop professional salespeople. A professional salesperson has two main qualities: complete product knowledge and creativity. The professional knows the product line from A to Z and understands what each item can and cannot do. He or she also understands how to apply the product to meet customers' needs. For instance, a sales rep might find a way to install conveyor equipment that will lower the cost of moving products in the prospective customer's plant.

Professional salespeople develop long-term relationships with their clients. Most rely on repeat business, which depends, of course, on trust and honesty. Most professional selling is not high pressured. Instead, the sales process is more a matter of one professional interacting with another, such as a salesperson working with a purchasing agent. Professional salespeople are largely sources of information and creative problem solvers. They cannot bully a professional buyer into making an unwanted purchase.

Sales Positions

Postsecondary graduates have many opportunities in sales. Among them are the following.

- *Selling to wholesalers and retailers*. When a firm buys products for resale, its main concerns are buying the right product and getting it promptly. Often retailers expect the manufacturer's salesperson to stock the merchandise on the shelves and to set up promotional materials approved by the store. Sometimes these sales jobs are entry-level training positions that can lead to better opportunities.

Exhibit 15.4 | Steps in Making a Successful Sale

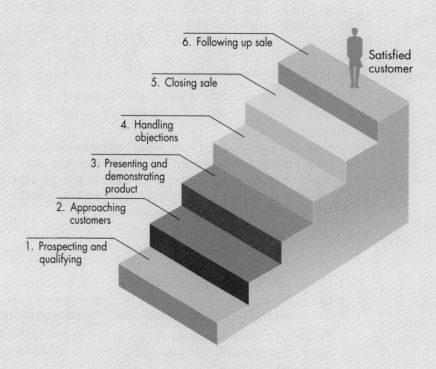

- *Selling to purchasing agents.* Purchasing agents are found in government agencies, manufacturing firms, and institutions (hospitals and schools). Purchasing agents look for credibility (Can the salesperson deliver merchandise of the proper quality when needed?), service after the sale, and a reasonable price. The message the salesperson must get across is one of complete dependability and reliability.

- *Selling to committees.* The form of selling that might demand the most professionalism and creativity is selling to a buying committee. When a purchase decision is so important that it will have a big impact on the buyer's long-run success, it is usually made by a committee. A committee sales presentation requires careful analysis of the potential buyer's needs. It commonly includes an audiovisual display.

The Selling Process

Selling is a process that can be learned. Scholars have spelled out the steps of the selling process, shown in Exhibit 15.4, and professional salespeople use them all the time. The steps are as follows:

Step 1: *Prospecting and qualifying.* To start the process, the salesperson looks for **sales prospects**, those companies and people who are most likely to buy the seller's offerings. This activity is called **prospecting**. Because there are no sure-fire ways of finding prospects, most salespeople try many methods.

For many companies, the inquiries generated by advertising and promotion are the most likely source of prospects. Inquiries are also known as sales leads. Leads usually come in the form of letters, cards, e-mail addresses, or telephone calls. Some

sales prospects

The companies and people who are most likely to buy a seller's offerings.

prospecting

The process of looking for sales prospects.

companies supply salespeople with prospect lists compiled from external sources, such as Chamber of Commerce directories, newspapers, public records, club membership lists, Internet inquiries, and professional or trade publication subscription lists. Meetings, such as professional conventions and trade shows, are another good source of leads. Sales representatives attend such meetings to display and demonstrate their company's products and to answer the questions of those attending. The firm's files and records can be another source of prospects. Correspondence with buyers can be helpful. Records in the service department can identify people who already own equipment and might be prospects for new models. Finally, friends and acquaintances of salespeople can often supply leads.

One rule of thumb is that not all prospects are "real." Just because someone has been referred or has made an inquiry does not mean that the person is a genuine prospect. Salespeople can avoid wasting time and increase their productivity by qualifying all prospects. **Qualifying questions** are used to separate prospects from those who do not have the potential to buy. The following three questions help determine who is a real prospect and who is not:

qualifying questions
Inquiries used by salespeople to separate prospects from those who do not have the potential to buy.

- Does the prospect have a need for our product?
- Can the prospect make the buying decision? and
- Can the prospect afford our product?

Step 2: *Approaching customers.* After identifying a prospect, the salesperson explains the reason for wanting an appointment and sets a specific date and hour. At the same time, the salesperson tries to build interest in the coming meeting. One good way to do this is to impart an interesting or important piece of information—for instance, "I think my product can cut your shipping and delivery time by two days."

Step 3: *Presenting and demonstrating the product.* The presentation and demonstration can be fully automated, completely unstructured, or somewhere in between. In a fully automated presentation, the salesperson shows a movie, slides, or uses a laptop computer and data projector, and then answers questions and takes any orders. A completely unstructured presentation has no set format. It might be a casual conversation, with the salesperson presenting product benefits that might interest the potential buyer.

Making Ethical Choices

DOES IT REALLY DO THAT?

Your business and creative talents have come together in your work as a copywriter for an advertising company. In the few years since you started working, your assignments have been on products that encourage weight loss and enhance physical fitness. You've written ads for dietary supplements and diet pills guaranteeing immediate and permanent weight loss. Now you've been asked to head the creative team to promote exercise equipment from a manufacturer that guarantees toned "abs" in two weeks after using the product for only 20 minutes per day.

As an advocate for keeping fit, you are curious about the claims on the fact sheet from the maker of the exercise product for which you're the creative-team lead. You wonder how best to motivate the team when you are not sure you believe the product's claims. In addition to doing research about

continued

the claims, you buy the exercise equipment for your older sister and ask her to follow the company's recommendation. She's overweight, and you are concerned, especially given the recent findings that carrying extra weight in one's midsection is a contributing factor to cancer.

After following the recommended exercise program for the machine you provide her with, your sister doesn't seem to have toned up or slimmed down. Your research reveals that "spot reduction ... isn't physiologically possible" using exercise machines. An independent council on exercise found that most claims that ab machine manufacturers make are greatly exaggerated.

ETHICAL DILEMMA

Can you continue serving as the lead of the creative team knowing that you'd be producing false advertising?

SOURCES: "Fad Diets and Exercise Machines as They Relate to Fat Loss," *Weight Loss and Diet Facts*, 2001, http://www.weightloss-and-diet-facts.com/exercise-machines; Nancy Hellmich, "Being Overweight Linked to Dying of Cancer," *USA Today*, April 24, 2003, http://www.usatoday.com/life; Nat Ives, "Fast Food and the Obesity Problem," *New York Times*, December 4, 2002, http://www.nyt.com; Joe Skorupa, "Crunch Time: Ab Machines Promise Washboard Stomachs in Minutes a Day, But Do They Really Work?" *Popular Mechanics*, http://www.popularmechanics.com/science/sports.

Step 4: *Handling objections.* Almost every sales presentation, structured or unstructured, meets with some objection. Rarely does a customer say "I'll buy it" without asking questions or voicing concerns. The professional salesperson tries to anticipate objections, so they can be countered quickly and with assurance.

Often employed in business, the "higher authority" objection is frequently used when one of the parties says, "This agreement looks good, but I'll have to run it by my committee" (or wife or any other "higher authority"). The result is that that sales presentation turns out to be just a preliminary, non-binding round. After the higher authority responds, often disapproving the agreement, the sale goes into a second round or starts all over again.

The next time you buy a house, car, or anything expensive, watch carefully how the salesperson will say, "If we find the house (or car) that you really like, is there any reason you could not make the purchase today?" Once they get the green light, the salesperson will spend whatever time it takes to find you the right product. However, if you say your uncle has to give the final approval, as he will be loaning you the money, the salesperson will try to set up an appointment when the uncle can be present.[7]

Step 5: *Closing the sale.* After all the objections have been dealt with, it's time to close the sale. Even old pros sometimes find this part of the sales process awkward. Perhaps the easiest way to close a sale is to ask for it: "Ms. Jones, may I write up your order?" Another technique is to act as though the deal has been concluded: "Mr. Bateson, we'll have this equipment in and working for you in two weeks." If Mr. Bateson doesn't object, the salesperson can assume that the sale has been made.

Step 6: *Following up on the sale.* The salesperson's job isn't over when the sale is made. In fact, the sale is just the start. The salesperson must write up the order properly and turn it in promptly. Often this part of the job is easy, but an order for a complex piece of industrial equipment might include a hundred pages of detail. Each detail must be carefully checked to ensure that the equipment is exactly what was ordered.

After the product is delivered to the customer, the salesperson must make a routine visit to see that the customer is satisfied. This follow-up call might also be a chance to make another sale. But even if it isn't, it will build goodwill for the salesperson's company and might bring future business. Repeat sales over many years are the goal of professional salespeople.

concept check

What are the advantages of personal selling?

Describe the professional salesperson.

Explain the selling process.

SALES PROMOTION

6 learning goal

sales promotions
Marketing events or sales efforts—not including advertising, personal selling, and public relations—that stimulate buying.

Sales promotion helps make personal selling and advertising more effective. **Sales promotions** are marketing events or sales efforts—not including advertising, personal selling, and public relations—that stimulate buying. Today, sales promotion is a $300 billion industry and growing. Sales promotion is usually targeted toward either of two distinctly different markets: Consumer sales promotion is targeted to the ultimate consumer market, whereas trade sales promotion is directed to members of the marketing channel, such as wholesalers and retailers. In a survey, 5,100 marketing managers in all industries were asked, "What sales promotion tactics are most important to your overall promotion strategy?" The replies were: co-marketing (37 percent); special events (31 percent); sampling (22 percent); coupons (22 percent); games, contests, and sweepstakes (20 percent); sponsorships (20 percent); the Internet (14 percent); trade shows (14 percent); and premiums (13 percent).[8] **Co-marketing** occurs when two or more companies promote each other's products and services. In 2003, General Motors entered into a co-marketing program with Genmar, the world's largest recreational-boat builder (Aquasport, Champion, Crestliner, Glastron, Ranger, and others). GM profiled Genmar boats in many of its advertising and promotion programs, and Genmar did the same to cross-promote GM's products.[9]

co-marketing
When two or more companies promote each other's products or services.

The goal of the promotion tactics cited above is immediate purchase. Therefore, it makes sense when planning a sales promotion campaign to target customers according to their general behaviour. For instance, is the consumer loyal to your product or to your competitor's? Does the consumer switch brands readily in favour of the best deal? Does the consumer buy only the least expensive product, no matter what? Does the consumer buy any products in your category at all?

The objectives of a promotion depend on the general behaviour of target consumers, as described in Exhibit 15.5. For example, marketers who are targeting loyal users of their product don't want to change behaviour. Instead, they want to reinforce existing behaviour or increase product usage. Frequent-buyer programs that reward consumers for repeat purchases can be effective in strengthening brand loyalty. Other types of promotions are more effective with customers prone to brand switching or with those who are loyal to a competitor's product. Cents-off coupons, free samples, or an eye-catching display in a store will often entice shoppers to try a different brand.

HOT *Links*

Advertising Age magazine http://www.adage.com has a wealth of information about the latest in advertising, including videos and ratings of new ads.

Sales promotion offers many opportunities for entrepreneurs. Entrepreneurs design contests and sweepstakes, fabricate displays, manufacture premiums, and deliver free samples, among other things. One successful entrepreneurial venture started when two friends were having a drink together in Paris. They created a company called Impact Diffusion, which provides tabletops to restaurants that incorporate areas that the restaurants can use to promote their suppliers' products.

concept check

How does sales promotion differ from advertising?

Describe several types of sales promotion.

Exhibit 15.5 | Types of Consumers and Sales Promotion Goals

TYPE OF BEHAVIOUR	DESIRED RESULTS	SALES PROMOTION EXAMPLES
Loyal customers: People who buy your product most or all of the time	Reinforce behaviour, increase consumption, change purchase timing	Loyalty marketing programs, such as frequent-buyer cards or frequent-shopper clubs Bonus packs that give loyal consumers an incentive to stock up or premiums offered in return for proof-of-purchase
Competitor's customers: People who buy a competitor's product most or all of the time	Break loyalty, persuade to switch to your brand	Sweepstakes, contests, or premiums that create interest in the product.
Brand switchers: People who buy a variety of products in the category	Persuade to buy your brand more often	Sampling to introduce your product's superior qualities compared to their brand
Price buyers: People who consistently buy the least expensive brand	Appeal with low prices or supply added value that makes price less important	Any promotion that lowers the price of the product, such as coupons, cents-off packages, and bonus packs Trade deals that help make the product more readily available than competing products Coupons, cents-off packages, refunds, or trade deals that reduce the price of the brand to match that of the brand that would have been purchased

PUBLIC RELATIONS HELPS BUILD GOODWILL

7 *learning goal*

public relations
Any communication or activity designed to win goodwill or prestige for a company or person.

publicity
Information about a company or product that appears in the news media and is not paid for directly by the company.

Like sales promotion, public relations can be a vital part of the promotional mix. **Public relations** is any communication or activity designed to win goodwill or prestige for a company or person. Its main form is **publicity**, information about a company or product that appears in the news media and is not directly paid for by the company. Publicity can be good or bad. Reports of children overeating fast food leading to obesity is an example of negative publicity.

Naturally, firms' public relations departments try to create as much good publicity as possible. They furnish company speakers for business and civic clubs, write speeches for corporate officers, and encourage employees to take active roles in such civic groups as the United Way. The main tool of the public relations department is the *press release*, a formal announcement of some newsworthy event connected with the company, such as the start of a new program, the introduction of a new product, or the opening of a new plant. Public relations departments may perform any or all of the functions described in Exhibit 15.6.

New-Product Publicity

Publicity is instrumental in introducing new products and services. It can help advertisers explain what's different about their new product by prompting free news stories or positive word of mouth about it. During the introductory period, an especially innovative new product often needs more exposure than

Toronto, stung by the SARS outbreak and the World Health Organization's travel advisory, launched a public relations campaign in 2003 to reassure business and vacation travellers that Toronto is a safe city to visit.

© DIAPHOR AGENCY / INDEX STOCK IMAGERY

conventional, paid advertising affords. Public relations professionals write press releases or develop videos in an effort to generate news about their new product. They also jockey for exposure of their product or service at major events, on popular television and news shows, or in the hands of influential people.

HOT *Links*

What should a media kit for the press include? 101 Public Relations, http://www.101publicrelations.com, provides the answer, along with other good information about getting publicity for your company.

Event Sponsorship

Public relations managers might sponsor events or community activities that are sufficiently newsworthy to achieve press coverage; at the same time, these events reinforce brand identification. Sporting, music, and arts activities remain the most popular choices of event sponsors. Many sponsors are also turning to more specialized events that have tie-ins with schools, charities, and other community service organizations.

Exhibit 15.6 | The Functions of a Public Relations Department

PUBLIC RELATIONS FUNCTION	DESCRIPTION
Press relations	Placing positive, newsworthy information in the news media to attract attention to a product, a service, or a person associated with the firm or institution
Product publicity	Publicizing specific products or services
Corporate communications	Creating internal and external messages to promote a positive image of the firm or institution
Public affairs	Building and maintaining national or local community relations
Lobbying	Influencing legislators and government officials to promote or defeat legislation and regulation
Employee and investor relations	Maintaining positive relationships with employees, shareholders, and others in the financial community
Crisis management	Responding to unfavourable publicity or a negative event

FACTORS THAT AFFECT THE PROMOTIONAL MIX

8 *learning goal*

Promotional mixes vary a great deal from product to product and from one industry to the next. Advertising and personal selling are usually a firm's main promotional tools. They are supported by sales promotion. Good public relations help develop a positive image for the organization and its products. The specific promotional mix depends on the nature of the product, market characteristics, available funds, and whether a push or a pull strategy is used.

The Nature of the Product

Selling toothpaste differs greatly from selling overhead industrial cranes. Personal selling is most important in marketing industrial products and least important in marketing consumer non-durables (consumer products that get used up). Broadcast advertising is used heavily in promoting consumer products, especially food and other non-durables. Print media are used for all types of consumer products. Industrial products might be advertised through special trade magazines. Sales promotion, branding, and packaging are roughly twice as important (in terms of percentage of the promotional budget) for consumer products as for industrial products.

Market Characteristics

When potential customers are widely scattered, buyers are highly informed, and many of the buyers are brand loyal, the promotional mix should include more advertising and sales promotion and less personal selling. But sometimes personal selling is required, even when buyers are well informed and geographically dispersed, as is the case with mainframe computers. Industrial installations and component parts might be sold to knowledgeable people with much education and work experience, yet a salesperson must still explain the product and work out the details of the purchase agreement.

Salespeople are also required when the physical stocking of merchandise—called **detailing**—is the norm. Milk and bread, for instance, are generally stocked by the person who makes the delivery rather than by store personnel. This practice is becoming more common for convenience products, as sellers try to get the best display space for their wares.

detailing
The physical stocking of merchandise at a retailer by the salesperson who delivers the merchandise.

HOT *Links*
How can you find the right magazine in which to advertise? The MediaFinder Web site, at http://www.mediafinder.com, has a searchable database of thousands of magazines.

push strategy
A promotional strategy in which a manufacturer uses aggressive personal selling and trade advertising to convince a wholesaler or retailer to carry and sell its merchandise.

Available Funds

Money, or the lack of it, is one of the biggest influences on the promotional mix. A small manufacturer with a tight budget and a unique product might rely heavily on free publicity. The media often run stories about new products.

If the product warrants a sales force, a firm with little money might turn to manufacturers' agents. They work on commission, with no salary, advances, or expense accounts. Duncan Parking Technologies, which makes parking meters, is just one of the many that rely on manufacturers' agents.

Push and Pull Strategies

Manufacturers may use aggressive personal selling and trade advertising to convince a wholesaler or a retailer to carry and sell their merchandise. This approach is known as a **push strategy**. The wholesaler, in turn, must often push the merchandise forward by persuading the retailer to handle the goods. A push strategy relies on extensive personal selling to channel members, or trade advertising, and price incentives to wholesalers and retailers. The retailer then uses advertising, displays, and other promotional forms to convince the consumer to buy the "pushed" products. This approach also applies to services. For example, the Jamaican Tourism Board targets promotions to travel agencies, which are members of its distribution channel.

At the other extreme is a **pull strategy**, which stimulates consumer demand to obtain product distribution. Rather than trying to sell to wholesalers, a manufacturer using a pull strategy focuses its promotional efforts on end consumers. As they begin demanding the product, the retailer orders the merchandise from the wholesaler. The wholesaler, confronted with rising demand, then places an order from the manufacturer. Thus, stimulating consumer demand pulls the product down through the channel of distribution. Heavy sampling, introductory consumer advertising, cents-off campaigns, and couponing may all be used as part of a pull strategy. For example, using a pull strategy, the Jamaican Tourism Board might entice travellers to come to its island by offering discounts on hotels or airfare. The push and pull promotional strategies are illustrated in Exhibit 15.7.

Rarely does a company use a pull or a push strategy exclusively. Instead, the mix will emphasize one of these strategies. For example, pharmaceutical company Marion Merrell Dow uses a push strategy, emphasizing personal selling and trade advertising, to promote its Nicoderm patch nicotine withdrawal therapy to physicians. Sales presentations and advertisements in medical journals give physicians the detailed information they need to prescribe the therapy to their patients who want to quit smoking. Marion Merrell Dow supplements its push promotional

pull strategy
A promotional strategy in which a manufacturer focuses on stimulating consumer demand for its product rather than on trying to persuade wholesalers or retailers to carry the product.

Exhibit 15.7 | Push and Pull Promotional Strategies

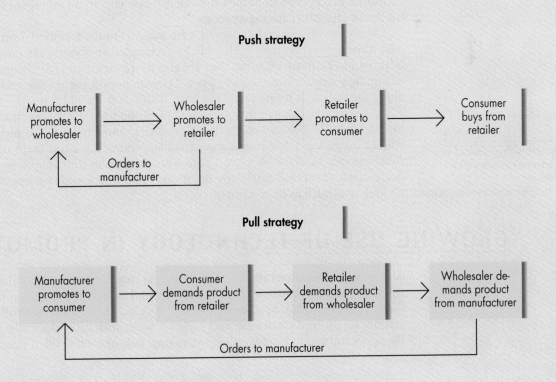

strategy with a pull strategy targeted directly to potential patients through advertisements in consumer magazines and on television. The advertisements illustrate the pull strategy in action: Marion Merrell Dow directs consumers to ask their doctors about the Nicoderm patch.

concept check

Explain how the nature of the product, market characteristics, and available funds can affect the promotional mix.

Distinguish between push and pull strategies.

Trends in Promotion

 learning goal

Companies are adopting new promotional strategies to hone their marketing message and reach more customers. They are also using new technology to make promotion more effective. The explosive growth of Internet advertising, the application of technology, and guerrilla marketing are discussed in this section.

THE GROWTH OF WEB ADVERTISING

HOT *Links*

One good site for the latest news and views on Internet advertising is the Internet Advertising section of Internet.com,
http://www.internetnews.com/

The explosive growth of the Internet has led to similar growth in Web advertising. For companies whose businesses are based on the Internet, building a recognized brand name is important. With nothing to pick up or touch, and hundreds of similar-sounding sites to choose from, on-line consumers have little to go on except a familiar name. In cyberspace, anyone with enough resources to rent space on a server and build some buzz for its brand is a potentially dangerous competitor.

A new study of on-line advertising has shown that it can positively influence consumer perceptions of brands and can increase sales by an average of 6.6 percent for major consumer packaged goods.[10]

Many on-line advertisers are moving away from the traditional small banner ads. Although bigger ads, such as large rectangles or skyscrapers (large vertical ads) tend to be more effective, they are also more expensive. ESPN.com promises 4.5 million impressions (views) for a 24-hour period for a wide rectangle run along the top of its home page. The cost is $100,000 for 24 hours.

HOT *Links*

See the savings you can enjoy by receiving coupons via the Internet at
http://www.happycoupons.com.

One study has shown that 12 percent of all shoppers use the Internet to download coupons.[11] Delivery methods for on-line coupons vary. Consumers who are willing to answer a few marketing survey questions can print them out directly from manufacturers' Web sites. Those who prefer one-stop shopping—and also don't mind answering marketing questions—can find a wide variety of coupons on Web sites such as happycoupons.com.

GROWING USE OF TECHNOLOGY IN PROMOTION

All forms of promotion are applying more and more technology to enhance effectiveness. The downtowns of European cities tend to have much greater foot traffic than those of Canada. As a result, street posters tend to be used more often. A typical size might be 4 metres tall and 2 metres wide, with full-colour ads. Now, with the application of technology, the posters sing, talk, or even smell. A London poster ad for an energy drink called Purdeys played "chilled out" wind chimes at bus stops. With the touch of a button on a poster, London pedestrians can get a whiff of Procter & Gamble's new shampoo Head & Shoulders Citrus Smell.[12]

First introduced in North America in California, electronic billboards are profiling drivers as they go by and then instantly personalizing the highway ads. For example, if the highway were packed with country music listeners, the billboards might make a pitch for casinos. If CBC Radio were on, the billboards could change to ads for a high-quality car or a gourmet grocery.

The billboards pick up which radio stations are being played and then instantly access a vast databank of information about the people who typically listen to those stations. The electronic ads will then change to fit listener profiles.[13]

GUERRILLA MARKETING

guerrilla marketing
Proactive efforts to spread positive word-of-mouth information and to encourage product usage.

Guerrilla marketing (also called *street marketing* and *diffusion marketing*) refers to proactive efforts to spread positive word-of-mouth information and to encourage product usage. Guerrilla marketing is designed to create a buzz about a product or service so that people start spreading the word. For example, the PT Cruiser was planted in rental fleets in trendy Miami to get people talking. Vespa hired sleek-looking models to buzz up to hot cafés and clubs in trendy Los Angeles neighbourhoods on their scooters.

Sony Ericsson used street marketing to create buzz for its T68i mobile phone, one of the first that could double as a digital camera. In one initiative, dubbed Fake Tourist, 60 trained actors and actresses hung around tourist attractions such as the Empire State Building in New York and the Space Needle in Seattle. Working in teams of two or three and behaving as if they were actual tourists, the actors and actresses asked unsuspecting passers-by to take their pictures. Presto: instant product demonstrations.

A second stunt involved the use of "leaners"—60 actresses and female models with extensive training in the phone's features who frequented trendy lounges and bars without telling the establishments what they were up to. The women received scripted scenarios designed to help them engage strangers in conversation. One involved having an actress's phone ring while she's in the bar—and having the caller's picture pop up on the screen. In another scenario, two women sit at opposite ends of the bar playing an interactive version of the Battleship game on their phones. Consumer activists decried the campaign as deceptive.[14]

concept check

Describe the advantages of Web advertising and why most large, traditional advertisers now run ads on-line.

How does technology improve the effectiveness of advertising?

When is it appropriate to use guerrilla marketing?

Great Ideas to Use Now

Two important points from this chapter apply directly to you now. By understanding how advertising is changing to benefit you, you will be a better informed consumer. By realizing the importance of selling yourself, you will be better able to take advantage of life's opportunities.

ADVERTISING WILL BE MORE BENEFICIAL TO YOU

More and more advertising dollars will be directed to on-line promotion in the future. For the on-line advertiser, the challenge is to educate, entertain, or otherwise give you a benefit. Advertisers know that no one can be compelled to pay attention on-line—they must deliver benefits up front. If Colgate Palmolive wants to advertise toothpaste on-line, it needs more than photogenic lovers with toothy smiles. Unilever has created a Web site for Mentadent toothpaste that offers potential customers the chance to order a free sample, get oral-care advice, and send questions to a dental hygienist. Every week airlines send e-mails to millions of subscribers listing rock-bottom fares for undersubscribed flights on the coming weekend. You can and should expect to receive benefits from on-line advertisers.

E-mail advertising is also becoming more personal and more valuable to you. Although users of e-mail have long complained about unwanted direct marketing—commonly called spam—that hasn't stopped companies from looking for new and improved ways to exploit e-mail as a marketing tool. Now, by using sophisticated data-mining techniques to develop far more tailored messages, marketers might well be succeeding. Lured by the speed, cost savings, and personalized pitches that are possible on-line, companies such as 1-800-Flowers and Amazon.ca are testing the tactic. Amazon.ca e-mails you if a favourite author is conducting an on-line chat or has published a new work. It's a far cry from impersonal mass advertising. This is strictly for you.

ALWAYS SELL YOURSELF

If you stop and think about it, all of us must be salespeople. If you are going to be successful in business, and in life in general, you must be a salesperson. You must be able to explain and sell your plans, ideas, and hopes effectively. A straight "A" student who can't do this will not be successful. Conversely, a "C" student who can will be successful. *Always* be prepared to sell yourself and your ideas. It's the best way to get ahead in business and in life.

CUSTOMER SATISFACTION AND QUALITY

The relationship between promotion and customer satisfaction and quality is very straightforward. If you are going to claim something about your product or service, you had better deliver. Nothing hurts a company more than promising what it can't deliver. Many years ago, one of the authors saw an ad for Pop Tarts when they first arrived on the market. It talked about their great taste, convenience, and so forth. He bought a box, ate one, and hasn't eaten one since. Moreover, he has told others about his experience. Certainly the product has been improved over the years, but nothing could coax him into trying one again. Unmet promises create dissatisfied customers and negative word-of-mouth promotion.

JetBlue (a U.S. low-cost airline) was recently named *Advertising Age's* "Marketer of the Year." Amy Curtis-McIntyre, vice president of marketing, says,

Advertising is the last thing you bring into the mix. You start by getting your product right, getting your employee attitude right, getting everyone internally understanding the mission. Then you move to telling your story through public relations. You build your advertising last."

JetBlue's focus is both price and great service. Offering live TV on every flight created great coverage in the media. Even offering Hain Celestial Terra Blue Chips generated a lot of free press. A *60 Minutes* producer was so impressed with JetBlue that *60 Minutes* did a segment on the company. The free publicity was worth millions.

SUMMARY OF LEARNING GOALS

1   What are the goals of promotional strategy?

Promotion aims to stimulate demand for a company's goods or services. Promotional strategy is designed to inform, persuade, or remind target audiences about those products. The goals of promotion are to create awareness, get people to try products, provide information, keep loyal customers, increase use of a product, and identify potential customers.

2   What are the elements of the promotional mix, and what is integrated marketing communications?

The unique combination of advertising, personal selling, sales promotion, and public relations used to promote a product is the promotional mix. Advertising is any paid form of non-personal promotion by an identified sponsor. Personal selling consists of a face-to-face presentation in a conversation with a prospective purchaser. Sales promotion consists of marketing activities—other than personal selling, advertising, and public relations—that stimulate consumers to buy. These activities include coupons and samples, displays, shows and exhibitions, demonstrations, and other selling efforts. Public relations is the marketing function that links the policies of the organization with the public interest and develops programs designed to earn public understanding and acceptance. Integrated marketing communications (IMC) is being used by more and more organizations. It is the careful coordination of all of the elements of the promotional mix to produce a consistent, unified message that is customer focused.

3   What is advertising and what are the different types of advertising?

Institutional advertising creates a positive picture of a company. Advocacy advertising takes a stand on controversial social or economic issues. Product advertising features a specific good or service. Comparative advertising is product advertising in which the company's product is compared with competing, named products. Reminder advertising is used to keep a brand name in the public's mind.

4   What are the advertising media, and how are they selected?

The main types of advertising media are newspapers, magazines, radio, television, outdoor advertising, direct mail, and the Internet. Newspaper advertising delivers a local audience but has a short life span. Magazines deliver special-interest markets and offer good detail and colour. Radio is an inexpensive and highly portable medium but has no visual capabilities. Television reaches huge audiences and offers visual and audio opportunities, but it can be very expensive. Outdoor advertising requires short messages but is only moderately expensive. Direct mail can reach targeted audiences, but it is only as good as the mailing list. The Internet is global in scope and can offer a personalized message response by e-mail, but as yet not everyone is on the Net. Media are evaluated on a CPM (cost per thousand contacts) basis and by reach and frequency.

5   What is personal selling?

Personal selling enables a salesperson to demonstrate a product and tailor the message to the prospect; it is effective in closing a sale. Professional salespeople are knowledgeable and creative. They also are familiar with the selling process, which consists of prospecting and qualifying, approaching customers, presenting and demonstrating the product, handling objections, closing the sale, and following up on the sale.

6 What are the goals of sales promotion, and what are several types of sales promotion?

Immediate purchase is the goal of sales promotion whether it is aimed at consumers or the trade (wholesalers and retailers). The most popular sales promotions are coupons, samples, premiums, contests, and sweepstakes. Trade shows, conventions, and point-of-purchase displays are other types of sales promotion.

7 How does public relations fit into the promotional mix?

Public relations is mostly concerned with getting good publicity for companies. Publicity is any information about a company or product that appears in the news media and is not directly paid for by the company. Public relations departments furnish company speakers for business and civic clubs, write speeches for corporate officers, and encourage employees to take active roles in civic groups. These activities help build a positive image for an organization, which is a good backdrop for selling its products.

8 What factors affect the promotional mix?

The factors that affect the promotional mix are the nature of the product, market characteristics, available funds, and whether a push or a pull strategy is emphasized. Personal selling is used more with industrial products, and advertising is used more heavily for consumer products. With widely scattered, well-informed buyers and with brand-loyal customers, a firm will blend more advertising and sales promotion and less personal selling into its promotional mix. A manufacturer with a limited budget might rely heavily on publicity and manufacturers' agents to promote the product.

9 What are three important trends in promotion?

Web advertising can positively influence consumer perceptions of brand and has been proven to increase sales of major consumer packaged goods. Increasingly, consumers are looking to the Web for more product information and sales promotions, such as coupons. Technology will continue to improve the effectiveness of advertising by personalizing promotional messages and delivering product information. Guerrilla marketing is designed to create a buzz about a product or service, so that people start spreading the word.

EXPERIENTIAL EXERCISES

1. **Sell yourself.** Go to **http://www.amazon.ca** and under the search engine type "selling yourself." Order one or more of the books available to improve your selling skills. Also, consider a Dale Carnegie training course. For more information, go to **http://www.dale-carnegie.com**.

2. **Protect your privacy on-line.** Here are some pointers to protect yourself against spam.

   • Use free Web-based e-mail services like Microsoft's Hotmail.com to create a second e-mail address to give out when shopping at an e-commerce site. This will prevent your corporate or primary account from being deluged with targeted spam.

   • Use Web sites like http://www.spychecker.com to check if you have unwittingly downloaded spyware—nettlesome programs that are secretly installed when you download many free programs. Visitors to Spychecker are prompted to enter the names of programs, and the site tells them whether the software contains spyware.

   • Activate your Web browser's security functions to block out cookies or alert you when a site is trying to install one on your computer. In Internet Explorer, you would go to Tools, and then click on the Internet Options command. That brings up a series of tabs, including one for Security. Moving the sliding bar to its highest setting will disable all cookies. This, however, might make it difficult to visit many popular Web sites, as the sites tend to require the ability to install cookies on your machine.

   • Use e-mail re-mailers like the one at **http://www.gilc.org/speech/anonymous/remailer.html** to bounce your message through a series of computers that forward it on, in theory making it untraceable. Sending anonymous e-mail through these re-mailers also reduces the odds of its being read by hackers, who try to monitor data traffic to and from companies and sites like Hotmail.

   • Use privacy software to shield the content and addresses of the Web sites you visit from employers and other prying eyes. One of the best such programs is available at **http://www.anonymizer.com**.

3. **Think of a product that you use regularly.** Find several examples of how the manufacturer markets this product, such as ads in different media, sales promotions, and publicity. Assess each example for effectiveness in meeting one or more of the six promotional goals described in the chapter. Then analyze them for effectiveness in reaching you as a target consumer. Consider such factors as the media used, the style of the ad, and ad content. Present your findings to the class.

4. **Choose a current advertising campaign for a beverage product.** Describe how the campaign uses different media to promote the product. Which medium is used the most, and why? What other promotional strategies does the company use for the product? Evaluate the effectiveness of the campaign. Present your results to the class.

5. **Apply what you learned in this chapter to a real-world business situation.** Assume the role of the Marketing and Sales Department Manager for Cameron Balloons, a company in Bristol, England. Spend some time at its virtual factory site, **http://www.bized.ac.uk/virtual/cb/welcome.htm**, where you will learn about the company and its major business functions. After familiarizing yourself with the company, focus on the marketing and sales pages. Develop a promotional strategy for the company. Be sure to explain the basis for the strategy, the target market(s), which promotional channels you will use and why (not all might be appropriate), and whether you recommend a push or a pull strategy.

6. The Zenith Media site at **http://www.zenithmedia.com** is a good place to find links to Internet resources on advertising. At the site, click on "Leading Corporate and Brand Sites." Pick three of the company sites listed and review them, using the concepts in this chapter.

7. Go to the *Sales and Marketing* magazine site at **http://www.salesandmarketing .com**. Read several of the free recent articles from the magazine, as well as on-line exclusives, and prepare a brief report on current trends in one of the following topics: sales strategies, marketing strategies, customer relationships, or training.

8. Does a career in marketing appeal to you? Start your journey at Careers in Marketing, **http://www.careers-in-marketing.com**, and explore the five areas listed there: Advertising & Public Relations, Market Research, Non-Profit, Product Management, and Retailing. Which one appeals to you most, and why? Briefly describe the type of work you would be doing, the career path, and how you will prepare to enter this field (courses, part-time jobs, etc.).

9. Entrepreneurs and small businesses don't always have big sales promotion budgets. The Guerrilla Marketing Web page, at **http://www.gmarketing.com**, has many practical ideas for those with big ideas but small budgets. After exploring the site, explain the concept of guerrilla marketing. Then list five ideas or tips that appeal to you and summarize why they are good marketing strategies.

10. Press releases are a way to get free publicity for your company and products. Visit several of the following sites to learn how to write a press release: **http://www.ereleases.com/howtowrite.html**; **http://www.press-releases .com/write-a-press-release.html**; **http://www.publicityinsider.com**; or **http://www.netpress.org/careandfeeding.html**. Which sites were most helpful, and why? Develop a short "how-to" guide on press releases for your classmates. Then write a press release that announces the opening of your new health food restaurant, Zen Foods, located just two blocks from campus.

REVIEW QUESTIONS

1. What are the goals of promotion?
2. What is the promotional mix, and what options are available in this mix?
3. Explain integrated marketing communications (IMC).
4. What are the various types of advertising available?
5. What do marketers need to consider before choosing the advertising media?
6. Discuss the strengths and weakness of the major media.
7. Explain the importance of personal selling.
8. What are some of the opportunities for postsecondary graduates in sales?
9. Describe the steps in making a successful sale.
10. What are the functions of a public relations department?
11. List the factors that affect the promotional mix.
11. What are some of the trends in promotion, and how do they affect marketing?

CREATIVE THINKING CASE
Quiksilver Goes Low Key to Stay Cool

In a 2¹/₂ minute biopic shot by the marketing department at Quiksilver Inc., surf champion Kelly Slater recalls the "heaviest" day of his life. He saw a surfer fatally swallowed by a giant wave; then he realized it was his best friend. "I just want to say one last thing, man," Mr. Slater says, his voice cracking. "I should have paddled back out to get you."

Mr. Slater endorses Quiksilver wetsuits and T-shirts, but all you see is his face. The name "Quiksilver" is nowhere to be found. Still, starting in September Quiksilver will be broadcasting the vignette, and three or four others like it, on Fox Sports Network twice an hour during the day in hopes of drawing more attention to the "board sports" it mentions.

Because Quiksilver is never explicitly mentioned—one of the vignettes even centres on a skateboarder who is sponsored by a competing apparel company—Fox Sports is running the spots free of charge. The video segments are part of the Huntington Beach, California, company's "tread lightly" approach to marketing. Although the company, which stated that it expects to post between $685 million and $690 million in revenue for the fiscal year ended October 2002, has been by far the biggest "breakout brand" in the close-knit, surf shop-centric "board sports" industry, it doesn't like to draw too much attention to itself. Danny Kwock, a Quiksilver cofounder, says, "We don't want to slap our name on everything like we're this big company, you know? Big is the enemy of cool."

The goal of the Fox Sports deal, and of the entertainment division that Quiksilver launched this year to start a video-on-demand channel for extreme-sports programming, is to "grow these sports," Mr. Kwock explains.

Quiksilver has made board shorts and wetsuits since the 1970s, and it has video-taped the exploits of the surfers and skateboarders it pays to endorse their products for almost as long. The company also has pioneered some creative marketing stunts: It branded all of the skaters in Activision Inc.'s wildly popular "Tony Hawk: Pro Skater" video game. This year, it teamed up with Nextel Communications, Inc., on a cell phone targeted at teenage girls that flips open to a pink screen emblazoned with the logo of Roxy, its surf wear line for girls.

But Quiksilver restricts its traditional promotion mainly to the sponsorship of surfing and skateboarding events and ads in magazines.

CRITICAL THINKING QUESTIONS

1. Do you think that Quiksilver is promoting the brand properly?
2. Wouldn't it be better to spend more money on network television to reach a wider audience?
3. What other forms of sales promotion could Quiksilver use?

SOURCE: Creative Thinking Case: Adapted from Maureen Tkacik, "Quicksilver Keeps Marketing to a Minimum," Wall Street Journal (August 28, 2002), p. B4. Reprinted by permission of the Wall Street Journal, Copyright © 2002 Dow Jones & Company, Inc. All Rights Reserved Worldwide.

Video Case
Cell Phone Secrets

Probably most of us would think we are pretty much aware of what we are getting when we buy a product, but are we? Let's look at cell phones. We go to the mall, find the kiosk, pick out a cool phone, and sign up for a plan. Simple? On the surface, maybe. But let's look at what can really happen. Did you know that you could get voice mail spam? Did you know there is a system access fee? What about dead zones? Can you get out of a contract because of dead zones? Just because a phone looks fabulous, does that mean it can do fabulous things? No. We also ignore the long distance information, if there is any. We'll never use it…but what if we do? Do we really want an $800 cell phone bill for one month? And finally, does your carrier bill by the minute or by the second? This can make a *huge* difference! Many sales reps give not only incomplete but also incorrect information.

Most of us don't even read the contract. Sales reps comment that many customers don't want the details. We are standing at the booth, anxious for our new phone, and we sign whatever is placed in front of us. How many people actually compare the various plans presented to them, let alone do a comparison across providers? A wise consumer would walk away with a list of possible phones and plans, and go home and check them out on the Net. A quick look at the various providers would tell you who charges by the second, if anyone still does (possibly Fido). We could also read the contract to check for small print that can lead to a huge cell bill and possibly a call from the company's collections department.

CRITICAL THINKING QUESTIONS

1. Do you believe that sales people are encouraged to disclose complete information to potential customers?

2. Whose responsibility is it to ensure that complete information is exchanged: the employee, the company or the consumer?

SOURCE: CBC, *Marketplace*, "Five Cell Phone Secrets," January 23, 2005.

E-COMMERCE CASE
DoubleClick

New York-based DoubleClick (**http://www.DoubleClick.com**) is the largest Internet advertising firm, with revenues of more than $300 million a year. Yet DoubleClick doesn't create ads for its clients; instead, it offers two services: Internet ad sales and ad serving.

DoubleClick sells advertising space on more than 1,500 Web sites, including Travelocity and AltaVista. The Web site owners pay DoubleClick a commission for selling space to advertisers. DoubleClick's proprietary technology also "serves" more than 60 billion ads per month for advertisers, making sure each ad is delivered and displayed properly on Web sites. Behind the scenes, DoubleClick's software also tracks Web surfers as they move around the Internet, click on ads, make purchases, and look at on-line information.

In 1999, DoubleClick purchased Abacus, the largest consumer database firm in the United States. Abacus has detailed consumer profiles of 90 percent of American households, gathered from sources like department store records and magazine subscriptions, as well as a business-to-business database with information on more than 62 million business contacts. DoubleClick combined its knowledge of Web surfers' Internet behaviour with Abacus's powerful consumer database to create large amounts of personal information about consumers. As a result, Web surfers would no longer be anonymous. Marketers would be able to find out their names, addresses, demographics, and actual buying habits. This transactional data would be invaluable in identifying new customers and optimizing the profitability of their existing customer base.

Consumer groups immediately cried foul, calling DoubleClick's plan an invasion of privacy. "Companies like DoubleClick are taking advantage of the technology to rob people of their privacy, causing people to distrust the Internet," said one privacy rights expert. Many advertisers, however, had a different view. "For an advertiser, if you marry Abacus information with behavioral data online, you get nirvana," said Michele Slack, an analyst with Jupiter Communications. Others pointed out that many companies already collect massive amounts of personal information about consumers.

Such attacks were nothing new to DoubleClick, whose size and clout have made it the target of privacy advocates concerned about the company's use of "cookies," files placed on Web surfers' computers to track and record their on-line activities. This information allows DoubleClick to target advertising to those who have an interest in relevant areas. "There are always going to be controversies when people start using new technologies," says Kevin Ryan, DoubleClick's CEO. "When credit cards were introduced, people wouldn't use them because they were worried that the credit card companies would be tracking them. But they got over it."

To appease privacy advocates, DoubleClick revised its privacy policy and requested comments from consumers, public interest groups, and lawmakers. "DoubleClick is committed to executing its business in the most open manner possible," said DoubleClick Chief Privacy Officer Jules Polonetsky. The policy explains how the company uses cookies and includes detailed instructions for users who want to "opt out," or stop receiving cookies.

CRITICAL THINKING QUESTIONS

1. How can marketers use personal data combined with Web use information to promote goods and services more effectively?

2. Visit DoubleClick's Web site and read the company's privacy policy statement. Do you think it goes far enough in protecting consumers' privacy? Why? What other steps can DoubleClick take to improve this policy?

3. Should businesses use information gathered on the Internet to develop customer databases for marketing purposes?

SOURCES: D. Ian Hopper, "Web Sites Give Info to Ad Cos.," *AP Online*, June 13, 2000, http://www.business.elibrary.com; "DoubleClick Reports 4Q and Full-Year 2002 Results," company press release, January 21, 2003, http://www.doubleclick.com; M. Corey Goldman, "Unglamourous DoubleClick Clicks Along," *The Toronto Star*, April 21, 2003, http://library.bigchalk.com; Ralph King, "Kevin O'Connor Gives People the Willies," *Ecompany.com*, October 2000, http://www.ecompany.com; David McGuire "DoubleClick Asks for Feedback on New Privacy Policy," *Newsbytes News Network*, June 1, 2001, http://www.newsbytes.com; and Fred Vogelstein, "The Internet's Busybody," *U.S. News & World Report*, March 6, 2000, 39.

Making the Connection

Using Financial Information and Accounting

In the previous five chapters, we examined the functional areas of marketing and operations, and saw that they must work together in a very integrative way to achieve the goals of the company. It is obvious that these two areas affect the level of product *quality* and *innovativeness,* and thus the ability to *meet customer needs,* and that they therefore affect the ability of the company to achieve *financial success.* Of course, all of this is done with the aid of the human resource area, discussed in Chapter 9, helping to *gain commitment of the employees* toward the goals of the company. In this chapter we will begin to look more specifically at the last functional area of *finance,* starting with how a firm develops and uses financial information through the function of accounting.

It's clear from the beginning of this chapter that regardless of your position in an organization, you need to understand accounting. It is the "financial language of businesses," and all decisions that are made in an organization eventually have financial consequences and therefore show up in the accounting information. For example, on the income statement, you might find advertising expenses and sales revenue from *marketing,* production and operating costs from *operations,* payroll and training costs from *human resources,* and, of course, the interest costs on debt financing to pay for it all. On the balance sheet, you can also see

the impact of each area on the numbers. For example, in the accounts payable section, there might be payments outstanding for employee wages, for marketing expenses, and for operating expenses, as well as for interest on debt financing or dividends payable to shareholders. In the current assets sections, you might find marketable securities (money invested in financial products to earn a return for a short period—a financing decision), accounts receivable from customers for invoices they have not yet paid (a marketing decision), and inventories of goods on hand (an operating decision).

All areas of the company, and employees at all levels, must therefore understand the financial implications of the decisions they make. They must see the integration of their decisions with each area and eventually on the "bottom line." Internal accounting reports help functional areas to make these decisions; for example, marketing sales reports can be used to assess how well different marketing strategies are working, and production cost reports help in efforts to control operating costs.

On the other hand, external accounting reports, such as balance sheets and income statements, which are contained in annual reports to shareholders, are used by many outside *stakeholder* groups. Potential employees use them to assess the stability of a company, and therefore job security and job prospects, before taking job offers, and potential investors use them to assess investment opportunities, just as current shareholders use them to assess the investments they have already made. These stakeholder relationships cannot be dealt with casually, particularly in light of recent scandals that have called into question the integrity of the accounting profession. The impact that these scandals, such as those involving WorldCom and Enron, as discussed in the opening vignette to the chapter, have had on the financial markets (*economic* environment) demonstrate quite clearly the far-reaching integrative impact of financial information and the importance of operating with the highest ethical standards. In fact, this demand for greater ethical conduct (*social* environment) has resulted in many new regulations (*political* environment) governing what firms can and cannot do in reporting accounting information.

The other aspect of the external environment that affects this functional area is *technology*. The advances in technology today have sped up the pace with which accounting information can be gathered and disseminated throughout an organization, thus giving all areas an opportunity to examine the impact of their decisions in an integrative way and focus more on the analysis of the information to make better decisions. In the remaining chapters, we'll continue with the finance area and look at these decisions in more detail.

16

00 Smith Street

Using Financial Information and Accounting

learning goals

1 Why are financial reports and accounting information important, and who uses them?

2 What is the difference between public and private accountants?

3 What are the six steps in the accounting cycle?

4 In what terms does the balance sheet describe the financial condition of an organization?

5 How does the income statement report a firm's profitability?

6 Why is the statement of cash flows an important source of information?

7 How can ratio analysis be used to identify a firm's financial strengths and weaknesses?

8 What major trends affect the accounting industry today?

Enron Drills through Accounting Rules

Once a high-flying energy company that ranked seventh on the 2000 Fortune 500, Enron (http://www.enron.com) is now the poster child for corporate financial wrongdoing. A boring pipeline company that became the world's largest wholesale energy trader, Enron was ultimately brought down by corporate greed—dragging its prestigious accounting firm, Arthur Andersen, along with it. Enron's top executives were brought to trial accused of fraud, money laundering, conspiracy, and obstruction of justice, among other charges.

Enron had a long history of playing fast and loose with accounting principles. It almost went under in 1987, when its oil traders reported more than $1 billion in false transactions to show higher volume and earn larger bonuses. During the 1990s, Chairman Kenneth Lay and President Jeffrey Skilling promoted a corporate culture that favoured innovative new ventures, whether or not they made sound business sense. To the public, the company was a major success story.

But underneath its glitzy surface Enron was manipulating accounting rules to create the illusion of growth, enhance its bottom line, and serve its own agenda. For example, the company obtained Securities and Exchange Commission (SEC) (the agency responsible for administrating the security laws in the United States) approval to use an accounting method that allowed it to report the total amount a project was expected to earn over its lifetime as current revenue. This encouraged managers to close deals quickly and then inflate future earnings estimates to reach profit goals and fatten their bonuses. For example, in 1999 the company reported income of more than $65 million on projected natural gas sales from an as-yet-unbuilt pipeline project.

Enron also formed a series of special-purpose entities to cover up losses in high-risk ventures and hide massive amounts of debt. A quirk in the law allowed Enron to borrow from the partnerships and not disclose the debt on Enron's corporate financial statements. These financial games and phantom earnings made the company's financial condition look solid, and its stock price rose to more than $90 per share in August 2000. Yet during 2000, its trickery represented about 96 percent of Enron's reported net income of over $979 million. The company also reported debt of only $10.2 billion rather than the full $22.1 billion for which it was responsible.

Enron did have review procedures in place, but they were often brushed aside. Enron employees and Andersen accountants who raised concerns about accounting irregularities were considered disloyal. In fact, Enron management pressured Andersen staffers and members of its internal risk management team to sign off on complicated deals or controversial accounting practices or risk losing their jobs.

Despite quarterly profits that continued to climb through July 2001, Enron's financial house of cards began tumbling down. In November 2001, Enron admitted to overstating profits by more than $586 million between 1997 and 2000, and also revealed that its declining financial condition triggered repayment on $690 million of debt hidden in the off-the-books companies. Investors, alarmed at how Enron had obscured financial information in its published financial reports, questioned the overall reliability of its corporate financial reporting. By December 2001, the stock was trading at 60 cents a share, and the company had filed for bankruptcy.[1]

Critical Thinking Questions

As you read this chapter, consider the following questions as they relate to Enron:

1. What role should Enron's independent accounting firm, Arthur Andersen, have played in stopping Enron's wrongdoing? What actions could it have taken?

2. Make some recommendations to Enron's new board of directors for procedures to prevent accounting problems in the future.

3. Do you think the government should get involved in setting accounting regulations, or should the accounting profession and companies self-regulate and enforce? Explain your answer.

The losses resulting from the Enron bankruptcy were more than $60 billion! And Enron was just the first in a series of companies whose stories hit the front pages as news of their disregard for accepted accounting procedures became public.

These cases raise critical concerns about the independence of those who audit a company's financial statements, integrity and public trust, and financial reporting standards. Investors suffered as a result, because the crisis in confidence sent stock prices tumbling. Companies lost billions in value.

So it's no surprise that more people are paying attention to accounting topics these days! We now recognize that accounting is the backbone of any business, providing a framework for understanding the firm's financial condition. Reading about accounting irregularities, fraud, audit (financial statement review) shortcomings, out-of-control business executives, and bankruptcies, we have become very aware of the importance of accurate financial information and sound financial procedures.

All of us—whether we are self-employed, work for a local small business or a multinational Fortune 100 firm, or are not currently in the workforce—benefit from knowing the basics of accounting and financial statements. We can use this information to educate ourselves about companies before interviewing for a job or buying a company's shares or bonds. Employees at all levels of an organization use accounting information to monitor operations. They must also decide which financial information is important for their company or business unit, what those numbers mean, and how to use them to make decisions.

Financial information is central to every organization. To operate effectively, businesses must have a way of tracking income, expenses, assets, and liabilities in an organized manner. Financial information is also essential for decision-making. Managers prepare financial reports using *accounting*, a set of procedures and guidelines for companies to follow when preparing financial reports. Unless you understand basic accounting concepts, you will not be able to "speak" the standard financial language of businesses.

We start this chapter by discussing why accounting is important for businesses and for users of financial information. We then provide a brief overview of the accounting profession and recent problems in the industry, and the new regulatory

Financial accounting information, such as asset values, sales, and inventory, helps managers in all types of organizations make business decisions that enhance organizational effectiveness and efficiency.

© BONNIE KAMIN / PHOTOEDIT

environment. Following that, we present an overview of accounting procedures, followed by a description of the three main financial statements: the balance sheet, the income statement, and the statement of cash flows. Using these statements, we then demonstrate how ratio analysis of financial statements can provide valuable information about a company's financial condition. Finally, we will explore current trends affecting the accounting profession.

ACCOUNTING: MORE THAN NUMBERS

1 learning goal

accounting

The process of collecting, recording, classifying, summarizing, reporting, and analyzing financial activities.

Accounting is the process of collecting, recording, classifying, summarizing, reporting, and analyzing financial activities. It results in reports that describe the financial condition of an organization. All types of organizations—businesses, hospitals, schools, government agencies, and civic groups—use accounting procedures. Accounting provides a framework for looking at past performance, current financial health, and possible future performance. It also provides a framework for comparing the financial positions and financial performances of different firms. Understanding how to prepare and interpret financial reports will enable you to evaluate two computer companies and choose the one that is more likely to be a good investment.

As Exhibit 16.1 shows, the accounting system converts the details of financial transactions (sales, payments, purchases, and so on) into a form that people can use to evaluate the firm and make decisions. Data become information, which, in turn, becomes reports. These reports describe a firm's financial position at one point in time and its financial performance during a specified period. Financial reports include *financial statements,* such as balance sheets and income statements, and special reports, such as sales and expense breakdowns by product line.

WHO USES FINANCIAL REPORTS?

managerial accounting

Accounting that provides financial information that managers inside the organization can use to evaluate and make decisions about current and future operations.

financial accounting

Accounting that focuses on preparing external financial reports that are used by outsiders such as creditors, lenders, suppliers, investors, and government agencies to assess the financial strength of a business.

generally accepted accounting principles (GAAP)

The financial accounting rules, standards, and usual practices followed by accountants in Canada when preparing financial statements.

The accounting system generates two types of financial reports, as shown in Exhibit 16.2: internal and external. Internal reports are used within the organization. As the term implies, **managerial accounting** provides financial information that managers inside the organization can use to evaluate and make decisions about current and future operations. For instance, the sales reports prepared by managerial accountants show how well marketing strategies are working. Production cost reports help departments track and control costs. Managers might prepare very detailed financial reports for their own use and provide summary reports to top management.

Financial accounting focuses on preparing external financial reports that are used by outsiders, that is, people who have an interest in the business but are not part of management. Although these reports also provide useful information for managers, they are primarily used by shareholders (the owners of the company), lenders, suppliers, investors, and government agencies to assess the financial strength of a business.

To ensure accuracy and consistency in the way financial information is reported, accountants in Canada follow **generally accepted accounting principles (GAAP)** when preparing financial statements. The professional association responsible for setting the standards for all Canadian accountants is the Canadian Institute of Chartered Accountants (CICA).

At the present time, there are no international accounting standards. Because accounting practices vary from country to country, a multinational company must make sure that its financial statements conform to both its own country's accounting standards and those of the parent company's country. Often another country's standards are quite different from Canadian GAAP. The International

Exhibit 16.1 | The Accounting System

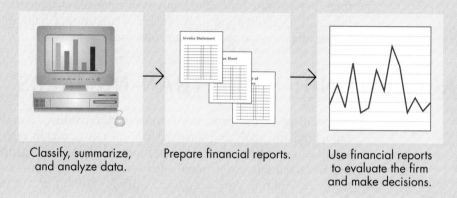

Classify, summarize, and analyze data.

Prepare financial reports.

Use financial reports to evaluate the firm and make decisions.

Accounting Standards Committee (IASC) has been working for years to develop global accounting standards that make it easier to compare financial statements of foreign-based companies.

Financial statements are the chief element of the **annual report,** a yearly document that describes a firm's financial status. Annual reports usually discuss the firm's activities during the past year and its prospects for the future. Three primary financial statements included in the annual report discussed and illustrated later in this chapter are

- the balance sheet,
- the income statement, and
- the statement of cash flows.

annual report

A yearly document that describes a firm's financial status and usually discusses the firm's activities during the past year and its prospects for the future.

HOT Links

Check out what is new at the International Accounting Standards Committee: http://www.iasb.org.

concept check

Explain who uses financial information.

Differentiate between financial accounting and managerial accounting.

Exhibit 16.2 | Reports Provided by the Accounting System

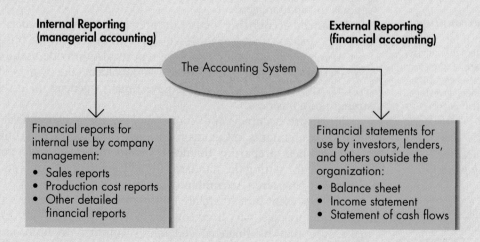

Internal Reporting (managerial accounting)

External Reporting (financial accounting)

The Accounting System

Financial reports for internal use by company management:

- Sales reports
- Production cost reports
- Other detailed financial reports

Financial statements for use by investors, lenders, and others outside the organization:

- Balance sheet
- Income statement
- Statement of cash flows

THE ACCOUNTING PROFESSION

2 *learning goal*

When you think of accountants, do you picture someone who works alone in a back room, hunched over a desk, scrutinizing pages and pages of numbers? Although today's accountants still must love working with numbers, they now work closely with their clients not only to prepare financial reports but also to help them develop good financial practices. Computers have taken the tedium out of the number-crunching and data-gathering parts of the job and now offer powerful analytical tools as well. Therefore, accountants must keep up with information technology trends. The accounting profession has grown due to the increased complexity, size, and number of businesses and the frequent changes in the tax laws. The more than 150,000 accountants in Canada are classified as either public or private (corporate) accountants.

The Accounting Designations

In Canada there are three accounting associations that grant professional designations. They are the Canadian Institute of Chartered Accountants (CICA), the Society of Management Accountants of Canada (CMA Canada), and the Certified General Accountants Association of Canada (CGA-Canada). Each of the professional accounting associations provides specialized services and has

The financial information contained in the CIBC Annual Accountability Report is prepared using financial accounting standards. Lenders, suppliers, investors, and government agencies refer to the annual report to assess the financial strength of a business.

Annual Accountability Report 2005

CIBC
For what matters.

COURTESY CIBC

HOT Links

To find out more about the accounting profession, visit the Canadian Institute of Chartered Accountants site at http://www.cica.ca, the CMA Canada site at http://www.cma-canada.org, or the Certified General Accountants site at http://www.cga-canada.org.

chartered accountant (CA)

An accountant who has completed an approved bachelor's degree program, completed an educational program, and passed a comprehensive examination.

certified management accountant (CMA)

An accountant who works primarily in industry and focuses on internal management accounting.

certified general accountant (CGA)

An accountant who focuses primarily on external financial reporting.

certain educational and work experience requirements for the accountant to be granted the professional designation.

A **chartered accountant (CA)** typically provides tax, audit, and management services. CAs focus on the external reporting and provide an opinion as to whether the financial statements accurately reflect the company's financial health (this can also be provided by a CGA—discussed below). Most CAs first work for public accounting firms and later become private accountants or financial managers.

CAs generally work in four key areas: public practice, industry, government, or education. In public practice they provide accounting and business advice to clients such as small business taxation, auditing, information technology, personal finance planning, business valuation, receivership, insolvency, and forensic investigation. In industry, CAs develop financial and administrative policies, analyze information, and provide strategic leadership.

A **certified management accountant (CMA)** works primarily in industry and focuses on internal management accounting. CMAs combine their accounting expertise and business know-how with professional management skills to provide strategic financial management, strategic planning, sales and marketing, information technology, human resources, finance, and operations. According to CMA Canada,

> They monitor, interpret, and communicate operating results, evaluate performance, control operations, and make decisions about the strategic direction of the organization. They also bring a strong market focus to strategic management and resource deployment and analyze both financial and non-financial management to develop total business solutions, identify new market opportunities and maximize shareholder value.[2]

Certified general accountant (CGA) roles have far expanded from the primary focus on external financial reporting. CGAs also provide tax and financial advice to individuals and businesses. Many own their own accounting business, whereas others are employed in industry and government. According to CGA Canada, "A CGA offers the highest standards of expertise in taxation, finance, information technology and strategic business management."[3]

The requirements to become a CA, CMA, or CGA are quite extensive. Each requires a degree plus additional professional studies that cover the full spectrum of financial and business management. Candidates must also complete a period of articling (that results in real-world skills and development of practical problem-solving abilities) and, finally, pass comprehensive exams that demonstrate their knowledge of the profession.

The accountants add value to organizations as CEO/president, treasurer/VP finance, controller, or systems developer. All areas of government require accounting expertise to guide the financial planning and to maintain fiscal control. Additionally, many of Canada's top educators are accountants.

A CA, CMA, or a CGA can be either a public accountant or a private accountant.

public accountants

Independent accountants who serve organizations and individuals on a fee basis.

auditing

The process of reviewing the records used to prepare financial statements and issuing a formal auditor's opinion indicating whether the statements have been prepared in accordance with accepted accounting rules.

Public Accountants

Independent accountants who serve organizations and individuals on a fee basis are called **public accountants.** Public accountants offer a wide range of services, including preparation of financial statements and tax returns, independent auditing of financial records and accounting methods, and management consulting. **Auditing,** the process of reviewing the records used to prepare financial statements, is an important responsibility of public accountants. They provide a formal auditor's opinion indicating whether the statements have been prepared in accordance with accepted accounting rules. This written opinion is an important part of the annual report. Presently, only CAs and CGAs can provide the auditor's opinion on a firm's financial statements.

Private Accountants

private accountants
Accountants who are employed to serve one particular organization.

Accountants employed to serve one particular organization are **private accountants.** Their activities include preparing financial statements, auditing company records to ensure that employees follow accounting policies and procedures, developing accounting systems, preparing tax returns, and providing financial information for management decision-making.

concept check

What are the three accounting designations in Canada?

Compare the responsibilities of public and private accountants.

BASIC ACCOUNTING PROCEDURES

3 *learning goal*

Using generally accepted accounting principles, accountants record and report financial data in similar ways for all firms. They report their findings in financial statements that summarize a company's business transactions over a specified time period. As mentioned earlier, the three major financial statements are the balance sheet, income statement, and statement of cash flows.

People sometimes confuse accounting with bookkeeping. Accounting is a much broader concept. *Bookkeeping,* the system used to record a firm's financial transactions, is a routine, clerical process. Accountants take bookkeepers' transactions, classify and summarize the financial information, and then prepare and analyze financial reports. Accountants also develop and manage financial systems and help plan the firm's financial strategy.

The Accounting Equation

assets
Things of value owned by a firm.

liabilities
What a firm owes to its creditors; also called *debts.*

owners' equity
The total amount of investment in the firm minus any liabilities; also called *net worth.*

The accounting procedures used today are based on the three main accounting elements of assets, liabilities, and owners' equity. **Assets** are things of value owned by a firm. They might be *tangible,* such as cash, equipment, and buildings, or *intangible,* such as a patent or trademarked name. **Liabilities**—also called *debts*—are what a firm owes to its creditors. **Owners' equity** is the total amount of investment in the firm minus any liabilities. Another term for owners' equity is *net worth.*

The relationship among these three elements is expressed in the accounting equation:

$$\text{Assets} = \text{Liabilities} + \text{Owners' equity}$$
$$\text{(own)} \qquad \text{(owe)} \qquad \text{(net worth)}$$

The accounting equation must always be in balance (that is, the total of the elements on one side of the equals sign must equal the total on the other side).

Suppose you start a bookstore and put $10,000 in cash into the business. At that point, the business has assets of $10,000 and no liabilities. This would be the accounting equation:

$$\text{Assets} = \text{Liabilities} + \text{Owners' equity}$$
$$\$10,000 = \$0 \qquad + \$10,000$$

double-entry bookkeeping
A method of accounting in which each transaction is recorded as at least two entries, so that the accounts or records are changed.

The liabilities are zero, and owner's equity (the amount of your investment in the business) is $10,000. The equation balances.

To keep the accounting equation in balance, every transaction must be recorded as at least two entries. As each transaction is recorded, there is an equal and opposite event so that the accounts or records are changed. This method is called **double-entry bookkeeping.**

Software programs such as QuickBooks help small businesses consolidate and simplify accounting and financial tasks. These programs walk users through the basics to create financial databases, prepare a budget, design customized forms, pay bills, invoice customers, track expenses, manage inventory, and print reports.

Suppose that after starting your bookstore with $10,000 cash, you borrow an additional $10,000 from the bank. The accounting equation will change as follows:

Assets	=	Liabilities	+	Owners' equity	
$10,000	=	$0	+	$10,000	Initial equation
$10,000	=	$10,000	+	$0	Borrowing transaction
$20,000	=	$10,000	+	$10,000	Equation after borrowing

Now you have $20,000 in assets—your $10,000 in cash and the $10,000 loan proceeds from the bank. The bank loan is also recorded as a liability of $10,000, because it's a debt that you must repay. Making two entries keeps the equation in balance.

The Accounting Cycle

The *accounting cycle* refers to the process of generating financial statements, beginning with a business transaction and ending with the preparation of the report. Exhibit 16.3 shows the six steps in the accounting cycle. The first step in the cycle is to analyze the data collected from many sources. All transactions that have a financial impact on the firm—sales, payments to employees and suppliers, interest and tax payments, purchases of inventory, and the like—must be documented. The accountant must review the documents to make sure they're complete.

Next, each transaction is recorded in a *journal,* a listing of financial transactions in chronological order. Then the journal entries are recorded in *ledgers,* which show increases and decreases in specific asset, liability, and owners' equity accounts. The ledger totals for each account are summarized in a *trial balance,* which is used to confirm the accuracy of the figures. These values are used to prepare financial statements and management reports. Finally, individuals analyze these reports and make decisions based on the information in them.

Computers in Accounting

Computerized accounting programs do many different things. Most accounting packages offer six basic modules that handle general ledger, sales order, accounts receivable, purchase order, accounts payable, and inventory control functions. Tax programs use accounting data to prepare tax returns and tax plans. Computerized point-of-sale terminals used by many retail firms automatically record sales and do some of the bookkeeping.

Accounting and financial applications typically represent one of the largest portions of a company's software budget. Accounting software ranges from off-the-shelf programs for small businesses to full-scale customized enterprise resource planning systems for major corporations. Besides the accounting packages mentioned above, many large accounting firms have customized accounting software developed for them and their clients.

concept check

Explain the accounting equation.

Describe the six-step accounting cycle.

What role do computers play in accounting?

Exhibit 16.3 | The Accounting Cycle

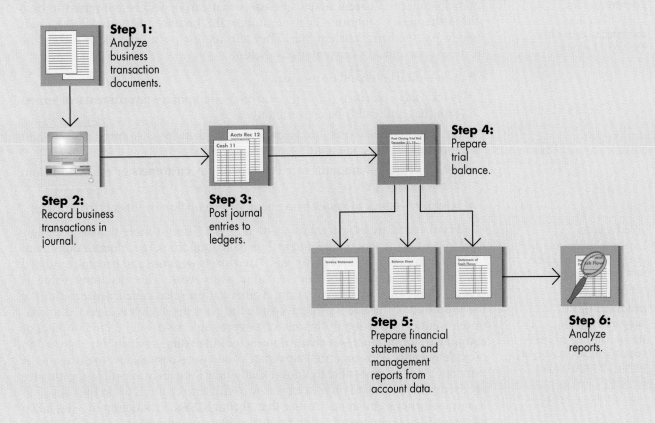

Step 1:
Analyze business transaction documents.

Step 2:
Record business transactions in journal.

Step 3:
Post journal entries to ledgers.

Step 4:
Prepare trial balance.

Step 5:
Prepare financial statements and management reports from account data.

Step 6:
Analyze reports.

THE BALANCE SHEET

learning goal

balance sheet
A financial statement that summarizes a firm's financial position at a specific point in time.

liquidity
The speed with which an asset can be converted to cash.

The **balance sheet**, one of three financial statements generated from the accounting system, summarizes a firm's financial position at a specific point in time. It reports the resources of a company (assets), the company's obligations (liabilities), and the difference between what is owned (assets) and what is owed (liabilities), or owners' equity.

The assets are listed in order of their **liquidity**, the speed with which they can be converted to cash. The most liquid assets come first, and the least liquid are last. Because cash is the most liquid asset, it is listed first. Buildings, on the other hand, have to be sold to be converted to cash, so they are listed after cash. Liabilities are arranged similarly: Liabilities due in the short term are listed before those due in the long term.

The balance sheet at December 31, 200x, for Production Inc., an imaginary manufacturer, is illustrated in Exhibit 16.4. The basic accounting equation is reflected in the three totals highlighted on the balance sheet: assets of $148,900 equal the sum of liabilities and owners' equity ($70,150 + $78,750). The three main categories of accounts on the balance sheet are explained below.

Assets

Assets can be divided into three broad categories: current assets, fixed assets, and intangible assets. **Current assets** are assets that can or will be converted to cash within the next 12 months. They are important, because they provide the funds used to pay the firm's current bills. They also represent the amount of money the firm can raise quickly. Current assets include

- *cash*—funds on hand or in a bank;
- *marketable securities (trading securities)*—temporary investments of excess cash that can readily be converted to cash;
- *accounts receivable*—amounts owed to the firm by customers who bought goods or services on credit;
- *notes receivable*—amounts owed to the firm by customers or others to whom it lent money; and
- *inventory*—stock of goods being held for production or for sale to customers.

Fixed assets are long-term assets used by the firm for more than a year. They tend to be used in production and include land, buildings, machinery, equipment, furniture, and fixtures. Except for land, fixed assets wear out and become outdated over time. Thus, they decrease in value every year. This declining value is accounted for through amortization. **Amortization (also called depreciation)** is the allocation of the asset's original cost to the years in which it is expected to produce revenues. A portion of the cost of a depreciable asset—a building or piece of equipment, for instance—is charged to each of the years in which it is expected to provide benefits. This practice helps match the asset's cost against the revenues it provides. As it is impossible to know exactly how long an asset will last, estimates are used. They are based on past experience with similar items or on the Canadian Revenue Agency's guidelines. Notice that, through 200x, Production Inc. has taken a total of $16,000 in amortization on its production equipment.

Intangible assets are long-term assets with no physical existence. Common examples are patents, copyrights, trademarks, and goodwill. *Patents* and *copyrights* shield the firm from direct competition, so their benefits are more protective than productive. For instance, no one can use more than a small amount of copyrighted material without permission from the copyright holder. *Trademarks* are registered names that can be sold or licensed to others. One of Production Inc.'s intangible assets is a trademark valued at $4,500. *Goodwill* occurs when a company pays more for an acquired firm than the value of its tangible assets. Production Inc.'s other intangible asset is goodwill of $7,000.

Liabilities

Liabilities are the amounts a firm owes to creditors. Those liabilities coming due sooner—current liabilities—are listed first on the balance sheet, followed by long-term liabilities.

Current liabilities are those due within a year of the date of the balance sheet. These short-term claims can strain the firm's current assets because they must be paid in the near future. Current liabilities include the following.

- *Accounts payable.* This is the amount that the firm owes for credit purchases due within a year. This account is the liability counterpart of accounts receivable.
- *Notes payable.* These are short-term loans from banks, suppliers, or others that must be repaid within a year. For example, Production Inc. has a six-month, $15,000 loan from its bank that is a note payable.
- *Accrued expenses.* These represent expenses, typically for wages and taxes, that have accumulated and must be paid at a specified future date within the year, although no bill has been received by the firm.

---

current assets

Assets that can or will be converted to cash within the next 12 months.

fixed assets

Long-term assets used by a firm for more than a year, such as land, buildings, and machinery.

amortization (depreciation)

The allocation of an asset's original cost to the years in which it is expected to produce revenues.

intangible assets

Long-term assets with no physical existence, such as patents, copyrights, trademarks, and goodwill.

current liabilities

Short-term claims that are due within a year of the date of the balance sheet.

Exhibit 16.4 | Balance Sheet for Production Inc.

PRODUCTION INC.
BALANCE SHEET AS OF DECEMBER 31, 200X

Assets

Current assets:

Cash		$15,000
Marketable securities		4,500
Accounts receivable	$45,000	
Less: Allowance for doubtful accounts	1,300	43,700
Notes receivable		5,000
Inventory		15,000
Total current assets		
Fixed assets:		
Production equipment	$56,000	
Less: Accumulated amortization	16,000	$40,000
Furniture and fixtures	$18,450	
Less: Accumulated amortization	4,250	14,200
Total fixed assets		
Intangible assets:		
Trademark		$ 4,500
Goodwill		7,000
Total intangible assets		
Total assets		

Liabilities and Owners' Equity

Current liabilities:

Accounts payable	$30,650	
Notes payable	15,000	
Accrued expenses	4,500	
Income taxes payable	5,000	
Current portion of long-term debt	5,000	
Total current liabilities		$60,150
Long-term liabilities:		
Bank loan for production equipment	$10,000	
Total long-term liabilities		10,000
Total liabilities		
Owners' equity:		
Common shares (10,000 shares outstanding)		$30,000
Retained earnings		48,750
Total owners' equity		
Total liabilities and owners' equity		

On its balance sheet, a bakery would list its bakery equipment, furniture, and fixtures as fixed assets. The amount it owes its vendors for supplies would appear as a current liability—accounts payable—and its bank loan would be under long-term liabilities. On the income statement, you'll find a summary of revenues and expenses for a particular time period.

© CHARLES GUPTON / CORBIS

- *Income taxes payable.* These are taxes owed for the current operating period but not yet paid. Taxes are often shown separately when they are a large amount.
- *Current portion of long-term debt.* This represents any repayment on long-term debt due within the year. Production Inc. is scheduled to repay $5,000 on its equipment loan in the coming year.

long-term liabilities

Claims that come due more than one year after the date of the balance sheet.

Long-term liabilities come due more than one year after the date of the balance sheet. They include bank loans (such as Production Inc.'s $10,000 loan for production equipment), mortgages on buildings, and the company's bonds sold to others.

Owners' Equity

Owners' equity is the owners' total investment in the business after all liabilities have been paid. For sole proprietorships and partnerships, amounts put in by the owners are recorded as capital. In a corporation, the owners provide capital by buying the firm's common shares. For Production Inc., the total common shares investment is $30,000. **Retained earnings** are the amounts left over from profitable operations since the firm's beginning. They are total profits minus all dividends (distributions of profits) paid to shareholders. Production Inc. has $48,750 in retained earnings.

retained earnings

The amounts left over from profitable operations since the firm's beginning; equal to total profits minus all dividends paid to shareholders.

concept check

What is a balance sheet?

What are the three main categories of accounts on the balance sheet, and how do they relate to the accounting equation?

How do retained earnings relate to owners' equity?

THE INCOME STATEMENT

5 *learning goal*

income statement

A financial statement that summarizes a firm's revenues and expenses, and shows its total profit or loss over a period of time.

The balance sheet shows the firm's financial position at a certain point in time. The **income statement** summarizes the firm's revenues and expenses and shows its total profit or loss over a period of time. Most companies prepare monthly income statements for management and quarterly and annual statements for use by investors, creditors, and other outsiders. The primary elements of the income statement are revenues, expenses, and net income (or net loss). The income statement for Production Inc. for the year ended December 31, 200x, is shown in Exhibit 16.5.

Revenues

revenues

The dollar amount of a firm's sales plus any other income it received from sources such as interest, dividends, and rents.

gross sales

The total dollar amount of a company's sales.

net sales

The amount left after deducting sales discounts and returns and allowances from gross sales.

expenses

The costs of generating revenues.

cost of goods sold

The total expense of buying or producing a firm's goods or services.

Revenues are the dollar amount of sales plus any other income received from sources such as interest, dividends, and rents. The revenues of Production Inc. arise from sales of its products. Revenues are determined starting with **gross sales,** the total dollar amount of a company's sales. Production Inc. had two deductions from gross sales. *Sales discounts* are price reductions given to customers that pay their bills early. For example, Production Inc. gives sales discounts to restaurants that buy in bulk and pay at delivery. *Returns and allowances* is the dollar amount of merchandise returned by customers because they didn't like a product or because it was damaged or defective. **Net sales** is the amount left after deducting sales discounts and returns and allowances from gross sales. Production Inc.'s gross sales were reduced by $4,500, leaving net sales of $270,500.

Expenses

Expenses are the costs of generating revenues. Two types are recorded on the income statement: cost of goods sold and operating expenses.

The **cost of goods sold** is the total expense of buying or producing the firm's goods or services. For manufacturers, cost of goods sold includes all costs directly related to production: purchases of raw materials and parts, labour, and factory overhead (utilities, factory maintenance, and machinery repair). For wholesalers and retailers, it is the cost of goods bought for resale. For all sellers, cost of goods sold includes all the expenses of preparing the goods for sale, such as shipping and packaging.

Production Inc.'s cost of goods sold is based on the value of inventory on hand at the beginning of the accounting period, $18,000. During the year, the company spent $109,500 to produce its manufactured goods. This figure includes the cost of raw materials, labour costs for production workers, and the cost of operating the production area. Adding the cost of goods manufactured to the value of beginning inventory, we get the total cost of goods available for sale, $127,500. To determine the cost of goods sold for the year, we subtract the cost of inventory at the end of the period:

$$\$127{,}500 - \$15{,}000 = \$112{,}500$$

gross profit

The amount a company earns after paying to produce or buy its products but before deducting operating expenses.

operating expenses

The expenses of running a business that are not directly related to producing or buying its products.

net profit (net income)

The amount obtained by subtracting all of a firm's expenses from its revenues, when the revenues are more than the expenses.

net loss

The amount obtained by subtracting all of a firm's expenses from its revenues, when the expenses are more than the revenues.

The amount a company earns after paying to produce or buy its products but before deducting operating expenses is the **gross profit.** It is the difference between net sales and cost of goods sold. As service firms do not produce goods, their gross profit equals net sales. Gross profit is a critical number for a company, because it is the source of funds to cover all the firm's other expenses.

The other major expense category is **operating expenses.** These are the expenses of running the business that are not related directly to producing or buying its products. The two main types of operating expenses are selling expenses and general and administrative expenses. *Selling expenses* are those related to marketing and distributing the company's products. They include salaries and commissions paid to salespeople and the costs of advertising, sales supplies, delivery, and other items that can be linked to sales activity, such as insurance, telephone and other utilities, and postage. *General and administrative expenses* are the business expenses that cannot be linked to either cost of goods sold or sales. Examples of general and administrative expenses are salaries of top managers and office support staff; utilities; office supplies; interest expense; fees for accounting, consulting, and legal services; insurance; and rent. Production Inc.'s operating expenses totalled $115,100.

Net Profit or Loss

The final figure—or bottom line—on an income statement is the **net profit** (or **net income**) or **net loss.** It is calculated by subtracting all expenses from revenues. If revenues are more than expenses, the result is a net profit. If expenses exceed revenues, a net loss results.

Exhibit 16.5 | Income Statement for Production Inc.

PRODUCTION INC.
INCOME STATEMENT FOR THE YEAR ENDED DECEMBER 31, 200X

Revenues

Gross sales		$275,000
Less: Sales discounts		2,500
Less: Returns and allowances		2,000
Net Sales		

Cost of Goods Sold

Beginning inventory, January 1		$ 18,000
Cost of goods manufactured		109,500
Less: Ending inventory December 31		15,000
Cost of goods sold		

Gross profit

Operating Expenses

Selling expenses		
Sales salaries	$31,000	
Advertising	16,000	
Other selling expense	18,000	
Total selling expenses		$ 65,000
General and administrative expenses		
Professional and office salaries	$20,500	
Utilities	5,000	
Office supplies	1,500	
Interest	3,600	
Insurance	2,500	
Rent	17,000	
Total general and administrative expenses		50,100
Total operating expenses		

Net profit before taxes
Less: Income taxes

Net profit

Several steps are involved in finding net profit or loss. (These are shown in the right-hand column of Exhibit 16.5.) First, the cost of goods sold is deducted from net sales to get the gross profit. Then total operating expenses are subtracted from gross profit to get the net profit before taxes. Finally, income taxes are deducted to get the net profit. As shown in Exhibit 16.5, Production Inc. earned a net profit of $32,175 in 200x.

It is very important to recognize that profit does not represent cash. The income statement is a summary of the firm's operating results during some time period. It does not present the firm's actual cash flows during the period. Those are summarized in the statement of cash flows, which is discussed briefly in the next section.

concept check

What is an income statement? How does it differ from the balance sheet?

Describe the key parts of the income statement. Distinguish between gross sales and net sales.

How is net profit or loss calculated?

THE STATEMENT OF CASH FLOWS

6 *learning goal*

statement of cash flows
A financial statement that provides a summary of the money flowing into and out of a firm during a certain period, typically one year.

Net profit or loss is one measure of a company's financial performance. However, creditors and investors are also keenly interested in how much cash a business generates and how it is used. The **statement of cash flows,** a summary of the money flowing into and out of a firm, is the financial statement used to assess the sources and uses of cash during a certain period, typically one year. All publicly traded firms must include a statement of cash flows in their financial reports to shareholders. The statement of cash flows tracks the firm's cash receipts and cash payments. It gives financial managers and analysts a way of identifying cash flow problems and of assessing the firm's financial viability.

Using income statement and balance sheet data, the statement of cash flows divides the firm's cash flows into three groups:

- *cash flow from operating activities*—those related to the production of the firm's goods or services;
- *cash flow from investment activities*—those related to the purchase and sale of assets; and
- *cash flow from financing activities*—those related to debt and equity financing.

Production Inc.'s statement of cash flows for 200x is presented in Exhibit 16.6. It shows that the company's cash and marketable securities have increased over the last year. Furthermore, during the year, the company generated enough cash flow to increase inventory and fixed assets and to reduce accounts payable, accruals, notes payable, and long-term debt.

HOT *Links*

Choose any public Canadian company. Search its Web site for their financial statements, and review the balance sheet and income statement.

concept check

What is the purpose of the statement of cash flows?

Why has cash flow become such an important measure of a firm's financial condition?

What situations can you cite from the chapter that support your answer?

ANALYZING FINANCIAL STATEMENTS

7 *learning goal*

ratio analysis
The calculation and interpretation of financial ratios using data taken from the firm's financial statements to assess its condition and performance.

Individually, the balance sheet, income statement, and statement of cash flows provide insight into the firm's operations, profitability, and overall financial condition. By studying the relationships among the financial statements, however, one can gain even more insight into a firm's financial condition and performance.

Ratio analysis involves calculating and interpreting financial ratios using data taken from the firm's financial statements to assess its condition and performance. A financial ratio states the relationship between financial data on a percentage of three to five years. A firm's ratios can also be compared to industry averages or to

Exhibit 16.6 | Statement of Cash Flows for Production Inc.

PRODUCTION INC. STATEMENT OF CASH FLOWS FOR 200X		
Cash Flow from Operating Activities		
Net profit after taxes	$27,175	
Amortization	1,500	
Decrease in accounts receivable	3,140	
Increase in inventory	(4,500)	
Decrease in accounts payable	(2,065)	
Decrease in accruals	(1,035)	
Cash provided by operating activities		$24,215
Cash Flow from Investment Activities		
Increase in gross fixed assets	($ 5,000)	
Cash used in investment activities		($ 5,000)
Cash Flow from Financing Activities		
Decrease in notes payable	($ 3,000)	
Decrease in long-term debt	(1,000)	
Cash used by financing activities		($ 4,000)
Net increase in cash and marketable securities		**$15,215**

basis. For instance, current assets might be viewed relative to current liabilities or sales relative to assets. The ratios can then be compared over time, typically to those of another company in the same industry. Period-to-period and industry ratios provide a meaningful basis for comparison, so that we can answer questions such as, "Is this particular ratio good or bad?"

How is Best Buy doing this quarter compared to historical results? With ratio analysis, managers can track performance. For example, the net profit margin shows how much profit is left after all expenses.

© AP/WORLD WIDE PHOTOS

It's important to remember that ratio analysis is based on historical data and might not indicate future financial performance. Ratio analysis merely highlights potential problems; it does not prove that they exist. However, ratios can help managers monitor the firm's performance from period to period, to understand operations better and identify trouble spots.

Ratios are also important to a firm's present and prospective creditors (lenders), who want to see if the firm can repay what it borrows and assess the firm's financial health. Often loan agreements require firms to maintain minimum levels of specific ratios. Both present and prospective shareholders use ratio analysis to look at the company's historical performance and trends over time.

Ratios can be classified by what they measure: liquidity, profitability, activity, and debt. Using Production Inc.'s 200x balance sheet and income statement (Exhibits 16.4 and 16.5), we can calculate and interpret the key ratios in each group. In Exhibit 16.7, we have summarized the calculations of these ratios for Production Inc. We will now discuss how to calculate the ratios and, more important, how to interpret the ratio value.

Liquidity Ratios

Liquidity ratios measure the firm's ability to pay its short-term debts as they come due. These ratios are of special interest to the firm's creditors. The three main measures of liquidity are the current ratio, the acid-test (quick) ratio, and net working capital.

The **current ratio** is the ratio of total current assets to total current liabilities. Traditionally, a current ratio of 2 ($2 of current assets for every $1 of current liabilities) has been considered good. Whether it is sufficient depends on the industry in which the firm operates. Public utilities, which have a very steady cash flow, operate quite well with a current ratio well below 2. A current ratio of 2 might not be adequate for manufacturers and merchandisers that carry high inventories and have lots of receivables. The current ratio for Production Inc. for 200x, as shown in Exhibit 16.7, is 1.4. This means little without a basis for comparison. If the analyst found that the industry average was 2.4, Production Inc. would appear to have low liquidity.

The **acid-test (quick) ratio** is like the current ratio except that it excludes inventory, which is the least liquid current asset. The acid-test ratio is used to measure the firm's ability to pay its current liabilities without selling inventory. The name *acid-test* implies that this ratio is a crucial test of the firm's liquidity. An acid-test ratio of at least 1 is preferred, but again, what is an acceptable value varies by industry. The acid-test ratio is a good measure of liquidity when inventory cannot easily be converted to cash (for instance, if it consists of very specialized goods with a limited market). If inventory is liquid, the current ratio is better. Production Inc.'s acid-test ratio for 200x is 1.1. Because Production Inc. does not carry large inventories, the values of its acid-test and current ratios are fairly close. For manufacturing companies, however, inventory typically makes up a large portion of current assets, so the acid-test ratio will be lower than the current ratio.

Net working capital, though not really a ratio, is often used to measure a firm's overall liquidity. It is calculated by subtracting total current liabilities from total current assets. Production Inc.'s net working capital for 200x is $23,050. Comparisons of net working capital over time often help in assessing a firm's liquidity.

Profitability Ratios

To measure profitability, a firm's profits can be related to its sales, equity, or shares value. **Profitability ratios** measure how well the firm is using its resources to generate profit and how efficiently it is being managed. The main profitability ratios are net profit margin, return on equity, and earnings per share.

net profit margin

The ratio of net profit to net sales; also called *return on sales*. It measures the percentage of each sales dollar remaining after all expenses, including taxes, have been deducted.

return on equity (ROE)

The ratio of net profit to total owners' equity; measures the return that owners receive on their investment in the firm.

earnings per share (EPS)

The ratio of net profit to the number of shares of common shares outstanding; measures the number of dollars earned by each share.

The ratio of net profit to net sales is the **net profit margin,** also called *return on sales.* It measures the percentage of each sales dollar remaining after all expenses, including taxes, have been deducted. Higher net profit margins are better than lower ones. The net profit margin is often used to measure the firm's earning power. "Good" net profit margins differ quite a bit from industry to industry. A grocery store usually has a very low net profit margin, perhaps below 1 percent, whereas a jewellery store's net profit margin would probably exceed 10 percent. Production Inc.'s net profit margin for 200x is 11.9 percent. In other words, Production Inc. is earning 11.9 cents on each dollar of sales.

The ratio of net profit to total owners' equity is called **return on equity (ROE).** It measures the return that owners receive on their investment in the firm, a major reason for investing in a company's shares. Production Inc. has a 40.9 percent ROE for 200x. On the surface, a 40.9 percent ROE seems quite good, but the level of risk in the business and the ROE of other firms in the same industry must also be considered. The higher the risk, the greater the ROE investors look for. A firm's ROE can also be compared to past values to see how the company is performing over time.

Earnings per share (EPS) is the ratio of net profit to the number of shares of common shares outstanding. It measures the number of dollars earned by each share. EPS values are closely watched by investors and are considered an important sign of success. EPS also indicates a firm's ability to pay dividends. Note that EPS is the dollar amount earned by each share, not the actual amount given to shareholders in the form of dividends. Some earnings may be put back into the firm. Production Inc.'s EPS for 200x is $3.22.

Activity Ratios

activity ratios

Ratios that measure how well a firm uses its assets.

inventory turnover ratio

The ratio of cost of goods sold to average inventory; measures the speed with which inventory moves through a firm and is turned into sales.

Activity ratios measure how well a firm uses its assets. They reflect the speed with which resources are converted to cash or sales. A frequently used activity ratio is inventory turnover.

The **inventory turnover ratio** measures the speed with which inventory moves through the firm and is turned into sales. It is calculated by dividing cost of goods sold by the average inventory. (Average inventory is estimated by adding the beginning and ending inventories for the year and dividing by 2.) Based on its 200x financial data, Production Inc.'s inventory, on average, is turned into sales 6.8 times each year, or about once every 54 days (365 days ÷ 6.8). The acceptable turnover ratio depends on the line of business. A grocery store would have a high turnover ratio, maybe 20 times a year, whereas the turnover for a heavy equipment manufacturer might be only 3 times a year.

Debt Ratios

debt ratios

Ratios that measure the degree and effect of a firm's use of borrowed funds (debt) to finance its operations.

debt-to-equity ratio

The ratio of total liabilities to owners' equity; measures the relationship between the amount of debt financing and the amount of equity financing (owner's funds).

Debt ratios measure the degree and effect of the firm's use of borrowed funds (debt) to finance its operations. These ratios are especially important to lenders and investors. They want to make sure the firm has a healthy mix of debt and equity. If the firm relies too much on debt, it might have trouble meeting interest payments and repaying loans. The most important debt ratio is the debt-to-equity ratio.

The **debt-to-equity ratio** measures the relationship between the amount of debt financing (borrowing) and the amount of equity financing (owners' funds). It is calculated by dividing total liabilities by owners' equity. In general, the lower the ratio, the better, but it is important to assess the debt-to-equity ratio against both past values and industry averages. Production Inc.'s ratio for 200x is 89.1 percent. The ratio indicates that the company has 89 cents of debt for every dollar the owners have provided. A ratio above 100 percent means the firm has more debt than equity. In such a case, the lenders are providing more financing than the owners.

Exhibit 16.7 Ratio Analysis for Production Inc. at Year-End 200x

RATIO	FORMULA	CALCULATION	RESULT
Liquidity Ratios			
Current ratio	Total current assets	$83,200	1.4
	Total current liabilities	$60,150	
Acid-test (quick) ratio	Total current assets − inventory	$83,200 − $15,000	1.1
	Total current liabilities	$60,150	
Net working capital	Total current assets − Total current liabilities	$83,200 − $60,150	$23,050
Profitability Ratios			
Net profit margin	Net profit	$132,175	11.9%
	Net sales	$270,500	
Return on equity	Net profit	$32,175	40.9%
	Total owners' equity	$78,750	
Earnings per share	Net profit	$32,175	$3.22
	Number of shares of common shares outstanding	10,000	
Activity Ratio			
Inventory turnover	Cost of goods sold		
	Average inventory		
	Cost of goods sold	$112,500	
	(Beginning inventory + Ending inventory)/2	($18,000 + $15,000)/2	
		$112,500	6.8 times
		$16,500	
Debt Ratio			
Debt-to-equity ratio	Total liabilities	$70,150	89.1%
	Owners' equity	$78,750	

concept check

How can ratio analysis be used to interpret financial statements?

Name the main liquidity and profitability ratios, and explain what they indicate.

What kinds of information do activity ratios give? Why are debt ratios of concern to lenders and investors?

Making Ethical Choices

SUPERMARKETS SHELVE REVENUES AND CAN AUDITORS

As the assistant controller of a major supermarket company, you work closely with the company's independent auditor. Overall, you have been pleased with your auditor's performance and believe that the firm has shown high standards of integrity.

During this year's review of your firm's financial reports and its internal controls, the auditor raised a question about the timing of incentive payments received from vendors and when they would be recognized as revenue. The issue of such incentive payments from vendors is a big one in the grocery industry. Several of your competitors recorded vendor payments received of $2 to $3 billion in 200x—more than those companies' operating profits. You are aware that your chain uses these payment receipts to manipulate earnings, choosing the supplier that offers the largest up-front incentive payments for shelf space to boost quarterly earnings by a sizable amount. Although this is legal, it is a practice that has come under closer scrutiny in the wake of investigations of other accounting irregularities.

You are called into a meeting with the CFO and the controller to discuss what to do about the warning from the audit firm that it might have a "reportable condition" relating to this situation. The CFO wants to fire the audit firm and hire another one. The controller asks for your opinion.

ETHICAL DILEMMA
Should you go along with the CFO and recommend firing the audit firm?

SOURCES: David Henry, "Accounting Games in the Grocer's Aisle," *Business Week*, April 14, 2003, 64; and Stephen Taub, "D&T Warned A&P Dismissed," *CFO.com*, September 19, 2002, http://www.cfo.com.

Trends in Accounting

8 *learning goal*

HOT Links
Learn more accounting terms at Small Business: Canada, http://sbinfocanada.about .com/od/accounting/ or http://sbinfocanada.about .com/cs/businessinfo/a/ biztermsall.htm.

The role of accountants has been changing and expanding. Although accountants still perform the important task of assuring that a company's financial reporting conforms to GAAP, they have become a valuable part of the financial team and consult with clients on information technology and other areas as well.

The increasing complexity of today's business environment creates additional challenges for the accounting profession. The information explosion means that the CICA must consider a greater number of new regulations and develop more position statements to keep up with the pace of change. The CICA also has an emerging issues task force that studies ways to make accounting standards more relevant for today's companies.

No longer can a company's assets be measured solely in terms of its bricks and mortar. Knowledge assets—brand names, patents, research and development (R&D) costs, and similar expenses—make up a large portion of the value of many information technology companies. As yet, however, there are few accepted ways of valuing those assets; indeed, there is disagreement over whether companies should even try. In other areas, GAAP is either unclear or subject to different interpretations.

ACCOUNTANTS EXPAND THEIR ROLE

Moving beyond their traditional task of validating a company's financial information, accountants now take an active role in advising their clients on systems and procedures, accounting software, and changes in accounting regulations. They also delve into operating information to discover what's behind the numbers. By examining the risks and weaknesses in a company, they can help managers develop financial controls and procedures to prevent future trouble spots. For example, auditors in a manufacturing company might spend a significant amount of time on inventory, a likely problem area.

Accounting firms have greatly expanded the consulting services they provide clients. As a result, accountants have become more involved in the operations of their clients. This raises the question of potential conflicts of interest. Can auditors serve both the public and the client? Auditors' main purpose is to certify financial statements. Will they maintain sufficient objectivity to raise questions while auditing a client that provides significant consulting revenues? Can they review systems and methods that they recommended? According to one expert, "If the financial markets don't believe in a firm's audit, the firm has nothing."

VALUING KNOWLEDGE ASSETS

As the world's economy becomes knowledge- rather than industrial-based, more of a company's value might come from internally generated intangible intellectual assets. Intellectual capital is an important resource to any organization, but are we serious about actually attaching a dollar value to it? Dr. Nick Bontis, a researcher and practitioner in knowledge management, intellectual capital, and organizational learning at McMaster University in Hamilton, Ontario, discovered that the main reason cited by his research subjects for leaving their employment was that they felt they were underutilized. With voluntary turnover in Canadian organizations reaching 15 percent, we are watching these knowledge assets walk out the door.[4]

Whether and how to value intangibles are controversial issues. Some people believe that because intangibles are uncertain and risky, they do not belong on the balance sheet. Costs related to intangibles might bear no relationship to their actual value. On the other hand, placing a value on intangibles allows companies to know whether they are earning adequate returns on R&D, whether patents are worth renewing, and whether they should invest more to build brands. Clearly, there are no quick and easy solutions to this issue, which will continue to be studied in the coming years.

TIGHTENING THE GAAP

Although GAAP is supposed to ensure uniformity in Canadian companies' financial reporting, in reality companies have some discretion in how they interpret certain accounting standards. Companies appear to be taking advantage of loopholes in GAAP to manipulate numbers, and there have been examples of companies accused of fraudulently inflating income by claiming inflated revenues. Many companies are pushing accounting to the edge—and over it—to keep earnings rising to meet the expectations of investment analysts, who project earnings, and investors, who panic when a company misses the analysts' forecasts. This has raised serious concerns about the quality of earnings and questions about the validity of financial reports.

One of the most common issues involves write-offs of certain large, one-time charges. What is a legitimate one-time charge, and what are normal operating costs that are written off as they are incurred? GAAP doesn't provide a clear answer. In this category are charges like restructuring charges (combining several years of expected future expenses and writing them off at once) and costs associated with acquisitions, such as "in-process R&D," the estimated value of R&D at an acquired company. The acquirer can write off the estimated value of products still in development. The benefits of this R&D are unknown and might be worthless in the future, so companies must take the charge against earnings now.

What new roles are accountants playing? Do you see any potential problems from these new roles?

What are knowledge assets, and why have they become so important?

How can large one-time write-offs distort a company's financial results?

What problems might the declining quality of financial reporting present for investors, lenders, and the economy in general?

Great Ideas to Use Now

By now it should be very clear that basic accounting knowledge is a valuable skill to have, whether you start your own company or work for someone else. Analyzing a company's financial statements before you take a job there can tell you quite a bit about its financial health. Once you are on the job, you need to understand how to read financial statements and how to develop financial information for business operations. It's almost impossible to operate effectively in a business environment otherwise. Especially in a small company, you will wear many hats, and having accounting skills may help you get the job. In addition, accounting will help you manage your personal finances.

If you own your own firm, you can't rely on someone else to take charge of your accounting system. You must decide what financial information you need to manage your company better and to track its progress. If you can't understand the reports your accountant prepares, you will have no idea whether they are accurate.

CUSTOMER SATISFACTION AND QUALITY

The recent upheaval in corporate financial reporting makes customer satisfaction and quality very relevant to financial statement preparation and the accounting profession. As noted earlier, auditing firms often gave good reports to companies later charged with accounting irregularities.

The customers for financial reports are not just the corporate clients who hire the auditors. The investing public—both institutions who buy large blocks of shares and individuals—rely heavily on the quality and reliability of reported financial information to make investment decisions. They are demanding that auditors and corporations demonstrate their compliance with higher standards.

Companies are now giving new respect to the external auditing process. "If you want an audit that will detect management fraud, you must be willing to pay more for it and pay far greater attention to the process and what will be included and analyzed," says Robert G. Eccles, PricewaterhouseCoopers senior fellow and coauthor of *Building Public Trust: The Future of Corporate Reporting.* "The audit committee must be the

customer for the audit, and this will require more time on the part of the audit committee."[5]

Better quality control will result from new corporate governance standards and financial disclosure practices. Management at Airgas Inc., an industrial gases distributor, now spends more time on these issues. It was already in compliance with the latest legislative and regulatory reforms. Recently the company implemented a more formal approach to financial quality control. The audit committee will hold a special meeting every year to review current business issues. "This focus is closely tied to our growth strategy," says Roger Millay, Airgas's senior vice president and CFO. "Good governance, and the perception and understanding of good governance, are important to our growth strategy. The market's confidence in our governance is essential to attracting capital."

SOURCE: Outlook 2003: More Changes, Greater Challenges, www.businessfinancemag.com December 2002. Reprinted with permission from Penton Media.

SUMMARY OF LEARNING GOALS

1 Why are financial reports and accounting information important, and who uses them?

Accounting involves collecting, recording, classifying, summarizing, reporting, and analyzing a firm's financial activities according to a standard set of procedures. The financial reports resulting from the accounting process give managers, employees, investors, customers, suppliers, creditors, and government agencies a way of analyzing a company's past, current, and future performance. Financial accounting is concerned with the preparation of financial reports using generally accepted accounting principles. Managerial accounting provides financial information that management can use to make decisions about the firm's operations.

2 What is the difference between public and private accountants?

Public accountants work for independent firms that provide accounting services—such as financial report preparation and auditing, tax return preparation, and management consulting—to other organizations on a fee basis. Private accountants are employed to serve one particular organization and may prepare financial statements, tax returns, and management reports.

3 What are the six steps in the accounting cycle?

The accounting cycle refers to the process of generating financial statements. It begins with analyzing business transactions, recording them in journals, and posting them to ledgers. Ledger totals are then summarized in a trial balance that confirms the accuracy of the figures. Next, the accountant prepares the financial statements and reports. The final step involves analyzing these reports and making decisions.

4 In what terms does the balance sheet describe the financial condition of an organization?

The balance sheet represents the financial condition of a firm at one moment in time, in terms of assets, liabilities, and owners' equity. The key categories of assets are current assets, fixed assets, and intangible assets. Liabilities are divided into current and long-term liabilities. Owners' equity, the amount of the owners' investment in the firm after all liabilities have been paid, is the third major category.

5 How does the income statement report a firm's profitability?

The income statement is a summary of the firm's operations over a stated period of time. The main parts of the statement are revenues (gross and net sales), cost of goods sold, operating expenses (selling and general and administrative expenses), taxes, and net profit or loss.

6 Why is the statement of cash flows an important source of information?

The statement of cash flows summarizes the firm's sources and uses of cash during a financial-reporting period. It breaks the firm's cash flows into those from operating, investment, and financing activities. It shows the net change during the period in the firm's cash and marketable securities.

7 How can ratio analysis be used to identify a firm's financial strengths and weaknesses?

Ratio analysis is a way to use financial statements to gain insight into a firm's operations, profitability, and overall financial condition. The four main types of ratios are liquidity ratios, profitability ratios, activity ratios, and debt ratios. Comparing a firm's ratios over several years and comparing them to ratios of other firms in the same industry or to industry averages can indicate trends and highlight financial strengths and weaknesses.

8 What major trends affect the accounting industry today?

The accounting industry is responding to the rise in information technology in several ways. The role of accountants has expanded beyond the traditional audit and tax functions and now includes management consulting in areas such as computer systems, human resources, and electronic commerce. A major issue facing the industry is how to treat key intangible assets—knowledge assets such as patents, brands, and research and development—and whether they should be valued and included on a company's balance sheet. In addition, the CICA has raised concerns about the quality of reported earnings. Loose interpretation of GAAP has given companies leeway in how they deal with items like restructuring charges and write-offs resulting from acquisitions.

EXPERIENTIAL EXERCISES

1. Learn to read financial statements. To become more familiar with annual reports and key financial statements, head for IBM's "Guide to Understanding Financials" at **http://www.ibm.com/investor/financialguide/.** The material offers a good overview of financial reporting and shows you what to look for when you read these documents.

2. **Prepare personal financial statements.** One of the best ways to learn about financial statements is to prepare them. Put together your personal balance sheet and income statement, using Exhibits 16.4 and 16.5 as samples. You will have to adjust the account categories to fit your needs. Here are some suggestions:

   - Current assets—cash on hand, balances in savings, and chequing accounts.

   - Investments—shares and bonds, retirement funds.

   - Fixed assets—real estate, personal property (cars, furniture, jewellery, etc.).

   - Current liabilities—credit card balances, loan payments due in one year.

   - Long-term liabilities—auto loan balance, mortgage on real estate, other loan balances that will not come due until after one year.

   - Income—employment income, investment income (interest, dividends).

   - Expenses—housing, utilities, food, transportation, medical, clothing, insurance, loan payments, taxes, personal care, recreation and entertainment, and miscellaneous expenses.

   After you complete your personal financial statements, use them to see how well you are managing your finances. Consider the following questions:

   - Should you be concerned about your debt ratio?

   - Would a potential creditor conclude that it is safe or risky to lend you money?

   - If you were a company, would people want to invest in you? Why or why not? What could you do to improve your financial condition?

3. Your firm has been hired to help several small businesses with their year-end financial statements.

a. Based on the following account balances, prepare the Marbella Design Enterprises balance sheet as of December 31, 200x:

Cash	$30,250
Accounts payable	28,500
Fixtures and furnishings	85,000
Notes payable	15,000
Retained earnings	64,450
Accounts receivable	24,050
Inventory	15,600
Equipment	42,750
Accumulated amortization on fixtures and furnishings	12,500
Common shares (50,000 shares outstanding)	50,000
Long-term debt	25,000
Accumulated amortization on equipment	7,800
Marketable securities	13,000
Income taxes payable	7,500

b. The following are the account balances for the revenues and expenses of the Windsor Gift Shop for the year ending December 31, 200x. Prepare the income statement for the shop.

Rent	$15,000
Salaries	23,500
Cost of goods sold	98,000
Utilities	8,000
Supplies	3,500
Sales	195,000
Advertising	3,600
Interest	3,000
Taxes	12,120

4. During the year ended December 31, 200x, Lawrence Industries sold $2 million worth of merchandise on credit. A total of $1.4 million was collected during the year. The cost of this merchandise was $1.3 million. Of this amount, $1 million has been paid, and $300,000 is not yet due. Operating expenses and income taxes totalling $500,000 were paid in cash during the year. Assume that all accounts had a zero balance at the beginning of the year (January 1, 200x). Write a brief report for the company controller that includes calculation of the firm's (a) net profit and (b) cash flow during the year. Explain why there is a difference between net profit and cash flow.

5. A friend has been offered a sales representative position at Draper Publications, Inc., a small publisher of computer-related books, but wants to know more about the company. Because of your expertise in financial analysis, you offer to

help analyze Draper's financial health. Draper has provided the following selected financial information:

Account balances on December 31, 200x:

Inventory	$ 72,000
Net sales	450,000
Current assets	150,000
Cost of goods sold	290,000
Total liabilities	180,000
Net profit	35,400
Total assets	385,000
Current liabilities	75,000
Other information	
Number of common shares outstanding	25,000
Inventory at January 1, 200x	48,000

Calculate the following ratios for 200x: acid-test (quick) ratio, inventory turnover ratio, net profit margin, return on equity (ROE), debt-to-equity ratio, and earnings per share (EPS). Summarize your assessment of the company's financial performance, based on these ratios, in a report for your friend. What other information would you like to have to complete your evaluation?

6. Two years ago, Rebecca Mardon started a computer consulting business, Mardon Consulting Associates. Until now, she has been the only employee, but business has grown enough to support an administrative assistant and another consultant this year. Before she adds staff, however, she wants to hire an accountant and computerize her financial record keeping. Divide the class into small groups, assigning one person to be Rebecca and the others to represent members of a medium-sized accounting firm. Rebecca should think about the type of financial information systems her firm requires and develop a list of questions for the firm. The accountants will prepare a presentation, making recommendations to her as well as explaining why their firm should win the account.

7. Do annual reports confuse you? Many Web sites can take the mystery out of this important document. See IBM's "Guide to Understanding Financials" at **http://www.prars.com/ibm/ibmframe.html.** Moneychimp's "How to Read an Annual Report" features an interactive diagram that provides a big picture view of what the report's financial information tells you: **http://www.moneychimp .com/articles/financials/fundamentals.htm.** Which site was more helpful to you, and why?

8. Can you judge an annual report by its cover? What are the most important elements of a top annual report? Go to Sid Cato's Official Annual Report Web site, **http://www.sidcato.com,** to find his 15 standards for annual reports and read about the reports that receive his honours. Then get a copy of an annual report and evaluate it using Cato's 135-point scale. How well does it compare to his top picks?

REVIEW QUESTIONS

1. What is accounting? What is the difference between managerial and financial accounting?

2. What is GAAP? What is its function?

3. Discuss the accounting profession in terms of public versus private account-ants, CAs, CMAs, and CGAs.

4. What is the accounting equation?

5. Explain the various categories of a balance sheet.

6. What is the purpose of the income statement? What does it include?

7. What is the purpose of a statement of cash flows?

8. What is ratio analysis?

9. Name and provide the formulas of the liquidity ratios mentioned in the chapter.

10. What do profitability ratios tell us? What are those that are mentioned in the chapter?

11. What are activity ratios and which ones are mentioned in the chapter?

12. What do debt ratios measure? What does the debt-to-equity ratio measure?

13. What trends are happening in the accounting field?

CREATIVE THINKING CASE
Accounting: Who Are We Responsible To?

Arthur Andersen started the accounting firm that bore his name in 1913. From the start, he embraced the highest business ethics, refusing to manipulate unsatisfactory financial results at a client's request. Andersen's motto, "Think straight, talk straight," was the foundation of the company's culture of honesty and integrity. The company was known for its disciplined and strict attention to accounting standards.

By the 1990s, the Andersen culture had strayed far from its founder's philosophy. Andersen was "a place where the mad scramble for fees had trumped good judgment," says Barbara Ley Toffler, author of *Final Accounting: Ambition, Greed and the Fall of Arthur Andersen*. These fees came not only from auditing but increasingly from the rapidly growing consulting practices of Andersen and its industry colleagues. Business units competed with each other and were rewarded for bringing in revenues, not for evaluating a deal's risks.

The growth of consulting revenues was in itself a problem. Andersen often provided business services to the same companies it audited, earning as much from consulting as auditing. This conflict of interest placed pressure on the auditors to go along with aggressive accounting practices, to preserve the consulting relation-ships and earnings.

Andersen's culture also placed a loyalty to the firm before loyalty to clients or shareholders. Partners who raised questions were penalized. This attitude went straight down the line, as Toffler discovered when leading a meeting of young Andersen employees. She asked how they would respond if a supervisor told them to do something they consider wrong. Only one person spoke up: "If he insisted I do it, yes, I would." Toffler then asked if he would tell anyone about it: "No. It could hurt my career."

Turning a blind eye to accounting irregularities at clients was a common prac-tice. Says Toffler, who—ironically—ran Andersen's business ethics consulting practice from 1995 to 1999, "High-level members of that organization knew much of what was going on." As Enron's wrongdoings became public, the firm's top man-agement became Enron's partner in duplicity instead of demonstrating the industry leadership its founder would have expected.

In June 2002, Andersen was convicted of obstruction of justice in the Enron case for shredding documents. Later that summer, the doors shut at the accounting firm that once set the standards to which other firms aspired.

1. Toffler says that Andersen executives expected that aggressive accounting would have an impact when the economy tanked but issued few warning memos and did nothing to change the culture of greed. With the benefit of hindsight, what steps could Andersen's leadership have taken to preserve the firm as the accounting scandals unfolded?

2. Andersen's Enron audit team was aware of monkey business as early as 1987, when management covered up the oil-trading scandal mentioned in the chapter opener. It also caved in to pressure to sign off on questionable deals and participated in document destruction that led to its obstruction-of-justice conviction. Suggest procedures that auditors and corporations should adopt and enforce to prevent these abuses.

3. Discuss why providing consulting services to audit clients in such areas as business strategy, financial strategy, human resources, and information technology systems planning, design, and implementation can create a conflict of interest.

SOURCES: Greg Farrell, "Former Andersen Exec Tells of Stressful Internal Culture," *USA Today*, March 3, 2003; William J. Holstein, "Lessons of a Fallen Rival for Accounting's Big 4," *The New York Times*, February 23, 2003; and Rob Walker, "Inside a Culture of Greed," *Newsday*, March 6, 2003.

VIDEO CASE
Doug Hall Fixes Tofino

Tofino is a remote community on the west coast of Vancouver Island. Many of the small businesses there depend on the tourism industry, which is, to a large degree, seasonal. Doug Hall is a successful business consultant who has been hired to advise three of Tofino's entrepreneurs on how to be more profitable. The operations include a fish/ice-cream market, Mike's Market; a whale-watching/museum company, and a cleaning business, Dust Bunnies. Each enterprise is able to cover its expenses and make a bit of money, but the profits are small, and there is virtually no growth. The owners report working long hours at their respective endeavours and are interested in what a high-profile American consultant might suggest.

The fish market owner has several other businesses and lacks focus. The whale-watching entrepreneur has tried to differentiate by offering whale bones for the tourists to admire as part of his museum. The owner of the cleaning service, although successful, is simply tired of cleaning toilets.

An analysis of each balance sheet might show a reasonable current ratio and acid-test ratio but nothing particularly strong. The ROE ratios might not look very good for the fish market and the whale-watching, as each of these probably has significant owner's equity. To help these businesses increase their cash flow, Doug Hall suggests strategies such as diversification for the whale-watching business, greater focus and branding for the fish/ice-cream market, and the addition of a totally new operation for the owner of the cleaning business.

In an area that depends heavily on tourism, it is more difficult to have money coming in regularly, and the stress of having to make enough money in the summer to last the entire year is enormous. The whale-watching does occur year-round, but summer is the busiest time. Dust Bunnies primarily cleans vacation rentals, and Mike's Market, although serving the locals, depends on the tourists as well.

Doug Hall makes excellent recommendations to the owners, and the results are interesting.

CRITICAL THINKING QUESTIONS

1. If these three entrepreneurs were to implement Doug's suggestions, how would they finance the changes?

2. Why would having significant owner's equity negatively affect the ROE for the market and the whale-watching businesses?

3. Which of the three companies profiled in the video found a strategy to allow year-round income? Check **http://www.tofinotime.com/main** and look at Bodi Bikes. Also look at **www.tofinowhalecentre.com.**

SOURCE: CBC, *Venture*, "Doug Hall Fixes Tofino Part 1, 2, and 3," February 20, 2005.

E-COMMERCE CASE
Accounting for the Dollars Spent on the Gun Registry.

Whether you disagree philosophically with the Canadian gun registry or not, most Canadian taxpayers would certainly disagree with the amount of tax dollars spent on it.

Criticisms of the gun registry have been voiced for years, but recently the auditor general, Sheila Fraser, has reported that the accounting decision to allow the Canada Firearms Centre to carry more than $22 million in computer development costs to present a better financial picture is questionable. The government accounting policies require computer development costs to be recorded in the year in which they are incurred rather than when they are payable. This is consistent with GAAP. Generally, costs are recorded when incurred, and revenue recorded when earned.

The Conservatives have been quick to comment on Liberal corruption, and the hunt is on for whoever made the decision to defer the costs. The costs to develop the computer system—$39 million in 2002–03 and $21.8 million in 2003–04—probably seem excessive to most taxpayers no matter when they are recorded on the books. Unfortunately, record keeping with respect to meetings and decision-making is such that it is very difficult to track the decision process and hence determine accountability. The ongoing debate as to whether the top bureaucrats or the politicians are ultimately responsible for a situation such as this might be solved by the Conservatives' accountability bill, which would designate the deputy minister as the "accounting officer" of his or her department (see information on this at **http://www.faa-lfi.gc.ca**).

As the costs of this program hover around the $2 billion dollar mark, one might ask, "Is it reasonable to spend more tax dollars just to determine who to blame for the already massive amount of money spent?"

CRITICAL THINKING QUESTIONS

1. By establishing an "accounting officer" in government departments, will the government be able to prevent incidents such as this?

2. Check out the Canadian Institute of Chartered Accountants' Web site at **http://www.cica.ca** for more information on GAAP, taking particular note of the "Public Sector Accounting" section. Have these practices been adhered to with respect to the Canada Firearms Centre?

SOURCES: Kathryn May, "MPs Hunt Gun-Registry Cover-Up Report," *The Ottawa Citizen*, May 19, 2006; and Barney Morehouse, "Gun Registry Must Go", *Ontario Out of Doors*, 38, no. 3 (April 2006), 8.

17

Making the Connection

Managing the Firm's Finances

In this chapter we will continue to look at the finance area of business. The primary role of the financial manager is to maximize the value of the firm for the owners. This is to achieve the main critical success factor of *financial performance*. This, we know, cannot be done without the other four success factors, reiterating the need for the managers in all departments to work closely with one another and the finance area in particular.

As we saw in Chapter 16, the relationship between finance and the major *stakeholders*, particularly the owners, is a difficult but important one. Among the many important decisions that finance managers must make regarding the acquisition, disposition, and management of financial resources is how much of the company's profit will be distributed to the shareholders in the form of a dividend. The shareholders expect a return, so if a regular dividend is not paid, then they expect the return in the form of an increased share price. This can happen only if the investing community sees potential in the value of the shares. If neither of these happens, the price of the shares will fall as shareholders sell their shares. The company must therefore consider the stakeholder response to the decisions it makes, as they will affect its ability to maximize the value of the firm for the owners.

As we also saw in Chapter 16, all decisions have financial consequences, but financial decisions have consequences in other areas as well. For

example, policies for granting credit affect *marketing's* ability to generate sales. Just imagine if Chrysler did not offer financing packages on its vehicles. Furthermore, money spent on research and development or new production facilities has an impact on what *operations* is capable of doing, just as the company's policies on payroll costs have an impact on attracting and keeping key employees (*human resources*). To make money, the firm must first spend money, but it must also control that money to continue to be profitable and stay viable. A fine balance must be achieved between taking the risks and reaping the rewards—one that the finance manager must consider and that affects all areas of the company.

Cash flow provides an example of this need for integration and balance. To aid marketing in selling the firm's products, the supply chain must be set up to make sure that inventory is available for customers and that credit is generally extended. However, that means that finance must balance the time that it takes to sell the inventory and then collect the accounts receivable from customers with the payments on that inventory and other expenses. If it does not do this, the company will not have enough cash coming in to pay its bills and will go bankrupt! Another example is with inventory. The operations area needs raw materials on hand to avoid delays in production, and marketing needs enough finished goods on hand to *satisfy customers*, but finance must balance these needs with the cost of carrying inventory, and therefore tries to keep inventory levels at a minimum. In Chapter 11 we discussed techniques for dealing with inventory and saw that technology provides many new options.

Technology is just one of the many environmental factors that must be taken into account in making financial decisions. For example, as market demand changes (*social* environment), funds need to be shifted between projects. The social environment has also had a significant impact on changing the role of the typical CFO in an organization—from being "just numbers people" to helping to develop and implement the firm's overall *strategy* and "re-establish public trust" in the wake of recent financial scandals. As interest and exchange rates fluctuate (*economic* environment), some projects and methods of financing projects either will need to be abandoned or will become more possible. General economic conditions in domestic and world markets might cause firms to speed up or slow down the rate of investment in different projects, and government policies in the home and foreign countries (*political* environment) might make investment in certain projects more attractive than others. Finally, as *technology* advances and costs drop, some projects become more accessible.

In the internal business environment, when budgets are set, the finance area must work with the other functional areas to develop *plans* for financing the company that help it meet its strategic goals. Each area has a role to play in helping the organization achieve its strategic goals, and the resources they will need must be considered. Finance uses various forecasts, as discussed in the chapter, to develop financial plans for the business.

SHIRLEY A. ROSE

Chapter 17

Managing the Firm's Finances

learning goals

1 What roles do finance and the financial manager play in the firm's overall strategy?

2 How does a firm develop its financial plans, including forecasts and budgets?

3 What types of short- and long-term expenditures does a firm make?

4 What are the main sources and costs of unsecured and secured short-term financing?

5 How do the two primary sources of long-term financing compare?

6 What are the major types, features, and costs of long-term debt?

7 When and how do firms issue equity, and what are the costs?

8 What is risk, and how can it be managed? What makes a risk insurable?

9 What types of insurance coverage should businesses consider?

10 What trends are affecting the practice of financial management?

Managing Risk in the Land Development Industry

Carl Cheverie has been in the land development and venture capital fields for more than 30 years and has seen the good, the bad, and the ugly aspects of the industry first-hand. Carl's responsibilities ranged from regional manager at Carma Developers LP, responsible for 6,000 acres of property, to his current position as president of Birchwood Properties Corp. During his career, he has experienced the industry from three distinct angles: as a seeker of investors willing to provide funds, as a lender of the venture capital, and as a borrower for his own projects.

The process for a development project generally follows these steps:

1. The developer obtains financing and buys the raw land.

2. The developer procures the appropriate approvals; for example, planning approvals, zoning approvals, land-use approvals, and various bylaw approvals.

3. The developer installs all utilities, roads, and parks within the parameters of the registered plan.

4. Lots are sold to builders or individuals with approximately 15 percent down, with the balance usually due in 6 to 12 months.

5. Once the title is transferred to the builder or the individual, the developer gets paid for the lot.

As Carl points out, there is a lot of money in flux as the project progresses. Are there substantial risks in the development business? It depends a great deal on the economy. If interest rates are on the rise, the risks are greater. The memory of the early '80s is still fresh in Carl's mind. As interest rates soared to 19 to 20 percent, builders simply walked away from the lots they had agreed to buy from the developer and left the 15 percent down payment on the table. Another risk is not getting the density you had planned on, and there are others as well. If these problems do occur, the developer can be left with a parcel of land partially serviced and a huge loan with a floating interest rate. This would definitely be one of the ugly aspects of the business.

However, when things are good, they can be very good, with lots selling out before the services are even in place and builders with enough cash flow to pay for each lot outright. In many parts of Canada, the housing market is strong, and because of Canada's national banking system, developers can move around to where the demand is greatest. For example, Toronto-based Dundee Realty Management Corporation is one of the many companies Carl does business with. Dundee operates in centres from St. John's to Vancouver. As economic conditions change, a national organization such as Dundee can simply put its resources into the strongest market area.

Carl feels the greatest danger is overextending and taking on too much debt, forgetting that the economy is cyclical. In the '80s many people were slow to catch on to the seriousness of the situation, and those who were overextended, no matter what the industry, were in trouble. What goes up must come down, eventually!

Critical Thinking Questions

1. How can a developer lower his or her risk if interest rates begin to rise?

2. Recall the chapters you have read. What other challenges might result from increasing interest rates?[1]

In today's fast-paced global economy, managing a firm's finances is more complex than ever. For Birchwood Properties' financial managers, a thorough command of traditional finance activities—financial planning, investing money, and raising funds—is only part of the job. Financial managers are more than number crunchers. As part of the top-management team, chief financial officers (CFOs) need a broad understanding of their firm's business and industry, as well as leadership ability and creativity. They must never lose sight of the primary goal of the financial manager: *to maximize the value of the firm to its owners.*

Financial management—spending and raising a firm's money—is both a science and an art. The science part is analyzing numbers and flows of cash through the firm. The art is answering questions like these: Is the firm using its financial resources in the best way? Aside from costs, why choose a particular form of financing? How risky is each option?

In this chapter, we focus on the financial management of a firm. We'll start with an overview of the role of finance and of the financial manager in the firm's overall business strategy. Next we consider the basics of financial planning: forecasts and budgets. Discussions of short- and long-term uses of funds and sources of short- and long-term financing follow. The importance of understanding and managing risk and insurance is examined, and finally, we will look at key trends affecting financial management.

THE ROLE OF FINANCE AND THE FINANCIAL MANAGER

1 learning goal

financial management
The art and science of managing a firm's money so that it can meet its goals.

Finance is critical to the success of all companies. It might not be as visible as marketing or production, but management of a firm's finances is just as much a key to the firm's success.

Financial management—the art and science of managing a firm's money so that it can meet its goals—is not just the responsibility of the finance department. All business decisions have financial consequences. Managers in all departments must work closely with financial personnel. If you are a sales representative, for example, the company's credit and collection policies will affect your ability to make sales.

Any company, whether it's a two-lawyer law partnership or Petro-Canada, needs money to operate. To make money, it must first spend money—on inventory and supplies, equipment and facilities, and employee wages and salaries.

Revenues from sales of the firm's products should be the chief source of funding, but money from sales doesn't always come in when it's needed to pay the bills. Financial managers must track how money is flowing into and out of the firm (see Exhibit 17.1). They work with the firm's other department managers to determine how available funds will be used and how much money is needed. Then they choose the best sources to obtain the required funding.

For example, a financial manager will track day-to-day operational data such as cash collections and disbursements to ensure that the company has enough cash to meet its obligations. Over a longer time horizon, the manager will thoroughly study whether and when the company should open a new manufacturing facility. The manager will also suggest the most appropriate way to finance the project, raise the funds, and then monitor the project's implementation and operation.

HOT *Links*

What challenges do today's financial managers face? To find out, browse through recent issues of *CFO* magazine at http://www.cfo.com.

Because all business decisions have financial consequences, managers in all departments must work closely with financial personnel. A company's credit and collection policies, for example, might impact a sales representative's ability to close a sale.

© ROYALTY-FREE/CORBIS

Financial management is closely related to accounting. In most firms both areas are the responsibility of the vice president of finance or the CFO (many of whom have an accounting designation). But the accountant's main function is to collect and present financial data. Financial managers use financial statements and

Exhibit 17.1 | How Cash Flows through a Business

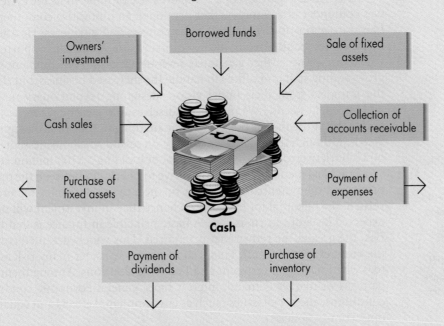

other information prepared by accountants to make financial decisions. Financial managers focus on **cash flows,** the inflows and outflows of cash. They plan and monitor the firm's cash flows to ensure that cash is available when needed.

The Financial Manager's Responsibilities and Activities

Financial managers have a complex and challenging job. They analyze financial data prepared by accountants, monitor the firm's financial status, and prepare and implement financial plans. One day they might be developing a better way to automate cash collections; the next they might be analyzing a proposed acquisition. The key activities of the financial manager are

- *financial planning*—preparing the financial plan, which projects revenues, expenditures, and financing needs over a given period;
- *investment (spending money)*—investing the firm's funds in projects and securities that provide high returns in relation to their risks; and
- *financing (raising money)*—obtaining funding for the firm's operations and investments and seeking the best balance between debt (borrowed funds) and equity (funds raised through the sale of ownership in the business).

HOT Links

When you come across a finance term you don't understand, visit the Hypertextual Finance Glossary at http://www.duke.edu/~charvey/Classes/wpg/glossary.htm.

The Goal of the Financial Manager

How can financial managers make wise planning, investment, and financing decisions? The main goal of the financial manager is *to maximize the value of the firm to its owners.* The value of a publicly owned corporation is measured by the share price of its shares. A private company's value is the price at which it could be sold.

To maximize the firm's value, the financial manager has to consider both short- and long-term consequences of the firm's actions. Maximizing profits is one approach, but it should not be the only one. Such an approach favours making short-term gains over achieving long-term goals. What if a firm in a highly technical and competitive industry did no research and development? In the short run, profits would be high, because research and development are very expensive, but in the long run, the firm might lose its ability to compete because of its lack of new products.

This is true regardless of a company's size or point in its life cycle. David Deeds was cofounder of a company that developed an innovative computer-aided design hardware and software package for architects and engineers. He and his partners made some decisions early in the company's life to pursue opportunities such as consulting projects that generated revenue quickly. The company saw its profits grow, adding staff and offices to handle the increased business, but this sidetracked the founders from their initial vision: designing revolutionary new products to address client needs. "We managed ourselves into a niche where we could survive and make a little money but never offer anything unique or grow significantly," says Deeds. Although they built a reasonably successful small business, the desire for the quick buck overrode the long-term goal of building a $100 million company.[2]

Financial managers constantly strive for a balance between the opportunity for profit and the potential for loss. In finance, the opportunity for profit is termed **return**; the potential for loss, or the chance that an investment will not achieve the expected level of return, is **risk.** A basic principle in finance is that the higher the risk, the greater the return that is required. This widely accepted concept is called the **risk-return trade-off.** Financial managers consider many risk and return factors when making investment and financing decisions. Among them are changing patterns of market demand, interest rates, general economic conditions, market conditions, and social issues (such as environmental effects and equal employment opportunity policies).

What is the role of financial management in a firm?

How do the three key activities of the financial manager relate?

What is the main goal of the financial manager? How does the risk-return trade-off relate to the financial manager's main goal?

FINANCIAL PLANNING: LOOKING AHEAD

2 *learning goal*

As we learned in Chapter 7, companies use several types of plans to determine how to achieve organizational objectives. A company's *financial plan* is part of the overall company plan and guides the firm toward its business goals and the maximization of its value. The financial plan enables the firm to estimate the amount and timing of its investment and financing needs.

To prepare a financial plan, the financial manager must first consider existing and proposed products, the resources available to produce them, and the financing needed to support production and sales. Forecasts and budgets are essential to the firm's financial planning. They should be part of an integrated planning process that links them to strategic plans and performance measurement.

Forecasting the Future

The financial-planning process starts with financial forecasts, or projections of future developments within the firm. The estimated demand for the firm's products (the sales forecast) and other financial and operating data are key inputs. At Ford Motor Company, economic analysts estimate expected production and sales for each line of cars and trucks. Then financial analysts prepare detailed short- and long-term financial forecasts based on these assumptions.

Short-term forecasts, or *operating plans,* project revenues, costs of goods, and operating expenses over a one-year period. Using short-term forecasts, Ford's financial managers estimate the next year's expenses for inventory, labour, advertising, and other operating activities. These estimates form the basis for cash budgets, described next, which forecast cash inflows and outflows over the same period.

Long-term forecasts, or *strategic plans,* cover a period that is longer than a year, typically 2 to 10 years, and take a broader view of the firm's financial activities. With these forecasts, management can assess the financial effects of various business strategies: What would be the financial results of investing in new facilities and equipment? Of developing new products? Of eliminating a line of business? Of acquiring other firms? Long-term forecasts also show where the funding for these activities is expected to come from.

Lenders typically ask potential borrowers for forecasts that cover the period the loan will be outstanding. "We're obviously asking so we understand the risk of a deal," says John L. Daniels, senior vice president, commercial banking, at a major financial firm. "We're looking for the cash-flow perspective and how we're getting paid. We build our loan agreements and covenants on that information."[3] (Covenants are requirements that the company comply with certain operating and financial measures during the loan period.)

Budgets

Firms prepare **budgets** to plan and control their future financial activities. Budgets are formal written forecasts of revenues and expenses that set spending limits based on operational forecasts. All budgets begin with forecasts. Budgets provide a way to control expenses and compare the actual performance to the forecast.

short-term forecasts
Projections of revenues, costs of goods, and operating expenses over a one-year period.

long-term forecasts
Projections of a firm's activities and the funding for those activities over a period that is longer than a year, typically 2 to 10 years.

budgets
Formal written forecasts of revenues and expenses that set spending limits based on operational forecasts; include cash budgets, capital budgets, and operating budgets.

Companies use capital budgets to forecast the costs of equipment like that shown here. Budgets of all types help companies plan and control their future financial activities.

© AP/WORLD WIDE PHOTOS

Firms use several types of budgets, most of which cover a one-year period.

- **Cash budgets** forecast the firm's cash inflows and outflows, and help the firm plan for cash surpluses and shortages. Because having enough cash is so critical to their financial health, many firms prepare annual cash budgets subdivided into months or weeks. Then they project the amount of cash needed in each shorter time period.
- **Capital budgets** forecast outlays for fixed assets (plant and equipment). They usually cover a period of several years and ensure that the firm will have enough funds to buy the equipment and buildings it needs.
- **Operating budgets** combine sales forecasts with estimates of production costs and operating expenses to forecast profits. They are based on individual budgets for sales, production, purchases of materials, factory overhead, and operating expenses. Operating budgets then are used to plan operations: dollars of sales, units of production, amounts of raw materials, dollars of wages, and so forth.

Budgets are routinely used to monitor and control the performance of a division, a department, or an individual manager. When actual outcomes differ from budget expectations, management must take action.

cash budgets
Budgets that forecast a firm's cash inflows and outflows and help the firm plan for cash surpluses and shortages.

capital budgets
Budgets that forecast a firm's outlays for fixed assets (plant and equipment), typically covering a period of several years.

operating budgets
Budgets that combine sales forecasts with estimates of production costs and operating expenses to forecast profits.

concept check

What is a financial plan? Name two types of financial-planning documents.
Distinguish between short- and long-term forecasts. How are both used by financial managers?
Briefly describe three types of budgets.

HOW ORGANIZATIONS USE FUNDS

3 *learning goal*

To grow and prosper, a firm must keep investing money in its operations. The financial manager decides how best to use the firm's money. Short-term expenses support the firm's day-to-day activities. For instance, an athletic-apparel maker regularly spends money to buy raw materials such as leather and fabric and to pay employee salaries. Long-term expenses are typically for fixed assets. For the athletic-apparel maker, these would include outlays to build a new factory, buy automated manufacturing equipment, or acquire a small manufacturer of sports apparel.

Short-Term Expenses

Short-term expenses, often called *operating expenses,* are outlays used to support current selling and production activities. They typically result in current assets, which include cash and any other assets (accounts receivable and inventory) that can be converted to cash within a year. The financial manager's goal is to manage current assets so the firm has enough cash to pay its bills and to support its accounts receivable and inventory.

Cash Management: Assuring Liquidity Cash is the lifeblood of business. Without it, a firm could not operate. An important duty of the financial manager is **cash management,** or making sure that enough cash is on hand to pay bills as they are due and to meet unexpected expenses.

Businesses use budgets to estimate the cash requirements for a specific period. Many companies keep a minimum cash balance to cover unexpected expenses or changes in projected cash flows. The financial manager arranges loans to cover any shortfalls. If the size and timing of cash inflows closely match the size and timing of cash outflows, the company needs to keep only a small amount of cash on hand. A company whose sales and receipts are fairly predictable and regular throughout the year needs less cash than a company with a seasonal pattern of sales and receipts. A toy company, for instance, whose sales are concentrated in the fall, spends a great deal of cash during the spring and summer to build inventory. It has excess cash during the winter and early spring, when it collects on sales from its peak selling season.

Because cash held in current accounts earns little, if any, interest, the financial manager tries to keep cash balances low and to invest the surplus cash. Surpluses are invested temporarily in **marketable securities,** short-term investments that are easily converted into cash. The financial manager looks for low-risk investments that offer high returns. Three of the most popular marketable securities are Treasury bills, certificates of deposit, and commercial papers. (**Commercial paper** is unsecured short-term debt—an IOU—issued by a financially strong corporation.)

In addition to seeking the right balance between cash and marketable securities, the financial manager tries to shorten the time between the purchase of inventory or services (cash outflows) and the collection of cash from sales (cash inflows). The three key strategies are to collect money owed to the firm (accounts receivable) as quickly as possible, to pay money owed to others (accounts payable) as late as possible without damaging the firm's credit reputation, and to turn inventory quickly to minimize the funds tied up in it.

Managing Accounts Receivable **Accounts receivable** represent sales for which the firm has not yet been paid. Because the product has been sold but cash has not yet been received, an account receivable amounts to a use of funds. For the average manufacturing firm, accounts receivable represent about 15 to 20 percent of total assets.

The financial manager's goal is to collect money owed to the firm as quickly as possible while offering customers credit terms attractive enough to increase sales. Accounts receivable management involves setting *credit policies,* guidelines on offering credit, and *credit terms,* specific repayment conditions, including how long customers have to pay their bills and whether a cash discount is given for quicker payment. Another aspect of accounts receivable management is deciding on *collection policies,* the procedures for collecting overdue accounts.

---

cash management
The process of making sure that a firm has enough cash on hand to pay bills as they are due and to meet unexpected expenses.

marketable securities
Short-term investments that are easily converted into cash.

commercial paper
Unsecured short-term debt—an IOU—issued by a financially strong corporation.

accounts receivable
Sales for which a firm has not yet been paid.

Setting up credit and collection policies is a balancing act for financial managers. On the one hand, easier credit policies or generous credit terms (a longer repayment period or larger cash discount) result in increased sales. On the other, the firm has to finance more accounts receivable, and the risk of uncollectible accounts receivable rises. Businesses consider the impact on sales, timing of cash flow, experience with bad debt, customer profiles, and industry standards when developing their credit and collection policies.

Companies that want to speed up collections actively manage their accounts receivable, rather than passively letting customers pay when they want to. Companies that take this approach can collect from anyone.

Technology plays a big role in helping companies improve their credit and collections performance. When the tech sector fell on hard times, Cisco saw its global days sales outstanding (DSO) climb to a high of 47 days in January 2001. The company then developed Web-based reporting tools that improved overall cash management. Managers received frequently updated accounts receivable and cash collection reports, along with real-time collection and credit reports. The new system also flagged potential problems with customers. Within nine months of implementation, Cisco exceeded its goal of reducing DSO to 30 days, slashing that number to 24 days.[4]

Inventory One use of funds is to buy inventory needed by the firm. In a typical manufacturing firm, inventory is nearly 20 percent of total assets. The cost of inventory includes not only its purchase price but also ordering, handling, storage, interest, and insurance costs.

Production, marketing, and finance managers usually have differing views about inventory. Production managers want lots of raw materials on hand to avoid production delays. Marketing managers want lots of finished goods on hand, so that customer orders can be filled quickly, but financial managers want the least inventory possible without harming production efficiency or sales. Financial managers must work closely with production and marketing to balance these conflicting goals. Techniques for reducing the investment in inventory—inventory management, the just-in-time system, and materials requirement planning—were described in Chapter 11.

Long-Term Expenditures

capital expenditures

Investments in long-lived assets, such as land, buildings, machinery, and equipment, that are expected to provide benefits that extend beyond one year.

A firm also uses funds for its investments in long-lived assets, such items as land, buildings, machinery, equipment, and information systems. These are called **capital expenditures.** Unlike operating expenses, which produce benefits within a year, the benefits from capital expenditures extend beyond one year. For instance, a printer's purchase of a new printing press with a usable life of seven years is a capital expenditure. It appears as a fixed asset on the firm's balance sheet. Paper, ink, and other supplies, however, are expenses. Mergers and acquisitions, discussed in Chapter 5, are also considered capital expenditures.

Firms make capital expenditures for many reasons. The most common are to expand and to replace or renew fixed assets. Another reason is to develop new products. Most manufacturing firms have a big investment in long-term assets. Boeing Company, for instance, puts millions of dollars a year into airplane-manufacturing facilities.

capital budgeting

The process of analyzing long-term projects and selecting those that offer the best returns while maximizing the firm's value.

Because capital expenditures tend to be costly and have a major effect on the firm's future, the financial manager must analyze long-term projects and select those that offer the best returns while maximizing the firm's value. This process is called **capital budgeting.** Decisions involving new products or the acquisition of another business are especially important. Managers look at project costs and forecast the future benefits the project will bring—for example, from increased productivity, staff reductions, and other cost savings—to calculate the firm's estimated return on the investment.

For instance, consider the period during which Air Canada or WestJet Airlines is planning for new aircraft. Before going ahead, the company must consider not only its present aircraft and load factors (i.e., how many seats are typically full during any of its routes) but also the actual acquisition costs, maintenance costs, how to finance the aircraft (i.e., debt capital or equity capital), the amount that the aircraft will actually be flying (and therefore making revenue), and the anticipated payback period (i.e., how long will it take for the revenue the aircraft will generate to pay off the costs of the aircraft).

concept check

Distinguish between short- and long-term expenses.

What is the financial manager's goal in cash management? List the three key cash management strategies.

Describe the firm's main motives in making capital expenditures.

OBTAINING SHORT-TERM FINANCING

4 learning goal

How do firms raise the funding they need? They borrow money (debt), sell ownership shares (equity), and retain earnings (profits). The financial manager must assess all of these sources and choose the one most likely to help maximize the firm's value.

Like expenses, borrowed funds can be divided into short- and long-term loans. A short-term loan comes due within a year; a long-term loan has a maturity greater than one year. Short-term financing is shown as a current liability on the balance sheet and is used to finance current assets and support operations. Short-term loans can be unsecured or secured.

Unsecured Short-Term Loans

unsecured loans
Loans for which the borrower does not have to pledge specific assets as security.

Unsecured loans are made on the basis of the firm's creditworthiness and the lender's previous experience with the firm. An unsecured borrower does not have to pledge specific assets as security. The three main types of *unsecured short-term loans* are trade credit, bank loans, and commercial paper.

trade credit
The extension of credit by the seller to the buyer between the time the buyer receives the goods or services and when it pays for them.

Trade Credit: Accounts Payable When Goodyear sells tires to General Motors, GM does not have to pay cash on delivery. Instead, Goodyear regularly bills GM for its tire purchases, and GM pays at a later date. This is an example of **trade credit:** The seller extends credit to the buyer between the time the buyer receives the goods or services and when it pays for them. Trade credit is a major source of short-term business financing. The buyer enters the credit on its books as an **account payable.** In effect, the credit is a short-term loan from the seller to the buyer of the goods and services. Until GM pays Goodyear, Goodyear has an account receivable from GM, and GM has an account payable to Goodyear.

accounts payable
Purchase for which a buyer has not yet paid the seller.

Bank Loans Unsecured bank loans are another source of short-term business financing. Companies often use these loans to finance seasonal (cyclical) businesses. For instance, a swimwear manufacturer has strong sales in the spring and summer and lower sales during the fall and winter. It needs short-term bank financing to increase inventories before its strongest selling season and to finance accounts receivable during late winter and early spring, as shown in Exhibit 17.2. The company repays these bank loans when it sells the inventory and collects the receivables.

line of credit
An agreement between a bank and a business that specifies the maximum amount of short-term borrowing the bank will make available to the business or an individual.

Unsecured bank loans include lines of credit and revolving credit agreements (although in Canada most are secured). A **line of credit** is an agreement between a bank and a business or an individual. It specifies the maximum amount of short-term borrowing the bank will make available to the firm or the individual. This allows the borrower to obtain a number of loans without reapplying each time, as long as they do not exceed the prearranged amount.

Exhibit 17.2 | Swimwear Manufacturer's Seasonal Cash Flows

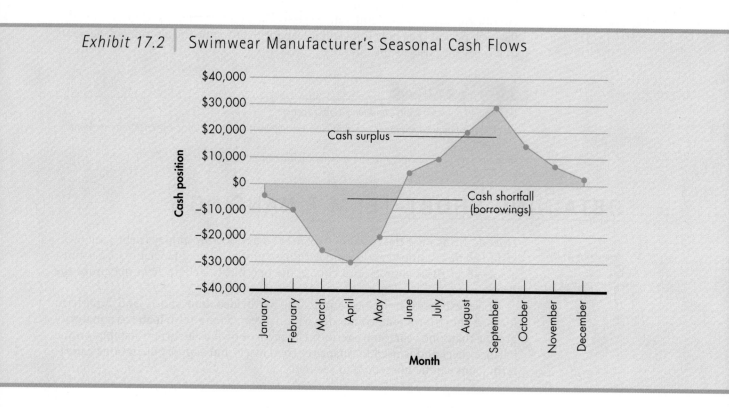

---

revolving credit agreement (or revolving line of credit)

A line of credit that allows the borrower to have access to funds again once it has been repaid.

Most lines of credit are a **revolving credit agreement (or revolving line of credit)**. A revolving credit agreement allows the borrower to continue to have access to funds as long as the maximum has not been exceeded. Therefore, the business or individual can pay off the line of credit and have access to the available funds again. Most credit cards offer revolving lines of credit.

Firms often obtain annual lines of credit based on their expected seasonal needs. Then they can quickly borrow without having to reapply to the bank each time funds are needed. Suppose the swimwear manufacturer projected a cash shortfall of $80,000 for the period from February to June. The financial manager might get a $100,000 line of credit from the bank. (The extra $20,000 would be there to cover any unexpected outlays.) The firm could borrow funds as needed—$10,000 in February, $25,000 in March, $30,000 in April. Then it could gradually repay the loan as it collects cash during the summer months.

Commercial Paper As noted earlier, *commercial paper* is an unsecured short-term debt—an IOU—issued by a financially strong corporation. Thus, it is a short-term investment for firms with temporary cash surpluses, and it is a financing option for major corporations. Corporations issue commercial paper in multiples of $100,000 for periods ranging from 3 to 270 days. Many big companies use commercial paper instead of short-term bank loans because the interest rate on commercial paper is usually 1 to 3 percent below bank rates.

Secured Short-Term Loans

secured loans
Loans for which the borrower is required to pledge specific assets as *collateral*, or security.

Secured loans require the borrower to pledge specific assets as *collateral*, or security. The secured lender can legally take the collateral if the borrower doesn't repay the loan. Chartered banks and commercial finance companies are the main sources of secured short-term loans to business. Borrowers whose credit is not strong enough to qualify for unsecured loans use these loans.

Typically, the collateral for secured short-term loans is accounts receivable or inventory. Because accounts receivable are normally quite liquid (easily converted to cash), they are an attractive form of collateral. The appeal of inventory—raw materials or finished goods—as collateral depends on how easily it can be sold at a fair price.

factoring
A form of short-term financing in which a firm sells its accounts receivable outright at a discount to a *factor*.

Another form of short-term financing using accounts receivable is **factoring.** In this case, a firm sells its accounts receivable outright to a *factor*, a financial institution (usually a chartered bank or commercial finance company) that buys accounts receivable at a discount. Factoring is widely used in the clothing, furniture, sporting goods, and appliance industries. Factoring allows a firm to turn its accounts receivable into cash without worrying about collections. Because the factor assumes all the risks and expenses of collecting the accounts, firms that factor all of their accounts can reduce the costs of their credit and collection operations. Factoring is more expensive than a bank loan, however, because the factor buys the receivables at a discount from their actual value. Often a company has no choice, however, because it has neither the track record to get unsecured financing nor other collateral to pledge as security for a loan.

HOT Links

When working capital is a problem, one option is factoring. Learn more about factoring by searching Export Development Canada's Web site at http://www.edc.ca.

concept check

Distinguish between unsecured and secured short-term loans.

Briefly describe the three main types of unsecured short-term loans.

Discuss the two ways in which accounts receivable can be used to obtain short-term financing.

RAISING LONG-TERM FINANCING

5 *learning goal*

A basic principle of finance is to match the term of the financing to the period over which benefits are expected to be received from the associated outlay. Short-term items should be financed with short-term funds, and long-term items should be financed with long-term funds. Long-term financing sources include both debt (borrowing) and equity (ownership). Equity financing comes either from selling new ownership interests or from retaining earnings.

Debt versus Equity Financing

Say that the Bombardier plans to spend $2 billion over the next four years to build and equip new factories to make regional jets. The company's top management will assess the pros and cons of both debt and equity and then consider several possible sources of the desired form of long-term financing.

financial risk
The chance that a firm will be unable to make scheduled interest and principal payments on its debt.

The major advantage of debt financing is the deductibility of interest expense for income tax purposes, which lowers its overall cost. In addition, there is no loss of ownership. The major drawback is **financial risk:** the chance that the firm will be unable to make scheduled interest and principal payments. The lender can force a borrower that fails to make scheduled debt payments into bankruptcy. Most loan agreements have restrictions to ensure that the borrower operates efficiently.

Equity, on the other hand, is a form of permanent financing that places few restrictions on the firm. The firm is not required to pay dividends or repay the investment. However, equity financing gives common shareholders voting rights that provide them with a voice in management. Equity is more costly than debt. Unlike the interest on debt, dividends to owners are not tax-deductible expenses. Exhibit 17.3 summarizes the major differences between debt and equity financing.

Exhibit 17.3 | Major Differences between Debt and Equity Financing

	Debt Financing	**Equity Financing**
Voice in management	Creditors typically have none, unless borrower defaults on payments. Creditors may be able to place restraints on management in event of default.	Common shareholders have voting rights.
Claim on income and assets	Debt holders rank ahead of equity holders. Payment of interest and principal is a contractual obligation of the firm.	Equity owners have a residual claim on income (dividends are paid only after interest and any scheduled principal payments are paid) and assets. The firm has no obligation to pay dividends.
Maturity	Debt has a stated maturity and requires repayment of principal by a specified maturity date.	The company is not required to repay equity, which has no maturity date.
Tax treatment	Interest is a tax-deductible expense.	Dividends are not tax-deductible and are paid from after-tax income.

Financial managers try to select the mix of long-term debt and equity that results in the best balance between cost and risk. If a company's debt load gets too high, in the view of investors and securities analysts, the costs of borrowing will rise. Company policies about the mix of debt and equity vary. Some companies have high debt compared to equity. Debt as a percentage of equity is 177 percent at International Paper, a capital-intensive manufacturer. Others keep debt to a minimum. The long-term debt-to-equity ratio for Nike is about 19 percent; Oracle, 6 percent; and Starbucks and Microsoft, 0 percent.

The media giant created when AOL and Time Warner joined forces started its life with a legacy of debt. About two-thirds of the total debt in early 2003—about $20 billion of $27 billion—came along with Time Warner at the time of the January 2001 merger. Much of that debt resulted from the 1990 merger between Time Inc. and Warner Communications. Chief executive officer Dick Parsons acknowledged the dangers of such high debt levels. "While our balance sheet remains strong, we have a lot of debt," he said. His immediate goal was to reduce debt by $2 billion by year-end 2003 and to $20 billion by 2005. Because AOL Time Warner's debt load is high for a company with a low cash position and net loss at year-end 2002, the company will have problems accessing the debt markets. If it finds willing lenders, it will have to pay higher interest rates to compensate for the additional risk lenders take.[5]

concept check

Discuss the major differences between debt and equity financing.
What is financial risk?

Long-Term Debt Financing

6 learning goal

Long-term debt is used to finance long-term (capital) expenditures. The initial maturities of long-term debt typically range between 5 and 20 years. Three important forms of long-term debt are term loans, bonds, and mortgage loans.

A **term loan** is a business loan with an initial maturity of more than one year. Term loans generally have 5- to 12-year maturities and can be unsecured or secured. They are available from chartered banks, insurance companies, pension funds, commercial finance companies, and manufacturers' financing subsidiaries. A contract between the borrower and the lender spells out the amount and maturity of the loan, the interest rate, payment dates, the purpose of the loan, and other provisions, such as operating and financial restrictions on the borrower to control the risk of default. Term loans may be repaid on a quarterly, semiannual, or annual schedule. The payments include both interest and principal, so the loan balance declines over time. Borrowers try to arrange a repayment schedule that matches the forecast cash flow from the project being financed.

Bonds are long-term debt obligations (liabilities) issued by corporations and governments. Like term loans, corporate bonds are issued with formal contracts that set forth the obligations of the issuing corporation and the rights of the bondholders. Most bonds are issued in multiples of $1,000 (par value) with initial maturities of 10 to 30 years. The stated interest rate, or *coupon rate*, is the percentage of the bond's par value that the issuer will pay each year as interest.

A **mortgage loan** is a long-term loan made against real estate as collateral. The lender takes a mortgage on the property, which lets the lender seize the property, sell it, and use the proceeds to pay off the loan if the borrower fails to make the scheduled payments. Long-term mortgage loans are often used to finance office buildings, factories, and warehouses. Life insurance companies are an important source of these loans. They make billions of dollars' worth of mortgage loans to businesses each year.

term loan
A business loan with an initial maturity of more than one year; can be unsecured or secured.

bonds
Long-term debt obligations (liabilities) issued by corporations and governments.

mortgage loan
A long-term loan made against real estate as collateral.

concept check

What is a long-term loan used for?

What is a term loan? A bond? A mortgage loan?

Equity Financing

7 learning goal

Equity is the owners' investment in the business. In corporations, the preferred and common shareholders are the owners. A firm obtains equity financing by selling new ownership shares (external financing), by retaining earnings (internal financing), or, for small and growing, typically high-tech companies, through venture capital (external financing).

Selling New Issues of Common Shares **Common shares** are securities that represent an ownership interest in a corporation. In March 2006, Tim Hortons offered 29 million shares of common shares at the initial price of $27 and began trading on the Toronto Stock Exchange and the New York Stock Exchange.

Tim Hortons's offering is an example of a company *going public*—its first sale of shares to the public. Usually, a high-growth company has an *initial public offering* (IPO), because it needs to raise funds to finance continuing growth. (Companies that are already public can issue and sell additional common shares to raise equity funds.) An IPO often enables existing shareholders, usually employees, family, and friends who bought the shares privately, to earn big profits on their investment.

But going public has some drawbacks. For one thing, there is no guarantee an IPO will sell. It is also expensive. Big fees must be paid to investment bankers, brokers, attorneys, accountants, and printers. And once the company is public, it is

common shares
A security that represents an ownership interest in a corporation.

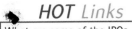

HOT Links

What are some of the IPOs available today? Check out the premium investor resource centre at http://ipo.investcom.com.

watched closely by regulators, shareholders, and securities analysts. The firm must reveal information such as operating and financial data, product details, financing plans, and operating strategies. Providing this information is often costly.

Going public can be successful when a company is well established and market conditions are right. Strong equity markets in the late 1990s and into 2000 prompted many companies, especially very young Internet-related companies, to go public. Frequently companies that were only a year or two old rushed to go public to take advantage of market conditions. Their prices popped up to what many believed were unrealistic levels. When the dot-com bubble burst and capital markets dried up, far fewer companies were willing to brave the IPO waters. Instead they turned to other financing sources to tide them over until the market for new issues picked up.

Dividends and Retained Earnings **Dividends** are payments to shareholders from a corporation's profits. A company does not have to pay dividends to shareholders, but if investors buy the shares expecting to get dividends and the firm does not pay them, the investors might sell their shares. If too many sell, the value of the shares decreases. Dividends can be paid in cash or in shares. **Share dividends** are payments in the form of more shares. Share dividends may replace or supplement cash dividends. After a share dividend has been paid, more shares have a claim on the same company, so the value of each share often declines.

At their quarterly meetings, the company's board of directors (with the advice of its financial managers) decides how much of the profits to distribute as dividends and how much to reinvest. A business's basic approach to paying dividends can greatly affect its share price. A stable history of dividend payments indicates good financial health. If a firm that has been making regular dividend payments cuts or skips a dividend, investors start thinking it has serious financial problems. The increased uncertainty often results in lower share prices. Thus, most firms set dividends at a level they can keep paying. They start with a relatively low dividend payout ratio, so that they can maintain a steady or slightly increasing dividend over time.

Retained earnings, profits that have been reinvested in the firm, have a big advantage over other sources of equity capital: They do not incur underwriting costs. Financial managers strive to balance dividends and retained earnings to maximize the value of the firm. Often the balance reflects the nature of the firm and its industry. Well-established and stable firms and those that expect only modest growth, such as public utilities, financial services companies, and large industrial corporations, typically pay out much of their earnings in dividends.

Most high-growth companies, like those in technology-related fields, finance much of their growth through retained earnings and pay little or no dividends to shareholders. However, in January 2003, Microsoft and Qualcomm, two technology companies, began paying dividends.

In the case of Microsoft, its business throws off a huge amount of cash—about $1 billion a month—and its cash account had grown to more than $43 billion by 2003. However, it was not finding suitable growth companies and business lines to acquire. The announcement also reflected Microsoft's coming of age in its company life cycle, as it joined notable dividend-paying tech firms such as IBM, Hewlett-Packard, and Intel.[6] Qualcomm, on the other hand, had been using retained earnings to build up market share for its patented wireless technology (CDMA). As its CDMA standard gained acceptance, licensing payments boosted its cash reserves to $3.7 billion. "The company can return some of its cash to shareholders without impacting future revenue and earnings growth or restricting strategic opportunities," said chairman and chief executive Irwin Jacobs.[7]

dividends

Payments to shareholders from a corporation's profits.

share or stock dividends

Payments to shareholders in the form of more shares; can replace or supplement cash dividends.

retained earnings

Profits that have been reinvested in a firm.

Making Ethical Choices

THE FRIENDS AND FAMILY IPO PLAN

As a financial analyst at an up-and-coming high-technology firm, you are involved in your most exciting project to date: helping to prepare pro forma financial statements (pro forma is a projection or estimate of what will happen in the future based on what is happening now) for the prospectus for the firm's initial public offering.

During your visits to various departments, you hear rumours about promises of IPO shares for favoured customers and suppliers. Researching if this is legal, you learn your company can give up to 5 percent of its offering to anyone it chooses. Because this price is not offered to the general public, inviting these "friends and family" to buy shares at the IPO price presents an attractive opportunity. At the height of the bull market, IPO share prices were jumping an average of 65 percent on the first day. Even though times are more normal now, the growth prospects make these shares a good buy. "Companies are continuing to be approached for shares by analysts and others who wield influence," says David Helfrich, a venture capitalist.

However, some legal experts believe that allocating IPO share to customers and vendors borders on bribery and creates conflicts of interest. Those receiving shares could feel pressured to send business to your firm. Yet such practices are common; other businesses in your industry use shares to gain a competitive advantage (perhaps as a way of saying "thank you" or of obtaining obligations from people who they want to help them in the future).

If your company is giving out only small allocations of shares, such as 100 to 200 shares, and the offering price is $18 to $20, the profit from flipping the shares on the first days is negligible and the potential for conflicts of interest reduced. If the invitation is for larger amounts, at what point does it become a problem?

ETHICAL DILEMMA

Should you bring this situation to your superiors' attention and urge them to develop a corporate policy that covers offers to sell shares at special prices?

SOURCES: Linda Himelstein, "CEOs to Eliot Spitzer: 'Give It Back? No Way!'" *Business Week*, June 9, 2003, 113; and Linda Himelstein and Ben Elgin, "High Tech's Kickback Culture," *Business Week*, February 10, 2003, 74–77.

---

preferred shares
Equity securities for which the dividend amount is set at the time the shares are issued.

Preferred Shares Another form of equity is **preferred shares.** Unlike common shares, preferred shares usually have a dividend amount that is set at the time the shares are issued. These dividends must be paid before the company can pay any dividends to common shareholders. Furthermore, if the firm goes bankrupt and sells its assets, preferred shareholders get their money back before common shareholders do. Preferred shares are described in greater detail in Chapter 18.

Like debt, preferred shares increase the firm's financial risk because it obligates the firm to make a fixed payment, but preferred shares are more flexible. The firm can miss a dividend payment without suffering the serious results of failing to pay back a debt.

Preferred shares are more expensive than debt financing, however, because preferred dividends are not tax-deductible. Furthermore, because the claims of preferred shareholders on income and assets are second to those of debt holders, preferred shareholders require higher returns to compensate for the greater risk.

HOT Links

Which companies are getting funding from venture capital firms? For this and other information, visit vFinance.com at http://www.vfinance.com.

HOT Links

Find out about the Canada's Venture Capital & Private Equity Association at http://www.cvca.ca.

Venture Capital As we learned in Chapter 6, *venture capital* is another source of equity capital. It is most often used by small and growing firms that aren't big enough to sell securities to the public. This type of financing is especially popular among high-tech companies that need large sums of money.

Venture capitalists invest in new businesses in return for part of the ownership, sometimes as much as 60 percent. They look for new businesses with high growth potential, and they expect a high investment return within 5 to 10 years. By getting in on the ground floor, venture capitalists buy shares at a very low price. They earn profits by selling the shares at a much higher price when the company goes public. Venture capitalists generally get a voice in management through a seat on the board of directors.

Getting venture capital is difficult, even though there are many private venture capital firms in this country. Most venture capitalists finance only about 1 to 5 percent of the companies that apply. Venture capital investors, many of whom experienced losses from their investments in failed dot-coms, are less willing nowadays to take risks on very early-stage companies with unproven technology. They are looking for companies with high growth potential that are already on a demonstrated track to profitability.

As a result, other sources of venture capital, including private foundations, governments, and wealthy individuals (called *angel investors*), are helping start-up firms find equity capital. These private investors are motivated by the potential for earning a high return on their investment. Accountants, attorneys, business associates, financial consultants, bankers, and others can help the small firm find an angel.

concept check

Define each of the following:

- *Common shares*
- *Dividends*
- *Share or stock dividends*
- *Retained earnings*
- *Preferred shares*
- *Venture capital*

MANAGING RISK AND INSURANCE

8 learning goal

Every day, businesses and individuals are exposed to many different kinds of risk. Investors who buy shares or speculate in commodities can earn a profit, but they also take the risk of losing all or part of their money. Illness is another type of risk, involving financial loss from not only the cost of medical care but also the loss of income.

Businesses, too, are exposed to many types of risk. Market risks, such as lower demand for a product or worsening economic conditions, can hurt a firm. Other risks involve customers, who could be injured on a company's premises or by a company's product. Like homes and cars owned by individuals, business property can be damaged or lost through fire, floods, and theft. Businesses must also protect themselves against losses from theft by dishonest employees. The loss of a key employee is another risk, especially for small firms.

It is impossible to avoid all risks, but individuals and businesses can minimize risks or buy protection—called insurance—against them. Although some risks are uninsurable, many others are insurable. Let's now look at basic risk concepts and the types of insurance available to cover them.

Risk Management

Every business faces risks like the ones previously listed. **Risk management** involves analyzing the firm's operations, evaluating the potential risks, and figuring out how to minimize losses in a cost-efficient manner. In today's complex business environment, the concern for public and employee welfare and the potential for lawsuits have both increased. Risk management thus plays a vital role in the overall management of a business.

Types of Risk Individuals and firms need to protect themselves against the economic effects of certain types of risk. In an insurance sense, risk (sometimes called *pure risk*) is the chance of financial loss due to a **peril** (a hazard or a source of danger). Insurable risks include fire, theft, auto accident, injury or illness, a lawsuit, or death. **Speculative risk** is the chance of either loss or gain. Someone who buys shares in the hope of later selling it at a profit is taking a speculative risk and cannot be insured against it.

Strategies to Manage Risk Risk is part of life. Nevertheless, people have four major ways of dealing with it.

- *Risk avoidance.* This means staying away from situations that can lead to loss. A person can avoid the risk of a serious injury by choosing not to go sky-diving. A daycare centre could avoid risk by not transporting children to and from the facility or taking them on field trips. Manufacturers who wish to avoid risks could produce only goods that have a proven track record, but these risk-avoidance strategies could stifle growth in the long run. Thus, risk avoidance is not good for all risks.

- *Self-insurance.* This is the willingness to bear a risk without insurance, also called *risk assumption*. This offers a more practical way of handling many types of risks. Many large firms with warehouses or stores spread out over Canada might choose not to insure them. They assume that even if disaster strikes one location, the others won't be harmed. The losses will probably be less than the insurance premiums for all of the locations. Many companies self-insure, because it is cheaper to assume some risks than to insure against them. Some choose to pay small claims and insure only for catastrophic losses. Others "go naked," paying for all claims from company funds. This is clearly the most risky strategy. A big claim could cripple the firm or lead to bankruptcy.

- *Risk reduction.* This is done by adopting techniques to prevent financial losses. For example, companies adopt safety measures to reduce accidents. Construction workers are required to wear hard hats and safety glasses. Airlines keep their aircraft in good condition and require thorough training programs for pilots and flight attendants. Hotels install smoke alarms, sprinkler systems, and firewalls to protect guests and minimize fire damage.

- *Risk transference.* This means paying someone else to bear some or all of the risk of financial loss for certain risks that can't be avoided, assumed, or reduced to acceptable levels. The way to transfer risk is through **insurance.** Individuals and organizations can pay a fee (a *premium*) and get the promise of compensation for certain financial losses. The companies that take on the risks are called *insurance companies*.

concept check

What is risk management?

What are the types of risk?

What are some strategies for managing risk?

risk management
The process of identifying and evaluating risks and selecting and managing techniques to adapt to risk exposures.

peril
A hazard or a source of danger.

speculative risk
The chance of either loss or gain, without insurance against the possible loss.

HOT *Links*

Learn about how Reuters Risk Management Services, at http://risk.reuters.com, helps companies with global operations identify, measure, and manage financial risk.

insurance
The promise of compensation for certain financial losses.

Insurance Concepts

insurance policy
A written agreement that defines what the insurance covers and the risks that the insurance company will bear for the insured party.

underwriting
A review process of all insurance applications and the selection of those who meet the standards.

insurable interest
An insurance applicant's chance of loss if a particular peril occurs.

insurable risk
A risk that an insurance company will cover. It must meet certain criteria.

law of large numbers
Insurance companies' predictions of the likelihood that a peril will occur; used to calculate premiums.

Companies purchase insurance to cover insurable risks. An **insurance policy** is the written agreement that defines what the insurance covers and the risks that the insurance company will bear for the insured party. It also outlines the policy's benefits (the maximum amount that it will pay in the event of a loss) and the premium (the cost to the insured for coverage). Any demand for payment for losses covered by the policy is a *claim*.

Before issuing a policy, an insurance company reviews the applications of those who want a policy and selects those that meet its standards. This **underwriting** process also determines the level of coverage and the premiums. Each company sets its own underwriting standards based on its experience. For instance, a life insurance company might decide not to accept an applicant who has had a heart attack within the previous five years (or to charge a 50 to 75 percent higher premium). A property insurer might refuse to issue a policy on homes near brush-filled canyons, which present above-average fire hazards.

To get insurance, the applicant must have an **insurable interest:** the chance of suffering a loss if a particular peril occurs. In most cases, a person cannot insure the life of a friend, because the friend's death would not be considered a financial loss. But business partners can get life insurance on each other's lives, because the death of one of them would have a financial impact on their firm.

Insurable Risks Insurance companies are professional risk takers, but they won't provide coverage against all types of risk. Some risks are insurable; some are not. For instance, changes in political or economic conditions are not insurable. An **insurable risk** is one that an insurance company will cover. For a risk to be insurable, it must meet these criteria.

- *The loss must not be under the control of the insured.* The loss must be accidental—that is, unexpected and occurring by chance. Insurance companies do not cover losses purposely caused by the insured party. No insurance company will pay for the loss of a clothing store that the insured set on fire, nor will most companies pay life insurance benefits for a suicide.

- *There must be many similar exposures to that peril.* Insurance companies study the rates of deaths, auto accidents, fires, floods, and many other perils. They know about how many of these perils will occur each year. The **law of large numbers** lets them predict the likelihood that the peril will occur and then calculate premiums.

Suppose that an insurance company has 150 policies in a city. The company knows from past experience that these policyholders are likely to have a total of 12 car accidents a year and that the average payment for a claim in this city has been $1,000. The total claims for one year's car accidents in the city would be $12,000 (12 accidents × $1,000). Thus the company would charge each policyholder a premium of at least $80 ($12,000 ÷ 150). Profits and administrative expenses would make the premium somewhat higher.

- *Losses must be financially measurable.* The dollar amount of potential losses must be known, so that the insurance company can figure the premiums. Life insurance is for a fixed amount specified at the time the policy is bought. Otherwise, the company and the beneficiary (the one who gets the funds) would have to agree on the value of the deceased's life at the time of death. Premiums have to be calculated before then, however.

- *The peril must not be likely to affect all the insured parties at the same time.* Insurance companies must spread out their risks by insuring many people and businesses in many locations. This strategy helps minimize the chance that a single calamity will wipe out the insurance company.

deductibles
The amounts that the
insured must pay before
insurance benefits begin.

- *The potential loss must be significant.* Insurance companies cannot afford to insure trivial things for small amounts. Many policies have **deductibles,** amounts that the insured must pay before insurance benefits begin.
- *The company must have the right to set standards for insurance coverage.* Insurance companies can refuse to cover people with health problems such as AIDS, cancer, or heart trouble, a poor driving record, or a dangerous job or hobby. They can also charge higher premiums because of the higher risks they are covering.

Premium Costs Insurance policies must be economical—relatively low in cost compared to the benefits—so that people will want to buy them. Yet the premiums must also cover the risks that the insurance company faces. Insurance companies collect statistics on many perils. Then specially trained mathematicians called *actuaries* use the law of large numbers to develop actuarial tables, which show how likely each peril is. Actuarial tables are the basis for calculating premiums. For example, actuaries use a mortality table showing average life expectancy and the expected number of deaths per 1,000 people at given ages to set life insurance premiums.

Almost every homeowner buys insurance to cover the perils of fire, theft, vandalism, and other home-related risks. With such a large pool of policyholders, homeowners' policies are usually inexpensive. Annual premiums are about 0.5 percent (or less) of the value of the home. This low cost encourages people to buy policies and thereby helps spread the insurance companies' risk over many homes throughout the country.

When setting premiums, insurers also look at the risk characteristics of certain groups to assess the probability of loss for those groups. For instance, smokers tend to die younger than non-smokers do and thus pay higher life insurance premiums. Female drivers under the age of 25 have a lower rate of accidents than male drivers, so their car insurance premiums are lower.

Insurance Providers Insurers can be either public or private. Public insurance coverage is offered by specialized government agencies (e.g., provincial health care plans and employment insurance). Private insurance coverage is provided by privately organized (nongovernment) companies.

Public Insurance Government-sponsored insurance can be regulated by either the provinces or the federal government. These are some of the main programs.

employment
insurance
Payment of benefits to laid-
off workers while they seek
new jobs.

- *Employment Insurance (EI).* The **employment insurance** program pays laid-off workers weekly benefits while they seek new jobs. Persons who terminate their employment voluntarily or are fired for cause are generally not eligible for employment insurance. These programs also provide job counselling, education opportunities, and placement services. The size of the weekly benefit depends on the workers' previous income. Employment insurance is funded by the employees and through contributions by the employers.

workers'
compensation
Payments to cover the
expenses of job-related
injuries and diseases,
including medical costs,
rehabilitation, and job
retraining if necessary.

- *Workers' compensation.* The provinces and territories have laws requiring employers in many industries to fund **workers' compensation** insurance to cover the expenses of job-related injuries and diseases, including medical costs, rehabilitation, and job retraining if necessary. It also provides disability income benefits (salary and wage payments) for workers who can't perform their job. Employers can buy workers' compensation policies or self-insure. A company's premium is based on the amount of its payroll and the types of risks present in the workplace. For instance, a construction company would pay a higher premium for workers' compensation insurance than would a jewellery store.

Canada Pension Plan
Insurance that provides
retirement, disability, death,
and health benefits.

- *Canada Pension Plan (CPP).* The **Canada Pension Plan** provides retirement, disability, survivor benefits, and death benefits. CPP is funded by equal contributions from workers and employers. Canadians that have paid into the plan can collect as early as age 60. The province of Quebec administers its own pension plan.

- *Provincial health care.* Health care is provided to all Canadians through their respective **provincial health care** programs. In some provinces the premiums are not collected separately but are included in other taxes, and in others there are direct payments to the provincial health care insurance program.

Private Insurance Companies Private insurance companies sell property and liability insurance, health insurance, and life insurance. Generally they can be either not-for-profit (e.g., Blue Cross) or shareholder insurance companies (e.g., Manulife Financial).

For example, all eligible residents in every province and territory can obtain Blue Cross coverage through their provincial/territorial independent member plan. Blue Cross provides products such as health care, dental care, life insurance, and disability income.

Just like other publicly owned corporations, *shareholder insurance companies* are profit-oriented companies owned by shareholders. The shareholders do not have to be policyholders, and the policyholders do not have to be shareholders. Their profits come from insurance premiums in excess of claim payments and operating expenses and from investments in securities and real estate.

Types of Insurance

Most companies offer group health and life insurance plans for their employees as a fringe benefit. Employers typically pay some of the health insurance premiums, and employees pay the rest. The cost is usually considerably less than for individual policies, although it pays to check before signing up. For example, companies might pay for the entire cost of life insurance equal to one or two times the employee's annual salary, with an option to purchase more under the group plan, but the premiums might be more expensive than buying an individual policy.

key person life insurance

A term insurance policy that names the company as beneficiary.

Businesses often insure the lives of key employees, such as top executives, salespeople, inventors, and researchers, whose death could seriously limit the income or value of a firm. To protect themselves, businesses buy **key person life insurance,** a life insurance policy that names the company as beneficiary. In the case of a partnership, which is dissolved when a partner dies, key person insurance is often bought for each partner, with the other partner named as the beneficiary, so that the surviving partner can buy the partnership interest from the estate of the deceased and continue operating.

Property and Liability Insurance Property and liability insurance is important for businesses that wish to protect against losses of property and lawsuits arising from harm to other people. *Property insurance* covers financial losses from damage to or destruction of the insured's assets as a result of specified perils, whereas *liability insurance* covers financial losses from injuries to others and damage to or destruction of others' property when the insured is considered to be the cause. It also covers the insured's legal defence fees up to the maximum amount stated in the policy. Automobile liability insurance is an example. It would pay for a fence damaged when the insured person lost control of his or her car. Commercial and product liability insurance also fall into this category.

Commercial liability insurance covers a variety of damage claims, including harm to the environment from pollution. In the case of *product liability,* if a defective furnace exploded and damaged a home, the manufacturer would be liable for the damages. If the manufacturer were insured, the insurance company would cover the losses or pay to dispute the claim in court.

Property and liability insurance is a broad category. Businesses buy many types of property and liability insurance. These protect against loss of property due to fire, theft, accidents, or employee dishonesty, and financial losses arising from liability cases. Landlords and owners of business property buy *building insurance,* a type of property coverage, for protection against both property damage and liability losses. For instance, if a person broke an arm slipping on a wet floor in a hardware store, the business's insurance policy would cover any claim.

Insurance policies usually include a coinsurance clause. **Coinsurance** requires the insured to pay a certain percentage of the claim. For example, if your dentist charges $1,400 for a crown, your insurance company might cover only 80 percent of the charges, leaving you as the insured to cover the remaining 20 percent.

Special Types of Business Liability Insurance Businesses also purchase several other types of insurance policies, depending on their particular needs.

- *Business interruption insurance.* This optional coverage is often offered with fire insurance. It protects business owners from losses occurring when the business must be closed temporarily after property damage. **Business interruption insurance** might cover costs such as rental of temporary facilities, wage and salary payments to employees, payments for leased equipment, fixed payments (for instance, rent and loans), and profits that would have been earned during the period. *Contingent business interruption insurance* covers losses to the insured in the event of property damage to a major supplier or customer.

- *Theft insurance.* Businesses also want to protect their property against financial losses due to crime. **Theft insurance** is the broadest coverage and protects businesses against losses from an act of stealing. Businesses can also buy more limited types of theft insurance.

- *Fidelity and surety bonds.* What if a firm has a dishonest employee? This situation is covered by a *fidelity bond*, an agreement that insures a company against theft committed by an employee who handles company money. If a restaurant manager is bonded for $50,000 and steals $60,000, the restaurant will recover all but $10,000 of the loss. Banks, loan companies, and retail businesses that employ cashiers typically buy fidelity bonds.

  A *surety bond,* also called a *performance bond,* is an agreement to reimburse a firm for non-performance of acts specified in a contract. This form of insurance is most common in the construction industry. Contractors buy surety bonds to cover themselves in case the project they are working on is not completed by the specified date or does not meet specified standards. In practice, the insurance company often pays another contractor to finish the job or to redo shoddy work when the bonded contractor fails to perform.

- *Title insurance.* A title policy protects the buyer of real estate against losses caused by a defect in the title—that is, a claim against the property that prevents the transfer of ownership from seller to purchaser. It eliminates the need to search legal records to be sure that the seller was actually the owner of (had clear title to) the property.

- *Professional liability insurance.* This form of insurance covers financial losses (legal fees and court-awarded damages up to specific limits) resulting from alleged malpractice by professionals in fields like medicine, law, architecture, and dentistry. *Directors and officers insurance* is a type of **professional liability insurance** designed to protect top corporate management, who have also been the target of malpractice lawsuits. It pays for legal fees and court-awarded damages up to specific limits.

coinsurance
Insurance coverage that requires the insured to pay a portion of the claim.

business interruption insurance
Covers costs such as rental of temporary facilities, wage and salary payments to employees, payments for leased equipment, fixed payments, and profits that would have been earned during that period.

theft insurance
A broad insurance coverage that protects businesses against losses for an act of stealing.

professional liability insurance
Insurance designed to protect top corporate management, who have been the target of malpractice lawsuits.

concept check

What is an insurance policy? Underwriting? Insurable interest?

What are premiums and deductibles?

What types of insurance policies are available? What is the purpose of each?

10 *learning goal*   Many of the key trends shaping the practice of financial management echo those in other disciplines. For example, technology is improving the efficiency with which financial managers run their operations. The "Customer Satisfaction and Quality" box, on page 556, describes how Dell Computer uses technology to improve its cash forecasts. The continued expansion of the financial manager's role in risk management is a natural outgrowth of the new regulations in the United States, as Canadian companies that trade on the United States exchanges must adhere not only to Canadian law but also American standards (e.g., the Sarbanes-Oxley Act).

THE CHANGING ROLE OF THE CFO

Enron's Andy Fastow, Tyco's Mark Swartz, and WorldCom's Scott Sullivan focused the spotlight on CFOs—for the wrong reasons. Their misdeeds changed the public's perception of CFOs for the worse. Other holders of this title now find themselves on the defence, assuring board members, shareholders, and others that most CFOs are honest and operate with the highest standards of integrity. As Ed Moneypenny, 7-Eleven's CFO, says, "I've never had anyone put pressure on me to fudge the numbers."

During the 1990s, CFOs expanded their jobs beyond the ordinary finance responsibilities. No longer just numbers people, they joined top management in developing and implementing the firm's strategic direction. Negotiating billion-dollar mergers and finding creative financing vehicles were all part of the day's work. They were the company's face to the Bay Street analysts, who watched to see if the company would meet each quarter's earnings estimates.

CFOs now must take the central role in re-establishing public trust, moving quickly to assure stakeholders that their company's transactions and reporting are honest. "My job is still to say, 'No, no, no!' whenever something doesn't make sense financially," says Home Depot CFO Carol Tomé. At the same time, the CFO should provide insight on the affairs of the company and its businesses to the CEO and the board.

"Every single aspect of my job is more difficult today than it was a year ago," says Dan Berce, CFO of a finance company. Investor relations now takes up 25 to 50 percent of his time, compared to almost none five years ago. He meets with investors, analysts, and mutual fund managers to review his company's business and financial statements. For example, he explains changes in accounting procedures to allay investor fears of possible impropriety.

In addition to all their additional responsibilities, however, CFOs are gaining a higher profile with their companies' boards. The increased status might mean higher compensation, as well as greater opportunities to move into a top executive job.[8]

WEIGHING THE RISKS AFTER SEPTEMBER 11, 2001

The job of managing a company's risk became even more difficult after the September 11, 2001 terrorist attacks in the United States. No one had ever imagined an event of this magnitude, one that would bring business operations at New York companies to a halt and would also have such an enormous effect on the rest of the world. The ripple effect reached firms in all industries. Yet how do you prepare for these events? Adding to the challenge was the volatility of the economy and financial markets both at home and abroad.

How can a company anticipate catastrophic events like September 11, 2001, and minimize the devastating impact on business? Many companies have created a new position, chief risk officer, to study risk potential and coordinate risk management procedures throughout the company.

Companies face a wide range of risks, including

- *credit risk*—exposure to loss as a result of default on a financial transaction or a reduction in a security's market value due to decline in the credit quality of the debt issuer;

- *market risk*—risk resulting from adverse movements in the level or volatility of market prices of securities, commodities, and currencies; and

- *operational risk*—the risk of unexpected losses arising from deficiencies in a firm's management information, support, and control systems and procedures.

Ford Motor Company implemented new procedures and systems to consolidate the company-wide risk exposure of its many subsidiaries. It started with a Web-based tool to calculate credit exposure at different levels. Next came evaluation of exposure limits and monitoring and reporting policies to identify problems and minimize risk. With the system fully operational, Ford can see its total credit risk exposure. This allows managers to forestall potential problems and be more proactive in managing risks.[9]

Because a failure in a company's risk control procedures can lead to substantial financial losses, financial managers continue to be key players in risk management, the process of identifying and evaluating risks and selecting and managing techniques to adapt to risk exposures. Many companies have created a new position, chief risk officer (CRO), to coordinate risk management procedures throughout the company. Companies are also using risk management in response to new corporate governance guidelines. Better risk management procedures are important to shareholders in the post-Enron era. They want to know that companies have taken steps to minimize risks that would affect the company's values.[10]

concept check

How has the role of CFO changed since the passage of the Sarbanes-Oxley Act?

Why are improved risk management procedures important to shareholders?

Great Ideas to Use Now

Whether you are a marketing manager, purchasing agent, or systems analyst, knowledge of finance will help you to do your job better. You'll be able to understand your company's financial statements, its financial condition, and management's investment and financing decisions. Financial information also provides feedback on how well you are doing and identifies problems. On a more practical note, you might be asked to prepare a budget for your department or unit. Employees who understand the financial decision-making process will be able to prepare proposals that address financial concerns. As a result, they will be more likely to be given the resources they require to accomplish the firm's goals.

If you own a business, you must pay close attention to financial management. Without financial plans, you might find yourself running out of cash. It's easy to get so caught up in growing sales that you neglect your billing and collection methods. In fact, managing accounts receivable is often one of the more challenging aspects of running a young company. But you can't rely on revenue increases to solve your cash flow problems. Good receivables practices start with credit policies. Be choosy when it comes to offering trade credit, and check customers' credit references and payment history thoroughly. Set the initial credit limit fairly low until the customer establishes a prompt payment history. Here are some other ways to improve collections.

- Bill frequently, not just at the end of the month, so that money flows in throughout the month. Send bills when milestones are reached, such as making a presentation or completing a phase of a project.
- Clearly state payment terms, and make sure that the language on the invoice matches the contract.
- Establish regular and frequent follow-up procedures. Some companies call to notify the customer that the bill has been sent and to make sure the customer is satisfied. Weekly calls are in order for late payments.
- Try to get a firm date by which you will be paid, and be prepared to say what you will do if you aren't paid on time—for example, stopping work on a project or not shipping the next part of the order.
- Keep detailed notes of all conversations relating to a collection: your contact, date of the call, what was promised, and what you replied. You can then e-mail this as confirmation of your understanding and as another reminder.
- Monitor results of outstanding receivables collection.
- Don't fill new orders from customers who are continually delinquent.[21]

CUSTOMER SATISFACTION AND QUALITY

Because an organization's finance department affects every other area of the firm, it must adhere to the highest quality standards. "Our decision-making needs to be near-perfect, if not perfect," says Ruth Ann M. Gillis, former CFO of Exelon, an electric utility company.

Reliable and consistent financial reports and analyses are critical for managers throughout the firm and also to investors, creditors, suppliers, and customers. Because CEOs and CFOs must now certify the company's financial reports under the Sarbanes-Oxley Act (although this is American legislation, Canadian companies listed on U.S. exchanges must also adhere to the act), they are demanding that their managers adhere to strict quality control procedures and guidelines. To minimize risks of errors, companies are establishing formal rules and procedures for corporate finance. Some CFOs, including Home Depot's Carol Tomé and Consolidated Edison's Joan Freilich, ask key finance managers to sign personal statements that the financial statements they submit are correct.

Financial managers are continually looking for ways to improve the quality of their forecasts and budgets. Unhappy with the level of accuracy in its cash forecasts, Dell Computer developed the Enzo Liquidity Forecasting Tool. It chose the name in honour of race car designer Enzo Ferrari, to underscore the speed of Dell's cash forecasts. Complex cash flow forecasts now take one person an afternoon to prepare instead of three people working for two days. Accuracy is extremely high: The variance is less than $30 million on an accounts payable balance of $5 billion, a 99.4 percent accuracy level. Better cash forecasts were one reason Dell was able to raise its investment income about $1.5 million annually. In addition, Enzo's sophisticated analytical powers give financial managers a broader view of the cash picture. "Any question you can have about a scenario, you can answer," says Nathan Brunner, senior finance consultant at Dell.

SOURCES: Joseph Weber, "CFOs on the Hot Seat," *Business Week,* March 17, 2003, 67–70; and "Stand Back! Enzo Has Arrived," in Jay Sherman and Susan Kelly, "Uphill Racer—The 2002 Alexander Hamilton Award Winners," *Treasury & Risk Management,* October 2002, http://www.treasuryandrisk.com.

SUMMARY OF LEARNING GOALS

1

What roles do finance and the financial manager play in the firm's overall strategy?

Finance is the art and science involved in managing the firm's money. The financial manager must decide how much money is needed and when, how best to use the available funds, and how to get the required financing. The financial manager's responsibilities include financial planning, investing (spending money), and financing (raising money). Maximizing the value of the firm is the main goal of the financial manager, whose decisions often have long-term effects.

2 How does a firm develop its financial plans, including forecasts and budgets?

Financial planning enables the firm to estimate the amount and timing of the financial resources it needs to meet its business goals. The planning process begins with forecasts based on the demand for the firm's products. Short-term forecasts project expected revenues and expenses for one year. They are the basis for cash budgets, which show the flow of cash into and out of the firm and are used to plan day-to-day operations. Long-term forecasts project revenues and expenses over more than a year, typically 2 to 10 years. These strategic plans allow top management to analyze the impact of different options on the firm's profits.

3 What types of short- and long-term expenditures does a firm make?

A firm invests in short-term expenses—supplies, inventory, and wages—to support current production, marketing, and sales activities. The financial manager manages the firm's investment in current assets, so that the company has enough cash to pay its bills and support accounts receivable and inventory. Long-term expenditures (capital expenditures) are made for fixed assets such as land, buildings, machinery, and equipment. Because of the large outlays required for capital expenditures, financial managers carefully analyze proposed projects to determine which offer the best returns.

4 What are the main sources and costs of unsecured and secured short-term financing?

Short-term financing comes due within one year. The main sources of unsecured short-term financing are trade credit, bank loans, and commercial paper. Secured loans require a pledge of certain assets, such as accounts receivable or inventory, as security for the loan. Factoring, or selling accounts receivable outright at a discount, is another form of short-term financing.

5 How do the two primary sources of long-term financing compare?

Financial managers must choose the best mix of debt and equity for their firm. The main advantage of debt financing is the tax-deductibility of interest, but debt involves financial risk, because it requires the payment of interest and principal on specified dates. Equity—common and preferred shares—is considered a permanent form of financing on which the firm might or might not pay dividends. Dividends are not tax-deductible.

6 What are the major types, features, and costs of long-term debt?

The main types of long-term debt are term loans, bonds, and mortgage loans. Term loans can be secured or unsecured and generally have 5- to 12-year maturities. Bonds usually have initial maturities of 10 to 30 years. Mortgage loans are secured by real estate. Long-term debt usually costs more than short-term financing because of the greater uncertainty that the borrower will be able to make the scheduled loan payments.

7 When and how do firms issue equity, and what are the costs?

The chief sources of equity financing are common shares, retained earnings, and preferred shares. The cost of selling shares includes issuing costs and potential dividend payments. Retained earnings are profits reinvested in the firm. For the issuing firm, preferred shares are more expensive than debt, because its dividends are not tax-deductible and its claims are secondary to those of debt holders, but less expensive than common shares. Venture capital is often a source of equity financing for small and growing, typically high-tech companies.

8 What is risk and how can it be managed? What makes a risk insurable?

Risk is the potential for loss or the chance that an investment will not achieve the expected level of return. Risk can be managed by identifying and evaluating the potential risks and selecting and managing techniques to adapt to risk exposures.

To get insurance, the applicant must have an insurable interest: the chance of suffering a loss if a particular peril occurs. An insurable risk is one that an insurance company will cover. To qualify, the following conditions must be met: The loss must not be under the control of the insured; there must be many similar exposures to that peril; losses must be financially measurable; the peril must not be likely to affect all the insured parties at the same time; the potential loss must be significant; and the company must have the right to set standards for insurance coverage.

9 What types of insurance coverage should businesses consider?

The main types of insurance that businesses should consider include property and liability, commercial liability, business interruption, theft, fidelity and surety bonds, title insurance, and profession liability insurance.

10 What trends are affecting the practice of financial management?

The role of the CFO has changed, with CFOs taking the central role in overseeing corporate compliance with the various regulations and re-establishing public trust. They must balance the roles of corporate cop and strategic planner. The continued expansion of the financial manager's role in risk management is a natural outgrowth as companies face a wide range of risks, including credit, market, and operational risk. More companies are adopting risk management to identify and evaluate risks and select techniques to control and reduce risk.

EXPERIENTIAL EXERCISES

1. Prepare a personal budget. A personal budget is one of the most valuable tools for personal financial planning. It will help you evaluate your current financial situation, spending patterns, and goals. Use the following steps to create your budget.

2. Using credit card receipts, cheque records, and other documents, record your income and expenses for the past 30 days. Based on this information, develop a personal budget for the next month. Record your budget in the "Planned" column of the worksheet in Exhibit 17.4. Include scholarships or grants as other income sources.

3. Track your actual income and expenses for one month. Write down *everything* you spend on a daily basis, or you will forget little things (like snacks) that add up over the course of a month. Record your actual totals in the "Actual" column of the worksheet.

4. At the end of the budget period, compare your budget to your actual results. Record any differences between the "Planned" and "Actual" values in the "Variance" column of the worksheet. How close were you to your budget estimates? In what categories did you overspend? Where did you under spend? Did creating the budget have any impact on how you allocated your money to different categories and how you spent your money?

5. Optional: Use the results of your first month's budget to project next month's income and expenses. Repeat the monitoring process.

6. The head of your school's finance department has asked you to address a group of incoming business students about the importance of finance to their overall business education. Develop an outline with the key points you would cover in your speech.

7. As a financial manager at Nature's Food Company, you are preparing forecasts and budgets for a new line of high-nutrition desserts. Why should the finance department prepare these plans for the product development group? What factors would you consider in developing your projections and assessing their impact on the firm's profits?

8. You are the cash manager for a chain of sporting goods stores facing a cash crunch. To date, the chain has always paid accounts payable within the credit period. The CFO wants to consider extending payments beyond the due date. Write a memo that discusses the pros, cons, and ethics of stretching accounts payable as well as other cash-saving options to investigate.

9. You are the chief financial officer of Discovery Labs, a privately held, five-year-old biotechnology company that needs to raise $3 million to fund the development of a new drug. Prepare a report for the board of directors that discusses the types of long-term financing available to the firm, their pros and cons, and the key factors to consider in choosing a financing strategy.

10. GetSmart (**http://www.getsmart.com**) is an information service that offers advice on business as well as personal loans. Click on Business Finance Center, and move through the various types of loans. Try the questionnaires in each area, using different answers, to see what is necessary to qualify for that financing option.

11. If factoring accounts receivable is still a mystery to you, visit the 21st Financial Solutions site, **http://www.21stfinancialsolutions.com.** Follow the links on the home page to answer these questions: What are factoring's advantages? What are the additional benefits, and what types of companies can use factoring to their advantage? Then summarize the factoring process.

12. Visit your bank's Web site to learn about the bank's products and services for corporate customers. Describe briefly each type of loan it offers. Then do the same for another financial institution.

13. Read the "Sources of Capital and Implication for Industry Structure" by MacDonald & Associates Limited at **http://www.fin.gc.ca/taskforce/research/pdf/rr18_e.pdf.**

14. Visit the Treasury Board of Canada Secretariat Web site at **http://www.tbs-sct.gc.ca/pubs_pol/dcgpubs/RiskManagement/siglist_e.asp** to learn more about risk management.

Exhibit 17.4 | Monthly Budget Worksheet

Name: _____

Month of _____

	Planned	**Actual**	**Variance**
Income			
Wages (take-home pay)			
Support from relatives			
Loans			
Withdrawals from savings			
Other _____			
Other _____			
(1) Total Available Income			
Expenses			
Fixed Expenses			
Housing			
Automobile payment			
Insurance			
Loan repayment			
Savings for goals			
Tuition and fees			
Other _____			
Subtotal, Fixed Expenses			
Flexible Expenses			
Food			
Clothing			
Personal care			
Entertainment and recreation			
Transportation			
Telephone			
Utilities (electricity, gas, water)			
Cable TV			
Medical and dental			
Books, magazines, educational supplies			
Gifts			
Other _____			
Other _____			
Subtotal, Flexible Expenses			
(2) Total Expenses			
Cash Surplus (Deficit) [(1)–(2)]			

REVIEW QUESTIONS

1. What is financial management?
2. List the responsibilities of the financial manager.

3. What is the goal of the financial manager? What are risk, return, and the risk-return trade-off?

4. What is the purpose of the three types of budgets mentioned in this chapter?

5. What is cash management, and why is it important in business?

6. How can technology be used to help companies improve their credit and collection performance?

7. What are the sources of short-term financing?

8. How do companies obtain long-term financing?

9. Describe the major differences between debt and equity financing.

10. What are dividends and retained earnings?

11. What is the difference between common shares and preferred shares?

12. What is risk management? What are some strategies to manage risk?

13. What are the various types of insurance available to businesses?

CREATIVE THINKING CASE
Fitter International Keeps Its Balance

It was the breakthrough Louis Stack had been waiting for: a chance to sell his company's balance-related fitness products at Target Stores. Fitter International's high-end products, long popular with sports trainers and physical therapists, were starting to appear in specialty outdoor and sports stores. Adding Target as a channel would greatly increase Fitter's sales and profit potential.

As wonderful as the deal sounded, however, there was a catch: Target's buyers wanted a three-product, branded line priced at about half his current prices. Stack weighed the pros and cons. His company, located in Calgary, Alberta, would have to change drastically to meet Target's price requirements. He would have to totally redesign his "wobble board" with lower cost materials, find a new manufacturer for the board, negotiate better pricing for the "sitting disk" products, and find a less expensive supplier of fitness balls. The costs of moving to a larger facility, re-engineering the wobble board, hiring more staff, developing new packaging, and marketing the products would run to $315,000 or more.

Spending such a large amount was daunting to Stack, who after 14 years of operating on a shoestring was finally on solid financial footing. On the other hand, greater sales volume and the new vendors would let him reduce the cost of his products by about 40 percent. "As long as we can keep our ratios in line, we can get debt financing," he figured. He also worried that the new lower priced retail brand might pull sales away from his high-quality professional line.

Nike and Reebok had introduced similar balance products, indicating to Stack that there was a large market to tap, but there were definite risks as well. Would Target be calling all the shots? How would its payment terms affect Fitter's cash flow? Could the company handle the larger sales volume? Stack was worried that growing too quickly could throw the company off balance, yet he realized that not doing so could cost him market leadership.

Stack decided to take the (fitness) ball and run with it. He increased his line of credit with RBC from $150,000 to $225,000, obtained a $100,000 term loan, and moved ahead with his plans. Then, just as the pieces were coming into place, the buyer who was sponsoring Fitter products left Target, placing the deal in jeopardy.

Stack quickly regrouped, deciding to capitalize on Fitter's success with specialty stores. Sales took off, and Fitter products began appearing in a variety of stores, from Road Runner Sports, the world's largest running store, to the Discovery Channel Store. Yet the idea of working with Target still has some appeal, and Stack wonders about the impact on Fitter of entering the mass market.

CRITICAL THINKING QUESTIONS

1. How would Stack use capital budgeting techniques to analyze the original Target proposal? List the type of information he would need to evaluate whether to proceed.

2. Fitter International's revenues would go up significantly as a result of its agreement with Target. So why would the company need a larger bank credit facility?

3. What questions should Stack ask in deciding whether to go after Target's business again? What are the risks and rewards?

SOURCES: Donna Fenn, "The Offer You Almost Can't Refuse," *Inc.*, January 1, 2003, http://www.inc.com; and Fitter International Web site, http://www.fitter1.com; and "Picture Still Sharp Despite Rapid Acquisition," *DSN Retailing Today*, January 7, 2002; "Tweeter Home Entertainment Group Launches Phase One of a Major Strategic Repositioning Initiative," *Business Wire*, May 29, 2003; and "Tweeter Home Entertainment Group Reports Results for Its Second Fiscal Quarter Ended March 31, 2003," *Business Wire*, April 24, 2003; all from http://www.findarticles.com.

VIDEO CASE
Debt Nation

Many Canadians are finding themselves in deep financial trouble, even though they make a reasonable income. The primary contributing factor seems to be credit card debt. Many items purchased with major credit cards are intangible, which means that you have nothing to show for it when the bill comes in. For example, trips, restaurant meals, shows, and gas are often purchased with credit cards. And the credit card companies are pushing hard.

In 2003, there were approximately 23.9 million *retailer-issued* credit cards in circulation in Canada. These are the ones at 28.8 percent interest (e.g., HBC/Zellers). Students often start out in debt simply from educational expenses, with the average amount being $22,700 for four-year programs. Add that to a credit card (or two, or three), and financial trouble can follow.

Family 1, Wayne and Theresa, are not that unusual, and many Canadians behave in a similar manner—the ostrich approach: If I can't see it, it's not a problem. Family 2, Joanne and Travis, admit that Joanne is a shopaholic. Some people get a genuine high from shopping, similar to that of drugs and alcohol. For Family 3, Hanna Laura might have to forgo her trip to England to curb her debt. How did this happen to ordinary Canadians? In 2001, Canadians received 208.3 million credit card solicitations. If you pay your monthly amount regularly, what happens? The credit card company probably raises your limit! This is a very slippery slope. With an increase in credit card debt of 90 percent between 1997 and 2001, as well as an estimated household debt owed by Canadians in 2003 of $731 billion compared to saving of $9.39 billion, it is obvious we need to step back and look at what we are doing.

CRITICAL THINKING QUESTIONS

1. If a large number of Canadians suddenly stopped using their credit cards (and did not have the cash to make intended purchases) what effect would this have on the Canadian economy?

2. Are the credit card companies acting responsibly by encouraging Canadians to accept more cards? How might they build their business in a more ethical matter?

SOURCES: CBC, *Marketplace*, "Debt Nation Part 1," January 15, 2006.

CBC, *Marketplace*, "Debt Nation Part 2," January 22, 2006.

E-COMMERCE CASE

Investing Your Money: Is the Target of Your Investment Managing Risk Adequately?

An important aspect of managing a firm's finances (the chapter title) involves understanding and managing risk. Do we have enough assets to cover our liabilities? Currently some Canadian corporate pension plans do *not* have enough assets to cover the value of the current pension plan obligations. In fact, these plans are underfunded. For example, Bombardier has pension plan obligations of $6.2 billion (USD), based on pension plan assets of $3.9 billion, a shortfall of $2.3 billion.

Investors in pension plans are sometimes unaware of this problem, as it is not readily apparent from the financial statements. An item such as pension plan underfunding would have to be discovered by examining the off–balance sheet obligations of the company.

What are the implications of an underfunded plan for the investor? A cash infusion might be required in a few cases; however, there is an impact on the share value. Keeping in mind that the asset value of the fund is an estimate, as is the value of future obligations, is this really a serious problem? It depends. Interest rates are relatively low right now—as this book is being printed—and when they rise, the current value of future obligations will decrease. Furthermore, the assets supporting the plan should appreciate in value, causing the underfunding gap to disappear. Again, given that the numbers reflect management estimates, of greater concern might be the trust in the firm's management.

Al Rosen, a commentator for *Canadian Business Online*, feels that attention needs to be given to the lack of accounting principles that might prevent the pension plan underfunding issue. In his opinion, the inadequacy of a system that does not look out for the interests of investors is the problem, with the pension issues being only a symptom.

CRITICAL THINKING QUESTIONS

1. Do you agree or disagree with Al Rosen's point of view? Why?

2. Choose a Canadian company at random, and see if you can tell from the financial statements whether the pension plan is adequately funded. Does the result of the exercise change your answer to question 1?

SOURCES: Al Rosen, "Time Bombs," *Canadian Business*, 79 no. 10 (Summer 2006), 23; Al Rosen, "The Pension Fun Never Stops," *Canadian Business*, 76 no. 13 (July 7–21, 2003), 23; April 29, 2003; and Boston Beer Company corporate Web site, http://www.bostonbeer.com (accessed May 1, 2003).

Making the Connection

Understanding Money, Financial Institutions, and the Securities Markets

In this chapter we will conclude our look at the finance area by examining where the money to run a successful business comes from. It would be wonderful if all the capital needed to operate and grow a business came from income alone. However, to move past a company's current level of income and to grow it to new heights, implementing its chosen *strategy* to achieve its *vision*, it typically must bring fresh capital in from outside. In the chapter, we introduce the role of money and financial institutions as well as the securities markets, which provide the fuel for companies—an arena for raising capital.

Among the major *stakeholders* in any business are the owners. As discussed in previous chapters, companies must consider the impact on stakeholders of any decisions they make. Certainly the choice of how a business is financed has a tremendous impact on the owners. Particularly in the publicly traded corporation, it is critical that financial managers consider this seriously, as there is a very integrative relationship between this major stakeholder and the firm's financing. Much of the firm's financial resources will come from investments from its owners—the shareholders—through the purchase of stocks or shares in the company. However, how those financial resources are managed will, in turn, affect the value of the company and the owners'

stake in it, and therefore whether they would consider the company worth continuing to invest in. This affects the company's ability to raise additional money through the sale of more shares.

If the financial manager does not focus on the first of the critical success factors—*achieving financial performance*—then the shareholders will be less inclined to invest further and perhaps even sell their shares, which could, if there is enough selling activity, drive down the price of the shares on the stock market, making the stock even less appealing to most investors. The ability to raise additional funds through the sale of stock will then be hindered. However to achieve financial performance, we know that it is essential to achieve the other success factors as well—*meeting customer needs, providing quality, encouraging innovation,* and *gaining employee commitment*—because they are all related. So all the functional area managers—*marketing, operations,* and *human resources,* as well as *finance,* are responsible for making sure the company is successful for its stakeholders. They all have an impact on financial performance.

Companies, of course, have other options for raising capital. In the securities markets, one of the major options besides selling equity investments—a piece of ownership through shares—is to sell bonds. Selling bonds is essentially borrowing money and so is debt rather than equity financing. The balancing act that the company plays between the amount of debt it uses to finance the company and the amount of equity also has an impact on the financial performance of the firm and, again, on its ability to raise more capital.

Whatever amount of debt it chooses to use versus equity, or the amount of bonds it sells as opposed to stock, the external environment will have an enormous impact, just as we've seen with all other aspects of the business. The external environment forms the context in which the company operates and thus affects its decisions and its success. For example, the *political* environment lays the foundation for how the company can raise capital—regulations exist surrounding the criteria that a company must meet to be able to sell its stock to the public—as well as the composition of the Board of Directors, the highest level of *management* in the firm, whose main job is to protect the interests of the shareholders. The *economic* environment certainly has an impact, both from a competitive standpoint, as firms compete not only for customers but for investors as well, and from a purely economic one, as the economy affects what investments are the most attractive to investors (influencing what type of financing is likely to be the more marketable—

selling stocks or bonds) and the cost of debt financing to the company through interest rates. The *social* environment also impacts a company's financing. This is evident in the popularity of ethical funds—mutual funds that invest in companies that have a strong social conscience. And finally, the impact of the *technological* environment was very obvious and extreme a few years back, when technological companies were the darlings of the stock market, before the "bubble burst" and they just as dramatically fell in value. But the impact of technology is also felt in how the market operates. Each year, more and more advances are made to automate the securities exchanges. Gone are the days of traders shouting across trading floors.

For investors, though, the markets are still exciting and offer an opportunity for ordinary people like you and me to become part owners in a company and share in its success. This is all made possible by companies' entering the market to raise capital to operate their businesses and, in turn, increase value for the owners, their primary stakeholders.

SHIRLEY A. ROSE

Chapter

18

Understanding Money, Financial Institutions, and the Securities Markets

learning goals

1   What is money, what are its characteristics and functions, and what are the parts of the Canadian money supply?

2   What are the basic functions of the Bank of Canada, and what tools does it use to manage the money supply?

3   What are the key financial institutions, and what role do they play in the process of financial intermediation?

4   How does the Canada Deposit Insurance Corporation protect depositors' funds?

5   What role do Canadian banks play in the international marketplace?

6   How do common shares and preferred shares differ as investments?

7   What are bonds, and what investment advantages and disadvantages do they offer?

8   What other types of securities are available to investors?

9   What is the function of the securities markets?

10   Where can investors buy and sell securities?

11   What trends are reshaping the financial industry?

The Changing Role of Banking

Ron Munaweera is the Senior Vice President and Chief Financial Officer of Bank West, a subsidiary of the Western Financial Group, Inc. Ron's career has spanned more than 30 years in the banking and insurance industries, in positions ranging from teller at the BC Teachers' Credit Union, through Coronado Mortgage Corporation, Seaboard Life and People's Trust, to his current position as VP and CFO. The Western Financial Group, Inc., has more than 600 employees and gross revenues of $63.6 million. The WFG provides insurance, financial, and banking services to more than 250,000 customers through WFG Agency Network, Western Life Assurance Company, and Bank West. The group owns and operates 56 offices and partners with other companies in 21 more offices.

As Ron has moved forward in his career, he has seen many changes in the Canadian banking industry. In the 1970s, when Ron began his banking career, there were numerous financial institutions but only the six major banks. Today there are 19 domestic banks, 23 foreign bank subsidiaries, and 21 foreign bank branches in Canada. Institutions such as Canadian Tire Bank and Manulife Bank of Canada are both domestic banks. Over the years, there have been trust company mergers as well as bank acquisitions of trust companies (e.g., TD Canada Trust, part of the TD Financial Group). These institutions manage approximately $1.8 trillion in assets.

In addition to the expansion occurring in the industry, there have been many changes in the focus of banking. Ron has identified three very important trends that have definitely changed the flavour of banking over the years. First, the regulation of the industry with respect to proper governance is stronger. Second, there is an emphasis on anti-terrorist financing and anti-money laundering financing. The banks must know their clients and also know where the clients are getting their money. Third, there is movement toward strengthening the international banking system to ensure consistent and proper measurement of risk. The Bank for International Settlements (BIS), which is a group of bankers from the developed countries, is developing a framework for international standards known as Basel II. As well, any financial institution traded on an American exchange must comply with the Canadian equivalent of Sarbanes-Oxley, known in the Canadian industry as SOX North.

These trends toward greater regulation have tremendously increased the compliance effort required, leading to time-consuming and complex decision making. But Ron finds it a very exciting time to be an executive in the industry—a role far removed from the "old-time" bank manager of the '70s, '80s, and '90s.[1]

Critical Thinking Questions

1. Given the trends toward increased regulation in the industry, is banking a reasonable career goal for a business student?

2. Research the Basel II accord. What can you see as possible problems if emerging economic powers such as China do not join BIS?

Principles of Money, Financial Institutions, and the Securities Markets

Imagine using your cell phone to open a bank account! The financial services industry is, indeed, moving in new directions. Advanced technology, globalization of markets, and the relaxation of regulatory restrictions are accelerating the pace of change in financial services. The changes are giving businesses and consumers new options for conducting their financial transactions. The competitive landscape for financial institutions is also changing, as they develop new ways of increasing their market share and boosting profits.

Because financial institutions connect people with money, we begin this chapter with a discussion of money, its characteristics and functions, and the components of the Canadian money supply. Next we explain the role of the Bank of Canada (Canada's central bank—first introduced in Chapter 1) in managing the money supply. Then we describe different types of financial institutions and their services, and the organizations that insure customer deposits. We continue with a discussion of international banking and the securities markets. Finally, we look at trends in the banking industry.

SHOW ME THE MONEY

1 *learning goal*

money
Anything that is acceptable as payment for goods and services.

Money is anything that is acceptable as payment for goods and services. It affects our lives in many ways. We earn it, spend it, save it, invest it—and often wish we had more of it. Business and government use money in similar ways. Both require money to finance their operations. By controlling the amount of money in circulation, the Bank of Canada can promote economic and financial well-being in Canada. For this reason, money has been called the lubricant for the machinery of our economic system. Our banking system was developed to ease the handling of money.

Characteristics of Money

For money to be a suitable means of exchange, it should have these key characteristics.

- *Scarcity*. Money should be scarce enough to have some value but not so scarce as to be unavailable. Pebbles, which meet some of the other criteria, would not work well as money, because they are widely available. Too much money in circulation increases prices. Central banks control the scarcity of money by limiting the quantity of money produced.

- *Durability*. Any item used as money must be durable. A perishable item such as a banana becomes useless as money when it spoils. Even early societies used durable forms of money, such as metal coins and paper money, that lasted for a long time.

- *Portability*. Money must be easily moved around. Large or bulky items, such as boulders or heavy gold bars, cannot be transported easily from place to place.

- *Divisibility*. Money must be capable of being divided into smaller parts. Divisible forms of money help make possible transactions of all sizes and amounts.

HOT Links

How durable is Canadian printed money? To discover the life expectancy of Canadian bills, visit http://www.bankofcanada.ca/en/banknotes/facts.html.

Functions of Money

Using several types of goods as money would be confusing. Thus, societies develop a uniform money system to measure the value of goods and services. For money to be acceptable, it must function as a medium of exchange, as a standard of value, and as a store of value.

As a *medium of exchange*, money makes transactions easier. Having a common form of payment in each country is much less complicated than having a barter system—where goods and services are exchanged for other goods and services. Money allows the exchange of products to be a simple process.

Money also serves as a *standard of value*. With a form of money whose value is accepted by all, goods and services can be priced in standard units. This makes it easy to measure the value of products and allows transactions to be recorded in consistent terms.

As a *store of value*, money is used to hold wealth. It retains its value over time. Someone who owns money can keep it for future use rather than exchange it today for other types of assets.

currency
Bank notes and coins used as a medium of exchange

demand deposits
Money kept in chequing accounts that can be withdrawn by depositors on demand.

time deposits
Money invested for a specific period of time.

term deposits
Deposits at a bank or other financial institution that pay interest but cannot be withdrawn on demand.

The Canadian Money Supply

The Canadian money supply has three parts: currency, demand deposits, and time deposits. The amount of money in circulation in Canada can be measured in various ways. The most common measurements are called the monetary aggregates and include these:

M1 is the narrowest measure. MI includes all **currency** (bank notes and coins) plus **demand deposits** (personal chequing accounts) and other current accounts at banks. Other forms of currency include traveller's cheques, cashier's cheques, and money orders.

M2 is a broader measure that includes not only M1 but also personal savings accounts, other chequing accounts, term deposits, and non-personal deposits that require notice before the money can be withdrawn.

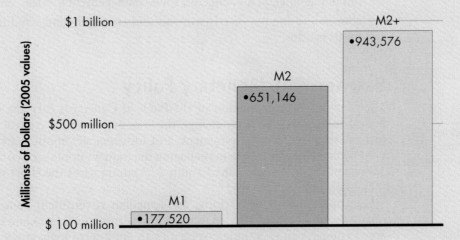

Exhibit 18.1 Three Measures of the Money Stock for the Canadian Economy

SOURCE: Statistics Canada, "Exchange Rates, Interest Rates, Money Supply and Stock Prices," http://www40.statcan.ca/101/cst01/econo07.htm (accessed March 21, 2006).

Because banks are not the only providers of deposit facilities, we can use an even broader measurement of money, *M2+ (also known as M3)*. This includes not only M1 and M2 but also all deposits at non-bank deposit institutions, such as money-market mutual funds and life insurance companies. Exhibit 18.1 shows these three measurements of the Canadian money supply.

Credit cards, sometimes referred to as "plastic money," are used as a substitute for cash and cheques. Credit cards are simply a form of borrowing. When RBC issues a credit card to a small business owner, it gives a short-term loan to the business by directly paying the seller for the business's purchases. The business pays RBC when it receives its monthly statement. Credit cards do not replace money; they simply defer payment.

concept check

What is money, and what are its characteristics?

What are the main functions of money?

What are the components of the Canadian money supply?

THE BANK OF CANADA

2 *learning goal*

Before the 20th century, there was very little government regulation of the Canadian financial system. In 1934 the Bank of Canada (also discussed in Chapter 1) was founded as a privately owned corporation. In 1938 it became a Crown corporation belonging to the federal government, with all shares held by the federal minister of finance.

The Bank of Canada is the sole issuer of bank notes in Canada and is responsible for facilitating the management of Canada's financial system. As an independent institution, the Bank of Canada has the power to create money, which is separate from the government's power to spend the money.

The Bank of Canada promotes the economic and financial welfare of Canada by

- conducting monetary policy in a way that fosters confidence in the value of money,
- supplying quality bank notes that are readily accepted and secure against counterfeiting (see Exhibit 18.1),
- promoting the safety and efficiency of Canada's financial system,
- providing efficient and effective funds management services, and
- communicating its objectives openly and effectively, and standing accountable for its actions.[2]

Carrying Out Monetary Policy

HOT *Links*

To learn more about how the Bank of Canada works, visit http://www.bankofcanada.ca.

open market operations

The purchase or sale of Canadian government securities by the Bank of Canada to stimulate or slow down the economy.

The most important function of the Bank of Canada is carrying out monetary policy. It uses its power to change the money supply to control inflation and interest rates, increase employment, and influence economic activity. Two tools used by the Bank of Canada in managing the money supply are open market operations and the overnight rate. Exhibit 18.3 summarizes the short-term effects of these tools on the economy.

In **open market operations,** the Canadian government issues securities to obtain the extra money needed to run the government (if taxes and other revenues aren't enough). In effect, these securities are long-term loans made by businesses and individuals to the government. When the Bank of Canada buys securities, it puts money into the economy. Banks have more money to lend so they reduce interest rates, and lower rates generally stimulate economic activity. The opposite occurs when the Bank of Canada sells government securities.

Exhibit 18.2 | Security of the $20 Bill

All security features
for this note:

- Holographic Stripe
- Watermark Portrait
- Windowed
  Security Thread
- See-Through
  Number
- Raised Print
  (Intaglio)
- Fine-Line Printing
- Fluorescence
- Serial Number
- Colours

Exhibit 18.3 | The Bank of Canada's Monetary Tools and Their Effects

TOOL	EFFECT ON ACTION	EFFECT ON MONEY SUPPLY	EFFECT ON INTEREST RATES	ECONOMIC ACTIVITY
Open market operations	Buy government securities	Increases	Lowers	Stimulates
	Sell government securities	Decreases	Raises	Slows Down
Overnight rate	Raise overnight rate	Decreases	Raises	Slows Down
	Lower overnight rate	Increases	Lowers	Stimulates

bank rate

The interest rate that the Bank of Canada charges on one-day loans to financial institutions.

target for the overnight rate

The signal to the major participants in the money market as to what the Bank of Canada is aiming for when participants borrow and lend one-day funds to each other.

Although the **bank rate** still exists, the Bank of Canada is now putting more emphasis on the **target for the overnight rate.** The bank rate is the interest rate that the Bank of Canada charges member banks that borrow from the Bank of Canada. On the other hand, the target for the overnight rate is a signal from the Bank of Canada to the major participants in the money market as to what rate the Bank of Canada is aiming for in the market for overnight funds.[3] The target for the overnight rate is more relevant to the Canadian monetary policy. It is the average interest rate that the Bank of Canada wants to see in the overnight market (one-day loans). Under the current system, the Bank of Canada will always change the target for the overnight rate and the bank rate at the same time and in the same amount.

concept check

What are the key functions of the Bank of Canada?

What tools does the Bank of Canada use in managing the money supply, and how does each affect economic activity?

THE CANADIAN FINANCIAL SYSTEM

3 *learning goal*

The well-developed financial system in Canada supports our high standard of living. The system allows those who wish to borrow money to do so with relative ease. It also gives savers a variety of ways of earning interest on their savings. For example, a computer company that wants to build a new headquarters in New Brunswick might be financed partly with the savings of families in British Columbia. The British Columbians deposit their money in a local financial institution. That institution looks for a profitable and safe way to use the money and decides to make a real estate loan to the computer company. The transfer of funds from savers to investors enables businesses to expand and the economy to grow.

Households are important participants in the Canadian financial system. Although many households borrow money to finance purchases, they supply funds to the financial system through their purchases and savings. Overall, businesses and governments are users of funds. They borrow more money than they save.

Sometimes those who have funds deal directly with those who want them. A wealthy realtor, for example, might lend money to a client to buy a house. But most often, financial institutions act as intermediaries—or go-betweens—between the suppliers of and demanders for funds. The institutions accept savers' deposits and invest them in financial products (such as loans) that are expected to produce a return. This process, called **financial intermediation,** is shown in Exhibit 18.4. Households are shown as suppliers of funds, and businesses and governments are shown as demanders, but a household, business, or government can be either a supplier or a demander, depending on the circumstances.

Financial institutions are the heart of the financial system, as they are convenient vehicles for financial intermediation. They can be divided into two broad groups: depository institutions (those that accept deposits) and non-depository institutions (those that do not accept deposits).

financial intermediation

The process in which financial institutions act as intermediaries between the suppliers and demanders of funds.

Exhibit 18.4 | The Financial Intermediation Process

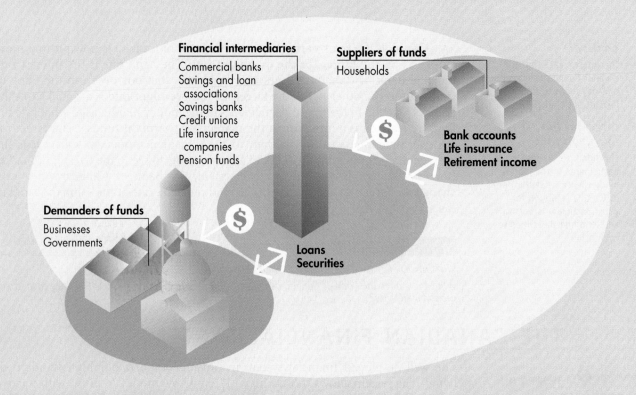

Financial intermediaries
Commercial banks
Savings and loan associations
Savings banks
Credit unions
Life insurance companies
Pension funds

Suppliers of funds
Households

Bank accounts
Life insurance
Retirement income

Demanders of funds
Businesses
Governments

Loans
Securities

Depository Financial Institutions

Not all depository financial institutions are alike. Most people call the place where they save their money a "bank." Some of those places are, indeed, banks, but other depository institutions include trust companies and credit unions.

Chartered Banks A **chartered bank** is a profit-oriented financial institution that accepts deposits, makes business and consumer loans, invests in government and corporate securities, and provides other financial services. There are about 14 domestic banks, 33 foreign bank subsidiaries, and 20 foreign bank branches operating in Canada. These banks operate through approximately 8,000 branches and manage more than $1.7 trillion in assets. Collectively, the chartered banks account for more than 70 percent of the total assets of the Canadian financial services sector.[4]

Customers' deposits are a commercial bank's main source of funds; the main use of those funds is loans. The differences between the interest earned on loans and the interest paid on deposits, plus fees earned from other financial services, pay the bank's costs and provide a profit. Chartered banks are corporations owned and operated by individuals or other corporations. In Canada banks are regulated through the Bank Act.

See Exhibit 18.5 for a list of the top five Canadian chartered banks by revenues and profits for 2004.

Trust Companies A **trust company** is the only financial institution allowed to administer trusts, such as those set up to manage estates. Like banks, they operate through a network of branches and may operate either under provincial or federal

---

chartered banks
Profit-oriented financial institutions that accept deposits, make business and consumer loans, invest in government and corporate securities, and provide other financial services.

HOT Links

Did you know that there is money unclaimed by depositors in Canada? Check out ucbswww.bank-banque-canada.ca/ to determine if you have deposits that you have forgotten about.

trust companies
A financial institution that conducts the same activities as a bank but can also administer estates, trusts, pension plans, and agency contracts.

Exhibit 18.5   Top Five Canadian Chartered Banks by Revenues and Profits for 2004

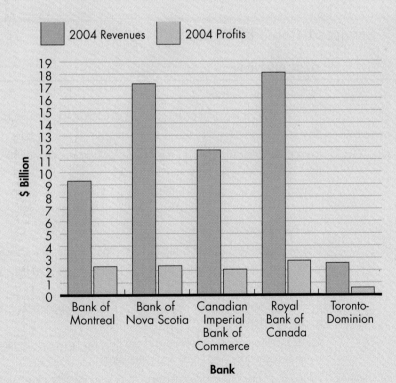

SOURCE: "Scotiabank Fears Q1 Will be Hard to Match," The Calgary Herald, Wednesday, March 2, 2005. Reprinted with the permission of The Calgary Herald.

One of the most popular services offered by depository institutions is the automated teller machine. ATMs on college campuses make it easy for students to deposit and withdraw money.

HOT Links

Checkout the services offered by TD Canada Trust at http://www.tdcanadatrust.com/

credit unions and caisses populaires

Not-for-profit, member-owned financial cooperatives.

legislation. When the Canadian government radically changed the financial regulations in the 1990s, this allowed banks to purchase trust companies (e.g., Toronto Dominion Bank purchased Canada Trust to become TD Canada Trust). There are few remaining independent trust companies, and those that do exist deal primarily in mortgage lending.[5]

Credit Unions and Caisses Populaires **Credit unions**, or **caisses populaires**, are not-for-profit, member-owned financial cooperatives that operate for the benefit of the members. They are subject to provincial regulation and are usually small and locally owned, and members typically have something in common—their employer, union, professional group, or church, for example. There were approximately 3,600 cooperative institutions in Canada at the end of 2002.[6]

Chartered banks, trust companies, and credit unions offer a wide range of financial services for businesses and consumers. Typical services offered by depository institutions are listed in Exhibit 18.6. These services play an important role in helping to fuel the Canadian economy and foster individual financial security. One of the newest bank services is on-line banking.

Non-Depository Financial Institutions

Some financial institutions provide a few banking services but do not accept deposits. These non-depository financial institutions include insurance companies, pension funds, brokerage firms, and finance companies. They serve both individuals and businesses.

Insurance Companies Insurance companies are major suppliers of funds. Policyholders make payments (called *premiums*) to buy financial protection from the insurance company. Insurance companies invest the premiums in stocks, bonds, real estate, business loans, and real estate loans for large projects.

Exhibit 18.6 | Services Offered by Depository Institutions

SERVICE	DESCRIPTION
Savings accounts	Pay interest on deposits
Chequing accounts	Allow depositors to withdraw any amount of funds at any time up to the amount on deposit
Money market deposit accounts	Savings accounts on which the interest rate is set at market rates
Certificates of deposit (CDs)	Pay a higher interest rate than regular savings accounts, provided that the deposit remains for a specified period
Consumer loans	Loans to individuals to finance the purchase of a home, car, or other expensive items
Business loans	Loans to businesses and other organizations to finance their operations
Money transfer	Transfer of funds to other banks
Electronic funds transfer	Use of telephone lines and computers to conduct financial transactions
Automated teller machines (ATMs)	Allow bank customers to make deposits and withdrawals from their accounts 24 hours a day
Debit cards	Allow customers to transfer money from their bank account directly to a merchant's account to pay for purchases
Smart cards	Cards that store monetary value and can be used to buy goods and services instead of using cash, cheques, and credit and debit cards
On-line and telephone banking	Allows customers to conduct financial transaction via the Internet or through a dial-in line that operates with a bank's software

pension funds
Large pools of money set aside by corporations, unions, and governments for later use in paying retirement benefits to their employees or members.

Pension Funds Corporations, unions, and governments set aside large pools of money for later use in paying retirement benefits to their employees or members. These **pension funds** are managed by the employers or unions themselves or by outside managers, such as life insurance firms, chartered banks, and private investment firms. Pension plan members receive a specified monthly payment when they reach a given age. After setting aside enough money to pay near-term benefits, pension funds invest the rest in business loans, stock, bonds, or real estate. They often invest large sums in the stock of the employer.

Brokerage Firms A *brokerage firm* buys and sells securities (stocks and bonds) for its clients and gives them related advice. Many brokerage firms offer some banking services. They might offer clients a combined chequing and savings account with a high interest rate and also make loans, backed by securities, to them.

Finance Companies A *finance company* makes short-term loans for which the borrower puts up tangible assets (such as an automobile, inventory, machinery, or property) as security. Finance companies often make loans to individuals or businesses that cannot get credit elsewhere. To compensate for the extra risk, finance companies usually charge higher interest rates than banks do. *Consumer finance companies* make loans to individuals.

concept check

What is the financial intermediation process?

What are the types of depository institutions, and what services do they offer?

What are the main types of non-depository institutions?

INSURING BANK DEPOSITS

4 *learning goal*

Canada Deposit Insurance Corporation (CDIC)
The Canada Deposit Insurance Corporation is a federal Crown Corporation created in 1967 to provide deposit insurance and contribute to the stability of Canada's financial system.

The **Canada Deposit Insurance Corporation (CDIC)** is a federal Crown corporation created in 1967 to provide deposit insurance and to contribute to the stability of Canada's financial system. The CDIC insures eligible deposits at member institutions and reimburses depositors for the amount of their insured deposits when a member institution fails. Until the federal budget announcement in 2005, the amount insured at a single member institution was $60,000; now it has been increased to $100,000.

CDIC is governed by the Canada Deposit Insurance Corporation Act and is accountable to Canada's Parliament through the Minister of Finance. Since its creation, 43 member institutions have failed, at a cost of about $4.7 billion. No member has failed since June 1996.[7]

Today, depositors are automatically insured for their deposits (to the maximum) if their deposits are with a member institution and in Canadian currency. As of April 30, 2004, CDIC had insured approximately $376 billion in deposits.[8]

HOT Links

To find out if your institution is a member of the CDIC or to see any new announcements, visit http://www.cdic.ca.

concept check

What is the CDIC, and what are its responsibilities?

How does this encourage confidence in the Canadian economy?

INTERNATIONAL BANKING

5 *learning goal*

The financial marketplace spans the globe, with money routinely flowing across international borders. Multinational corporations need many special banking services, such as foreign currency exchange. Many Canadian banks have started expanding into trans-border and overseas markets by opening offices in the United States, Europe, Latin America, and the Far East. They provide better customer service than local banks in many countries and have access to more sources of funding.

Competing against foreign banks can be difficult. Foreign banks are subject to fewer regulations, making it easier for them to undercut Canadian banks on the pricing of loans and services to multinational corporations and governments. Some governments protect their banks against foreign competition. In Singapore, for example, the government prohibits foreign banks from acquiring domestic banks, which are mostly family-owned businesses. Until recently, Singapore limited foreign ownership to 40 percent. By eliminating that restriction and permitting a limited number of foreign banks to open branches in Singapore and to install ATMs, the government is now allowing more competition from foreign banks.[9]

International banking can be profitable, but it's also a high-risk business. For example, poorly regulated banking activities in East Asian countries caused an economic crisis in 1997 that Singapore Prime Minister Goh Chok Tong called "Asia's worst crisis since the Second World War." Some Asian banks made loans to finance highly speculative real estate ventures and corporate expansions that were fuelling a booming economy in the Pacific Rim, which attracted many foreign investors. International banks made billions of dollars worth of loans to Thailand, Indonesia, Malaysia, and Korea, and these bank loans and foreign investments made the balance sheets of the Asian banks and their customers look better than they actually were. When investors started taking their money out of the Asian banks, the banks' assets plummeted, which forced currency devaluations. The situation severely injured the economies of several Asian countries, resulting in high inflation and deep debt. Lacking capital, Asian banks could not get loans to conduct business, and companies couldn't get loans to finance the production and export of their products.[10]

Canadian banks play an important role in global business by providing loans to foreign governments and businesses. They also offer trade-related services. For example, Scotiabank's global cash management services help firms manage their cash flows to improve their payment efficiency and reduce their exposure to operational risks. The bank's advanced information systems enable corporate customers to access their accounts electronically throughout the world. Other Canadian banks are taking advantage of their technological expertise and information systems to sell more financial services throughout the world.

HOT Links

Scotiabank is Canada's most international bank, with more than 2,000 branches and offices in 50 countries. Check out their Web site at http://www.scotiabank.com/cda/index/0,,LIDen_SID15,00.html.

concept check

What is the role of Canadian banks in international banking?

What challenges do Canadian banks face in foreign markets?

INVESTOR'S CHOICE: STOCKS AND BONDS

6 *learning goal*

securities

Investment certificates issued by corporations or governments that represent either equity or debt.

As we discussed in Chapter 17, a central concern of most businesses is raising capital to finance operations and expansion. Many corporations use securities as a source of long-term financing. **Securities** are investment certificates that represent either equity (ownership in the issuing organization) or debt (a loan to the issuer). Corporations and governments sell securities to investors, who, in turn, take on a certain amount of risk with the hope of receiving a profit from their investment. Although we discussed equity and debt securities from the corporation's perspective in Chapter 17, let's review the advantages of these and other types of securities from an investor's viewpoint.

Sharing the Wealth—and the Risks

Equity securities, commonly called *shares,* represent ownership in a corporation. A share is issued for each unit of ownership, and the shareholder (owner) gets a stock certificate to prove ownership. If you own a share in General Electric, for example, you are a partial owner of GE. Your ownership interest isn't very big, because GE has billions of shares outstanding, but your ownership gives you certain rights and potential rewards. The two types of equity securities are common shares and preferred shares. Each has advantages and disadvantages for investors.

Common Shares *Common shares* are the most widespread form of ownership. Holders of common shares receive the right to vote on many important corporate decisions, such as who should sit on the company's board of directors and whether the firm should merge with another company. In most cases, common shareholders get one vote for each share they own. Common shares also give investors the opportunity to share in the company's success, through either dividends or share price increases.

As discussed in Chapter 17, *dividends* are the part of corporate profits that the firm distributes to shareholders. Dividends for common shares can be paid either in cash or in additional shares (called *stock dividends*). Common share dividends are usually declared either annually or quarterly (four times a year) by a corporation's board of directors. However, these dividends are paid only after all other obligations of the firm—payments to suppliers, employees, bondholders, and other creditors, plus taxes and preferred share dividends—have been met. Some firms, especially rapidly growing companies and those in high-technology industries, choose not to pay any dividends on their common shares. Instead, they reinvest their profits in more buildings, equipment, and new products in hope of earning greater profits in the future. As noted in Chapter 17, these reinvested profits are called *retained earnings.*

One advantage of common shares ownership is its liquidity: Many common shares are actively traded in securities markets and can be bought and sold quickly. An investor can benefit by selling common shares when the price increases, or *appreciates,* above the original purchase price. For example, in 2000, Procter & Gamble's stock was trading at a low of $52 a share. Soon after, P&G chief executive A. G. Lafley launched a new strategy for the consumer products firm. Instead of constant—and costly—new-product introductions, P&G refocused its marketing efforts on its most successful and established products, including brands like Tide, Crest, and Pampers. As profits rose, so did the company's share price. By early 2003, P&G's share price had soared to $85 a share, a more than 60 percent increase.[11]

Although the returns from common share dividends and price appreciation can be quite attractive, common shareholders have no guarantee that they will get any return on their investment. Share prices are subject to many risks related to the economy, the industry, and the company. Like any commodity, the price of a specific company's stock is affected by supply and demand. The supply of shares is limited by the number of shares a company has issued, whereas demand is created by the number of investors who want to buy the shares from those who already own them. Factors that can increase demand for shares—and their price—include strong financial reports, new-product market opportunities, and positive industry trends. However, demand can fall—and a share's price drop—when negative events occur.

The threat of a lawsuit or increased government regulation of a firm's industry can send stock prices downward. Market conditions can also affect a company's share price. For example, video game manufacturers have faced tough competition and a slowing market in the past few years. Electronic Arts, the publisher of popular games like Madden NFL and The Sims, saw its share price drop nearly 33 percent in just three months in early 2003. The reason? Sales of Electronic Arts' much-anticipated Sims Online interactive game didn't live up to sales expectations, forcing the firm to cut the software's retail price drastically.[12]

Factors like these can hold down a common share's dividends and its price, making it hard to predict the share's return.

Preferred Shares *Preferred shares* are a second form of corporate ownership. Unlike common shareholders, preferred shareholders do not receive voting rights. However, preferred shares provide several advantages to investors that common shares do not, specifically in the payment of dividends and the distribution of assets if the firm is liquidated.

The dividend for preferred shares is usually set at the time the shares are issued, giving preferred shareholders a clearer picture of the dividend proceeds they can expect from their investment. This dividend can be expressed either in dollar terms or as a percentage of the share's par (stated) value. As with common shares, the company's board of directors might decide not to pay dividends if the company encounters financial hardships. However, most preferred shares are *cumulative preferred shares*, which means that preferred shareholders must receive all unpaid dividends before any dividends can be paid to common shareholders. Suppose, for example, that a company with a $5 annual preferred dividend misses its quarterly payment of $1.25 ($5.00 ÷ 4). The following quarter, the firm must pay preferred shareholders $2.50—$1.25 in unpaid preferred dividends from the previous quarter plus the $1.25 preferred dividend for the current quarter— before it can pay any dividends to common shareholders. Similarly, if the company goes bankrupt, preferred shareholders are paid off before common shareholders.

Investors like preferred shares because of the fixed dividend income. Although companies are not legally obligated to pay preferred dividends, most have an excellent record of doing so. However, the fixed dividend can also be a disadvantage, because it limits the cash paid to investors. Thus, preferred shares have less potential for price appreciation than common shares.

Cashing in with Bonds

Bonds are long-term debt obligations (liabilities) of corporations and governments. A bond certificate is issued as proof of the obligation. The issuer of a bond must pay the buyer a fixed amount of money—called **interest,** stated as the *coupon rate*—on a regular schedule, typically every six months. The issuer must also pay the bondholder the amount borrowed—called the **principal,** or *par value*—at the bond's maturity date (due date). Bonds are usually issued in units of $1,000—for instance, $1,000, $5,000, or $10,000. The two sources of return on bond investments are interest income and gains from sale of the bonds.

Unlike common and preferred shareholders, who are owners, bondholders are creditors (lenders) of the issuer. In the event of liquidation, the bondholders' claim on the assets of the issuer comes before that of any shareholders.

Bonds do not have to be held to maturity. They can be bought and sold in the securities markets. However, the price of a bond changes over its life as market interest rates fluctuate. When the market interest rate drops below the fixed interest rate on a bond, it becomes more valuable, and the price rises. If interest rates rise, the bond's price will fall.

Corporate Bonds *Corporate bonds*, as the name implies, are issued by corporations. They usually have a par value of $1,000. They may be secured or unsecured, include special provisions for early retirement, or be convertible to common shares.

---

7 *learning goal*

interest

A fixed amount of money paid by the issuer of a bond to the bondholder on a regular schedule, typically every six months; stated as the *coupon rate*.

principal

The amount borrowed by the issuer of a bond; also called *par value*.

high-yield (junk) bonds
High-risk, high-return bonds.

secured bonds
Corporate bonds for which specific assets have been pledged as collateral.

mortgage bonds
Corporate bonds that are secured by property, such as land, equipment, or buildings.

debentures
Unsecured bonds that are backed only by the reputation of the issuer and its promise to pay the principal and interest when due.

convertible bonds
Corporate bonds that are issued with an option that allows the bondholder to convert them into common shares.

bond ratings
Letter grades assigned to bond issues to indicate their quality, or level of risk; assigned by rating agencies such as Moody's and Standard & Poor's (S&P).

High-yield, or **junk, bonds** are high-risk, high-return bonds that became popular during the 1980s, when they were widely used to finance mergers and takeovers. Today, they are used by companies whose credit characteristics would not otherwise allow them access to the debt markets. Because of their high risk, these bonds generally earn 3 percent or more above the returns on high-quality corporate bonds.

Corporate bonds can be either secured or unsecured. **Secured bonds** have specific assets pledged as collateral, which the bondholder has a right to take if the bond issuer defaults. **Mortgage bonds** are secured by property, such as land, equipment, or buildings. **Debentures** are unsecured bonds. They are backed only by the reputation of the issuer and its promise to pay the principal and interest when due. In general, debentures have a lower risk of default than secured bonds and therefore have lower interest rates. Of course, a debenture issued by a financially shaky firm probably has greater default risk than a mortgage bond issued by a sound one.

Corporate bonds may be issued with an option for the bondholder to convert them into common shares. **Convertible bonds** generally allow the bondholder to exchange each bond for a specified number of shares. For instance, a $1,000 par value convertible bond might be convertible into 40 shares—no matter what happens to the market price of the common shares. Because convertible bonds could be converted to shares when the price is very high, these bonds usually have a lower interest rate than non-convertible bonds.

Government Securities Both the federal government and provincial governments also issue bonds to finance programs. When the government of Canada borrows money on a short-term basis, it issues Treasury bills (T-bills); whereas bonds are meant to be held for a longer period.

Bond Ratings Bonds vary in quality, depending on the financial strength of the issuer. Because the claims of bondholders come before those of shareholders, bonds are generally considered less risky than shares. However, some bonds are, in fact, quite risky. Companies can *default*—fail to make scheduled interest or principal payments—on their bonds.

Investors can use **bond ratings,** letter grades assigned to bond issues to indicate their quality or level of risk. Ratings for corporate bonds are easy to find. The two largest and best-known rating agencies are Moody's and Standard & Poor's (S&P), whose publications are in most libraries and in stock brokerages. Exhibit 18.7 lists the letter grades assigned by Moody's and S&P. A bond's rating can change with events.

Exhibit 18.7

BOND RATING CODES

RATING	S&P	MOODY'S
Highest quality	AAA	Aaa
High quality	AA	Aa
Upper medium quality	A	A
Medium grade	BBB	Baa
Somewhat speculative	BB	Ba
Low grade, speculative	B	B
Low grade, default possible	CCC	Caa
Low grade, partial recovery possible	CC	Ca
Default, recovery unlikely	C	C

SOURCE: Moody's Investor's Service http://www.cftech.com/BrainBank/FINANCE/BndRtgs.html, accessed Dec 1, 2006

Mutual funds pool investor funds into professionally managed, diversified share or bond portfolios, which can reduce risk for investors. However, as this ad for the Vanguard Group discusses, investors should consider the fees and expenses charged by mutual fund companies before choosing a fund.

8   learning goal

mutual fund
A financial service company that pools its investors' funds to buy a selection of securities that meet its stated investment goals.

futures contracts
Legally binding obligations to buy or sell specified quantities of commodities or financial instruments at an agreed-on price at a future date.

What are the advantages and disadvantages of common share for investors and corporations?

What is a preferred share, and how is it different from a common share?

Describe the common features of all bonds and the advantages and disadvantages of bonds for investors.

PLAYING THE MARKET WITH OTHER TYPES OF SECURITIES

In addition to equity and debt, investors have several other types of securities available to them. The most popular are mutual funds, futures contracts, and options. Mutual funds appeal to a wide range of investors. Futures contracts and options are more complex investments for experienced investors.

Mutual Funds

Suppose that you have $1,000 to invest but don't know which shares or bonds to buy, when to buy them, or when to sell them. By investing in a mutual fund, you can buy shares in a large, professionally managed *portfolio*, or group, of shares and bonds. A **mutual fund** is a financial service company that pools its investors' funds to buy a selection of securities—marketable securities, shares, bonds, or a combination of securities—that meet its stated investment goals.

Each mutual fund focuses on one of a wide variety of possible investment goals, such as growth or income. Many large financial service companies sell a wide variety of mutual funds, each with a different investment goal. Investors can pick and choose funds that match their particular interests. Some specialized funds invest in a particular type of company or asset: in one industry, such as health care or technology; in a geographical region, such as Asia; or in an asset, such as precious metals.

Mutual funds appeal to investors for three main reasons:

- They are a good way to hold a diversified and, thus, less risky, portfolio. Investors with only $500 or $1,000 to invest cannot diversify much on their own. Buying shares in a mutual fund lets them own part of a portfolio that might contain 100 or more securities.
- Mutual funds are professionally managed.
- Mutual funds might offer higher returns than individual investors could achieve on their own.

Futures Contracts

Futures contracts are legally binding obligations to buy or sell specified quantities of commodities (agricultural or mining products) or financial instruments (securities or currencies) at an agreed-on price at a future date. An investor can buy commodity futures contracts in cattle, pork bellies (large slabs of bacon), eggs, coffee, flour, gasoline, fuel oil, lumber, wheat, gold, and silver. Financial futures include Treasury securities and foreign currencies, such as the British pound or Japanese yen.

Futures contracts do not pay interest or dividends. The return depends solely on favourable price changes. These are very risky investments, because the prices can vary a great deal.

Options

options

Contracts that entitle holders to buy or sell specified quantities of common shares or other financial instruments at a set price during a specified time.

Options are contracts that entitle holders to buy or sell specified quantities of common shares or other financial instruments at a set price during a specified time. As with futures contracts, investors must correctly guess future price movements in the underlying financial instrument to earn a positive return. Unlike futures contracts, options do not legally obligate the holder to buy or sell and the price paid for an option is the maximum amount that can be lost. However, options have very short maturities, so it is easy to lose a lot of money quickly with them.

concept check

Why do mutual funds appeal to investors? Discuss some of the investment goals pursued by mutual funds.

What are futures contracts? Why are they risky investments?

How do options differ from futures contracts?

ON THE TRADING FLOOR: SECURITIES MARKETS

learning goal

institutional investors

Investment professionals who are paid to manage other people's money.

Stocks, bonds, and other securities are traded in securities markets. These markets streamline the purchase and sales activities of investors by allowing transactions to be made quickly and at a fair price. They make the transfer of funds from lenders to borrowers much easier. Securities markets are busy places. On an average day, individual and institutional investors trade billions of shares in more than 10,000 companies through securities markets. They also trade bonds, mutual funds, futures contracts, and options. *Individual investors* invest their own money to achieve their personal financial goals. **Institutional investors** are investment professionals who are paid to manage other people's money. Most of these professional money managers work for financial institutions, such as banks, mutual funds, insurance companies, and pension funds. Institutional investors control very large sums of money, often buying stocks in 10,000-share blocks. They aim to meet the investment goals of their clients. Institutional investors are a major force in the securities markets, accounting for about half of the dollar volume of equities traded.

Businesses and governments also take part in the securities markets. Corporations issue bonds and shares to raise funds to finance their operations. They are also among the institutional investors that purchase corporate and government securities.

HOT Links

You have probably heard of buying on margin. Find out how this works at http://www.investopedia.com/university/margin/margin1.asp.

investment bankers

Firms that act as intermediaries, buying securities from corporations and governments and reselling them to the public.

underwriting

The process of buying securities from corporations and governments and reselling them to the public, with the aim of reselling at a higher price; the main activity of investment bankers.

stockbroker

A person who is licensed to buy and sell securities on behalf of clients.

The Role of Investment Bankers and Stockbrokers

Two types of investment specialists play key roles in the functioning of the securities markets. **Investment bankers** help companies raise long-term financing. These firms act as intermediaries, buying securities from corporations and governments and reselling them to the public. This process, called **underwriting,** is the main activity of the investment banker, which acquires the security for an agreed-on price and hopes to be able to resell it at a higher price to make a profit. Investment bankers advise clients on the pricing and structure of new securities offerings, as well as on mergers, acquisitions, and other types of financing. Most Canadian banks now offer investment banking services.

A **stockbroker** is a person who is licensed to buy and sell securities on behalf of clients. Also called *account executives*, these investment professionals work for brokerage firms and execute the orders customers place for shares, bonds, mutual funds, and other securities.

© HUREWITZ CREATIVE / CORBIS

Stockbrokers are the link between public companies and the investors interested in buying their shares. Before investing in securities, investors must select a stock brokerage firm, select a stockbroker at that firm, and open an account. Investors are wise to seek a broker who understands their investment goals and can help them pursue their objectives.

Brokerage firms are paid commissions for executing clients' transactions. Although brokers can charge whatever they want, most firms have fixed commission schedules for small transactions. These commissions usually depend on the value of the transaction and the number of shares involved.

On-line Investing

Improvements in Internet technology have made it possible for investors to research, analyze, and trade securities on-line. Although traditional brokerage firms still dominate the investment industry, many investors use on-line brokerage firms for their securities transactions. On-line brokerages are popular with "do-it-yourself" investors, who choose their own shares and don't want to pay a full-service broker for these services. Lower transaction costs are a major benefit. Fees at on-line brokerages range from $8 to $20 to buy 200 shares of a $20 share, compared to about $115 using a traditional firm's brokers. However, many traditional brokerage firms now have added on-line trading options to their list of services.

Linking investors and public companies, stockbrokers serve a vital role in the securities marketplace. Today, most customer buy-sell orders are transacted electronically.

HOT Links

Check on-line investment information at the following: http://www.questrade.com, http://www.bmoinvestorline .com, and http://www .tradefreedom.com.

primary market
The securities market where new securities are sold to the public, usually with the help of investment bankers.

secondary market
The securities market where old (already issued) securities are bought and sold, or traded, among investors.

Types of Markets

Securities markets can be divided into primary and secondary markets. The **primary market** is where *new* securities are sold to the public, usually with the help of investment bankers. In the primary market, the issuer of the security gets the proceeds from the transaction. A security is sold in the primary market just once—when it is first issued by the corporation or government.

Later transactions take place in the **secondary market,** where *old* (already issued) securities are bought and sold, or traded, among investors. The issuers generally are not involved in these transactions. The vast majority of securities transactions take place in secondary markets, which include the organized stock exchanges, the over-the-counter securities market, and the commodities exchanges. You'll see announcements of both primary and secondary shares and bond offerings in *The Globe and Mail* and other newspapers.

concept check

How do securities markets help businesses and investors? How does an investment banker work with companies to issue securities?

How is on-line investing changing the securities industry?

Distinguish between primary and secondary securities markets.

BUYING AND SELLING AT SECURITIES EXCHANGES

10 *learning goal*

organized share exchanges
Organizations on whose premises securities are resold using an auction-style trading system.

The two key types of securities markets are organized stock exchanges and the over-the-counter market. **Organized stock exchanges** are organizations on whose premises securities are resold. They operate using an auction-style trading system. All other securities are traded in the over-the-counter market.

Trading in an organized stock exchange is done by exchange members, who act as agents for individual and institutional investors. To make transactions in an organized stock exchange, an individual or firm must be a member and own a

© AP/WORLD WIDE PHOTOS

Once a customer order is transmitted to the trading floor, getting the most competitive price for the customer is the job of the brokerage's floor broker. Floor brokers must act quickly and aggressively to outbid other brokers.

HOT *Links*

To learn more about the Toronto Stock Exchange, the TSX Venture Exchange, how companies get listed on the exchanges, and the most current stock price quotes, visit http://www.tsx.ca.

HOT *Links*

The Montreal Exchange trades primarily in the options, futures, and derivative markets. To find out more about these, visit http://www.m-x.ca.

over-the-counter (OTC) market

A sophisticated telecommunications network that links dealers and enables them to trade securities.

National Association of Securities Dealers Automated Quotation (NASDAQ) system

The first electronic-based stock market and the fastest-growing part of the stock market.

"seat" on that exchange. Owners of the limited number of seats must meet certain financial requirements and agree to observe a broad set of rules when trading securities.

The Primary Canadian Stock Exchanges

The cornerstone of the Canadian financial system is the TSX Group. The TSX Group owns and operates the two national stock exchanges, the Toronto Stock Exchange and the TSX Venture Exchange. The Toronto Stock Exchange serves the senior equity market (a broad range of established businesses from across Canada, the United States, and other countries), and the public venture equity market is served by the TSX Venture Exchange (which provides emerging companies with access to capital).

Other Exchanges Important to Canadian Businesses

Of all the foreign exchanges, the New York Stock Exchange (NYSE) is the most important to Canadian business. Canadian companies that are listed on the NYSE have access to a greater pool of potential investors because of the sheer number of people who live and invest in the United States. Only companies that meet certain minimum requirements are eligible to be listed on the NYSE.

Global Trading and Foreign Exchanges

Improved communications and the elimination of many legal barriers are helping the securities markets go global. The number of securities listed on exchanges in more than one country is growing.

Stock exchanges also exist in foreign countries. The London and Tokyo Stock Exchanges rank behind the NYSE and NASDAQ (described below). Other important foreign stock exchanges include those in Buenos Aires, Zurich, Sydney, Paris, Frankfurt, Hong Kong, and Taiwan.

The Over-the-Counter Market

Unlike the organized share exchanges, the **over-the-counter (OTC)** market is not a specific institution with a trading floor. It is a sophisticated telecommunications network that links dealers. The **National Association of Securities Dealers Automated Quotation (NASDAQ)** system, the first electronic-based stock market, is the fastest-growing part of the stock market. It provides up-to-date bid and ask prices on about 3,500 of the most active OTC securities. Its sophisticated electronic communication system is the main reason for the popularity and growth of the OTC market.

The securities of many well-known Canadian companies, some of which could be listed on the organized exchanges, trade on the OTC market, for example Research in Motion. Although there are Canadian companies listed on NASDAQ, most companies are American.

What makes the NASDAQ different from an organized exchange? On the TSX, one specialist handles all transactions in a particular stock, but on the NASDAQ system, a number of dealers handle ("make a market in") a security. For instance, about 40 dealers make a market in Apple Computer shares. Thus, dealers compete, improving an investor's ability to get a good price.

The TSX and the NASDAQ face a competitive threat from the emergence of other electronic exchanges called *electronic communications networks (ECNs)*. ECNs allow institutional traders and some individuals to make direct transactions without using brokers, securities exchanges, or the NASDAQ, in what is called the *fourth market*. Because they deal mostly in NASDAQ shares, ECNs are taking trading volume away from the NASDAQ. ECNs are most effective for high-volume, actively traded shares. Money managers and institutions such as pension funds and mutual funds with large amounts of money to invest like ECNs because they cost less than other trading venues.

Market Conditions: Bull Market or Bear Market?

bull markets

Markets in which securities prices are rising.

bear markets

Markets in which securities prices are falling.

Two terms that often appear in the financial press are "bull market" and "bear market." Securities prices rise in **bull markets.** These markets are normally associated with investor optimism, economic recovery, and government action to encourage economic growth. In contrast, prices go down in **bear markets.** Investor pessimism, economic slowdown, and government restraint are all possible causes. As a rule, investors earn better returns in bull markets; they earn low, and sometimes negative, returns in bear markets.

Bull and bear market conditions are hard to predict. Usually, they can't be identified until after they begin. Over the past 50 years, the stock market has generally been bullish, reflecting general economic growth and prosperity. Bull markets tend to last longer than bear markets.

concept check

How do the organized share exchanges differ from the OTC market?

Explain a bull market and a bear market.

Trends in the Financial Industry

11 *learning goal*

Once a highly regulated industry offering limited services, the banking industry continues to change. Trends influencing the direction of banking are on-line banking, consolidation, and the integration of banking with brokerage and insurance services.

ON-LINE BANKING

HOT Links

To learn more about Canadian banks on-line, visit http://www.businessjeeves.ca/Banks.html.

Banks are using Internet technology to expand their services. "Online banking may be the critical service that enables banks to maintain their role as the dominant provider of financial services," says Paul Johnson, an analyst with International Data.[13]

One service that offers banks tremendous profit potential is on-line bill presentment and payment. The service will benefit many businesses, such as utility firms, because it will eliminate the time-consuming and costly process of printing bills, mailing them to customers, and waiting for the cheques to arrive and clear.[14]

ONE-STOP FINANCIAL SHOPPING

In 1992, the federal government reduced the various barriers and created a new framework for competition. These far reaching changes include the ability for banks to offer a wider range of services to their customers. The deregulation of the financial industry saw financial services being consolidated, and now banks offer many of the services that were traditionally offered by industry-specific institutions. For example, insurance, brokerage services, and so on were not offered by the banks prior to the deregulation.

concept check

How has technology changed the way we bank?

How have the changes in legislation governing financial institutions changed the way they do business?

Making Ethical Choices

TRIALS AND MANIPULATIONS

You have just joined a prestigious investment banking firm as a junior securities analyst covering the pharmaceutical industry. Eager to make a good impression on your boss, you diligently monitor the companies your group follows and search for unique ways to get the scoop on new drugs currently under development. Rumour has it that a biotechnology firm has come out with a new drug for insomnia with the potential to be a blockbuster. You've heard that other analysts, posing as doctors or patients, have called the managers of clinical trials to get inside information or have paid doctors involved in the trials to disclose confidential data. They then use what they learn in their share reports, making recommendations that can significantly impact the price of the share.

Why not go a step further, you wonder, and participate in the trial for the insomnia drug yourself? After all, you've had many sleepless nights and believe you'd

qualify for the study. Not only would you help the cause of science, but you'd also get the chance to talk to doctors about the other patients in the study to find out more about the results of the trial so far.

With your boss's approval, you apply for the trial. When you arrive for your first appointment, you are asked to sign a confidentiality agreement to not disclose any treatment information based on your experiences or anything you learn about other patients.

ETHICAL DILEMMA

Should you honour the confidentiality agreement or share your findings with your boss to use in writing the share report?

SOURCES: Getta Anand and Randall Smith, "Biotech Analysts Strive to Peek Inside Clinical Tests of Drugs," *Wall Street Journal*, August 8, 2002; and Penni Crabtree, "Firm Fined for 'Creative' Research on Neurocrine," *San Diego Union-Tribune*, October 29, 2002.

Great Ideas to Use Now

After reading this chapter, you might be wondering if investing in shares or bonds is right for you. Like millions of others, you've probably read headlines about the markets' rise and fall. How can you minimize the risks while reaping the benefits of securities investments? The basic information presented in this chapter is a good starting point. It's also important to understand some of the key strategies used by successful investors.

THE TIME IS NOW

As the Dow Jones Industrial Average (Dow) fell after nearly a decade of nonstop growth, many investors panicked. They rushed to sell off their shares—often at a loss—because they believed doing otherwise would spell financial ruin.

These investors fell prey to some common mistakes of novice investors. For one thing, they got caught up in the mystique of the Dow. Although it is the most publicized market indicator, it represents the activity of just 30 large industrial stocks. A milestone on the Dow is just another number. It doesn't tell investors where their individual investments are going or how long the market will stay at a particular level.

The stock market has always been cyclical in nature. Share prices rise and fall depending on many factors. A bull markets is almost invariably followed by a bear market. Although every investor dreams of buying a share at its low point and selling it at its peak, predicting the market's ups and downs is impossible.

Successful investors think of the stock market as a long-term investment. They know that it's important to let their investments grow over time, and they avoid falling into the trap of thinking that they should sell their shares whenever there's a market downturn. They also recognize that the best time to buy stock is when the market is at a low point.

Financial advisers suggest investing small amounts over time. Start early and invest regularly, whether the market is up or down. Don't immediately panic if the market takes a nosedive. The highs and lows will average out over time, and you'll find yourself with long-term gains.

Another reason many investors lost money in recent years is that they failed to diversify their investment portfolios. Many poured money into technology shares while ignoring the stocks of businesses in other industries. When the technology boom ended, these investors were hit the hardest. Building a portfolio of individual shares in different industries can help cushion losses. Investing in mutual funds can also help spread your risk over a broad group of securities. Also, consider investing in

---

CUSTOMER SATISFACTION AND QUALITY

Some would say that the first obligation of a public corporation is to make money for its shareholders. Of course, companies have many stakeholders—employees, customers, and the communities where they operate—but building shareholder value has been front and centre of the concerns facing most corporate executives for the past 20 years.

As the stock markets boom, corporations face tremendous pressure from shareholders to keep pace. Many CEOs made strategic decisions that were focused mainly on pushing the share price. Unfortunately, as investors at companies like Enron and WorldCom eventually discovered, some corporate executives responded to the pressure by making unscrupulous choices.

Shareholder value will always be a central concern of publicly traded companies, but now many chief executives have discovered that providing shareholder value means more than just inflated share prices. It also means serving investors with financial results built on honesty and realistic expectations. It means keeping an eye on the basic principle of business: Make your customers happy first.

Procter & Gamble's chief executive A. G. Lafley sums it up best when asked how P&G shares have soared nearly 60 percent in value since 2000. "Over the last half of the 1990s, we were a little bit too shareholder focused, too growth-at-any-cost focused," he says. "I tried to get people to flip that around. If we create brands that make a difference to our customers and focus on the fundamentals, ultimately shareholder growth will take care of itself."

SOURCES: Joseph Nocera, "Value Judgments," *Money*, December 2001, http://www.business2.com; and Nicholas Stein, "America's Most Admired Companies," *Fortune*, March 3, 2003, 81.

a mix of shares and bonds. Bonds tend to rise in value as share prices drop, and vice versa, further lessening the risk of losing it all when one investment vehicle declines.

Most important, do your homework. Don't make investment decisions based only on what you find on a Web site or in a single magazine. It's easy to be taken in by someone hyping a stock. To avoid investment scams, do your own research. Investigate the company's standing with the TSX, and look at its historic performance over a number of years. Remember, if it sounds too good to be true, it probably is!

SUMMARY OF LEARNING GOALS

1 What is money, what are its characteristics and functions, and what are the parts of the Canadian money supply?

Money is anything accepted as payment for goods and services. For money to be a suitable means of exchange, it should be scarce, durable, portable, and divisible. Money functions as a medium of exchange, a standard of value, and a store of value. The Canadian money supply consists of currency (coins and paper money), demand deposits (chequing accounts), and time deposits (interest-bearing deposits that cannot be withdrawn on demand).

2 What are the basic functions of the Bank of Canada, and what tools does it use to manage the money supply?

The Bank of Canada promotes the economic and financial welfare of Canada, by

- conducting monetary policy in a way that fosters confidence in the value of money,

- supplying quality bank notes that are readily accepted and secure against counterfeiting,

- promoting the safety and efficiency of Canada's financial system,

- providing efficient and effective funds management services, and

- communicating their objectives openly and effectively and standing accountable for their actions.

The Bank of Canada uses the Monetary Policy to manage the money supply.

3 What are the key financial institutions, and what role do they play in the process of financial intermediation?

Financial institutions can be divided into two main groups: depository institutions and non-depository institutions. Depository institutions include chartered banks, trust companies, and credit unions and caisses populaires. Non-depository institutions include insurance companies, pension funds, brokerage firms, and finance companies. Financial institutions ease the transfer of funds between suppliers and demanders.

4 How does the Canada Deposit Insurance Corporation protect depositors' funds?

The CDIC is a Crown corporation that insures eligible deposits at member institutions and reimburses depositors for the amount of their insured deposits when a member institution fails.

5 **What role do Canadian banks play in the international marketplace?**

Canadian banks provide loans and trade-related services to foreign governments and businesses. They also offer specialized services such as cash management and foreign currency exchange.

6 **How do common shares and preferred shares differ as investments?**

Common and preferred shares represent ownership—equity—in a corporation. Common shareholders have voting rights, but their claim on profits and assets ranks behind that of holders of other securities. Preferred shareholders receive a stated dividend. It must be paid before any dividends are distributed to common shareholders.

Common shares are more risky than preferred shares. They offer the potential for increased value through growth in the stock price and income through dividend payments. However, neither price increases nor dividends are guaranteed. Preferred shares are usually bought for their dividend income rather than potential price appreciation.

7 **What are bonds, and what investment advantages and disadvantages do they offer?**

Bonds are a form of debt and may be secured or unsecured. Bondholders are creditors of the issuing organization, and their claims on income and assets rank ahead of those of preferred and common shareholders. The corporation or government entity that issues the bonds must pay interest periodically and repay the principal at maturity. Bonds provide a steady source of income and the potential for price appreciation if interest rates fall below the coupon rate. However, investors also bear the risk that rising interest rates might erode the bond's price.

8 **What other types of securities are available to investors?**

Mutual funds are financial service companies that pool the funds of many investors to buy a diversified portfolio of securities. Investors choose mutual funds because they offer a convenient way of diversifying and are professionally managed. Futures contracts are legally binding obligations to buy or sell specified quantities of commodities or financial instruments at an agreed-on price at a future date. They are very risky investments, because the price of the commodity or financial instrument can change drastically. Options are contracts that entitle the holder to buy or sell specified quantities of common shares or other financial instruments at a set price during a specified time. They, too, are high-risk investments.

9 **What is the function of the securities markets?**

Securities markets allow shares, bonds, and other securities to be bought and sold quickly and at a fair price. New issues are sold in the primary market. After that, securities are traded in the secondary market. Investment bankers specialize in issuing and selling new security issues. Stockbrokers are licensed professionals who buy and sell securities on behalf of their clients.

10 **Where can investors buy and sell securities?**

Securities are resold on organized share exchanges, such as the Toronto Stock Exchange and regional share exchanges, and in the over-the-counter market, a telecommunications network linking dealers throughout North America. The most actively traded securities are listed on the NASDAQ system, so dealers and brokers can perform trades quickly and efficiently.

11 What trends are reshaping the financial industry?

By using Internet technology, banks are delivering more services on-line. Mergers and acquisitions in the financial industry continue to consolidate the industry, helping financial institutions to improve their operating efficiency, reduce costs, and extend their geographic reach. Recent passage of bank reform legislation that allows banks to market securities and insurance products will help banks compete with non-depository institutions and with banks in other countries.

EXPERIENTIAL EXERCISES

1. Is it really free? How much is your chequing account really costing you? Maybe more than you think. Even "free" chequing accounts aren't always a good deal when you add up extra costs such as ATM fees, lost interest, bounced-cheque charges, and other hidden expenses. Take a closer look at your current chequing account, and then comparison shop to see if you could be getting a better deal elsewhere. Here's how.

   - Ask yourself how you really use your chequing account. What's the average balance you keep in your account? How many cheques do you write in a typical month? What time of day do you do most of your banking, and where do you prefer to do it?

   - Zero in on the real cost of your current chequing account. Once you know how you use your chequing account, you can get a clearer idea of its true cost—beyond just the monthly account fee. Do you write more cheques per month than allowed by your "free" account? What is the cost of each cheque? How many times do you use the ATM instead of a branch? How much does it cost each time? Do you pay extra for overdraft protection? What does your bank charge for bounced cheques? Add in any bonuses you receive with your chequing account as well. For example, does your bank waive your credit card's annual fee for keeping your chequing account with them?

   - Comparison shop. Check the websites of the major banks and credit unions in your area. Could you pay lower fees elsewhere? Could you earn interest on your chequing account at a credit union? Would you be better off paying a monthly fee with unlimited cheque-writing privileges? Crunch the numbers to find the best deal.

2. Compare brokerages. Visit the sites of two on-line brokerages, such as E*Trade (http://www.etrade.ca) or BMO (https://www.bmoinvestorline.com), or any others you know. Compare them for ease of use, quality of information, and other criteria you select. Summarize your findings. Which firm would you prefer to use, and why?

3. Track stock prices. Pick a portfolio of five companies in at least three different industries. Choose companies you know, read the financial press to find good candidates, or follow the stock on the TSX. Set up a table to track the stock prices. Record the end-of-month prices for the past six months, and track the daily price movements for at least two weeks (longer is even better!). Visit the Web sites of these companies to view their investor relations information. Finally, monitor economic and market trends and other events that affect market conditions. Share the performance of the portfolio with your classmates. Explain your basis for selecting each stock, and analyze its price changes.

4. Research the trends in the initial public offering (IPO) marketplace from 2000 to present. Then select two IPO success stories and two failures. Prepare a report for the class on their performance. What lessons about the securities markets can you learn from their stories?

5. What role do a CEO's actions/strategies have in influencing a company's stock performance? Prepare a class presentation that answers this question using both positive and negative examples from at least three companies covered in recent business news. In your presentation, discuss what your recommendations for each CEO would be.

6. At the Vanguard Group's site, http://www.vanguard.com, go to the page for "Personal Investors," then to the "Planning & Education" section. Read about investor education and mutual funds. After learning about the fundamentals of mutual funds, prepare a presentation for the class based on the materials.

7. You've been asked to address your investment club on socially responsible investing and how companies qualify as socially responsible. Research this topic at the Web sites of the Social Investment Forum, http://www.socialinvest.org. Prepare a detailed outline of the key points you would include in the speech. How can your personal financial decisions have a positive impact on communities and the environment? Do you support socially responsible investing?

REVIEW QUESTIONS

1. What are the characteristics of money?
2. What are the functions of money?
3. Differentiate between M1, M2, and M2+ (M3).
4. What are the roles of the Bank of Canada?
5. What are chartered banks, and what are their roles?
6. What are some of the non-depository financial institutions?
7. What agency protects depositors, and to what limit?
8. Discuss the differences between common and preferred shares.
9. Discuss the use of bonds as a form of liability.
10. What are some other types of securities (other than common shares, preferred shares, and bonds)?
11. What are the security markets? What are the two key securities markets?
12. What is the role of investment bankers and stockbrokers?
13. What are the current trends in financial institutions?

CREATIVE THINKING CASE
ING Direct Serves up Coffee, Tea, and Mortgages

ING Direct's mission is clear, says president and CEO Arkadi Kuhlmann: to challenge the traditional banking industry by offering consumers a new option. He says,

> Look at an airline such as Southwest. People like them because they make it easy to fly. They also make you feel as if they're on your side by cracking jokes and not wearing standard uniforms. We're trying to do that with banking. We want to make people feel proud about saving their money— even make them feel that it's a cool thing to do.

Step into one of ING Direct's three branch offices, and you hardly know you're in a bank. Dubbed ING Direct cafés, their façades are made of glass, and the colour scheme inside is bright orange. Behind the counters, sales associates serve up cappuccino and biscotti along with information on mortgages, savings accounts, and CDs. Customers take a seat at nearby café-style tables to sip their coffee and do their actual banking at Internet stations.

The cafés are all part of a strategy that have helped ING rocket to $10 billion in assets since its founding in September 2000. With more than a million customers and new assets streaming in at more than $500 million a month, the Wilmington, Delaware, financial institution is now one of the 50 biggest banks in the country.

Kuhlmann says ING focuses on the things customers really want—high interest rates on deposits and radically simplified loans—while eliminating the high-cost services that customers can do without. As a result, ING doesn't have an ATM network, and customers are urged to do most of their banking via the Internet or over the phone. Marketing focuses on low-cost, high-return campaigns. Sales associates (unlike at traditional banks ING doesn't call customer contact personnel customer service representatives) are trained to develop upbeat, positive relationships with customers but also earn steep commissions. Customers are ING's biggest selling tool. Nearly 40 percent of new accounts are generated by word of mouth when happy customers tell others about ING.

CRITICAL THINKING QUESTIONS

1. Do you agree with Kuhlmann, that most banking customers would choose higher interest rates and simplified loans over extra banking services? Why or why not?

2. Compare the structure and economics of the airline industry to the financial services industry. How are they alike? How are they different? ING Direct's CEO compares the company to Southwest Airlines. Do you think this is a fair comparison? Why? What challenges might ING Direct face that are different from those encountered by Southwest Airlines in its early history?

3. How might ING Direct's current strategy affect its future growth?

SOURCES: Scott Kirsner, "Would You Like a Mortgage with Your Mocha?," *Fast Company*, March 2003, http://www.fastcompany.com; and Stephanie Milloti, "Coffee, Tea, or IRA," *Business 2.0*, June 2002, http://www.business2.com.

VIDEO CASE
Card Tricks

Can't wait for your new credit card to arrive in the mail? A little trip to Mexico on spring break? Or how about Fort Lauderdale?

Stop right there! Have you read the agreement? Most of us never do. Credit card agreements are written by lawyers, for lawyers. The lender is in charge of this relationship. You are simply borrowing from them. Interest is charged on the entire balance if you do not pay it in full. Hard to do on your 20 hours a week at Starbucks.

Credit card companies will often start you out at perhaps 1.5 percent interest for six months. What happens at the end of six months? Unfortunately the interest rate is not tied to the prime rate in any way. The lender can change your rate at its discretion and without any warning. You might also be charged an extra fee for using your card in another country, in addition to the currency conversion fee rolled into your exchange rate. If you do make your minimum monthly payment on time, the credit card company might increase your spending limit. But is this really a problem?

It most definitely is. There are more than *50 million* Visa and MasterCards in circulation in Canada with more than 22 million of these carrying a balance. Canadians owe approximately $50 billion on their Visa and MasterCards. Interest rates on the Visa and MasterCards can vary widely, but some department store cards are at an interest rate of almost 30 percent!

So what do we do to avoid trouble? The first and best course of action is to pay off the balance each month. However that is not always possible. Other options include the use of a personal line of credit, which has a lower interest rate, or, at the very least, finding a credit card that has a lower rate. Check out http://www.fcac.gc.ca/, an interactive site of the Financial Consumer Agency of Canada, for a credit card comparison table. You might be surprised by what you see.

CRITICAL THINKING QUESTIONS

1. Assume you charge your spring break trip on your Visa. If the trip costs $1,500, and your interest rate is 17.9 percent, how much would you actually pay if you make regular payments of $125 per month for one year? Do you still owe a balance? How much?

2. Using the PEST model, what environment factors can impact your ability to handle your debt?

SOURCE: CBC, *Marketplace*, "Card Tricks," February 27, 2005.

E-COMMERCE CASE
Canadian Banks' International Presence

Canadian banks want to evolve and expand, but how they do this has been the subject of much debate and controversy. One obvious strategy would be horizontal integration, through merger or acquisition, involving banks, credit unions, or insurance companies. The Canadian Bankers Association supports allowing this strategy, as do the major banks and some of the large insurance companies, whereas Sun Life and Great-West Life want a ban on such mergers. Given the limited opportunities for growth in Canada, the big banks are looking at foreign markets.

The Bank of Montreal purchased the Harris Bank of Chicago in 1984 and has been building up its U.S. presence ever since. The Royal Bank is visible in the southern United States. The Bank of Nova Scotia has been visible in Latin America and the Caribbean for decades and in 2005 acquired two banks in Peru. Toronto-Dominion is the majority shareholder of TD Banknorth, and more acquisitions are planned in the U.S. northeast.

However, all ventures into the United States have not been pretty. The drop in the technology sector of North America contributed to a net loss for TD in 2002, and CIBC's long-standing relationship with Enron cost the bank $80 million in settlement payments to the U.S. Securities and Exchange Commission and $2.4 billion in settlement of a class action suit by Enron investors. Fortunately for the Canadian banks, they have strong retail banking operations in Canada and have relied on this stable income source to buoy their bottom line when things have soured south of the border.

It seems we have a classic catch-22 situation. The Canadian banks argue that they need to expand outside of Canada, but if they are to be able to gain greater access to foreign markets, then Canada must allow foreign access to the domestic market. If this is allowed, competition will increase, supporting the Canadian banks' argument for domestic consolidation. The Bloc, Liberals, and Conservatives are generally on the same side of the debate, with the NDP teetering on the edge. Positions range from advocating on behalf of the banks, to allowing domestic mergers, to blocking any mergers until protection is assured for bank employees and consumers. Major reforms suggested are in the areas of transparency, accountability, community reinvestment, credit card interest rates, as well as consumer and employee protection. However, a very important point is the fact that the Canadian public is not supportive of bank mergers, with small and large businesses both finding the idea less than appealing. If bank reforms are instituted requiring more transparency and accountability, we might just see more Canadian mergers in the financial sector.

CRITICAL THINKING QUESTIONS

1. What are the arguments for and against the merger of banks in Canada?

2. Look once again at the PEST model, and identify which environmental factors could impact, either positively or negatively, Canadian banks operating domestically and internationally.

SOURCES: Murray Cole, "The Bank Merger Debate in the Harper Era," *Canadian Dimension*, 40, no.3 (May/June 2006), 20; and Matthias Rieker, "TD Banknorth on Naming of President," *American Banker*, 171, no. 123 (June 28, 2006), 1. Steve Bliss, "TD to Give TSYS 55% of Canada Market," *American Banker*, 170, no. 206 (October 26, 2005), 12.

Appendix

Making the Connection

Corporate Governance, the Legal Environment, and Taxation

In this appendix we're back to our PEST model. Corporate governance, the legal environment, and taxes fit most directly in the *political* environment, as the government at all levels regulates business activity. It lays out the laws for business to follow and taxes businesses in many different ways.

However, these laws are not shaped by the political environment alone. The political environment responds to the changing needs of the social, economic, and technological environments, changing laws and creating new ones as appropriate. You'll read in this appendix, for example, about laws relating to the natural environment, as the *social* environment becomes increasingly aware and protective of the natural environment; laws relating to employment equity, as the workforce becomes more diverse; laws relating to competition (the *economic* environment) to protect consumers from businesses engaging in anticompetitive behaviour; and laws relating to privacy issues and the Internet (the *technological* environment). An interesting integrative example is in the economic trend toward deregulation—removing regulations

governing competition in certain industries, as opposed to creating new regulations. This practice has led to one of the major trends discussed in Chapter 6—the increase in the number of new small and entrepreneurial businesses in the economy as opportunities have opened up in deregulated industries. For these reasons, business needs to see the whole of the external environment in an integrative and proactive way to stay within the boundaries created by the legal system.

There are many examples in this appendix of how the legal system affects decisions made by business and therefore, ultimately, the success of the business. For example, in the area of *operations,* the law of negligence requires that "businesses comply with industry standards in the manufacture" of products or "liability to consumers may result." This makes it extremely critical to monitor product *quality* (one of our critical success factors) to prevent strict liability resulting from defective products or packaging. In the area of *human resources,* the Employment Standards Act covers minimum wage, hours of work, and other workplace regulations. In the area of *marketing,* the Trademarks Act applies to all businesses and affects the ability of the company to create a unique brand in the customer's mind. Patent law also affects the ability to create a competitive advantage and *meet customer needs* by protecting *innovations* from competitive threats (more critical success factors). And finally, there is the tax system, which, of course, affects the *financial* area of business and cannot be ignored. If not managed correctly, the amount of taxes that a business is required to pay can severely affect its ability to *achieve financial success.*

Associations, industry, and governments are working closely together to protect the *stakeholders of business.* Clearly, as with the changes in the other areas of the external environment, the legal and tax environment of a business is a certain yet virtually uncontrollable factor that must be monitored and managed in an integrative way, for the business to achieve success in all areas.

Appendix

Corporate Governance, the Legal Environment, and Taxation

learning goals

1 What is corporate governance, and why is it important?

2 How does the legal system govern business transactions and settle business disputes?

3 What are the required elements of a valid contract, and what are the key types of business law?

4 What are patents, copyrights, and trademarks? How do these help businesses?

5 What are Employment Standards Acts?

6 What are the most common taxes paid by businesses?

A Basic Understanding of Canadian Business Law and the Tax System Adds Certainty

According to Sandra Malach, LLB, LLM, the law has an effect on how business is conducted in Canada, because it sets standards, defines business risks, and defines business relationships. As an instructor of business law, securities, and corporate tax, as well as being a contributing author on legal issues in small-business publications, Sandra believes that a business law course for management students is invaluable, because it provides a background to areas that are not, in the strictest sense, day-to-day management issues but affect managers and the way they conduct their operations, both internally and externally. "Managers need to be aware of the laws that affect their day-to-day operations," she says. "And more importantly, that they can recognize legal issues and contact the appropriate professional to resolve the issue."

"Many businesspeople see the law as solely establishing rules regarding permissible and illegal business activities. But the law goes beyond dictating what can and what cannot be done. By understanding the basics of the laws as they affect business, it can add certainty to business activity, particularly with regard to activities that affect third parties. For example, the law of contract allows businesses to know when they have formed an enforceable contract allowing them to seek compensation if the contracting party does not fulfill its obligations." Sandra continues, "The law of negligence has established that businesses must comply with industry standards in the manufacture and inspection of their products or liability to consumers may result. Regulations establish standards for the import of certain products and the conduct of certain kinds of business."

"The Employment Standards Act is one of the most important areas for any employer. Each of the provinces has its own act that covers topics such as minimum wage, allowable deductions, hours of work, and so on. Without the knowledge of the act (or in some cases its existence) business owners may be violating laws that they are not aware of, which could amount to considerable costs if violations occur."

Another vital area to have at least some knowledge of is the tax system and the obligations of a corporation and its directors. "Often when businesses are having financial difficulties, they will not remit their payroll deduction amounts and the directors are often surprised to find out that they are personally responsible," she says.

In a final thought, Sandra states, "As a result, it is important for businesspeople to become familiar with the laws, as it affects their business, so that they can minimize their risk exposure through proper conduct of the operational aspects of their business."[1]

Critical Thinking Questions

As you read this appendix, consider Sandra Malach's thoughts on why it is important for employees, business owners, and corporations to have at least a basic understanding of Canadian business law and the tax system. Consider the following:

1. Why are there laws that relate to external business practices?
2. How do contracts help the parties to the contract?
3. What laws apply to the business when it has employees?
4. How are consumers protected by the laws?
5. Why is the tax system important to Canada and its society?

Principles of Corporate Governance, the Legal Environment, and Taxation

1 learning goal

corporate governance
The way in which an organization is governed, directed, and administered.

Corporate governance refers to the way in which an organization is governed, directed, and administered.[2] As discussed in Chapter 5, the board of governors is responsible for the organization's being managed in the best interest of the corporation. Recent experiences in Canada, the United States, and around the world have highlighted the outcome of poor corporate governance on the organization's performance and survival. Increasingly, stakeholders are looking at the corporate governance and control systems of businesses to ensure that they are being managed with the interests of the stakeholders in mind. Although the debate has focused primarily on the financial position and reporting of companies, other concerns are being discussed (honesty in other information, respect for the environment, etc.).

Since the early 1990s, the debate on corporate governance has been flourishing, and regulators in Canada have been setting guidelines to address this issue. This has been in response to worldwide incidents that have raised questions about boards of directors' performance and alleged management incompetence. Most notable have been the WorldCom and Enron scandals (where financial statements proved to be inaccurate), but Canada has not escaped its own examples (e.g., Bre-X and YBM).[3] As well, companies are expected to be socially responsible in their investing. According to Brian A. Schofield and Blair W. Feltmate in *Sustainable Development Investing,*

> Stakeholders now require that companies be committed to minimizing environmental disruptions and to contribute to the economic and social advancement of the communities in which they operate, known as sustainable development.[4]

In July 2002, the Canadian Institute of Chartered Accountants, the Canadian Securities Administrators, and the Office of the Superintendent of Financial Institutions announced the creation of the Canadian Public Accountability Board (CPAB). Its mission is to "contribute to public confidence in the integrity of financial reporting of public companies by promoting high-quality, independent auditing."[5]

So what has brought about the need to create the CPAB? There have been many successful attempts by associations to regulate their industries. The provincial legal associations, medical associations, faculty associations, accounting associations, and others have developed strict guidelines that control the responsibilities and actions of their members, but this does not guarantee that every member will follow the guidelines. Typically, when there are serious violations, government bodies react and enact regulations (in the form of laws) to protect society, or, in some cases, governments have been proactive in anticipation of violations.

HOT Links

For more news and updated events, search the Office of the Superintendent of Financial Institutions' Web site at http://www.osfi-bsif.gc.ca.

THE LEGAL SYSTEM

2 learning goal

Our legal system affects everyone who lives and does business in Canada. The smooth functioning of society depends on the law, which protects the rights of people and businesses. The purpose of law is to keep the system stable while allowing orderly change. The law defines which actions are allowed or banned and regulates some practices. It also helps settle disputes. The legal system both shapes and is shaped by political, economic, and social systems. All three levels of government—federal, provincial, and municipal—regulate various business activities as set out in the laws of Canada and the provinces.

In any society, **laws** are the rules of conduct created and enforced by a controlling authority, usually the government. They develop over time in response to the changing needs of people, property, and business. The legal system in Canada is thus the result of a long and continuing process. In each generation, new social problems occur, and new laws are created to solve them. For instance, the Combines Investigation Act and its successor, the Competition Act, were enacted to protect consumers in areas such as misleading advertising and abusive marketing practices. These acts also contain provisions that can be grouped under three categories: conspiracies, monopolies, and mergers.

Environmental law is an area over which the federal and provincial governments have concurrent jurisdiction. Increased awareness of pollution and a social movement toward the protection of our environment has made this area an important public issue. The appropriate federal and provincial Environmental Protection Acts apply to all the elements of the environment: air, land, and water.

Another area of law that is important to businesses is the Employment Equity Act. Passed in the late 1980s, the act initially applied to all employers with 100 or more employees. Employment rights go beyond requiring employers to treat potential and existing employees equally, regardless of their personal characteristics. The employers, at a minimum, were encouraged to make their workforce reflect various underrepresented peoples (i.e., their organizations should reflect society as much as possible). Because of the increase of businesses geared toward social responsibility, not only did employers with 100 or more employees try to follow the Employment Equity standards, smaller organizations did so as well.

The Employment Equity Act was amended in 1996 to include that every employer (not only those with 100 or more employees) shall implement employment equity. The amendment also states that all employers shall make reasonable accommodations to persons of one of the four designated groups (i.e., women, persons with disabilities, Aboriginal people, and visible minorities) to achieve a degree of representation that is consistent with their representation in the Canadian workforce. The Act allows employers to consider the potential employee's availability to meet reasonable occupational requirements.

laws

The rules of conduct in a society, created and enforced by a controlling authority, usually the government.

Statute laws at the federal level are the end result of the legislative process in Ottawa.

© PHOTODISC COLLECTION/GETTY IMAGES

Today new areas of law are developing to deal with the Internet. The increasing use of the Internet, as discussed in Chapter 4, requires that industry and the governments respond to various applicable issues, such as privacy.

Public and Private Law

Public law is the law relating to the relationship between the individual or business and the government (or its agencies). The Criminal Code and the Income Tax Act are two examples at the federal level. Liquor laws are an example of public law at the provincial level.

Private law is the law relating to the relationship between individuals, businesses, or individuals and businesses. Statutes that protect one person from the harm of another are private laws.

The Main Sources of Law

Common law is the body of unwritten law that has evolved out of judicial (court) decisions rather than being enacted by legislatures. It is also called case law. It developed in England and applies to most of the English-speaking world. Common law is based on community customs that were recognized and enforced by the courts. Therefore, it is based on previous decisions. The reliance on previous decisions creates certainty and predictability.

Civil code is a body of written law that sets out the private rights of the citizens. In Quebec much of what would be found in the common law of other provinces has been codified and is known as the Civil Code.

Statute law (or statutory law) is written law enacted by legislatures at all levels, from municipal and provincial governments to the federal government. Statutes are the end result of the legislative process. Statutory laws are the elected representatives of the people's wishes. The particular advantage of statute law over common law is the relative ease that the statutes can be changed.

Related to statutory law is **administrative law**, or the rules, regulations, and orders passed by boards, commissions, and agencies of municipal, provincial, and federal governments. The scope and influence of administrative law has expanded as the number of these government bodies has grown. Examples of the activities of regulatory agencies include the sale of securities by public companies, employment standards, and broadcasting.

Business Law

Business law is the body of law that governs commercial dealings. These laws provide a certainty within which businesses can operate, serving as guidelines for business decisions. Every businessperson should be familiar with the laws governing his or her field. Some laws, such as the Trade-marks Act, apply to all businesses. Other types of business laws might apply to a specific industry, such as the Canadian Radio-television and Telecommunications Commission Act, which regulates and supervises all aspects of the Canadian broadcasting system and regulates telecommunications carriers and service providers that fall under federal jurisdiction.

The Court System

Canada has a highly developed court system. There are four levels of courts in Canada. The trials of most business disputes are heard in the Provincial/Territorial Superior Courts. These courts also hear appeals from Provincial Court judgments and judgments from the Provincial Administrative Tribunals. Appeals of these decisions are made to the Provincial Court of Appeal and subsequently to the Supreme Court of Canada. The Federal Court, Trial Division, and the Court of

---

public law

The law relating to the relationship between the individual or business and the government (or its agencies).

private law

The law relating to the relationship between individuals, businesses, or individuals and businesses.

common law

The body of unwritten law that has evolved out of judicial (court) decisions rather than being enacted by a legislature; also called *case law*.

civil code

A body of written law that sets out the private rights of the citizens.

statute law (or statutory law)

Written law enacted by a legislature (municipal, provincial, or federal).

administrative law

The rules, regulations, and orders passed by boards, commissions, and agencies of government (municipal, provincial, and federal).

business law

The body of law that governs commercial dealings.

Appeals hear appeals of federally regulated Administrative Tribunals. The highest court in Canada is the Supreme Court of Canada and it is the final court of appeal from all other Canadian courts. Also, there are specialized Federal Courts, including the Tax Court of Canada, where individuals and companies have an opportunity to settle matters relating to federal tax and revenue legislation. See Exhibit A-1 for an outline of Canada's court system.[6]

Nonjudicial Methods of Settling Disputes

Settling disputes by going to court is both expensive and time-consuming. Even if the case is settled prior to the trial, a sizable legal expense can be incurred in preparing for trial. Therefore, many companies now use private arbitration and mediation firms as alternatives to litigation. Private firms offer these services, which are a high-growth area within the legal profession.

With **arbitration,** the parties agree to present their case to an impartial third party and are required to accept the arbitrator's decision. **Mediation** is similar, but the mediator intervenes with the view of persuading the parties to adjust or settle their dispute. The mediator might or might not offer a resolution, but even if the mediator does offer a solution, neither party is bound by the mediator's decision. The mediator may suggest alternative solutions and primarily tries to help the parties negotiate a settlement. Mediation is more flexible than arbitration and allows for compromise. If the parties cannot reach a settlement, they can then go to court, an option not available in most arbitration cases.

arbitration

A method of settling disputes in which the parties agree to present their case to an impartial third party and are required to accept the arbitrator's decision.

mediation

The intervention of a third party with a view to persuading the parties to adjust or settle their dispute.

Exhibit A-1 Outline of Canada's Court System

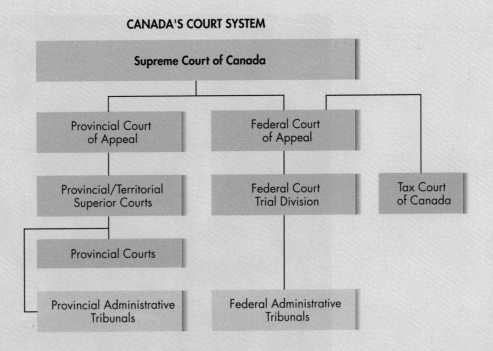

CANADA'S COURT SYSTEM

Supreme Court of Canada

Provincial Court of Appeal

Federal Court of Appeal

Provincial/Territorial Superior Courts

Federal Court Trial Division

Tax Court of Canada

Provincial Courts

Provincial Administrative Tribunals

Federal Administrative Tribunals

SOURCE: "Outline of Canada's Court System—Figure," Dept. of Justice Canada, 2003. http://canada.justice.gc.ca/en/dept/pub/trib/page3.html. Reproduced with the permission of the Minister of Public Works and Government Services, 2003.

Corporate Governance, the Legal Environment, and Taxation

contract

An agreement that sets forth the relationship between parties regarding the performance of a specified action; creates a legal obligation and is enforceable in a court of law.

express contract

A contract in which the terms are specified in either written or spoken words.

implied contract

A contract that depends on the acts and conduct of the parties to show agreement; the terms are not specified in writing or orally.

In addition to saving time and money, corporations like the confidentiality of testimony and settlement terms in these proceedings. Arbitration and mediation also allow businesses to avoid the risks associated with going to trial. Generally speaking, once court action is initiated, the information is then public.

Contract Law

A **contract** is an agreement that sets forth the relationship between parties regarding the performance of a specified action. The contract creates a legal obligation and is enforceable in a court of law. Contracts are an important part of business law. Contract law is also incorporated into other fields of business law, such as property and agency law, which we'll discuss later. Some of the business transactions that involve contracts are buying materials and property, selling goods, leasing equipment, and hiring consultants.

A contract can be an **express contract,** which specifies the terms of the agreement in either written or spoken words, or an **implied contract,** which depends on the acts and conduct of the parties to show agreement. An example of an express contract is the written contract an employee might sign that outlines the obligations of the employee and the employer. On the other hand, an implied contract exists when you order and receive a sandwich at Jason's Grill. You and the restaurant have an implied contract that you will pay the price shown on the restaurant's menu in exchange for an edible sandwich.

Michelle Sales, a 22-year-old owner of a small cosmetics company, is looking for a supplier to provide her store with inventory. She found a supplier she had confidence in, and after some negotiating, she and the supplier agree on a price of $11,000. The supplier writes up a contract, which they both sign. Has Michelle legally bought the inventory for $11,000? The answer is yes, because the transaction meets all the requirements for a valid contract.

A contract may be verbal or written, express or implied.

© ALISTAR BERG/PHOTODISC/GETTY IMAGES

CONTRACT REQUIREMENTS[7]

3 *learning goal*

Businesses deal with contracts all the time, so it's important to know the requirements of a valid contract. For a contract to be legally enforceable, all of the following elements must be present.

- *Mutual agreement.* This is evidenced by the offer of one party being accepted by another party. Each party to the contract must have entered into it freely, without duress. Using physical or economic harm to force the signing of the contract—threatening injury or refusing to place another large order, for instance—invalidates a contract. Likewise, fraud—misrepresenting the facts of a transaction—makes a contract unenforceable. Telling a prospective used-car buyer that the brakes are new when, in fact, they have not been replaced makes the contract of sale invalid.

- *Capacity of the parties.* This refers to the legal ability of a party to enter into contracts. Under the law, minors (those who have not attained the age of majority according to the law of their province or territory), people who are mentally incompetent, and those addicted to drugs or alcohol cannot enter into contracts.

- *Legal consideration.* This is the exchange of something of legal value or benefit between the parties. Consideration can be in the form of money, goods, or a legal right given up. Suppose that an electronics manufacturer agrees to rent an industrial building for a year at a monthly rent of $1,500. Its consideration is the rent payment of $1,500, and the building owner's consideration is permission to occupy the space. But if you offer to type a term paper for a friend for free and your offer is accepted, there is no contract. Your friend has not given up anything, so you are not legally bound to honour the deal.

- *Lawful object (legal purpose).* This means absence of illegality. The purpose of the contract must be legal for it to be valid. A contract cannot require performance of an illegal act. A contract to smuggle a banned substance into Canada for a specified amount of money would not be legally enforceable.

- *Legal form.* A contract can be in oral or written form, as required. Many can be oral (although a written contract provides an accurate record to the parties of their obligations). For instance, an oral contract exists when Bridge Corp. orders office supplies by phone from Ace Stationery Store and Ace delivers the requested goods. Written contracts include leases, sales contracts, and property deeds. Some types of contracts must be in writing to be legally binding.

As you can see, Michelle's inventory purchase meets all the requirements for a valid contract. Both parties have freely agreed to the terms of the contract. Michelle is not a minor and presumably does not fit any of the other categories of incapacity. Both parties are giving consideration, Michelle by paying the money and the supplier by delivering the inventory. The purchase of the inventory is a legal activity, and the written contract is in the correct form, because the cost of the inventory is over the legal amount that requires a written contract (this varies by province).

Breach of Contract

breach of contract
The failure by one party to a contract to fulfill the terms of the agreement without a legal excuse.

A **breach of contract** occurs when one party to a contract fails (without legal excuse) to fulfill the terms of the agreement. The other party then has the right to seek a remedy in the courts. There are three legal remedies for breach of contract.

- *Payment of damages*—money awarded to the party who was harmed by the breach of contract, to cover losses incurred because the contract wasn't fulfilled. Suppose that Ajax Roofing contracts with Fred Wellman to fix the large hole in the roof of his factory within three days, but the roofing crew doesn't show up as promised. When a thunderstorm four days later causes $45,000 in damage to Wellman's machinery, Wellman can sue for damages to cover the costs of the water damage, because Ajax breached the contract.

- *Specific performance of the contract*—a court order that requires the breaching party to perform the duties under the terms of the contract. Specific performance is a common method of settling a breach of contract. Wellman might ask the court to direct Ajax to fix the roof at the price and conditions in the contract.

- *Restitution*—cancelling the contract and returning both parties to the situation that existed before the contract. If one party fails to perform under the contract, neither party has any further obligation to the other. Because Ajax failed to fix Wellman's roof under the terms of the contract, Wellman does not owe Ajax any money. Ajax must return the 50 percent deposit it received when Wellman signed the contract.

WARRANTIES

Express warranties are specific statements of fact or promises about a product by the seller. This form of warranty is considered part of the sales transaction that influences the buyer. Express warranties appear in the form of statements that can be interpreted as fact. The statement "This machine will process 1,000 gallons of paint per hour" is an express warranty, as is the printed warranty that comes with a computer or a telephone answering machine.

Implied warranties are neither written nor oral. These guarantees are imposed on sales transactions by statute or court decision. They promise that the product will perform up to expected standards. For instance, a man bought a used car from a dealer, and the next day the transmission fell out as he was driving on the highway. The dealer fixed the car, but a week later the brakes failed. The man sued the car dealer. The court ruled in favour of the car owner, because any car without a working transmission or brakes is not fit for the ordinary purpose of driving. Similarly, if a customer asks to buy a copier to handle 5,000 copies per month, she relies on the salesperson to sell her a copier that meets those needs. The salesperson implicitly warrants that the copier purchased is appropriate for that volume.

PATENTS, COPYRIGHTS, AND TRADEMARKS

4   *learning goal*

patent
A form of protection (limited monopoly) established by the government to inventors; gives an inventor the exclusive right to manufacture, use, and sell an invention for 20 years.

copyright
A form of protection established by the government for creators of works of art, music, literature, or other intellectual property; gives the creator the exclusive right to use, produce, and sell the creation during the lifetime of the creator and for 50 years thereafter.

Canadian law protects authors, inventors, and creators of other intellectual property by giving them the rights to their creative works. Patents, copyrights, and registration of trademarks are legal protection for key business assets.

A **patent** gives an inventor the exclusive right to manufacture, use, and sell an invention for 20 years. The Patent Act grants patents for ideas that meet its requirements of being new, unique, and useful. The physical process, machine, or formula is what is patented. Patent rights—pharmaceutical companies' rights to produce drugs they discover, for example—are considered intangible personal property (i.e., they do not have physical form but are of value).

The government also grants copyrights. A **copyright** is an exclusive right, shown by the symbol © (but does not necessarily need it), given to a writer, artist, composer, or playwright to use, produce, and sell her or his creation. This protection is automatic. Works protected by copyright include printed materials (books, magazine articles, lectures), works of art, photographs, and movies. Under current copyright law, the copyright is issued for the life of the creator plus 50 years after the creator's death. Patents and copyrights, which are considered intellectual property, are the subject of many lawsuits today.

A **trademark** is a design, name, or other distinctive mark that a manufacturer uses to identify its goods in the marketplace. Apple Computer's multicoloured apple logo (symbol) is an example of a trademark.

Trademarks are valuable because they create uniqueness in the minds of customers. At the same time, companies don't want a trademark to become so well known that it is used to describe all similar types of products. For instance, Coke is often used to refer to any cola soft drink, not just those produced by the Coca-Cola Company. Companies spend millions of dollars each year to keep their trademarks from becoming generic words, terms used to identify a product class rather than the specific product. Coca-Cola employs many investigators and files 70 to 80 lawsuits each year to prevent its trademarks from becoming generic words.

Once a trademark becomes generic (which a court decides), it is public property and can be used by any person or company. Names that were once trademarked but are now generic include aspirin, thermos, linoleum, and zipper.

TORT LAW

A **tort** is a civil, or private, act that harms other people or their property. The harm might involve physical injury, emotional distress, invasion of privacy, or defamation (injuring a person's character by publication of false statements). The injured party may sue the wrongdoer to recover damages for the harm or loss. A tort is not the result of a breach of contract, which would be settled under contract law. Torts are part of common law. Examples of tort cases are medical malpractice, slander (an untrue oral statement that damages a person's reputation), libel (an untrue written statement that damages a person's reputation), product liability (discussed in the next section), professional negligence, and fraud.

A tort is generally not a crime, although some acts can be both torts and crimes. (Assault and battery, for instance, is a criminal act that would be prosecuted by the government and is also a tort because of the injury to the person.) Torts are private wrongs and are settled in courts. Crimes are violations of public law punishable by the government in the criminal courts. The purpose of criminal law is to punish the person who committed the crime. The purpose of tort law is to provide remedies to the injured party.

For a tort to exist and damages to be recovered, the harm must be done through either negligence or deliberate intent. Negligence occurs when reasonable care is not taken for the safety of others. For instance, a woman attending a baseball game was struck on the head by a foul ball that came through a hole in the screen behind home plate. The court could rule that a sports team charging admission has an obligation to provide structures free from defects and seating that protects spectators from danger. Therefore, the baseball organization could be found negligent. Negligence does not apply when an injury is caused by an unavoidable accident, an event that was not intended and could not have been prevented even if the person used reasonable care. This area of tort law is quite controversial, because the definition of negligence leaves much room for interpretation.

PRODUCT–LIABILITY LAW

Product liability refers to manufacturers' and sellers' responsibility for defects in the products they make and sell. It has become a specialized area of law combining aspects of contracts, warranties, torts, and statutory law.

An important concept in product-liability law is **strict liability**. A manufacturer or seller is liable for any personal injury or property damage caused by defective products or packaging that does not meet industry standards.

BANKRUPTCY AND INSOLVENCY ACT

bankruptcy

The legal procedure by which individuals or businesses that cannot meet their financial obligations are relieved of some, it not all, of their debt.

It might be possible to save a business, even though it is insolvent, by using the provisions under the Bankruptcy and Insolvency Act. **Bankruptcy** is the legal act by which individuals or businesses that cannot meet their financial obligations are relieved of some, if not all, of their debt. Working through a Trustee in Bankruptcy, the company (or individual) files a Proposal ("offer") to the company's creditors asking them to accept less than the actual monies owed so that the company can survive.

COMPETITION ACT

HOT Links

For more information on corporate bankruptcy, see the Web site that helps people and businesses get a fresh financial start at http://www.BankruptcyCanada.com.

cartel

An agreement between enterprises to lessen competition.

monopoly

A situation where there is no competition and the benefits of a free market are lost.

As stated earlier in this appendix, the Competition Act was enacted to protect consumers and provide provisions that can be grouped under three categories: conspiracies, monopolies, and mergers. Each of these three categories is briefly discussed below.

Many measures have been taken to try to keep the marketplace free from influences that would restrict competition. The Competition Act sets out the basic prohibition against cartels, (the expression that is often used is *antitrust law*), among other issues. A **cartel** is an agreement between enterprises to lessen competition. If it can be proven that enterprises entered into an agreement or arrangement (a conspiracy) to lessen competition, they can be charged with a criminal offence.

Some of the more common methods of reducing or eliminating competition are

- *parallel pricing*—competing firms adopt similar pricing strategies;
- *setting quotas*—imposing limits of production;
- *market sharing*—dividing the market based on a geographical basis; and
- *product specialization*—whereby each firm agrees to specialize its products.

According to the free market economy (as discussed in Chapter 1), the essential characteristic of an efficient market is competition. If customers have a choice of products to purchase (i.e., competition), prices will be generally lower, and quality will be better, or both. A **monopoly** is a situation when there is no competition and the benefits of a free market are lost.

For various reasons (e.g., small population, large geographical area) some monopolies are allowed to exist in Canada. Some examples have been utilities and telecommunications services, but these have been governed by regulatory agencies (e.g., utility boards) that protected the consumers' rights. These *natural monopolies* have been disappearing in the past decade as government regulations have promoted more competition in reaction to the stronger move to increased competition.

The third area where the Competition Act protects the consumer is mergers and acquisitions. As discussed in Chapter 6, mergers and acquisitions are often an important means of seeking efficiencies in business. The Competition Act allows the government to stop any mergers and acquisitions that might lessen competition.

EMPLOYMENT STANDARDS ACTS

5 learning goal

One issue that many businesses face is the ability to recruit good employees. Furthermore, each province has an Employment Standards Act (or an equivalent, such as an Employment Standards Code) that outlines the minimum terms of employment in such areas as minimum wages, payment of earnings, hours of work, overtime, general (statutory) holidays, vacations, maternity and parental leaves, termination, layoff and recall, and the employment of children.

Without the knowledge of these minimum standards, employers can potentially be violating the standards and can incur considerable costs if action is taken against them. Particularly at risk are the smaller organizations that do not have a human resource department with professional human resource personnel.

CONSUMER PROTECTION

consumerism
A movement that seeks to increase the rights and powers of buyers vis-à-vis sellers.

Consumerism reflects the struggle for power between buyers and sellers. Specifically, it is a movement seeking to increase the rights and powers of buyers vis-à-vis sellers, often resulting in consumer protection laws. Sellers' rights and powers include the right

- to introduce into the marketplace any product, in any size and style, that is not hazardous to personal health or safety, or, if it is hazardous, to introduce it with the proper warnings and controls;
- to price the product at any level they wish, provided they do not discriminate among similar classes of buyers;
- to spend any amount of money they wish to promote the product, so long as the promotion does not constitute unfair competition;
- to formulate any message they wish about the product, provided that it is not misleading or dishonest in content or execution; and
- to introduce any buying incentives they wish.

Meanwhile, buyers have the rights and powers

- to refuse to buy any product that is offered to them,
- to expect products to be safe,
- to expect a product to be essentially as the seller represents it, and
- to receive adequate information about the product.

DEREGULATION OF INDUSTRIES

deregulation
The removal or rules and regulations governing business competition.

Since the 1980s, the Canadian governments (federal and provincial/territorial) have actively promoted deregulation, the removal of rules and regulations governing business competition. **Deregulation** has drastically changed some once-regulated industries (especially the transportation, telecommunications, and financial services industries) and created many new competitors. The result has been entries into and exits from some industries.

TAXATION OF BUSINESS

 6 learning goal

Taxes are sometimes seen as the price we pay to live in this country. Taxes are assessed by all levels of government on both business and individuals, and they are used to pay for the services provided by government.

Income Taxes

income taxes
Taxes that are based on the income received by businesses and individuals.

Income taxes are based on the income received by businesses and individuals. Most personal income taxes are progressive, meaning that rates increase as income increases (one exception is the flat tax for individuals in Alberta). The tax rates for the federal government apply to all Canadians (with few exceptions) equally, but the provinces are free to set their own rates. Income taxes for businesses are flat (i.e., same rate regardless of income).

As we discussed in Chapter 5, the net income for sole proprietorships and partnerships are included in the personal income taxes of the owners. For corporations, taxes are the responsibility of the corporation.

Other Types of Taxes

Besides income taxes, individuals and businesses pay a number of other taxes. The four main types are property taxes, payroll taxes (only as a remittance), sales taxes, and excise taxes.

Property taxes are assessed on real property, based on its assessed value. Most jurisdictions tax land and buildings. Property taxes may be based on fair market value (what a buyer would pay), a percentage of fair market value, or replacement value (what it would cost today to rebuild or buy something like the original). The value on which the taxes are based is the *assessed value.*

Any individual that is employed is required to pay federal and provincial taxes on the money that he or she earns (after the personal exemption is deducted), called income taxes. These taxes must be paid on wages, salaries, and commissions. The employer deducts the income taxes from the employee's pay and remits them to the federal government, where they are called **payroll taxes.**

Sales taxes are levied on goods when they are sold and are a percentage of the sales price. These taxes are imposed by the federal government (the goods and services tax, or GST) and most provincial governments in the form of a provincial sales tax (PST). (One exception is that there is no provincial sales tax in Alberta.) Some provinces now have a harmonized sales tax (HST), which is a combination of the GST and the PST. The PSTs vary in amount and in what is considered taxable. Sales taxes increase the cost of goods to the consumer. Businesses are responsible for collecting sales taxes and remitting them to the government.

Excise taxes are placed on specific items, such as gasoline, alcoholic beverages, and tobacco. They can be assessed by federal and provincial governments. In many cases, these taxes help pay for services related to the item taxed. For instance, gasoline excise taxes are often used to build and repair highways. Other excise taxes—like those on alcoholic beverages and tobacco—are used to control practices that can cause harm.

property taxes
Taxes that are imposed on real and personal property based on the *assessed value* of the property.

payroll taxes
Income taxes that are collected by the employer and remitted to the federal government, usually in the form of a deduction from the employee's pay.

sales taxes
Taxes that are levied on goods and services when they are sold; calculated as a percentage of the price.

excise taxes
Taxes that are imposed on specific items such as gasoline, alcoholic beverages, and tobacco.

Summary

This appendix has been about businesses governing themselves in a legal manner to respond to their stakeholders. Corporate governance is increasingly becoming important, and it is necessary for businesses to be aware of their ethical and legal responsibilities.

Our environment is always changing, and businesses must be proactive in responding to the changes, or governments are forced to act. Associations can encourage strict adherence to the ethical standards that they set out, but these have little power to stop someone from acting unethically, or even illegally, often until it is too late.

Organizations, associations, industry, and government are increasingly working together to protect the stakeholders to ensure that business is governed in an ethical and legal manner.

SUMMARY OF LEARNING GOALS

1   What is corporate governance, and why is it important?

Corporate governance is the way in which an organization is governed, directed, and administered. Increasingly, organizations must be seen as acting in the interests of its various stakeholders, or its survival could be in jeopardy. If a corporation is acting in a perceived unethical manner, it could lose sales, have regulations imposed on it, have difficulty attracting employees, and so on.

2   How does the legal system govern business transactions and settle business disputes?

Laws are the rules governing a society's conduct that are created and enforced by a controlling authority. The Canadian court system governs the legal system and includes both federal and provincial courts, each organized into three levels. The courts settle disputes by applying and interpreting laws. Most cases start in trial courts. Decisions can be appealed to appellate courts. The Supreme Court of Canada is the nation's highest court and the court of final appeal. To avoid the high costs of going to court, many firms now use private arbitration or mediation as alternatives to litigation.

3   What are the required elements of a valid contract, and what are the key types of business law?

A contract is an agreement between two or more parties that meets five requirements: mutual agreement, capacity of the parties, legal consideration, lawful object (legal purpose), and legal form. If one party breaches the contract terms, the remedies are damages, specific performance, or restitution.

Tort law settles disputes involving civil acts that harm people or their property. Torts include physical injury, mental anguish, and defamation. Product-liability law governs the responsibility of manufacturers and sellers for product defects. Bankruptcy law gives business or individuals who cannot meet their financial obligations a way of being relieved of their debts. Some laws are designed to keep the marketplace free from influences that would restrict competition, such as price fixing and deceptive advertising. Laws protecting consumer rights are another important area of government control.

4   What are patents, copyrights, and trademarks? How do these help businesses?

A patent is a form of protection (limited monopoly) established by the government to protect inventors. It gives an inventor the exclusive right to manufacture, use, and sell an invention for 20 years. A copyright is established by the government to protect creators of works of art, music, literature, or other intellectual property. It gives the creator the exclusive right to use, produce, and sell the creation during his or her lifetime and for 50 years thereafter. A trademark is a design, name, or other distinctive mark that a manufacturer uses to identify its goods in the marketplace.

Patents, copyrights, and trademarks help businesses protect their rights for the exclusive use of their inventions, creations (e.g., music), names, and designs.

5   What are Employment Standards Acts?

Each province has an Employment Standards Act (or an equivalent act) that outlines the minimum terms of employment in such areas as minimum wages, payment of earnings, hours of work, overtime, statutory holidays, vacations, maternity and parental leaves, termination, layoff and recall, and the employment of children.

6 What are the most common taxes paid by businesses?

Income taxes are based on the income received by businesses and individuals. They are paid to both the federal and provincial governments, who are responsible for setting their own rates. In addition to income taxes, individuals and businesses also pay property taxes (assessed on real property), payroll taxes (employers are responsible for collecting the income taxes from their employees and remitting them to the federal government), sales taxes (e.g., GST and HST, which are levied on goods and services), and excise taxes (levied on specific products such as gasoline, alcoholic beverages, and tobacco).

glossary

A

absolute advantage The situation when a country can produce and sell a product at a lower cost than any other country or when it is the only country that can provide the product.

accounting The process of collecting, recording, classifying, summarizing, reporting, and analyzing financial activities.

accounts payable Purchase for which a buyer has not yet paid the seller.

accounts receivable Sales for which a firm has not yet been paid.

acid-test (quick) ratio The ratio of total current assets excluding inventory to total current liabilities; used to measure a firm's liquidity.

acquisition The purchase of a corporation by another corporation or by an investor group; the identity of the acquired company can be lost.

activity ratios Ratios that measure how well a firm uses its assets.

administrative distribution system A vertical marketing system in which a strong organization takes over as leader and sets policies for the distribution channel.

administrative law The rules, regulations, and orders passed by boards, commissions, and agencies of government (municipal, provincial, and federal).

advertising Any paid form of non-personal presentation by an identified sponsor.

advertising agencies Companies that help create ads and place them in the proper media.

advertising media The channels through which advertising is carried to prospective customers; includes newspapers, magazines, radio, television, outdoor advertising, direct mail, and the Internet.

Advertising Standards Canada The Canadian advertising industry's self-regulatory body.

advocacy advertising Advertising that takes a stand on a social or economic issue; also called *grassroots lobbying*.

affirmative action programs Those that give preference to certain groups of individuals, for example members of minorities or people with disability, as a way of countering past or ongoing discrimination against them.

agency shop A company where employees are not required to join the union but must pay it a fee to cover its expenses in representing them.

agents Sales representatives of manufacturers and wholesalers.

amortization (depreciation) The allocation of an asset's original cost to the years in which it is expected to produce revenues.

angel investors Individual investors or groups of experienced investors who provide funding for start-up businesses.

annual report A yearly document that describes a firm's financial status and usually discusses the firm's activities during the past year and its prospects for the future.

application service providers (ASPs) A service company that buys and maintains software on its servers and distributes it through high-speed networks to subscribers for a set period and price.

application software Software that is *applied* to a real-world task; used to perform a specific task or to solve a particular problem.

apprenticeship A form of on-the-job training that combines specific job instruction with classroom instruction.

arbitration A method of settling disputes in which the parties agree to present their case to an impartial third party and are required to accept the arbitrator's decision.

assembly process A transformation process in which the basic inputs are either combined to create the output or transformed into the output.

assets Possessions of value owned by a firm.

Association of Southeast Asian Nations (ASEAN) Organization initially established in 1967 to promote economic growth, social progress, and cultural development in the region; currently has 10 members.

attitude Learned tendency to respond consistently toward a given object, idea, or concept.

audience selectivity An advertising medium's ability to reach a precisely defined market.

auditing The process of reviewing the records used to prepare financial statements and issuing a formal auditor's opinion indicating whether the statements have been prepared in accordance with accepted accounting rules.

authority Legitimate power, granted by the organization and acknowledged by employees, that allows an individual to request action and expect compliance.

autocratic leaders Directive leaders who prefer to make decisions and solve problems on their own with little input from subordinates.

B

baby boomers People born between the late 1940s (after World War II) and the mid-1960s.

backward integration The acquisition of the production process by a wholesaler or retailer.

balance of payments A summary of a country's international financial transactions showing the difference between the country's total payments to and its total receipts from other countries.

balance of trade The differences between the value of a country's exports and the value of its imports during a certain time.

balance sheet A financial statement that summarizes a firm's financial position at a specific point in time; also known as the *statement of financial position*.

Bank of Canada Canada's central bank whose objective is to "promote the economic and financial well-being of Canada."

bank rate The interest rate that the Bank of Canada charges on one-day loans to financial institutions.

bankruptcy The legal procedure by which individuals or businesses that cannot meet their financial obligations are relieved of some, if not all, of their debt.

barriers to entry Factors, such as technological or legal conditions, that prevent new firms from competing equally with a monopoly.

batch processing A method of updating a database in which data are collected over some time period and then processed together.

bear markets Markets in which securities prices are falling.

belief An organized pattern of knowledge that an individual holds as true about the world.

benefit segmentation The differentiation of markets based on what a product will do rather than on customer characteristics.

bill of material A list of the items and the number of each required to make a given product.

board of directors A group of people elected by the shareholders to handle the overall management of a corporation, such as setting corporate goals and policies, hiring corporate officers, and overseeing the firm's operations and finances.

bond ratings Letter grades assigned to bond issues to indicate their quality, or level of risk; assigned by rating agencies such as Moody's and Standard & Poor's (S&P).

bonds Securities that represent long-term debt obligations (liabilities) issued by corporations and governments.

brainstorming A method of generating ideas in which group members suggest as many possibilities as they can without criticizing or evaluating any of the suggestions.

brand A company's product identifier that distinguishes the company's products from those of competitors.

brand equity The value of company and brand names.

brand loyalty A consumer's preference for a particular brand.

breach of contract The failure by one party to a contract to fulfill the terms of the agreement without a legal excuse.

breakeven point The price at which a product's costs are covered, so additional sales result in profit.

breaking bulk The process of breaking large shipments of similar products into smaller, more usable lots.

brokers Go-betweens that bring buyers and sellers together.

browser Software that allows users to access the Web with a graphical point-and-click interface.

budgets Formal written forecasts of revenues and expenses that set spending limits based on operational forecasts; include cash budgets, capital budgets, and operating budgets.

bull markets Markets in which securities prices are rising.

bundling The strategy of grouping two or more related products together and pricing them as a single product.

business An organization that strives for a profit by providing goods and services desired by its customers.

business cycles Upward and downward changes in the level of economic activity.

Business Development Bank of Canada (BDC) Bank that provides small and medium-sized businesses with flexible financing, affordable consulting services, and venture capital.

business interruption insurance Covers such costs as rental of temporary facilities, wage and salary payments to employees, payments for leased equipment, fixed payments, and profits that would have been earned during that period.

business law The body of law that governs commercial dealings.

business plan A formal written statement that describes in detail the idea for a new business and how it will be carried out; includes a general description of the company, the qualifications of the owner(s), a description of the product or service, an analysis of the market, and a financial plan.

business-to-business (B2B) e-commerce Electronic commerce that involves transactions between companies.

business-to-consumer (B2C) e-commerce Electronic commerce that involves transactions between businesses and the end user of the goods or services; also called *e-tailing*.

business-to-enterprise (B2E) Electronic collecting, storing, updating, and using of information within the business.

buyer behaviour The actions people take in buying and using goods and services.

C

CAD/CAM systems Linked computer systems that combine the advantages of *computer-aided design* and *computer-aided manufacturing*. The system helps design the product, control the flow of resources, and operate the production process.

caisses populaires Credit unions operating in Québec and other areas of Canada with francophone populations.

Canada Deposit Insurance Corporation (CDIC) The Canada Deposit Insurance Corporation is a federal Crown Corporation created in 1967 to provide deposit insurance and contribute to the stability of Canada's financial system.

Canadian Charter of Rights and Freedoms Legislation that guarantees the rights and freedoms of Canadians.

Canada Pension Plan Insurance that provides retirement, disability, death, and health benefits.

capital The tools, machinery, equipment, and buildings used to produce goods and services and get them to the consumer are known as capital. Sometimes the term *capital* is also used to mean the money that buys machinery, factories, and other production and distribution facilities.

capital budgeting The process of analyzing long-term projects and selecting those that offer the best returns while maximizing the firm's value.

capital budgets Budgets that forecast a firm's outlays for fixed assets (plant and equipment), typically for a period of several years.

capital expenditures Investments in long-lived assets, such as land, buildings, machinery, and equipment, that are expected to provide benefits over a period longer than one year.

capital products Large, expensive items with a long life span that are purchased by businesses for use in making other products or providing a service.

cartel An agreement between enterprises to lessen competition.

cash budgets Budgets that forecast a firm's cash inflows and outflows and help the firm plan for cash surpluses and shortages.

cash flows The inflow and outflow of cash for a firm.

cash management The process of making sure that a firm has enough cash on hand to pay bills as they come due and to meet unexpected expenses.

cash-and-carry wholesaler A limited-service merchant wholesaler that does not offer credit or delivery services.

category management Suppliers manage the inventory of a category of products for a retailer.

cellular manufacturing Production technique that uses small, self-contained production units, each performing all or most of the tasks necessary to complete a manufacturing order.

centralization The degree to which formal authority is concentrated in one area or level of an organization.

certified general accountant (CGA) An accountant that focuses primarily on external financial reporting.

certified management accountant (CMA) An accountant that works primarily in industry and focuses on internal management accounting.

chain of command The line of authority that extends from one level of an organization's hierarchy to the next, from top to bottom, and makes clear who reports to whom.

chartered accountant (CA) An accountant who has completed an approved bachelor's degree program, completed an educational program, and passed a comprehensive examination. Only a CA can issue an auditor's opinion on a firm's financial statements.

chartered banks Profit-oriented financial institutions that accept deposits, make business and consumer loans, invest in government and corporate securities, and provide other financial services.

chief information officer (CIO) An executive with responsibility for managing all information resources in an organization.

circular flow The movement of inputs and outputs among households, businesses, and governments; a way of showing how the sectors of the economy interact.

civil code A body of written law that sets out the private rights of the citizens.

closed shop A company where only union members can be hired.

code of ethics A set of guidelines prepared by a firm to provide its employees with the knowledge of what the firm expects in terms of their responsibilities and behaviour toward fellow employees, customers, and suppliers.

coercive power Power that is derived from an individual's ability to threaten negative outcomes.

cognitive dissonance The condition of having beliefs or knowledge that are internally inconsistent or that disagree with one's behaviour.

coinsurance Insurance coverage that requires the insured to pay a portion of the claim.

collective bargaining The process of negotiating labour agreements that provide for compensation and working arrangements mutually acceptable to the union and to management.

co-marketing Where two or more companies promote each other's products or services.

command economy An economic system characterized by government ownership of virtually all resources and economic decision-making by central government planning; also known as a *planned economy*.

commercial paper Unsecured short-term debt (an IOU) issued by a financially strong corporation.

committee structure An organizational structure in which authority and responsibility are held by a group rather than an individual.

common law The body of unwritten law that has evolved out of judicial (court) decisions rather than being enacted by a legislature; also called *case law*.

common shares Securities that represent one form of ownership interest in a corporation.

comparative advertising Advertising that compares the company's product with competing, named products.

competitive advantage A set of unique features of a company and its products that are perceived by the target market as significant and superior to those of the competition; also called *differential advantage*.

component lifestyle A lifestyle made up of a complex set of interests and choices.

computer network A group of two or more computer systems linked together by communications channels to share data and information.

computer virus A computer program that copies itself into other software and can spread to other computer systems.

computer-aided design (CAD) The use of computers to design and test new products and modify existing ones.

computer-aided manufacturing (CAM) The use of computers to develop and control the production process.

computer-integrated manufacturing (CIM) The combination of computerized manufacturing processes (such as robots and flexible manufacturing systems) with other computerized systems that control design, inventory, production, and purchasing.

conceptual skills A manager's ability to view the organization as a whole, understand how the various parts are interdependent, and assess how the organization relates to its external environment.

conglomerate merger A merger of companies in unrelated businesses; done to reduce risk.

consensual leaders Leaders who encourage discussion about issues and then require that all parties involved agree to the final decision.

consultative leaders Leaders who confer with subordinates before making a decision but who retain the final decision-making authority.

consumer fraud The practice of deceiving customers by such means as failing to honour warranties or other promises or selling goods or services that do not meet advertised claims.

consumer price index (CPI) A measure of retail price movements that compares a representative "shopping basket" of goods and services.

consumerism A movement that seeks to increase the rights and powers of buyers vis-à-vis sellers.

consumer-to-business (C2B) e-commerce Electronic commerce that involves transactions between consumers and businesses initiated by the consumer.

consumer-to-consumer (C2C) e-commerce Electronic commerce that involves transactions between consumers.

contingency plans Plans that identify alternative courses of action for very unusual or crisis situations; typically stipulate the chain of command, standard operating procedures, and communication channels the organization will use during an emergency.

contingent workers Persons who prefer temporary employment, either part- or full-time.

continuous improvement A constant commitment to seeking better ways of doing things to achieve greater efficiency and improve quality.

continuous process A production process that uses long production runs lasting days, weeks, or months without equipment shutdowns; generally used for high-volume, low-variety products with standardized parts.

contract An agreement that sets for the relationship between parties regarding the performance of a specified action; creates a legal obligation and is enforceable in a court of law.

contract manufacturing The practice in which a foreign firm manufacturers private-label goods under a domestic firm's brand name.

contractionary policy The use of monetary policy by the Bank of Canada to tighten the money supply by selling government securities or raising interest rates.

contractual distribution system A vertical marketing system in which a network of independent firms at different levels (manufacturer, wholesaler, retailer) coordinate their distribution activities through a written contract.

controlling The process of assessing the organization's progress toward accomplishing its goals; includes monitoring the implementation of a plan and correcting deviations from the plan.

convenience products Relatively inexpensive items that require little shopping effort and are purchased routinely without planning.

conventional ethics The second stage in the ethical development of individuals in which people move from an egocentric viewpoint to consider the expectations of an organization of society; also known as social ethics.

convertible bonds Corporate bonds that are issued with an option that allows the bondholder to convert them into common shares.

cooperatives Legal entities typically formed by people with similar interests, such as customers or suppliers, to reduce costs and gain economic power. A cooperative has limited liability, an unlimited life span, an elected board of directors, and an administrative staff; all profits are distributed to the member-owners in proportion to their contributions.

copyright A form of protection established by the government for creators of works of art, music, literature, or other intellectual property; gives the creator the exclusive right to use, produce, and sell the creation during the lifetime of the creator and for 50 years thereafter.

corporate campaign A union strategy in which a union disrupts a corporation's relations with its shareholders or investors as a means of attacking the company.

corporate culture The set of attitudes, values, and standards of behaviour that distinguishes one organization from another.

corporate distribution system A vertical marketing system in which one firm owns the entire distribution channel.

corporate governance The way in which an organization is being governed, directed, and administered.

corporate open house Persons are invited to an open house on the premises of the corporation. Qualified applicants are encouraged to complete an application before leaving.

corporate philanthropy The practice of charitable giving by corporations; includes contributing cash, donating equipment and products, and supporting the volunteer efforts of company employees.

corporation A legal entity with an existence and life separate from its owners, who therefore are not personally liable for the entity's debts. A corporation has many of the same legal rights and responsibilities as that of a person: it can own property, enter into contracts, sue and be sued, and engage in business operations.

corrective advertising An advertisement run to correct false impressions left by previous ads.

cost competitive advantage A firm's ability to produce a product or service at a lower cost than all other competitors in an industry while maintaining satisfactory profit margins.

cost of goods sold The total expense of buying or producing a firm's goods or services.

cost per thousand (CPM) Cost per thousand contacts is a term used in expressing advertising costs; refers to the cost of reaching 1,000 members of the target market.

cost-of-living adjustment (COLA) A provision in a labour contract that calls for wages to increase automatically as the cost of living rises (usually measured by the consumer price index).

cost-push inflation Inflation that occurs when increases in production costs push up the prices of final goods and services.

costs Expenses incurred in creating and selling goods and services.

countertrade A form of international trade in which part or all of the payment for goods or services is in the form of other goods and services.

credit unions Not-for-profit, member-owned financial cooperatives.

critical path In a critical path method network, the longest path through the linked activities.

critical path method (CPM) A scheduling tool that enables a manager to determine the critical path of activities for a project—the activities that will cause the entire project to fall behind schedule if they are not completed on time.

cross-functional teams Teams of employees who are from about the same level in the organizational hierarchy but from different functional areas; for example, task forces, organizational committees, and project teams.

crowding out The situation that occurs when government spending replaces spending by the private sector.

Crown corporations Companies that only the provincial and federal government can set up.

culture The set of values, ideas, attitudes, and other symbols created to shape human behaviour.

currency Bank notes and coins used as a medium of exchange.

current assets Assets that can or will be converted to cash within the next 12 months (within the next fiscal year).

current liabilities Short-term claims that are due within a year of the date of the balance sheet.

current ratio The ratio of total current assets to total current liabilities; used to measure a firm's liquidity.

custom regulations Regulations on products that are different from generally accepted international standards.

customer departmentalization Departmentalization that is based on the primary type of customer served by the organizational unit.

customer satisfaction The customer's feeling that a product has met or exceeded expectations.

customer value (in economics) The customer's perception of the ratio of benefits (functionality, performance, durability, design, ease of use, and serviceability) to the sacrifice (of money, time, and effort) necessary to obtain those benefits.

customer value (in marketing) The ratio of benefits to the sacrifice necessary to obtain those benefits, as determined by the customer; reflects the willingness of customers to buy a product.

customization The production of goods or services one at a time according to the specific needs or wants of individual customers.

cyclical unemployment Unemployment that occurs when a downturn in the business cycle reduces the demand for labour throughout the economy.

D

data The many facts that together describe a company's status and/or its environment.

database An electronic filing system that collects and organizes data and information.

database marketing The creation of a large computerized file of the profiles and purchase patterns of customers and potential customers, usually required for successful micro-marketing.

data mart Special subset of a data warehouse that deals with a single area of data and is organized for quick analysis.

data warehouse An information technology that combines many databases across a whole company into one central database that supports management decision-making.

dealer brands Brands that are owned by the wholesaler or retailer rather than the manufacturer.

debentures Unsecured bonds that are backed only by the reputation of the issuer and its promise to pay the principal and interest when due.

debt A form of business financing consisting of borrowed funds that must be repaid with interest over a stated time period.

debt ratios Ratios that measure the degree and effect of a firm's use of borrowed funds (debt) to finance its operations.

debt-to-equity ratio The ratio of total liabilities to owners' equity; measures the relationship between the amount of debt financing and the amount of equity financing.

decentralization The process of pushing decision-making authority down the organizational hierarchy.

decision support system (DSS) An interactive, flexible, computerized information system that allows managers to make decisions quickly and accurately; used to conduct sales analyses, forecast sales, evaluate advertising, analyze product lines, and keep tabs on market trends and competitors' actions.

decisional roles A manager's activities as an entrepreneur, resource allocator, conflict resolver, or negotiator.

deductibles The amounts that the insured must pay before insurance benefits begin.

delegation of authority The assignment of some degree of authority and responsibility to persons lower in the chain of command.

demand The quantity of a good or service that people are willing to buy at various prices.

demand curve A graph showing the quantity of a good or service that people are willing to buy at various prices.

demand deposits Money kept in chequing accounts that can be withdrawn by depositors on demand.

demand-pull inflation Inflation that occurs when the demand for goods and services is greater than the supply.

democratic leaders Leaders who solicit input from all members of the group and then allow the members to make the final decision through a vote.

demographic segmentation The differentiation of markets through the use of categories such as age, education, gender, income, and household size.

demography The study of people's vital statistics, such as their age, race and ethnicity, and location.

demotion The downgrading or reassignment of an employee to a position with less responsibility.

departmentalization The process of grouping jobs together so that similar or associated tasks and activities can be coordinated.

depreciation (amortization) The allocation of an asset's original cost to the years in which it is expected to produce revenues; also referred to as *amortization*.

deregulation The removal or rules and regulations governing business competition.

detailing The physical stocking of merchandise at a retailer by the salesperson who delivers the merchandise.

devaluation A lowering of the value of a nation's currency relative to other currencies.

differential advantage A set of unique features of a product that the target market perceives as important and better than the competition's features.

differential competitive advantage A firm's ability to provide a unique product or service that offers something of value to buyers besides simply a lower price.

direct foreign investment Active ownership of a foreign company or of manufacturing or marketing facilities in a foreign country.

distribution centres Warehouses that specialize in changing shipment sizes rather than in storing goods.

distribution channel The series of marketing entities through which goods and services pass on their way from producers to end users.

distribution strategy The part of the marketing mix that involves deciding how many stores and which specific wholesalers and retailers will handle the product in a geographic area.

diversity Employee differences in age, race and ethnicity, gender, educational background, and work experience.

dividends Payments to shareholders from a corporation's profits.

division of labour The process of dividing work into separate jobs and assigning tasks to workers.

double-entry bookkeeping A method of accounting in which each transaction is recorded as two entries so that two accounts or records are changed.

dumping The practice of charging a lower price for a product in foreign markets than in the firm's home market.

E

earnings per share (EPS) The ratio of net profit to the number of common shares outstanding; measures the number of dollars earned by each share.

economic growth An increase in a nation's output of goods and services.

economic system The combination of policies, laws, and choices made by a nation's government to establish the systems that determine what goods and services are produced and how they are allocated.

economics The study of how a society uses scarce resources to produce and distribute goods and services.

efficient consumer response (ECR) A method of managing inventory and streamlining the movement of products from supplier to distributor to retailer; relies on electronic data interchange to communicate information such as automatic shipping notifications, invoices, inventory data, and forecasts.

electronic business (e-business) The entire process that involves the full value chain (the entire value-adding process, from the raw materials to the eventual end user, including the disposing of the packaging after use) and how all units of a business operate.

electronic commerce (e-commerce) The actual transaction of selling a product or service via the Internet.

electronic data interchange (EDI) The electronic exchange of information between two trading partners.

embargo A total ban on imports or exports of a product.

employee orientation Training that prepares a new employee to perform on the job; includes information about job assignments, work rules, equipment, and performance expectations, as well as about company policies, salary and benefits, and parking.

employment insurance Payment of benefits to laid-off workers while they seek new jobs.

empowerment The process of giving employees increased autonomy and discretion to make decisions, as well as control over the resources needed to implement those decisions.

enterprise portal A customizable internal Web site that provides proprietary corporate information to a defined user group, such as employees, supply chain partners, or customers.

enterprise resource planning (ERP) A computerized resource planning system that includes information about the firm's suppliers and customers as well as data generated internally.

entrepreneurs People with vision, drive, and creativity who are willing to take the risk of starting and managing a new business to make a profit or of greatly changing the scope and direction of an existing firm.

environmental scanning The process in which a firm continually collects and evaluates information about its external environment.

e-procurement The process of purchasing supplies and materials on-line using the Internet.

equilibrium The point on the supply and demand curve at which quantity demanded equals quantity supplied.

equity A form of business financing consisting of funds raised through the sale of stock in a business.

equity theory A theory of motivation that holds that worker satisfaction is influenced by employees' perceptions about how fairly they are treated compared with their coworkers.

ethics A set of moral standards for judging whether something is right or wrong.

European Union (EU) An organization of 15 European nations (as of early 2004) that works to foster political and economic integration in Europe; formerly called the European Community.

exchange The process in which two parties give something of value to each other to satisfy their respective needs.

exchange controls Laws that require a company earning foreign exchange (foreign currency) from its exports to sell the foreign exchange to a control agency, such as a central bank.

excise taxes Taxes that are imposed on specific items such as gasoline, alcoholic beverages, and tobacco.

exclusive distribution A distribution system in which a manufacturer selects only one or two dealers in an area to market its products.

executive information system (EIS) A management support system that is customized for an individual executive; provides specific information for strategic decisions.

expansionary policy The use of monetary policy by the Bank of Canada to increase the growth of the money supply.

expectancy theory A theory of motivation that holds that the probability of an individual acting in a particular way depends on the strength of that individual's belief that the act will have a particular outcome and on whether the individual values that outcome.

expense items Items, purchased by businesses, that are smaller and less expensive than capital products and usually have a life span of less than one year.

expenses The costs of generating revenues.

experiment A marketing research method in which the investigator changes one or more variables—price, packaging, design, shelf space, advertising theme, or advertising expenditures—while observing the effects of these changes on another variable (usually sales).

expert power Power that is derived from an individual's extensive knowledge in one or more areas.

expert system A management support system that gives managers advice similar to what they would get from a consultant; it uses artificial intelligence to enable computers to reason and learn to solve problems in much the same way humans do.

exporting The practice of selling domestically produced goods to buyers in another country.

exports Goods and services produced in one country and sold in other countries.

express contract A contract in which the terms are specified in either written or spoken words.

express warranty Specific statement of fact or promises about a product by the seller.

extensive decision-making Purchasing an unfamiliar, expensive, infrequently bought item.

extranet A private computer network that uses Internet technology and a browser interface but is accessible only to authorized outsiders with a valid user name and password.

F

factoring A form of short-term financing in which a firm sells its accounts receivable outright at a discount to a *factor*.

factors of production The resources that are necessary to produce goods and services: labour, capital, entrepreneurs, physical resources, and information.

federal budget deficit The condition that occurs when the federal government spends more for programs than it collects in taxes.

financial accounting Accounting that focuses on preparing external financial reports that are used by outsider stakeholders such as creditors, suppliers, investors, and government agents to assess the financial strength of a business.

financial intermediation The process in which financial institutions act as intermediaries between the suppliers and demanders of funds.

financial management The art and science of managing a firm's money so that it can meet its goals.

financial risk The chance that a firm will be unable to make scheduled interest and principal payments on its debt.

fiscal policy The government's use of taxation and spending to affect the economy.

fixed assets Long-term assets used by a firm for more than a year, such as land, buildings, and machinery; also referred to as *capital assets* or *property, plant, and equipment (PPE)*.

fixed costs Costs that do not vary with different levels of output; for example, rent.

fixed-cost contribution The selling price per unit (revenue) minus the variable costs per unit.

fixed-position layout A facility arrangement in which the product stays in one place and workers and machinery move to it as needed.

flexible manufacturing system (FMS) A system that combines automated workstations with computer-controlled transportation devices—automatic guided vehicles (AGVs)—that move materials between workstations and into and out of the system.

floating exchange rates A system in which prices of currencies move up and down based upon the demand for and supply of the various currencies.

focus group A group of 8 to 12 participants led by a moderator in an in-depth discussion on one particular topic or concept.

formal organization The order and design of relationships within a firm; consists of two or more people working together with a common objective and clarity of purpose.

forward integration The acquisition by a market intermediary of another marketing intermediary closer to the customer.

four Ps (4Ps) Product, price, promotion, and place (distribution), which together make up the marketing mix.

franchise agreement A contract setting out the terms of a franchising arrangement, including the rules for running the franchise, the services provided by the franchisor, and the financial terms. Under the contract, the franchisee is allowed to use the franchisor's business name, trademark, and logo.

franchisee In a franchising arrangement, the individual or company that sells the goods or services of the franchisor in a certain geographic area.

franchising A form of business organization based on a business arrangement between a franchisor, which supplies the product concept, and the franchisee, who sells the goods or services of the franchisor in a certain geographic area.

franchisor In a franchising arrangement, the company that supplies the product concept to the franchisee.

free-rein (laissez-faire) leadership A leadership style in which the leader turns over all authority and control to subordinates.

free trade The policy of permitting the people of a country to buy and sell where they please without restrictions.

free trade zone An area where the nations allow free, or almost free, trade among each other while imposing tariffs on goods of nations outside the zone.

frequency The number of times an individual is exposed to an advertising message.

frictional unemployment Short-term unemployment that is not related to the business cycle.

friendly takeover A takeover that is supported by the management and board of directors of the targeted company.

fringe benefits Indirect compensation such as pensions, health insurance, and vacations.

full employment Situation when the economy is producing to its maximum sustainable capacity, using labour, technology, land, capital, and other factors of production to their fullest potential.

full warranty The manufacturer's guarantee to meet certain minimum standards, including repair or replacement of the product or refunding the customer if the product does not work.

full-service merchant wholesalers Wholesalers that provide many services for their clients, such as providing credit, offering promotional and technical advice, storing and delivering merchandise, or providing installation and repairs.

functional departmentalization Departmentalization that is based on the primary functions performed within an organizational unit.

futures contracts Legally binding obligations to buy or sell specified quantities of commodities or financial instruments at an agreed-on price at a future date.

G

Gantt charts Bar graphs plotted on a time line that show the relationship between scheduled and actual production.

general partners Partners who have unlimited liability for all of the firm's business obligations and who control its operations.

general partnership A partnership in which all partners share in the management and profits. Each partner can act on behalf of the firm and has unlimited liability for all its business obligations.

generally accepted accounting principles (GAAP) The financial accounting standards followed by accountants in Canada in preparing financial statements.

Generation X Those born between the mid-1960s and the late 1970s.

Generation Y People born from the early 1980s to the mid 1990s.

generic products Products that carry no brand name, come in plain containers, and sell for much less than brand name products.

geographic departmentalization Departmentalization based on the geographic segmentation of the organizational units.

geographic segmentation The differentiation of markets by region of the country, city or county size, market density, or climate.

global management skills A manager's ability to operate in diverse cultural environments.

global vision The ability to recognize and react to international business opportunities, be aware of threats from foreign competition, and use international distribution networks effectively to obtain materials and move finished products to customers.

goal-setting theory A theory of motivation based on the premise that an individual's intention to work toward a goal is a primary source of motivation.

goods Tangible items manufactured by businesses.

grievance A formal complaint, filed by an employee or by the union, charging that management has violated the contract.

gross domestic product (GDP) The total market value of all final goods and services produced within a nation's borders each year.

gross national product (GNP) The total market value of all final goods and services produced by a country regardless of where the factors of production are located.

gross profit The amount a company earns after paying to produce or buy its products but before deducting operating expenses.

gross sales The total dollar amount of a company's sales.

group cohesiveness The degree to which group members want to stay in the group and tend to resist outside influences.

guerrilla marketing Proactive efforts to spread positive word-of-mouth information and to encourage product usage.

H

Hawthorne effect The phenomenon that employees perform better when they feel singled out for attention or feel that management is concerned about their welfare.

high-yield (junk) bonds High-risk, high-return bonds.

horizontal merger A merger of companies at the same stage in the same industry; done to reduce costs, expand product offerings, or reduce competition.

host computer The central computer for a Web site that stores services and data used by other computers on the network.

hostile takeover A takeover that goes against the wishes of the target company's management and board of directors.

human relations skills A manager's interpersonal skills that are used to accomplish goals through the use of human resources.

human resource (HR) planning Creating a strategy for meeting future human resource needs.

human resource management (HRM) The process of hiring, developing, motivating, and evaluating employees to achieve organizational goals.

hygiene factors Extrinsic elements of the work environment that do not serve as a source of employee satisfaction or motivation.

hypertext A file or series of files within a Web page that links users to documents at the same or other Web sites.

I

ideal self-image The way an individual would like to be.

implied contract A contract that depends on the acts and conduct of the parties to show agreement; the terms are not specified in writing or orally.

implied warranty An unwritten guarantee that a product is fit for the purpose for which it is sold.

import quota A limit on the quantity of a certain good that can be imported; also known as a *quantitative restraint*.

imports Goods and services that are bought from other countries.

income statement A financial statement that summarizes a firm's revenues and expenses and shows its total profit or loss over a period of time; also referred to as a *profit and loss statement* or *statement of earnings*.

income taxes Taxes that are based on the income received by businesses and individuals.

industrial distributors Independent wholesalers that buy related product lines from many manufacturers and sell them to industrial users.

inflation The situation in which the average of all prices of goods and services is rising.

informal organization The network of connections and channels of communication based on the informal relationships of individuals inside an organization.

information A meaningful and useful representation or interpretation of data.

informational labelling A type of product label that provides product information to aid consumers in making product selections and minimize cognitive dissonance after the purchase.

information system (IS) The hardware, software, people, data, and so on, that provide information about all aspects of a firm's operations.

information technology (IT) The equipment and techniques used to manage and process information.

informational roles A manager's activities as an information gatherer, an information disseminator, or a spokesperson for the company.

infrastructure The basic institutions and public facilities upon which an economy's development depends.

initial public offer (IPO) A company's first issuance of shares to the public.

institutional advertising Advertising that creates a positive picture of a company and its ideals, services, and roles in the community.

institutional investors Investment professionals who are paid to manage other people's money.

insurable interest An insurance applicant's chance of loss if a particular peril occurs.

insurable risk A risk that an insurance company will cover. It must meet certain criteria.

insurance The promise of compensation for certain financial losses.

insurance policy A written agreement that defines what the insurance covers and the risks that the insurance company will bear for the insured party.

intangible assets Long-term assets with no physical existence, such as patents, copyrights, trademarks, and goodwill.

integrated marketing communications (IMC) The careful coordination of all promotional activities—media advertising, sales promotion, personal selling, and public relations, as well as direct marketing, packaging, and other forms of promotion—to produce a consistent, unified message that is customer focused.

intensive distribution A distribution system in which a manufacturer tries to sell its products wherever there are potential customers.

interest A fixed amount of money paid by the issuer of a bond to the bondholder on a regular schedule, typically every six months; stated as the *coupon rate*.

intermittent process A production process that uses short production runs to make batches of different products; generally used for low-volume, high-variety products.

International Monetary Fund (IMF) An international organization, founded in 1945, that promotes trade, makes short-term loans to member nations, and acts as a lender of last resort for troubled nations.

Internet A worldwide computer network that includes both commercial and public networks and offers various capabilities, including e-mail, file transfer, on-line chat sessions, and newsgroups.

Internet service provider (ISP) A commercial service that connects companies and individuals to the Internet.

interpersonal roles A manager's activities as a figurehead, company leader, or liaison.

intranet An internal corporate-wide area network that uses Internet technology to link employees in many locations and with different types of computers.

intrapreneurs Entrepreneurs who apply their creativity, vision, and risk taking within a large corporation, rather than starting a company of their own.

inventory The supply of goods that a firm holds for use in production or for sale to customers.

inventory management The determination of how much of each type of inventory a firm will keep on hand and the ordering, receiving, storing, and tracking of inventory.

inventory turnover ratio The ratio of cost of goods sold to average inventory; measures the speed with which inventory moves through a firm and is turned into sales.

investment bankers Firms that act as underwriters, buying securities from corporations and governments and reselling them to the public.

involvement The amount of time and effort a buyer invests in the searches, evaluations, and decision processes of consumer behaviour.

ISO 14000 A set of five technical standards of quality management created by the International Organization for Standardization to provide a uniform way of determining whether manufacturing plants and service organizations conform to sound quality procedures.

ISO 9000 A set of technical standards designed by the International Organization for Standardization to promote clean production processes to protect the environment.

J

job analysis A study of the tasks required to do a particular job well.

job description The tasks and responsibilities of a job.

job enlargement The horizontal expansion of a job by increasing the number and variety of tasks that a person performs.

job enrichment The vertical expansion of a job by increasing the employee's autonomy, responsibility, and decision-making authority.

job fair An event, typically one day, held at a convention centre to bring together thousands of job seekers and hundreds of firms searching for employees.

job rotation Reassignment of workers to several different jobs over time so that they can learn the basics of each job; also called *cross-training*.

job sharing A scheduling option that allows two individuals to split the tasks, responsibilities, and work hours of one 40-hour-per-week job.

job shop A manufacturing firm that produces goods in response to customer orders.

job specification A list of the skills, knowledge, and abilities a person must have to fill a job.

joint venture An agreement in which a domestic firm buys part of a foreign firm to create a new entity.

justice What is considered fair according to the prevailing standards of society; in the 21st century, an equitable distribution of the burdens and rewards that society has to offer.

just-in-time (JIT) A system in which materials arrive exactly when they are needed for production, rather than being stored on site.

K

key person life insurance A term insurance policy that names the company as beneficiary.

knowledge The understanding or awareness of information about a subject.

knowledge management (KM) A worker who develops or uses knowledge, contributing to and benefiting from information used in performing various tasks, including planning, acquiring, searching, analyzing, organizing, storing, programming, producing, distributing, marketing, or selling functions.

knowledge worker A worker who develops or uses knowledge, contributing to and benefiting from information used in performing various tasks, including planning, acquiring, searching, analyzing, organizing, storing, programming, producing, distributing, marketing, or selling functions.

L

labour union An organization that represents workers in dealing with management over issues involving wages, hours, and working conditions.

law of large numbers Insurance companies' predictions of the likelihood that a peril will occur, used to calculate premiums.

laws The rules of conduct in a society, created and enforced by a controlling authority, usually the government.

layoff A temporary separation of an employer from the organization; arranged by the employer, usually because business is slow.

leader pricing The strategy of pricing products below the normal markup or even below cost to attract customers to a store where they would not otherwise shop.

leadership The process of guiding and motivating others toward the achievement of organizational goals.

leadership style The relatively consistent way that individuals in leadership positions attempt to influence the behaviour of others.

lean manufacturing Streamlining production by eliminating steps in the production process that do not add benefits that customers are willing to pay for.

legitimate power Power that is derived from an individual's position in an organization.

leveraged buyout (LBO) A corporate takeover financed by large amounts of borrowed money; can be done by outside investors or by a company's own management.

liabilities What a firm owes to its creditors; also called *debts*.

licensing The legal process whereby a firm agrees to allow another firm to use a manufacturing process, trademark, patent, trade secret, or other proprietary knowledge in exchange for the payment of a royalty.

limited decision-making Situation in which a consumer has previous product experience but is unfamiliar with the current brands available.

limited liability partnership (LLP) In a limited liability partnership, each individual partner is protected from responsibility for the acts of other partners, and each party's liability is limited to harm resulting from that party's own actions.

limited partners Partners whose liability for the firm's business obligations is limited to the amount of their investment. They help to finance the business and/or promote the business, but do not participate in the firm's day-to-day operations.

limited partnership A partnership with one or more general partners, who have unlimited liability, and one or more limited partners, whose liability is limited to the amount of their investment.

limited-service merchant wholesalers Wholesalers that typically carry a limited line of fast-moving merchandise and do not offer many services to their clients.

line extension A new flavour, size, or model using an existing brand name in an existing category.

line of credit An agreement between a bank and a business that specifies the maximum amount of unsecured short-term borrowing the bank will allow the firm over a given period, typically one year.

line organization An organizational structure with direct, clear lines of authority and communication flowing from the top managers downward.

line positions All positions in the organization directly concerned with producing goods and services and which are directly connected from top to bottom.

line-and-staff organization An organizational structure that includes both line and staff positions.

liquidity The speed with which an asset can be converted to cash.

liquidity ratios Ratios that measure a firm's ability to pay its short-term debts as they come due.

local area network (LAN) A network that connects computers at one site, enabling the computer users to exchange data and share the use of hardware and software from a variety of computer manufacturers.

local union A branch or unit of a national union that represents workers at a specific plant or in a specific geographic area.

lockout An employer tactic in a labour dispute in which the employer refuses to allow workers to enter a plant or building to work, which means that the workers do not get paid.

logistics management The management of the physical distribution process.

long-term forecasts Projections of a firm's activities and the funding for those activities over a period that is longer than a year; from a financial point typically covers 2 to 10 years.

long-term liabilities Claims that come due more than one year after the date of the balance sheet.

loss leader A product priced below cost as part of a leader pricing strategy.

loyalty cards Cards issued by a manufacturer, service organization, or retailer that give discounts to loyal and frequent shoppers.

M

Maastricht Treaty A 1993 treaty concluded by the members of the European Community (now the European Union) that outlines plans for tightening bonds among the members and creating a single market; officially called the Treaty on European Union.

macroeconomics The sub-area of economics that focuses on the economy as a whole by looking at aggregate data for large groups of people, companies, or products.

make-or-buy decision The determination by a firm of whether to make its own production materials or buy them from outside sources.

management The process of guiding the development, maintenance, and allocation of resources to attain organizational goals.

management information system (MIS) The methods and equipment that provide information about all aspects of a firm's operations

management support system (MSS) A dynamic information system that helps managers make decisions by allowing them to analyze data, identify business trends, make forecasts, and model business strategies.

managerial accounting Accounting that provides financial information that managers inside the organization can use to evaluate and make decisions about current and future operations.

managerial hierarchy The levels of management within an organization; typically includes top, middle, and supervisory management.

managing diversity Fully utilizing the potential of all employees in a work environment.

manufacturer A producer; an organization that converts raw materials to finished products.

manufacturer brands Brands that are owned by national or regional manufacturers and widely distributed; also called *national brands*.

manufacturers' representatives Salespeople who represent non-competing manufacturers; also called *manufacturers' agents*.

manufacturing resource planning II (MRPII) A complex computerized system that integrates data from many departments to control the flow of resources and inventory.

market economy An economic system based on competition in the marketplace and private ownership of the factors of production (resources); also known as the *private enterprise system* or *capitalism*.

market segmentation The process of separating, identifying, and evaluating the layers of a market to design a marketing mix.

market structure The number of suppliers in a market.

marketable securities Short-term investments that are easily converted into cash.

marketing The process of discovering the needs and wants of potential buyers and customers and then providing goods and services that meet or exceed their expectations.

marketing concept Identifying consumer needs and then producing the goods or services that will satisfy them while making a profit for the organization.

marketing database Computerized file of customers' and potential customers' profiles and purchase patterns.

marketing intermediaries Organizations that assist in moving goods and services from producers to end users.

marketing mix The blend of product offering, pricing, promotional methods, and distribution system that brings a specific group of consumers superior value.

marketing research The process of planning, collecting, and analyzing data relevant to a marketing decision.

markup pricing A method of pricing in which a certain percentage (the markup) is added to the product's cost to arrive at the price.

Maslow's hierarchy of needs A theory of motivation developed by Abraham Maslow; holds that humans have five levels of needs and act to satisfy their unmet needs. At the base of the hierarchy are fundamental physiological needs, followed in order by safety, social, esteem, and self-actualization needs.

mass customization A manufacturing process in which modules are mass-produced and then assembled to meet the needs or desires of individual customers.

mass production The ability to manufacture many identical goods or provide many identical services at once.

master brand A brand so dominant that consumers think of it immediately when a product category, use, attribute, or customer benefit is mentioned.

materials requirement planning (MRP) A computerized system of controlling the flow or resources and inventory. A master schedule is used to ensure that the materials, labour, and equipment needed for production are at the right places in the right amounts at the right times.

matrix structure (project management) An organizational structure that combines functional and product departmentalization by bringing together people from different functional areas of the organization to work on a special project.

mechanistic organization An organizational structure that is characterized by a relatively high degree of job specialization, rigid departmentalization, many layers of management, narrow spans of control, centralized decision-making, and a long chain of command.

mediation The intervention of a third party with a view to persuading the parties to adjust or settle their dispute.

mentoring A form of on-the-job training in which a senior manager or other experienced employee provides job- and career-related information to a protégé.

merchant wholesaler An institution that buys goods from manufacturers (takes ownership) and resells them to businesses, government agencies, other wholesalers, or retailers.

Mercosur A trade agreement among Argentina, Brazil, Paraguay, and Uruguay that eliminates most tariffs among the member nations.

merger The combination of two or more firms to form a new company, which often takes on a new corporate identity.

microeconomics The sub area of economics that focuses on individual parts of the economy such as households or firms.

middle management Managers who design and carry out tactical plans in specific areas of the company.

mission An organization's purpose and reason for existing; its long-term goals.

mission statement The formalized statement of an organization's purpose and reason for existing.

mixed economies Economies that combine several economic systems; for example, an economy where the government owns certain industries but others are owned by the private sector.

monetary policy The measures taken by the Bank of Canada to regulate the amount of money in circulation to influence the economy.

money Anything that is acceptable as payment for goods and services.

monopolistic competition A market structure in which many firms offer products that are close substitutes and in which entry is relatively easy.

monopoly A situation in which there is no competition and the benefits of a free market are lost.

mortgage bonds Corporate bonds that are secured by property, such as land, equipment, or buildings.

mortgage loan A long-term loan made against real estate as collateral.

motivating factors Intrinsic job elements that lead to worker satisfaction.

multiculturalism The condition when all major ethnic groups in an area, such as a city, county, or province, are about equally represented.

multinational corporations Corporations that move resources, goods, services, and skills across national boundaries without regard to the country in which their headquarters are located.

mutual fund A financial service company that pools its investors' funds to buy a selection of securities that meet its stated investment goals.

mutual-aid pact An agreement by companies in an industry to create a fund that can be used to help cover fixed costs of any member company whose workers go on strike.

N

National Association of Securities Dealers Automated Quotation (NASDAQ) system The first electronic-based stock market and the fastest-growing part of the stock market.

national debt The accumulated total of all of the federal government's annual budget deficits.

national union A union that consists of many local unions in a particular industry, skilled trade, or geographic area and thus represents workers throughout an entire country.

nationalism A sense of national consciousness that boosts the culture and interests of one country over those of all other countries.

net loss The amount obtained by subtracting all of a firm's expenses from its revenues, when the expenses are more than the revenues.

net profit (net income or net earnings) The amount obtained by subtracting all of a firm's expenses from its revenues, when the revenues are more than the expenses.

net profit margin The ratio of net profit to net sales; also called *return on sales*. It measures the percentage of each sales dollar remaining after all expenses, including taxes, have been deducted.

net sales The amount left after deducting sales discounts and returns and allowances from gross sales.

net working capital The amount obtained by subtracting total current liabilities from total current assets; used to measure a firm's liquidity.

niche competitive advantage A firm's ability to target and effectively serve a single segment of the market within a limited geographic area.

non-programmed decisions Responses to infrequent, unforeseen, or very unusual problems and opportunities where the manager does not have a precedent to follow in decision-making.

North American Free Trade Agreement (NAFTA) An agreement, launched in 1994, creating a free-trade zone including Canada, the United States, and Mexico.

not-for-profit organization An organization that exists to achieve some goal other than the usual business goal of profit.

O

observation research A marketing research method in which the investigator monitors respondents' actions without interacting directly with the respondents; for example, by using cash registers with scanners.

odd-even (psychological) pricing The strategy of setting a price at an odd number to connote a bargain and at an even number to suggest quality.

office automation system An information system that uses information technology tools such as word processing systems, e-mail systems, cellular phones, pagers, and fax machines to improve communications throughout an organization.

oligopoly A market structure in which a few firms produce most or all of the output and in which large capital requirements or other factors limit the number of firms.

one-person corporation A corporation with only one person as the shareholder; common in professional practices (e.g., medical doctors, accountants, or lawyers).

one-to-one marketing Creating a unique marketing mix for every customer.

on-line (real-time) processing A method of updating a database in which data are processed as they become available.

on-the-job training Training in which the employee learns the job by doing it with guidance from a supervisor or experienced coworker.

open market operations The purchase or sale of Canadian government securities by the Bank of Canada to stimulate or slow down the economy.

open shop A company where employees do not have to join the union or pay dues or fees to the union; established under right-to-work laws.

operating budgets Budgets that combine sales forecasts with estimates of production costs and operating expenses to forecast profits.

operating expenses The expenses of running a business that are not directly related to producing or buying its products.

operational planning The process of creating specific standards, methods, policies, and procedures that are used in specific functional areas of the organization; helps guide and control the implementation of tactical plans.

operations management The design and management of the transformation process.

operations planning The aspect of operations management in which the firm considers the competitive environment and its own strategic goals in an effort to find the best methods.

operations The creation of products and services by transforming inputs, such as natural resources, raw materials, human resources, and capital, into outputs, products, and services.

opinion leader Those who influence others.

options Contracts that entitle holders to buy or sell specified quantities of common shares or other financial instruments at a set price during a specified time.

organic organization An organizational structure that is characterized by a relatively low degree of job specialization, loose departmentalization, few levels of management, wide spans of control, decentralized decision-making, and a short chain of command.

organization chart A visual representation of the structured relationships among tasks and the people given the authority to do those tasks.

organized share exchanges Organizations on whose premises securities are resold using an auction-style trading system.

organizing The process of coordinating and allocating a firm's resources to carry out its plans.

outsourcing The assignment of various functions, such as human resources, accounting, or legal work, to outside organizations. Also refers to the purchase of items from an outside source rather than making them internally.

over-the-counter (OTC) market A sophisticated telecomunications network that links dealers and enables them to trade securities.

owners' equity The total amount of investment in the firm minus any liabilities; also called *net worth*.

P

participative leadership A leadership style in which the leader shares decision-making with group members and encourages discussion of issues and alternatives; includes democratic, consensual, and consultative styles.

partnership An association of two or more persons who agree to operate a business together for profit.

patent A form of protection (limited monopoly) established by the government to inventors; gives an inventor the exclusive right to manufacture, use, and sell an invention for 20 years.

payroll taxes Income taxes that are collected by the employer and remitted to the federal government, usually in the form of a deduction from the employee's pay.

penetration pricing The strategy of selling new products at low prices in the hope of achieving a large sales volume.

pension funds Large pools of money set aside by corporations, unions, and governments for later use in paying retirement benefits to their employees or members.

perception The process by which we select, organize, and interpret stimuli into a meaningful and coherent picture.

perfect (pure) competition A market structure in which a large number of small firms sell similar products, buyers and sellers have good information, and businesses can be easily opened or closed.

performance appraisal A comparison of actual performance with expected performance to assess an employee's contributions to the organization.

peril A hazard or a source of danger.

perpetual inventory A continuously updated list of inventory levels, orders, sales, and receipts.

personal selling A face-to-face sales presentation to a prospective customer.

personality A way of organizing and grouping how an individual reacts to situations.

persuasive labelling A type of product label that reinforces or repeats a promotional theme or logo.

physical distribution (logistics) The movement of products from the producer to industrial users and consumers.

picketing Union members parade in front of the employer's plant carrying signs and trying to persuade non-striking workers to stop working and customers and suppliers from doing business with the company.

planning The process of deciding what needs to be done to achieve organizational objectives, identifying when and how it will be done, and determining by whom it should be done.

postconventional ethics The third stage in the ethical development of individuals in which people adhere to the ethical standards of a mature adult and are less concerned about how others view their behaviour than about how they will judge themselves in the long run; also known as *principled ethics*.

power The ability to influence others to behave in a particular way.

preconventional ethics A stage in the ethical development of individuals in which people behave in a childlike manner and make ethical decisions in a calculating, self-centred, way, based on the possibility of immediate punishment or reward; also known as *self-centred ethics*.

preferential tariff A tariff that is lower for some nations than for others.

preferred shares Equities for which the dividend amount is set at the time the stock is issued.

prestige pricing The strategy of increasing the price of a product so that consumers will perceive it as being of higher quality, status, or value.

price skimming The strategy of introducing a product with a high initial price and lowering the price over time as the product moves through its life cycle.

pricing strategy The part of the marketing mix that involves establishing a price for the product based on the demand for the product and the cost of producing it.

primary data Information collected directly from the original source to solve a problem.

primary market The securities market where *new* securities are sold to the public.

principal The amount borrowed by the issuer of a bond; also called *par value*.

principle of comparative advantage The concept that each country should specialize in the products that it can produce most readily and cheaply and trade those products for those that other countries can produce more readily and cheaply.

private accountants Accountants who are employed to serve one particular organization.

private corporation Corporation that does not trade publicly and, therefore, is not listed on a stock exchange.

private law The law relating to the relationship between individuals, businesses, or individuals and businesses.

problem-solving teams Teams of employees from the same department or area of expertise and from the same level of the organizational hierarchy who meet regularly to share information and discuss ways to improve processes and procedures in specific functional areas.

process The way a good is made or a service provided.

process departmentalization Departmentalization that is based on the production process used by the organizational unit.

process layout A facility arrangement in which work flows according to the production process. All workers performing similar tasks are grouped together, and products pass from one workstation to another.

process manufacturing A transformation process in which the basic input is broken down into one or more outputs (products).

producer price index (PPI) An index of the prices paid by producers and wholesalers for various commodities such as raw materials, partially finished goods, and finished products.

product In marketing, any good or service, along with its perceived attributes and benefits, that creates value for the customer.

product (assembly line) layout A facility arrangement in which workstations or departments are arranged in a line with products moving along the line.

product advertising Advertising that features a specific good or service.

product departmentalization Departmentalization that is based on the goods or services produced or sold by the organizational unit.

product liability The responsibility of manufacturers and sellers for defects in the products they make and sell.

product life cycle The pattern of sales and profits over time for a product or product category; consists of an introductory state, growth stage, maturity, and decline (and death).

product manager The person who develops and implements a complete strategy and marketing program for a specific product or brand.

product strategy The part of the marketing mix that involves choosing a brand name, packaging, colours, a warranty, accessories, and a service program for the product.

production The creation of products and services by turning inputs, such as natural resources, raw materials, human resources, and capital, into outputs, which are products and services.

production orientation An approach in which a firm works to lower production costs without a strong desire to satisfy the needs of customers.

production planning The aspect of operations management in which the firm considers the competitive environment and its own strategic goals in an effort to find the best production methods.

production process The way in which a good is made.

professional liability insurance Insurance designed to protect top corporate management, who have been the target of malpractice lawsuits.

profit The money left over after all expenses are paid.

profit maximization A pricing objective that entails getting the largest possible profit from a product by producing the product as long as the revenue from selling it exceeds the cost of producing it.

profitability ratios Ratios that measure how well a firm is using its resources to generate profit and how efficiently it is being managed.

program evaluation and review technique (PERT) A scheduling tool that is similar to the CPM method but assigns three time estimates for each activity (optimistic, most probable, and pessimistic); allows managers to anticipate delays and potential problems and schedule accordingly.

programmed decisions Decisions made in response to frequently occurring routine situations.

programmed instruction A form of computer-assisted off-the-job training.

promotion (in employment) An upward move in an organization to a position with more authority, responsibility, and pay.

promotion (in marketing) The attempt by marketers to inform, persuade, or remind consumers and industrial users to engage in the exchange process.

promotion strategy The part of the marketing mix that involves personal selling, advertising, public relations, and sales promotion of the product.

promotional mix The combination of advertising, personal selling, sales promotion, and public relations used to promote a product.

property taxes Taxes that are imposed on real and personal property based on the assessed value of the property.

prospecting The process of looking for sales prospects.

protectionism The policy of protecting home industries from outside competition by establishing artificial barriers such as tariffs and quotas.

protective tariffs Tariffs that are imposed to make imports less attractive to buyers than domestic products are.

provincial health care Health insurance programs provided by the provinces.

psychographic segmentation The differentiation of markets by personality or lifestyle.

public accountants Independent accountants who serve organizations and individuals on a fee basis.

public corporation Corporation that has the right to issue shares to the public.

public law The law relating to the relationship between the individual or business and the government (or its agencies).

public relations Any communication or activity designed to win goodwill or prestige for a company or person.

publicity Information about a company or product that appears in the news media and is not directly paid for by the company.

pull strategy A promotional strategy in which a manufacturer focuses on stimulating consumer demand for its product rather than on trying to persuade wholesalers or retailers to carry the product.

purchasing The process of buying production inputs from various sources; also called *procurement*.

purchasing power The value of what money can buy.

pure monopoly A market structure in which a single firm accounts for all industry sales and in which there are barriers to entry.

push strategy A promotional strategy in which a manufacturer uses aggressive personal selling and trade advertising to convince a wholesaler or retailer to carry and sell its merchandise.

Q

qualifying questions Inquiries used by salespeople to separate prospects from those who do not have the potential to buy.

quality Goods and services that meet customer expectations by providing reliable performance.

quality control The process of creating standards for quality and then measuring finished products and services against them.

quality of life The general level of human happiness based on such things as life expectancy, educational standards, health, sanitation, and leisure time.

R

ratio analysis The calculation and interpretation of financial ratios taken from the firm's financial statements to assess its condition and performance.

rational branding A tactic for advertising on the Internet that combines the emotional aspect of traditional brand marketing with a concrete service that is offered only on-line.

reach The number of different target consumers who are exposed to a commercial at least once during a specific period, usually four weeks.

real self-image How an individual actually perceives him- or herself.

recession A decline in GDP that lasts for at least two consecutive quarters.

recruitment The attempt to find and attract qualified applicants in the external labour market.

re-engineering The complete redesign of business structures and processes to improve operations.

reference groups Formal and informal groups that influence buyer behaviour.

referent power Power that is derived from an individual's personal charisma and the respect and/or admiration the individual inspires.

relationship management The practice of building, maintaining, and enhancing interactions with customers and other parties to develop long-term satisfaction through mutually beneficial partnerships.

relationship marketing A strategy that focuses on forging long-term partnerships with customers by offering value and providing customer satisfaction.

reminder advertising Advertising that is used to keep a product's name in the public's mind.

resignation A permanent separation of an employee from the organization, done voluntarily by the employee.

retailers Firms that sell goods to consumers and to industrial users for their own consumption.

retained earnings (in accounting) Profits that have been reinvested in a firm.

retained earnings (in financial management) The amounts left over from profitable operations since the firm's beginning; equal to total profits minus all dividends paid to shareholders.

retirement The separation of an employee from the organization at the end of his or her career.

return The opportunity for profit.

return on equity (ROE) The ratio of net profit to total owners' equity; measures the return that owners receive on their investment in the firm.

revenues The money a company earns from providing services or selling goods to customers.

revolving credit agreement (revolving line of credit) A guaranteed line of credit whereby a bank agrees that a certain amount of funds will be available for a business to borrow over a given period.

reward power Power that is derived from an individual's control over rewards.

risk The potential for loss or the chance that an investment will not achieve the expected level of return.

risk management The process of identifying and evaluating risks and selecting and managing techniques to adapt to risk exposures.

risk–return trade-off A basic principle in finance that holds that the higher the risk, the greater the return that is required.

robotics The technology involved in designing, constructing, and operating computer-controlled machines that can perform tasks independently.

routine response behaviour Purchase of low-cost, frequently bought items with little search or decision-making.

routing The aspect of production control that involves setting out the workflow—the sequence of machines and operations through which the product or service progresses from start to finish.

S

sales promotions Marketing events or sales efforts—not including advertising, personal selling, and public relations—that stimulate buying.

sales prospects The companies and people who are most likely to buy a seller's offerings.

sales taxes Taxes that are levied on goods and services when they are sold; calculated as a percentage of the price.

scanner-based research System for gathering information from a single group of respondents by continuously monitoring the advertising, promotion, and pricing they are exposed to and the things that they buy.

scheduling The aspect of production control that involves specifying and controlling the time required for each step in the production process.

scientific management A system of management developed by Frederick W. Taylor and based on four principles: developing a scientific approach for each element of a job, scientifically selecting and training workers, encouraging cooperation between workers and managers, and dividing work and responsibility between management and workers according to who can better perform a particular task.

seasonal unemployment Unemployment that occurs during specific seasons in certain industries.

secondary data Information that has already been collected for a project other than the current one but that can be used to solve the current problem.

secondary market The securities market where (already issued) old securities are traded among investors; includes the organized stock exchanges, the over-the-counter market, and the commodities exchanges.

secured bonds Corporate bonds for which specific assets have been pledged as collateral.

secured loans Loans for which the borrower is required to pledge specific assets as collateral, or security.

securities Investment certificates issued by corporations or governments that represent either equity or debt.

selection The process of determining which persons in the applicant pool possess the qualifications necessary to be successful on the job.

selection interview An in-depth discussion of an applicant's work experiences, skills and abilities, education, and career interests.

selective distribution A distribution system in which a manufacturer selects a limited number of dealers in an area (but more than one or two) to market its products.

selective exposure The process of deciding which stimuli to notice and which to ignore.

selective strike strategy A union strategy of conducting a strike at (shutting down) a critical plant that supplies parts to other plants.

self-concept How people perceive themselves.

self-managed work teams Highly autonomous teams of employees who manage themselves without any formal supervision and take responsibility for setting goals, planning and scheduling work activities, selecting team members, and evaluating team performance.

separation The departure of an employee from the organization; can be a layoff, termination, resignation, or retirement.

servers Computers that store data and "serve" information to other computers called clients, on request.

services Intangible offerings of businesses that can't be held, touched, or stored.

share or stock dividends Payments to shareholders in the form of more shares; can replace or supplement cash dividends.

shareholders The owners of a corporation, who hold shares of stock that provide certain rights; also known as *stockholders*.

shop steward An elected union official who represents union members to management when workers have issues.

shopping products Items that are bought after considerable planning, including brand-to-brand and store-to-store comparisons of price, suitability, and style.

short-term forecasts Projections of revenues, costs of goods, and operating expenses over a one-year period.

sick-out A union strategy in which a group of employees claim they cannot work because of illness, thereby disrupting the company.

Six Sigma A quality control process that relies on defining what needs to be done to ensure quality, measuring and analyzing production results statistically, and finding ways of improving and controlling quality.

small business A business that is independently owned, is owned by an individual or a small group of investors, is based locally, and is not a dominant company in its industry.

social investing The practice of limiting investments to securities of companies that behave in accordance with the investor's beliefs about ethical and social responsibility.

social marketing The application of marketing techniques to social issues and causes.

social responsibility The concern of businesses for the welfare of society as a whole; consists of obligations beyond those required by law or contracts.

socialism An economic system in which the basic industries are owned either by the government itself or by the private sector under strong government control.

socialization process The passing down of cultural norms and values to children.

software The general term for various programs used to operate computers; a set of instructions that directs a computer's activities.

sole proprietorship A business that is established, owned, operated, and often financed by one person.

span of control The number of employees a manager directly supervises; also called span of management.

specialization The degree to which tasks are subdivided into smaller jobs.

specialty products Items for which consumers search long and hard and for which they refuse to accept substitutes.

speculative risk The chance of either loss or gain, without insurance against the possible loss.

staff positions Positions in an organization held by individuals who provide the administrative and support services that line employees need to achieve the firm's goals.

stakeholders Individuals or groups (including organizations) to whom the business has a responsibility; including the investors or shareholders (those with a financial interest), employees, customers, suppliers (business partners), governments, local communities, the environment, and society as a whole.

standard of living A country's output of goods and services that people can buy with the money they have.

statement of cash flows A financial statement that provides a summary of the money flowing into and out of a firm.

statute law (or statutory law) Written law enacted by a legislature (municipal, provincial, or federal).

stock dividends Payments to shareholders in the form of more shares; may replace or supplement cash dividends.

stockbroker A person who is licensed to buy and sell securities on behalf of clients.

strategic alliance A cooperative agreement between business firms; sometimes called a *strategic partnership*.

strategic giving The practice of tying philanthropy closely to the corporate mission or goals and targeting donations to regions where a company operates.

strategic planning The process of creating long-range (one to five years), broad goals for the organization and determining what resources will be needed to accomplish those goals.

strict liability A concept in products-liability laws under which a manufacturer or seller is liable for any personal injury or property damage caused by defective products or packaging that do not meet industry standards.

strike replacements Non-union employees hired to replace striking union members; also known as *scabs*.

structural unemployment Unemployment that is caused by a mismatch between available jobs and the skills of available workers in an industry or region; not related to the business cycle.

supervisory management Managers who design and carry out operational plans for the ongoing daily activities of the firm.

supply The quantity of a good or service that businesses will make available at various prices.

survey research A marketing research method in which data are gathered from respondents in person, by telephone, by mail, at a mall, or through the Internet to obtain facts, opinions, and attitudes.

supply chain The entire sequence of securing inputs, producing goods, and delivering goods to customers.

supply chain management The process of using information along the supply chain so that the firm can satisfy its customers with quality products and services; includes working closely with suppliers.

supply curve A graph showing the quantity of a good or service that a business will make available at various prices.

system software Software that controls the computer and provides instructions that enable applications programs to run on a particular computer.

T

tactical planning The process of beginning to implement a strategic plan by addressing issues of coordination and allocating resources to different parts of the organization; has a shorter time frame (less than one year) and more specific objectives than strategic planning.

target for the overnight rate The signal to the major participants in the money market as to what the Bank of Canada is aiming for when participants borrow and lend one-day funds to each other.

target market The specific group of consumers toward which a firm directs its marketing efforts.

target return on investment A pricing objective where the price of a product is set so as to give the company the desired probability in terms of return on its money.

tariff A tax imposed on imported goods.

technical skills A manager's specialized areas of knowledge and expertise, as well as the ability to apply that knowledge.

telecommuting An arrangement in which employees work at home and are linked to the office by phone, fax, and computer.

term deposits Deposits at a bank or other financial institution that pay interest but cannot be withdrawn on demand.

termination A permanent separation of an employee from the organization, arranged by the employer.

term loan A business loan with a maturity of more than one year; can be unsecured or secured.

test marketing The process of testing a new product among potential users.

theft insurance A broad insurance coverage that protects business against losses for an act of stealing.

Theory X A management style, formulated by Douglas McGregor, that is based on a pessimistic view of human nature and assumes that the average person dislikes work, will avoid it if possible, prefers to be directed, avoids responsibility, and wants security above all.

Theory Y A management style, formulated by Douglas McGregor, that is based on a relatively optimistic view of human nature; assumes that the average person wants to work, accepts responsibility, is willing to help solve problems, and can be self-directed and self-controlled.

Theory Z A theory developed by William Ouchi that combines U.S. and Japanese business practices by emphasizing long-term employment, slow career development, moderate specialization, group decision-making, individual responsibility, relatively informal control over the employee, and concern for workers.

time deposits Interest-bearing deposits that cannot be withdrawn on demand.

top management The highest level of managers; includes CEOs, presidents, and vice presidents, who develop strategic plans and address long-range issues.

tort A civil, or private, act that harms other people or their property.

total cost The sum of the fixed costs and the variable costs.

total profit Total revenue minus total cost.

total quality management (TQM) The use of quality principles in all aspects of a company's production and operations.

total revenue The selling price per unit times the number of units sold.

trade credit The extension of credit by the seller to the buyer between the time the buyer receives the goods or services and when it pays for them.

trade deficit An unfavourable balance of trade that occurs when a country imports more than it exports.

trade surplus A favourable balance of trade that occurs when a country exports more than it imports.

trademark The legally exclusive design, name, or other distinctive mark that a manufacturer uses to identify its goods in the marketplace.

training and development Activities that provide learning situations in which an employee acquires additional knowledge or skills to increase job performance.

transaction processing system (TPS) An information system that handles the daily business operations of a firm. The system receives and organizes raw data from internal and external sources for storage in a database.

transfer A horizontal move in an organization to a position with about the same salary and at about the same organizational level.

transmission control protocol/Internet protocol (TCP/IP) A communications technology that allows different computer platforms to communicate with each other to transfer data.

trust companies Financial institutions that conduct the same activities as a bank but can also administer estates, trusts, pension plans, and agency contracts.

U

underwriting The process of buying securities from corporations and governments and reselling them to the public; the main activity of investment bankers.

unemployment rate The percentage of the total labour force that is not working but is actively looking for work.

union shop A company where non-union workers can be hired but must then join the union.

unsecured loans Short-term loans for which the borrower does not have to pledge specific assets as security.

unsought products Products that either are unknown to the potential buyer or are known but the buyer does not actively seek them.

Uruguay Round A 1994 agreement by 117 nations to lower trade barriers worldwide.

utilitarianism A philosophy that focuses on the consequences of an action to determine whether it is right or wrong; holds that an action that affects the majority adversely is morally wrong.

V

value pricing A pricing strategy in which the target market is offered a high-quality product at a fair price and with good service.

value-stream mapping Routing technique that uses simple icons to visually represent the flow of materials and information from suppliers through the factory and to customers.

variable costs Costs that change with different levels of output; for example, wages and cost of raw materials.

variable pay A system of paying employees in which a portion of an employee's pay is directly linked to an individual or organizational performance measure.

vendor-managed inventory A system of managing inventory in which the supplier manages the distributor's inventory, thereby reversing the traditional arrangement.

venture capital Financing obtained from investment firms that specialize in financing small, high-growth companies and receive an ownership interest and a voice in management in return for their money.

vertical marketing system An organized, formal distribution channel in which firms are aligned in a hierarchy such as from manufacturer to wholesaler to retailer.

vertical merger A merger of companies at different states in the same industry; done to gain control over supplies of resources or to gain access to different markets.

vestibule training A form of off-the-job training in which trainees learn in a scaled-down version or simulated work environment.

virtual corporation A network of independent companies linked by information technology to share skills, costs, and access to one another's markets; allows the companies to come together quickly to exploit rapidly changing opportunities.

virtual private networks (VPNs) Private corporate networks connected over a public network, such as the Internet. VPNs include strong security measures to allow only authorized users to access the network.

virtual teams Teams of employees in different geographic or organizational locations who come together as a team via a combination of telecommunications and information technologies.

volume segmentation The differentiation of markets based on the amount of the product purchased.

W

warranty A guarantee of the quality of a good or service.

web portal A Web site that provides a starting point, or gateway, to other resources on the Internet or on an intranet.

Web sites Locations on the World Wide Web consisting of a *home page* and, possibly, other pages with documents and files.

whistle blower An employee, former employee, or any other member of an organization that reports misconduct by others in the organization that have the power to take corrective action.

wholesalers Firms that sell finished goods to retailers, manufacturers, and institutions.

wide area network (WAN) A network that connects computers at different sites via telecommunications media such as phone lines, satellites, and microwaves.

wildcat strike A strike by a group of union members or an entire local union without the approval of the national union while the contract is still in effect.

work groups Groups of employees who share resources and coordinate efforts so as to help members perform their individual duties and responsibilities better. The performance of the group can be evaluated by adding up the contributions of the individual group members.

work teams Groups of employees who not only coordinate their efforts, but also collaborate by pooling their knowledge, skills, abilities, and resources in a collective effort to attain a common goal, causing the performance of the team to be greater than the sum of the members' individual efforts.

workers' compensation Payments to cover the expenses of job-related injuries and diseases, including medical costs, rehabilitation, and job retraining if necessary.

World Bank An international bank that offers low-interest loans, as well as advice and information, to developing nations.

World Trade Organization (WTO) An organization established by the Uruguay Round in 1994 to oversee international trade, reduce trade barriers, and resolve disputes among member nations.

World Wide Web (WWW) A subsystem of the Internet that consists of an information retrieval system composed of *Web sites*.

Y

yield management system Mathematical software that helps companies adjust prices to maximize revenue

endnotes

Introduction

1. *Worldwide Quality of Life Survey* (London: Mercer Consulting Group, 2002).
2. These factors are adapted from Fry, Stoner, and Hattwick, *Business: An Integrative Framework* (New York: McGraw-Hill, 1998).

Prologue

1. Marlene Caroselli, Interpersonal Skills (South-Western, a Division of Thomson Learning, 2003), 1. The section entitled "Getting Ahead in Business and Life" is also adapted from the above text.
2. Adapted from, Investing in Your Future (South-Western, a Division of Thomson Learning, 2001), 1–10.
3. The material on "going to college" is adapted from Abby Marks-Beale, Success Skills: Strategies for Study and Lifelong Learning (South-Western, a Division of Thomson Learning, 2002).
4. Julie Griffin Levitt, Your Career: How to Make It Happen, 5th ed. (South-Western, a Division of Thomson Learning, 2003), 2–4.
5. Levitt, Your Career, 36.
6. "Get Your Career in Site," Fast Company, March 2000, 218–230.
7. Barbara Ling, http://www.riseway.com
8. CBS, "Web Largely Untapped by Job Seekers," http://MarketWatch.com (accessed January 24, 2003).
9. Levitt, Your Career, 100.
10. Levitt, Your Career, 189–205.
11. Levitt, Your Career, 205.

Chapter 1

1. Lester Thurow, "Changing the Nature of Capitalism," in *Rethinking the Future*, ed. Rowan Gibson (London: Nicholas Brealey, 1997), 228.
2. Olga Chudakova, "Executive Commentary," *Academy of Management Executive* (November 2001).
3. Don Clark, "In Setting Up Its New Plants, Chip Maker Clones Older Ones Down to the Paint on the Wall," *Wall Street Journal*, October 28, 2002. © 2002 by Dow Jones & Co. Inc. Reproduced with permission of Dow Jones & Co. Inc., in the format Textbook via Copyright Clearance Center.

Chapter 2

1. Steven Erlanger, "Ach! The Viennese Lap Up Starbucks," *International Herald Tribune*, June 3, 2002.
2. Statistics Canada, "Imports, Exports and Trade Balance of Goods on a Balance-of-Payments Basis, by Country or Country Grouping," http://www40.statcan.ca/l01/cst01/gblec02a.htm (accessed April 5, 2006).
3. "Armchairs, TVs and Expresso—Is It McDonald's?" *Wall Street Journal*, August 30, 2002. © 2002 by Dow Jones & Co. Inc. Reproduced with permission of Dow Jones & Co. Inc., in the format Textbook via Copyright Clearance Center.
4. Government of Canada, Department of Foreign Affairs and International Trade, "Trade Negotiations and Agreements—Why Trade Matters," http://www.dfait.maeci.gc.ca/tna-nac/text-e.asp (accessed June 4, 2002).
5. "Trade Negotiations and Agreements—Why Trade Matters."
6. Government of Canada, "Team Canada—What Is Team Canada," http://www.tcm-mec.gc.ca/what-e.asp (accessed June 4, 2002).
7. "Team Canada—What Is Team Canada."
8. "Trade Negotiations and Agreements—Why Trade Matters."
9. What's at Stake," *Business Week*, October 22, 2001, 34–37.
10. Statistics Canada, "Study: Canada's Place in World Trade", http://www.statcan.ca/Daily/English/060316/d060316b.htm (accessed April 20, 2006).
11. "The Americas: Another country; Argentina," *The Economist* (London) 376, no. 8436 (2005): 50.
12. "Anti-Trade/Pro-Poverty," Fortune, January 10, 2000, 40.
13. "Anti-Trade/Pro-Poverty," 40
14. "The Pros and Cons of Globalization," Business Week, April 24, 2000, 41.
15. "Globalization: What Americans Are Worried About," *Business Week*, April 24, 2000, 44.
16. Government of Canada, Department of Foreign Affairs and International Trade, "About EPD, Export and Import Controls Bureau," http://www.dfait-maeci.gc.ca/~eicb/eicbintro-e.htm (accessed June 4, 2002).
17. Association of Southeast Asian Nations, "Overview," http://www.aseansec.org/64.htm (accessed April 19, 2006).
18. "How the Chevy Name Landed on an SUV Using Russian Technology," *Wall Street Journal*, February 20, 2001, A1, A8.
19. "How Well Does Wal-Mart Travel?" *Business Week*, September 3, 2001, 82–84.
20. "War of the Superstores," *Business Week*, September 23, 2002, 60.
21. "Wal-Mart's European Beachhead," *International Herald Tribune* March 13, 2001.
22. BBC News, "China Emerges as Global Consumer," http://news.bbc.co.uk/2/hi/asia-pacific/4272577.stm (accessed April 8, 2006).
23. "Survey: Coming Out," *The Economist* (London), 378, no. 8470 (2005): 4.
24. "India's Coming Eclipse of China," Far *Eastern Economic Review*, 169, no. 2 (2006): 12-18.
25. "Payment System Lets Customers Choose Currency," *Information Week*, April 2, 2001, 33.
26. Hal Lancaster, "Global Managers Need Boundless Sensitivity, Rugged Constitutions," *Wall Street Journal*, October 13, 1998.

Chapter 3

1. Canadian Business for Social Responsibility, "CBSR—What Is CSR," http://www.cbsr.bc.ca/what_is_csr/index.cfm (accessed May 23, 2002).
2. Interview with Randy Gossen, May 17, 2006.
3. Statistics Canada, "Canadian Statistics—Employment by Age, Sex, Type of Work, Class of Worker and Province (Monthly)," http://www40.statcan.ca/l01/cst01/labr66a.htm (accessed March 21, 2006).
4. Research Briefs," http://www.mediapost.com," (accessed July 16, 2002).
5. "The Roxy Echo–It's a Girl Thing," *The Star Ledger* (Newark, NJ), September 9, 2001.
6. Christy Harvey, "A Guide to Who Holds the Purse Strings," *Wall Street Journal*, June 22, 2000.
7. Statistics Canada, "Average Total Income by Economic Family Type," http://www40.statcan.ca/l01/sct01/famil05a.htm (accessed March 21, 2006).
8. Linda Morton, "Targeting Generation Y," *Public Relations Quarterly*,-2002), 46–49.

9. "The Gen-X Budget," *American Demographics*, 24 no. 7 (2002), S5.
10. Canadian Policy Research Network, "Population Projections for 2017," http://www.cprn.com/en/ diversity-2017.cfm (accessed April 10, 2006).
11. Canadian Heritage, Government of Canada, "What is Multiculturalism," http://www.pch.gc.ca/progs/multi/ what_e.cfm (accessed July 11, 2006).
12. Alain Belanger and Eric Caron Malenfant, "Ethnocultural Diversity in Canada: Prospects for 2017," *Canadian Social Trends*, 79 (2005), http://www.statcan.ca/english/freepub/ 11-008-XIE/0030511-008-XIE.pdf (accessed October 9, 2006).
13. Statistics Canada, "Births and Birth Rate, by Province and Territory," http://www40.statcan.ca/101/cst01/ demo04a.htm (accessed March 21, 2006).
14. "Births and Birth Rate."
15. Marianne Moody Jennings, *Case Studies in Business Ethics*, 2nd ed. (St. Paul, MN: West Publishing Company, 1996 pp xx-xxiii)
16. Milton Borden, "The Three R's of Ethics," *Management Review*, (1998), 59–61.
17. Canadian Tire Corporation, "Canadian Tire & The Community," http://www2.canadiantire.ca/ CTenglish/enreop_wrd.html (accessed May 23, 2002).
18. Manulife Financial, "Corporate Giving," http://www.manulife.com/corporate/ Corporate2.nsf/Public/corporategiving .html (accessed April 11, 2006).
19. *Business Ethics Online*, http://www.business-ethics.com.

Chapter 4

1. Drew Robb, "Case Study: Care Group Health System," *Computerworld*, December 16, 2002, http://www .computerworld.com .
2. "Executive Guides: Intranet/Extranet," *Darwin Executive Guides*, http://guide.darwinmag.com/ technology/web/intranet/index.html (accessed January 30, 2003).
3. "Executive Guides: Wireless," *Darwin Executive Guides* http://guide.darwinmag .com/technology/communications/ wireless/index.html (accessed January 31, 2003); and "Wi-Fi," Webopedia, http://www.webopedia.com
4. Find VPN.com, "(VPN) Virtual Private Network FAQs," http://findvpn.com/ articles/faq.php (accessed January 31, 2003); and About.com: Computer Networking, "VPN Tutorial,"

http://compnetworking.about.com/ library/weekly/aa010701a.htm (accessed January 24, 2003).
5. "Executive Guides: Data Warehouse," *Darwin Executive Guides*, http://guide.darwinmag.com/ technology/enterprise/data/index.html (accessed February 3, 2003).
6. Kathleen Melymuka, "Far from the Mother Ship," *Computerworld*, December 9, 2002, http://www .computerworld.com
7. "Executive Guides: Knowledge Management," *Darwin Executive Guides*, http://guide.darwinmag.com/ technology/enterprise/knowledge/ index.html (accessed January 31, 2003).
8. Tom Standage, "When the Door Is Always Open" (Survey of Digital Security, Special Section), *Economist*, October 26, 2002, 16–17.
9. Office of the Privacy Commissioner of Canada, Federal Government of Canada, "Personal Information Protection and Electronic Documents Act," http://www.privcom.gc.ca/. (accessed May 31, 2006).
10. "Egghead Files for Chapter 11," *New York Times*, August 6, 2001; and Daniel F. Lohmeyer and Jim McCrory, "Managing Information Security," Inc., July 1, 2002, http://www.inc.com
11. Donna Howell, "New Tactics Could Stave off Digital Pirates," *Investor's Business Daily*, December 16, 2002, http://www.investors.com
12. Michael Liedtke, "Critics See TurboTax's Anti-Piracy Activation Code as Anti-Consumer," *San Diego Union-Tribune*, January 13, 2003.
13. Jon Surmacz, "Ante Virus," Darwin, January 29, 2003, http://www.darwin.com
14. Alex Salkever, "The Big Lessons of a Little Worm," *Business Week Online*, January 31, 2003, http://www .businessweek.com
15. "Security Policies 101," *Intranet Journal*, January 6, 2003, http://www.intranetjournal.com
16. Tom Standage, "The Weakest Link" (Survey of Digital Security, Special Section), *Economist*, October 26, 2002, 11–16.
17. Tech Trends 2002, Volume 2 (City: Deloitte & Touche LLP, Technology, Media and Telecommunications Group, http://www.deloitte.com
18. We're missing an end note, which might be 17 or 18, as the note above doesn't indicate the content. End note 17 should relate to privacy legislation in Canada. Note 18 should relate to HP and / or use of web portals. See also Note 9, which might

fit in here, in which case a new note would be needed for 9, also related to privacy.
19. Spencer E. Ante, "The New Blue," *Business Week*, March 17, 2003; Bruce V. Bigelow, "Gateway Launches On-Demand Computing," *The San Diego Union-Tribune*, December 11, 2002; Sami Lais, "Grid Computing," *Computerworld*, December 23, 2002, http://www.computerworld.com; Darnell Little and Ira Sager, "Who Needs Supercomputers?" B*usiness Week Online*, June 3, 2002; and Irving Wladawsky-Berger and Ira Sager, "Info Tech's 'Post-Technology Phase,'" *Business Week Online*, December 31, 2002, http://www.businessweek.com
20. Office of the Privacy Commissioner of Canada, "Identity Theft: What It Is and What You Can Do about It," http://www.privcom.gc.ca/fs-fi/ 02_05_d_10_e.asp (accessed October 13, 2005).

Chapter 5

1. Christopher Halpin, personal communication, April 10, 2005.
2. Anne Stuart, "Where Do Great Ideas Come From?" *Inc.*, October 2002, 43, 45.
3. Clodhoppers, "*About Us*", http://www .clodhopppers.tv/about.html (accessed July 26, 2006).
4. Mike Hofman, "The Bad Boy," *Inc.*, September 2002, 78–80.
5. Canadian Co-Operative Association. "About Co-operatives," http://www .coopscanada.coop/aboutcoop/ (accessed November 1, 2005).
6. "About Co-operatives."
7. Hydrocarbons Technology, "Syncrude 21 Expansion Project, Alberta, Canada," http://www.hydrocarbons-technology. com/projects/syncrude/ (accessed November 1, 2005).
8. "Worldwide Refinishing Announces Expansion into Korea," *Franchise Handbook Online NewsBytes*, http:// www.franchise1.com/articles/newsbyte .html (accessed January 7, 1999).
9. Cynthia E. Griffin, "Ladies in Waiting," *Entrepreneur Magazine*, November 2002, http://www.entrepreneur.com.
10. Devlin Smith, "One Big Happy Family," January 2003, http://www.entrepreneur.com.
11. Kenneth Klee, "Mergers and Accusations," *Inc.*, October 2002, 48–49.
12. Caliber Collision Centers Web site, http://www.calibercollision.com; and Justin Martin, David Birch, "Slump? What Slump?" *Fortune Small Business*, December 2002/January 2003, http://www.ask.elibrary.com; Robert

McGarvey, "When It Comes to Customer Service Actions Speak Louder than Words," *Entrepreneur Magazine*, January 1997, http://www.entrepreneur.com.

13. Jane Applegate, "Novelty Pillow Catches Manufacturer's Eye," February 2002, http://www.entrepreneur.com ; Carolyn Morton, e-mail correspondence, January 17 and 24, 2003; and Peeramid Web site, http://www.peeramid.com.

Chapter 6

1. Personal interview with Gino Panucci, November 2005.
2. Andreea Dulipovici, "Small Business—Big Picture", Canadian Federation of Independent Business, http://www.cfib.ca (accessed February 9, 2006).
3. "The 411 on OGIO," OGIO International Web site, http://www.ogio.com; and Anne Stuart, "Where Do Great Ideas Come From?" *Inc. 500*, October 15, 2002, 40, 42–43.
4. April Y. Pennington, "Entrepreneurial Snapshot: Katrina Markoff," *Entrepreneur*, November 2002, http://www.entrepreneur.com
5. David Shook, "Jeff Bezos: Finally Relaxing?" *Business Week Online*, October 1, 2002, http://www.businessweek.com.
6. SMEI Academy of Achievement, "Jim Pattison," http://www.academyofachievement.org/honorees/jim_pattison.htm (accessed July 26, 2006).
7. Dean Takahashi, "Reinventing the Intrapreneur," *Red Herring*, September 2000, http://www.red_herring.com.
8. Michael Arndt, "Whirlpool Taps Its Inner Entrepreneur," *Business Week Online*, February 7, 2002, http://www.businessweek.com.
9. "Got ID?" *Entrepreneur*, November 2002, http://www.entrepreneur.com (accessed DATE).
10. "Are You Building an Inc. 500 Company?" *Inc. 500*, October 15, 2002, http://www.inc.com/inc500.
11. "Are You Building an Inc. 500 Company?"
12. Strategis, Industry Canada, http://strategis.ic.gc.ca.
13. Industry Canada, "*Small Business Research and Policy—II. The Importance of Small Business in Canada*, http://strategis.ic.gc.ca/epic/internet/insbrp-rppe.nsf/en/rd00022e.html (accessed June 7, 2006).

14. Justin Martin and David Birch, "Slump? What Slump?" *Fortune Small Business*, December 2002/January 2003, http://ask.elibrary.com.
15. "*Small Business—Big Picture*."
16. Dun & Bradstreet, "D&B 21st Annual Small Business Survey Summary Report," http://www.dnb.com.
17. Ellen Roseman, "The Vision Thing Helps When Starting a Business," *Toronto Star*, May 5, 2002, http://ask.elibrary.com.
18. "Are You Building an *Inc.* 500 Company?" *Inc.* 500.
19. David Noonan, "Be Your Own Master," *Newsweek*, September 23, 2002, 61.
20. Kimberly McCall, "Then There Were Two: Should You Hire a Staff?" Startup *Journal.com*, November 4, 2002, http://www.inc.com.
21. Cara Cannella, "Keeping It Flexible," *Inc.* 500, October 15, 2002, 76.
22. Jeff Bailey, "Growing Up," *Wall Street Journal*, March 27, 2002, R6; Case, "Trading Places," 74–82; Brenda L. Moore, "Changing Classes," *Wall Street Journal*, March 27, 2002, R8; and "Be Your Own Master."
23. Paul D. Reynolds, Nancy M. Carter, William B. Gartner, Patricia G. Greene, and Larry W. Cox. *The Entrepreneur Next Door: Characteristics of Individuals Starting Companies in America.* (Kansas City, MO: E. M. Kauffman Foundation, 2002).
24. Gisela M. Pedroza, "Survival of the Fittest," *HomeOffice*, November 2002, http://www.entrepreneur.com.
25. "Be Your Own Master."
26. Geoff Williams, "Looks like Rain," *Entrepreneur*, September 2002, http://www.entrepreneur.com.
27. "Got ID?"
28. Kate O'Sullivan, "Six Ways to Outrun the Competition," *Inc.* 500, October 15, 2002, 56–58.

Chapter 7

1. "Now for the Hard Part," *Fortune*, November 18, 2002, 95–106.
2. Katrina Brooker and Julie Schlosser, "The un-CEO," *Fortune* (September 16, 2002), 88–94.
3. "Jim Kilts Is Old-School Curmudgeon," Fortune, December 30, 2002, 95–102.
4. Jeffrey Garten, "Jack Welch: A Role Model for Today's CEO," *Business Week*, September 10, 2001, 32.
5. "Jim Kilts Is....," *Fortune*.
6. Max Messmer, "Surviving and Thriving as a New Manager," *National Public Accountant*, June 2000, 22–24.

7. WestJet Airlines Press Release, "WestJet's Corporate Culture Most Admired in Canada Independent Study Reveals," October 20, 2005, http://www2.ccnmatthews.com (accessed July 5, 2006).
8. Orit Gadiesh, "Transforming Corner-Office Strategy into Frontline Action," *Harvard Business Review*, May 2001, 72–90.
9. Tom McDonald, "A World of Challenges," *Successful Meetings*, July 2002, 25.
10. Robert Ramsey, "What Will You Do if the Worst Case Scenario Really Happens?" *Supervision*, June, 2002, 6–7.
11. "The Shiniest Reputations in Tarnished Times," *Fortune*, March 4, 2002, 70–72.
12. Cora Daniels, "The Last Taboo: It's Not Sex. It's Not Drinking. It's Stress—And It's Soaring," *Fortune*, October 28, 2002, 136–140 and David Noonan, Jill Sieder, and Kevin Peraino, "Stop Stressing Me," *Newsweek*, January 29, 2001, 54–56.
13. Betsy Morris, "Can Ford Save Ford?" *Fortune*, November 18, 2002, 52–60.

Chapter 8

1. Brian Garrity and Carolyn Horwitz, "BMG Realigns Management Units," *Billboard*, October 2001, 5; and Wolfgang Spahr, "BMG Is Fit and Ready for Expansion," *Billboard*, April 2002, 49.
2. Timothy Aeppel, "On Factory Floors, Top Workers Hide Secrets to Success," *The Wall Street Journal*, July 1, 2002, A1, A10.
3. "Building the Right Team," *Maclean's*, October 28, 2002, 31.
4. Paul Sweeney, "Ford's Better Idea: A Centralized Treasury," *Treasury & Risk Management*, March 2000, 12.
5. Stephane Fitch, "Reengineering 101: Phil Condit Sees Salvation in Services," *Forbes*, May 13, 2002, 82–84.
6. Bradley L. Kirkman, Benson Rosen, Cristina B. Gibson, Paul E. Tesluk and Simon O. McPherson, "Five Challenges to Virtual Team Success: Lessons from Sabre, Inc.," *Academy of Management Executive*. 16 no. 3.
7. "Managing Virtual Teams," *Workforce*, June 2001, 60-65.
8. Frederick Reichhold, "Putting Customers First Is Rewarded," *Wall Street Journal*, September 10, 2002, A1.
9. Kelly Barron, "Stormy Weather," *Forbes*, February 19, 2001, 66.

Chapter 9

1. Michelle Neely Martinez, "Get Job Seekers to Come to You," *HR Magazine*, 45 (August 2000), 44–52.
2. "Gore-Text," *Fast Company*, January 1999, 160.
3. Melanie Peacock, personal interview, conducted March 31, 2006.
4. Betty Sosnin, "Is a Video in Your Vision?" *HR Magazine*, 46 (February 2001), 100–106.
5. Statistics Canada, "Average Hourly Wages of Employees by Selected Characteristics and Profession, Unadjusted Data, by Province (Monthly)," http://www40.statcan.ca/101/cst01/labr69a.htm (July 27, 2006).
6. Janice Revall, "Mo' Money, Fewer Problems," *Fortune*, March 31, 2003, 34.
7. "The GM Layoffs and the Logic of Neoliberalism (Sam Gindin)," *Canadian Dimension*, http://canadiandimension.com/articles/2005/11/29/221/ (accessed July 27, 2006).
8. Mark Heinzl and Norihiko Shironzu, "Canadian Union Reaches Accord with Ford Motors," *Wall Street Journal*, October 1, 2002, A2, A14.
9. Diane Cadrain, "An Acute Condition: Too Few Nurses," *HR Magazine*, 47 (December 2002), 69–71.

Chapter 10

1. UPS Web site, http://www.ups.com; Keith Hammonds, "Handle with Care," *Fast Company*, August, 2002, 102–107.
2. Kim Clark, "No Pink Slips at the Plant," *U.S. News & World Report*, February 2002, 40.
3. Clint Willis, "The 100 Highest Rollers," Forbes, April 2, 2001, 78.
4. Kayte Vanscoy, "The Hiring Crisis," *Smart Business for the New Economy*, July 2000, 84–94.
5. The section on "Motivation Is Culture Bound" is from Nancy J. Alder, *International Dimensions of Organizational Behaviour*, 4th ed. (City: South-Western, a division of Thomson Learning, 2002), 174–181.
6. From Alder, *International Dimensions*, 174–181.
7. "Preventive Medicine," *Ward's Auto World*, June 1, 2002.
8. Martin Rosenthal, "High-Performance Teams," *Executive Excellence*, October 2001, 6.
9. Julie Filatoff and Thomas Zamiara, "Secrets of Teambuilding Gurus," *On Wall Street*, October 2000, 10–16.

10. Robert Levering and Milton Moskowitz, "The 100 Best Companies to Work for in America," *Fortune* (January 20, 2003), pp. 127–144.
11. Laird Harrison, "We're All the Boss," *Time* (April 8, 2002), 10–11.
12. "ESOP Companies Outperform Stock Market," *PR Newswire*, August 19, 2002.
13. "Knowledge Work," *Executive Excellence*, October 1, 2002, 12.
14. "Strategies for Developing an Effective Employee Absenteeism Policy," *HR Focus*, September 11, 2001, 5.
15. Jeffrey Marshall, "Employee Retention Linked to Better Customer Service," Financial Executive, March/April 2001, 11–12; and Gary Wallace, "Satisfied Employees Help Attract and Retain Members," *Credit Union Magazine*, September 2002, 32.

Chapter 11

1. Mark Haines and David Farber, "Harley-Davidson—CEO Interview," *CNBC/Dow Jones Business*, Video, October 11, 2002; Tim Stevens, "Technologies of the Year—DFM Concurrent Costing Version 2.0," *Industry Week*, December 12, 2002, http://www.industryweek.com; John Teresko, "Technology Leader of the Year—Fueled by Innovation," *Industry Week*, December 1, 2002, http://www.industryweek.com; and John Teresko, "Driven by Cost," *Industry Week*, September 1, 2002, http://www.industryweek.com.
2. Jill Jusko, "Locations—Globe Motors Turns to Portugal," *Industry Week*, November 1, 2002, http://www.industryweek.com.
3. Jill Jusko, "Locations."
4. John S. McClenahen, "The World's Best," *Industry Week*, April 16, 2001, http://www.industryweek.com.
5. John S. McClenahen, "The World's Best."
6. Michael A. Verespej, "E-Procurement Explosion," *Industry Week*, March 1, 2002, http://www.industryweek.com.
7. John S. McClenahen, "Best Plants 2002," *Industry Week*, n.d., http://www.industryweek.com.
8. John S. McClenahen, "Best Plant Winners 2002," *Industry Week*, n.d., http://www.industryweek.com.
9. Doug Bartholomew, "Faster CAD Design Called a Lifesaver," *Industry Week*, June 4, 2001, http://www.industryweek.com.

10. John Teresko, "Robots Evolution," *Industry Week*, April 1, 2002, http://www.industryweek.com.
11. Gene Bylinsky, "Elite Factories: They're Setting Lofty Standards in Quality Control, Preventive Maintenance, and Automation," *Fortune*, September 2, 2002, 172B.
12. Gene Bylinsky, "Elite Factories."
13. Tim Stevens, "Factories of the Future—Integrated Product Development," *Industry Week*, June 1, 2002, http://www.industryweek.com.
14. Tim Stevens, "Factories of the Future."

Chapter 12

1. Statistics Canada, "Population Characteristics," http://www.statcan.ca (accessed March 21, 2006).
2. Sally Beatty, "Avon Is Set to Call on Teens," *Wall Street Journal*, October 17. © 2002 by Dow Jones & Co. Inc. Reproduced with permission of Dow Jones & Co. Inc., in the format Textbook via Copyright Clearance Center.
3. "Caring for the Customer Pays Off for Lexus Again," *Essex Chronicle Series*, May 10, 2002.
4. American Marketing Association Web site, http://www.marketingpower.com (accessed August 28, 2003).
5. Ann D'Innocenzio, "Stores Putting Data from Loyalty Cards to Work," *Fort Worth Star Telegram*, March 25, 2003.
6. "GM's Winning Vision: Staff First, Profit Follows," *Hotels*, March 2003, 14.
7. "The Persuaders—Cold Is Hot," *Business 2.0*, November 2002, 115. © 2002-Time Inc. All rights reserved.
i http://www.marketingpower.com (August 28, 2003).

Chapter 13

1. "Less Power to You," *Newsweek*, January 27, 2003, 72; "Kids Need to Brush up on Oral Care Habits, Crest SpinBrush Survey Finds," *PR Newswire*, January 16, 2003; "Why P&G's Smile Is So Bright," *Business Week*, August 12, 2002, 58; and Daniel Eisenberg, "A Healthy Gamble; How Did A. G. Lafley Turn Procter & Gamble's Old Brands into Hot Items?" *Time*, September 16, 2002.
2. "Brand Loyalty Loses to Price, Quality and Promotions in All Categories but Pet Food," *Research Alert*, October 18, 2002.

3. Carl Franklin, "The Last 30 Years Have Seen Great Advances in Marketing Techniques," *The Business,* April 7, 2002.
4. Yumiko Ono, "Overcoming the Stigma of Dishwashers in Japan," *Wall Street Journal,* May 19, 2000.© 2000 by Dow Jones & Co. Inc. Reproduced with permission of Dow Jones & Co. Inc., in the format Textbook via Copyright Clearance Center.
5. Conversation with Jerry Thomas, CEO of Decision Analyst, April 14, 2003.
6. Michael Mendano, "Priced to Perfection," *Business2.com,* March 6, 2001, 40–41.
7. "Colour by Numbers," *American Demographics,* February 2002, 31–35.
8. "Making the Most of eBay," *Business 2.0* (June 2002), 129–130. © 2002-Time Inc. All rights reserved.
9. Cris Prystay and Meeyoung Song, "Fragrant Fabrics: Peppermint 3-Piece Is Hot in Hong Kong," *Wall Street Journal,* October 21, 2002. © 2002 by Dow Jones & Co. Inc. Reproduced with permission of Dow Jones & Co. Inc., in the format Textbook via Copyright Clearance Center.

Chapter 14

1. Human Resources Development Canada, Retail Salespersons and Sales Clerks—Ontario Job Futures, www1.on.hrdc-drhc.gc.ca (accessed March 29, 2006).
2. Part of the section on supply chain management is adapted from Charles Lamb, Joe Hair, and Carl McDaniel, Marketing, 7th ed. (South-Western, a division of Thomson Learning, 2002), 392–394.
3. David Maloney, "Rite Place, Rite Time, Rite Aid," *Modern Materials Handling,* May 2002, 6–9.
4. Andrew Raskin, "Who's Minding the Store," *Business 2.0,* February 2003, 70–74.
5. Adapted from Kim Cross, "Fill It to the Brim," *Business 2.0* (March 6, 2001), pp. 36–41.
6. "Oracle Puts Priority on Customer Service, *Wall Street Journal,* January 21, 2003.

Chapter 15

1. Suzanne Vranica, "New Beetle Takes on a Bug Problem," *Wall Street Journal,* October 31, 2002. © 2002 by Dow Jones & Co. Inc. Reproduced with permission of Dow Jones & Co. Inc., in the format Textbook via Copyright Clearance Center.

2. Strategis, *The Consumer Trends Report—Industry Canada Research Paper,* http://www.strategis.gc.ca (accessed March 30, 2006).
3. "World Ad Outlays Seen Rising 2.9% During Next Year," *Wall Street Journal,* December 9, 2002.
4. Leading National Advertiser's database, http://www.advertisingage.com.
5. Jung Jeon and Sharon Beatty, "Comparative Advertising Effectiveness in Different National Cultures," *Journal of Business Research,* November 2002, 908–913.
6. Charles Lamb, Joe Hair, and Carl McDaniel, *Marketing,* 7th ed. (City: South-Western, a division of Thomson Learning, 2002), 537.
7. Bob Oros, "Remove the Roadblock to a Successful Sale," ID: *The Information Source,* March 2002.
8. "Promotion Trends 2002: A Glass Half Full," *Promo Magazine,* March 14, 2002.
9. "General Motors and Genmar Holdings to Develop Co-Marketing Programs," *PR Newswire,* January 21, 2003.
10. "Online Ads Proven to Boost Brand Awareness and Sales," *New Media Age,* April 18, 2002, 18.
11. "Click and Clip," *Wall Street Journal,* October 21, 2002.
12. "Advertisers Hope Fragrant Posters Are Nothing to Sniff At," *Wall Street Journal,* October 10, 2002.
13. "High Tech Billboards Tune in to Driver's Taste," *San Francisco Chronicle,* December 22, 2002.
14. "That Guy Showing Off His New Phone May Be a Shill," *Wall Street Journal,* July 31, 2002.

Chapter 16

1. Peter Behr and April Witt, "Visionary's Dream Led to Risky Business," *Washington Post,* July 28, 2002; "Dream Job Turns into a Nightmare," *Washington Post,* July 29, 2002; and "Concerns Grow Amid Conflicts," *Washington Post,* July 30, 2002; all from http://www.washingtonpost.com; John R. Emshwiller, "Enron Improperly Transferred up to $5 Billion, a Report Finds," *Wall Street Journal,* March 6, 2003, http://www.wsj.com; "Enron's Accounting," *HoustonChronicle.com,* February 25, 2003, http://www.chron.com/content/news/photos/02/03/18/enron/popup2/htm; Tom Fowler, "The Pride and the Fall of Enron," *Houston Chronicle,* October 20, 2002, http://www.houstonchronicle.com; and "Understanding Enron's Partnerships,"

HoustonChronicle.com, February 25, 2003, http://www.chron.com/content/news/photos/02/01/25/partnership/popup2/htm.
2. CMA Canada, "What Is a CMA" and "About CMA," http://www.cma-canada.org (accessed July 8, 2003).
3. CGA Canada, "Become a CGA," http://www.cga-canada.org (accessed July 8, 2003).
4. Anne Papmehl, "Accounting for Knowledge: Measuring Our Intellectual Assets Helps Us Manage Them Effectively," *CMA Management,* March 2004, http://www.allbusiness.com (accessed April 1, 2006).
5. Fay Hansen, "Outlook 2003: More Changes, Greater Challenges," *Business Finance,* December 2002, http://www.businessfinancemag.com.

Chapter 17

1. Personal interview with Carl Cheverie, August 2, 2006.
2. David Deeds, "Extra! Extra!" *Inc.,* September 2002, 110–112.
3. Kris Frieswick, "The Five-Year Itch," *CFO,* February 1, 2003, http://www.cfo.com.
4. Jay Sherman and Susan Kelly, "Uphill Racer—The 2002 Alexander Hamilton Award Winners," *Treasury & Risk Management,* October 2002, http://www.treasuryandrisk.com.
5. "Profile: AOL Time Warner," *Yahoo! Finance,* biz.yahoo.com/p/a/aol.html (accessed March 26, 2003); and Doug Tsuruoka, "AOL's Real Bogeyman Is Debt, Not Its Ailing Internet Service." *Investor's Business Daily,* February 25, 2003, http://www.investors.com.
6. Steve Lohr, "Microsoft Says It Will Start Paying Dividend," *San Diego Union-Tribune,* January 17, 2003; and Amey Stone, "Microsoft's Lonely Dividend Bandwagon," *Business Week Online,* January 28, 2003, http://www.businessweek.com.
7. Jennifer Davies, "Qualcomm to Reward Shareholders with Dividend," *San Diego Union-Tribune,* February 12, 2003.
8. Section based on Deloitte Consulting, "Deloitte Consulting/BusinessWeek Survey Finds Ambiguity in Who Leads Charge in Response to New Disclosure Rules," March 7, 2003, http://www.dc.com; Jeremy Kahn, "The Chief Freaked-Out Officer," *Fortune,* December 3, 2002, http://www.fortune.com; and Joseph Weber, "CFOs on the Hot Seat," *Business Week,* March 17, 2003, 67–70.

9. "A Long-Range Radar for Risk," in Jay Sherman and Susan Kelly, "Uphill Racer—The 2002 Alexander Hamilton Award Winners," *Treasury & Risk Management*, October 2002, http://www.treasuryandrisk.com.
10. Jerry Miccolis, "ERM Lessons across Industries," *IRMI.com*, March 2003, http://www.irmi.com.

Chapter 18

1. Personal interview with Ron Munaweera, June 8, 2006.
2. http://www.bankofcanada.ca/en/central .htm (accessed February 2, 2005).
3. http://www.bankofcanada.ca/en/ glossary/ glosstragrate.htm (accessed March 8, 2005).
4. Statistics Canada, "Chartered Banks," http://142.206.72.67/03/03e/03e_001a _e.htm (accessed March 8, 2005).
5. Statistics Canada, "Trust Companies," http://142.206.72.67/03/03e/03e_001b _e.htm (accessed March 8, 2005).
6. Statistics Canada, "Credit Unions," http://142.206.72.67/03/03e/03e_001c _e.htm (accessed March 8, 2005).
7. Canada Deposit Insurance Corporation, "About Us," http://www.cdic.ca/?id=4 (accessed March 8, 2005).

8. Canada Deposit Insurance Corporation, "Home," http://www.cdic.ca/?id=100 (accessed March 8, 2005).
9. "Singapore's Little Bang," *The Economist*, May 22, 1999, 86.
10. Jim Rohwer, "Asia's Meldown: The Risks Are Rising," *Fortune*, February 16, 1998, 84–90; Brian Bremmer, Pete Engardio, Dean Foust, Kerry Capell, and Bruce Einhorn, "What to Do about Asia," *Business Week*, January 26, 1998, 26–30; and "Reality Hits Japan," *The Economist*, November 29, 1997, 15–16.
11. Nicholas Stein, "America's Most Admired Companies," *Fortune*, March 3, 2002, 81.
12. Adam Lashinsky, "Game Over?," *Fortune*, March 3, 2003, 156.
13. "Online Banking Booming, Says IDC," http://www.electronicbanker.com (accessed June 2, 1999).
14. Reuters, "Top Banks Plan Online Billing Network," *The Sheboy-gan Press*, June 24, 1999, C5.

Appendix

1. Personal interview with Sandra Malach, April 13, 2003.
2. Mohammed B Hemraj, "Preventing Corporate Failure: The Cadbury Committee's Governance Report," *Journal of Financial Crime*, October 2002.

3. Colin P. MacDonald, "Where Were the Directors?" *Business Credit*, January 2003.
4. Adapted in part from Brian A. Schofield and Blair W. Feltmate, "Sustainable Development Investing," *Employee Benefits Journal*, March 2003.
5. Government of Canada, Canadian Public Accountability Board (CPAB), Office of the Superintendent of Financial Institutions Web site, http://www.osfi-bsif.gc.ca/eng/issues/ cpab_e.asp (accessed July 10, 2003).
6. Canada, Department of Justice, "Canada's Court System," http://www .canada.justice.gc.ca/en/dept/pub/trib/ page3.html.
7. Adapted from the notes of Robert Malach, LLB, LLM.

company index

subject index

C

CAD/CAM systems, 353
Cain, Jim, 245
caisses populaires, 574
Canada Business Corporations Act, 144
Canada Firearms Centre, 529
Canada Pension Plan (CPP), 551
Canada Trade Missions, 41
Canadian Auto Workers Union, 282
Canadian Bankers Association, 592
Canadian Business for Social Responsibility (CBSR), 71
Canadian Charter of Rights and Freedoms, 81
Canadian Code of Advertising Standards, 476
Canadian Franchise Association, 55
Canadian Human Rights Act, 278
Canadian Information Processing Society, 83
Canadian Institute of Chartered Accountants (CICA), 503–6, 520
Canadian Public Accountability Board (CPAB), 598
Canadian Union of Public Employees (CUPE), 282
capital, 6
    budgeting/budgets, 538, 540
    expenditures, 540
    investment, 18
    markets, 103
    partnerships and, 141
    sole proprietorships and, 139
capitalism, 7
capital products, 404–5
career planning, 290
cartels, 606
cash, 509–10
    budgets, 538
    flows, 515, 530–31, 535–36
    management, 539
    surplus, 539
cash-and-carry wholesalers, 448–49
category management, 457
cellular manufacturing, 344
cellular phones, 110, 117, 495–96
census, 131–32
centralization, 239–40
Certified General Accountants Association of Canada (CGA-Canada), 505–6
certified general accountants (CGAs), 506
certified management accountants (CMAs), 506
chain of command, 237
Chambers, Jeff, 306
Chambers, John, 231
chartered accountants (CAs), 506
chartered banks, 573
Chavez, Julz, 188
chequebook philanthropy, 92

Cheverie, Carl, 533
chief executive officers (CEOs), 276
chief financial officers (CFOs), 534, 554
chief information officers (CIOs), 107, 227–28
chief knowledge officers, 118
chief risk officers (CROs), 555
China
    auto manufacturing in, 68
    entrepreneurship in, 29
    international trade and, 61
    multinational social responsibilities and, 94
    trade with, 43
Chirac, Jacques, 8
Chudakova, Olga, 29
Ciandrini, Paul, 458
circular flow, economics as, 3, 10–11
civil code, 600
Clark, Ed, 297
closed shops, 282
Clyde, Rob, 120
code of ethics, 86–88
coercive power, 210
coffee, fair trade in, 99–100
cognitive dissonance, 391
Cohen, Ben, 85
coinsurance, 553
collaboration, 316
collateral, 543
collection policies, 539–40
collective bargaining, 281–82
colour, 423–26
co-marketing, 483
Combines Investigation Act, 599
command economy, 7–8, 9
commercial liability insurance, 552
commercial paper, 539, 542
commissions, sales, 274
commitment
    employee, 201, 258, 298–99
    in entrepreneurship, 174
committee buying, 480
committee structure, 243, 255
common law, 600
common shares, 545–46, 577–78
Companies Act, 144
comparative advertising, 474
compensation, 259
    employee, 273–76
    executive, 276–77
competition, 7
    in free markets, 24–25
Competition Act, 154, 476, 599, 606
Competition Bureau, 154, 476
competitive advantage, 279, 373, 470
competitive workplaces, 28
component lifestyles, 71, 74–75
component parts and materials, 405
compressed workweek, 313
computer-aided design (CAD), 353, 363

computer-aided manufacturing (CAM), 353
Computer Ethics Institute (CEI), 82
computer-integrated manufacturing (CIM), 354
computers
    literacy, 126–27
    networks, 108
    protection of, 119–23
    viruses, 121
conceptual skills, 219
Condit, Phil, 246
confiscation, 57
conglomerate mergers, 155
consensual leaders, 211
consultants, in small business management, 184–85
consultative leaders, 211
consumer durables, 403
consumer finance companies, 575
consumerism, 607
consumer non-durables, 403
consumer price index (CPI), 15
consumer products, 403–4
consumer protection, 607
contingency plans, 208
contingent workers, 264–65
continuous improvement, 351
continuous process, 338
contractionary policy, 17
contract manufacturing, 55
contracts, 602–4
contractual distribution systems, 445
controlling, 214–16
    production, 335
convenience products, 404
conventional ethics, 82
convertible bonds, 579
Conway, Craig, 130
Cooper, Cynthia, 288
cooperatives, 149–50, 449
copyrights, 510, 604
corporate bonds, 578–79
corporate campaigns, 287
corporate culture, 213
corporate distribution systems, 445
corporate governance, 594, 598
Corporate Knights, 71
corporate open houses, 267
corporate philanthropy, 91–92
corporate responsibility, 73
corporations, 143–49
    advantages vs. disadvantages, 146–47
    crown, 149
    finance, 575
    officers of, 145
    one-person, 148
    public vs. private, 143–44
    structure of, 145–46
cost competitive advantage, 373
cost of goods sold, 513

E

earnings per share (EPS), 518
e-business, 103, 105
e-commerce, 61–62, 227–28, 451
    and customization, 433–34, 463–64
economic communities, 51–53
economic environment, 2–3
    global, 37
    and global marketplace, 58–59
    political environment and, 36
economic growth, 12–13
economic responsibilities, 88–89
economics, 3, 10
    as circular flow, 3, 10–11
economic systems, 6–9
Edwards, Jeff, 355
efficient consumer response (ECR), 451
electronic billboards, 489
electronic bulletin boards, 117
electronic data interchange (EDI), 347, 451
Ellison, Larry, 257
El-Mansy, Youssef Aly, 33
e-mail, 62, 116, 490
embargoes, 49
Emery, Chris, 140
employee motivation, 298, 302. *See also*
  motivation
    and customer satisfaction, 322
    external environment and, 299
    operations management and, 331
    trends in, 319–21
employees
    absenteeism, 320–21
    commitment, 201, 231, 258,
      298–99, 498
    compensation, 259, 273–77
    contingent, 264–65
    of corporations, 147
    customer orientation of, 371
    education, 319
    empowerment of, 212, 220, 314
    group insurance for, 552
    orientation, 270–71
    ownership, 319
    recruitment of, 265–68
    responsibility to, 90
    retention of, 290
    selection of, 268–70
    of small businesses, 185, 191
    social contract with, 93
    sole proprietorships and, 139
    technology and, 102
    training and development of, 259,
      270–72, 319
    turnover of, 298
Employment Equity Act, 280, 599
employment insurance, 551
Employment Standards Acts, 606–7
empowerment, 212, 220, 314
encryption, 122

enterprise portals, 124
enterprise resource planning (ERP), 107–8,
    127, 130, 331, 346, 362
entrepreneurs, 6, 171
    classic, 171–72
    growth-oriented, 171–72
    opportunities for, 188–89
    personality of, 174, 198–99
    sales promotion and, 483
entrepreneurship, 7, 70, 170–73
    demographic changes and, 187
    PEST model, 166–67
    small business vs., 171
    success in, 173–75
    trends in, 187–90
environmental protection, 91, 599
environmental scanning, 372
e-procurement, 347
equilibrium, 21
equitability, 81
equity financing, 182, 543–44, 545–48,
    564–65
equity securities, 577–78
equity theory, 310
e-quotient, 268
ethics, 74
    accounting and, 527
    codes of, 86–88
    computers and, 82–83
    development of, 82
    global, 93–94
    individual, 80–85
    organizational, 85–88
    PEST model and, 70–71
    problem resolution in, 95–96
    and success, 70–71
    training programs, 85
    unethical activities, 83–85
euro, 53
European Community Bank, 53
European Union (EU), 52–53
event sponsorship, 485
exchange controls, 49
exchange rate, 45–46
exchanges, marketing, 368
excise taxes, 608
exclusive distribution, 446
executive compensation, 276–77
executive information systems (EISs), 116
executive search firms, 267
expansionary policy, 17
expectancy theory, 309–10
expense items, 404–5
expenses, 513
experiments, 387
expert power, 210
expert systems, 116
Export Development Canada (EDC), 185
exports, 41, 42–45, 54
    management companies (EMCs), 186
    trading companies, 186

express contracts, 602
express warranties, 410, 604
expropriation, 57
extensive decision-making, 382

F

factoring, 543
factors of production, 6–7
fairness, 81
fair trade, 99–100
families
    marketing and, 379
    two-income, 75–76
Fastow, Andy, 554
fax systems, 117
federal budget deficit, 18
feedback, 311
    control and, 215
    customer, 392
Feltmate, Blair W., 598
fidelity bonds, 553
Filo, David, 195, 256
financial accounting, 503
financial institutions, 572
    depository, 573–74
    non-depository, 574–75
financial intermediation, 572
financial management, 534–37
    accounting and, 535–36
    and stakeholders, 564
    trends in, 554–55
financial managers, 530, 534–37
financial performance
    organizational structures and, 230
    success and, 530, 564
financial planning, 536–38
financial reports, 502, 503–4
financial risk, 543
financial statements, 503–4, 515–19
financial system, Canadian, 571–75
financing, 536
    corporations and, 146–47
    debt vs. equity, 543–44, 564–65
    and external environment, 565
    long-term, 543–48
    short-term, 541–43
    of small business, 182
Fine, Deborah I., 367
Finnson, Larry, 140
Fiorina, Carly, 206
firewalls, 110, 122
fiscal policy, 17–18
fixed assets, 510
fixed-cost contribution, 419
fixed costs, 419
fixed-position layouts, 344
flexible manufacturing system (FMS), 353
flextime, 313

liability
>corporations and, 146
>insurance, 552
>partnerships and, 141
>sole proprietorships and, 139

licensing, 54–55
life insurance, 552
limited decision-making, 381
limited liability partnerships (LLPs), 141–42
limited partnerships, 140–42
limited-service merchant wholesalers, 448–49
line-and-staff organizations, 243–44
line extensions, 411
line organization, 242–43
line organizations, 242–43
line positions, 243–44
lines of credit, 541–42
liquidity, 509, 539, 543
>ratios, 517
local area networks (LANs), 108–10
local unions, 282
location, 339–42
>in retailing, 453
>of warehouses, 455–56
lockouts, 287
logistics, 454
London Stock Exchange, 583
long-term expenditures, 540–41
long-term financing, 543–48
long-term forecasts, 537
long-term liabilities, 512
losses
>corporations and, 147
>net, 513–15
>sole proprietorships and, 140
loss leaders, 421
Lowe, Graham, 297
loyalty
>in accounting, 527
>cards, 390
>programs, 371
>promotion and, 471
>sales promotion and, 483
lumber dispute, Canada-U.S., 67
Lundquist, Scott, 395
Lynas, Robin, 105

M

macroeconomics, 10
Maiffret, Marc, 143
make-or-buy decisions, 344
management, 204
>conflicts with labour, 286–87
>control in, 200
>crisis, 221
>in entrepreneurship, 174–75
>external environment and, 200

global, 63–64
IT and, 220–21
Japanese philosophy of, 307
multinational cultures and, 221
of partnerships, 141
PEST model and, 200–1
planning, 200–1, 205–8
pyramid, 237
role of, 204–5
of small businesses, 184–86
of sole proprietorships, 139
span of, 238–39
stress, 222–23
time, 222
management information systems (MIS), 107, 112–17
management support systems (MSSs), 113, 115
managerial accounting, 503
managerial hierarchy, 230–31, 237–38, 255
managers
>decision-making, 216, 218
>example-setting, 221
>involvement of, 221
>roles, 216, 217
>skills, 218–20
Manning, Jeff, 99
manufacturer brands, 408
manufacturers, 440
manufacturers' representatives/agents, 448–49
manufacturing environment, location and, 341
manufacturing resource planning II (MRPII), 331, 346
Marderosian, Karen, 469
marketable securities, 510, 539
market density, 384
market economies, 7–9, 19, 24–25
marketing, 368
>communications directors, 472–73
>concept, 368–71
>databases, 390
>demographic changes and, 79
>direct-response, 450–51
>external environment of, 364–65, 372
>families and, 379
>guerrilla, 489
>intermediaries, 440–42
>location and, 340
>mix, 375, 402, 453
>by not-for-profit organizations, 377
>operations management and, 436
>PEST model and, 364–65
>research for, 385–88, 392, 395–96
>research surveys on, 391
>social factors in, 379
>strategy, 372–75, 412, 415
>technology and, 103
>trends in, 388–91

market penetration, 475
market risk, 555
market segmentation, 365, 383–85
market sharing, 606
market structure, 24
Markfield, Roger, 237
Markoff, Katrina, 171
markup pricing, 418–19
Marshall, Sir Colin, 369
Martinez, Arthur, 279
Maslow, Abraham, 303
Maslow's hierarchy of needs, 304–6, 311
mass customization, 336–37
mass production, 336, 368, 453
master brands, 406
materials
>handling systems, 456
>requirement planning (MRP), 346
matrix structure, 244–45
Mayo, Elton, 303–4
McCullough, Stuart, 369
McGregor, Douglas, 306
mechanistic organizations, 241
mediation, 285, 601
mentoring, 271
merchant wholesalers, 448
Mercosur, 52
mergers, 154–55, 157, 159–60
>global, 250–51
Messmer, Max, 201, 212
Mexico
>NAFTA and, 51
>Wal-Mart in, 56
microeconomics, 10, 19–23
micromarketing, 390
micropreneurs, 171
middle management, 209
migration, 78
Millay, Roger, 522
mission/mission statement, 206
Mitnick, Kevin, 122
Mitterand, François, 8
mixed economies, 8–9
modular production, 355
monetary policy, 16–17, 570–71
money, 568–70
>supply, 17, 569–70
Moneypenny, Ed, 554
monopolies, 606
monopolistic competition, 24
Moore, Gordon, 33
Morgan, Kelly, 99
Morgan, Tim, 203
mortgage bonds, 579
mortgage loans, 545
Morton, Carolyn, 163
motivation. See also employee motivation
>behaviour reinforcement and, 312
>contemporary theories, 309–12
>cultural aspects, 311–12
>employee empowerment and, 314

Polonetsky, Jules, 497
portfolios, 580, 586–87
positive reinforcement, 312
postconventional ethics, 82
posters, street, 488–89
power, 210
Pratt, Dale, 249
Pratt, Mike, 170–71
preconventional ethics, 82
preferential tariffs, 51
preferred shares, 547, 578
premiums, insurance, 551, 574
press releases, 484
prestige pricing, 422
price(s)
    and consumer decision-making, 398
    demand and supply interaction and,
      21–23
    macroeconomics and, 14–16
    microeconomics and, 19
    and product life cycle, 415
    quality and, 398
    setting, 418–20, 453
    share, 577
    skimming, 420
    stability, 14–16
    tariffs and, 49
pricing
    breakeven analysis and, 419
    and external environment, 399
    leader, 421
    markup, 418–19
    odd-even, 421–22
    parallel, 606
    penetration, 420
    prestige, 422
    of products, 415–18
    for profit maximization, 416–17
    and revenues, 423
    strategies, 375, 420–22
    as target return on investment, 417
    of tickets, 432–33
    value, 418
primary data, 387
primary market, 582
principal, 578
principle of comparative advantage, 46–47
private accountants, 507
private corporations, 144
private enterprise system, 7
private law, 600
problem-solving teams, 316–17
process departmentalization, 236
process layouts, 342
process manufacturing, 338
procurement, 455
producer price index (PPI), 16
production, 7, 12–13, 334–35
    automation of, 112
    control, 335, 347–50

layout, 342–44
modular, 355
multinationals and, 60
and operations management, 335
orientation, 368–69
PEST model and, 398–99
planning, 335–36
process, 336
resource planning, 344–46
scheduling, 455
technology and, 353–54
timing, 338
product managers, 413–14
product(s), 402–3. *See also* new products
    advertising, 474
    as blend of goods and services, 403
    branding of, 406–9
    business, 404–5
    colours of, 423–26
    consumer, 403–4
    departmentalization, 236
    design, 356
    development, 411
    and external environment, 399
    layouts, 344
    liability, 552, 605
    life cycle, 399, 414–15
    new, 408, 410–14
    offering, 451
    packaging, 409–10
    presentation and demonstration of,
      481–82
    pricing of, 415–18
    promotional mix and, 486
    prototype development, 412
    returns policies, 459
    specialization, 606
    strategy, 375
    tangible vs. intangible attributes
      of, 402
professional liability insurance, 553
profit, 7
    cooperatives and, 150
    corporations and, 147
    maximization, 416–17
    net, 513–15
    partnerships and, 142
    sharing, 275, 315
    sole proprietorships and, 139
profitability ratios, 517–18
program evaluation and review technique
    (PERT), 349–50
programmed decisions, 216
programmed instruction, 272
project management approach, 244
promotional mix, 466, 471–73, 486–88
promotion(s), 259, 277, 466, 470. *See also*
    advertising
    customer satisfaction and, 490–91
    external environment and, 467

goals of, 470–71
informative, 470–71
quality and, 490–91
strategies, 376, 452, 466
technology in, 488–89
timing of, 472–73
property
    insurance, 552–53
    taxes, 608
prospecting, 480–81
protectionalism, 47
protective tariffs, 48
psychographic segmentation, 384–85
psychological pricing, 421–22
public accountants, 506
public corporations, 143–44, 545–46
publicity, 485–86
public law, 600
public relations, 471, 484–85, 486
public utilities, 25
pull strategies, 487–88
purchasing, 344
    agents, 480
    power, 14, 26
pure monopoly, 25
push strategies, 486–88

Q

qualifying questions, 481
quality, 351
    control, 331, 351
    customer satisfaction and, 428
    financial management and, 556
    in global marketplace, 63
    international standards, 352
    operations management and, 361–62
    price and, 398, 453
    promotion and, 490–91
    small business and, 192
    technology and, 102
Quebec Pension Plan (QPP), 551
quota setting, 606

R

rack jobbers, 449
ratio analysis, 515–17
raw materials, 405
reach, 475
recessions, 12
recruitment, 266–67
re-engineering, 246
reference groups, 379
referent power, 210
reinforcing behaviour, 312

vertical marketing systems, 444–45
vertical mergers, 155
vestibule training, 272
Vincent, Terri, 328
virtual assistants, 327–28
virtual corporations, 231, 248, 251
virtual private networks (VPNs), 109, 111
virtual teams, 249
visible minorities, 261. *See also* diversity
    in small business, 166–67, 187
vision
    in entrepreneurship, 174
    global, 36–37, 40
voice mail, 117
volume segmentation, 385
voluntary reductions in pay, 277
voluntary time off, 277–78

W

wages, 284
    hourly, 274
    and inflation, 15

Wallace, Gary, 322
warehouses, 455–56
warranties, 410, 604
Watkins, Sherron, 288
web portals, 124
Welch, Jack, 208
whistle blowers, 92, 288
Whitwam, David R., 172
wholesaling, 441, 447–49, 479
wide area networks (WANs), 108–10
Wi-Fi, 110
wildcat strikes, 286
Winchester, Jim, 222
wireless technology, 109–10, 117
wireless WANs (WWANs), 109
Wladawsky-Berger, Irving, 125
Wolf, Amy, 190
women
    earnings, 75
    in small business, 166–67
    working, 71, 75–76
Woods, Tiger, 389
workers' compensation, 551
work groups, 316
work-life benefits, 299, 319–20

work teams, 316–18
World Bank, 47, 50–51
World Trade Organization (WTO), 47, 50, 62

Y

Yang, Jerry, 256
Yates, Davin, 401
yield management systems (YMS), 423
York, Charlie, 163

Z

Zarate, Steve, 220–21
Zuckerman, Ethan, 101